Center Township
from
Moon Township
Beaver County

Including its pioneer families
and diverse history
of surrounding rural areas.

Volume I of II

By Sandy Davis

All rights reserved. No part of this publication may be reproduced, distributed, or transmitted in any form or by any means, including photocopying, recording, or other electronic or mechanical methods, without the prior written permission of the author, except in the case of brief quotations embodied in critical reviews and certain other noncommercial uses permitted by copyright law- 2021 by Sandy Davis.

ISBN 978-0-9992452-2-4

Contents

Map Index 6

PREFACE / INTRODUCTION 9

BEAVER COUNTY 12

HISTORY and PHYSICAL ASPECTS 12

MOON TOWNSHIP 21

CENTER TOWNSHIP 23

    Municipal Buildings and Officials 27

    Law Enforcement 31

    Police Department 33

        Center Township Police Department 33

        Potter Township Police Department 35

    Fire Departments 37

        Moon Township Fire Department 37

        Center Township Volunteer Fire Units 38

        Potter Township Volunteer Fire Department 41

    Water Authority 42

    Sanitary Authority 48

    Road Department 52

ROADS 52

PRIOR TO BRIDGES 97

    Ferry Businesses 97

COVERED BRIDGE 110

    (Potter Township) 110

STREETCAR 111

CREEKS, WATERWAYS, RIVER 113

MISCELLANEOUS TOWNSHIP INFORMATION 118

    Community Garden 118

    Cable Television Services 118

    Food Distributions Programs 119

    Land Fill Area 119

    Miscellaneous and General Facts for Potter Township 120

MEDICAL 121

    Beaver County Tuberculosis Sanatorium 121

    Beaver County General Hospital   aka   Rochester General Hospital ..126

    Aliquippa Hospital 127

    Beaver County Home   aka   County Poor Farm 129

    Beaver Valley Geriatric Center   aka   Friendship Ridge 137

Gateway Rehabilitation Center aka Gateway Farms 138
Allegheny Health Network Cancer Institute - Beaver 139
Heritage Valley Health System 139
Earlier Physicians 140
Physicians and other related medical facilities and businesses 142
Pharmacies 147
Christmas Seals 148
Illnesses 149
Old Time Cures 150
Epidemics and/or Illnesses 150

ACTIVITIES and ORGANIZATIONS 159

Center Grange Hall 159
    Center Grange Youth Club 163
4-H Clubs 163
    Center Township 163
    Potter Township 4-H Clubs 164
Various Organizations and Groups 165
    Center Township P.T.A. 171

POST OFFICES 174

Mail Carriers 180

FINANCIAL INSTITUTES 183

EDUCATION 186

One-Room School Houses 189
Schools located on current Monaca Heights 193
As the One-Room Schools were being phased out 195
Jointures / Mergers 201
    The little known or forgotten Jointure of 1957 201
Central Valley School District 204
Miscellaneous educational information 206
    Supervisory Positions 207
Teachers 208
Potter Township Schools 209
Student Transportation 213
Universities and Colleges 214
Other colleges and higher education institutes 223

CHURCHES and CEMETERIES 228

CHURCHES 228
Miscellaneous other Early Local Churches 237
Cemeteries 240

- ENTERTAINMENT and RECREATION ... 250
  - Dancing ... 250
  - Fishing ... 252
  - Golf ... 253
  - Township Fairs ... 262
  - Park Areas ... 263
  - Township Recreation ... 265
  - Swimming ... 269
  - Roller Skating ... 274
  - Bowling ... 276
  - Car Racing ... 276
- MOVIE THEATERS ... 277
  - Drive-In Theaters ... 282
- AMUSEMENT and PICNIC PARKS ... 284
- HOTELS ... 299
- NEWSPAPERS - NEWS STANDS - PRINTING ... 304
  - Reporters ... 305
  - Newspapers ... 306
- WEATHER ... 317
  - Tornados ... 317
  - Major Snow Falls of the Area ... 319
  - Drought and Flooding ... 321
- WAR TIMES ... 328
  - Veterans Memorials ... 343
    - Day Air Raid Test ... 344
  - Rationing Programs ... 346
  - War Bonds ... 357
- GREAT DEPRESSION ... 365
  - W.P.A. C.C.C.   New Deal ... 365
- ADS and INTERESTING ARTICLES ... 369
  - Events/happenings between 1914 and 2017 ... 380
- INDUSTRIAL BUSINESSES ... 398
  - Unions and Industrial Groups ... 418
- HOUSING PLANS and AREAS ... 419
  - Luxuary apartment complexes ... 440
- Contents for Volume II ... 446

Map Index

(Volume I)

Formation of Beaver County – 1781, 1788, 1800, current	14-15
Original Beaver County townships – Smith, Robinson, Hanover	16
1800 Map of Beaver County with First and Second Moon	17
1812 Map including Hopewell, Moon, Green & Hanover Townships	18
1888 Map of Beaver County	19
Current map of Beaver County	20
1860 Landowners map of Moon Township	22
Outline of Center Township	25
Plat map of Mona Manor area	67
Plat map of pre BV Mall area	68
Moffett Run Road area	70
Old Pleasant Drive area	70
Snippets of Monaca Road former layout (Vankirk)	72
Former Route 115 (18) and Route 76 (51/Brodhead Road)	89
1900 map with Narrows Road	91
1925 plat map	91
Area maps indicating Bellowsville Ferry site	102
Maps showing bridges across Raccoon Creek	114
Map showing older Post Office locations	180
Snippet of 1898 Outline Map of Beaver County (Post Offices)	181
Location of Potter #1 / Independent School	210
Layout of former Raccoon Golf Course	256, 257
1925 plat map of Sylvan Crest area	424, 426, 427
2017 map of new area behind Beaver Valley Mall "Bluffs at Glade Path"	445

Map Index

The following maps may be found in Volume II.

Drawing of Hostetter Estate – Potter Township

Sample of old maps showing rods, posts, trees, et cetera

1860 landowners' map

1876 landowners' map

1870s map of Moon Township

Braden ownership map

Snippet of 1860 map with Burneson farm

Snippet of 1876 map with Craig farms

Snippet of 1876 map with Davis farms

Snippet of 1876 map with Deens farms

Snippet of 1876 map with Douds farms

Snippet of 1876 map with Elliott farm

Snippet of 1876 map Baker farms

Snippet of 1876 map with Johnston farms

Snippet of 1876 map with Keller farm

Snippet of 1876 map with Laubscher farm

Snippet of 1876 map with Springer farm

Map indicating Todd farms

Map indicating Uselton farms

Map of brick works along Ohio River

Snippet of 1876 map indicating Crail's Steam Saw Mill

Snippet of 1876 map indicating Braden's Salt works and a Saw Mill

Snippet of 1876 map indicating J. R. Stewart's Grist Mill

Snippet of 1876 map indicating J. J. Anderson's Grist Mill

ACKNOWLEDGMENTS

"We must find time to stop and thank the people who make a difference in our lives."
-John F. Kennedy

I want to personally thank the following persons for all the patience and time they extended to me with my researching and collecting information and pictures for this book. They shared personal memories, pictures, and/or special information with me. If some names or information did not come to mind easily, many of them contacted others to obtain addition information, too. Without all this help, this book would be missing many important details, locations, businesses, and/or family listings.

John Bickerton
Cindy Stuehling
Vesta Davis
Jenette Fiejdasz
Linda D'Antonio
Ellen Glasser
Amy Coombs
Alice Phillis
Debbie Huffmyer
The Floyd and Douds Families
Michael "Jerry" Michaluk
Al and Diane Wenzig
Gary and Branell Lowery
Woody Aaron
Al Cwynar
Lucci Kitchen and Bath
Center Township personnel, including John Plutko and Frank Vescio

The Beaver County Historical Research and Landmarks Foundation for their collections and archived materials.

The Beaver Area Heritage Foundation for their archived materials and collection of information.

All the libraries and other historical locations and organizations for being so willing to share and aid in my research.

To the many persons not listed who came forward and shared tidbits while we were engaged in casual conversation, they may not have realized at the time how much information they provided just by conversing with me; so, I thank all these persons.

I also had the pleasure of sharing time, information, pictures, and/or having conversations with several persons who have since passed away.
    Richard Temple   Joann Biship   Robert Bickerton
    James Mateer   Denver Walton   Bill Pyle

A special thank you to Woody and Jo Anne Aaron for all the proof-reading assistance.

"The best kind of people are the ones that come into your life and make you see the sun where you once saw clouds. The people that believe in you so much, you start to believe in you too. The people that love you, simply for being you. The once in a lifetime kind of people." -Anonymous

Sandy

PREFACE / INTRODUCTION

I have always found local history of great interest. Other than a small pamphlet type of information prepared in the 1960s by Mrs. Mildred Dyke and another smaller paperback booklet published during Center Township's centennial celebration, there has been no attempt at providing a more complete and informative history on Moon Township. Moon Township was the parent township prior to the erection of Center Township. I was born and raised and still currently live in Center Township, thus why I decided to take on this project.

History must of necessity be a thing of the past for the real evaluation of men and their work must be left to those who follow them. As we come nearer to the present day, I do admit that the newer and/or most recent businesses will not be well represented, nor did I center much attention on them. My goal was concentrating and gathering the earlier history of the Moon and Center Townships. That being said, the more recent, current, and future is a matter of your knowledge and I leave a more thorough and accurate recording of all to those who come after the writing of this book. It can be a task of someone in the future to capture as "history;" to research and show how the area changed and moved forward from the point I leave off in this book.

History books tend to state that "Moon" became Center Township, which is truthful for the most part, but a bit misleading because there is a bit more to this statement. Moon Township was indeed the parent township for Center, but also other townships were formed from Moon. Raccoon Township was formed in 1837 and Phillipsburg Borough in 1840 (now Monaca), then Potter Township was formed in 1912 from a lower portion of Moon and upper portion of Raccoon Township. In 1914, a large, lower portion of Moon Township was formed to erect Center Township, and in 1932, the last remaining smaller, upper portion of Moon Township, between the Borough of Monaca and Center Township, became annexed to Monaca. For this reason, plus the fact that boundaries tended to "float" and change during the earlier years, readers may find tidbits of information throughout the book regarding all these areas. Potter Township will be mentioned the most, mostly since even today, if you use any one of the lesser traveled, secondary roads, it is hard to tell if you are actually in Center Township or Potter Township. Even early census enumerators would easily include residents truly from one township on another township's area, which was not only confusing, but could be misleading. I felt it better to include as much information as possible rather than exclude or segregate any businesses or individuals. I also chose to pull and/or duplicate some limited information from my two-volume book on Monaca (*Monaca aka Phillipsburg*) since it involved some information on Moon/Center and Potter Townships and was also applicable to this book. Regardless of if and when I include another township's information, businesses, or residents, please remember that each township should be remembered and respected for their own history and they have and still stand proudly on their own.

I will also take this time to apologize for all misspellings and possible errors in the information in this publication. Everything was read, reread, cross referenced, and doubled checked to the best of my ability, but I am only human. The biggest fluctuation will be found in the spelling of first and surnames. I spelled these exactly as they were found in any specific document. Many times, these names were spelled phonetically on census sheets and other referenced documents, but not personally knowing these persons or families, I did not feel comfortable or qualified in altering any spellings from the original findings.

Speaking of references, there is a complete list of all resources at the end of Volume II of this book. By listing all at the end of the book, I felt this made the book flow much easier rather than have everything cluttered with multiple specific references with each business or entry, since information may have been extracted from many sources. I found most of my information from endless hours of reading historical publications, archived newspapers spanning over more than a hundred years, archived tax records, and an unnumbered amount of deeds, wills, and other legal transactions. Regarding newspaper publications, specific dates, and pages of where the information was extracted, these are not listed. I only included the names and time frames for each of the papers which were used. This was also done to streamline the list of reference information.

A diligent search of all existing records was made in the preparation of this book. Many times, within the material presented is information largely based on documented evidence and yet some on tradition that is believed to be entirely true. Information is provided "as is" without warranty of any kind, either expressed or implied. While I strive for accuracy in the factual content, I cannot offer any guarantee of accuracy. Information could include technical inaccuracies or errors of omission. Opinions and commentary are those of myself or other individuals who shared with me and do not necessarily represent the views of anyone else. Doubtless inaccuracies have crept in resulting in errors in names and dates, but I took great pains to have them as nearly correct as possible with the material at hand. Many pictures were shared with me from others or found in archived materials. Often they were sent to me anonymously so there will be no mention as to the contributor or if any copyright was in place. It is not my intention to usurp any copyright holders' rights but only to promote the older material as purely educational. I do not bear any responsibility for any consequences resulting from the use of this or any other information provided.

I know no better way to sum up my efforts in this writing of the history of Moon/Center Township except to quote Rev. J. R. Thomson:

> "In the old days on the farm they use to boil sap and manufacture maple sugar. It was a complicated and tedious process, the sap had to be gathered from the maple trees, previously tapped. It had to be carried to the place of manufacture, placed in pans or kettles over the fire, boiled down into molasses and later sugared off. During this time much straining had to be done, and there had also to be a continual skimming off of the froth. The residue in the form of sugar was always an uncertain quantity.
> Such has been the preparation of this history, it has been a tapping, gathering, warming up, boiling down, and skimming off process. Perhaps I have skimmed off what you wanted left in, perhaps I have left in what you might have wanted strained out, but here is the result. The residue you will now be permitted to sample."

I invite all reading this book to sit back and enjoy learning how the open wilderness of the area was settled, how the early residents turned the wilderness into homesteads, and how these persons and the descendants of those pioneers and others helped with the early and current development of Moon/Center Township.

~ ~ ~

Front Cover images are of currently existing township structures: (large, background) on W. Woodland Drive – formerly Baker/Short/Blair homes, (smaller, left) on Chapel Road – formerly Henry Davis homestead, (smaller, right) on Pleasant Drive - formerly Douds farm.

METHOD TO MY MADNESS

I have divided the many venues and information of Center Township into sections to hopefully help the reader easily find any business or activity. In each of the different categories/sections of this book, I have included as many known or found business, people, facts, notes, explanations, ads, and pictures. The businesses listed under any specific section or category are usually loosely listed alphabetically, but occasionally you may find a sub-section by 'type' of business. Within all sections or categories, I used the following design or setup for each business's information:

First will be listed......
    Although not in every section, within various business / occupations sections, if a business is known to be "current," then the name will be in **bold** print.
    If found or known, the address(es) will follow a business's name.
        Note: Throughout the book, when an address was found to be on Brodhead Road, I tried to include what the number was prior to the renumbering of all Brodhead Road's addresses, as well as the new/current assigned number if that was known.
        It may also aid the reader for orienting the location of places along Brodhead Road to know....
            Even numbers on Brodhead Road are on the left coming from Monaca and heading toward Aliquippa. Odd numbers are on the right.

Right under the name and address will be....
    A few of the years I found information on this business will be listed to give an estimate of when the business was in operation. Unless otherwise stated, any date(s) listed under a business's name does NOT indicate the only year(s) of operation. The date(s) is only to provide a general idea of time frames.
        Note: I did not include every year of when information was found, just a few random years to verify the business existed.

Following any year(s) or dates that may be listed will be ....
    Miscellaneous found information about the business – opening date, closing date, any owner(s) and/or other pertinent details.

And lastly....
    If there was a picture and/or sampling of any advertisements available, it is included.

There will also be random "Fact" or "Fun fact" inserts throughout both volumes of this book.

~ ~ ~

Beaver County - Moon Township - Center Township

BEAVER COUNTY
HISTORY and PHYSICAL ASPECTS

This section will give the history of the area prior to and into the erection of Beaver County, all being many years before what would become Center Township out of Moon Township. I have tried to uncover and find as much information as possible as to the types of occupations, the business, homes in the township, roads, and many of the earlier people/families who lived in the section of Moon Township that became Center Township. But knowing what happened prior to Moon Township and Center Township is also very important including the layout and erection information of Beaver County, particular portions of the county that came to include Moon Township, and what occurred prior to the majority of the settlers coming to this area. As readers continue through this section, the importance of this background information will come to surface and it will be more apparent as to why it is being included at this time. So, with all that being said, here is my condensed history lesson. ☺

I chose to begin with quoting a statement from an article in 2015 by Travis Jeffries of Koppel who so eliquently stated,

> "The fabric of our history was woven through the Native Americans ... so much of our history, our government," he noted. "Without possibly Native American influence and intervention, the country itself may not have existed or may not have started obviously the way it started or when it started." "We owe so much to them and to the culture and history."

I do make mention periodically within this book regarding the Native Americans who populated the area. But, in this section, I am including more detailed information. I believe it may be hard for current township residents to remember what is now Center Township, was once pure wilderness and unsettled land. It was first populated by the Native Americans, then the pioneers began to move into the area.

Pennsylvania was populated by various native Indian nations through history, but the Lenni Lenape or Delaware were the most populous nation within the area that became Beaver County. The native Indians of this area have been best known as Woodland Indians. The Lenni Lenape or Delaware were a fiercely independent people. They had little national cohesion and no conception at all of labor organized on the scale necessary for the construction of public works of any size. The native Indian society was not one large group that occupied any specific area, but instead their society was "atomistic," that is, broken up into many small, autonomous communities, with each family possessing its own fields and its own hunting territory. These independent and sovereign territories were quite large tracts of land. They were not measured in square feet or even acres but were described as "extending as far back into the woods as one walks in a day and a half." Without official markers or posts or surveyors, each nation just "knew" where their boundaries were and the majority of the time, each respected these boundaries.

> *Fun facts:*
> *…. On the site of Beaver, where the Beaver River (then known as Big Beaver Creek) meets the Ohio River, there was a Delaware village that was locally known as Sawkunk.*
>
> *…. There is one well-known archaeological site in Beaver County located on the north shore of the Ohio River, west of Vanport Township. In the 1950s they began excavations there and the archaeologists found artifacts dating back to 7,000 B.C. The official number of this site is 36BV9. There were many items found by the Monongahela inhabitants who lived in that area between the years 900 to 1600. The findings prove that this area was the scene of apparent violence since individuals found buried there appear to have been murdered. Other items found were shell beads, bone pendants, stone anvils, hammers, pipes, and pottery.*

It should be remembered that for the most part, "white man," who came to America did not renounce the ways or culture of the native Indians. Instead, they more often espoused many aspects of it. Almost one half of today's world's agricultural products are from plants that were first domesticated by native Indians. Today's society is still using products thanks to the use of the Indians' corn, potatoes, tobacco, cocoa, quinine. Outside the food products, there are also the hammock, canoe, toboggan, military strategy, democratic thinking, and highways.

In western Pennsylvania, including the nowadays Center Township area, where much of the land is cut up into a jumble of hills and glens without any discernible pattern, the Indian paths were thoughtfully laid out and followed the highest ridges because they alone offered a more continuously level course. The pioneers and settlers, who came into these areas, were not always on foot or horseback as the Indians were, but often also used wagons and carts. As a result, ignoring how well thought out, mapped, and engineered the Indian trails really were, the settlers sometimes chose to break off and create new roads rather than widen the original Indian paths. Yet, on the other hand, as "white man" became more numerous in areas, many of the Indian trails were used, at least being widened into bridle paths adequate for horses carrying two-hundred-pound packs. By the time of the Revolutionary War, the Conestoga wagon had cause for men to convert old trails into even wider roadways as far as Pittsburgh. After the Revolutionary War, the movement for converting trails into more improved roads continued west "towards the setting sun" and into Ohio, Indiana, and "beyond to the Western Sea."

The evolution of the Indian trails into those used by settlers as a bridle path, wagon road, and later, motor highway was a slow, continuous process. The courses of most original Indian paths were so well chosen that not until the invention of the internal combustion engine, was there any occasion for many changes in their' routes. Often when a roadway broke away from the original Indian's ridge routes, it would merely be for the purposes of serving any mill towns that had been built. Many of the new roads the settlers chose to create and follow that were not original Indian routes were affected by wet weather and proved to be very troublesome to many travelers with many quite soft/muddy places. These changes have produced proof as to why the Indians chose higher grounds for their paths. In the valleys the slopes tend to be gushing with springs. These inconveniences just reinforce how well engineered the Indian trails were. Some things never really change, even with "paved" roadways nowadays. We still have areas of trouble and discomfort occasioned by road surfaces that are frost-broken during the months of February and March (potholes), areas affected by landslides, and even flooding.

One of the well-known, and possibly one of the oldest of the Indian trails was the *Catawba*, or *Cherokee Trail* leading from Georgia through Virginia, western Pennsylvania, and western New York to Canada. The *Catawba* and the *Warrior Branch* (from Kentucky into Fayette County) were the most important trails that ran north and south. The trails that ran east and west were even more traveled, the best known of these was the *Kettanning*. It traveled from Maryland, running to Pittsburgh, and continued into what became Beaver County where it was known as the *Tuscarawas Trail*, then on to Lake Erie. The Beaver and Butler road in Beaver County is supposed to follow this trail in a great part of its length.

There is much written on another Indian "roadway" in Western Pennsylvania called *Glade Path*. *Glade Path* was quite widely used as it ran from Bedford to Washington, Pa., much the same way as the road still does today. This roadway being Pennsylvania Route 31 (PA 31), a 74-mile-long state highway that parallels U.S. Route 30 and the Pennsylvania Turnpike for most of its length. In fact, the name found associated with Route 31 is Glade Pike. Glade Path connected or crossed several other trails. It became a favorite route for many early white settlers to reach familiar destinations.

The road leading into Murdocksville from the south was along that portion of Raccoon Creek and was known as *Bigger Road*. In 1700s and 1800s, it was often simply called the *Creek Road*. Before the white settlers came it was also known as the "*Hunters' Path*." The Indian path that led from Fort Pitt, through the present New Sheffield area of Aliquippa, PA, to the Ohio River, opposite Fort McIntosh, became Brodhead Road. It was used during the Revolutionary War for providing supplies to Fort McIntosh from Pittsburgh. (See Roads section for more on Brodhead Road.)

Fun fact: Modern day billboards are not all that original when it comes to spreading any news. Native Indians use to strip a ring of bark off a tree and would then paint on the exposed surface of that stripped area with red ochre and charcoal to paint "the news of the day." All Indians of Pennsylvania, whatever their spoken language, could read these pictures, which told of war heroes or gave the latest gossip of local hunting parties. These "original billboards" were used for many purposes. During the Braddock campaign, the French Indians painted trees with defiant and derisive symbols where the English were bound to see them. In the vicinity of some Moravian Indian towns, trees were even painted with Scripture texts. It is reported that some of these tree paintings remained visible for as long as fifty years. So......" Billboards" of today may not be painted on a tree trunk, but they definitely are not anything new in American advertising of events.

In 1792, a law was passed that opened the territory north and west of the Ohio River that allowed settlers to occupy this land area. Times could not have been too easy for any of these earliest settlers because the Indians were still very hostile on into the 1790s. The roads that formed from the well-used Indian paths led right through the heart of many of the Indians' valued hunting grounds, which reached from the shores of the Monongahela on the east, on past the Ohio River on the west. As the settlers crossed the Alleghenies and began chopping down trees and building permanent homes, the Indians rightfully became alarmed and angry at seeing their hunting grounds gradually grow smaller and smaller, justifying their hostilities. After many conflicts and uprisings, and the General Wayne's Treat of Greenville in 1795, history shows the Indians conceded and moved on, leaving the settlers to build their homes and clear more land, thus forming all the counties, townships, boroughs, towns, and cities of the areas we know today.

I would be remised if I didn't explain what the land mass was originally prior to eventually becoming Beaver County and ultimately including Moon/Center Township. This all involves explaining how the counties in Pennsylvania were formed and the time period involved in these formations. Here are some random maps from various years to show many of these formations:

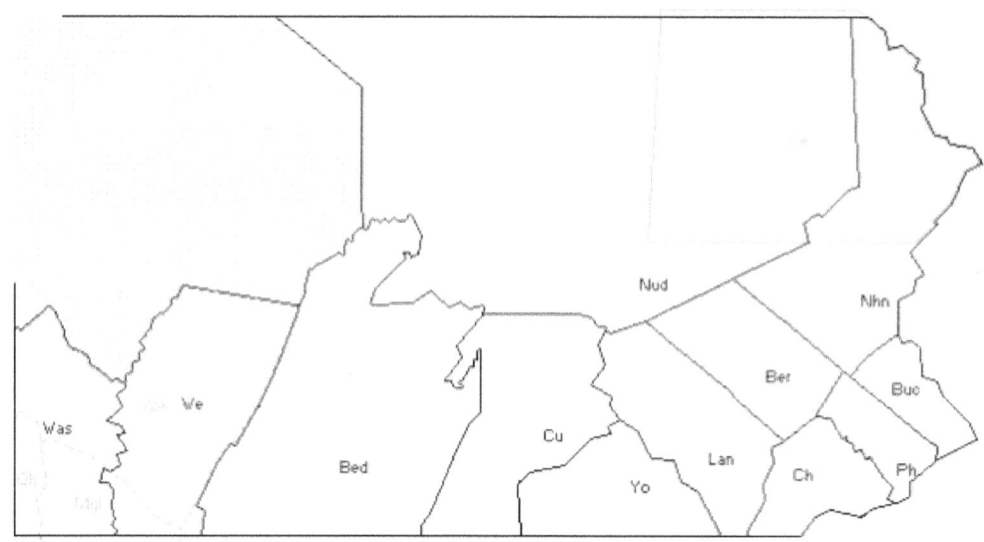

1781

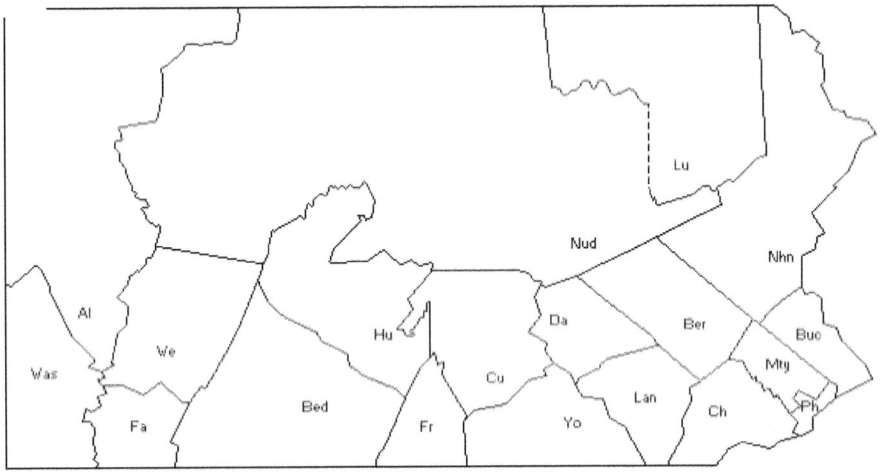

1788

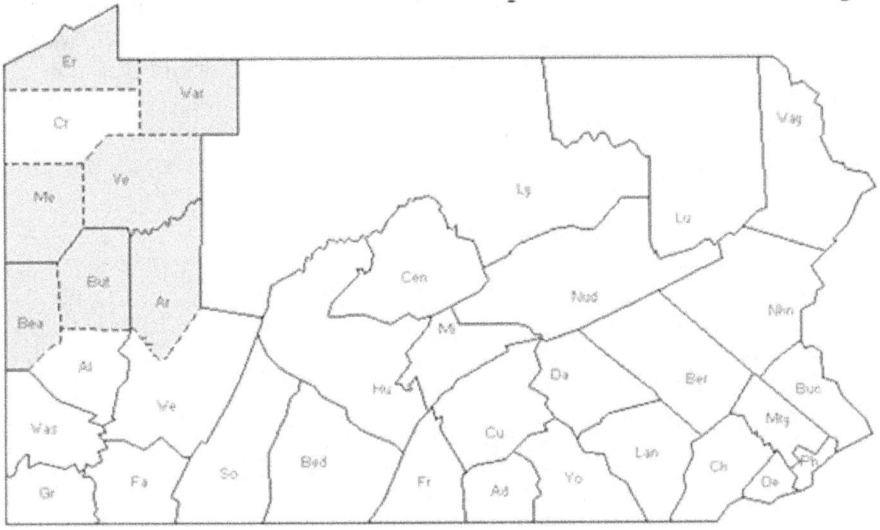

1800

Beaver, Crawford, Armstrong, Butler, Erie, Mercer, and
Venango were all formed from Allegheny County.

Current

~ ~ ~

As for the formation of Beaver County, I will concentrate on the townships south of the Ohio River. This is being done not because the townships of the northern portion of Beaver County are not of significance, but rather only because the northern townships really do not relate to what became any part of Moon /Center Township.

Previous to 1786 all of what is now the south side (lower portion) of Beaver County lay in the then Washington County and were then the townships of Smith (all that portion west of Raccoon Creek) and Robinson (all that portion to the east of Raccoon Creek). Smith Township was the last one of the original thirteen Washington County Townships set off (it was named for Rev. Joseph Smith). On Mar 11, 1786, Smith Township was divided. The northern part, using the Ohio River as the northern and eastern boundaries (See Map 1 further), then became Hanover Township (see Map 2 further).

There was an important Indian and traders' town known as Logstown. There was a French post erected at Logstown in 1754. The English built Fort McIntosh in 1778 and one of the first of the nation's training camps was established by General Anthony Wayne at Legionville (outside of Ambridge). The importance of the Beaver River itself added to that of the Ohio River which formed in what is currently Allegheny County from the Allegheny and Monongahela Rivers at what is now Pittsburgh. The convenience of waterway communication and transportation quickly became important factors in the development of Beaver County. Also, many found that only a small portion of what was to become Beaver County was unsuitable for agriculture. The Ohio River basin and all the tributary streams provided access to what were considered naturally fertile lands, and often known as "river bottom lands."

These two maps are pre-1800 views of what was to become the lower, left corner of Beaver County.

Map 1   Map 2
(Note: These two maps extend to the Virginia Line and are NOT just of the current lower Beaver County.)

To orient places on the two maps and on any additional maps, note White's Mill in the center of each of the above maps. Once all the counties were established, White's Mill became the point of intersection of the boundary lines of Beaver, Washington, Allegheny Counties. It intersected the following townships - Hanover & Independence Townships (Beaver County), Hanover & Robinson Townships (Washington County), and Findlay Township (Allegheny County). (See Map 3 further.)

1800s

Beaver County was erected Mar 12, 1800, from parts of Allegheny and Washington Counties. Tradition states that it took its name from the Beaver River ("Beaver" being a translation of an Indian name for the stream). Thanks to the wise decision of Beaver County officials to retain and store all past census enumerations, tax books, warrant, and survey books for future generations to review, we know there were originally six townships - North Beaver, South Beaver, Sewickley, First Moon, Second Moon, and Hanover. At its formation in 1800, the population of Beaver County totaled 5,776 with each township's being, North Beaver (east and west of Big Beaver Creek) – 338; Sewickley (east of Big Beaver Creek) – 853; South Beaver (west of Big Beaver Creek) – 2,581; First Moon – 527; Hanover – 421; and Second Moon – 1,056.

Once the settlers became more numerous in the soon to be area of Beaver County, agriculture became the major force, eventually followed by industry combined to provide prosperity to the area. While farming was prevalent, almost all the major agricultural crops were being produced. Sandstone quarries provided building stones and were also used to provide materials to form crushed stone for roadways. Mining in the area produced sand, gravel, coal, shale, and clay which provided materials for brick making. Soon to follow were added metal product producing industries.

I tried to simplify all the information on the forming of Beaver County and then Moon Township without making this a formal history lesson. From the whole area in the lower left corner of Pennsylvania, the land south of the Ohio, there were three differently shaped townships formed – First Moon, Second Moon, and Hanover. Rather than just giving the general name of "Moon Township" to the original larger land area and the county seats, they were called First Moon and Second Moon. With there being such great areas and distances between the voting places of these three townships, it was decided in 1812 that four townships would be formed from these three larger, oddly shaped townships. These four townships became Greene, Hanover, Hopewell, and Moon.

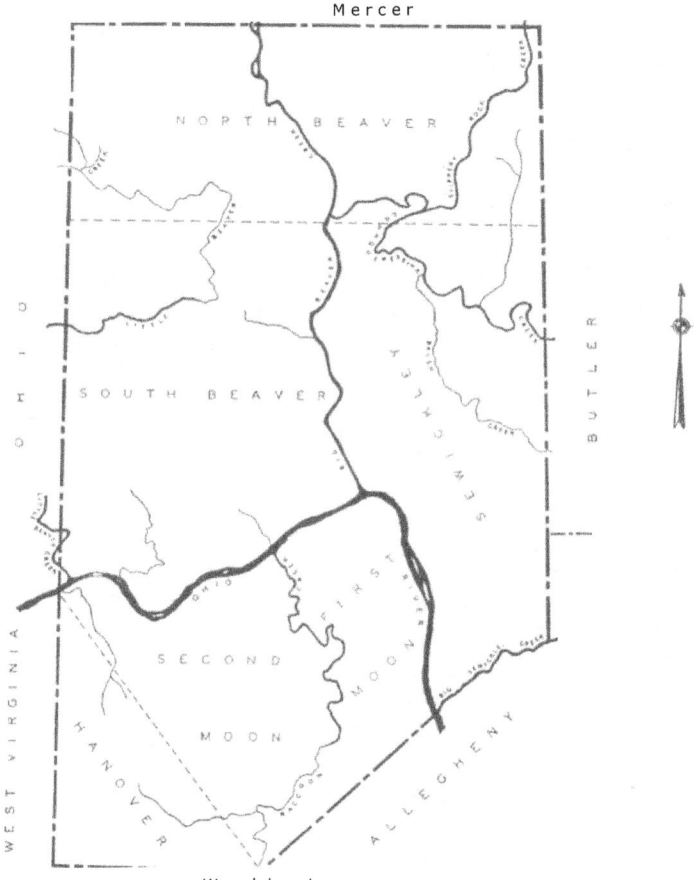

1800 map of Beaver County
(Map 3)

On the previous 1800 map of Beaver County (Map 3), note the location of Raccoon Creek running between Second and First Moon. It was used as the guideline or unofficial dividing line between the properties of these two townships. That is to say, the majority of tracts of land listed in First Moon were bound on the west by the Raccoon Creek and tracts of land listed as being in Second Moon were basically bound on the east by Raccoon Creek.

This next map is from 1812 showing the formation of the southern section of Beaver County after its official erection in 1800.

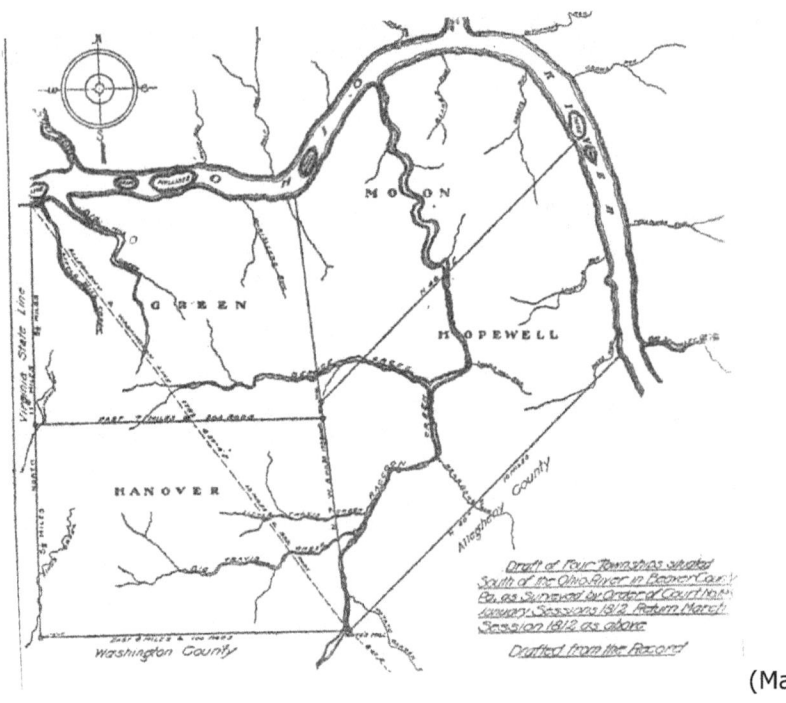

(Map 4)

As previously stated, the southern townships were reorganized into four almost equal quarters and became Hopewell, Moon, Greene, and Hanover Townships. (For orientation purposes, again, note on Map 4, Raccoon Creek which runs through lower Green, part of Hopewell, and near the middle of Moon Township.) Through the years, Moon Township of Beaver County was subdivided into smaller communities, forming Raccoon Township in 1833, Phillipsburg in 1840, and Potter Township in 1912. On Nov 24, 1914, after a second election, the court decreed that the remaining, larger southern section of Moon be known as Center Township. Eighteen years later, the remaining portion of Moon in the north was annexed by Monaca, becoming that borough's Fourth and Fifth Wards (Monaca Heights and Colona Heights).

> *Fun facts:* The "South Side" of Beaver County (including Moon/Center Township) can take claim to:
> ... the first settler(s) in the county -- Dungans and/or Bakers
> ... the first church – Mill Creek
> ... the first theological school, and the only one – Eudolpha Hall
> ... the first superintendent of common schools – Thomas Nicholson
> ... the first circulating library – Frankfort
> ... the first public highway – <u>Brodhead Road</u>, from Pittsburgh to Fort McIntosh
> ... the first justice of the peace – Wm. Glasgrow
> ... the biggest Indian fight – Poe and Bigfoot

The division of the northern portion of Beaver County was a bit more complicated.

Just for general information....... In 1801, Sewickley Township was divided into North Sewickley and New Sewickley Townships. South Beaver Township was first divided in 1802 to form Little Beaver, Big Beaver, and South Beaver Townships. But, in 1804, the small area in the southeast corner of South Beaver Township, which was known as Beaver Borough, separated off and became Borough Township. Borough Township held that name until 1970 when it was renamed Vanport Township. In 1805, the portion of South Beaver Township that remained became Ohio and South Beaver Townships. In 1816, the townships of Ohio and South Beaver became divided into four portions. Ohio and Brighton Township were to the north of the Ohio River. South Beaver and Chippewa Townships were above them, further north.

I found The Beaver County Tourism site to have the best explanation for how Beaver County came to be named such, so I will just quote them:

"The name "Beaver" was given to the county from the stream and town called at the time of its earliest settlers, and the town had been named for the stream. As to the origin of the name of the stream itself, we need not be in any doubt. It was a translation into English of the Indian word for beaver, the much-prized animal after which the local Indians had named the stream. The Delaware called the stream Amockwi-sipu, or literally, "beaver stream." They gave this name to the creek because of its being a favorite home of the beaver.

The French, who were the first whites to reach this region, merely translated the Indian name for the stream calling it, as we have learned from a map in Pouchot's memoirs, River au Castor, (Beaver River), and the English when they arrived, called it the same name."

(They go on to explain how the town of Beaver received its name and how it became the *"county seat of the new county in its beginning stage of development.)*

Thus, it was natural that when the time came for the creation of the county, it should receive a name associated with the most important stream and locality belonging distinctively to its territory, and was accordingly called "Beaver."

~ ~ ~

The following map is not very clear at all, especially with smaller details, but, although difficult, the basic townships and boroughs can be read. It is included only to provide the concept of the layout of Beaver County in 1888. It reflects Moon and Raccoon Township prior to Potter Township being erected from portions of both of these townships.

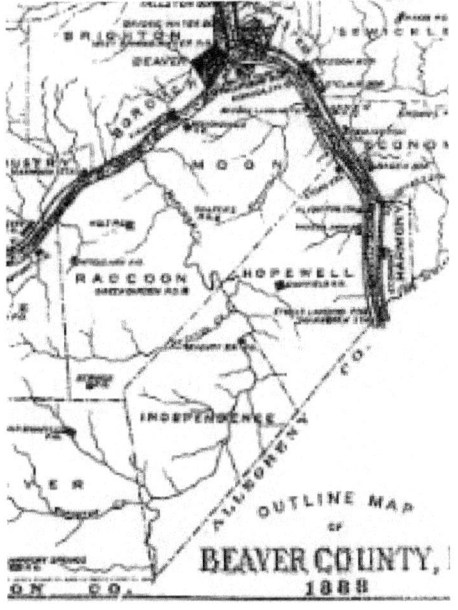

Beaver County currently is bordered by Lawrence County at the top (north) and Butler County on the right (east). Allegheny is still along the slanted lower line (southeast). Washington also is still along the bottom portion (south). West Virginia and Ohio border the left side (west).

Beaver County now contains:

TOWNSHIPS (as of 1990): Brighton, Center, Chippewa, Darlington, Daugherty, Franklin, Greene, Hanover, Harmony, Hopewell, Independence, Marion, New Sewickley, North Sewickley, Patterson, Potter, Pulaski, Raccoon, Rochester, South Beaver, Vanport, White.

BOROUGHS (as of 1990): Aliquippa (town), Ambridge, Baden, Beaver, Beaver Falls (town), Big Beaver, Bridgewater, Conway, Darlington, East Rochester, Eastvale, Economy, Ellwood City, Fallston, Frankfort Springs, Freedom, Georgetown, Glasgow, Homewood, Hookstown, Industry, Koppel, Midland, Monaca, New Brighton, New Galilee, Ohioville, Patterson Heights, Rochester, Shippingport, South Heights, West Mayfield.

Fun fact: Part of Beaver County was taken to form Lawrence County by an Act of the Legislature in 1849.   This caused almost 9000 residents to then be known as no longer living in Beaver County, but now Lawrence County, yet none of them ever moved even one board or stone of their homes.

Seldom was there any listing of streets to verify exactly where some of the families lived within Moon/Center Township on the census sheets. Also, township boundaries varied greatly through the years, therefore many of the names mentioned on various older census sheets may not have been "considered" to have been living within Moon/Center Township boundaries during certain census years. This means, depending on the year of the census, depending on where the census enumerator "thought" the township boundaries were, and/or who the census enumerator was, he/she may have placed that family in either the current areas of Monaca, Potter, Raccoon, or a portion of Hopewell when the families were actually living in "Moon Township." I have tried my best to sort out who was who and to correctly credit Center Township based families with being such. Keeping all this in mind………..Phillipsburg/Monaca, Center Township, Potter Township areas, and even some areas of Raccoon and Hopewell all just seem to flow back and forth into each other in many ways through the earlier years as the boundaries fluctuated, not to mention as do the families and their connections.

~ ~ ~

Beaver County's
MOON TOWNSHIP

Monaca, Center, and Potter areas and the residents have comfortably been quite intertwined throughout the years, yet each area having their own unique qualities and history. Again, without making this a complete, long, and formal history lesson, I will do my best to simplify it all in a condensed form and will be concentrating on only the southern portion of the county -- Moon Township of Beaver County.

Again, First and Second Moon Townships were subdivided over the years and eventually came to be known as Hopewell Township (being reduced in 1948 for Independence Township to be formed), Raccoon Township (reduced to help form Potter Township), and Phillipsburg (now Monaca). (See Map 4 previous.) The remaining area after these townships were formed became known simply as Moon Township, then Potter Township was formed from an upper portion of Raccoon and lower portion of Moon Townships. The remaining larger lower portion of Moon Township officially created Center Township, and the remaining northern portion became annexed by Monaca.

Moon Township was a very sparsely populated area for many years. It was just open land, with substantial amounts of acres between neighbors. The future land of Center Township remained primarily unchanged through the mid 1700s, 1800s and into the earlier 1900s, being first known as an agricultural community with only unpretentious homesteads being spread throughout. Almost all of the occupations of the original homeowners and families in Moon Township were essentially that of farmers in some capacity. Although finding the straightforward occupation of "farmer" listed, one must understand that this was just a general listing of the occupation. Since the land was used for many different commodities, the "farmers" were also very different. Some specialized in growing fruit, vegetables, and/or hay/grains, while others raised/bred cattle or other live-stock, poultry, and still others engaged in wool or dairy products. Each farmer owned, maintained, and worked hundreds of acres of land. These farms and homesteads were much, much more than what many people today call a "large back yard."

The 1850 census enumeration showed a total of 916 residents living in Moon Township (469 males, 417 females). From this census, the trend was for the number of residents to grow and grow each year. One book on the history of Beaver County states that in 1880, the population of Moon Township was 1,124. There are other publications that have a lower number and state in 1890, Moon Township was recorded as only having a population of 1,092. By 1900, the population was 1,095. There was a noticeable change between 1880 and 1890. This is probably due to the changing boundaries and formation of other townships. In 1900, Moon Township had 355 taxable properties, 10,029 acres of cleared land, and 1,978 acres of "timber land". Records of 1900 have real estate valued at $552,189 ($518,564 worth of taxable and $33,625 exempt from taxation).

Here is a copy of an 1860 map of Moon Township with landowners listed. Note the vast and open spaces separating most of the landowners. Although some names can be read, this map is not meant to actually permit readability of landowners but is included simply to show the vast areas between and of the land owned.

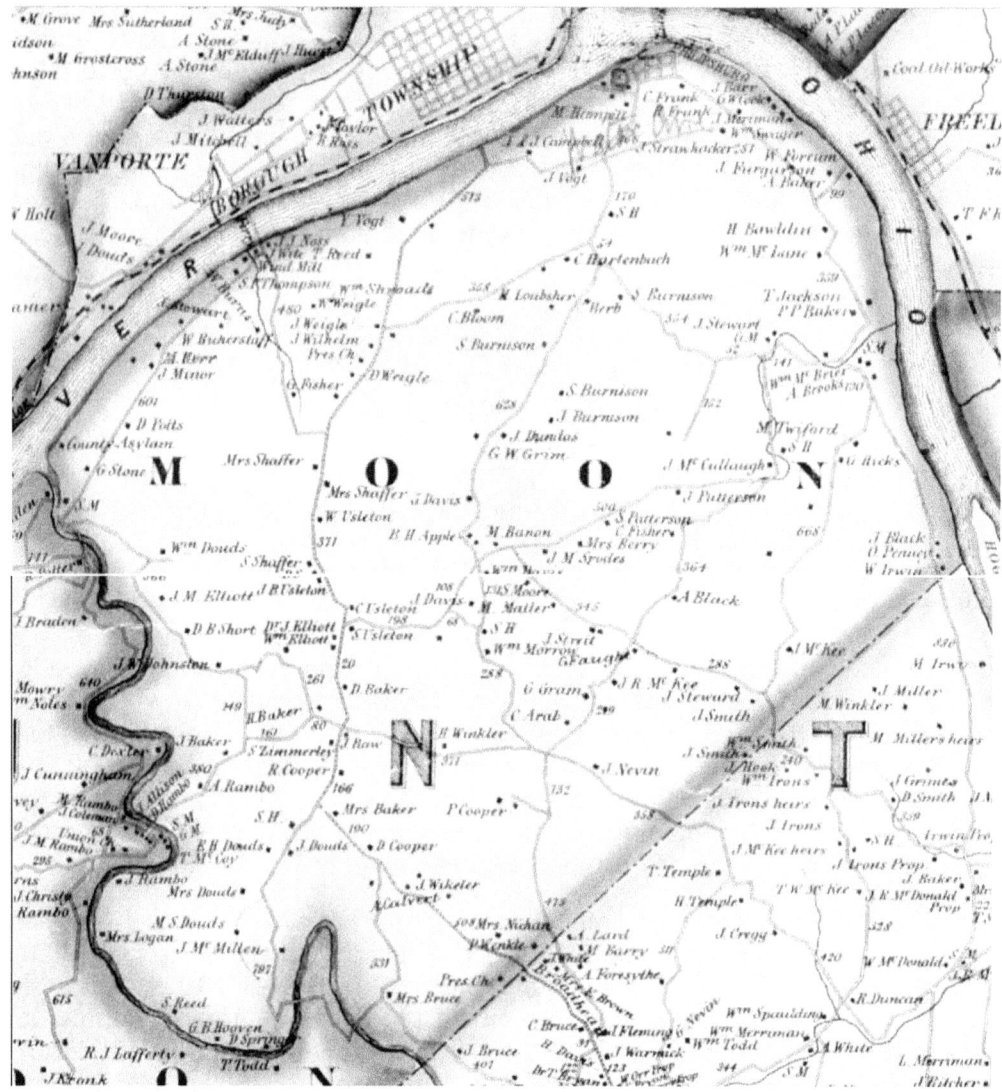

Before the erection of Center Township, as previously stated, Moon Township was basically a large and vast accumulation of open acreage. Farms were scattered east, north, west, and south within its borders. When you drive around the once Moon Township, now Center Township area and surrounding communities, "older residents" may remember, but younger and/or newer residents may find it hard to comprehend, that this same area was once a pure haven for farmers. A person could ride a roadway for quite a distance before seeing another home or building. Farming was the major industry not only in Moon/Center Township, but in the whole county for many years. Owning vast homesteads was for reasons of survival and/or profit. Trying to envision much sparser homesteads with wide open surrounding lands and acre after acre of open fields or large herds of livestock grazing is hard do with all the modern shopping plazas, large hospitals, nuclear power plants, and major industry, not to mention the many housing projects and apartment type complexes, and so much asphalt and concrete now consuming the once producing farmlands. In those very early years, there were no planes flying over, high power lines, multiple natural gas lines, township water or sewers, air conditioning, telephones, or televisions. It was very much a simpler lifestyle.

~ ~ ~

Out of Moon Township came....

CENTER TOWNSHIP

Now comes the history of the erection of Center Township. I will include information on Center Township's municipality in general, residents, and lifestyles. In other sections I have included as much information as possible to elaborate on and provide as to the types of occupations and former businesses. When found, there will be facts on homes in the township, organizations, and many of the people and families who made up earlier Moon/Center Township and even before its onset.

A dispute among the Moon Township residents split the township into two areas. One area was the more heavily populated suburban section to the north, the second and lower larger area was the more sparsely populated section to the south and west. The lower and larger area became Center Township while the smaller northern portion eventually became annexed to Monaca, now best known as Monaca Heights.

So............ from Moon Township, Center Township was erected................

THE DAILY TIMES

ONE CENT A COPY.   BEAVER, PA., WEDNESDAY EVENING, NOVEMBER 25, 1914. $3.00 A YEAR.

MOON TOWNSHIP TO BE DIVIDED, COURT'S ORDER

Judge Richard S. Holt made a decree today for the division of Moon township. It is decreed that the township be divided to the lines marked out and returned by the commissioners; that the name of the township thereby formed lying northeasterly of said line retain the name of Moon township, and that the larger part of the original township, lying southwesterly of said line, be called Center township.

The two election districts in Moon township as now constituted are to remain, the district designated as the "Fourth District" to be changed to the "Second District," and the one designated as the "First District" in the original township to be known and designated as the first election district of Moon. The place for holding the general election in the township of Center will remain as fixed at Shaffer's residence.

The following officers have been appointed for Center township, to serve until the next general election: Elmer Sohn, constable; James E. Smith, tax collector; James E. Smith, assessor; Benjamin Forsythe, Frank McTeer, James Cochran, supervisors; Henderson Davidson, Armstrong Gorsuch, William Kugel, John Cooper, J. A. Patterson, school directors; Charles P. Blair, George F. Douds, Fred Meany, auditors. The following are named election officers: Michael Mateer, judge; Jacob Streit, majority inspector; David Figley, minority inspector.

The township of Moon as now constituted, is declared a school district of the fouth class and the township of Center is also declared a school district of the fouth class.

News article from Nov 25, 1914.

After many subdivisions of Moon Township, late in 1914, Center Township was on the records and officially formed as part of Beaver County. As far as townships go, Center is considered a quite "young" one. With an agricultural background, the local Grange group was among the first to be organized in Center Township with the Center Grange Hall erected by 1922. Many of the individual aspects of maintaining a new and official township began to take place through the years including township officials, taxes, roads, police, businesses, then water and sewage service, et cetera. Finding specific information on Center Township from 1914 through the earlier 1950s proved quite difficult, yet I did manage to piece together some of this information. With very few official records now attainable through the township's offices, I have still tried to recreate, include, and provide as much information as could be found from various other sources.

Center Township lies in the northeastern corner of the south side in Beaver County, bordering for a short distance close to the bend along the Ohio River with Potter, Raccoon, Monaca, and Hopewell for its neighbors. In addition to the Ohio River there are several familiar smaller waterways that pass-through Center Township, with Raccoon Creek the largest of any having major volume or size. Raccoon Creek winds through Center Township at different points to the south of the township and bounds the township towards the west. It is used as a more common separator from the current townships of Potter and/or Raccoon. Besides Raccoon Creek and several small runs, Center Township also has that advantage of some access to that great river, the Ohio, running along a portion of its domain. (See the section on Streams and Creeks for more information.)

With Center Township being a young township by comparison, it must be remembered that any and all buildings erected in the 1800s are quite noteworthy and even those built from 1900 to 1919 may be considered only to be a bit over one hundred (100) years old today, but are some of the few remaining to hold the township's history. Although these homes, former schools, and a few other structures are not currently marked as "historical," I would personally like to help anyone living in one of these structures by providing them with the proper paperwork and will help with submitting the information to have a home or building approved and on record as being officially a "historical" building within the township. If you already know or find you are living in one of these structures from information you will find throughout this book and would like to have the building/home officially registered as historical, please do not hesitate to contact me for assistance.

Fun fact: The 1859 tax list included a total of assessments at the end of that year's listing. Note what were included to be of value to be included with these assessments:
Real Estate - $105,116
Personal - $10,444   \
Occupations - $4,400   Total of $124,974 (an increase of $378 from 1858)
Money in interest - $4,416 /
Carriages - $488
Watches - $110

Progress and additional residents just seemed to continually flood into the township over the years. For many years, much of the growth was a welcomed and needed updating and changing within the township. From its meager status at the time of erection, by 1980 there was a total of 3,403 units occupied in the township. In 1990 the total grew to 3,879 units. Rented housing progressed enough to be included with separate totals, those being, 1980 - 525 units for rent, 1990 - a total of 729, and in 2000 – 781. Single family dwellings continue to be the predominant type of housing in the township, but their total numbers actually declined when all of the total types of housing are considered. This decline was the result of two likely factors. 1) older residents had passed their properties on to younger family members and these younger persons just did/do not have the same passion for the value of owning larger homesteads/property, therefore selling off the property to developers of business properties. 2) developers erected condo type structures, gated communities, and/or apartment complexes. All this has aided to the increase in once large family properties of multiple acreage being just one single-family homestead, to now having multifamily spaces or many structures/homes being built on land. The United States Census Bureau now states that Center Township is made up of "a total area of 15.4 square miles (39.8 km^2), of which 15.1 square miles (39.0 km^2) is land and 0.31 square miles (0.8 km^2) or 1.95%, is water".

Between the 1950s and 1960s, people began moving from the more urban areas within Beaver County, to enjoy the more rural environment of Center Township. This environment was short lived and has continued to change throughout Center Township. It is now like a very much denser suburban community rather than being quieter and rural. Employment centers were permitted to develop within the township and currently Center Township has changed from its rural community beginnings to be a semi-suburban community with multiple employment centers, multiple hotels, a few higher education institutes. For the most part, all this occurred beginning in the 1960s.

Population of the current Center Township continues to grow as more and more of the rural lands are being bought and developed.   Populations have been recorded at:

1950 – 3,995	1970 – 10,598	1990 – 10,742
1960 - 7,113	1980 – 10,733	2000 – 11,492

Today, too much of the once open, undeveloped farmland has been greatly reduced. It has been replaced with one after another of housing developments, small and larger businesses and stores, gasoline stations, numerous mini-open air plazas, a large indoor shopping mall, industrial districts, abnormal number of hotels, massive parking lots, and countless other general changes.

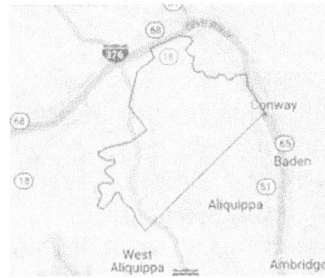 A simple outline of Center Township to give a visual view of its layout.

Fun fact: Whether Moon Township or Center Township, the actual location of the land was many, many times been referred to as to being "back of Monaca on the improved road." The number of miles referenced would vary depending on where or what they were referring to, but it always said "back of Monaca." The "improved road" would be Brodhead Road, which in the early 1900s was improved compared to other roadways, but not even close to what nowadays we would call improved. In these older references, with Moon/Center being a true rural area and not a "town," it was associated with the nearest town which was usually Monaca.   So, if you are reading any other early references to the Moon/Center Township area and find "back of Monaca," you should know they mean this area that is now Center Township.

Fun fact: Tradition is that Center Township received its name from being the "center property" of the original Moon Township after Raccoon and Potter Townships, including what was to become Monaca Heights, were all formed. The property remaining from the original Moon Township thus became the remaining land in the c<u>enter</u> of all this --- Center Township.

I have also attempted to bring to light how the creation of law enforcement and fire departments, residents moving from wells, outhouses, and septic systems to public water supplies and sewage service, and the development and maintenance of roads. Many, many of the residents settled and developed what was still Moon Township and continued into the erection of Center Township. From this, I will move on to some of the early homeowners and homesteads within Moon/Center Township. Following all this information will be the housing developments, then the businesses. Once the readers peruse through the information in this book, my hope is that it will be understood how so many of the early residents not only lived within what was Moon Township, but how they started various businesses and left the footprints that helped form the importance of the township of Center. After researching and knowing who many of the very early residents were, it is no surprise to myself that they still have descendants who have chosen to continue to live within the township – some even still living on former family land.

There are many noteworthy homes still standing in Center Township. In a separate section further, I have given descriptions of some of the first homes/houses as well as some information on various residents and families who either built or were early owners. (See the Homes and Families section of this book.)   It is surprising how many of the very early homes that were built in Moon Township from the mid 1800s to the early 1900s are still standing today, most still being used as residential homes.   A few of the former one room schoolhouses are also still standing. Their descriptions and locations may be found in the Education section of this book.

As I previously mentioned, Center Township itself has had a few smaller writings done on it. There was one smaller booklet written by Mrs. Mildred Dyke. Another was done by the township as a centennial booklet which included pictures and information provided by Denver Walton. Both booklets captured the more recent "past" of Center Township, sharing the businesses beginning from the mid 1900s and how some of the same families stayed and grew within the township. Each of them provides quite interesting information. Yet they had no thorough or formal recording of the very early people and pre 1950 businesses that gave Center Township its foothold and importance in Beaver County. These booklets are what gave me the appetite to explore more on the very early history of Moon/Center Township, do deeper researching, and bring to light the importance of many of the original residents.

Although progress, change, development, and modernization are inevitable and to some extent necessary, I am sure our ancestors and the first settlers/people/families to this township, and many other rural areas for that matter, would be quick to remind those making these current decisions that some respect, former history, and originality to all areas should never be simply tossed aside. These ancestors would agree that turning too much, and what is being proven disastrous in many cases, of the open land into concrete and asphalt, and only looking for the money aspect of things, is absolutely going to come back to haunt many very soon. History is history and if it is not preserved and respected, many will find you can never recreate natural and undeveloped land as it was presented to us when first created. (Sadly, those making the current decisions to approve any and all bits of land into some form of a "development" will not be alive to see the results and destruction they have "approved.")

Another purpose of writing this book, as well as my belief and my hope, is that everyone have a healthy respect for the past. We must recognize the importance of those that came before us and the care and respect they showed to the land and environment. In doing this, then township residents can see to it that our local officials have more respect, due diligence, and much better skepticism in understanding and for making their decisions. They need to consider how these decisions will truly impact current residents and future generations. Progress is important and keeps us moving forward, **but** more importantly, disrespect and forgetting the past is a dangerous and destructive path to take.

~ ~ ~

Once again, let me emphasize, there will be grayer areas with some of the boundaries of townships never being clear and much less defined from the boundaries as they are currently. This will be reflected in the various categories in this book that contain information on roads, residents, businesses, organizations, schools, and churches in Center Township, along with specifics of the township itself. This means that there may be mentions of some of the same category information and for some residents, both being from the then Potter, Raccoon, and Hopewell Township, as well as Monaca. Many people lived in one area and had a business in one of the others and vice versa. Many businesses could have serviced people from all these areas. Also, homesteads spanned over boundaries of one township into another. The census sheets are a very good example of how boundaries were not clearly defined. i.e. The Poor Farm census would be within the Moon/Center Township sheets for quite a few years, then found listed with Potter Township's for a few other years. This reflects how census enumerators tended to cross over township lines listing residents in one township one year, yet in another township the next. With all this, I wanted to make readers aware that they will find some sprinkling of surrounding areas' information and residents throughout this book. If readers are interested in knowing more specific details, there have been a few histories written on Potter Township. Readers may go to the Potter Township web site to read and learn more of the details on that township. Additionally, there are other publications on Raccoon and Hopewell Townships, as well as some formation of Beaver County.

CENTER TOWNSHIP'S
Municipal Buildings and Officials

The first township / municipal building was erected on Wilhelm Drive in the later 1950s. The building was constructed of large cement blocks. John Davidson made the donation of 4.33 acres on Wilhelm Drive to the township on May 22, 1950 (deeded the property to the township for $1.00), then in late Oct 1950, Ralph and Jayne Davis also donated another small parcel of adjacent land (also deeded for $1.00). The township supervisors planned to also use this building to house road equipment, trucks, and other equipment for maintenance throughout the township. This block building's looks have changed to some degree, but still stands today and is now the headquarters for the CT Road Department.

This building on Wilhelm Drive housed the township offices until the new building was built and dedicated at 224 Center Grange Road. The 14-acre plot of property on Center Grange Road was bought in 1970, with plans for 12.4 acres of this plot to be developed into recreational facilities (See Recreation section). Groundbreaking for the new municipal building was started in Feb 1973. Carl G. Baker and Associates were the architects for the project. The new township building was dedicated in Sep 1975. The building now houses a public meeting room, the Police Department, the Township Secretary and Administrative Staff Offices, the Water Authority, the Sewer Authority and storage and utility areas. Prior to 1993, the Water Authority had constructed an addition onto the rear of the building.

Former township office building on Wilhelm Drive, now home to the CT Road Department.

Center Township's Municipal Building (2019) – 224 Center Grange Road

At the time this book was being written, there were rumors of plans for a new township municipal building to be built, but I have no further information on this subject.

~ ~ ~

During the years prior to 1978, there was a total of only three supervisors that governed the township. The move to expand the board was sponsored by Center Citizens for Action and the Fourth District Democratic Committee. The voters approved a new five-member board in the 1977 general election. In Oct 1978, the Center Township voters followed through with their decision that "five heads are better than three" and the board of supervisors was expanded to five members. The township's Board of Supervisors currently still consists of five members. Though not a complete or official list at all, I did find various names for a few men who served as earlier township supervisors. (I apologize for any misspelled or omitted names.)

Some of the very early Moon Township names found include:
- 1805 – First Moon...John Baker and James McClelland; Second Moon...Ben
- 1806 – Second Moon...Benoni Dawson and James Craig
- 1807 – First Moon...Jonas Figley and John Baker; Second Moon...John Engles and John Thompson
- 1808 – First Moon...James McClelland and Robert Graham; Second Moon...Thomas Dawson and Samuel Wilson
- 1809 – First Moon...James McClelland and Robert Graham; Second Moon...Samuel Wilson and Thomas Dawson
- 18?? - John M. Stewart, Jr.
- 1885 – Charles Kugel
- 1898 – Christian Haller

When Judge Holt made the decree Nov 25, 1914, to form Center Township, the following officers were appointed to serve until the next general election, Constable-Elmer Sohn, Tax Collector-James E. Smith, Assessor-James E. Smith, Supervisors-Benjamin Forsythe, Frank Mateer, James Cochran, and Auditors-Charles P. Blair, George F. Douds, and Fred Meany. Additionally, there were the following election officers appointed, Judge-Michael Mateer, Majority Inspector-Jacob Streit, and Minority Inspector-David Figley. The official decree of division with Moon Township stated Shaffer's Post Office location would remain the fixed placed for holding elections. Center was also then declared a school district of the fourth class with School Directors-Anderson Davidson, Armstrong Gorsuch, William Kugel, John Cooper, J. A. Patterson.

For many of the earlier years, the supervisors held their meetings in the Monaca Bank in downtown Monaca, but in the 1950s, they began holding the meetings at the CT Water Authority building that was, and is still, located on the authority's property adjacent to the current Beaver Valley Mall area (at the far end of the parking lot area, behind the current Arby's and Burger King restaurants).

Between the years of 1929 and the 1990s, some of the names found of those serving as a supervisor in Center Township included (alphabetically), Anthony Amadio, Woodrow Aaron, Joseph E. Babich, Jr., Albert Bartosh, Edward Cochran (22 years), James Cochran, William DiCioccio, Sr., Fred Glasser, Henry Hartenbach, Sidney Huffmyer (28 years), Edward Kalinoski (1950s), Frank Kalinoski, Howard Kalinoski, James C. Lindey, Samuel Lucci, Burton McPherson, Frank Mateer, Martin M. Meiter, Mike Meiter, William Milne, Hilliary Milne, William Milne, R. A. Myers, George Setters, David E. Stewart, Fred Taddeo, Frank Vescio, David Weigle, Robert Wyres, Joseph Yezzi, and Joseph Zupsic.

Center Township Board of Supervisors as of mid-2019: William DiCioccio, Jr – Chairman, Dr. Michael Sisk – Vice Chairman, and members, Richard George, George Warzynski, and Lesa Mastrofrancesco.

Some other very early offices that were held in First and Second Moon Townships were:

First Moon
- 1805 – Overseers – Alexander Culberson, Daniel Weigle.
    - Auditors – David Scott, George Bruce, Jonas Figley, Daniel Christy.
    - Appraisers – William McGee, William Thompson.
- 1806 – Overseers – Matthias Hook, James Eaton.
    - Auditors – John Rainey, John Stanford, Benjamin Anderson, Samuel Searight.
- 1807 – Overseers – James Hutchison, Joseph Kerr.
    - Auditors – Samuel Law, John Rutherford, Alexander Walker, Robert Robertson.
- 1808 – Overseers – Wm. Connor, Edward Crail.
    - Auditors – Samuel Kennedy, David Smith, Michael Baker, Wade Barnes.
    - Appraisers – James Ewing, David Gordon.
- 1809 – Overseers – James Hutchinson, David McCoy.
    - Auditors – David Patton, David School, Samuel Law, Samuel Graham.

Second Moon
- 1805 – Overseers – Thomas Dawson, Samuel Searight.
  - Auditors – John Cain, Michael Baker, Robert Laughlin, James Eaton.
  - Appraisers – John Nelson, Andrew Poe.
- 1806 – Overseers – Mattias Hook, James Eaton.
  - Auditors – John Rainey, John Stanford, Benjamin Anderson, Samuel Searight.
- 1807 – Overseers – Andrew Poe, Robert Parks.
  - Auditors – James Anderson, Michael Baker, Isaac Barnes, Samuel Searight.
  - Appraisers – Samuel Christho, Elias Elliott.
- 1809 – Overseers – John Nelson, Mathias Hooke.
  - Auditors – Samuel Kennedy, David Smith, Wm. Little, Samuel Searight.
  - Appraisers – Andrew Poe, James Eaton.

In 1898, the Moon Directory listed:
- Clerk – W. S. Dunn
- Treasurer – J. S. Calvert
- Justices of Peace - James S. Calvert and James Prentise
- Constable – O. B. Elliott

I have no exact years, but prior to 1859, James S. Calvert was listed as serving as a Justice of the Peace. In the later 1800s, James Davis became an auditor and justice of the peace in the township. Samuel Burneson was also listed as serving in several township offices between c1836 and c1859. John P. Cooper served as a township auditor for six years in the very early 1900s.

Victor Bortnick, George M. Elish, and Lorretta J. McCon were among a few of the earlier township secretaries. Bernard Rabik was also found to have served as a township solicitor for several years.

As of mid 2019, the various township positions included, Plan Development Coordinator–Frank Vesscio, Planning Commission-Frank Vescio, Patrick McMullen, Dave Ambrose, Richard Gradisek, Karen Hall, Michael Dyrwal, Jack Smith, Dennis Morrison, John Peterson, Zoning Officer-John Plutko, Township Solicitor-Nicholas Urick, District Justice-Joseph Schafer, Township Engineer-Ned Mitrovich of Lennon Smith Souleret Engineering, Planning Consultant-Carolyn Yagle of Environmental Planning Consultant, Zoning Hearing Board-William Battisti, John McCracken, Robert Martini, George Paich, Jack Morrison, Secretary/Treasurer-Rachel DelTondo, and Asst. Secy/Treas-Virginia Schafer.

~ ~ ~

When Center Township was officially formed in 1914, James E. Smith was appointed to serve as the Tax Collector and the Assessor until the next general election. At age 74, his death certificate stated he was still serving as a tax collector. Some of the other various tax collectors for Center Township in later years have included……. George Huffmyer, David Lewis, Stanley Brobeck, Woodrow Aaron, and Dick Huff. Dick Huff was not only a former tax collector for Center but also for Potter Township, holding that position until 1977 until John Espey was voted in as tax collector in Potter Township.

The following names do not begin to cover all the years nor all the tax collectors or miscellaneous other officials of Center Township, but in going through earlier information and publications, these names surfaced so I wanted to include them (I indicated the year(s) if I found the information):
- …… Loretta J. McCon was a past township secretary
- ….. Larry Souleret was a past township engineer
- …… Eugene Morris was a past township solicitor
- …… 1910 - James Smith - tax collector (lived and had his office on "Sheffield Road" (Chapel Road)
- ….. late 1950s - Mrs. David Weigle – wage tax collector (lived on and had office on Center Grange Road)
- ….. 1960s – John Espey – tax collector for Potter Township
- ….. 1968 - Evelyn Salasky – township secretary and wage and earnings tax collector
- ….. 1970s and 1980s - Dick Huff – occupational tax collector

….. 1970s/1980s - Beulah Hallisey – mercantile tax collector
….. May 1988 – Bernadette Becker – appointed occupational tax collector
….. 1989 - Ann Simmons – Potter Township's occupational tax collector
….. 1991 - Bernadette Becker Girata – occupational tax collector
         Beulah Hallisey – mercantile tax collector
         Mary Cellini – wage tax collector
….. 1990s to 2019 - Bernadette Becker Bowser - tax collector
….. 2019 – the firm of Berkheimer of Lehigh Valley, PA now collects township taxes

~ ~ ~

Prior to the current Municipal/Township offices being located on Center Grange Road, there were no established or permanent offices for many of the officials of the township. In the late 1950s, I found residents would have to pay their accounts and taxes via many different locations and to specific individuals. Most established locations were either within a private home or in a place of business. Some of the early tax information found included…….
   …… water bills were paid at McCartney's Service Station
   …… taxes and streetlight assessments were paid to Woodrow Aaron who lived on Center Grange
        Road
   …… wage taxes were paid to Mrs. David Weigle who lived on Center Grange Road
   ….. fire hydrant assessments were paid to Mrs. George Setters at her home
   …… Lawrence Figley lived on Brodhead Road, and this is where you would obtain building permits.

The Municipal Building on Center Grange Road is now the central location for contacting many of all township officials for the paying of taxes, water and sewage bills, obtaining permits, contacting the C.T. Police Department, and the meeting location of township supervisors and other township departments.

~ ~ ~

CENTER TOWNSHIP'S
Law Enforcement

During the earlier years, many times there was no typical designation between Justice of the Peace, Magistrate and/or Squire. They all were part of the those who help enforce peace, heard local cases, and helped keep laws enforced. Often, nowadays a Justice of the Peace is also known as magisterial district judges.

When Beaver County was first formed, the governor of Pennsylvania appointed the first constables, then after, various positions in each township/area were elected. Listed below are some of the very early people who held the office of Constable in what were either portions of or what became Moon and/or Center Township:

... James Jordon came to Moon Township in 1784 and was the first constable of Moon Township.

... 1804 appointed positions:
  First Moon: Samuel Allison – Constable.   Second Moon: Thomas Dawson - Constable.

... 1805 elected positions:
  First Moon: James Jordan - Constable.   Second Moon: John Thompson – Constable.

... 1806 elected positions:
  First Moon: Samuel Wilson and George Baker – Constables
  Second Moon: John Thompson – Constable

... 1807 elected positions:
  First Moon: William Thompson-Constable.   Second Moon: John Crail – Constable.

... 1808 elected positions:
  First Moon: Robert Hood – Constable.   Second Moon: Noah Potts – Constable.

... 1809 elected positions:
  First Moon: Robert Hood – Constable.   Second Moon: Nathaniel Blackmore–Constable

Prior to 1803, there was but one sheriff who served a specific term for all of Beaver County.
Note – this is an accumulated list -- not all listed were Moon/Center Township residents and may have been from all over Beaver County, yet would have serviced Moon Township.

- 1803-06 – William Henry
- 1806-09 & 1812-15 – Jonathan Coulter
- 1809-12 – Samuel Power
- 1815-18 & 1833-36 – William Cairns
- 1818-21 – James Lyon
- 1821-24 – Thomas Henry
- 1824-27 - John Dickey
- 1827-30 – David Porouter
- 1830-33 – J. A. Sholes
- 1836-39 – Matthew T. Kennedy
- 1839-42 – David Somers
- 1842-45 – Milo Adams
- 1845-48 – James Kennedy, Jr.
- 1848-51 – Robert Wallace
- 1851-54 – George Robinson
- 1854-57 – James Darragh
- 1857-60 – William W. Irwin
- 1860-63 – John Roberts
- 1863-66 – Joseph Ledlie
- 1866-69 – J. S. Little/Littell
- 1869-72 – John Graebing
- 1872-75 – Chamberlin White
- 1875-78 – J. P. Martin
- 1878-81 – Mark Wisener
- 1881-84 – Henry E. Cook
- 1884-87 – John D. Irons
- 1893-96 – Oliver Molter
- 1899-1902 – J. Henry Geer
- 1903-   - Howard Bliss

I also found listings through previous years for the following who were Moon/Center Township residents, but many have no specific dates or years of terms attached. (listed alphabetically)

--- James L. Aultman – Justice of the Peace - Brodhead Road (James L. was born in c1891.) He served for 18 years (probably in mid 1900s). When he unexpectedly died, his wife …
--- Frances A. Aultman served the remaining years of her husband's term.
--- Walter J. Cochran, Jr. – Justice of the Peace – Brodhead Road (mid to later 1900s).
--- Art Coombs - elected Beaver County Commissioner in 1920. Served as commissioner for 28 years–7 terms.
--- James Davis - Squire - was a justice of the peace for many years. (mid 1800s to 1906).
--- Louis D. Hibar – became Center Township Constable in 1952, then police officer/chief.
--- James Irons - justice of the Peace beginning 1883, also served at least two terms as Burgess of Water Cure.
--- Joseph Lakas – Justice of the Peace – lived on Brodhead Road (1980s).
--- George W. Shroads of Bellowsville held many township offices in the mid to later 1800s including constable for 15 years and justice of the peace.
--- Dan Swantko – Justice of the Peace – Ivy Lane.
--- William Shroads was a Constable for 15 years and Justice of the Peace for 30 years. He was also the county commissioner (1859-1860) and held the position of steward of the county home for 13 years. (all in the mid-1800s to early 1900s).
--- Daniel B. Short was the county commissioner - 1862-63.
--- G. W. Shroads was the county commissioner – 1875-78.
--- James Todd was elected county commissioner – 1888-91.

When Center Township was official formed from Moon Township, Elmer Sohn was appointed to serve as the Constable until the next general election.

Up until 1975, commissioners served only two year terms, then under the Constitution of 1874 the term was made three years.
--- Joseph Liberati – District Magistrate / lawyer – Gee Bee Plaza (in 1970s) / then Brodhead Road. With the rental fee for Joseph Liberati's office in the Gee Bee Plaza being raised, the county wanted to find a new more affordable office space found. Beaver County Commissioners tabled actions being taken for a court recommendation to relocate the office of Center's district justice of the peace to a space in the A & R Complex on Brodhead Road but in Oct 1977, there was a five-year lease proposed for the space.

There was a law in effect which prohibited magistrates and police from being housed in the same building, so, the Beaver County District Court #36-3-03 is currently located in its own building in Center Township, built at 226 Center Grange Road, adjacent to the Township Building. Joseph Shaffer - District Justice - 2006 to current.

Fun fact: Nov 1946 – the whole township had but one polling place. Voting was done at the Center Grange Hall.   That same year, Potter Township also only had one polling place – the County Home Hospital.

~ ~ ~

Police Department
Center Township Police Department

Among all the information I read through, there were several listings of who was either chief of police, acting police chief, or assistant police chief. The names and/or positions changed and often crossed over through the years.......
    ..... at least the 1940s to 1955 –Louie Hibar, Police Chief
    ..... 1955 through 1958 – Dante Colaluca, Police Chief
    ..... 1958 through 1966 – Dante Colaluca, Assistant Police Chief
    ..... 1958 through 1965 – Louie Hibar, Police Chief
    ..... 1966 through 1996 – Dante Colaluca, Police Chief
    ..... Jul 1958 – Michael Mezmar, acting police chief while Chief Hibar was on a 3-week vacation

Fun facts: In Feb 1952, Constable Louis D. Hibar posted his own statement in the local paper that residents were to keep their dogs confined or be subject to a fine and costs. His action was prompted by complaints of several township residents. He also issued a warning to motorists who had been passing stopped school buses and that this practice was endangering the lives of children. He stated that several drivers had already received fines of $25 and that a crackdown on this violation would be enforced.

Louis D. Hibar

The first records of Center Township having a police chief found was in around the mid-1940s -- he was Louis Hibar. For many years, Chief Hibar not only served as the police chief, but he was the only officer and just doubled as the chief. When Chief Hibar began as police chief, and for close to twenty more years, times were a bit different. There were no official vehicles provided through the township, so he had to work out of his own car. With the area still being quite rural, he would get such important calls as escaped cows or chickens needing to be chased down. With only 100+ families living in the township, it was quite easy for there to be a very personal connection between Chief Hibar and all the people in the township. He even knew the names of each child in the township.

    There were no radios for communication between surrounding areas, so, except for a telephone call, the police in Monaca or Aliquippa had no up-to-date idea what was happening in Center Township, and vice versa. Chief Hibar would have to walk to the closest home and knock on someone's door to use their phone or he would use his own in his home. If he broke down somewhere, needed to call county control to retrieve or supply information, to request assistance, or to call for an ambulance if needed in the case of an accident was far from as easy as just using a radio in the car. Mr. Hibar was listed as also holding the position of constable in 1952. He was married to Helen, and they had a son and two daughters.

~ ~ ~

Dante Colaluca

Dante Colaluca, more commonly and fondly known as Danny, began to work with the township police department when still quite a young man. Moving up from being the assistant Police Chief, Danny became listed as the Police Chief in Center Township as early as 1955. It was considered a part-time position and at that time, his monthly salary was $125.00, yet he was expected to be more or less "on call" as needed. Danny graduated from Aliquippa High School and signed up for the military police. While serving for 18 months in Frankfurt, Germany, he worked with the German police. Danny has stated that this provided the foundation for his career. Several months after his discharge from the service in 1955, he was accepted with the state police. At that time, they did not permit you to get married and you could be transferred anywhere at will. He was not fond of those conditions, so he chose to answer an ad by Center Township for a chief of police. In an interview, Mr. Colaluca stated that he remembered meeting with three supervisors after making his application for the position, and he was hired. He had to purchase his own outfit. He could not find a hat, but bought a shirt, a gun, and his leather gun belt. He also got a siren from a nearby funeral director and installed it in his car. As stated above and was the practice with former Chief Hibar, Chief Colaluca also had to work out of his own car and had to pay for all the gasoline he used. Even in the mid to late 1950s, there were still less than 200 families in the township, and Chief Colaluca also knew all the people by name. Danny Colaluca married Janet and they had a son and a daughter.

1988

Danny served as the police chief until 1958 when politics changed in the township. He was then demoted to patrolman. There were only three officers working in the township at that time. Between 1958 and 1966, many articles reflected that Danny was assistant police chief. In 1966, he was once again placed in the position of Police Chief but this time he was the first full-time chief for the township. There were still only three officers in the department. The township had purchased a police car for the department by 1966. For many years, Center Township did not have an office for the police chief, nor a lock up facility, so they used the Monaca jail on an as need basis.

The police department grew and improved greatly thanks to Chief Colaluca's dedication to the department. He was responsible for the department receiving weapons training courses through the county. Eventually, he became a certified instructor and would then qualify other officers on the shooting range. Chief Colaluca never wavered in his dedication to the township or his position. He received countless accommodations and awards, including FBI training course on narcotics and drugs. In Jan 1988, he was inducted into the International Police Association's Hall of Fame, being selected because "he has so many unusual qualities in his background." "...the (selection) committee felt he was one cop who was above the crowd."

Being Chief of Police is not always an easy and uneventful position. Mid Aug 1982, Chief Colaluca applied for a job in Sarasota, Fla. after being involved in a reported public disagreement with a then township supervisor who discussed a "confidential and privileged" report regarding the security at the Beaver Valley Mall, making the information of the report public. Chief Colaluca was very upset because the discussion disclosed a report that detailed what kind of security measures and patrols were being done. He felt the exposure of all this information could endanger the public in general.

Fortunately, Chief Colaluca did not resign or take the job in Florida but remained as chief of police until he retired in 1996. Upon retiring, Chief Colaluca appointed John Swogger as acting police chief until the supervisors appointed a new Chief of Police. In 1997, many citizens made it known that they were very upset that the supervisors did not appoint Mr. Swogger to the position of Police Chief permanently. The citizens stated that he had been a resident and taxpayer in the township for 25 years, was a policeman in Center for 20 years, had a degree in criminology, and was the acting police chief after Danny Colaluca retired. The township supervisors approved hiring Mr. Barry Kramer of Economy Township as the new Police Chief of Center Township. Chief Kramer is still currently serving as Center Township's Chief of Police (2019).

Police Officers................

In lieu of the rise in certain crimes within the township, in the spring of 1984, the township's supervisors appointed patrolman Steve Drobac as a full-time criminal investigator (at the same rate as he earned being a full-time policeman). Mr. Drobac would be investigating both adult and juvenile crimes. Part-time patrolman Maxim Strano was promoted to full-time to replace Drobac. At the same meeting, the supervisors also hired two new part time patrolmen – Phillip Sciaretta and James Chernko, both township residents (each had either completed the 480 hours of state-mandated police training or were in the process of completing the training at that time).

As a result of the steel mill shutdowns, the Board of Supervisors was forced to lay off nine police officers in 1984 for budgetary reason, but by 1985, there were ten full-time and twelve part-time officers included on the Center Township Police force. The Center Township Police Department has grown over the years to accommodate the growth of the residents and businesses in the township. As stated, since 1997, Mr. Barry Kramer has served as Chief of Police. The CTPD now has approximately 30 officers and more than twelve vehicles. One recent addition to the police department happened in 2011. Sgt. Cindric was certified as the first Center Township Police K-9 handler and was assigned to "Ingo" (a German Shephard) as his new partner. Ingo and Sgt. Cindric have been responsible for hundreds of thousands of dollars of drug seizures, and they were awarded the Howard Murray award in 2013 for outstanding police service.

The protection and services of the CTPD has been more than sufficient for all residents and the entire task force is congratulated on their excellent services provided to the township. Unfortunately, the more recent lack of many police involved incidents being published or included in the local newspaper or made available to the general public makes it impossible to include any deserving accounts in this book. In all previous years, there were numerous informational articles and publications available to keep residents abreast of precautions and/or happenings within the township but in conversation, one older resident stated that she feels the township is not as much of the utopia as it appears to be since there is now the lack of sharing such information – be it good or bad news/information. Many residents still feel happenings should be made available to current residents and the public. It would be very informative to know of a rash of break-ins or vandalization to homes, cars, mailboxes, businesses, et cetera. This type of notice of ongoing happenings and actions would help keep residents much better informed and prepared. Again, in general, all appears to show that the CTPD has and is doing a very fine job of maintaining as safe an environment as possible whether residents of the township are informed or not.

Fact: Beaver County's waterways have many various amounts of commerce passing through them daily and also are considered as being the largest recreational area in the county. Therefore, the establishment of a jointly owned and operated patrol boat partnership for the Beaver and Ohio Rivers was being discussed with the police departments of Beaver Borough and Center Township, including the municipalities of Center and Vanport Township. This project was to be the beginning of forming a task force between the municipalities with the water waterways of Beaver County. The boat used was a law enforcement model Boston Whaler, fully equipped including a trailer and a tow vehicle.

~ ~ ~

Potter Township Police Department

This book is intended to provide information on Center Township, but with the close ties to Potter Township, I chose to include the following information. This is in no way a "history" of The Potter Township Police Department, but to simply provide some information.

Potter Township Police Department was started in 1950, with Danny Huskins being the first police chief. The department was in the municipal building but moved in Aug of 1976, to the building that last housed the Potter Beer Distributor on Frankfort Road. The garage building beside the municipal building was renovated and the police department then moved to that location.

The Potter Township Board of Supervisors "shut down" the Potter Township Police Department in 1998. At the time the department was suspended, there was an investigation being conducted for providing coverage of Potter Township, the state police had been responding to calls in Potter. Potter officials were going to review contracting Vanport, Center, and/or Raccoon Townships to provide their services. Jun 10, 1999, with the Potter Township Police Department disbanded, the Potter Township Board of Supervisors approved a Joint Municipal Agreement for Law Enforcement Services between the Township of Potter and the Township of Center. This basically meant that the Center Township Police Department was contracted to also provide coverage in Potter Township.

Bits and pieces of information found:
    Thomas Malloy was justice of peace in Potter Township in 1953.
    Bob George was the Chief of Potter Police for several years (at least in 1970s)
    1981 – Terry Walton was a Potter Township officer

~ ~ ~

Fire Departments

Moon Township Fire Department

Prior to the erection of Center Township and the formation of the Center Township Fire Department was the Moon Township Fire Department. The current Monaca Fire Department No. 4 was at one time called the Moon Township Fire Department. The original Moon Township Fire Department was organized Nov 17, 1912 and Chartered Jun 5, 1925. On Jun 1, 1913, a 50-gallon chemical engine was purchased from funds that had been raised. A small fire house was built, and they bought a fire bell from Heckman Bros. Hardware (downtown Monaca). Soon a 24' x 40' building was erected on a lot they purchased at the corner of Taylor Avenue and Bechtel Street. A bell tower was attached, and the fire bell installed. In Jun 1925 they purchased a new truck with four, 40-gallon chemical tanks, two hose reels, and a 1000 foot of hose. In 1930, the now Monaca Heights area of Moon Township became annexed to the Monaca Borough. Monaca added two more volunteer fire departments following this annex of the area, both providing protection and servicing the new Monaca Heights area. In Dec 1930, a water supply now being assured, the truck was changed into a combination chemical and hose equipment.

Following this annex, the name of the fire department became the Monaca Heights Fire Company – Fourth Ward with the address of 1031 Bechtel Street. This firehall is now called Monaca Heights Volunteer Fire Department – No. 4. They then built a new building in 1964 at 913 Taylor Avenue and the old one storey frame fire hall was sold to the highest bidders of Ronald and Joan Ciccozzi. The Ciccozzis planned on using it for storage and display purposes for their refrigerating and air conditioning business. Over time there was also a pizza business in the front of the building.

The first officers were President-Frank Rambo, Secretary-E.E. Elmer, Treasurer-W. A. Dalzell, and Chief-R.M. Winkle. There was a Ladies Auxiliary to the Moon Township Fire Department/Monaca Heights Fire Department. It was organized by six women Apr 14, 1914, Mrs. Charles Pike, Mrs. Thomas, Mrs. Winkle, Mrs. Dalzell, Mrs. Clarence Panner, Mrs. Wadatz, Mrs. Elizabeth Davis, and Mrs. Creese (1st Pres.).

1913 Little Beaver Historical Society

Former station building at corner of Bechtel Street and Taylor Avenue.

current – Taylor Avenue

Center Township Volunteer Fire Units

Center Township is currently serviced by all volunteer fire fighters. There are three companies located within the township – Stations 36, 37, and 38.

The Center Township Fire Department was organized in the Bluebird Dance Hall on Brodhead Road in 1929/1930. (This dance hall stood in the vicinity of the current Lincoln Homes area – tradition has it on Mike Meiter's property.) They were chartered on Nov 25, 1930. Jack Coombs was elected as the first President of the company and Mike Meiter was named the first fire chief. The fire station members then used Rosa (Cochran) Engle's garage on Brodhead Road for the first few months after they were chartered. Rosa's garage and property were listed very close to that of Mike Meiter on the 1930 census. Rev. W. J. Engle owned property around the former Golden Dawn supermarket and Lincoln Drive. (With his property near the current Lincoln Homes and Snowy White Cleaners, then the James O. and Rosa Engle farm evidently was not very far from that location.)

Some of the known officers included Albert C. Solkovy-President (1950s) and Fire Chief (1972), Woodrow V. Aaron-President, A. B. Miller-Vice president, Robt. E. Merriman-Secretary, Robert Bickerton-Treasurer, and Line Officers (all in 1950s). Additional names found were Stanley Boden, Evertt Patterson, and Leo Parrish. One article stated that Evertt Patterson served as a former fire chief for about twenty years.

The first fire truck was built in 1931 from a Chevrolet truck.

This picture was published in the local newspaper in Oct 1956. Underneath this picture was a statement that the officials of the three volunteer fire units in Center Township were upset over the condition of the truck in the picture. The three units were behind a drive to convince the township voters to approve a two-mill increase in their property tax which would be used to help the units purchase needed equipment. The men in this picture are – L to right – E. M. Patterson-President of Fire Company No. 1, Paul Gillin-assistant chief of Company No. 3, and L. A. Morris-assistant chief of Company No. 2.

They then purchased a 1951 Federal Fire Truck, which was in use for over 50 years.

Center Township Fire Co. No 1 –   Station 36 - 3385 Brodhead Road (corner of Main Street/Brodhead Road)

A new fire hall was erected on part of the Sohn farm, that building was razed late in the 1950s or in the early 1960s. The new station, a block building, was completed in 1964 at the same location - the corner of Main Street and Brodhead Road. The company had two trucks, and a new siren was installed on the tower of their building at this time.

The Ladies Auxiliary for Fire Company No. 1 was organized in August of 1938. The first president of the group was Mrs. Josephine Prosser.

Engines are currently (2019) all royal blue and white. As of mid-2019, officers of the CTVFD included, Daniel McHattie-President, William D. Brucker-Vice President, James Arner-Treasurer, Sophia Zeiber-Secretary, William D. Brucker-Chief, Ed Kallen-Assistant Chief, Rod Biskup, Sr.-Fire Police Chief, and James Warner-Fire Police Lieutenant. The CTVFD relies heavily on donations. All which are used entirely for providing fire service to the township, so, remember to donate to the CTVFD as often as possible to help support funds needed beyond what is covered by taxpayer dollars.

Current building (2018)
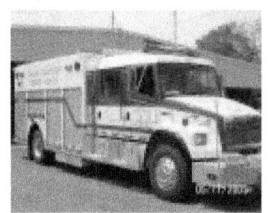

Center Township Fire Co. No 2 – Station 37 - 108 Grandview Avenue

The need for a fire company in the Sylvan Crest neighborhood was realized when the Mchaffey home burned in 1943, therefore this company was organized Mar 9, 1943.   Homer Morgan gave a piece of land to the Company on Grandview Avenue. Well-known businessman in Monaca and then in Rochester, Morris Barnett's home was moved to Sylvan Crest when the Monaca-Aliquippa Boulevard was being built over the Barnett property. This house became the first building of the Volunteer Fire Company No. 2 Sylvan Crest when it was donated in 1944 by the County Commissioners. In 1948, the men bought cement blocks and built the current front part of the fire hall. They purchased their first truck from the Ohioview Fire Company, and the Center Township Fire Company No. 1 donated the first siren to this company.   The siren was installed at the Lawrence Morris home.   Mrs. Morris would sound this siren each day at noon.   The original two stall garage/station was completed in 1971 and has since been remodeled.

First officers elected at CT Fire Co. No. 2 were Russell Butts-Pres., John Grimes-Vice Pres., James Irwin-Secy, Gerald Crizer-Financial Secy, Charles Harper-Fire Chief, and Lawrence Morris-Asst. Fire Chief. Some of the members included Spencer Boyer, William Milne, David Milne, Clarence Bailes, Joseph Harper, James Harper, and John Stainecker.   The 1950s officers included James Matthews-President, John Close-Vice president, Charles Derflinger-Secreatary, Richard Walker-Treasurer; line officers included Joseph Harper, John Fleishman, and L. Morris.

The Ladies Auxiliary to Company No. 2 was organized on Jan 9, 1946.   This auxiliary was chiefly responsible for this fire company obtaining their funds and they also raised the money to modernize the fire hall.   The first officers were Mrs. W. Edmonds-Pres., Mrs. Frances Boyer Vice Pres., Mrs. James Irwin-Secy, Mrs. David Milne, Treas, Mrs. Ina Swan, Mrs. Margie Bailes, Mrs. Ray

Johnson, Mrs. William Milne, Sr., Mrs. William Milne, Jr., Mrs. Lawrence Morris, Mrs. Alice Crizer, Mrs. Delores Mchaffey, Mrs. Spencer Boyer, Mrs. Hugo Eder, and Mrs. Annabele Pratt. Two other surnames of the auxiliary charter members were Smith and Reese.

Center Township Fire Co. No 2 – 108 Grandview Avenue..................

Then

Current

Center Township Fire Co. No 3 – Station 38 - 110 Vankirk Road

This company held their organizational meeting in July of 1946 in the Vankirk Lutheran Church. The first members included John Egyud, Earl, Ed, and Emil Erickson, Abe Fath, Nathan Moore, Walter Reynolds, Steve Perun, George Sahayda, Garlnd Wells, Martin Winkle, and William Zeiber. In 1948, the fire hall was erected on Monaca Road in the Vankirk area and was remodeled late in the 1950s/early 1960s. Henry Erickson was the first president and John Zupsic the first fire chief. The current building was erected on Vankirk Road.

The Ladies Auxiliary to Fire Company No. 3 was organized with 14 members in Nov of 1946.

The former firehall building on Monaca Road.

This building is still standing.

Early picture of firehall building

and

current view of firehall building built on Vankirk Road.

1960 – all three of Center Township's fire departments organized into one unit to operate more efficiently instead of as three separate companies. They became the Center Township Volunteer Fire Department but still have the three separate station numbers, separate locations of the fire halls, and separate trucks at each station. The first officers of the combined departments were Woodrow V. Aaron-President, Ronald Winkle-Vice president, Robt. E. Merriman-Secretary, Albert C. Solkovy-Treasurer, and Donald Erickson-Chief. It was a great help to these companies when the township citizens voted to provide them with funding through taxes.

~ ~ ~

Potter Township Volunteer Fire Department

Organized Jun 9, 1952, and was originally housed on Frankfort Road in the building last and best known as the home to the Potter Beer Distributors. This same building was once a private residence and then Koppers owned it. By using the building for their fire truck, it also insured Koppers' safety. They moved in 1966 when the addition to the municipal building was completed. In 2003, a new fire department building was started on land that had been donated to the Township by ZCA on the corner of Bauer Road and Mowry Road. Their current address is 247 W Mowry Road.

The original slate of officers was Andrew W. Factor-President, Joseph A. Parsons-Vice President, Robert A. Ritzmann-Secretary, Robert Dunn, Jr.-Treasurer, D. L. Merriman-Chief, and W. S. Carlton-Assistant Chief. Other known officers include A. F. Laughner-President, L. Harkins-Vice President, N. L. McCoy-Treasurer, J. Espey-Secretary, M. Short-Chief, and A. Cwynar-Assistant Chief. They operated a 1956, 500-gallon tank, mid-ship mounted pump truck, as well as a 1948 GMC 500-gallon tank truck with a bumper-mount pump.

~ ~ ~

Water Authority

Prior to Center Township providing their public water system, residents of the township always relied on well water. Wells were one of humans' earliest construction activities next to shelter. Most of the early farms and homesteads had a larger hole that was bored out and sometimes lined with brick. Most times, for safety reasons, a cover was placed over the hole, and some constructed a simple pulley type structure for raising and lowering buckets into the well.

Drilling a well in the 1800s was not an easy task. Many of the first wells were dug by hand, while others began to be dug with the use of a spring-pole and manual labor. A bit would be used and would have to forcibly hit the ground or rock. A spring pole system was only as reliable as the strength and endurance of the man/men operating it.

Spring-pole system

Walking beam

Following the spring-pole system, but before steam power engines became more common, wells were dug with a horse powered treadle rigged to a walking beam. A horse would be placed on a treadmill device which provided the power for the drill and did what the manual spring-pole did.

The cable-tool device was eventually used in place of the spring-pole and walking beam devices. The walking beam and cable-tool device concepts continued into the 1920s and sometimes the 1950s depending on the area even though there were drilling machines available then.

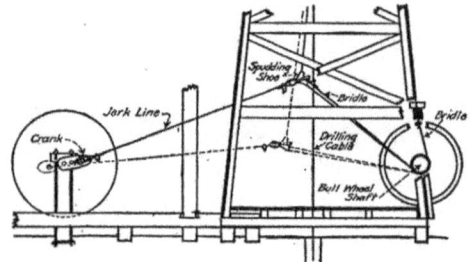
Cable-tool device

Each homestead had its own well that was drilled and maintained totally by that homeowner. Seldom did more than one home share a well. Often it would depend on where an adequate well of water could be found which would determine where the actual location of the house would be situated. It was important to have a well that was easily accessible to the house since a well had to provide enough water to meet the needs for drinking, cooking, showering/bathing, water for animals, crop irrigation, and if/when needed – fire protection.

As neighborhoods began to form and homes were built closer to each other, often this caused problems because a new homeowner would find a good well/water supply, but it was often the same source that supplied water to an adjacent or surrounding homes. This was a problem because that meant that more people were drawing water from that supply source of water and the "supply and demand" might cause a well to go dry when previously it supplied more than was needed by the first person to tap the source.

Fun Fact: The Stones, Spechts, Skelly, Dykes, and McCartney's all lived in the Pleasant Drive area.   The Dyke family property had a hand-dug well which was round, 16 feet deep, dug out of solid shale, and was walled up by Frank Mateer.   (Oh…. can you imagine going down in a tubular hole like that to work!!)

Hand pumps were being used as early as the 1800s.   Hand pumps were installed very close to, if not right over the borehole to a well.   They were manually operated, using human-power to draw the needed water from the well.

The manual pumps were eventually replaced with electric pumps. These were usually housed in an addition, a lean to, or separate "pump house" adjacent to the main home and instead of just providing water to the kitchen sink or an outside trough, would provide water to all desired areas of a home. Most electric pumps use suction to draw the water from the well.

Fun Fact: Almost every home had "rain barrels" for collecting and storing water. Rather than exhausting precious well water, the "rainwater" was used for washing clothes and cars, using in the yard/gardens, livestock and/or crop irrigation. A large barrel was placed under a down spout of a rain gutter and when one barrel would be filled, another would be put in its place.

Fact: In Aug 1930, there was a traveling laboratory located in Rochester by the Secretary of Health to service sections in this area of Pennsylvania. Any homeowner who was uncertain as to the purity of their private water supplies could notify Dr. John Stevens-County Medical Director or A.C. Brown-Pennsylvania Department of Health. These two gentlemen would notify this laboratory which would then send representatives to the source of the private water supply and run tests. There was no charge for this service.

The Citizens Council began to push for a water system in Center Township in Nov of 1951. The council chose to center their attention and time about water because it was the main topic most residents in the township were most interested in since many were experiencing difficulties with their existing wells (excessive minerals, taste, discoloration of laundry, wells running dry, et cetera).

Fact: Well waters tend to contain many minerals indigenous to an area. In Center Township, iron and probably manganese (since they are sister elements) were a problem. It would many times not react well with bleach when the laundry was done using the water from the well rather than rainwater. The bleach would oxidize the metals in the well water and caused a brownish tint to all the whites and very light-colored clothes. Also, an ongoing problem was the brownish/red ring that would form around the inside of a washing machine, wash basin, or white porcelain bathtubs or sinks.

A committee of residents was sent out to canvass the township's homeowners regarding the need for a public water system.   (For genealogy enthusiasts....) This committee consisted of Mrs. John Edmond, Mrs. Logan Brubaker, Mrs. Bryon Collins, Mrs. Elbert O. Cone, Joseph Reinish, Clair T. Allison, John C. Kier, Eugene Geist, H. R. Dickson, Eric Garing, J. D. Baker, A. T. Albright, G. E. Brock, C. Jane Brock, Michael Mikula, Robert Bickerton, R.R. Morris, Louis D. Hibar, George Belich, Eli Uzelac, Steve Chunchick, Carmine Celeste, Andrew Minzak, Jr., L. A. Roosa, Paul Marthens, Woodrow Aaron, Howard Roosa, and Elmer Carlson.   Between mid-1952 and Jan 1953, more than 700 homeowners were contacted and agreed to the proposed water system plan.

During 1953 and 1954, contracts were signed, mapping of where lines were to go was determined, and tap-in fees were collected from those residents who signed for water. The Citizens Council ordered $9,777.11 worth of copper pipe and valves to be used for water lines from the main trunk line and going into the residents' homes.

The council asked the supervisors (William Milnes, Fred Glasser, and Ed Kalinoski) for monies from the 1952 budget to be set aside to pay for half of a water survey, and the Beaver County Planning Commission was asked to cover the other half of the cost. In Mar of 1952, the supervisors and BC Planning Commission both agreed to pay their share of the water survey. There was a reduced tap in fee for those early prospective water users in 1953. The reduced fee was $60 and all those signing up after the set deadline of Oct 1, 1953, would have to pay $90. Once construction started and the pipeline was completed, the tap in fee would be $125. Homeowners also had to pay for their own personally needed copper pipe and hardware. The cost was 41 cents per foot for the pipe and a valve placed beyond the homeowner's meter was $1.50. Negotiations were also done with property owners for the location of storage tanks. By the date of the deadline for payment of tap-in fees, all residents involved had paid and were assured of a $6 per month water rate.

What seemed like overnight, Center Township residents started to see major work occurring along Brodhead Road with trenches being dug along roadways and through lawns to accommodate the new water lines. There were mounds of the massive pipeline everywhere just waiting to be laid.

With the cut-off date of Oct 1st quickly approaching, in mid Sep 1953, the Center Township Water Authority placed a notice in the Daily Times to make one last call to all township residents who had to-date not contracted for water services and thereby being able to take advantage of a reduced tap-in fee of $60.   After Oct 1st, residents were then charged the full $90 for contracts signed before the construction was started, after the pipeline was completed, they were charged $125. The township took full advantage of almost all families in Center having children attending school and distributed information to the residents by sending all information and updates with the children to give to parents. One such distribution was a compiled report by the water authority of the progress of the number of contracts for water services that were signed as of Oct 1st.

At the Citizens' Council meeting the end of Jan 1954, the bylaws of the Water Authority were read to all those in attendance at the meeting. Then at a meeting the end of Apr in 1954, the Citizens' Council announced that Randall Hewing would be doing ditch digging and back filling for water lines at a charge of 25 cents per foot.

By the end of May in 1954, the Center Township Water Authority and the Center Township Citizens' Council announced that the first well for the new water system had been dug.   The well was located adjacent to the St. Joseph Lead Company and reported as 104 feet in depth. They also stated that even without the actual pump testing, it was declared "unofficially successful".   The St. Joseph Company gave their permission and signed all the paperwork for water lines to cross its property.   Six hundred and twenty homeowners had signed for water and agreed to pay the tap-in fee and the council was out collecting tap-in fees with that deadline for payment approaching.   The Citizens' Council also reported that the deadline to order ¾ inch copper pipe would be Mar 15, 1955. The pipe could be purchased from the council as well as the valves. The valves were placed beyond the meter on the individual water line allowing the shutting on and off of water as needed. The first of Jul 1954, the Center Township Water Authority had placed an ad to receive bids on one 300,000-gallon steel reservoir, foundation for this reservoir, one 250,000-gallon elevated steel tank, foundation for elevated tank, domestic water meters, various lengths/ lineal feet of 2", 4", 6", and 8" water lines, two wells complete with pumps, and well pump control station.

Center Township residents now had public water……well, *almost* all residents…. the Stobo district of the township was not included in the water system as it was too far from the water lines. In 1958, the water authority was petitioned to see if these lines could be extended for Stobo. Some areas of Sylvan Crest were also excluded and received their water from the Borough of Monaca for many years. In May 1982, the Monaca Borough Council was asking for bids to supply around seventeen homes in the Sylvan Crest area of Center Township with water. Why… well, even though Sylvan Crest property owners live within Center Township, their water had been traditionally piped from Monaca's supply through former private lines in the development since around 1926.

There was a building erected off Brodhead Road for the water pumps and it also was used as a city building. A huge tank for water storage was located on the former Robert Good property, Gross Drive. Currently (2019), there are two water storage tanks located at this site. The second elevated storage tank was erected after the Water System Master Plan in c2004.

Two current towers/tanks adjacent to Gross Drive.

Fun Fact: It is evident that the Center Township Water Authority considered the elevation of this site on Gross Drive when they chose to erect each of these two township water storage tanks. The property in the area of these two water towers on Gross Drive was part of the original Baker estate, which was purchased by the Gross, then Good family, then, Robert Good sold this portion to the Turney family. According to a government geological survey, this is the highest point on the south side of the Ohio River. The location in Big Knob is reported the highest in Beaver County and is only 12 feet higher than this one in Center Township.

A tower once stood at this geological point and a cement marker was placed where the tower once stood. People who did get to climb the tower before it was removed reported the view was magnificent. At the time Robert Good sold the property to the Turneys, using the former tower, the surveyors of the property could spot a light at night from another geological point on Lilac Street, Squirrel Hill in Pittsburgh.

Next there was a 400,000-gallon water tank erected on a piece of property on a hill in the St. James Park housing plan. This piece of property is located just off the Brodhead Road, accessed from within St. James Park. The current water tanks are quite visible from many areas even outside the township since, like the location of the other tank(s), this property sits on one of the higher land areas in the township. The legality of a permit to erect the first, smaller water tank adjacent to the homes of St. James Park was challenged at first because the township zoning ordinance prohibited construction of the tank in that area.

Two tanks along Brodhead Road.

As additional housing and businesses kept growing within the township, so did water tap-ins, so, the Water Authority found they also needed to grow. In the summer of 1981, there were plans to construct a one-million-gallon water tank adjacent to the tank already situated in the St. James Park housing plan on Brodhead Road. Many of the residents in the area, especially the St. James housing area, opposed and again challenged the legality of an additional water tank being constructed. A few of the current township supervisors (Joseph Yezzi, William DiCicco, and Albert Bartosh) agreed to attend the zoning hearing in mid-Aug of 1981 to help voice the residents' concerns. The alternate site for another larger water tank was being considered on Chapel Road, but it was determined the location of the current 400,000-gallon tank near St. James was the best site due to its elevation. As of 1983, the water authority had one million dollars to build the new one-million-gallon water tank and tower and after many protests, court hearings, and voices being heard at many meetings, it is apparent that the water authority had it their way and the larger tank was erected adjacent to St. James Park.

Fun fact: Back when steam engines were being used by the railroads, there were also nonpublic drinking water tanks located along the roadway at Elkhorn Run Road just outside Monaca (heading toward Aliquippa). These were used to service the Pittsburgh and Lake Erie Railroad for many years. As the need for storing water for the railroad diminished, these tanks then became storage tanks for molasses. The molasses was brought in by barge on the Ohio River, then tanker trucks would haul it to these tanks and drain it into them by steam power. The molasses was then sold, pumped into tank trucks and taken to cattle feed mills in the valley to be mixed with feed for livestock.

From the 1951 drive of the Center Township Citizens' Council to establish a water system in Center Township, also came the first members of the Center Township Water Authority. As of Feb 1951, and through at least 1954, Gibson Brock was appointed chairman of the newly established Center Township Water Authority. Also named to serve on this new authority were Collins Greer, Sterling Lewis, Joseph Reimish, and Paul Marthens.

As of mid-2019, CTWA Board Members were Steven Drobac, Jr.-Chairman, William DiCicco, Sr.-Vice Chairman, William Mencanin-Treasurer, Carol A. Lancos-Secretary, and Danny D. Santia, Jr.-Asst. Secy/Treas. Other positions held include Ned Mitovich-Lennon, Smith, Souleret Engineering Firm, Bill DiCioccio, Jr.- CTWA Operational Supervisor, Vera Dugan Sisk-Office Manager, and Attorney Ronald J. DiGiorno-Solicitor. Through the years, the Water Authority has had their maintenance offices in the same location, being on Fairview Drive, located at the far end of the parking lot in the Beaver Valley Mall area.

Once the site of the new water intake system was completed, the water tank pictured above, that once stood adjacent to the Water Authority building at the far end of the parking lot of the Beaver Valley Mall (on what is known as Fairview Drive), was torn down (in 2018).

Did you know….
"Anyone opening Hydrants and utilizing Authority water without the expressed persmission of the Authority through appropriate channels will be in violation of Pennsylvania Law and subject to appropriate charges and sanctions." "Only Water Authority and Fire Department Personnel, during an emergency, for flushing pipe lines, or for filling tanks on fire trucks, are permitted to operate/open Fire Hydrants in the Township."

Fun Fact: A small drip from a faucet can waste as much as 75 liters of water a day.

Since those many years in the past, Center Township Water Authority and Supervisors have continued to add many updates to the water system, as well as installing fire hydrants throughout the township. In continuing to provide the township residents with the most updated sciences and safe water, the authority stated that they would once again be doing some updating. In 2015 talks and plans were underway between the Center Township Water Authority and Shell Chemicals regarding Center Township's water intake system. The existing site for the four groundwater wells water source intake system for Center Township was located within the plans on land that would become the site of the new Shell cracker plant. The authority assured residents that the existing wells had not been compromised during the over fifty years it had been in existence even though it was surrounded by a zinc processing/smelting facility, active railway, fly ash landfill, and an interstate highway. But, as stated by the CTWA, "It was determined early on that operation of a groundwater water supply source and construction/operation of an ethane processing facility were incompatible." It was therefore decided that a project would begin for the CTWA and Shell to do a "land swap" so the water authority could construct a completely new water intake system and then surrender their existing property of the groundwater wells to Shell.

With CTWA having constructed the existing wells in the 1950s and now servicing an estimated 18,000 people, they were nearing at capacity with the existing wells. Without going into any of the legal wording and details, the basic deal between the CTWA and Shell was reported -- Shell agreed to fund all but $3 million of the estimated $72 million project for the CTWA to have a new water intake site, a temporary water intake plant, and then a new water intake treatment plant. Because the old intake structure was located on land that was being developed by Shell, CTWA and Shell essentially swapped pieces of land. This action would allow the water authority availability for the new intake and water treatment plant on land behind/adjacent to the Beaver Valley Mall and give Shell full access to the land where the 1950s wells were located. It is reported that the CTWA paid Shell $10 for the new piece of land (just over 3 acres) that is described as located "east of the Vanport Bridge, on the south side of the Ohio River;" this property had a county-assessed value of $20,300 at the time the deed was filed. Upon completion of the permanent intake system, the authority was going to be selling the land they still owned and using to operate the then current groundwater wells (which again, were within the cracker plant site). The CTWA also made plans for a two-storey building to be erected along the banks of the Ohio River on the authority's new property with construction estimated to cost $3 million.

The CTWA finished the construction of the township's temporary intake system and continued with the completion of the permanent system which involved tunneling beneath the Ohio River to build that connection. As of 2017, the old well field and groundwater treatment plant was "decommissioned", and the interim facilities were being used. They are rated for 3 million gallons per day and the new permanent facility is expected to be rated at 5 million gallons per day.

So, when all was said and done, the CTWA was reported to be paying for the construction of the two-storey building and Shell would be paying an estimated $69 million to replace and create both the temporary and the permanent water intake and treatment facility. The new CTWA water intake system and facility were being completed with the intention of being "a long term, 50-plus year facility."

This picture is of the current Center Township Water Authority Treatment Plant located on Stoney Ridge Drive, off the Beaver Valley Mall Blvd. (behind the current Ollie's and Beaver Valley Auto Mall).

photo copied from 2017 CT Newsletter

Fun fact: Less than 1% of the water supply on earth can be used as drinking water.

~ ~ ~

Sanitary Authority

As expressed previously, Moon Township/Center Township was first a rural area. Together with earlier years and any rural environment came the absence of a formal sewer systems. Before actual septic tanks/systems and/or sewage systems, there were *outhouses*. For anyone who is not familiar with an outhouse, just think of a much cruder and stationary form of a current porta potty unit. As a rule, most outhouses structures were 3 or 4 feet square and had no electric light, no windows, no heat, and were situated somewhere close enough to a home to be conveniently accessed, yet far enough from the main house as to not be troublesome to the nose.

Having an outhouse required a deep hole manually being dug deep enough to sufficiently be used for the collection. Thinner layers of dirt were periodically added into the pits/holes to cover said collections. When the pits would become full, many found it much less of a stomach-turning process to simply dig a new hole, and move the outhouse structure over the new hole, than to try to remove what had been added to the current pit/hole. They would use the dirt excavated for the new pit to cover and fill in the former pit. Due to the obvious problem of odor, an outhouse would be constructed at least 40 feet or more from the main house. The door opening was always facing away from the house since the doors were usually left open when being used to provide ventilation. This also provided needed light while using the facility. Needless to say, when it came time to relieve oneself, it involved a stroll into the back yard, rain or shine, night, or day. In colder weather, it also involved bundling up. Lanterns were most likely required when the sun was not up yet or had already set. Remember, even after electricity was available, there were probably no electricity provided to the outhouse and most likely no porch lights to turn on to light the way.

 Pit and base for outhouse structure to be built on.

Fun fact: Did you know there is such a thing as outhouse digging? In the 1700s, 1800s, and earlier 1900s, outhouses were also used as a garbage disposal. Nowadays, if it is found there was an outhouse somewhere, interested persons will dig in this area with the hopes of finding vintage old medicine bottles, stoneware, whiskey bottles, and a variety of other items from days gone by.

Fun fact: Many outhouses used by the public would have either a crescent moon cutout or a star cutout on the door. These cutouts date back to the colonial days when few people could read. The crescent moon was used as the symbol for women, the star cutout was for men. The cutouts also let in just a little light to the windowless "bathroom." Most residential homes only had one outhouse for the entire family and tended to just use a crescent moon cutout on their facilities. When the outhouse was on private property, the crescent moon meant it was unisex.

Women's outhouses tended to survive much longer than the men's structures since the women took better care of them, while the men just seemed to let theirs fall into quite bad shape.

Fun fact: In pre-Christian Ireland, the Winter Solstice was an occasion to thoroughly clean one's home, very similar to how we do spring cleaning today. At some point in time, the tradition transformed into an annual Christmas Eve white washing of the outhouse. Nothing says Merry Christmas like a clean outhouse!

Some larger homesteads or those with numerous children may have even had a larger outhouse that had two holes in the seat area, one for the adults and one for the children. The smaller sized hole would be included because one of the children sitting on the bigger hole could easily result in very unpleasant consequences.

Outhouse structure/building.

Two seater – adult and children

Finding the most convenient way of relieving oneself has always been an ongoing process. An alternate to having to go out and use one's outhouse in the middle of the night, during inclement weather, or in the dead of winter, was to have the convenience of a chamber pot available in most bedrooms. Of course, someone had to have the wonderful task of emptying the pots each morning or as needed. If the pot did not have its own lid to contain its deposits, then a small piece of wood would be placed over the top. A chamber pot would usually be kept in a special cupboard called a *commode*.

Fancier chamber pot with its own lid

Simple pot

Fun fact: Real toilet paper was a true luxury for rural families so most families would use newspapers and/or old catalogue pages.

Rather than a daily event, bathing was a weekly affair, usually occuring on Saturday evening, so all family members would be clean for attending church on Sunday. It took a sufficient amount of water for bathing and a special effort for heating the needed water. In the earlier years, baths were taken in a large galvanized tub, which would be placed either in the kitchen or on a back porch. The entire family would share and take their turn in the tub with the same water. It was common practice for the man of the house to bath first, followed by the other family members to usually the babies being last to be given their baths. By the time the smallest child would be bathed, you can imagine how dirty the water would have been.

Fun fact: The common saying, "Don't throw the baby out with the bath water," comes from the fact that the bath water was so tainted by the time the youngest was bathed, that it would be easy to lose someone in it. Thus the saying became very popular to describe the error in which someone may actually eliminate something good (the baby), when trying to get rid of something bad (the dirty bath water).

Before actual bathrooms or closets were being added to homes, it became increasingly popular for bedrooms to often times have a bowl and pitcher for daily cleansing.

In the very early 1900s, it was being widely recognized that bacteria was a common culprit and diseases like cholera and typhoid were caused by unsanitary conditions. This prompted changes in households and individuals improving their hygiene practices. Cities were also beginning to implement sewer systems and sanitation projects to resolve the general public conditions, as well as stopping the practice of simply throwing things out into the street, including the contents of a chamber pot. Cleanliness has always been considered a virtue, but by as early as 1899 companies like Standard Sanitary Manufacturing were beginning to introduce porcelain fixtures. These easy to clean products were making the concept very desireable for adding a designated bathroom to many businesses and homes. By 1910 almost every house plan that was prepared included a specific bathroom closet area. Companies like Sears sold bathroom items for homes, but they were not for the lower-end or common rural home, infact, it was not very likely that many rural homes had indoor plumbing for several decades.

Between 1929 and 1954 an actual bathroom in a home was becoming very popular and new homes being built had this special room included in the construction. Just as popular was the remodeling of the pre-1900 homes to also include a bathroom. Many time, in the rural areas, this addition was no more than adding a toilet and a sink on a newly enclosed portion of the back porch. Some converted a larger closet to be used as a bathroom or made a sufficient enclosure/lean-to onto the existing house for the fixtures.

Public health was improving with the application of indoor plumbing, public water system, and a proper sewage system. Center Township was not to be left behind with implementing all these concepts. From small and wooden outhouses to chamber pots, to makeshift bathrooms, to actual bathrooms with all the fixtures, Moon / Center Township residents have come a long way. The Center Township Sewer Authority was established in 1966. On Sep 21, 2009, the name was changed from the Center Township Sewer Authority to The Center Township Sanitary Authority.

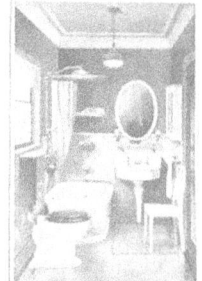
1920/30s   J. L. Mott Iron Works ad

Fun fact: A toilet seat was once called a closet seat and a sink was called a lavatory.

Prior to 1960, all wastewater from the majority of all households and businesses in Center Township was processed through individual septic systems. In 1956, the Citizen's Council was discussing and reviewing township sewage and septic tank regulations and building permit regulations due to the rapid growth of the township to raise the concern to establish a sewage system. In May 1956, the Center Township Supervisors adopted an ordinance (effective Jul 1) providing for issuance of building permits and setting of minimum requirements for sewage disposal systems, all recommended by the township planning commission. They set the fees for building permits to be $2 if no inspection was involved and $7 for those that required inspection. All new sewage disposal systems would have to comply with FHA requirements and then be inspected in two steps, a percolation test and final inspection. The supervisors had to appoint a sewer inspector to conduct these final two inspections. Center Township authorities started to formulate information regarding a sewer system in Jan of 1961. Beginning about 1964, there were petitions being signed by residents to have a sewage plan put in place so they could be included in the sewage system. Many septic systems were proving unsatisfactory and were failing. There were also many letters being sent to homeowners whose septic systems were now found to be draining onto roadways and causing major problems and/or health conditions. "In 1966, The Center Township Board of Supervisors, under the Municipality Act of 1945, established the Center Township Sewer Authority. The Sewer Authority is comprised of a five-member board appointed by The Center Township Supervisors."

To complicate matters, by the 1970s, where no sewer services were currently made available, residents with older failing septic systems, were required to replace all with quite expensive sand mound systems. The new sand mound septic systems were also required to be installed by all new residential constructions. Not even five years after many residents had spent so much for the sand mound systems, the township expanded the sewer system's coverage, and the same households were then told they now had to lay pipelines and tap into a sewage system. Understandably, these specific households were not happy having just spent upwards of eight to ten thousand dollars for a sand mound only to now be told they had to spend thousands more to install a public sewage system.

In 1971/72, with the growing occurrence of all the new construction of apartments, homes, and businesses, it was found that the lots were becoming increasingly smaller and were just not large enough for the required septic systems to be installed. With all this considered, a new network for collecting all this sewage was created, and in 1973, the Elkhorn Treatment Plant was put into use. The Elkhorn Treatment Plant is located off Biskup Lane/Elkhorn Road, along Elkhorn Run stream, thus its name. Then the Moon Run Treatment Plant was built in 1975 to accommodate the increasing demands. It received its name from the Moon Run stream that runs adjacent to this plant on Shade Hollow Road. In 1982 approval had been given. There was new construction at the Elkhorn Run treatment plant scheduled to begin and the capacity of the Moon Run plant was to be increased. Usage of the Moon Run and Elkhorn Run plants doubled the township sewage capacity. As of 1982, sewage collected at the Moon Run plant was trucked to the Elkhorn Run plant. Following a five-year evaluation of the sewage situation, the Supervisors and Sewer Authority made plans for the Moon Run sewage to be transported by pipeline to the Elkhorn plant by using State funds to construct the pipeline as soon as it became available.

> *Fun fact: In Jun of 1978, the township decided to accept proposals for the purchase of a piece of township-owned land off Skyview Drive.   This property was purchased and originally plans were for this property to be the site for a sewage treatment plant, but plans changed.   It was determined that the site was "not a buildable lot."   The Township sewer and water authorities stated they no longer had interest with it since "it couldn't even be used for recreation, the way it is laid out."*

Center Township continued to grow and by 1993 the Elkhorn Run Plant underwent major expansion to accommodate processing twice the volume needed per day. Slowly, the township continued to provided sewer services to more residents of Center. It was also planned to enlarge the existing Moon Run plant, installing over 47 miles of sewer line, and constructing four pumping stations.   All these improvements and additions would mean that approximately sixty per cent of the land area of the township would then have access to sewer services. As of 1993, only areas on Temple Road, parts of Bunker Hill Road, Raccoon Creek and Shade's Hollow were without service.

Usage of the Moon Run Plant was discontinued in 2002 and all processing is currently done at the Elkhorn Run Plant which processes wastewater and provides treatment services to Center Township as well as a small portion of Monaca. This plant uses the method for treatment known as Activated Sludge, "the plant utilizes physical and biological processes to remove the harmful pollution from the wastewater." After the wastewater is fully processed, it is released into the Ohio River.   The Elkhorn Run Water Pollution Control Plant is still located along Elkhorn Run Creek, off Biskup Lane, a short distance before it intersects with Vankirk Road. The current authority has stated that the collection of sanitary sewage consists of at least seventy (70) miles of lines and 15 square miles of sewage systems, in conjunction with ten (10) Lift Stations which are necessary to provide pumping assistance to the sewer lines that do not drain by gravity. As of 2017/2018, there were approximately 4,642 residential and commercial sewer connections to the township's system.

The sewage department originally had the name The Center Township Sewer Authority, but in 2009, the name was officially changed to The Center Township Sanitary Authority.   Samuel Rebich was chairman of the sewer authority in 1972. As of mid-2019, the CTSA Sanitary Board is made up of Richard Nicastro-Chairman, Frank Vescio-Vice Chairman, Marsha DeCenzo-Secretary, Joy George-Treasurer, Mario DiBello, Joe Elias, Richard Nicastro, Robert Martini-Operations Supervisor, Ned Mitrovich, PE-Lennon, Smith Souleret Engineering, and Joseph A. Askar, Esq.-Solicitor

~ ~ ~

Road Department

As with all the other departments in Center Township, the Road Department also plays an important part of the functioning and success of the township.

As of 2017, the Center Township Road Department had six full time employees. It is a time consuming task and large responsibility to keep the approximate 50 miles of roads in good condition. This department also is responsible for township storm drains, street signs, mowing, snow and/or ice removal, and mechanical maintenance of township-owned equipment and vehicles. As if that list is not large enough, the department also does periodic street sweeping.

Dave Foore was a well-known Road Foreman in the township for many years in Center. Joseph Perich is the current Road Foreman (2019).

> Reminder, when an address is included, it may help the reader to orient the location of a home, business, or roadway by remembering. Even numbers on Brodhead Road are on the left side of the road (coming from Monaca going toward Aliquippa, the side of the road toward the interior of the township. Odd numbers on are on the right side, the "river side" of Brodhead Road. The numbering of all other roadways within the township will basically be the same principal as far as odd numbers all on one side of a road, even all on the opposite side.

CENTER TOWNSHIP
ROADS

View of a typical road in early Center Township.

Fun facts: State roads in Beaver County were laid out by Acts of Legislature. There was one local state road that started along the Ohio River, opposite Vanport. This was known in the early years as Route 115 and nowadays it is Route 18. (See Frankfort Road and Routes 18 and 51 and 18 & 51 Intersection further.) It was twenty and a half miles long and ran through Moon Township, then through Raccoon (prior to Potter Township's erection) and Hanover Townships into Frankfort Springs. This is where the name "Frankfort" Road was derived. This roadway was the only one in Beaver County that had "mile-posts." These "mile-posts" were made of locust plants and were five feet long, 12 to 15 inches wide. Each post had the distances and names of places painted on them. It was said that some of these posts remained standing even after a period of 40 years. James Harper and William Hales were appointed and authorized by an Act of Assembly to build this roadway for $1,600. They received payment in silver and in turn paid the workmen in silver.

The old saying "as the crow flies" is usually applied when someone wants to indicate the shortest distance between two points. As with most forming communities, when Moon (Center) Township was being settled and formed, this "as the crow flies" straighter path thinking didn't always seem to be the case or applied when it came to private lanes or secondary roads being developed. There was no mountain moving equipment to simply cut out a lane or roadway, let alone make it "straighter" or more convenient in the earlier years. Actually, as long as a drive, lane, and/or roadway was passable and safe, nobody really noticed all the curves and bends it had. The curves and imperfections were tolerated if you could access your destination. As Moon/Center Township became much more settled and populated, land moving equipment became more accessible. Numerous roadways were changed, straightened, and/or altered to better accommodate traffic on them. Alterations were also made for accessing more and more residencies that were springing up everywhere, too. In the early years, only one entrance to a farm was needed for the family to enter or leave the property. As these farms were being sold and subdivided, multiply entrances were often needed.

Center Grange Road is a perfect example of some of these changes and alterations. At one-time Center Grange Road was nothing more than a very "curvy" and dirt driveway or lane that led to a small cluster of the Davis family homes. It was originally named Davis Lane. As this family grew and/or some of the properties being sold outside the family and slowly subdivided, the entrance to what we know as Center Grange Road was straightened to meet "squarely" onto Brodhead Road. (See Davis Lane aka Center Grange Road further and see section on Organizations for much more on the Center Grange Hall.)

Throughout Beaver County, between the years of 1920s and 1940s, many roads were updated from just dirt roadways, subsequently as much as possible throughout Center Township. Depending on the amount of traffic a dirt lane or roadway may have supported, it could be considered for updating from dirt to cement/asphalt. What roadways that were not updated to cement or asphalt were kept in fair condition for the residents by being tarred and chipped once a year, sometimes bi-yearly depending on the amount of traffic.

Fun fact: Though not in Center Township, the road near Darlington, Route 30, was the first such road to be on record as being updated with a mile of concrete being poured as an experiment. This first "one mile" of concrete soon turned into the thousands of miles of paved roadways today, including those in Center Township.

Roadways in Moon Township were once only traveled by foot, horse, and buggies. Currently motor vehicles are usually the sole form of transportation you will see on any given form of road. It is a rare sight to see anyone cycling or walking along the busier township roads nowadays. Of course, people should remember, with all the significant changes in transportation also comes air pollution and air quality concerns. Unfortunately, the once treasured "fresh air" has definitely been diminished greatly. One concern that should be addressed is that more and more trees and greenery are being removed or greatly reduced for "progress" just to satisfy the main goal to increase that almighty amount of tax monies in increasing housing and businesses. But this also greatly increases the amount of carbon dioxide being emitted from the increased number of gallons of gasoline being consumed by cars and trucks coming and going within the township. Less greenery and trees mean less natural filtration of all the health hazardous fumes and gasses – not a good thing for any living thing! I know, I know – some will say "but they plant new" or "they replant areas" ----- but until all those "new" and/or replacements reach the same maturity and "thickness" as what once stood, they cannot even begin to do the job the original growth was doing.

~ ~ ~

I found two very early listings for proposed roadways. There were no names of these roads, and no follow up information as to whether they were approved or ever became roadways.

> 1 March 1797.—A petition for a road to lead from Brodhead's road to Isaac Lawrence's ferry on the Ohio river opposite Samuel Johnston's in Beaver Town.
>> This would be for a road from _?_ and heading down over the hillside by the current Lowe's Plaza area. Lawrence's Ferry was along the river just below this area. This statement above does not say from what portion of Brodhead's road, so the origin or location is not clear, just that it would eventually lead down to the Ohio River (across from the current town of Beaver).

and

5 March 1803.—Petition for a road from William Guy's, Senior, in Moon township to Brodhead's road leading to Beaver Town and it is computed that distance will be two miles nigher than the best road.

> William Guy was a miller, which indicates to me that he lived along some type of waterway. He was also listed as living in Robinson Township, Allegheny County in 1800 and 1810. This petition would probably have only partly affected Moon (Center) Township but was important enough to connect to the more traveled Brodhead's road which ran through Moon Township.

~ ~ ~

Fun Fact: All Department of Highway roads prior to mid 1946 had either one solid line painted in the middle of the road to indicate a driver could not pass other cars, or they had a section of broken lines to indicate it could be crossed. It was announced the end of Aug 1946 that all State highways in Beaver County, along with all other roads in the 12,000-mile system under the jurisdiction of the Department of Highways would be painted with a new double line on hills and curves to help reduce motoring hazards in those areas. The two lines may be altered with one solid line and one broken line. This would indicate traffic could do passing since the right distance was sufficient to permit safe passing, but only the traffic on the side with the broken line could do the passing.

~ ~ ~

Although not unique to just this area, while researching Moon/Center Township, it was quite apparent that names of roads changed frequently, and new roadways were continually added to provide access within multiple housing plans/areas. With all the different names, lanes, drives, routes, whether state or locally maintained, it brings a familiar phrase to mind – the one from Shakespeare's play *Romeo and Juliet*...... "WHAT'S IN A NAME? THAT WHICH WE CALL A ROSE / BY ANY OTHER NAME WOULD SMELL AS SWEET." Loosely translated, it means "the importance of a person or thing is the way it is; not because of what it is called; the names of things cannot affect what they actually are." This one phrase is quite profound, suggesting that names are just labels to distinguish one thing from another. Neither has any worth, nor gives true meaning. I referenced this Shakespearian quote because it holds some weight to me when you know the history of why many of the current roadways were of importance to begin with, how they obtained their original names, and the homestead(s) on the original drive, lane, roadway. Keep this in mind as you read the information with roads in Moon/Center Township. ☺

I have listed a small sampling of many of the roads in Moon/Center Township that were in existence many years ago. Some may have been eliminated, altered, renamed, or even still retain their name and location nowadays. I chose the ones listed further for a few reasons... They have more of a history to them and many are still used frequently today. Their names may reflect a family or business from the past. Several of these roads are now defunct and/or may not be known by residents nowadays. There are many more that could have easily been included but many of them were created later as the housing plans were developed.

Note: those receiving their names from the original homestead owners' names obviously began as just drives or lanes that only led to that family's homestead. As portions of these former homesteads were subdivided and sold, many of those former private drives were taken over by the township and became an actual township road to access all the subdivisions. Thus, they gave access to other homes and connect to other areas of the township. As a result of this networking of roadways continually growing, the township found it necessary to properly name and improve many of the roadways. The original name or "familiar" name known for so many prior years was either officially approved, or in some cases, a decision for a name change was made.

I will sound like a damaged record/taping as you read through this listing of roads as I repeat "this roadway had a few different names," but with early residents giving more of a nickname to a road, it is sometimes hard to decipher exactly where a location may have been to current residents. More curious to some nowadays may be why the roadway received a particular name.

I will begin with Brodhead Road information since it is the main roadway that passes through the township. Following Brodhead Road's information will be a loosely alphabetized listing of other roadways within the township.

Brodhead Road

If someone was to pick a roadway that was the mainstay of the township, Brodhead Road would most likely win many of the votes. It has been the main roadway used since the 1700s to connect surrounding areas to one another and used to access all other areas from the early formation of Moon Township. Brodhead Road is listed as one of the earliest roads in the county. It was the military highway cut from Fort Pitt through the county on the "South Side" and used to supply provisions and other stores for Fort McIntosh.

Brodhead Road was one of these multi-named roads by local township residents. Through the years it had portions of it that would be labeled "Brodhead Road" and other portions labeled "Bye Road" and yet other mentions of "Main Road."   I can presume Main Road would be because it was the main road through the township, but I have yet to find the reasoning or explanation for "Bye Road."   Perhaps it was because it was the only major roadway to lead you out of the township -? –

Unidentified section of Brodhead Road - c. late 1800s to 1900

Throughout this book and in my *Monaca aka Phillipsburg* book, you find that I love to go off the beaten path and included miscellaneous information, but it all actually does apply to the subject matter in some form. That being said… within the next few paragraphs is an example of this as I give a mini history of Brodhead Road.

In 1778, Brodhead Road was an improved version of an Indian trail. Col. Daniel Brodhead and his 8th Regiment troops (*see *Fun fact* further) built the new roadway. I have chosen to use a direct quote that gives such a clear, yet condensed description of Brodhead Road………. In one of Gino Piroli's newspaper articles, he stated, "It began at the Monongahela River, traveled to what is now West Carson Street to Saw Mill Run (near/by the West End Bridge), crossed three ridges and descended into a beautiful valley, now Crafton. It then forded Chartiers Creek to the junction with Stuebenville Pike, reached Summitville (Moon Run) and went along what is now Beaver Grade Road before descending into the Montour Run and then Carnot.   Beyond Carnot, there was a mile-long dip in the valley of Flaugherty Run.   From there it went 4½ miles through Five Points in Hopewell into New Sheffield in Aliquippa, where the troops camped at Camp Raccoon, which had a large spring where Raccoon Cemetery is.   The road continued to what is now Center Township, past West Shaffer Road to North Branch Road along what is now Old Brodhead past the present site of the Penn State-Beaver campus, crossed a ridge near what is now the Sylvan Crest plan, then down to the river across from Fort McIntosh."   Mr. Piroli continues to also include a little more history…. "The river was about 1,200 feet wide and was fordable in dry weather but required ferry service in the spring and fall.   Fort McIntosh was built overlooking and guarding the river crossing of Brodhead Road with 6-pound artillery pieces mounted in each river bastion for protection."

This is an archived picture of officials of the former Great Arrow Historical Association on the portion of the original Brodhead Road that would have gone over the hillside before ending directly across the river from the site of Fort McIntosh (in Beaver). Indians, soldiers, and settlers could have easily crossed the river in those early years because it would have been quite shallow. There was consideration many years ago, for this site to be marked as a scenic and historical park. I have nothing further on the developments of this plan, if there were markers made, or why none of this seemed to ever occur.

It is not clear as to exactly what "road" or section of road the following petition is referencing, but it reflects that very early in time, residents were concerned with developing proper and very usable roadways in Moon (Center) Township. It clearly appears to be for a roadway connecting to what is the current Brodhead Road in Center Township. It may have even been simply an extension or improvement of a portion of the former Brodhead Road. This early petition was found and extracted from the Road Docket No. 1 of Allegheny County. There were several of the homeowners in the then Moon Township who submitted this application in 1799. It included:

"That a road is very much wanted from a road by the name of Broadhead road to a ferry over the Ohio river opposite a gut below the mouth of Big Beaver Creek, a road from here has been traveled for many years as it is the only road that wagons can travel from Pittsburgh or Washington to Beavertown as has been already of great utility to the Inhabitants of the Township of Moon and particularly so to persons emigrating to the settlements north and west of the Ohio river but this road has not yet been laid out by authority, in consequence of which it is greatly out of repair.

    Your petitioners therefore humbly pray the Court to appoint men to view the premises & if four or more of them shall see necessary that they lay out a road beginning on Brodhead's road from one to three miles from the River Ohio, and from that place to proceed on such a route as they may think best to the above described ferry, and your petitioners as in duty bound will every pray."

John Baker	John Douds
Henry Baker	John Oark
	William Cooly
his	Thomas Banks
Daniel X Waggle	Daniel Heart
mark	James Tod
	David McKeay
Daniel Waggle, Jun.	Wm. Jordan
John Waggle	Reuben Reion
John Baker, Sr.	John Smith
Andrew Johnston	James Smith
John Parkinson	William Gray

                          September 1799

(This petition may have led to what became known as Narrows Road or possibly an extension to what became Stone Quarry Road. With such broad description in the petition and no map to accompany the petition, it is too difficult to make a determination.)

~ ~ ~

In the fall of 1999, hundreds of homes and business were renumbered along Brodhead Road, beginning in the current Moon Township of Allegheny County, and continuing through Center Township to Monaca. All the homes and business in Center Township beginning close to the King's Restaurant, to just past Penn State Campus retained their original address numbers (which begin in the 1000s to the 1400s) and are referenced as "Old Brodhead Road." The remaining homes and business along Brodhead Road in Center Township were all renumbered and now begin with the 4100s (as soon as you exit Monaca) and end in the 2900/2800s (as you travel Brodhead toward Sheffield area of Aliquppa). It was stated that this would be a temporary "inconvenience" for those involved, but that it was long overdue. This renumbering was necessary since emergency services were finding it very difficult to find a home and/or business when responding to calls since the address involved did not appear in sequence and therefore were duplicated. At one time you could stand on Brodhead Road in Aliquippa/Hopewell area and be between one house with the address of 100 Brodhead Road and the other also at 100 Brodhead Road --- one would be considered *North* Brodhead, and one *South* Brodhead. Unless people were very careful to specify "North" or "South" in an emergency, the "two-roads-in-one status" created unnecessary confusion and responding personnel could easily go to the wrong home.

The "South" numbers went along the entire road into the current Moon Township of Allegheny County, which kept the same numbering sequence on into the West Hills area. The "North" numbers went through the Sheffield area of Aliquippa Borough, all through Center Township, and ended in Monaca. The new numbering now begins in Moon Township (Allegheny County) at Narrows Run Road and sequentially extends on into Beaver County. One example of the changes is the Beaver Valley Alloy (just outside Monaca) went from 1899 Brodhead Road to 4165 Brodhead Road. When Col. Brodhead and his 8th Regiment troops* improved the Indian trail that became Brodhead Road, I am sure they never imagined this much improvement would need to be involved on the roadway.

Although the renumbering was clearly a necessity, for all those affected by this renumbering it was indeed a very big inconvenience. Those affected by the switch had to go through all the hassles of basically updating all contact information but never even moving an inch off their present location. It affected business letterheads, financial documents, mailboxes, personal documents such as drivers' licenses, and all the other headaches that go along with having to change an address. Since the renumbering has been completed and all those involved now have their new addresses, the emergency personnel have a much more efficient method of finding anyone in need of their services and now many wonder why it was not considered and did not occur sooner.

With many of the business and even family information included in this book, you may see so many of the addresses simply say "along Brodhead Road" or some may reflect one of the former numbers as assigned prior to 1999. I have tried to indicate what, if any, the new number would now be, but this will not always be the case. This is due to the business or building no longer existing or a new building or plaza now being at that location which leaves no point of reference to one of the previous numbers.

*Fun fact: During the Revolutionary War, my Gr-Gr-Gr-Gr Grandfather, William Davis was among the men in the 8th Regiment under Col. Brodhead. He helped to build and improve that first roadway that became Brodhead Road. Many of the Regiments traveled to and from Fort McIntosh via this roadway.

*Fun fact: For many years there was a conflict with the spelling of Brodhead Road. It should be noted that the road received its name from Col. Brodhead who spelled his name with only one "a" in it. For multiple years, many would spell it B-r-o-**a**-d-h-e-a-d (as in a broad road) rather than after the proper name of the Revolutionary War colonial. Today, it is a fact that there are not two "a's" in its spelling, yet much of Allegheny County continues to add the extra "a."*

The section of roadway which still comes out of Monaca and blends into Center Township was once merely dirt, but it was greatly improved with crews pouring sections of concrete. There once was a culvert at the bottom of the hill (where the current traffic light on Route 18 and Old Brodhead intersects just outside Monaca). At this culvert was once a sign in the shape of a keystone with the date of 1921 indicating when the concrete was poured. For many years, the concrete on this roadway was only laid from Pennsylvania Avenue Extension (as you exit Monaca), then along the short stretch of Brodhead Road (to the current traffic light), and the concrete continued up the hill to the entrance of Union Cemetery and Chapel Road. From this point, the remaining portion of Brodhead Road's surface became just dirt again.

Photo courtesy Monaca Borough

This old photo gives a nice view of how Pennsylvania Avenue at the end of Monaca blended into Brodhead Road as it headed into Center Township. Note the direction of the roadway. The pointer is to show how Brodhead Road once led to the left before it was widened and straightened.

The pointer in this picture indicates how Pennsylvania Avenue was also widened and blends into Brodhead Road after it had been straightened and made into a four-lane highway. Construction on this project began Nov 1965. Note how the roadway now goes to the right after passing through the viaduct area instead of to the left (as seen in the previous picture).

Fun fact: For history buffs.... The Soldiers' Orphans' School buildings use to sit to the right of Pennsylvania Avenue, but all have long since been razed. The area to the right is now the site of Monaca's water treatment plant. The house and former gas station on left (which was Paul & Ted's Super Service) have both also been razed. The German Lutheran cemetery is on then left between the house and the railroad tunnel/viaduct. This section of Monaca's street was originally named Factory Street. When all the originally streets were renamed, this section became Pennsylvania Avenue Extension. Also, with the two previous pictures, to the bottom left (and not in the picture) would be what was originally known as Fourth Street, now Pennsylvania Avenue. To the right on the bottom (and out of this picture) was the former Hanover Street, now Fourth Street. (Many more pictures, maps and details of Monaca's history may be found in my Monaca aka Phillipsburg book.)

Old Brodhead Road
This is still the name attached to the portion of the remaining original Brodhead Road beginning at the main intersection (by current Kings Restaurant) and extends on past the current Monaca Turners, past the Penn State Beaver Campus, and to the intersection at the traffic light on Route 18.

Fun fact: Although they act as major roads in Center Township, the Old Brodhead Road (SR03002), Brodhead Road (SR03007), Chapel Road (SR03005), and Center Grange Road (SR03012) are listed as state routes. North Branch Road is still maintained by the state's road department, too, since it was originally part of the former/early Brodhead Road.

Aliquippa Road and Colona Road
(See *Colona Road* and *Monaca Road* further)

Baker Lane – currently Bonanni Drive
This Baker Lane is not to be confused with the former Baker Street, now Baker Road that leads to the Central Valley High School. There was a Baker Lane a short drive to the right of the current *The Healing Place* building. On some deeds from the early 1900s, this short drive can be found referenced as Baker Lane. I have no date as to when it was changed to Bonanni Drive, but it would appear both names were family surname choices of landowners.

Beaver County Sanitorium Road   now   **College Drive**
This was the roadway used to access the Beaver County Tuberculosis Sanitorium which was once in operation on the property where the current main administrative buildings now stand of Penn State Beaver Campus. The roadway first gave access to the Turnbull farm, then the Huffmyer homestead, followed by then giving access to the sanitorium property as well as property purchased by Dr. and Mrs. Mitchell. (See Medical section, see Huffmyer Family, see Hartenbach Family, see Education section.)

This roadway was renamed College Drive when the property was willed/granted to Penn State by the Hartenbach family. There is also still a private drive to the right a short distance after turning on to this roadway (which is also marked by two stone pillars). One of these homes was that of Dr. and Mrs. John A. Mitchell who then subdivided their property on which a few other homes were erected. All the homes on this semiprivate drive now have addresses of College Drive.

Beaver Run Road – defunct – Sylvan Crest area
This road was originally found on a 1920s plat map when the Sylvan Crest area was laid out into lots for the housing plan. (See Garland Heights Road; see Housing Plans section – Sylvan Crest.)

Beggs (Boggs) Avenue – defunct - in Sylvan Crest area
Went from Bridge Street to Jones. It appears to have been what is now Grandview from Bridge Street to near Cross Street. This road was sometimes found spelled B<u>o</u>ggs and sometimes B<u>e</u>ggs. It was originally listed on a 1920s plat map when the Sylvan Crest area was laid out into lots for the housing plan. (See Garland Heights Road; see Housing Plans section – Sylvan Crest.)

Bellowsville Road
Bellowsville was a small community of its own, including a cemetery, post office, a ferry landing, access to the railroad, stores, businesses, and homesteads. To access this community, one had to use what was known then as Bellowsville Road. This name was attached to the roadway because it led you into the community and area of Bellowsville. The 1876 Weyand & Reed's Beaver County Centennial Directory has Moon Township's post office listed as *Bellowsville*. Even after Bellowsville itself seem to fade away and no longer exist, the same road then led to what became known as Josephtown and shortly after, parts of the Kobuta community. (More on Bellowsville, Josephtown, and Kobuta in another section.) There were several families that lived along Bellowsville Road, including Frank Barnes, Joseph Phibbs, and William McClintock.

Berry Hollow Road - defunct
This drive/lane/roadway was located very close to Mamula's meat processing business but on the opposite side of Chapel Road. As was past practice, this road was most likely named for the family who lived there. Faint traces of the roadway can still be seen, and it appears to have come off Chapel Road and led to a home or homes that would have been down in/below what is now the Sky View plan (the same land is now accessible off East Shaffer Road).

Biskup Lane

The current Biskup Lane was originally simply more of a longer driveway taking you to a few family homesteads which eventually did include the Biskup family farm and home(s) as well as several other person's homesteads. It branched off the former extended portion of Davis Lane (now Center Grange Road). The first homes that were built on this former "drive" had the address of *Davis Lane* before the drive was renamed after multiple families began building homes on the properties. I found no official date for it becoming named *Biskup Lane.* As of the 1940 census, Biskup Lane was not yet named and homesteads along the roadway were simply listed as "off Center Grange Road." Extended family and friends' homes were built on this roadway so the length of this "lane" continued to grow and today Biskup Lane is much more than just a "driveway." It still branches off Center Grange Road, but now continues to connect with Vankirk Road in the Stobo area of the township. Although there is still quite a bit of land not yet developed along Biskup Lane, more than 70 homes can be found on the once very quiet and more sparsely populated drive/lane.

The township received a donation from George Gourley in Jul 1976 for the triangular piece of property at the intersection of Center Grange Road and Biskup Lane. Supervisors had sought the property to put in a short-paved road connecting Biskup Lane and Center Grange Road cutting behind the point of the triangle. Depending which direction you were traveling, vehicles had been using the slag and mud "cut through" as an easier way to access or exit Biskup Lane. In doing so, this had been encroaching on private property. By owning and paving this piece of roadway, the township felt confident this would stop any further damage to the adjacent private property.

Bunker Hill Road

Tried as I may, I found no documentation as to why the area of *Bunker Hill* received this name. As I stated elsewhere, it is "hilly" in that area and a short distance further along Brodhead Road from Bunker Hill Road, as you head toward New Sheffield, is one of the higher elevations of the township. This may give a clue to the word "Hill" being in the name of the road and area but is no help with "Bunker." Although the surname of "Bunker" exists, I found no family with this name recorded as living within or associated with Moon (Center) Township over the years. Now this does not mean they did not live here; it just means they are not listed on any official records. With a former school with that name, a roadway with that name, and such a large area being referenced as "Bunker Hill," one would think that if a family did live here by that name, some mention of them would be found in at least one of the historical records. I also found no references to any actual "bunker" being in the area during any of the conflicts through the earlier years. Now there may have been a block house built for protection from the Indians, but no evidence of this has been recorded or found either. Perhaps one of the early residents was a veteran and it reminded him of an area that did contain a "bunker" when he was serving, and he fondly made the reference which soon became a tradition. If anyone reading this book knows the answer to this, please contact me and share your information. (See Raccoon Creek Road further).

This is a view of Bunker Hill Road from many years ago

Bye Road

This road was listed on several of the census forms and in a few other documents. I am not sure why, but various sections of Brodhead Road were often called *Bye Road* through the years. In 1910, a section of Brodhead Road around the intersection of the current E. and W. Shaffer Roads was called *Bye Road*. Yet I found that even a portion of North Branch Road or very close to it was referenced as *Bye Road*. Oddly, the census sheets would specifically have Brodhead Road listed and then switch to list *Bye Road* for a few residents, then back to Brodhead Road with no rhyme or reason. Perhaps it was a means of indicating the residents' homes sat a distance back in and off Brodhead Road. Throughout the census sheets, some of the families listed as living along *Bye Road* included Weigel, Dunn, Staub, Streit, Blair, Goll, and Figley. (See *Brodhead Road previous*.)

Chapel Road
This road begins on Old Brodhead Road, across from the current Penn State Beaver Campus and adjacent to the entrance of Union Cemetery. It continues a fair distance, then crosses over Center Grange Road and again continues to the Borough of Aliquippa coming out on Brodhead Road by the current First United Methodist Church. Just as with Brodhead Road and several other well-traveled roadways, the "local" residents would give more of a nickname to a roadway for reference or to indicate where they would be going or where they were living. Chapel Road was no different, and portions of the road actually had several other names before the entire roadway was officially renamed. I have no exact date as to when the length of what is now Chapel Road was officially given its name, but today, regardless of where you are on that roadway, it is known as *Chapel Road*.

The portion of Chapel Road which begins on Old Brodhead Road by the current Penn State Campus, Union Cemetery, and Monaca Turners building and travels to near the area where Todd Lane currently meets Chapel Road, was first known as "Old Union Cemetery Road" or just "Union Cemetery Road." I found many old deeds and documents that stated Union Cemetery Road and at first thought there was some defunct roadway that led in, through, and out of the cemetery. My secondary thought was there may have been a forgotten cemetery somewhere in the township. I spent many fruitless hours reviewing old maps and doing research to find this mystery *Union Cemetery Road*. By comparing the names of families listed on this mystery roadway, it became apparent where the general area of it really was. I finally came across a deed that specifically stated, "Chapel Road (formerly known as Union Cemetery Road)." Even a blind squirrel finds a nut once in a while, and this squirrel was very happy with her find. (See Cemetery section.)

The portion of Chapel Road which extends from approximately where Todd Lane Road joins Chapel Road to the intersection with Center Grange Road, was known for many years as " 'the' chapel road." Logically, this section received its name due to the former McGuire Chapel church being located along the roadway. The chapel/church was located adjacent to the current McGuire Chapel Cemetery which is closer to the intersection of the current Chapel and Center Grange Roads. Evidently many people would simply refer to going to "the" chapel road meaning they were going to travel on the roadway past or in the area of this chapel. (See Church / Cemetery section.)

Until a little past the 1920s, the portion of Chapel Road from the intersection of Center Grange Road, heading toward Aliquippa/New Sheffield was known as "Sheffield Road" or "New Sheffield Road." Presumably, this name was used since that section of the road came out very close to the (New) Sheffield area of Woodlawn/Aliquippa. The census enumerators and deeds listed it as "Sheffield Road" for many years. Gilbert Sohn (a census enumerator) specifically used "Sheffield Road" on his 1910 census sheets and on the 1920 census Joshua A. Patterson (another enumerator) also referred to it as "Sheffield Road." Actually, this was the only road Joshua included or indicated on all the census sheets done by him that year. Sometime in the 1940s/1950s, regardless of what section of this roadway was being referenced, the current Chapel Road was fairly consistently called just that – Chapel Road. (See *Davis Lane* and *Center Grange Road*.)

Colona Road   --   Monaca Road   --   Aliquippa Road
I found articles, census, and deeds where two separate portions of what is now Monaca Road were frequently referred to by two different names. Until the 1930s, the section of Center Grange Road close to the current Reinish Drive to the intersection of Chapel Road was merely referred to as an extension of Davis Lane (now Center Grange Road). Then, as the area now known as Vankirk/ Stobo expanded and became more populated, the residents in that area found it easier to access the main sections of Moon Township by creating a more frequently used roadway that connected their area to Davis Lane. Thus, that portion of the current Center Grange Road was further developed and now intersects with Monaca Road. Nowadays, this section of Center Township on Monaca Road may be

accessed via Center Grange Road and/or off the divided roadway coming from Monaca and/or coming from a section of Aliquippa.

There was an area between Monaca and Moon Township, adjacent to the current Vankirk/Stobo area, known separately as Colona. This lends to the tradition of this roadway being called "Colona" and/or "Monaca" Road, and probably just more of nickname for the roadway because of where it originated from or led you to. Many early references were made to accessing the homes of this area on a roadway referred to as Colona Road. One year, census enumerators listed the homesteads along this roadway as Colona Road. The next year, it was listed as Monaca Road. Portions of the extended Davis Lane were also periodically referenced as one or the other of these roads. This indicates they were one in the same and would be listed by the most familiar name to the enumerator.

With Davis Lane being more formerly extended and renamed Center Grange Road, there were already several established homesteads in that area. It appears that when you traveled on the extended Davis Lane, then _turned left_ on what is currently Monaca Road, it would have taken you down into the area known as Colona at the outskirts of Monaca just as it still does nowadays. Another confirmation of the roads being the same, but just with different names would be --- A few of the homesteads listed along Davis Lane extension prior to 1910, then on "Colona Road" in 1910 would currently be listed on Center Grange Road. These included James Davidson, Fred Meany, James Hineman, Edward Reynolds, and George Mateer.

Turning right at the end of the extended Davis Lane/Center Grange Road where it intersects Monaca Road would have and still eventually takes you down into Aliquippa. This was most likely why it was referred to as "Aliquippa Road." A few homesteads listed in Moon/Center Township, but on "Aliquippa Road" in 1910 were Sam Polas, Fred Kugel, and Michael Morohowic.

The portion of Center Grange Road beginning off Brodhead Road to the current intersection of Chapel and Center Grange Roads remained known as Davis Lane until the 1940s. A short distance past this intersection, and on your left, there was another lane or drive for a few homesteads. With the Biskup's family homesteads on this lane/drive, it soon became officially named Biskup Lane. (See Davis Lane further and Biskup Lane previous.)

Creek Road   (See *Raccoon Creek Road* further.)

Center Grange Road (See *Davis Lane*)

Davis Lane   now   Center Grange Road
Originally, what became Center Grange Road was much "curvier" and was eventually straightened to meet "squarely" onto Brodhead Road. Center Grange Road was originally known as *Davis Lane* because in those early years it was nothing more than a private lane/drive which led to the Davis families' properties, farms, and homes from Brodhead Road. One author wrote of Davis Lane, stating, "...a few who will admit it was *Lovers' Lane* in the days when old dobbin knew the way home..." This "lane" began off Brodhead Road adjacent to the current Faith Lutheran Church/ Tri-State Pulmonary Medicine building. It originally only continued to just past the current intersection of Center Grange and Chapel Roads. Through the years, as the Davis properties were subdivided and more homesteads developed, Davis Lane continued to slowly be extended, past the drive that became Biskup Lane and by an 1888 map, it went on to connect to what is now Monaca Road at the current intersection of Y McDonald/Monaca Road.

By the 1930s, the remaining acreage along Davis Lane eventually began to be divided and sold into many much smaller lots with more homes being built along the roadway. In 1922, the Center Grange Hall building was erected toward the end of the roadway closest to Brodhead Road. The increased population and usage of this roadway made it necessary to also improve the entire roadway, including the extended portion. With the diversity of families and surnames increasing along Davis Lane since more of the farmlands began to be sold and even more homes were built, it was thought better to re-name the road more generically. By the later 1930s, with the most important building in the township being the Center Grange Hall, it was decided to rename the roadway Center Grange Road. Even after being officially named Center Grange Road, many deeds and addresses were still referencing the address/location as "Davis Lane." It was still called Davis Lane on the 1930 census sheets and there are deeds up to 1939 that reference it as Davis Lane. By the 1940 census sheets, it was listed as Center Grange Road but then after 1940, there were mentions of the Milton Young, Weigel, Biskup, Davis, and Meany families all living on *Davis Lane.* In fact, Davis Lane was still being referenced in 1949, 1952, and 1953. Just goes to prove that new names take some time to get used to.

This is the former Davis Lane (fondly called Lover's Lane), now Center Grange Road. Brodhead Road is going from left to right along the very bottom of the picture. This picture was taken from Brodhead Road and shows what the road looked like prior to it being straightened as it intersected with Brodhead Road. For orientation, the Center Grange Hall was located just past the far bend in this picture.

Doak Street / Baker Street ....now Baker Road

A large portion of both sides of the current Baker Road and Baker Road Extension had been the Samuel S. Doak farm. The current Baker Road was but a lane or drive that led to their farm, thus why it was called Doak Road. A Michael Baker family then came to own a large plot of land between Baker Road and along Christy Drive, therefore as the Doak farm was divided and sold, the roadway took on the name Baker Street.

The end of Jun 1956, land was deeded to the Township by residents then living along what was called Baker Street for the widening of the roadway (between Brodhead Road and the entrance to the current Central Valley School property) so it would be thirty-three (33) feet in width. On this deed, Doak Road and Baker Street are both included in the description of the roadway. The deed stated, "...known as Baker Street, formerly Doak Street..."

The last of the Doak farm between the current stop sign to the entrance to the current school campus was subdivided into lots in 1959 and again in 1962. Even at that time, this portion of the current Baker Road was still listed/known on deeds as *Doak Street*. By 1967 it was listed as *Baker Road / Baker Road Extension*. I did not find a beginning month or year for the original adoption of the name of this street/road changing from Baker "Street" to "Road."

Elkhorn Road

This road has definitely changed through the years, not only in its name, but also in its location. In the 1800s, this roadway started off along Brodhead Road and was originally named *Elkhorn Run Road*. There was another road with a similar name on the other end of the township closer to the Ohio River and just outside Monaca. This roadway was also called Elkhorn "Run" Road since the stream, Elkhorn Run, paralleled portions of the road. To designate which road was which, the current E. Shaffer Road simply became known as *Elkhorn Road*. The name was next changed to *Shaffer Road* sometime in the 1920s, and eventually the E. (for East) was added once W. (West) Shaffer was named.

Elkhorn Road started at the current intersection of Brodhead Road and W. & E. Shaffer Roads. As of an 1860 map, it followed the same basic layout of the current E. Shaffer Road until it meets with Chapel Road. It appears Elkhorn Road then made a curve or two and on to the other side of Chapel Road. It continued and followed the same path of the nowadays Elkhorn Road until it intersected with Center Grange Road (by the current Beaver Creek apartment/condo complex). On the 1876 map, it crossed over Center Grange Road, and continued until it reached the current Biskup Lane area (approximately somewhere between the current Shaffer's Auto Repair business and the current Oakland Heights Drive on Biskup Lane). In the 1800s, Biskup Lane ended at this point, but Elkhorn Road continued, basically following the creek (Elkhorn Run) and would have connected/intersected with the currently defunct section of Shade Hollow Road / Elkhorn Run Road. Nowadays, directly across Center Grange Road from where Elkhorn comes out at the apartment/condo complex, there is a driveway to a private home. After exploring the area, there are small sections of the former continuation of Elkhorn Road that can still be seen.

After reviewing several deeds and other documents, I found that there had been much earlier plans to improve and "finish" this now defunct portion of Elkhorn Road (on the other side of Center Grange Road) but this improvement and finishing never occurred. This portion of the former roadway just seems to have ceased to exist. As of 1876, the portion of the roadway that would have continued across Chapel Road (where E. Shaffer now intersects with Chapel Road) was slightly altered and changed to pass to the right of the current Mamula Meat Processing business and connect / come off Temple Road (as it still does nowadays).

To sum all up, currently (2019) an original portion of Elkhorn Road was renamed E. Shaffer Road. Elkhorn Road begins a short distance after turning onto Temple Road adjacent to Mamula Meat Packing business and continues until it reaches its end as it intersects with Center Grange Road, adjacent to the Beaver Creek apartment/condo complex. Elkhorn Run Road begins off Route 51, shortly after leaving Monaca, and continues for a distance, nearly paralleling the creek Elkhorn Run, with the remaining portion being defunct as it continues into the township. (See Elkhorn Run Road next.) Nowadays, E. Shaffer, Elkhorn Road, or Elkhorn Run Road are all separate roadways, and none currently connect on to Biskup Lane or Shade Hallow Roads or even each other.

Elkhorn Run Road
This road is accessed off Route 51, shortly after exiting Monaca and heading toward Aliquippa. This current roadway is now basically a "dead end" road. At one time it would have continued to snake through the valley and joined onto Shade (Schade) Hollow Road (off Chapel Road by the Union Cemetery – see Shade Hallow Road further). It was confusing trying to find residents on Elkhorn Run Road because in the 1870s, the census enumerators usually listed all residents on the Phillipsburg/ Monaca sheets. Then, sporadically through the 1850s, 1860s, 1880s the whole area was listed under Hopewell on some census or under Moon Townships on others. Remembering, none of these families had moved at all, it was just in the grey area/seemingly "floating" of the boundary lines of the townships. A McKee family was listed as living in this same area as early as 1830. This family lived around the Baker's Landing / Vankirk areas, both being along the Ohio River adjacent to the far end of Phillipsburg/ Monaca. In addition to the McKee family, there were also the Baker, Winkle, McDonald, McCullough, and Vankirk families who lived on or adjacent to Elkhorn Run Road.

The current Elkhorn Run Road begins in what is mapped as Center Township, portions of the middle of this road are mapped to travel within Monaca Borough, then the end of Elkhorn Run Road is again listed within Center Township. Remnants of the former continuation of Elkhorn Run Road can still be seen today on some areal mappings. (See Elkhorn Road previous.)

Frankfort Road   (See River Road further.)

Fairway Drive – Beaver Valley Mall
This roadway was much longer, but a portion of it is still located within what is currently the BV Valley Mall area (to the rear of the current Burger King and Arby's businesses). This smaller portion of the roadway now has the Center Township Water Authority Maintenance, the former Rainaldi

Restaurant, and leads to the Hampton Inn parking lot – all having addresses of Fairview Drive. It originally was the roadway that would have connected to Lombardy Street at one end and Oak Street on the other end (both now defunct). It was developed around the same time as Golfview Drive/Pettibon Lane and received its name when the golf course was developed since it traveled along one of the outer edges of the once Raccoon/Pettibon Golf Course. I am sure the name was selected since golf courses do have fairways. ☺ (See Golfview Drive, Oak Street, and Lombardy Street further.)

Franklin Avenue – in the Sylvan Crest area
In 1925, this roadway was just a continuation of the now defunct Sylvan Avenue.

Gillen Drive   (See McDonald Road / Monaca Road.)

Garland Heights Road - defunct
This roadway was off Stone Quarry Road and led to homes in the current Sylvan Crest area. On the 1930 and 1940 census, the census enumerator specifically listed "Garland Heights Road" for the residents living on this elevated part of the township. Any one of the roadways that led up to these homes in that area was most likely just called by/given this name. I do not believe that it was ever an official name of such a roadway within the township, but rather a "familiar" name used by locals and census enumerators to define the location.

For many years, the only residents who lived on the elevated area now known as Sylvan Crest were the Garland families who had their summer estates on this acreage. The Garlands named all their acreage/their estates *Sylvan Crest*. (See Summer Homes section.) After the brothers sold their estates, the area was subdivided, and other families began to purchase lots and erect homes. A new roadway (would have been either Wagner Road or another once called Sylvan Avenue which was around the current Franklin Avenue) was developed and used once the original private drive of the Garlands slowly became defunct. Because of the well-known previous part-time residents of the area, many people and census enumerators evidently just referred to the whole area as Garland Heights and whichever roadway led to the homes of the area as Garland Heights Road. Some families that were listed on the 1940 census as living along this road were Carpenter, Irvin, Bailies, Rambo, and Lloyd. A few of the other now defunct names of roads listed within "Garland Heights" / Sylvan Crest in the 1920s included Sylvan Avenue, Beaver Run Road, Beggs Avenue, Union Avenue, Short Street, and Jones Street. (See the plat map in the Housing Areas section – Sylvan Crest.)

Golfview Drive   aka   **Pettibon Lane**
Association, association, association – that seems to be the way most of the early roads in the township were named – by "association" to a better-known homestead or a business along that specific roadway. Pettibon Lane was originally the roadway that led into the former Pettibon's Raccoon Golf Course, currently the site of the Beaver Valley Mall. The name of this road was originally Pettibon Lane but was changed to Golfview Drive, probably just to a be a bit less "personal" and relate better to the actual golf course itself. Pettibon Lane/ Golfview Drive would have started along a section of Stone Quarry Road (as it still does nowadays) and led you directly onto the golf course property (now the entrance roadway of the BV Mall). Remember, there was no multi-lane highway at that time, so Golfview Drive would have continued straight across the area of the current highway and onto what is now the Beaver Valley Mall entrance roadway/property.

When the golf course was first erected with only 9 holes, the first Golfview Drive (after crossing over the area of the current multi-lane highway) would have veered/turned to the left. I believe it would have continued to almost parallel Lombardy Street (see further). This course of Golfview Drive would have led you to the first club house which was originally erected in the area approximately at the current Hampton Inn entrance / parking lot. Once the golf course was expanded and a new club house was erected on the opposite side of the golf course, this original (left) portion of Golfview Drive was no longer needed, so it appears it was just eliminated and became "greens." Once the golf course was expanded to 18 holes and the second club house was erected, Golfview Drive would have then veered to the right to lead to this new/second club house. (The second club house was in the area between the current Boscovs and former Best Buy store.)

As stated, there is still a small portion of Golfview Drive that exists today. It connects the current divided highway with a portion of Stone Quarry Road, directly across from the main entrance to the BV Mall, giving access to several businesses. These include The Pool Store, The Dollar Store, and Wendy's. (See Entertainment section for more on the golf course.) (Also see Fairview Drive, Oak Street, and Lombardy Street in this section.)

Grandview Avenue – in Sylvan Crest area
Originally was in a U shape from the middle of Bridge Street, wrapping around and continuing along the edge of hillside to meet the other end of Bridge Street.

Jones Street - defunct – Sylvan Crest area
This road was originally found on a 1920s plat map when the Sylvan Crest area was laid out into lots for the housing plan. (See Garland Heights Road; see Housing Plans section – Sylvan Crest.)

Lash Street – Sylvan Crest
This road was originally found on a 1920s plat map when the Sylvan Crest area was first laid out into lots for the housing plan. It appears to have been originally longer. It began on Grandview, as it still does, but went straight to meeting the other "U" shape of what was more of Grandview.

It is difficult to determine if it is still at its original location or if it has been altered through the years. (See Garland Heights Road; see Housing Plans section – Sylvan Crest.)

Lincolnshire Drive - name changed .... currently **Lincoln Drive**
This roadway is off Brodhead Road, across from the Snowy White Laundromat (below the two large white water storage tanks). This roadway was originally named *Ruhe Street* (1957) when the lots were first laid out for homes by the Ruhe family. It then became renamed Lincolnshire Drive and the name was changed again, currently named **Lincoln Drive**.

Lincoln Drive – defunct – Mona Manor area
(This is not to be confused with the current Lincoln Drive (see Lincolnshire Drive above.)
H. L. Grimmell was a real estate agent out of Monaca. He purchased 54 acres of the former 94 acres of the Dr. Turnbull property/farm (currently Penn State Campus and Mona Manor). The Grimmell's 54 acres included the land situated above the current water treatment plant at the traffic lights where Brodhead Road meets Route 18 just outside Monaca. They built their large frame home on the corner of this property and accessed their home from the now defunct Lincoln Road. They named their acreage / "estate" *Mona Manor*. (See Housing Plan section.) Mr. Grimmell completed making a new roadway to access his estate in mid Apr 1922. It led from Brodhead Road to his residence on his estate. By the mid 1920s, he then began to subdivide the remaining land of his 54 acres. With this subdivision/ on his original plat map, there was only Lafayette Road, Lincoln Road, and Lawrence Lane. (Lafayette Road is the only one that has remained almost exactly as it was when first laid out in 1926.)

Lincoln Drive, the original and only entrance to the Grimmell's estate (Mona Manor), began at the traffic light on Route 18 (to the side and slightly behind the current water treatment station) and went up the hill to the Grimmell estate. Once Mr. Grimmell began to subdivide his property, Lincoln Drive then was extended through the property coming out between Lafayette Drive and the current lower entrance to Penn State campus (almost exactly where a current private driveway leads to a home off Brodhead Road). As late as 1994, the lower section of Lincoln Drive (portion closest to the current traffic light) was still appearing on plat maps. It appears that after the 1930 plat map (see further) was approved/revised, the remaining portion of the planned Lincoln Drive was never developed any farther than approximately 275 feet off Brodhead Road. It only led to the Grimmell's home. With the steep hillside that was along that section of Lincoln Drive, the developing of lots, and to have a new and safer access to the property, all led to the beginning of Lincoln Drive being phased out and the new entrance to the property becoming Lafayette Drive. It is difficult to find an exact date for this Lincoln Drive becoming totally defunct because all further mention of accessing the Grimmell home was simply listed as "leading from Brodhead Road" which could have also meant the new Lafayette Drive entrance.   I will also mention there was a proposed small roadway that connected Lafayette Drive to the lower section of this Lincoln Drive. On a 1994 plat map the roadway called Perry Lane was listed but doesn't appear to have developed beyond that plat map. Next time you are sitting at the traffic light, headed toward the BV Mall or making the left-hand turn onto Old Brodhead, look on the edge of the hillside behind the small sewage plant that sits there. You will be able to make out the remnants of the former Lincoln Drive.   (See Mona Manor Drive further.)   See the following portion of 1926 plat map of "Mona Manor."

... The lower left arrow indicates the still current entrance from Brodhead Road onto Lafayette Drive.
... The upper left arrow indicates where Lincoln Drive was intended to originally continue to (adjacent to Penn State's lower entrance, by the stone pillars) and if you follow Lincoln Drive on the map, it continues on to the lower right corner. It would have come out by the current traffic light as described above.
... The lower right arrow indicates where the Grimmell's home was situated.
... Brodhead Road is the roadway indicated all along the left and bottom of the above map.
... For orientation purposes, Penn State Beaver Campus would be along the upper portion of the map.
... The former Alcorn One Room School House would have sat where the words "School District" are printed on the left of the map. The former Mateer home/current apartment/condo complexes and Marshal Road would be in the lower left-hand area of the map.

Lombardy Street – defunct – Beaver Valley Mall property
There was once a Lombardy Street that would have been along the very edge of the current Mall's property, running almost parallel to the divided/multi-lane highway (Route 18). It extended to meet with Stone Quarry Road. It started to the right of the current main entrance of the BV Mall and extended to just past the former Rainaldi restaurant.

In 1963, the State Department was planning the enlargement of the then Route 18 & 51 intersection and in the process, adding a two and four-tenths miles length of new highway—going past the current Walmart Plaza to the intersection. This meant Lombardy Street, all the homes (15 to 20), and all the land between Lombardy Street and the current multi-lane highway were condemned for the new roadway.

For orientation, at that time, these properties and homes would have spanned the area adjacent to the former Steak and Shake (which is close to where Stone Quarry Road would have been) and then as previously stated, continued on toward the intersection. (See information on Routes 18 and 51 for more on this area.)   I suspect Lombardy Street was there prior to Mr. Pettibon selling the main portion of the golf course property and it was completely eliminated about the same time as the BV Mall's property was developed.

Today, some maps still show outlines of the roadway, placing it within the BV Mall property. It seems to follow the current outer roadway of the mall as it passes by the current drive-to bank building and NTB Tires. I did not find any Lombardy families that lived in that area, so the origin of the name is unknown. (See Fairview Drive previous and Oak Street further.)

A portion of a 1959 plat map.

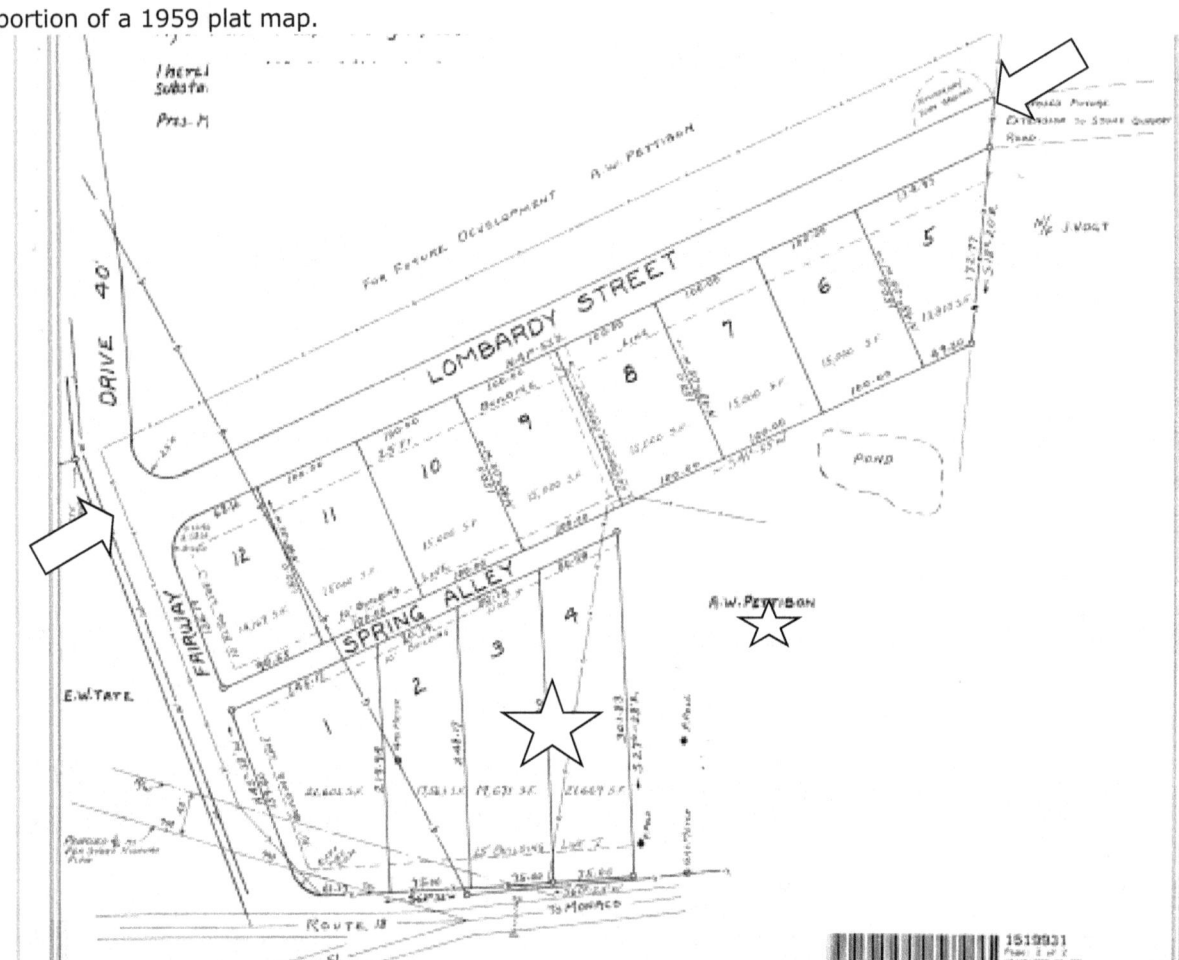

This 1959 plat map gives a layout of some of the properties that were affected by the current divided/multi-lane highway (between the left and right pointers). The larger star indicates approximately where the current Kings restaurant is located. The smaller star is approximately where the former Pettibon's home would have sat (the pond no longer exists) and the current Aaron's business is located.
Note: Fairway Drive, Lombardy Street, and Spring Alley are all listed on this plat map.

Main Road   aka   Brodhead Road
This was another name that was periodically used to reference Brodhead Road in the earlier years. Again, many times a census sheet would have "Main Road" for several residents, then have "Brodhead Road," before going back to "Main Road." Just as with the previously mentioned *Bye Road*, I have no sound reasoning to the variations of names except the suspicion of it being a choice made by local residents. (See Brodhead Road and Bye Road.)

Marshall Road
Marshall Road begins off Old Brodhead Road, just past the Penn State Campus. The portion of this road that goes past the new apartment/condo complexes (by the former Mateer's Auto Sales), and then continues toward the address of #231, are included within Center Township. All of Marshall

Road was once considered in Moon Township because the whole area, including Monaca Heights, was a part of the original Moon Township. The vast majority of Monaca Heights was annexed to the Monaca Boro while a small portion of the area became part of Center Township. Marshall Road was once a state-maintained roadway. In 1985/86, the township submitted required paperwork to transfer the road from PennDot to the township. Marshall Road was not a well-traveled road in the 1800s. I did not find any documentation as to when it became known officially as Monaca Road. It originally did not intersect with any other roadway except the Old Brodhead Road. It was only indicated with dotted lines on the 1876 map of Moon Township with it leading into the current Monaca Heights area and simply giving access to the Docktor, Patterson, and Eckhert homesteads. Nowadays, from the Old Brodhead Road, Monaca Road continues through Monaca Heights and ends at Jackson Avenue at the entrance to Allaire Park.

Mawson Lane
This very short, one lane, dead-end road is accessed off North Branch Road. It begins adjacent to and then partially parallels the beginning of Todd Lane. Mawson Lane is considered a private lane and not maintained by the township. Mawson Lane still provides access to two homes. It began as a mere drive leading to what was last known as the Tilly homestead and farm. At some point, after c1940, some of this land was subdivided, and it then was also used to give access to the Mawson home. With many of the roads and lanes developing their names from families who lived on the roads, Mawson Lane again echoes this pattern. This lane becomes a dead-end road, ending almost where the Tillie house once stood. (All the Tillie property was recently purchased and is now subdivided into yet another housing project. Access to this housing project is via a St. James housing road.)

Middle Road aka **Middles Quarry Road** (See Stone Quarry Road further.)
The 1876 map of the township shows this roadway paralleling Brodhead Road, beginning outside Monaca and heading toward the soon to be Potter Township boundaries. Some have stated it was called "the Middle Road," while some deeds referenced it as Middles Quarry Road, with it being situated between (or in "the middle") of the river and Brodhead Road. It seems to have been the section of roadway that began at the intersection and then went to the intersection of Stone Quarry Road, current North Branch Road, and Old Brodhead Road. Middle Road seemed to have been one of those roadways given a "nickname" for references only since I found no mention of this being an official roadway nor listed on any census sheets or deeds.

Milne Drive
I do not know when Milne Drive officially received its name, but it seems to have been added into the mix later, after Stone Quarry Road was severed to make way for the multilane. The name of the drive most likely is associated with the Milne family that lived in this area. All the homes and properties formerly along the section of Stone Quarry Road affected by the new multilane roadway being constructed were offered fair market value for their properties. All but one homeowner accepted the deal; the other homes and buildings were torn down. The one home that still stands is along the current Milne Drive and sits in front of the current Colonial Arms Apartment complexes. This one home and all those residents of the Colonial Arms Apartments now must use the entrance to the Walmart Plaza, Milne Drive to access their homes. (See Stone Quarry Road.)

Moffett Run Road aka **Moffett Mill Road** aka **Moffett Mill Run Road**
A few deeds and/or older plat maps place this road as beginning where the current W. Shaffer Road is located off Brodhead Road. It started off Brodhead Road, exactly where W. Shaffer Road still begins, continued the same path as W. Shaffer Road, went across the current Pleasant Drive, and traveled down into the valley to meet up with Raccoon Creek at the site of the Moffett's mill. Nowadays, W. Shaffer Road ends by Herda Drive and the Bunker Hill Church area. Prior to Route 376 (BV Expressway) being built, as stated, Moffett Mill Road continued to where the current Moffett Run Road now begins off Pleasant Drive. This road is not found to be specifically listed on any censuses up to and including the 1940 enumeration. Not meaning to repeat myself, but like so many others, this road obtained its name from the Moffett family. The Moffett Grist Mill is the only

mill shown on the 1876 atlas of Beaver County. (There is a picture of this grist mill in the Business Section of this book as well as more information on the mill's history.)

To complicate things with this roadway, many people in the earlier days would prefer to take shortcuts to travel to and from specific areas they frequented repeatedly. This was the case with this particular grist mill, and probably any other homesteads that sprang up in that area. There is a short section of roadway that comes off Brodhead Road immediately before you access Bunker Hill Road. This short section travels from Brodhead Road, goes behind the former O.C. Cluss property, and comes right back out on the current Pleasant Drive (approximately across from the current Dollar General store). This short segment of roadway is listed as both Pleasant Drive and Moffett Mill Road on many older plat maps. Nowadays, it is usually just listed as Old Pleasant Drive on maps. I would have to imagine since this former portion of Pleasant Drive intersected or led to the Moffett Mill Road, it would have been sometimes referenced simply as Moffett Mill Road. By using this "shortcut," it saved anyone traveling from the Aliquippa area to go further and continue on Brodhead Road to the beginning of the Moffett Mill Run Road/Moffett Mill Road (now W. Shaffer). This shortcut did save a few miles of travel. To further confirm this short roadway's name being Moffett Mill Road, there are a few writings and deeds that also make references to the Lowery family and Pompeani home being "on the corner of Brodhead Road and Moffett Mill Road." (The Pompeani home was built by Pearl Lowery. The site of this home became the same site of the former Cabinet World and Rebich Beer Distributor). (See Pleasant Drive.)

To condense all this, the original beginning of Moffett Mill Run Road/Moffett Mill Road came off Brodhead Road (now W. Shaffer Road), continued to the current Herda Drive by the Bunker Hill Community Church, continued and crossed land that is now that of the BV Expressway. It then continued to where it originally begins today (by the car wash business) and went down into the valley and across Raccoon Creek. Just a note, older references and plat maps label this roadway "Moffett Mill Run Road" but through the years, once the grist mill disappeared, the word "Mill" was dropped, and the roadway is now simply called "Moffett Run Road."

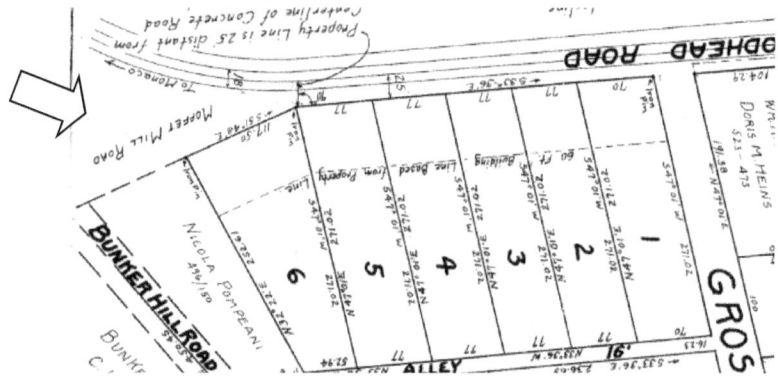

This 1945 plat map shows the small section of road that comes off Brodhead and passed behind the former O.C. Cluss business as being Moffett Mill Road (it is written upside down – see pointer). This small section of the former Pleasant Drive was often referred to as Moffett Mill Road/Moffett Mill Run Road.

Today, maps indicate this short roadway as *Old Pleasant Drive*.

Fun fact: **Moffett Mill Run Road Bridge**
The former metal bridge was considered "historic," yet it was destroyed and replaced with an open concrete bridge-way over the creek. The original metal bridge carried Moffett Mill Run Road over Raccoon Creek and was built in 1929 by Farris Engineering Company of Pittsburgh. This metal bridge was in such disrepair that it was demolished in 2012 and replaced with the open concrete structure.

McDonald Road - now a portion of Monaca Road
This was the name that local people gave to the drive/lane which eventually became named Monaca Road. During many of the earlier years, even deeds referenced the current Monaca Road as McDonald Road. Once again, I will say, it just became known as McDonald Road for all those years for the reason of being best known of giving access to the McDonald family homestead. McDonald Road was also referenced as Colona Road since it led down into what was known as the Colona area adjacent to Monaca.

Access to McDonald Road began by making a right turn off Route 51 after exiting Monaca (heading toward Aliquippa). You would go up the hill, where it would then level off to some extent, giving access to the McDonald farm and a few other adjacent homesteads. In those early years, the only access to these homes was by using this very narrow dirt drive/lane/road.

The McDonald farmhouse was the first home you came to at the top of the hill on the drive/lane. The William VanKirk and McDonald families were the first families to settle and erect their homes in this immediate area. Through the years, more homesteads developed in this area and the road was extended/lengthened accordingly. McDonald Road/Colona Road/Monaca Road was slowly lengthened to a point where it eventually extended toward Aliquippa (almost just as the current Monaca Road still does). This roadway extension that lead toward Aliquippa/Woodlawn was then known as Aliquippa Road. Also, through the years, this former McDonald Road/Colona Road/Monaca Road became intersected with the extension of Center Grange Road. This gave a formation in the shape of a "Y." This "Y" intersection of roads became well-known as a landmark and was called *Y McDonald*. Y McDonald became a place of reference for many people and is still referenced as such today by long-time residents of the area. (See Colona Road – Monaca Road - Aliquippa Road and Y McDonald information.)

As you reach the top of the hill after coming off Route 51/boulevard, the original layout of McDonald Road/Monaca Road has been changed through the years. Originally, you would come up the hill on the road and would have veered to the left and then made a sharper right turn before the road straightened more. Nowadays, Monaca Road goes up the hill and bends more of a right before it straightens some. The portion with all those previous bends/turns is now the roadway known as Gillen Drive. (See Monaca Road further for an earlier map showing the former bends in roadway.)

Slowly through the years, all along this roadway, pathways/drives were added to access newer homesteads, and as more homes were erected, those turn into lanes, and currently have turned into township roads. At some point in time, with the McDonald families no longer being present in the area due to the subdividing and selling of their lands, it was decided to officially change the name of the entire main road to Monaca Road.

(See snippet of 1937 plat map on next page.)

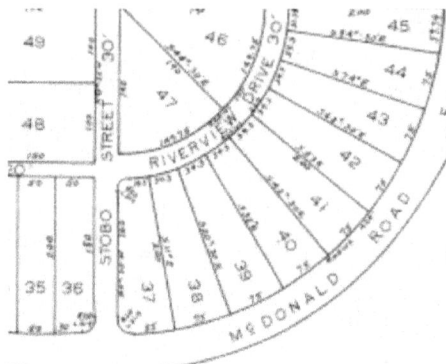

Snippet of 1937 plat map.

Monaca Road   (See *McDonald Road* and *Colona Road*)
As mentioned previously with McDonald Road, in viewing an 1876 map, Monaca Road traveled a different path than it does currently. As stated, it was also known by different names in the earlier years. In 1937, a plat map indicated the portion of Monaca Road that currently connects to Dorothy Street, Grimm Street, and Stobo Street as being *McDonald Road*, presumably called this because of all the McDonald properties in this area. The name of Monaca Road was logically given since it led down and into Monaca. Monaca Road was also found to be simply indicated as F.R.D. #1 on the 1940 census.

There is currently a Gillin Drive on your left as you come up Monaca Road off Route 51. Evidently, to make things easier, McDonald/Colona/Monaca Road was straightened, and this short section of the road's original path was more or less simply "removed" from the original roadway. This short, severed section of the former McDonald/Colona/Monaca Road became its own separate road which is now Gillin Drive.   (Also see Vankirk Road further.)

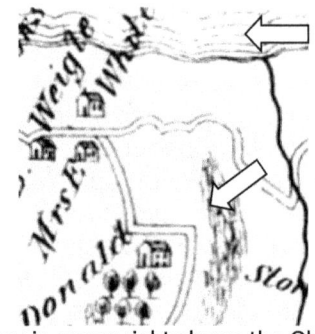

Arrow in upper right shows the Ohio River for orientation.
Arrow in the lower right shows the former path of Monaca Road prior to it being straightened.
   This particular portion the arrow is pointing to is now Gillin Drive.

Mona Manor Road - defunct
This road was more or less just a nickname for the actual road(s) that led into the estate of the Grimmell family (who named their estate *Mona Manor*). When the Grimmells subdivided their property into individual lots, more roads were added to the mix and currently the main road to access all the homes of Mona Manor is *Lafayette Drive*. In 1940, some of the families listed on Mona Manor Road were High, Anderson, Patterson, Calligan, Embree, Ademan, Feely, Sinclair, Stewart, and Elwood. (The Grimmell family had already sold their home and property prior to 1940 and moved from the area.)   (See Lincoln Drive previous.)

North Branch Road
North Branch Road was once a section of the original Brodhead Road. Following some improvement, upgrading, reconfiguring of Frankfort Road, Stone Quarry Road, and a portion of what was referred to as Middle Quarry Road, a new section was added to Brodhead Road. A slight curve was added to allow the new section of Brodhead Road to lead into the area of the current big intersection. Thus, eliminating the portion of the former Brodhead Road now known as the current North Branch Road. Once Brodhead Road was re-directed, as with so many of the roadways in rural communities, this old section of the former Brodhead Road was then referred to from the most popular domicile or commorancy on the road, in this case, North Branch Church. The township residents would have made reference to going to "North Branch road" which meant they were going to be using the road by the church and cemetery. So eventually, the official name of the road became North Branch Road.

Oak Street – defunct – Beaver Valley Mall area
This roadway was basically where the current Beaver Valley Mall Boulevard is located (which is the portion of the current lower entrance roadway into the BV Mall, beside the former ToysRUs). The whole roadway leading off Route 18 into the Mall was first given the name Valley View Road before being changed to Beaver Valley Mall Boulevard.

Pleasantview Drive
This drive was originally a private drive to the McMullen /Irons homestead. As other properties adjacent to the McMullens were purchased and additional homes were built, there were right of ways that occurred for usage of the drive. Eventually, in Sep 1949, the McMullen, Glasser, Moore, and Majzlik families all had a legal document drawn up that contained the verbiage and conditions necessary for the roadway to be maintained by these residents who had their homesteads or accessed their properties via this private road. This agreement stated all would equally pay a reasonable fee for sharing the expense of maintaining the road. Since this was a private road, all the residents at that time had their addresses simply as Chapel Road. The McMullen, Majzlik, Glasser, and Moore families then deeded the property of this road (and a turnaround area) to the Township the first of Aug 1950. This action changed it from a private road to one which would be maintained by the township. From that point forward, the roadway and addresses became Pleasantview Drive.

Poor House Run Road   and   Pleasant Drive
One would imagine this roadway received its original name of Poor House Run Road from the fact that there was an active small stream named Poorhouse Run which fairly paralleled the road's path. The Poor House Run stream was eventually moved into underground piping at the road's former intersection with Frankfort Road and then emptied into the Ohio River, not too far downstream from the former site of the Beaver County Home and Hospital aka "The Poor House." This roadway actually led down through the countryside and came out almost directly across Frankfort Road from the actual entrance drive of the county's poor house.

Through the early years, Pleasant Drive began off Brodhead Road a short distance from where it currently begins. The original beginning of Old Pleasant Drive was behind the former O.C. Cluss lumber business and then continued through to connect on to Frankfort Road. A short portion of this original roadway still exists today as you turn off Brodhead Road to access Bunker Hill Road. This short section continues and rejoins to the redesigned Pleasant Drive. In earlier years, once on Pleasant Drive you could also make a right or left turn off Pleasant Drive (by the current car wash and Women's Center) and would be on the former Moffett Mill Run Road (see W. Shaffer Road and Moffett Run Road). From the area by the car wash and Duquesne Light headquarters, Pleasant Drive would have then continued very close to its current path until it intersects with Main Street. From this intersection with Main Street, by turning left, you would have been on the section of roadway known as Poor House Run Road. Now it is the continuation of Pleasant Drive. When the Shell organization moved in and started their land moving process, the lower portion of the former Poor House Run Road/current Pleasant Drive was severed. You can no longer travel the road the distance to intersect with Frankfort Road. Also, during the earlier years, the former Simon Field

Road would have made its way through the valley of the township and came out near the lower and now defunct portion of Pleasant Drive. (See Simon Field Road.)

In late May 1954, Center Township Supervisors appointed Mr. Mike Chapes as the chairman of a committee who was to prepare a petition and send it to Harrisburg requesting that Poor House Run Road be renamed Pleasant Drive (Poor House Run Road was a state road prior to this petition). With all the paperwork approved, it was soon officially renamed Pleasant Drive. Even with the name change, for many more years, reference to this portion of Pleasant Drive was *Poor House Run Road*. In some paperwork on speed limits being adjusted in 1976, Poor House Run Road was still being mentioned. These documents stated it connected to Main Street – "*T-625, Main Street, at Poorhouse Run Road (LR-04043).*"

The Douds was a well-known family in the area and since their homestead/farm was along this roadway for so many years, the Poor House Run Road/Pleasant Drive was also often referred to as *Douds Road*. A 1961 deed between the Potter Township School District and St. Joseph Lead Co. stated, "on a public road called Douds Road or Poor House Run Road," which reflects how this road was known by several different names through the years. A few plat maps after the late 1970s had the roadway indicated as "the new Pleasant Drive," but there was no reference as to how much of it was considered "new." When the former open-air K-Mart plaza (currently the bus terminal plaza) and McDonald's restaurant were developed in the 1980s, the plat maps listed "New Pleasant Drive."

> *Fun fact: As mentioned above, one of the names considered in renaming the roadway once known as Poor House Run Road was using one of the "familiar" names that the local folks had already attached to the road – Douds Road. The Douds had a popular produce stand which many often patronized. The family chose not to have this tribute to them in the naming of the roadway and so it became known as Pleasant Drive. I have found no documentation to why the name Pleasant Drive was chosen but may have stemmed from the fact that, as stated in a few writings, while traveling on a road in this area, you could view beautiful scenery and it was a very pleasant experience to drive along. Although the roadway was not specifically named in the document that was found, it could have very well been why the name "Pleasant Drive" was selected.*

Poplar Avenue / Poplar Drive

Poplar Avenue already had its name by 1962. The new lots on a plan of homes which were approved in 1962 only had "future street" listed for what was to become Roosevelt and Truman. Poplar Drive did not become an official township road until after 1979.

Raccoon Creek Road   aka   Creek Road

This road closely followed Raccoon Creek and was in the lower area of the current Bunker Hill and Moffett Run Road areas. The Good, Zimmerman, Douds, Waxler, Johnson, Malloy, Schwarz, Kramer, Siebert, McCracken, Irons, and Moore families were among those listed as living on *Creek Road* in the earlier years. (See *Bunker Hill Road* and *Creek Road* previous.) There were many mentions of "Creek Road" in various histories of the area. Confusingly, it was not a name that was exclusive to Moon/Center Township. One description found stated, "*The road leading into Murdocksville from the south, along Raccoon Creek was known as Bigger Road; in even earlier generations it was simply called the "Creek Road."* Before the white settlers came it was the "Hunters' Path."

To the best I can decipher as for Creek Road in Moon (Center) Township, Bunker Hill Road is indicated on maps as blending into Raccoon Creek Road, with both roadways paralleling closely to the creek at various areas. If I had to decide whether it was Moffett Mill Run Road or Bunker Hill Road that was being referenced or would have been called "Creek Road" many years ago, I would say it was Bunker Hill Road since it tends to follow noticeably more of the creek. Moffett Mill/Moffett Run Road eventually leads down to a portion of Raccoon Creek but does not parallel the creek for any great length before it becomes the current Raccoon Creek Road. (During earlier years, it appears that Raccoon Creek Road had at one time been connected and crossed through the creek itself, but apparently without the use of a bridge. Today the depth and width and higher banks of the creek have eliminated this ford. Using many older maps and plat maps, I did not find any reference to any road's name as "formerly Creek Road." Creek Road evidently started as more of a "familiar name" which was applied to the roadway that would have led to many areas along Raccoon Creek. Then through the years, as with other roadways, the name was officially changed.

Red Gate Road

Red Gate Road was a familiar name given to a section of one of the township roads. The "Red Gate" name lends itself to a feature of a homestead which was located at the end of the road. This homestead was owned by Henry and Armida (Baker) Weigel (and later by his son Jennings and family). These families had an actual 'red gate' on the property by their house. It has not been determined if this gate was visible from Brodhead Road or Stone Quarry Road. The township has no record of this road which indicates Red Gate Road was never an official name of a road in the township, but as repeatedly stated, rather another "familiar name" given by local residents.

Knowing where the Weigel family farm was and the fact that their "red gate" was used as a common landmark, besides going by information found on a few early deeds in Moon Township, is what indicates that Red Gate Road was a section of Old Brodhead Road or Stone Quarry Road. If it was a section of Old Brodhead Road, it would be what comes down the hill, starting close to or a short distance past the current Penn State and Marshall Road. If Red Gate Road was a section of Stone Quarry Road, it could have been the section of road that came down and met up with Brodhead Road (very near the current site of the traffic light). In reviewing numerous deeds in this section of Moon/Center Township, I tend to lean toward Red Gate Road being a section of Old Brodhead Road. I have included a snippet from one particular deed I found, it does not make any mention of Stone Quarry Road and only references Brodhead Road. In the fifth line down, it specifically states "leading from a point **in** the Broadhead Road, known as the Red Gate, to a point **in** the Broadhead Road............"

> BEGINNING at a point, or hickory tree on the dividing line of tract herein conveyed, lands of John B. Weigle heirs and lands now or formerly of F.C. Hodkinson; thence along the dividing line between the tract herein conveyed and lands of John B. Weigle heirs, South 54° west, 119 perches to a point; thence north 9° east, 4 perches to a point in the center of the Public road leading from a point in the Broadhead Road, known as the Red Gate, to a point in the Broadhead Road at or near the North Branch Church; thence in a northwesterly direction along the center of said public road, 120 perches, more or less to a point on the dividing line between the lands herein conveyed and lands now or formerly of F.C. Hodkinson; thence along the dividing line between tract herein conveyed and lands now or formerly of F.C. Hodkinson, south 23° east, 40.6 perches to a point thence north 71° 45' east, 25.5 perches to a point; thence south 52° east, 27 perches to a point; thence south 19° east, 17.3 perches to a point and the place of beginning.

To help visualize the area, Brodhead Road now travels to where the traffic lights are currently located by the small water treatment plant. There were no lights or stops many years ago, instead it simply veered/made a turn to the right and headed into Monaca. This original portion of Brodhead Road would have been closer to the hillside on your right (as you are heading into Monaca). Also, by the current area of the traffic light in this area, would have been where Stone Quarry Road intersected with Brodhead Road. Since both roadways had very steep embankments as mentioned in some articles of Red Gate Road, either of these roadways could have been referenced by local residents as "Red Gate Road." Stone Quarry Road was never mentioned in any
of the articles or deeds yet was a popular roadway even prior to the 1920s. (Wagner Road had not been yet developed and did not have any steep embankments mentioned, so it is not considered in the mix of roadways.)

Next are a few bits and pieces from various reports and articles found regarding this Red Gate Road:

... In Mar 1920 there was a young woman who died because of injuries from a sleigh riding party at Red Gate. She went over a very steep embankment.
    (From this article it could lend to Old Brodhead Road or Stone Quarry Road because of steep embankments found on both roadways.)

> *Fact: This young lady was Bessie O. Mateer (d/o George A. Mateer, who was the s/o George A. and Mary Elizabeth (Baker) Mateer). The Mateers owned a large number of acres of land from the corner of Brodhead Road/Marshall Road. This land extended along the right side of Old Brodhead Road as you now travel down to the traffic light. Bessie O. had married George Harley.*

... Sep 1920 - It was reported that a five-ton motor truck from Woodlawn went over an eight-foot embankment at Red Gate in Center Township in the fog Tuesday morning. The truck was badly damaged. The report didn't state whether the driver or others were injured.
    (From this article, again, I lean toward that one section of Old Brodhead Road or Stone Quarry Road.)

... Jul 1936 - There were bids put out for resurfacing roads, "Redgate Road, extending westerly from Brodhead Road at foot of Monaca Hill."
    (What did they consider *Monaca Hill*? Was it the roadway that came down from Stone Quarry Road or Brodhead Road coming down after passing the current Penn State campus?)

... 1937 - Red Gate was reported to go "from the old Wagner Farm along the Brodhead Road to the end of that thoroughfare at the Jennings Weigel farm, also bordering on the Brodhead Road." (This section was describing the resurfacing of "Red Gate" in 1937.) The article also stated, "The scenery along this stretch of roadway is said to be that of some foreign country" because it was so beautiful.
    (This article once again could lend to being either Old Brodhead Road or Stone Quarry Road since it stated "the old Wagner Farm" and also "along the Brodhead Road <u>to the end of that thoroughfare</u>...")

... 1937 - "Mona Manor on *Red Gate Road*"
    (This statement definitely references that the Grimmell Estate of Mona Manor was accessible from Red Gate Road. This lends once again to Brodhead Road because the roadway of Lincoln Drive turned off Old Brodhead Road and not the Stone Quarry Road. There was never access to Mona Manor via Stone Quarry Road in the 1920s/1930s.)

I personally found no absolute proof or township documentation of the exact location of Red Gate Road, but the description in various deeds and the examples of the above news articles do seem to indicate it would be a section of Old Brodhead Road rather than Stone Quarry Road. Regardless of its location, we know its general location. It is also a conclusion that Red Gate Road was simply a "familiar name" that was used.

Ridge Road

On the 1910 census sheets, Gilbert Sohn was the enumerator and indicated two homes on this road, (1) Jane Short (widow) with her children and an older pair of siblings and (2) Elizabeth and George Holmes. Mr. Sohn had these names and this road sandwiched between New Sheffield Road (current Chapel Road) and Creek Road (near current Pleasant Drive). Although not an absolute guarantee, it does appear that Mr. Sohn did seem to simply follow the roadways as they were laid out in the township, moving one to the next. Using his pattern, this would place Ridge Road in this area. In 1900, Daniel and Jane Short and family were listed on the census adjacent to those on Creek Road. By 1920, Jane had died, but the children were still living in the same home, again listed somewhere in the current lower Pleasant Drive area. As for the Holmes siblings, they were also living in the same home in 1900 somewhere in the same area surrounding the current Pleasant Drive. I did not find either Elizabeth or George Holmes on the 1920 census. Conclusion, there is no definitive location of this roadway. It must have been just a familiar name applied to a portion of roadway that passed along a "ridge.".

River Road

River Road seems to be a more familiar name attached to what became the old Frankfort Road. In the 1800s, River Road/Frankfort Road followed a bit of a different path than it does today (see Frankfort Road previous). River Road came from Bellowsville and appears to have traveled a straight course, just a bit inland, above and fairly parallel to the shoreline of the Ohio River, before crossing the Raccoon Creek and continuing into then Raccoon Township (prior to Potter Township being formed). Raccoon Creek Road and Pleasant Drive/Poor House Run Road connected on to what was known as "River Road." Another reinforcement of River Road and Frankfort Road being one in the same were some of the earlier families found as living along River Road, in the area between the Bellowsville area and Raccoon Creek. They included Merriman, Potts, Reed, Anderson, Dunn, Springer, Trotter, Potter, and Hostetter.

Ruhe Street (changed)

This was the original name given to what is currently Lincoln Drive, off Brodhead Road. Eugene B. & Vera Humbert and Otto & Rose Mary Ruhe originally laid out a subdivision of land in 1957 with Ruhe Street the singular drive to these lots. It was all then deeded to A. Secontine Sylvester and the name of the road became Lincolnshire Drive before becoming the current Lincoln Drive. Lincoln Drive also has Winwood Drive and Oakcrest Drive now extending from it.

Shade Hollow Road

This road is located on your left a short distance after entering Chapel Road off Old Brodhead Road (near the rear parking lot area of the current Turners property). The actual surname of the family who had their homestead here was "S**c**had**e**." The "e" was omitted from the spelling of this road for many years before being recently rectified but for some reason the "c" was and is still omitted. The Schade family members were well-known dairy and general farmers in the township for many years. Some former families associated with Shade Hollow Road were Schade, Barto/McCartney, Champion, Harley, and Irons.

This is a fairly lengthy, unpaved, quite curvy, and dead-end road. With its many curves, there are even portions of Shade Hollow Road which veer into what is part of the Monaca Borough, with it officially ending within Center Township. If you have some form of a four-wheel drive vehicle, you could possibly even continue from the current seemingly end of Shade Hollow Road onto a crude course/path that eventually connects to Elkhorn Run Road, which begins from just outside Monaca off Route 51/Constitution Boulevard.

> SEVEN BRIDGES
> This was a reference by local township residents to the area accessible from Shade Hollow Road and/or Elkhorn Run Road. It was fondly referred to Seven Bridges because there were actually seven forms of bridges that provided travel over Elkhorn Run creek when traveling in this area.

Shaffer Roads -- East and West Shaffer Roads

There is an "East" and "West" Shaffer Road today. They intersect with Brodhead Road directly across from each other. From reviewing different documents, E. Shaffer Road appears to have had the surname "Shaffer" attached to it the longest.

The current E. Shaffer Road was originally named *Elkhorn Run Road*, with the name changed to just Shaffer Road by the late 1920s or early 1930s and eventually the "E." being added to it once W. Shaffer was named. It is apparent that this name change from Elkhorn Run Road came about from the tradition of people calling it Shaffer Road by the association while accessing the Shaffer Post Office and Shaffer's small store. Both the store and post office were formerly located on the corner lot at E. Shaffer and Brodhead Road. (See Elkhorn Run Road previous and the Post Office section.)

W. Shaffer Road was originally named *Moffett Mill Run Road* until what appears to be the late 1920s or early 1930s. Moffett Mill Run Road actually began off Brodhead Road just as W. Shaffer Road now does and continued on what is now called W. Shaffer Road. It then would have continued down into the valley (on the same path that nowadays is known as just Moffett Run Road, off Pleasant Drive). The original roadway named Moffett Mill Run Road was severed when the BV Expressway was constructed. The section coming off Brodhead Road was then named W. Shaffer and the remaining section (off Pleasant Drive) was named Moffett Run Road, with the word *Mill* being dropped from the name. At the far end of Moffett Run Road, there is now a bridge that allows it to pass over Raccoon Creek. The roadway then becomes Moffett Mill Road and/or Raccoon Creek Road. (See Moffett Mill Run Road previous.)

Shirley Drive – Sylvan Crest area
Originally the whole area was laid out with just lots.   This roadway was added after 1925.

Sheffield Road
This was the former name for the current section of Chapel Road between the intersection of Center Grange Road/Chapel Road to the end of the road where Chapel Road intersects with Brodhead Road by The First United Methodist Church.   (See *Chapel Road*)

Short Street - Sylvan Crest area
In the 1920s, there was another Short Street found on the plat map of Sylvan Crest when it was laid out into lots for housing.   This Short Street was just that – a short street – and was located along the edge/top of the hillside adjacent to the Monaca Borough boundary.   (See *Garland Heights Road previous; see Housing Areas-Sylvan Crest*.)

Currently, as you exit the Township Market Plaza (by Lowes), there is a small section of roadway between the stop signs by Eat 'n' Park and the traffic light at the entrance of Walmart Plaza that is found to be labeled on maps as "Short Street."

Simon Field Road
This road begins on the opposite side of Brodhead Road across from the two large water tanks and adjacent to the current Gentile's plaza.   It still travels down and beside the current Gentile's plaza, continuing down into that valley.   This roadway was another one to be severed by the construction of the BV Expressway. Today, both segments are dead-end roads.   Prior to the BV Expressway being built, Simon Field Road started on Brodhead Road and would wind through that valley coming out on the former Poor House Run Road/Pleasant Drive (just prior to reaching the former intersection with Frankfort Road/Route 18).   During the earlier years, Simon Field Road originally would have been another means for township residents to access the heart of the community of Bellowsville and to access the Beaver County Home.

As of 2018, I only found two homes along the portion of the roadway that begins off Brodhead Road.   Each are situated quite a distance down on this roadway.   Even in 1870s and 1880s, there were only three or four homesteads – J. Merkle (53 acres), G. Weygandt (41 acres), Jas. Wallace (36 acres), and possibly Mary McCoy. (Her home was on 13 acres between Pleasant Road and Simon Field Road, so it is hard to say which roadway she would have been considered to be living on.) (See Poor House Run Road and Pleasant Drive.)

There was once a one room schoolhouse called the Simon Field School House situated along Brodhead Road very close to the entrance of Simon Field Road (see Education section).   It is written the school received its name because it sat on the edge of a field which was owned by a man named Simon.   I would like to verify this information, but 1) I found nothing on who this Mr. Simon __ or Mr. __ Simon was or of either owning any land in that area, and 2) I could find no documentation as to the naming of the school.   Since most schoolhouses were named for a family or a road, was the road already named when the school was built or was the roadway unnamed and merely a drive? Perhaps Simon Field Road simply received its name because of the proximity to the Simon Field School house?

Spring Alley – defunct
This was a roadway that was eliminated/absorbed into the current divided highway between the intersection and the traffic light at the entrance of the BV Mall. (See map with Lombardy Street.)

Stone Quarry Road
When it comes to Stone Quarry Road, it is confusing when you go through some older deeds and other paperwork because other names were associated with this roadway, as was the case with many other roads. One of the roadways that seems to be mentioned consistently with Stone Quarry Road was called "Middles Quarries Road" or just the "Middles Road;" another was Milne Drive which was found to be referenced as being the "former Stone Quarry Road." It is presumed that Stone Quarry Road received its name due to the actual stone quarry that was operated on the Israel Wagner property which was accessed via this road.

Just as mentioned with several other roadways, Stone Quarry Road was yet another roadway to be severed because of a bigger highway being developed and constructed. This bigger highway was first referenced as simply the "New Road," but is now known as Route 18 (it is the divided highway which begins at the intersection, goes past the BV Mall and on into Monaca). When you take an aerial view of the area, you can see where the two ends of Stone Quarry Road would have met and how it was originally laid out. There are still faint traces that can be seen past where one section ends and the other section begins. Stone Quarry Road now begins off Old Brodhead Road at the current intersection of Old Brodhead and North Branch/Old Brodhead/Stone Quarry roads. It continues for a short distance before becoming a dead end just past Woods Avenue. Originally it would have continued to the area that is currently the entrance by the Aldi's store before then joining back up with Brodhead Road adjacent to the area by the current traffic light outside Monaca.

> *Fun fact: The stone quarry associated with this road was worked by powder shot being put into the rock formations in the area. The stones were then extracted and cut by hand and hauled out by horse and wagon. This was a sandstone quarry used by many local homeowners for constructing cellar walls. Other uses for this sandstone were for curbstones and/or the quarried stones were crushed and used for roadbeds. Many years ago, prior to paving, Penna. Avenue to Carey's Corner (current P-Dub's at Ninth Street in Monaca) was once made up of crushed stone from this quarry.*

> *Fun fact: On many of the deeds and transactions of properties along the area where they were "rerouting" Stone Quarry Road in the early 1900s, due to the developing and construction of a new road from the intersection and into Monaca, this new roadway was simply referred to as "the state boulevard." By the mid 1920s, the deeds and documents stated this roadway which led toward Monaca and met up with the Old Brodhead Road outside Monaca, would be known as or referenced as the "New Road."*

As stated, today, the portion of Stone Quarry Road becomes a dead end just past Woods Avenue. The second portion of the original Stone Quarry Road consists of the roadway begining at a stop sign along Wagner Road (across the road from the current Eat 'n' Park), then continues and provides access to a few homes and a set of three apartments/condos (across the road from the current Aldi's store) where it also becomes a dead end. A great deal of some of the original Stone Quarry Road has just disappeared. The missing portions are associated from between the stop sign along Wagner Road and heading toward Monaca. As you come out of Monaca, go through the first set of traffic lights, and head toward the next set of traffic lights at the Walmart plaza, you can make the first right-hand turn and be on Wagner Road. Once on Wagner Road, just a short distance straight ahead is a small section of road with four or five homes on it. This short section was all a former portion of the original Stone Quarry Road which would have continued to meet up with the original Brodhead Road.

This information discusses a roadway that was either a short section of Stone Quarry Road or Milne Drive……………………

In 1921, there was a group of residents that recorded a deed for the creation of a private road to their properties. The signers of this deed included James/Linnie Landis, Francis/Marie LeGoullon, Henry Miksch, Wm./Katherine Milne, Elmer/Anna Hicks, Paulis/Mary Koehler, Fred./Mary Bechtel, Wm./Nellie Bechtel, John/Martha Phillis, Clarence/Leva Ballis, Michael/Anna Zimm, and Nancy Phillis. The intention of this conveyance by all these residents listed was to maintain a vacated/changed public highway that gave access as a private way to all the homesteads of those residents. There was no mention of the name of the vacated roadway, but, being it was referenced as "a public highway" would lend itself to being one of the severed sections of Stone Quarry Road. This is only my theory though. This "private way" to the above-mentioned homesteads could have possibly been for a portion of Wagner Road or Milne Drive.

Sylvan Avenue - defunct – Sylvan Crest area
This now defunct roadway was once located within in the Sylvan Crest housing plans. It would have been approximately where Franklin Avenue is currently found. It was the entrance road which abutted to Bridge Street, then went straight and seems to have become Franklin Avenue. Sylvan Avenue wound its way up the hillside and was the former private drive, which was the entrance to the estates. (See pictures of this drive in the Summer Home section; see *Garland Heights Road;* see Housing Plans section – *Sylvan Crest*.)

Todd Lane   aka   **Todd Hollow Road**
Todd Lane, as with most roads in the township, was like a pathway or driveway through the farmland to access one or two homes and farms. These were originally listed simply as "off Chapel Road" in early years. There was no name attached to this lane since it was really just a "driveway." Eventually, this portion of the road/lane that now travels between Chapel Road and North Branch Road was given the name of "Todd Hollow Road;" many plat maps and deeds made reference to "Todd Lane, formerly known as Todd Hollow Road." Coming off Chapel Road was originally the only entrance to access the few homesteads, but as a few more homes were being built closer to the section/end by North Branch Road, that entrance soon developed. During the early 1900s, these homesteaders sought a shorter route to Brodhead Road (currently North Branch Road) to access North Branch Church. From repeated usage, these families had started to create a very crude lane that brought them out onto that portion of the then Brodhead Road.

As you come off the current North Branch Road onto Todd Lane, land on the right would have been owned originally by D. C. Bruce, then Christian and Mary Ann Docktor. This property bordered land of James Smith and butted against the Keller/Todd family property. On the left, the acreage would have been owned by John C. Erb, then by John Wilhelm. This property butted up to the other portion of the Keller/Todd land (which spread over both sides of the current Todd Lane).

The Landis/Lundis family and Keller family were two of the earliest of the three or four residents on the lane for many years. It was originally just a long drive off Chapel Road that took you into these homesteads. Around 1900, the Keller farm became the home of their daughter who had married James Todd. (See the Keller Family and Todd Family information.) William Irwin became the owner of a house on Todd Lane, directly across from where Edgewater intersects with Todd Lane. This house and 88 acres of land appears to have first been that of the Jacob Landis family. (See Landis Family and Irwin Family information.)

As of the 1940 census, the enumerator still did not indicate this lane as "Todd Hollow/Todd Lane." It was simply listed as "off Chapel Road." Either the lane was not yet officially a public township road or the census enumerator chose not to include the name. Again, as with other roads/lanes, its name obviously was generated from the most popular family surname of a resident living along the road/lane; in this case, the Todd family. Even though the 1940 census did not include a name for the road/lane, I found where it was first referenced as *Todd Hollow Road* from close to 1900. Into the 1950s and on some 1976 plat maps, it was listed as *Todd Hollow Road.* From this point, deeds and maps started to simply list *Todd Lane,* with a note for reference, "aka Todd Hollow Road" or "formerly Todd Hollow Road."

> *Fun fact: Until into the 1960s or 1970s, the entire length of Todd Lane was quite narrow. Whether traveling on Todd Lane from the North Branch Road entrance or from the Chapel Road entrance, it was all little more than a one lane road. This was especially noticeable along the former Todd homestead property where it makes a severe and blind bend (which is*

still on the lane). Before the road/lane was widened to a full two-lane road, only one car could pass along most portions of the road and especially the blind bend. When coming to this blind bend, great caution had to be observed. Especially in the 1950s and 1960s, it didn't matter which direction you would be traveling, you would have to stop a short distance from this bend, roll down your car window, toot your horn a few short times, and wait to hear a reply "tooting." If there was no return "tooting," you knew you could safely proceed (very slowly) around that bend. But...... if you had a reply toot, it meant there was another car at that blind bend heading toward you. Tradition for all the neighbors and people familiar with the lane was the car coming down the hill from the North Branch end of the road would have the "right of way." Sometimes, as a stranger would travel along Todd Lane, one of the residents of Todd Lane would find themselves face to face, more like bumper to bumper, with the stranger's car since they did not know the common "safety practice" at this bend. Even now, this bend commands respect from all traveling on Todd Lane.

Associated with this information of the blind and sharp bend on Todd Lane, I am certain this was and is not the only road/lane in the township with this condition. There are quite a few roadways still within the township that are not full two-lane roads. Most of these roadways are not considered "main roadways" since ninety eight percent of the traffic is from those with homes on them. Just as with Todd Lane, if you do meet another car traveling the opposite direction, you or the other car will have to pull as far off the road as possible. This is to allow the other to safely pass. Both cars share the burden and must slow down to a crawl, put the wheels on the passenger side of the cars off the road and into the "ditch" area to allot enough room to pass by each other.

The portion of Todd Lane that began off Chapel Road and led to the previously described blind bend was also a very locally traveled portion of the lane. There were only a few farms along this portion. It was also no more than a bit wider than a single lane road for many years. This portion of Todd Lane was more twisting and bending compared to today. In approximately 1969, the positioning of a portion of this end of the lane was greatly changed from its current appearance when plans were developed to eliminate another quite severe bend along this section of roadway. With the school district purchasing the acreage for the high school and the plans for Todd Lane Elementary, it was advantageous for that portion of Todd Lane to be moved and straightened. The portion of the lane effected was the section just past Edgewater up to the homes across from the current Todd Lane School building. Previously, as you passed Edgewater Drive, it went more to the right and wound its way with several twists and bends. it would have crossed the properties closer to where the current small athletic storage shed now sits, then would have curved back toward the homes that now sit across from the Todd Lane School.

Also, there once was a small wooden bridge close to the intersection with Edgewater Drive that allowed you to cross over the Moon Run stream. It was replaced with a large concrete pipe placed under the roadway. Many people today do not even realize there is a stream passing under the roadway.

Todd family members on Todd Hollow Road

Temple Road

Just as with Monaca Road, Elkhorn Run Road, Marshall Road, and other roadways that cross over into other townships or boroughs, parts of Temple Road are mapped to not only be in Center Township but have sections of the roadway that travel into Aliquippa and Hopewell Township. This was originally a lane to access the multiple Temple family homesteads that were spread out through all these townships, including Moon/Center. Current Center Township residents along Temple Road include addresses up to approximately #1043 Temple Road. From that point, they are considered residents of another township.

Union Avenue - defunct – Sylvan Crest area
This road was originally found on a 1920s plat map when the Sylvan Crest area was laid out into lots for the housing plan. It appears to have faded away over time. It would have run from Bridge Street to Jones (near the same site as the current Carpenter Street). (See Garland Heights Road; see Housing Plans section – Sylvan Crest.)

Union Cemetery Road
This was one of the early "applied" names to the portion of the current Chapel Road which begins off Old Brodhead Road (by the Union Cemetery) to approximately the Cochran Drive and Todd Lane area. (See Chapel Road previous.)

Wagner Road
Jacob and Israel Wagner owned their large homesteads adjacent to and between the BV Mall and current Sylvan Crest area.

Valley View Road - defunct – Beaver Valley Mall property
This was the name of the road of the lower entrance to the BV Mall leading off Route 18. It is currently known as *Beaver Valley Mall Boulevard*. (See Oak Drive.)

Y McDonald intersection (See *McDonald Road.*)

~ ~ ~

MISCELLANEOUS POST CARD......................
The wording on the top of this post cards is "Hollow Road, near Monaca, Pa;" it is calculated to be from 1910 or 1920.

This could be a picture of almost a dozen lanes throughout the township since many had the name "Hollow" attached to them. Since this states, "...near Monaca, PA." this indicates it was in the portion of Moon/Center Township closest to Monaca rather than Aliquippa. This could have easily been either Todd Hollow Road or Shade Hollow Road since both of those roads have a stream that crosses them and would have required a bridge. Elkhorn Road and the Shaffer roads also have streams crossing them. Whichever road/lane it actually is in the picture, the subject matter alone depicts how rural the whole area once was. The buggy and horse pictured on this post card are interesting enough to look at. A horse and buggy/wagon or just a horse was a common site in the township during those pre-1930 years. Even into the 1950s, seeing them was not considered totally unusual on any of the lesser used roads.

~ ~ ~

Routes 18 and 51 and 18 & 51 Intersection

This area was at one time a very simple meeting of two roadways. Then it progressed to an actual crossing of roadways. There were no traffic lights and there was not even a four-way stop area for several years. After it became a four-way meeting of roadways, it was often called and/or known as "The Point." Also referenced as being at The Point, was an entrance to the Matko's Tavern/Adam's Inn, Hank's Frozen Custard/hamburger business, and a service station.

The roadways known as Route 18 and Route 51 once intersected with Brodhead Road in Center Township. In fact, many long-time residents still refer to the intersection by the current Kings Restaurant as the "intersection of 18 & 51." Currently, it is known as the intersection of Route 18 and Brodhead Road. There are some people who still reference Route 51 as being the roadway that comes out of Monaca and continues up past the main entrance of the mall, goes through this intersection, and then continues as Brodhead Road into Aliquippa. This comes from many years of that roadway and Brodhead Road being labeled Route 51.

Some examples of references for the former Route 51: When Wendy's was opening, it was described as being on the corner lot of Golfview Drive and Route 51, with directions to Monaca being to "pass the Beaver Valley Mall and continue on Route 51...." In Mar 1960, it was stated "Route 51, passing Main Street and the C.T.V.F.D. #1 station..." Another in 1957, was referencing Pleasant Drive, "which runs between Routes 51 and 18." This is talking about it starting on Brodhead Road (Rte 51) and traveling to meet up with Frankfort Road (Rte 18). In Dec 1986, when speaking of the two routes meeting in Center Township, it stated, "that of 18 and 51..." A historical description stated, "Another branch of the Catawba trail came down the west side of the Ohio through New Sheffield and reached the Beaver River about a mile or so below what is now the town of Monaca. General Brodhead followed this portion of the trail when he built the Brodhead Road, now part of Route 51."

So, to those who never knew Brodhead Road was Route 51, it is quite apparent that Brodhead Road was indeed well-known as Route 51 and it is also clear to see that it once came out of Monaca, traveled through Center Township, then head into the Borough of Aliquippa.

Route 18 --
The roadway that still comes out of Monaca and goes past the mall to the intersection is now labeled as Route 18. It then turns/veers to the right just before the big intersection in Center and continues down the hill into Potter Township. Brodhead Road begins at the same big intersection but is simply labeled as "Brodhead Road" and not Route 51 any longer, but it is maintained as a state road.

Route 18 begins at the bottom portion of Pennsylvania, just outside Waynesburg University and travels eventually into Potter Township. It then enters Center Township, to the aforementioned big intersection, past the main entrance of the Beaver Valley Mall, down into Monaca, along Pennsylvania Avenue. Once in Monaca, it passes over the Ohio River via the Monaca-Rochester Bridge. Once on the Rochester side of the bridge, Route 18 then continues through Rochester, into New Brighton and Beaver Falls, through Wampum, continues into Hermitage, across the Shenango River/ Reservoir, and on to the intersection of Route 322 in Hartstown.

In 2015 and 2016, Route 18 was rerouted or "repositioned" in Potter Township for both infrastructure improvements and for widening because of the area being reconstructed for Shell's visions. The Royal Dutch Shell paid for all the realignment and related costs.

Route 51 -- It currently comes from the Pittsburgh area, paralleling the river and into Monaca (Constitution Boulevard) before now intersecting with Route 18 in Monaca and passing over the Ohio River. Once on the Rochester side of the Monaca-Rochester Bridge, Route 51 is listed as going to the right with the main portion of 51 continuing through Rochester a short distance. It then crosses the Beaver River, goes a few blocks through Bridgewater and turns into a four-lane road past the new Veteran's Bridge. It travels on toward Brady's Run, into Chippewa and to the Ohio state line.

Fun Fact: The Monaca-Rochester Bridge has the distinction of carrying both Route 18 and Route 51. Few bridges are host to two separate state routes.

Fun Fact: At a length of 205 miles (330 km), PA Route 18 is one of the few state routes in Pennsylvania, north to south or east to west, to traverse the entire state. It also has the distinction of being the longest state route in Pennsylvania.

Prior to the current view and layout of the original, current intersection of Route 18 and Brodhead Road, it was but simple cross-roads before having only a few stop signs added to control increasing traffic. The intersection was originally expanded prior to 1962. With this updating, a few buildings were altered and/or razed. Hank's, a small restaurant/frozen custard business, was eliminated, along with a popular gas station. Also, the original club house of the former golf course which had been converted into a private home of the Tate family was left standing but had to be cut in half to accommodate footage allowance for the hillside that was created.

As if this wasn't a big enough hit to these landowners, late in Dec of 1962 to early Jan 1963, there was a right of way determined which involved and affected even more properties adjacent to the intersection. Appraisal was given for 15 to 20 buildings/homes that would have to be condemned and then razed for construction of a two and four-tenths mile length of limited access roadway. This roadway and the affected properties included the area of the intersection that was then Route 51 starting in front of the former Tate Trailer Sales Co. (currently the Hampton Inn) to the current entrance of the mall. Also, the land and properties past Stone Quarry Road (currently between Walmart Plaza and Eat n Park) and heading toward Monaca.

Construction of this roadway began in 1964 and was completed Sep 1966. Not only did many people lose their homes with this "progress," the original/first club house of the golf course (then being the Tate's home) was once again targeted. Mr. Tate let them condemn the home and pay him for its value. Then, since he was determined not to have his home razed, he purchased the condemned building back at a very deep discount, built a new basement/foundation further in on his property, and had the house "rolled"/moved to its new location on top of that foundation where it stood until the Hampton Inn was built.

With this new roadway being completed and extended, additional traffic was created, therefore, the former intersection of then Routes 18 & 51 was becoming a very dangerous place. With there still only being two stop signs at the sight of the intersection, many accidents were occurring on a regular basis. In Sept 1966, the Center Township Supervisors requested the state's Highways Department to conduct a survey of the intersection. The supervisors did not receive the paperwork or forms for the survey until mid Oct. This paperwork was for approval to install two additional stop signs. It was felt that a traffic light would be justified, but until the permit for the light was reviewed and approved, the need for additional stop signs was immediately necessary. The time frame to have approval for the stop signs would be much shorter than for the lights. Therefore, authority from Harrisburg was solicited to add two more stop signs at the intersection due to the number of accidents that were occurring there. As of 2019, there are multiple traffic lights, each with designated lanes and green turning arrows aiding in the flow of traffic. There are added lanes for the loops leading into/out of the intersection, all creating an involvement of 24 lanes of traffic.

To summarize or help clarify what happens to the roads at the big intersection in Center Township:

- The intersection once was referenced as "18 & 51," is now known as *Route 18 and Brodhead Road*.

- Old Brodhead Road (SR 3002) begins at the intersection, continues through Center Township, past Penn State Beaver Campus, connecting again to Route 18 which then goes into Monaca.

- Brodhead Road coming from the Hopewell and Aliquippa area, continues through Center Township to the intersection, (facing toward the divided highway which goes past the main entrance of the BV Mall). Brodhead Road ends at this intersection, then becomes known as "Old Brodhead Road."

- Route 18 (Frankfort Road) comes up the hill from Potter Township, past the lower exit of the Mall and former ToysRUs, then to the intersection.

- At the intersection (coming from Potter Township), Route 18 would be followed by making a left, going to the light at the main entrance to the BV Mall, down the hill past Walmart, entering Monaca, and continuing over the Monaca-Rochester Bridge and on through Rochester.

This is a picture of the former intersection of Routes 18 & 51 in Oct of 1966.
These gentlemen in the picture are standing at what would be near the edge of the current King's restaurant parking lot. The current Hampton Inn would be behind the men on the left. The darker colored road beginning on the left of the picture and fading off in the distance is Route 18 going toward Potter Township. Not included in the picture --- to the left would be Brodhead Road (leading toward Aliquippa) and Old Brodhead Road (which would lead to Center Square/Center Stage.

Pictured left to right: Rev. Fred Simmel, pastor of Vankirk Faith Lutheran Church, Rev. Harold Bowman, pastor at North Branch Church, Rev. Paul A. Holzer, pastor at St. Francis Cabrini Church, Carl Weigle, Center Grange executive board member, and Dante Colaluca, Center Township Police Chief.

Fact: At the same time of application for this intersection's survey, the supervisors were also making application for a survey at the intersection of Wagner Road (currently the entrance to Lowes plaza area) where it joined the new roadway from the mall area leading into Monaca. They were seeking to provide smoother access in and out of Wagner Road which would provide Sylvan Crest residents with a safe entrance/exit from their residential area.

~ ~ ~

More information for the former intersection of 18 and 51... It was a common sight at the older big intersection for people to see road signs with arrow indicators showing which direction you were to go to follow Route 18 and which direction to follow Route 51. The only road signs that currently hold both Route 18 and Route 51 on them in Center will direct you toward Monaca. Once in Monaca, there are several signs as you come off the East Rochester Bridge or as you approach Ninth Street in Monaca before going onto the Monaca-Rochester Bridge. I am bringing up these road signs to emphasize how absolutely confusing it must be to figure out which way to go to find your way since both routes travel across the same bridge.

Fun Fact: During the times when there were no GPS devices, people did not have the means to have directions "fed" to them. It was probably quite confusing since even though road signs label a route "north" or "south," it does not mean that the road will be going in a "true" north or south direction.

Did you know that it is a rule of thumb that all highways that travel north to south are assigned an odd number, with the lowest numbers in the east, and highest in the west and these north to south routes have numbers ending in "1." East to west highways are typically even-numbered, with the lowest numbers in the north, and highest in the south. East–west routes have numbers ending in "0."

Also, three-digit numbered highways will most likely be a "spur route" of a parent highway (U.S. route 151 would be a spur off of U.S. Route 51).

Defunct portion of Route 51

Now known as Route 51, it begins in Monaca as Pennsylvania Avenue and turns into Beaver Avenue before being labeled Constitution Boulevard. This road was originally only a two-lane highway. Anyone who has traveled the four-lane highway, aka Constitutional Boulevard, between Monaca and Aliquippa, may have noticed that further up on the hillside (to your right as you are heading toward Aliquippa) there are still remnants of an old highway. This portion of the former two-lane highway had the hillside on one side, then there was a longer slope down to the railroad tracks before the land leveled off for various plants/companies whose properties bordered the Ohio River. By the mid 1950s, it was decided to expand this two-lane road into a four-lane highway which involved relocating it closer to the railroad tracks and mill properties. Therefore, the original portion of the roadway was abandoned. Elkhorn Run Road and Monaca Road are two means of accessing Center Township along this roadway. Both are still accessible from this four-lane Route 51.

Fact: As early as Oct 1907, there was a petition that the crude roadway between Aliquippa and Monaca be repaired after a heavy rain had washed a large portion of the roadway out. Horses were still the main form of transportation and without this roadway being accessible, it meant those wanting to reach Woodlawn/Aliquippa from Monaca or that side of what was known as Moon Township (now Center) had to travel at least an extra three miles out of their way.

Speaking of this defunct section of Route 51 –

Fun fact: In my younger years, I remember traveling on the former old two-lane portion of this highway. As a treat on a nice summer evening, my father would take us for a ride, and then pull over to the berm of this now defunct section of the road. Since at that time, the road sat quite a bit higher, it gave a perfect view of the railroad and steel mill property. We could watch them pouring the slag pots that were filled with molten hot slag at J & L Steel. It was fascinating to see the glowing golden liquid slag pour out of the pots. Once they did away with the elevated two-lane roadway and replaced it with the lower current four-lane roadway, the view of the steel plant yard was ruined.

If this were a full color photograph, it would make a much bigger impact because the liquid metal flowing over the hillside would be a brilliant, glowing golden yellow.

~ ~ ~

Fun fact: Did you know that there was a turnpike in Pennsylvania in the early 1800s? It was not only a toll road as today's turnpike still is, but it also had the same concept of "rest stops" every mile or two for travelers to use. This is a direct quote from the History of Beaver County book which describes this turnpike. I chose to use a quote for the very entertaining and flowery descriptions.

"A peculiar form of roadway in the early day was that known as the turnpike---sometimes corduroyed with timber and branches, sometimes made of plank, and sometimes of sand, gravel or stone. Two important institutions—adjuncts—were required to complete this thoroughfare, the tollgate and the inn. The latter was the merry place at which the heart of the weary traveler was made glad as he enjoyed the rich fare of the table, the tempting drink of the bar, the strains of enchanting music in the evening, and the companionship of others wending their weary way along the same track.........."

Fun fact: During the war of 1812, the turnpike was initially used as the main road for transporting grains and plaster. When the eastern county farmers of Northampton began to obtain plaster from New York, they transported it from New York down the Susquehanna River, then onto the turnpike on wagons and sleds. The transportation of plaster became the turnpike's legacy and therefore this gave the turnpike its popularity for not only travelers, but its importance as a commercial roadway.

Beaver Valley Expressway

Center Township currently has the Beaver Valley Expressway that bisects the township. Going opposite directions on the expressway from Center is about a fifteen-minute ride to either the Pittsburgh International Airport or the Pennsylvania Turnpike. In the late 1940s, the 60-mile long Expressway was first being considered. It was in the planning to become an important industrial artery and would connect the steel-producing centers of Pittsburgh to the Youngstown-Sharon areas.

In Dec of 1957, the Department of Highways of the Commonwealth (now PennDOT) approved the design and location of the new highway we now usually just call "the Expressway." Originally, I-79 was supposed to be located on the eastern portion of Beaver County, then pass through Lawrence and Mercer counties before reaching/ending in Erie. The Expressway was lobbied for by Pittsburgh officials to become an update interstate freeway being closer to the city and running through four counties, thus giving motorists an option to the hodge-podge of highways.

Construction of the project was started in Sep of 1964. There are 19 sections of the Expressway and the first was completed in Dec 1967, being the West Middlesex Interchange. Construction of the bridge over the Ohio River (at Vanport) began in 1966 and this Vanport Bridge was opened to traffic in Dec 1968, with the second major segment of the Expressway going over this bridge.

The Beaver Valley Expressway (Interstate 376) opened from the Vanport Bridge to the Pittsburgh International Airport the end of Jun 1971. In April of 2006 signs were being erected to reflect the new designation of the roadway as being Interstate 376 from the formerly known Route 60.

Opening of Beaver Valley Expressway
Photo by Pete Sabella

Beaver County "caravan" on the Expressway.

Fact: The Expressway has two distinctions, 1) having the first heated interchange ramp ever constructed in the state (600-foot-long electrically heated part of Route 18 interchange), 2) the Vanport Bridge was designed and built using curved steel girders.

The Allegheny Valley Expressway (SR 28) and one portion of the Beaver Valley Expressway (SR 60) both opened to traffic in Dec 1973. Both were designed by the Transportation Division of the Michael Baker Corp. at Harrisburg. In the summer of 1975, the section to Chippewa had been completed and was opened to traffic. In 1983, it was being discussed to complete a 16-mile link of the Expressway between the northern end of the Expressway and the Pennsylvania Turnpike. The Pennsylvania Turnpike Commission took over this project in 1990. It took until 1992 for the "end" portion of the Expressway to be completed going to New Castle. It was the missing link to connect to Route 60. This portion was made into a toll road when it opened and is still at that status today (2019). It is the only portion of this roadway that requires a toll.

Expressway Bridge

It was first stated in 1958 that a freeway would be constructed. With this freeway, a bridge would have to cross over the Ohio River at Vanport. This all would be part of a connecting road to link the Penn-Lincoln Parkway and the Pittsburgh Airport with the proposed Keystone Shortway. It was considered to be beneficial to a large segment of the state in contrast to the localized appeal of past bridges over the Ohio River. Michael Baker, Jr. assisted in the plans during the 1950s including those of the Beaver Valley Expressway.

Couroutesy BCHR&LF

The Ohio River is the dark area at the bottom of the picture with the Vanport Bridge passing over it. (For orientation, to the right is Vanport and the top of the picture indicates where the Expressway simply "ended" in 1968 since this is all that was completed as of the summer of 1975.

Fact: On Nov 20, 2003, there was heavy rain that created excessive flooding down the Ohio River causing 20 barges to break away further up the river. The Vanport Bridge along with three other nearby bridges were closed. Inspection crews found no serious damage was caused as the barges were carried by the flood waters into this bridge's piers.

~ ~ ~

Did you know that until around 1940, Route 18 was original labeled as Route 115 and Route 51 was originally Route 76?

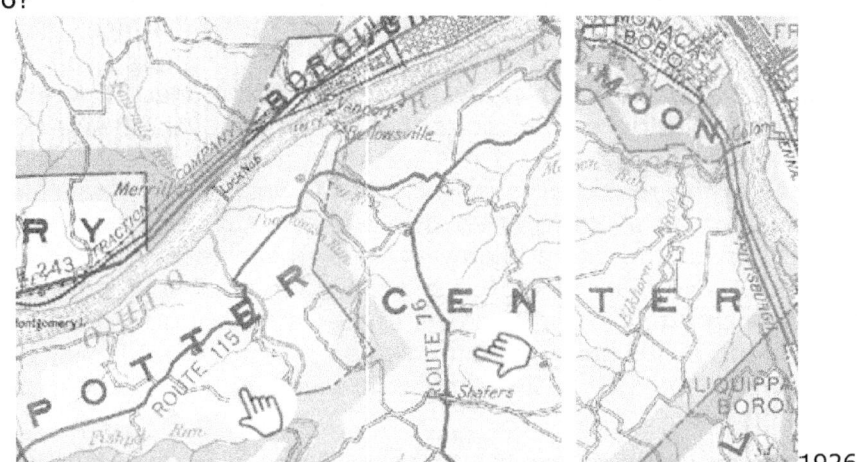
1926

The pointers indicate Route 115 (renamed 18, known as Frankfort Road) and Route 76 (which WAS Route 51, now simply Brodhead Road).

Fun fact: Confusing as it all is with the change of numbers of local routes, even in 1978, PennDOT was referencing the four-lane highway that comes from the BV mall, past Walmart (then Gee Bees) as LR 76. At that time, Penn Dot set the speed limit on that section of the road to be 40 mph.

This map shows the renamed Routes 18 and 51. Note: Bellowsville is still listed on this 1941 map (left side pointer) as is the Colona Station at the end of Monaca (right side pointer).

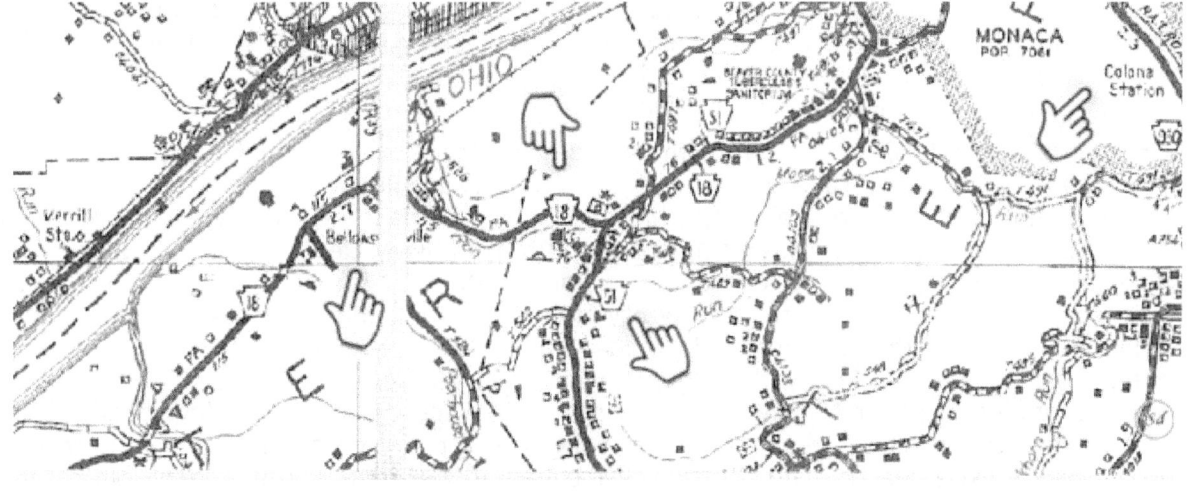

~ ~ ~

Narrows Road – defunct

Repeatedly I found information on a roadway called the Narrows Road. I could not absolutely locate such a road or current information to positively identify it for quite a while. Then as they say "even a blind squirrel finds a nut." Originally, I was leaning toward it being a roadway that may have been renamed. Maybe a road that we're all still driving upon, until I stumbled upon an old timer who distinctly remembered the road and remembered traveling on parts of it. From that point of actually having an idea of where it was located, using older maps, and finding many articles as a source, I finally verified Narrows Road.

Narrows Road was located along the shore of the Ohio River, paralleling the river from the end of Monaca, beginning approximately where the current railroad bridge crosses the Ohio River. It continued along the river's shoreline into the area of current Potter Township that was once known as Bellowsville before joining up with the former route/path of Frankfort Road. In short - Narrows Road was once a quite popular route which would have connected Monaca to the area of Bellowsville. (Bellowsville was considered the area very close to the former site of the Beaver County Home. Later and more familiar landmarks would be the areas of the former St. Joseph Lead/Horsehead Corp). Through the years, many of the residents in both Center Township and Monaca Borough addressed the issues in keeping this portion of Narrows Road in a usable condition. Investigations indicate it eventually was the decision of the State Highway Department to move and relocate a roadway further inland. This would have made it more useful to a larger population and having a roadway that did not require as much attention as Narrows Road was proving to need. This road was still periodically being used in the 1930s but was being treated as a private roadway that was maintained by a combination of individuals and/or businessmen. It was no longer listed or shown on any maps after a 1941 map I located.

Unfortunately, quite a bit of my research was halted dead in its tracks with all the current land moving and reshaping of the property in Potter Township by the Shell project, as well as all the redevelopment on the hillside by the BV Mall. This either directly involved the former roadway or land directly adjacent of where the roadway was located. Up until 2014, prior to all the land moving that occurred, you could look over either side of the Vanport Bridge of the Beaver Valley Expressway (while on the Center/Potter Township side) and still see some signs of the former Narrows Road (see pictures further.) If interested, you may still get a partial view and fair idea of where this roadway was once located if you go along River Road in Beaver and look across the Ohio River toward the lower hillside on either side of the area below the BV Mall when there is no or limited foliage growing.

There was a single railroad track that was laid and also went along the shoreline of the Ohio River, directly adjacent to the location of Narrows Road. By Apr 1938, Routes 115 and 76 had become Routes 18 and 51 respectively. Bellowsville's post office had been closed. Center Township, Potter Township, and Monaca residents and businessmen had numerous meeting and discussions. The State Highway Department was involved. The P & L E railroad was also involved, yet there was still no improvement or re-construction to the Narrows Road. If it were a contest, then the State won with their plan of abandoning the roadway and redirecting a new roadway.

Originally, Route 115/18 came from the bridge in Potter Township that crossed Raccoon Creek. Then it became curvy and traveled along the top of the hillside closer to the Ohio River before straightening and eventually going up the hill to meet up with Stone Quarry Road/Brodhead Road/ Route 51. Eventually a survey was completed, and the Highway Department had decided to drop / eliminate the Narrows Road and opted to straighten Route 115/Route 18 and improve a new roadway from the entrance area to the County Home. This all meant access to the County Home would be via a longer drive. Frankfort Road would then go up the hill to the current 18 and Brodhead Road intersection. From that point it would provide access to Monaca. For over 80 years most of the original path of Narrows Road was still in place as originally developed. Then Shell moved in and re-constructed the entire area making a larger portion of the roadway unrecognizable. There was also all the construction on the hillside behind the Beaver Valley Mall. Narrows Road is now but a memory.

This snippet of a 1900 map of Monaca, PA has two pointers indicating two possible ends of Narrows Road as it would have come into Monaca. (The current viaduct under the railroad and the German Lutheran/Monaca Cemetery are in the top left corner.)

In this 1911 cropped picture which was taken to show the demolition of the old Ohio River railroad bridge, you can see Narrows Road just above the shoreline along the riverbank. The absolute origin for developing this roadway was not found, but a fair guess would be for Narrows Road to provide access to all the mines along the hillsides of this area, to provide a means to transport the clay and coal from these mines, and/or allowing access to maintenance of the railroad tracks. (The roadway is indicated above by the pointers.)

This next illustration is a cropping from a 1925 plat map of the Sylvan Crest area which shows the land over the hillside along the river. In the very small print below the arrow, is a roadway and the writing states "public road to Monaca" …….this public road was Narrows Road. The NC&P railroad tracks are also indicated adjacent to Narrows Road in this drawing, both being adjacent/a short distance from the high water marking of the shoreline for the river.

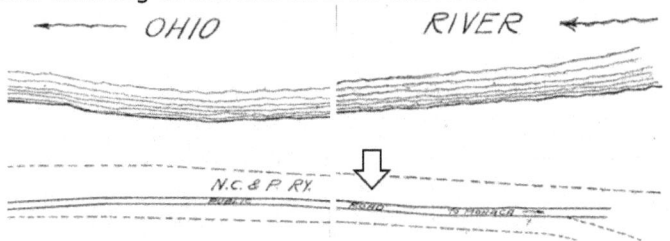

I have no exact date of when, but at some point, the Narrows Road was never further developed or maintained. Eventually all traffic was moved to Frankfort Road/Route 18 which was located at a higher elevation further inland. I have condensed quite a few articles to give as much information on locating the Narrows Road. Once you read all the information further, you will see why the actual location of Narrows Road surfaced.   Here are some snippets of information and quotes from older publications and newspaper articles related to Narrows Road.

1903 - There was an old shack or run-down former home that stood along the Narrows. (This surfaced to be close to the former Bellowsville area.)

1906 – "A force of men is at work putting the river road, known as the Narrows in good condition, a slide having occurred there a few days ago."

1907 – "The work of repairing the river road, commonly known as the Narrows is progressing rapidly and when completed the road will be in first class condition." John P. Potter, of Monaca was doing the work.

1911 – "The wagon road between Monaca and the County Home is almost impassable on account of mud."

Oct 1914 - (None of this first bit of information has to do with the Narrows Road, it is being included just to reflect how active this club was in the area.

"The South Side Good Roads Club was also involved in the success of having the paved road between Monaca and Aliquippa; it was a five-year project to attain the approval and success in the project. The base of the road was concrete and overlaid with brick; this continued over a two-and one-half-mile length of roadway. Once this section of roadway was paved, except for a small section between Woodlawn and South Heights, there would be an improved highway all the way from Monaca to Pittsburgh." Then the article went on to say, "With the success the Good Roads Club had seeing this road work being completed, they turned their attention to the Narrows roadway."

Another article found involving the Good Roads Club...

Voters decided not to allow the county commissioners to remove the County Home as was planned. With the Home remaining at its location, the Good Roads Club took up a campaign to improve the highway between Monaca and the Home. The commissioners wanted to move the Home since there were times it was inaccessible during very rainy weather or in the winter. The Club wanted a new road made for travel to the Home instead. The Club stated that the main route of travel to the Home was the Narrows Road which ran along the Ohio River's shore. They went on to say this road was bad in two ways. One, it was not kept up and two, it was subject to frequent landslides in the winter. To eliminate the possibilities of landslides, the Club proposed having another road made as the accepted route to the Poor Farm. They wanted the new road to be an extension to join the Brodhead Road, Red Gate Road, and Stone Quarry Road. It would then come from Monaca to the Israel Wagner and Hodgkinson farms, to the extension, then the County Home. The newer road meant no landslides were likely to occur as on the Narrows Road.

At a Monaca Women's Club meeting, Frank Batchelor, President of Council, spoke on various topics, one being securing a highway from Monaca to Washington which involved the relocation of Route 115 (now Frankfort Road/Route 18) and the Narrows.   He stated that with the growing industrial activity at Shippingport and the splendid town sites in the vicinity of Bellowsville, a new roadway was imperative. He led all in attendance at this meeting to believe that it was better to keep the location of the highway along the Narrows as opposed to doing as the state proposed. This entailed building a road through a deep valley from the North Branch Church (he was most likely referring to creating an extension of Frankfort Road or possibly even the Simon Field Road -?-).

Between 1914 and 1924, it appears that the state road department won the battle of moving the roadway once referred to as the Narrows Road.

….Jul 1924 - The topic of the Narrows Road needing resurfaced and improved continued, but in 1924 Monaca Council was surprised (and obviously previously uninformed) to find that the state considered Narrows Road no longer their property since they considered the roadway relocated. The Borough of Monaca was going to communicate with the State Highway Department in Harrisburg to find out where the road was moved. In 1924, the road ran from Bellowsville (Potter Township) to Monaca. It was found that in some manner, this road had been relocated and instead of going to Monaca, it then went from Bellowsville to a point on the Brodhead Road (either near the North Branch Church or Simon Field School) at least 3 miles, if not more, from Monaca.   Council wanted to know how and why this change in the road was made. Monaca needed this information before they could take any actions on the borough's responsibility of any portion of improving Narrows. They found the move came about because portions of the road were in such bad shape and the location of it made it impossible to safely improve and maintain.

Jan 1925 - An engineer of the State Highway Department was going to hold a conference with the Beaver County Commissioners to discuss the Narrows Road. Most of the commissioners favored the improvement of the Narrows Road if it could be done at a price that did not exceed the cost of the improvement of the Hill Road (could have been the name applied to the roadway coming past the former Toys R US). They felt that the improvement of the Narrows would open up one of the prettiest drives in Western Pennsylvania. It would give access to several clay and coal mines and provide one of the finest bathing beaches along the Ohio River (the beach area by Monaca Water Works). It could also furnish a direct route to the proposed Beaver power plant of the Duquesne Light Company at Shippingport.

The proposed Hill Road would leave Route No 115 (Route 18/Frankfort Road) at a point southeast of Bellowsville and would connect with Route No 76 (Brodhead Road) for a direct route to either Woodlawn or Monaca. It was decided in favor of the Narrows Road being built below the present new roadway at a very reasonable price. The businessmen of Rochester, Monaca, Freedom, and Beaver were also interested in the improvement of the Narrows Road. It was claimed that Woodlawn and Pittsburgh interests favored the new roadway over the hill.

Jan 1924 - The Monaca Council questioned where, why, how the change came about. It was decided that the State Highway Department would resurvey the Narrows Road before any further decisions would be made.

Feb 1925 - The highway engineers, county commissioner, and officials of the Beaver Valley and Duquesne Light Company all met and drove their automobiles (in the rain) to the junction of improved Route 76 with the proposed North Branch Road and the planned section to connect Route 76 with Route 115 one mile southeast of Bellowsville. From that point, the delegation inspected the route and the Middles Quarries Road (a section of Stone Quarry Road) which was also proposed as a substitute for the Narrows Road. They then inspected the actual Narrows Road from the County Home (in Potter Township/Bellowsville) to Monaca. They found that other than a few fallen trees from a recent storm, the road was in good condition. It was determined that it would not be affected by any high water of the river and although the cliffs on the opposite side of the road looked imposing (they were flatter than a 2 to 1 slope and therefore not hazardous to road building by reason of slides). The representatives for the State Highway Department promised to give the question of the road to be improved consideration and make a report later, so once again, a decision was delayed.

Mar 1930 - The county commissioners were discussing taking over the Narrows Road from Monaca to the Independence School House in Potter Township and along the bank of the Ohio River but it was obvious that these talks did not become what the Monaca Council would have liked since the Narrows Road did not become a state road and was never improved by the state. Instead, it was transferred to the P&LE railroad so construction of a spur track to the new St. Joseph Lead Co. could be completed.

Oct 1930 - Once it was known the state had transferred the Narrows Road area to the P&LE railroad, action of the Monaca council was taken to retain a right of way along the Narrows Road. This meant if in the future the road was needed, there would be a right of way on which to build.

Dec 1930 - It was reiterated once again how there was a need for a highway to replace the Narrows Road along the Ohio River. It was the understanding, and many were confident that another roadway would be built by the railroad company once they completed their new tracks, which were under way.

Apr 1938 - Monaca Council once again tried to have the P&LE railroad build the Narrows Road, asking the County Commissioners to cooperate in the manner. They stated that several years ago the right-of-way of the old Narrows Road was almost completely taken to build a spur railroad line from Monaca to the St. Joseph Lead Company Plant. It was understood at that time that in return for that right-of-way, the railroad company would eventually construct a new road adjacent to the spur line. Eight years later, this still had not occurred.

In conclusion, Narrows Road ceased to exist.

This photo was taken prior to all the land moving by Shell and is a view looking OVER the side of the expressway bridge and facing toward Potter. The Ohio River is seen on the right of the photo. A bit of the roadway can be seen in the left/middle of the picture by the pointer.

This photo was also taken prior to all the Shell land moving and looking OVER the other side of the expressway bridge facing toward Monaca with the Ohio River on the left of the photo - part of the road can be seen here, too.

With all this information of landslides, rising waters of the Ohio, et cetera, the conclusion of this roadway is that Narrows Road was definitely a well-known, important, and frequently used roadway to have commanded so much attention from the 1800s through at least the later 1930s. It was also definitely a separate roadway situated along the riverbank rather than a portion of the current Frankfort Road coming through Potter Township nor a part of Stone Quarry Road or any roads that met or were adjacent to the current intersection in Center Township.

~ ~ ~

Frankfort Road aka **Route 18** – Potter Township

Frankfort Road is only a portion of the roadway originally laid out by Acts of Legislature. Part of the twenty and a half mile long roadway that ran through Moon Township, Raccoon Township (prior to Potter Township's erection), Hanover Township, and into Frankfort Springs. The entire roadway was known in the early years as Route 115 and it is currently part of Route 18. Like many other roadways, it received more of a "familiar" name by long time residences. Since this section of Route 115 was best known for traveling to the Frankfort Springs area, it was given the name "Frankfort Road." (See Routes *18 and 51.*)

The portion of "old Frankfort Road" that was laid out in the current Potter Township was much curvier and originally was basically positioned closer to the Ohio River, much closer than most people may remember. (Of course, Shell's creativity has greatly changed even the most recent memories of how Frankfort Road was.)

In the earlier years as you were traveling toward Monaca on Frankfort Road, it crossed Raccoon Creek a very short distance further up the creek from the current bridge via a covered bridge. (This covered bridge was closer to the current, private boat launch area along the creek.) After crossing the creek, it would bear to the left (just prior to the few houses that many will remember being on the right side shortly after coming off the bridge) and then continued to go in a direction toward the river, more or less following the path of the creek to where it empties into the Ohio River. From this point, it then continued along the crest of the hillside above the river and led into the Bellowsville area.

This original layout of the roadway changed at some point. After the roadway crossed Raccoon Creek, it paralleled the creek for a brief distance, then made a slight right. It then began to parallel the river for another brief distance (along what is currently the back side of the current BASF Corporation property). The road curved again to the right, coming out by the main entrance gate to the BASF company. It would have then veered more to the left (across from the more recent trucking business building). Part of the original Frankfort Road was used as the "back" entrance to the former Midway Bar and Grill. It would have continued past the former Midway, made another curve or two toward the river. With a few more bends/curves to the right, It eventually made its way up the hill (past the former ToysRUs) and connected into the intersection.

Once the covered bridge was abandoned and the roadway became Route 18, Frankfort Road traveled across the new bridge. It was straightened to follow the "basic" layout as it still does today, traveling a straighter route which travels up the hill and to the intersection in Center Township. Most recently, when Shell purchased the properties in Potter Township (in 2016) for their new plant, permission was granted for both infrastructure improvements and widening in response to the Pennsylvania Shell ethylene cracker plant, with Royal Dutch paying for this construction and realignment. Poor River Road/ Frankfort Road/ LR-115/ Route 18 has been moved and re-routed quite a few times over the years.

The roadway that was the exit/entrance to the Midway Bar was listed as old Rte 18.

This picture shows the continuation of the former Route 115/Frankfort Road that would have led toward the Beaver County Poor House and the Bellowsville area.

For orientation ...   The bottom, right pointer indicates where you would have turned off Frankfort Road. After making this turn, you went a few feet and came to a stop sign. By making a left you could have gone to the Midway Bar, by making a right turn (see the pointer in the middle) you could have acessed a few private homes. You would then have come upon a gate that blocked traveling any further. To sum it all up, in the earlier years, that "back entrance" to the Midway Bar (see next picture) would have continued past the bar and then (again, see the middle and upper right pointer above) continued traveling more toward the river and past the entrance of the former Poor Farm/County Home before making a few bends and leading up the hill. Not even a glimpse of the former roadways, buildings, trees, layout of the land, former homes, et cetera exist on this section of the roadway today (2019). All this area has been "re-landscaped," leveled then redesigned, and Frankfort Road/Route 18 was once again re-shaped and moved to accommodate the Shell company's plans.

This is a view of an area in Potter Township prior to all the alterations that occurred in 2017. You would be coming from the Potter bridge and heading toward the Beaver Valley Mall. The pointer to the left is indicating an original portion of Frankfort Road which was the back entrance to the former Midway Bar and Grill. It would have then continued, going past what became the former Midway Bar and then past a few homes. Many years ago, it would have continued toward the former Beaver County Home before eventually curving more times and going up the hill into Moon/Center Township (see previous picture). Almost nothing on either side of this tract of property or Frankfort Road is now reconizable to those who traveled it all those years prior to the Shell company purchasing all the land.   They obtained authorization to move/alter/change the majority of the land and roadways in this area. The layout of the straighter section of Route 18 / Frankfort Road that comes up the hill into Center Township basically remains as it had been for many years.

Fun Fact: Portions of former LR 115/Route 18 / Frankfort Road in Potter Township have had quite a few changes over the years. At one time in the earlier 1920s, a portion of this roadway was originally what is now Mowry Road. It followed the basic route of the current Mowry Road, then connected onto what is now Bauer Road. It would have continued to connect with and/or become the then River Road (now Frankfort Road). During the early years, Frankfort Road gave access to the Potter #2/Badlam Place School (now considered on Mowry Road), to the Potter #1/Independent School also known as the St. Joe School, to the Kobuta community area during its years of operation (in the 1940s), and then to the entrance to the Poor Home and/or the former Bellowsville area.

~ ~ ~

Shell bought up all the properties in the area, moved in with their monstrous equipment and now none of the former area is as it EVER once was! The next picture depicts what was only the start to the "changes."

2014/2015

This view is looking at the whole area with the river being along the bottom and out of the picture. The Expressway and Center Township are to the left, Raccoon Creek and Potter Township are to the right. To anyone not familiar with the former area, there are no remaining recognizable landmarks to know where the former Bellowsville, Josephtown, Kobuta, the Beaver County Home, and more recently, Horsehead, Kobuta, St. Joe Lead, Kobuta Hotel, Midway Bar, Pleasant Drive, et cetera, ever were. Former hillsides have been flattened and other new hillsides created. All former vegetation was stripped, roadways were eliminated or moved as new ones were created. Small dips and valleys have been filled in with others created. In Jun 2016, it was confirmed there would definitely be a cracker plant erected on this property, as of 2019 the massive plant is well under construction. NOTE: since the 'creative landscaping' by Shell began, no<u>thi</u>ng depicted in the above photograph is even the same. The company continued to redesign/redefine the land and construction just keeps continuing to change on a regular basis! The entire area is now filled with multiple structures of the Shell plant.

~ ~ ~

PRIOR TO BRIDGES

Ferry Businesses

With many of the former Indian trails already very conveniently located and being used by the settlers as roadways, engineers and visionaries found these trails proved to be the best as far as placement, for traveling, and the shortest distance between many locations. Therefore, the majority of these trails were simply upgraded and made into proper roadways through the years. With more and more of the areas becoming settled and pioneers continuing to develop communities, towns, and rural areas, there were also new roads created. The Indian trails that led to and then crossed the rivers and creeks were of the next concern for settlers. During the earlier years when water levels were much lower in the rivers and/or creeks, while a person on foot or even on horseback could normally just wade through and cross with little problem, settlers with laden down horses and/or wagons found the task quite difficult to impossible. Continuing to cross these waterways was becoming a necessity to regularly reach other settled and growing areas alike. During periods of higher water levels or inclement weather the usual natural fords were found to be impassable. Thus, bridges were developing and also ferries began to be used. At first these ferries were simply canoes or cruder boats that provided passage for people only, but they developed through the years to also accommodate horses, then horses and buggies, and eventually motor vehicles.

Fun fact: The Ohio River was once known for its blue water and for being able to see the bottom of the river in many places up and down the river.

These ferries were very welcomed in all areas, yet I cannot help but think the Moon Township residents were probably even happier to have heard the news of the construction of the first suspension bridge between Rochester and Monaca which occurred in 1896. You may find it hard to believe by looking at the Ohio River as it is nowadays, but even into the earlier 1900s, during the summers the Ohio River would run only a little over one foot deep between Pittsburgh and Cincinnati. Especially in the winters or during periods of more drought like conditions the boat traffic would usually come to a complete halt. One finding stated that in 1881 all river traffic was halted when the portions of the Ohio River reached its lowest level on record of one foot, nine inches. During these times people could easily just walk through the very shallow water or across the frozen river water. The addition of the dams along the Ohio River increased its pool depths making it much deeper and more dependable and consistent for boating traffic. The Ohio River usually ran at least fourteen feet lower in its depth before the Montgomery Dam was built in the 1930s. Dredging of the Ohio River has dramatically changed the depth of the river and the current depth of the Ohio River is now known to up to ten to twelve feet deep closer to the banks most of the time but through the middle of the river, the depth can run up to sixty feet.

Monaca-Rochester Bridge   Little Beaver Historical Society
This picture reflects a very shallow Ohio River……note how the shoreline is extended from the normal riverbanks at Monaca.   (The pointer is indicating the actual more common river's edge.)

When one of the ferries would be out of commission due to weather, low waters, or whatever the reason, persons could choose to try to venture across one of the lower areas of the rivers or, as many chose to do, would take a longer route, and use other existing roadways to possibly access another ferried area or bridge. Even though it kept shoes and clothing much cleaner and drier as opposed to wading through water, using the round-a-bout route of roadways meant a much longer and rougher round trip. Remember, in those early years, most would either be walking, going by horseback, or in a wagon to their destinations. With bridges not being near as numerous as they are today, for the Moon (Center) Township residents, one alternate land route would have been a 22-mile walk or ride to the Chester-West Virginia bridge, then to East Liverpool-Ohio, and back into Pennsylvania. Although a 22-mile, one-way ride isn't usually given a second thought nowadays, while walking, in a wagon or on horseback or even in one of the earlier models of automobiles, it still would have been quite a venture, not to mention the time factor.

Residents of Moon Township found an interest and the necessity to cross waterways to reach other areas and towns for employment, trading, selling, buying, and seeing other family members. Therefore, crossing the township's waterways was accomplished in the very early years using canoes, then cruder rafts or small flat-bottomed boats. As stated previously, most ferries started and simply carried a few people at a time across the waterways. These quickly evolved and were then made to carry more people and even some supplies. Ultimately, the sizes and complexity of these water vehicles continued to change to accommodate horses and buggies, then motor vehicles across rivers and larger creeks.

There were several types of ferry boats through the years. Ferries were basically flat bottomed and would sit/ride along the surface of the water, right at water level, and had handrails made of some form of rope or cable that was strung along the sides to keep people and vehicles from pitching overboard. There was a simple type of lip or plank that would drop down and turn into a landing, loading, or exit ramp. As horses and buggies began to fade out, it was found that many of the same ferries could typically hold several automobiles, sometimes up to eight cars. In Moon (Center) Township and surrounding areas, the most common forms of early ferry vessels started with small boats propelled by oars or poles. They were replaced by large flatboats propelled by a form of long oar called a sweep. Depending on the location of the docking areas, the river's current itself sometimes greatly aided and/or provided the means of propulsion. A very popular type of ferry boat used in the area was called a cable ferry, chain ferry, or swing ferry. A cable made of either heavy rope or steel chains was eventually replaced with more durable heavier wire cable that was strung across the waterway between landings. A "ferryman," with the help of any willing passengers, would guide the ferry boat across the river by pulling, hand over hand, on the cable. With a cable strung across the waterway, it would be safe to say these types of ferries were only productive on waterways where larger steamboats did not have regular routes.

Before bridges eventually eliminated the need and use of ferry boats, the need for cables was replaced as the ferries began using engines that propelled the ferry boats across the waters. Although the first steam powered ferry was used on the Delaware River in 1790, it was many years later before these were used in the Moon Township area. With these engine driven ferries, there were also gas-powered "pushers" or "yachts" attached to the sides of the ferries. These would have a swivel type device on them so the ferry could travel in either direction without having to be turned around. Passengers could travel in the "pusher" or "yacht" area if desired, but weather permitting, it was more common to see them just standing on the decks.

Steam powered ferries also opened the door for ferries to not only simply cross from one side of a river to the other side, it gave the option of traveling up and down a river, too. Once the gas-powered engines became more commonly used, ferries would often take people from as far as Georgetown, up the Ohio River to Pittsburgh on a daily basis for work. These types of commutes definitely would have been quite time consuming since it would normally take approximately ten minutes just to make a simple crossing of the river. Most ferries ran from 6 am until 6 pm on what they called "slow time" (standard time) and from 6 am until 8 pm on "fast time" (daylight saving time). A typical load for a local ferry each day would be close to one hundred cars.

Through the years, you could find several ferry businesses up and down the Ohio River ---- from Sewickley to Coraopolis, Moon Township and Ambridge to the South Heights, Rochester, and Beaver to Monaca, Vanport to Bellowsville. The average fare on the ferries per wagon/car was thirty-five cents a car or a nickel per person on foot.

During the cross over years when bridges were slowly replacing the needs for ferry services, residents were still not always guaranteed an opportunity to cross one of the rivers. Even with the increasing appearance of bridges, there were many weather-related events which could easily interfere. An example of this is with the extremely high water in the 1930s that put many of the smaller bridges underwater and even totally destroyed several larger bridges. Of course, to be fair, often these same high and dangerous waters would have also put the functioning ferries out of commission for a period of time.

> *Fact: As with all modes of transportation, ferries were no different as far as occurrences of accidents. The Georgetown ferry landing is an example even though it wasn't actually the ferry boat that caused the accident. Late in the 1940s, there was a fatal accident late at night when a car sped onto the flat boat while the ferry was closed for the day. The car snapped both chains stretched across the entrance ramp, traveled straight across the deck of the ferry, and again snapped the chains on the exit ramp at the other end, plunging into deeper water since the river was running high at the time. It was not until the river level dropped that the top of the car was discovered with two couples found dead in the submerged car.*
>
> *Another deadly accident occurred in 1963 when there was one of the worse fogs in the area. A towboat with eleven empty barges (Consolidation Coal Co.) wrecked head on into the Shippingport Ferry boat. The ferry was completely full of eight cars and thirteen passengers. When the crash occurred, some people panicked, one person jumped onto an empty barge, and one jumped into the river. The Crucible worker from Pittsburgh who jumped into the river unfortunately died along with one other of the thirteen people aboard.*

Listed further are many of the more popular ferries/ferry businesses that Moon (Center) Township residents would have used through the years, sometimes on a more regular basis or at least more frequently for visiting out of the area families, for shopping, or even for going/returning for work.

Ferry crossings and businesses directly related to Moon/Center Township

Lawrence's Ferry

Lawrence's Ferry plied the Ohio River from Moon Township to Beaver Town (now Beaver) with the landing in Beaver Town in the vicinity of the Fort McIntosh site. This ferry's landing was in the area on Moon Township's side of the Ohio River just below the right side of the current Lowe's plaza -- which was where the original Brodhead Road was located and had a ford on the Ohio River. (See information on Brodhead Road.)

Isaac Lawrence is listed as the owner of this ferry in the very late 1700s and into the very early 1800s. Records listed Isaac's ferry business opposite on the river from the Samuel Johnston's Landing (which was on the Beaver Town side of the river – see further) which verifies there were two separately owned ferry businesses for the same ford. I could not find any further specifics on Isaac's ferry businesses such as whether it transported just people or could also accommodate horses. I also found no official dates for the startup or ending of Lawrence's Ferry except that Isaac's was still referenced as Lawrence's Ferry in Mar of 1797 on a road report.

Following is an excerpt taken from the minutes of the Court of Session (1793 to 1820).

> 1 March 1797.—A petition for a road to lead from Brodhead's road to Isaac Lawrence's ferry on the Ohio river opposite Samuel Johnston's in Beaver Town.

Samuel Johnston's Landing

As previously mentioned, Samuel Johnston's ferry business was in Beaver Town (now Beaver) in the area of the Fort McIntosh site. This ferry was opposite from Lawrence's Ferry and plied the Ohio River. From the previous excerpt, it is a fact that Samuel's ferry was at least in business in the very late 1700s and most likely into the earlier 1800s. Samuel's ferry was listed as being "a horse-ferry" which indicates he could transport more than just "humans" across the river. (Samuel lived in Beaver Town and in 1802 was also listed as owning 7 1/2 acres of land, had a slave, his own horse, four cows, and was an Esquire.)

It is quite clear that both the Lawrence and Johnston landings preceded the Bellowsville Ferry. Either these two landings became obsolete and thus the ferries further down the Ohio were started or the start of the Bellowsville and/or Vanport ferries were the demise of the Johnston and Lawrence ferries.

Bellowsville Ferry

There are a couple maps listed further (following the Vanport Ferry information) which show the location of the ferry landing that was in the defunct area known as Bellowsville (in Potter Township, close to the Moon/Center Township line). This ferry crossed the Ohio River to the Vanport landing on Ferry Street. It would have crossed the Ohio adjacent to where the Vanport Expressway Bridge spans the Ohio River (2019). Along with the reports of a ferry being operated out of Bellowsville, there were also reports stating a ferry was also operated out of Vanport. (See the Vanport ferry further).

As anyone who has been a longer time resident in the Monaca and Rochester areas already knows --- the Monaca-Rochester bridge is also known as the Rochester-Monaca bridge......all depending on which area you call home or are more loyal to. I mention this because I strongly suspect this was the case of the Bellowsville-Vanport ferry. There were financial reports submitted for the "Bellowsville and Vanport Ferry Company" as early as 1863 through 1909. This lends to these two ferries being connected by some means, most likely by the owner(s).

The Simon Field Road came out on the lower end of Pleasant Drive, which intersected with then *River Road* / now Frankfort Road area. These roadways gave access to property of William Flockers, Mrs. N. Eaton, Joseph B. Maxwell, Samuel Maxwell, D. Springer, Jonas Rambo, George Shrodes, and William Merryman who were all residents of Bellowsville in Moon Township. I mention this because I found a string of owners of this Bellowsville Ferry business which included George J. Shrodes, George W. Shrodes (s/o George J.), Jonas/John Rambo, Milo Rambo (s/o Jonas), and brothers - Samuel and Joseph B. Maxwell.

While doing research for my *Monaca aka Phillipsburg* book, I found a listing for "John Rainbow" who was listed in an 1841 Directory with his occupation *Ferryman*, but there was no location of such a business along the Ohio nor a specific name of the ferry. I originally thought Mr. Rainbow may have been employed by Mr. Volhardt who had a ferry business for a few years at the end of Monaca, by the current railroad bridge across the Ohio River or Mr. Rainbow possibly worked on or ran one of the shifts of the *Messenger (see further)*. Not until I began the research on Moon/Center Township did I discover there was no "Rainbo" or "Rainbow" person but was actually Jonas/John <u>Rambo</u> of Moon Township who had his own ferry business. Also, from the information found in Jonas Rambo's will, it verifies that his ferry business was not connected to any of the Monaca ferries, but instead was located further down river at Bellowsville and crossed the Ohio River to Vanport. Jonas Rambo was 71 in 1860 and by this time listed "retired" as his occupation while his son, Milo had "ferryman" as his occupation which indicates Milo had taken over for his father. Various other information also places and verifies the Rambo ferry business was in the exact location of the Vanport/ Bellowsville ferry site.

Additionally, to tie Jonas Rambo into this ferry business further, I found that George Jacob Shrodes/ Shroads (born 1770, died c1837) came to Bellowsville in around 1824. He also had a ferry business connected with "going to Vanport." George J.'s son, George W. also ferried at this location. Another connection to the Shroads and Rambo family was that Jonas/John's brother, Moses, had a daughter, Jane who married George W. Shroads, Sr. (born 1831 – s/o George J.).

Information on tax listings all lend to Robert Moffit/Moffett being the next owner of the ferry after the Rambos. The 1841 through 1845 tax listings had Moses Rambo with 43 acres and owning one grist mill and one sawmill, Robert Moffit was listed with 106 acres and one ferry. By the 1850 tax list, ownership was reversed – Moses had about 133 acres of land and then had a ferry and Robert had the grist mill and sawmill on about 50 acres (these tax listings had no mention as to the name of the ferry). The only tax list that was legible and/or available with information on Jonas Rambo was 1853 through 1863, with Jonas owning 55 acres and an additional 6 acres which included the ferry. As stated, following Jonas's death in 1868, his son Milo operated the ferry for a short time.

Other than a brief period of Robert Moffit being in the mix and listed as owning the ferry, the next to be connected to the Bellowsville Ferry was the Shrode family. After the Shrodes was the Maxwell brothers. When researching the Maxwell family information, I found that Samuel and Joseph B. Maxwell moved to Bellowsville between 1860 and 1870 and partnered to run a ferry business. With the time frame of Jonas Rambo's death (1868) and his daughter then getting her father's farm (she died by 1870), and Jonas's son, Milo getting the ferry business and 6-acres adjacent to it (Milo had moved from the area by 1870), it all adds up to Samuel and Joseph B. Maxwell being the next owners of this ferry business, the former Rambo property, as well as additional acreage. After Samuel Maxwell and his brother Joseph B. came to Bellowsville, they were said to have erected a substantial ferryboat which plied between Bellowsville and Vanport for at least ten years. Samuel had learned the trades of iron molder and then the blacksmith's bellows trade, an occupation the village of Bellowsville is said to have received its name.

Just as with the previously listed Lawrence and Johnston ferries, from various writings and information, it appears, at some point, there may have been two separate businesses that worked between Bellowsville and Vanport --- one based out of Bellowsville, the other based out of Vanport. There was also some information that also seemed to bind the two businesses together. Whether this was one business that ran between the two areas, or whether there were really two different ferry businesses and therefore separate boats, is not absolutely clear except for the information on a few persons who had a homestead in each area listing their occupations as ferry business owners. Yet, as said, there was that report of capital monies earned with the business which had the name listed of "Bellowsville and Vanport Ferry Company." The confusing part is that I also found reports stating the "Vanport ferry over Ohio River" was located in Vanport (1879) along with a few different pictures of what was specifically called the *Vanport ferry*. I did not find many official publications or documents that specifically had a listing of just the Bellowsville ferry nor any pictures of this specific ferry. Like I stated, it may simply have depended on which side of the river you were on and where you were headed when it came to the name or referencing of the ferry.

From the information that was found, the Bellowsville ferry business is on record as being incorporated in 1868. The transaction stated the Charter of the incorporation was an act to establish a ferry across the Ohio River. It included all boats, skiffs, ropes, tackle fixtures, derricks, and fixtures of every kind or character for the ferry Charter on the south side of the Ohio River in Moon Township (Bellowsville) and across the river at the Village of Vanport.

Joseph B. Maxwell died in 1877, then his brother, Samuel sold most of his own holdings in the Bellowsville area (including the ferry business) to his sister and brother-in-law, Nathaniel and Rhuanna Nelson in 1879. The Nelsons sold the Charter for the ferry business to Wm. Fisher and Elijah Barnes who then sold it to Jos. C. Fronk (of Moon Township) and Wm. J. Bickerstaff (of Phillipsburg) in 1881. Following the 1881 sale of the Charter for this ferry business, I found no other transactions or mention of this ferry business. J. C. Fronk and W. J. Bickerstaff also purchased 5+ acres from Nancy Eaton in Bellowsville in 1883. This partnership appears to have dissolved by 1889 because W. J. and his wife sold their share of 5+ acres to J. C. Fronk and his wife, but no specific information was listed of the business.

The pointer above indicates where the ferry crossing was located between Bellowsville and Vanport. The two Maxwell brothers had their homesteads and other businesses within Bellowsville, as did the Rambo and Shroads families who also conducted the Bellowsville ferry business.

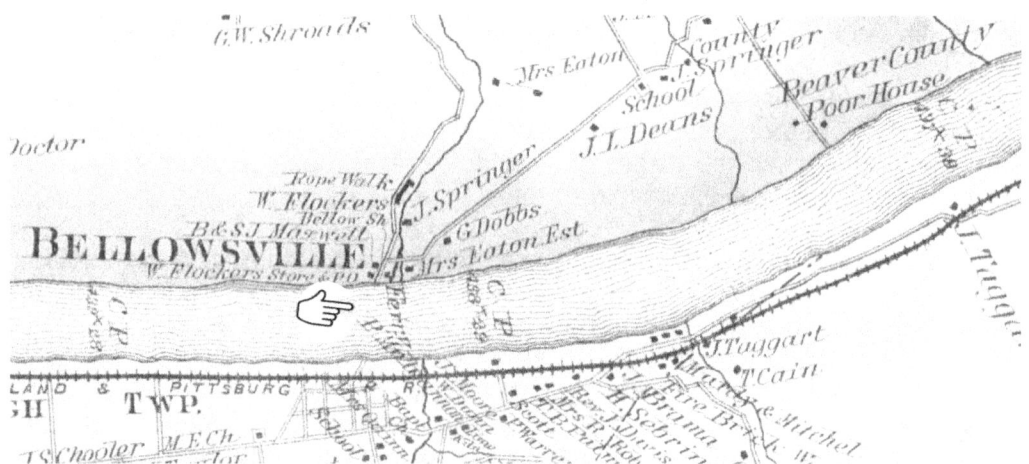

This is a segment of another map also showing the crossing of the ferry business between Bellowsville and Vanport.

Fun fact: Just a very short distance on the Ohio River from the former Bellowsville area, along the shore of the Ohio River, was a place known as Rag Run. This is where the Rag Run creek emptied into the Ohio. It was used as some type of port and was also the site of a small, local ferry that traveled a short distance to Bellowsville.

Fun Fact: F. Cuming wrote Sketches of a Tour to the Western Country. While in the area of the former Bellowsville area, he made entry in his journal that stated due to a very bad storm, they sought shelter on the left bank of the Ohio River. "We were received very hospitably in their small log house by Mr. and Mrs. Potts. ….entertaining us with some good songs, and long stories about his (Mr. Potts') travels." He also tells of sleeping on the floor only after refusing to take the Potts up on their offer of their own bed, their other one being filled with their five children. He states the Potts home was ten miles below Beaver and two and a half above Georgetown. He also noted three small islands in the distance called First, Second, and Grape Islands.

(F. Cuming kept a journal as he traveled along the Ohio River.)

Vanport Ferry

This ferry provided service between Ferry Street in Vanport and Bellowsville. In the History of Beaver County, it states this ferry was established around 1800. Information indicates that it was operated from at least 1807 to a bit beyond 1915. This ferry was an example of an underwater cable ferry. This type of cable was said to keep a ferry steady for its crossings. Vanport Ferry was well known for its forge. As stated previously, the actual crossing of this ferry over the river would have been very close to where the current (2019) Vanport Expressway Bridge now spans the Ohio River. In his travels, F. Cuming (who wrote *Sketches of a Tour to the Western Country*) made an entry that included he took a boat down the Ohio River and past this area of the ferry. In this writing, he alludes to the Vanport ferry as he saw and was describing the Ohio River in 1807– "A ferry two miles below Beaver is a handsome situation, beyond which the banks are high on both sides, and the river does not exceed one hundred and fifty yards wide."

Vanport ferry – 1915   courtesy BCHR&LF

Fun fact: Vanport was listed as a very active and bustling community. Prior to being "settled," Vanport was home to many Indian tribes who were said to "watch for enemies from the lookout point at Bear Hill." Thomas B. Boggs is credited with planning the town of Vanport in 1835 with the actual village being laid out by J. J. Noss, who built the first brick house there. Census sheets have Mr. Noss listed as a resident of Moon (Center) Township. The Vanport area grew and began to prosper, thus the need for the ferry was recognized. The piers were built were the Two-Mile Creek emptied into the Ohio River. (See information further on J. J. Noss.)

The following six men were all found to have listed their occupations as owning a ferry business on various documents. None of them were associated with a specifically named ferry business, so unless it was individually listed, it is pure speculation on my part in associating them with actually owning a ferry business. Each of these men could have merely owned a ferry boat which was leased, since the tax lists simply had "ferry" included under each man's assets. Although their ferry boat would have been a true asset, they could have simply been a ferryman for someone else's business. They were all listed as residents of Moon Township, so I chose to include the information I did locate.

David Stone

David Stone (s/o Adam Stone) was listed in 1842 through 1853 on the Moon Township tax lists as owning a ferry (and 50 acres). He may have owned it beyond 1853, but many years of the tax lists for Moon Township had either very light print which made it impossible to read or were simply missing. The Stone family lived in what became Potter Township in the area close to what would have been Bellowsville. I found no name of his ferry business, but perhaps he was one of the owners of the ferry business connected with the one at Rag Run.

Jacob J. Noss

Between 1847 and 1853, Jacob was listed on the Moon Township tax lists as owning a ferry. He also had rental value listed on the same lists for an Inn. I have no locations or names for either the ferry or the inn. By the 1863 tax list, Jacob was still listed, but there was no ferry or inn included within his assets. The Noss family lived in what became Potter Township in the area close to what would have been Bellowsville. I found no name of his ferry business, but perhaps he was one of the owners of the ferry business connected with Bellowsville or with Rag Run -?- (See previous Fun fact about Vanport and J. J. Noss.)

Jacob Baker
The Moon Township tax lists for 1842 through 1846 show Jacob Baker as owning a ferry. I believe this ferry would have been somewhere near the Bellowsville area because on some of the older maps, there was not only a "Baker's Landing" known to be at the far end of Phillipsburg/Monaca, but there was one also listed near Bellowsville. As already mentioned, there was a ferry known to travel between Rags Run and Bellowsville and perhaps this was where his ferry business operated. (See the Post Office section for a map showing the Baker Landing near Bellowsville.)

Joseph Craig
The 1843 Moon Township tax list is the only one where I found Joseph listed as owning a ferry.

Lewis Hoffman
The only legible Moon Township tax lists found with Lewis Hoffman as owning a ferry was for 1844 and 1845.

William Irwin
Mr. Irwin and family were known to live in or adjacent to the Bellowville area. The 1844 tax list shows him with 50 acres and one ferry.

You may wonder why I am including all this information on ferries. Well...... it is because, just like roadways, ferries were of great importance to many residents of Moon Township. As previously stated, prior to all the bridges, whether people lived in the towns or in the rural areas, they all relied on the ferry boats to provide transportation across the Ohio River and even portions of Raccoon Creek. There were many farmers who sold their commodities to the many "city folk" in what are now Beaver, Rochester, Beaver Falls, and New Brighton, they may have also wanted to visit family members who had moved to areas across the river, and yet others may have found employment in a business across the river. With it being a long ride from various areas of Moon Township into Phillipsburg/Monaca just to be able to use a ferry for access to places on the opposite side of the Ohio River, the ferries within Moon Township came from necessity. They made crossing the Ohio River more appealing and convenient.

> *Fun fact:* As of 2004, the closest place for Center Township residents interested in experiencing a ride across the Ohio River on a ferry was on the Sistersville Ferry. This ferry travels from Sistersville, W. VA to Fly, Ohio or vice versa. Sistersville is located along the Ohio River, about forty minutes south of Wheeling. The Sistersville ferry provides the only means of crossing the Ohio River within 30 miles either direction. If you were to live in this area, it would take nearly fifty minutes to drive to the nearest bridge while the ride on this ferry took only five minutes. Locals who work in the mills and hospitals on the other side of the river from Sistersville use the ferry on a more regular basis with tourists making up about ½ of the summer traffic. In 2004, the Sistersville ferry was listed to make runs between 6 a.m. to 6 p.m. and the rates were $3.00 per car, one-way, $2.00 for a motorcycle, and $1.00 for a pedestrian.

Depending on the destination, to access various areas as needed, Moon/Center Township residents could have and probably made trips using almost any of the additional ferries I have listed further. I have only included a few of the other ferries that existed over the span of time before being basically put out of business by the construction of railroad bridges and multiple pedestrian, vehicular, and street car accessible bridges. Following is some information on these ferries.

Niblow's Ferry
This ferry was located somewhere in the vicinity of where the Monaca P&LE RR bridge reaches the shoreline in Monaca. It was opposite the former Harmony warehouse in Beaver.

Volhardt's Ferry
Henry Volhardt was the operator of the first canoe/boat ferry for pedestrians between Phillipsburg and Beaver, beginning first as a simple canoe. He lived by the current Monaca-Beaver P&LE railroad bridge. Henry Volhardt's ferry was not used for anything but transporting persons.

Monaca – Rochester Ferry
I found only one statement making claim to *The Borough-Bee* being the ferryboat that made connection between Rochester and Phillipsburg prior to the bridge being constructed. I found no pictures, no dates of operation, or further information to verify this statement of *The Borough-Bee*. Other information states the first ferry in Phillipsburg was established in 1833 by the New Philadelphia Society and called the *Messenger*. This ferry was in service until about 1847, maybe a bit longer. It was eventually replaced by steam ferries -- the *W. C. Gray* and the *Mary C. Campbell* (see pictures further). The *Messenger* plied between Philipsburg and Rochester for many years and docked between the site of the water works plant and the Monaca- Rochester bridge. In 1862, the *W. C. Gray* was the only ferryboat found that traveled between Monaca and Rochester. It was rebuilt and re-named the *Mary C. Campbell*.

courtesy BCHR&LF

The picture on the left is of the *Messenger*. It was one of the first Monaca-Rochester ferry boats and is pictured sitting along the Ohio River shoreline in Monaca. (Rochester is in the background.)

The picture on the right is of the *Mary C. Campbell* plying the Ohio River at Monaca. This picture is a view looking toward the Monaca shore -– the pointer is indicating the building at the top, right – this was the old Shrodes/Point Breeze Hotel (now razed). The water works building would be just out of the picture to the right.

Logstown Run Ferry
Sheffield Road was built to be able to access this ferry at Logstown Run. As New Sheffield grew, there was a Pittsburgh to Beaver stagecoach line.

Unnamed Ferry
On the 1876 map, there is a ferry marked very lightly on the map. It appears to have been located in the area of the current Montgomery Dam, close to where the current Montgomery Dam Road would meet the Ohio River. This ferry may be one in the same as the Roger's Ferry/Industry-Safe Harbor Ferry (-?-) but there is no documentation for this statement.

Christler's Ferry
This ferry was in use in 1793. It was located in what is now Shippingport. There was a roadway that led from this landing to what was not yet named but referenced as Brodhead's road.

Cook's Ferry   aka   Shippingport-Midland Ferry   aka   Christler's Ferry
This ferry went from lower Industry (approximately at the Midland line) across the river to the borough of Shippingport. It was started in 1858 by George W. Cook. George W. was living in Phillipsburg in 1853 and did farming and basket making. He moved to Shippingport in 1858 and bought the ferry. George and his son William had this ferry company for well over thirty years and never had an accident as of 1888. William and his wife Harriet (Swaney) had seven children – five being sons. As stated, one of the sons continued in the ferry business, but I have no findings to

identify owners from 1888 through the mid 1960s. As of the mid 1960s, it was owned by Jack Morrow and a partner. This ferry was in use at the same time as the Roger's aka Industry ferry in the early 1900s which is verified by maps and drawings and listings in books as early as 1916. (Also see Roger's aka Industry ferry information.)

There were members of the Cook family located all along the river in the lower Industry, upper Midland areas beginning in the mid 1800s and the name of the ferry came from its founder. The village of Shippingport was originally known as Christler's Landing. In 1910 when the Borough of Shippingport was incorporated. Prior to the Shippingport Bridge, this ferry was used daily by many as a means of crossing the Ohio River by those going to or returning from places of employment. In Apr 1964, the equipment of the ferry company was impounded by the US Court, Pittsburgh from the owners at that time, Robert Christy and Jack Morrow. They were named defendants in a case stemming from the death of two men in Oct 1963 when the ferry boat struck a towboat owned by the Consolidation Coal Co, Pittsburgh. The owners had to post bond and obtain property and liability insurance which presented a problem since ferry boat insurance was hard to find with not many ferries still in operation at that time. In 1963 and 1964, more than 400 motorists still patronized the ferry daily or they would have had to drive to East Liverpool, Ohio, and Chester W.VA or to Rochester or Monaca to cross the river on a bridge. The Shippingport Bridge, built in 1964, most likely is what really sealed the fate of this business.

Cook's Ferry- late 50s/early 60s   Little Beaver Historical Society

Fun Fact: The high school aged children of the Shippingport area had to attend classes across the Ohio River in Midland during the earlier years. With no bridge across the Ohio River at that time, this meant that the children had to take the ferry to attend Midland's school. The school district had to pay for the students' ferry boat fares during these years.

Fun fact: Safe Harbor Road was in the Village / Borough of Shippingport, PA and disappeared from maps with the erection of the Bruce Mansfield Plant.

There were two ferries in Industry, one went to Shippingport prior to the Shippingport Bridge opening in 1964, and another ferry was in what is now a defunct area, Safe Harbor (currently the location of a boat mooring across the Ohio of where Wolfe's Run empties into the Ohio at Shippingport). Outside Industry, Route 68, there was Smith's Ferry in Georgetown. Smith's Ferry began to operate before the Civil War. Even though the actual ferry was a flat-bottomed boat, due to the depth of the Ohio River in the early years, it would be grounded until the winter's ice melted and the spring rains raised the water levels. Anyone familiar with local history should know of the story of Meriwether Lewis who had a noted voyage two-hundred years ago with his leaky boat which landed in Georgetown. There is still a road down to the bank of the river at the end of Market Street in Georgetown that leads to the former ferry stop.

Midland Ferry Company

The ferry navigated over the Ohio River near the foot of McCoy Street in the town of Midland, Ohio Township, PA. It went to a point opposite the south side of the river, near the end of Hookstown Road in Green Township. The ferry site was estimated at two miles from the Smith Ferry / Georgetown ferry and was also about two miles from Cooks Ferry. It was also nearly nine miles from the nearest bridge, ten miles from the Monaca/Rochester bridge, and six miles from the bridge in East Liverpool, Ohio.

Roger's Ferry aka Industry/Safe Harbor Ferry
This ferry was in Industry, PA. It crossed the Ohio River in the area just below Potter Township, a bit past the current Montgomery Dam.

Little Beaver Historical Society

This picture was indicated as "Roger's Ferry", but all findings indicated an "Industry Ferry" that went across the Ohio River to Safe Harbor. Roger may have been the first or last name of the man who operated the ferry.

The ferry between Industry and Safe Harbor would have been to the right of the Shippingport Bridge that spans the Ohio River (looking from Shippingport toward Industry). The Cook's Ferry / Shippingport Ferry would have been a little bit farther down-stream (to the left of the Shippingport Bridge).

Dawson's Ferry aka Smith's Ferry aka Georgetown Ferry
This ferry was referenced by several names. It appears that many times it was listed by the village's name where it was located and other times it was listed by the name of the owner of the ferry. As you read further, you will see why the name of this ferry may have varied so frequently.

Smith's Ferry was also the name of a village in the late 1700s. Thomas Smith came from Maryland around 1790 with his family, he was one of the first settlers at Georgetown. The Smith's Ferry community was named from this family. It is in the southwestern corner of Ohio Township and across the river from Georgetown. The two were connected by a ferry that was in operation at least by 1799 because it is "mentioned in a road petition presented to the court of Allegheny County in Dec of 1799 and described as being in the lower end of Moon Township...." The ferry was a means of communication between the southern and northern portions of the county.

The earliest documented report describing any ferry at this location was in 1794 when the troops from Burgettstown crossed the river on Dawson's ferry and marched along the Tuscarawas. There was also a steamboat landing known as Rock Port located close to a quarter mile above Smith's Ferry area. There was a stagecoach line that traveled from Pittsburgh through Georgetown with mail and passengers. It would cross the Ohio River by ferry at Smiths' Ferry to get to Cleveland, Ohio. There was a toll bridge erected about a mile from the mouth of the Little Beaver in summer/fall of 1809 on the road leading from Washington County to New Lisbon, Ohio.

Benjamin Dawson owned the ferry prior to and during 1817. Benjamin built the second house in the village of Smith's Ferry, the first was built by James Clark who was killed by Indians in 1792. Jesse Smith purchased the ferry boat from Benjamin Dawson in 1817. Jessie died in May 1818 and his sons Jesse and Thomas ran the ferry after his death. The ferry ceased operations in 1949 after more than 150 years of service. A gruesome accident involving the ferry occurred just prior to the decision to close the business. Even without the horrible accident, the building of more bridges and lack of usage surely contributed to its closing.

Little Beaver Historical Society   Photo by Nate Thomas

Fun Fact: Before the dam of the area was built raising the water levels near the community of Smiths Ferry, PA, there were Indian carvings in the rocks along the bank of the river. These are now totally submerged with the depth of the river being increased.

from a 1908 postcard

There were casts of these made prior to the rising waters of the Ohio River and can be seen at the Carnegie Museum in Pittsburgh.

Unidentified Ferry Boat crossing the Ohio River - 1907

This ferry was not identified, it simply stated it was crossing the Ohio River. I found this picture to provide many noteworthy views: the paddle wheel boat ("Charter #2) in the background, the smaller flat bottomed boat ("Sterling") also docked along the shoreline, the small boat on the side of the ferry, the front and rear ramps on the ferry for boarding and unloading, the ferry's simple construction, the horse and buggy, and the period clothing.

Fallston Ferry
This ferry crossed the Beaver River. Use of this ferry was eventually replaced by the Sharon Bridge.

Little Beaver Historical Society

This was a "cable ferry." I have enlarged this portion of the previous picture to show the actual cable. You can easily see the cable and a few of the men are working to pull the ferry across the river.

Once the Pennsylvania and Lake Erie Railroad came to Monaca, it did indeed bring in new factories, more residents, and other diverse businesses to all areas, as well as pedestrian/vehicular bridges being added to the mix. But these all also aided in proving the ferry businesses of the area to have outlived their life and usefulness. The opportunity to sit and watch a ferry cruise across the river, the excitement and wonder on the face of a person traveling on a ferry for the first time, and the livelihood of many ferry owners all joined the ranks of becoming but a memory.

~ ~ ~

COVERED BRIDGE
(Potter Township)

As of 1923, one of the few covered bridges remaining in Beaver County was the Potter Bridge over Raccoon Creek. Records indicate this covered bridge crossed Raccoon Creek a short distance inland from the present-day bridge. It carried the road across the creek in the area between the locations of the current private boat docks and truss bridge.

This wooden, covered bridge in Potter Township was built in 1865 and endured quite a bit of traffic which took a toll on the structure. It was closed in Jul 1923 for repairs. Despite some repairs being made, the weakened structure of this bridge caused it to collapse mid-day the first part of Aug 1923. A new bridge was constructed to replace it in 1924, then it was torn down in 1931/32 and replaced with an open truss bridge.

Former covered bridge that spanned the Raccoon Creek in Potter Township.

What became Route 18 and Frankfort Road continued to be heavily traveled. People from this area of Beaver County would frequently travel to and from Frankfort Springs, the Beaver County Home, relatives' homesteads, and various businesses. This roadway also provided access to other roadways when there was a need to travel to a "town" (meaning Monaca, Woodlawn, or even across the river to Rochester, Beaver, New Brighton and/or Beaver Falls). The demand to have a sturdier and well-constructed bridge was a necessity, therefore, the current truss bridge that crosses Raccoon Creek in Potter on Route 18 was constructed in 1932. In the fall of 1978, there was major repair work done to this bridge with one lane of the bridge remaining open during these repairs and reconstruction.

Current Potter Township truss bridge over Raccoon Creek.

~ ~ ~

STREETCAR

Many people associate street cars with providing transportation within towns and cities. I was very much surprised that a group of men had the vision of providing a multi-community/city electric street railway for some of the more rural residents. In 1907, F. G. Baker, J. B. Armstrong, J. J. Allen, W. B Dunlap, and M. D. Youtes proposed plans for an electric street railway to pass through a portion of Moon / Center Township. This streetcar business was to provide service traveling either direction between Fifteenth Street in Monaca, along the river into Bellowsville, cross over a proposed bridge into Vanport, continue through to Beaver, Bridgewater, Fallston, and into New Brighton. This was all proposed in a Charter made in June of 1907. The business was called the "Beaver County Electric Street Railway Company." It is evident that this electric street railway never developed as proposed since there is no mention of any streetcar tracks being laid, no bridge for the street car built over the river adjacent to Vanport, and no street cars that traveled along Narrows Road nor along Frankfort Road/Route 18, or through Bellowsville.

Following is the complete Charter Notice that was published in The Daily Times in June of 1907.

CHARTER NOTICE.

Notice is hereby given that an application will be made to the Governor of the State of Pennsylvania on the 19th day of June, 1907, at ten o'clock a m., by F. G. Barker, J. B. Armstrong, J. J. Allen, W. B. Dunlap and M. D. Youtes, under the Act of Assembly of the Commonwealth of Pennsylvania, entitled "An Act to provide for the incorporation and regulation of certain corporations, approved May 14th, 1889, and the amendments thereto, for the charter of an intended corporation to be called the "Beaver County Electric Street Railway Company," the character and object whereof is for the purpose of constructing, maintaining and operating a street railway for public use in the conveyance of passengers by power other than locomotives, in the County of Beaver and State of Pennsylvania.

Beginning at Fifteenth Street in the Borough of Monaca; thence along Virginia avenue in said borough in a westerly direction to Twelfth street; thence along Twelfth street to Atlantic avenue in said Borough; thence along Atlantic avenue to land now of the Pittsburg and Lake Erie Railroad Company; thence over the property of the Pittsburg and Lake Erie Railroad Company to land of the Welch-Bright Company; thence over the land of the Welch-Bright Company to the Monaca and Bellowsville public road in the Township of Moon; thence along said public road which follows down the south bank of the Ohio River, to the land of Alberta Boggs; thence over land of said Alberta Boggs to the south end of the approaches of a proposed bridge across the Ohio River; thence over said approaches and said proposed bridge to Walnut Alley in the village of Vanport in the Township of Borough; thence along Walnut Alley to Ferry Street; thence along Ferry Street to Jefferson Street; thence along Jefferson Street to land of S. D. Jones; thence across land of said Jones to Locust Alley; thence along said Locust Alley to Ohio Alley; thence along said Ohio Alley to Sassafras Alley; thence along Sassafras Alley to Euclid Avenue in the Groveland Plan of Lots in said Borough Township; thence along Euclid Avenue to the Borough of Beaver; thence along Second street in said Borough to Market Street; thence along Market Street to Fourth Street; thence along Fourth Street to Beaver Street; thence along Beaver Street to Wolf Lane, now Second Street extension; thence along said Second Street extension and Wolf Lane to the Bridgewater Borough Line; thence along Wolf Lane in the Borough of Bridgewater, to Market Street; thence along Market Street northerly to the Beaver and Mercer Road, sometimes called the Sharon Road; thence along said road to and across Water street to the land of the M. Darragh heirs; thence over land of the M. Darragh heirs, the Grove Foundry and Machine Company and others to Water street in the Borough of Bridgewater near the west end of the Sharon Bridge; thence along Water Street and the Beaver and Fallston Public Road, to the Fallston Borough Line; thence through the Borough of Fallston along the Beaver and Fallston Public Road to Front Street; thence along Front Street to the west end of the Fallston bridge; thence across the Fallston bridge to Ferry Street in the Borough of New Brighton; thence along said Ferry Street to the west end of Thirteenth Street; thence along Thirteenth Street to Fourth Avenue; thence along Fourth Avenue to Fifth street, return by the same line, and for these purposes to have, possess and enjoy all the rights, benefits and privileges of the said Act of Assembly and its supplements.

J. SHARP WILSON,
may25jun1-8. Solicitor.

Fun Fact: Although Center Township never did have a trolley car service, residents would encounter this type of transportation when visiting in a neighboring town of Monaca or Aliquippa or other areas. Many of the amusement parks were sponsored by trolley companies, too. (See Recreation / Entertainment section for lists of movie theatres, parks, and more.) Evidently many people didn't know how to conduct themselves where these trolleys were being used and the following was published numerous times in the local newspapers...............

Safety First, Last and Always

From the time you start to leave the car till you reach the sidewalk never stop looking for danger.

Don't hesitate in front of a car, it confuses the motorman. Go forward or back in a decided manner.

When you stop to think be sure to stop in a safe place.

Get in and out of a car quickly, but don't hurry--- hurrying is dangerous and sometimes fatal.

Don't let a child under eight cross a trolley car street alone.

If you don't warn and take care, your child may be maimed or killed, no matter how much we warn and take care.

Double your watchfulness when you cross a double-track street.

THE BEAVER VALLEY TRACTION COMPANY

~ ~ ~

Fun fact: Some pre PennDot and Drivers' Centers information ...

Automobile License
FOR 1914

can be had and executed in my office.

Notary Public

M. L. JACK
Brighton Ave., Rochester
Both Phones, Office and Home

Nov 1914

~ ~ ~

CREEKS, WATERWAYS, RIVER

Of the official 15.35 mi² area of Center Township, it can be defined to show about 15.1 square miles (39.0 km²) is land and 0.31 square miles (0.8 km²), or 1.95%, is water.

The Ohio River is the only river associated with the township, but there are quite a few streams, creeks, and runs of water throughout Center Township. Many of these have no name attached to them but a few are significant enough to have been named. Some of these streams and runs of water, whether named or not, provide and feed numerous natural and man-made small ponds and lakes. They all provide fish, amphibians, reptiles, wildlife, and/or fowls with much needed resources.

Ohio River

The Ohio River borders Center Township to the north. The actual frontage along the Ohio River associated with Center Township is limited and only includes the area below the current Sylvan Crest area to approximate the Cinamax and/or Petsmart plazas.

The Ohio River is formed by the confluence of the Allegheny and Monongahela rivers at Point State Park in Pittsburgh, Pennsylvania. The Ohio River then flows northwest through Allegheny and Beaver counties before it makes an abrupt turn to the south-southwest at the Pennsylvania – Ohio - West Virginia triple-state line. The Ohio River flows through or along the border of six (6) states, Illinois, Indiana, Kentucky, Ohio, West Virginia, and Pennsylvania. It is approximately 981 miles in length and is the 10th longest river in the United States.

> *Fun fact: Approximately 164 species of fish have been found in the Ohio River. However, the dams have drastically altered the habitat for river organisms as they prevent many fish and other organisms from moving up and down the river in their natural cycles. Pollution of the river water is another major factor for the aquatic life. There once were estimated to be eighty species of mussels who lived in the Ohio River, but currently only 50 species occur. At least 5 of those are in danger of extinction.*

Raccoon Creek

The largest waterway within Center Township is the Raccoon Creek. The lower boundary of Center Township to Raccoon and Potter Townships is more or less defined by the Raccoon Creek. Raccoon Creek is far from exclusive to these three townships. It flows from Hickory in Washington County to the Ohio River with the mouth of this creek in Potter Township.

Raccoon Creek has been of significance long before this area saw any white settlers and it still continues to prove its worth and value. In the early years, the waters of the creek supported many types of aquatic life. Turtles were harvested from this creek on a regular basis to make the popular turtle soup desired by many.

Raccoon Creek provided the natural power for numerous grist mill and sawmill businesses through the early years. Nowadays, Potter Township, unlike many other townships, has taken great efforts to acknowledge the importance of not approving every possible area "improved" or be transformed by some form of construction or covered in asphalt or concrete. This is especially evident along Raccoon Creek. In 2010, Horsehead Corporation donated two parcels "by deed restriction to low-impact, non-motorized public access to the banks and waters of Raccoon Creek." There is almost a half-mile long range along the creek by Potter Township's Tank Farm on Raccoon Creek Road that is known as Rocky Bottom Natural Area. Rocky Bottom area is being preserved and "is a special place – not only because generations of people have grown to love its quiet beauty – but because of its ecological value." This area is significant because of the forest habitat, the important birding area, wildlife habitat, scenic views, water supply, and many other natural values. It is the only free public access to lower Raccoon Creek.

Through the later 1800s and into the 1900s there were unnumbered mentions of families spending just a weekend to a lengthy visit at either a camp site or someone's residence along Raccoon Creek. Many groups and clubs were also known to hold numerous events along various areas of Raccoon Creek.

Unfortunately, the water quality of the main stem of Raccoon Creek has been considered degraded for many years due to AMD (abandoned mine drainage). Pennsylvania has a two-hundred-year industrial history which involved mining, in fact, the amount of abandoned surface mines has resulted in pollution of an estimated 2,300 miles of streams with AMD. There are many steps and projects currently underway to correct the damages of AMD and restore purity to the waters of the area, including Raccoon Creek.

The 1876 map of what was then considered Raccoon Township, now Potter Township, indicates a ford across Raccoon Creek - see map on the left below. Adjacent to this ford, there was a roadway between the confluence of the creek and the Ohio river and Frankfort Road (on the former Nova plant site). This roadway was much closer to the river, yet farther down creek from the former location of the covered bridge across the creek. The ford was indicated where this roadway met Raccoon Creek. Curiously, there was no indication of a roadway on the other side of the creek. O. R. Braden had his 194-acre homestead along this area adjacent to where the road met the creek at the ford. (Note - With the width and depth of the Ohio River being quite different in 1876, the mouth of Raccoon Creek depicted would have extended some distance past the current and visible mouth of the creek as it appears today.)

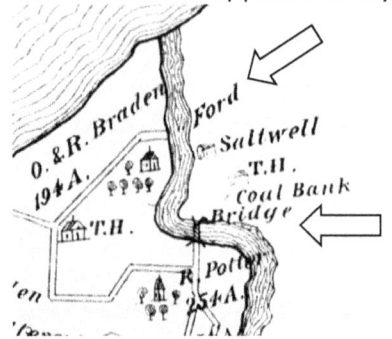

This is from the map of Raccoon Township (now Potter Township). The top arrow points to the "ford."

This is from the map of Moon Township - note there is no indication of the ford or a road which is indicated on the map of Raccoon Township.

The bottom arrow on both maps indicates the covered bridge across Raccoon Creek.

Moon Run - This is a stream that flows through a large portion of the township. Different areas of this stream have also been assigned "familiar" names through the years. This stream is significant because it supplies the water to several pools of water including one small pond along Todd Lane and one larger man-made lake along Edgewater Drive.

For orientation: Moon Run's course begins near the area of Lincoln Drive, it continues and then feeds the small pond along Todd Lane on the former Todd farmland, then flows under Todd Lane, continues along Edgewater Drive, feeding Lyons Lake, then travels along and under Chapel Road by Morgan Lane. Moon Run then flows behind St. John's Cemetery before making a bend and paralleling Shade Hollow Road. It continues from there until its confluence with the Ohio River along Constitution Blvd. just outside Monaca, PA. Moon Run is fed by several unnamed small flows of water on its path throughout the township. There is a small waterway that connects to Moon Run as it travels along Shade Hollow Road in the same general area as where the Elkhorn Run stream meets Moon Run (close to the end of Tank Road which is off Constitution Boulevard just past the end/boundary of Monaca Borough).

Duck Run - A small stream which eventually flows into the Elkhorn Run stream. It forms prior to reaching the Hall's Lake, feeds the current Hall's Lake, then passes under Chapel Road, and continues, then connecting with Shafers Run/Elkhorn Run.

Elkhorn Run - This is considered a "stream." It continues to wind and flow along Chapel Road and Elkhorn Run Road, passing under Center Grange Road, continuing to also pass under Biskup Lane, then along Elkhorn Run Road before it then joins onto and becomes part of Moon Run.

Fun fact: One tradition states the name "Elkhorn" came from the Indians of the area because the creeks that tie in with the current Elkhorn Run stream created so many branches that it resembled an elk's horn......... thus the name Elkhorn Run Creek and Elkhorn Run Road. Another tradition is that many, many years ago, there was an elk's horn found in that area, again.... thus, the name. Either of these are plausible explanations because there was a time prior to the mid 1800s when elk roamed freely throughout their native Pennsylvania range. With unregulated hunting and the increased settlement in the area that caused a loss of habitat, the state's native elk herd was wiped out.

Wood's Run – This stream is located to the right of the current Vankirk area of the township and empties into the Ohio River just past Monaca Road as you travel along Route 51 after exiting Monaca, not far from the location of Moon Run (which also empties into the Ohio River). It is found indicated (nameless) on late 1800 and early 1900 maps. Other than it being mentioned as a physical landmark on various old deeds, I found no other history or records for Wood's Run stream. Veiwing current maps, it still exists, but has no notable landmarks along its course to identify it with except the valley to the right of the current Monaca Road, the overhead industrial bridge along Constitution Boulevard, and the Ohio River Trail that passes over the stream prior to it emptying into the Ohio River.

Shafers Run – The stream now known as Shafers Run begins prior to the area between the Expressway and Broncho, Hillside, Main Street and tends to parallel the Expressway/Rte 376 until it passes under and parallels W. Shaffer Road, then under Brodhead Road to parallel E. Shaffer Road (forming a small pond in this path). It then passes under Chapel Road close to where East Shaffer Road joins Chapel Road. Shafers Run then continues to flow and often parallels along Elkhorn Road before eventually flowing into Elkhorn Run stream. In the early years, prior to the Shafer Post Office being established, this stream was known as Elkhorn Run. There are several unnamed streams that flow into Shafers Run prior to it crossing the Brodhead Road and again prior to connecting to Elkhorn Run stream.

Unnamed streams – There are quite a few unnamed streams that flow throughout the township. Some of these are significant in size, others are much smaller. All flow into either another unnamed stream or one of the named streams. Some of these unnamed streams are include further, but note, this list does not contain all of them.

#1 - Begins between Brodhead Road and the Center Manor Mobile Home Court. It then flows on, paralleling Old Brodhead Road, continuing on through the Penn State Campus, going under University Drive and then into the Duck Pond on Penn State's campus. This stream was well utilized by the Hartenbach families when they owned this land, now occupied by Penn State. They harvested ice as needed from this stream for use in conjunction with their dairy farm. From the Duck Pond area, it appears to leach along before resurfacing along Shade Hollow Road and joining with Moon Run.

#2 - Begins in the area between the Car Wash and Wilhelm Drive. It continues and feeds into the manmade Lyons Lake, which is also fed by Moon Run (on Edgewater Drive).

#3 - Begins in the McCracken Drive area (off Chapel Road), this stream supplies water to the two lakes between Cochran Road and McCracken Drive. It flows into another unnamed stream (which is fed by several other unnamed streams) and eventually into Moon Run.

#4 - Four small streams join to form another small stream that then travels quite a distance through the township. One small stream begins along Church Drive -- another one begins to the left of Sherwood Acres housing plan. These two streams flow together to form another small stream which is then also fed by a small stream that more or less parallels Poplar Drive. This combined unnamed stream then continues and is fed by the small stream that comes out of McCracken Drive area. There are also a few very small streams that feed into this combined stream before it feeds into Moon Run.

#5 - This is also another smaller unnamed stream which comes from the area between Billigen Street and Chapel Road. There is a small lake that sits down in a distance behind McGuire Cemetery and closer to/behind a house (whose driveway is off Chapel Road, just past the McGuire Cemetery). This stream either flows into or out of this small lake and connects to the unnamed stream #4.

#6 - This is yet another smaller stream that originates between Marshall Road and just past the end of Griener Street (Monaca Heights). Then it goes behind the new construction on the former Mateer property, continuing to flow parallel to Old Brodhead Road to that traffic light (outside Monaca) before flowing into Markey's Run (by the railroad bridges).

#7 - This stream begins in the area of the condo complex units by Brohios and Katerina Drives along Brodhead Road. It flows toward and under Frankfort Road. The current continuation of this stream is unknown with all the land moving by Shell in that area. At one time, it would have emptied into Poor House Run stream.

#8 – Begins behind the Rogan & Brobeck Cycles and Felouzis Auto Shops (Brodhead Road). This small stream flows down toward Pleasant Drive and into the Poor House Run stream.

Markey's Run – stream
It begins just past the Beaver Valley Mall, across from the parking lot of the current Target's store parking lot. There is a small natural pond/wet land area in this same area, along with two man made collection areas. Markey's Run continues, going under the Center Commons Blvd. roadway, and on toward the current Eat n Park restaurant where it travels under the divided multi-lane highway, resurfacing on the opposite side of the highway by the McDonald's restaurant. It then parallels the divided multi-lane highway, turning and passing back and forth under the highway a few times before paralleling the highway until just past the traffic light (at the end of Brodhead Road). From this point, it flows toward the viaduct just outside Monaca, once again passing under the roadway, and then flows further and into the Ohio River by the newer boat dock and railroad bridge in Monaca. It has been a notable stream and found indicated on maps of the late 1800s and early 1900s.

Logstown Run - considered a "stream"
This stream begins in the area where Ridgeview Drive turns off Brodhead Road, it continues and flows under Academy Drive, flowing on and under Chapel Road just before Imperial Drive and on into Aliquippa toward Kennedy Boulevard/Maratta Road.

McKees Run – considered a "stream"
This stream empties into the Ohio River in the Aliquippa area, at the upper end of the former Crows Island. It is found indicated by name on late 1800 and early 1900 maps. McKees Run was found to wind through some areas of Moon Township and used as a land marking on several old deeds.

~ ~ ~

Potter Township also has multiple streams throughout, but there are a few that were familiar with Moon (Center) Township residents and are still better known. These include the following.

Rag Run - considered a "stream"
This stream begins behind the Beaver Valley Mall and flows down into the Ohio River to the right of the current Expressway bridge. It would have been in the former Bellowsville area of Moon Township. This stream was found indicated on various maps of the late 1800s into the 1900s but usually had no name assigned to it. There was, however, mention of Rag Run on some documents and even a ferry business where Rag Run flows into the Ohio River. With Shell's land moving activities, it either finds its own path through underground springs or is contained in underground pipes since there are now areas which no longer permit or support a surface stream at this time.

Poorhouse Run - considered a "stream"
This stream is located in Potter Township and empties into the Ohio River a short distance up river to the right of the mouth of Raccoon Creek. Just as most of the surface run of Rag Run has faded away, the same applies with Poorhouse Run due to all the land moving activities in the area. The flow of this stream was found indicated on various maps of the late 1800s into the 1900s but usually with no name. (See information on Poor House Road/Pleasant Drive in the Road section.)

 Poorhouse Run (stream)

Fishpot Run - considered a "stream"
This stream is in Potter Township and flows under Raccoon Creek Road before emptying into Raccoon Creek. The confluence of Fishpot Run with Raccoon Creek is not very far from the designated Rocky Bottom Natural Area, Raccoon Creek Greenway, and the Tank Farm Recreational Area.

~ ~ ~

Watershed Areas
The following watershed areas were found listed on a survey map of the township. Each of the areas I found that were listed as a watershed area did have a significant stream and/or several small tributaries to these streams included in the area. I have no specific information on these areas or what the parameters were to qualify them as a watershed area.

- Ohio River Watershed
- Markeys Run Watershed
- Rag Run Watershed
- Poor House Run Watershed
- Lower Raccoon Creek Watershed
- Shafers Run Watershed
- Moon Run Watershed
- Elkhorn Run Watershed

~ ~ ~

Although Center Township does not rely, to any great extent, on any of the streams or waterways as a source for businesses nowadays, it is important for township supervisors and other township departments to realize and honor the significance and importance in preserving ALL these streams that do currently flow throughout the township. This also applies to all township residents who should be respectful of any stream that flows upon their properties and be vigilantly monitoring the decisions made by the township.

The highest priority should be extended to all these streams so they are preserved and all contamination to them eliminated. Maintaining their current and natural paths of flow should NEVER be compromised!

Physical beauty of the land is an environmental treasure that should be protected and preserved.

~ ~ ~

MISCELLANEOUS TOWNSHIP INFORMATION

Community Garden

Center Township had a municipal garden from about 1977 until at least 1986. Hank Bruce was the organizer of this project. The property was located on the campus of the Community College of Beaver County. The township would plow the ground in this garden area and then applications were accepted by residents interested in using a portion of this garden area for planting. Areas would then be cordoned off for residents who made the applications for their own plantings.

In 1977, the persons involved in the Community Garden project included Mrs. Ruth Slingluff of Economy, Community Gardens general chairman and representative of the Beaver County Federation of Women's Clubs; Nicholas Colafella–Dean of Community Education at CCBC; A. L. Curran of Brighton Township, Cooperative Extension Services; Jessie Council of Rochester Township., Soil Conservation Service; George T. Pettibon of Center Township, committee member and County Commissioner; and Hank Bruce of Center Township, Organizer of the Community Gardens Project.

Cable Television Services

Having a television was never even thought of by the first settlers of the area, let alone cable services. Before televisions, was the treasured radio. Being able to own a radio was actually a big deal and this was reflected on the 1930 census where there was actually a separate column for the enumerators to indicate which family had a radio. On the 1930 census for Center Township, approximately 119 of the 293 households were indicated as having a radio.

Local radio stations provided their listening areas with quite a bit of local news – announcing illnesses, births, deaths, farm news, weather, upcoming events, as well as turnouts and successes of local events. After many families were able to afford and have radios in their homes, the next milestone was being able to buy a television. (See LOOKING BACK in Volume I for more on the first television.) As the technology of televisions developed and became much more affordable, just as with radios, almost every home in the township eventually came to also have a television.

Reception devices for these televisions began with a simpler set of antennas called "rabbit ears;" they were connected to the television via a wire and either sat on top of the television console or very close to the console. As more channels became available, the use of a roof top antenna unit became very popular. With the technology continuing to advance, so came an alternate method of receiving the signals from the broadcasting networks. After many years of the rabbit ear antennas being the norm, then external antennas on a building, followed by cable television.

When the changes came for television signals to not only be broadcast over the air, but also through a cable, township residents did not have a choice of a company if they chose to take advantage of a cable service. The township would negotiate a contract with a franchise company and then that company would wire and connect all residents who could afford and wanted to use the cable service. Nowadays, township residents can choose which ever and whatever type of services they desire to obtain access to broadcasting stations and movies, not to mention internet connections.

The CATV industry itself had its origin in Pennsylvania in 1948. John Walson, Sr. is said to be one of the first cable operators in the nation and started the nation's first community antenna television system in Mahony City, Schuylkill County. It was regulated by the federal and local governments. CATV systems were franchised and became privately or municipally owned in the Commonwealth. The most probably reason that cable even became necessary was because in 1948, the FCC put a freeze on transmitting stations. The FCC was encountering considerable co-channel interference and it recognized the current plan just was not going to continue to work, therefore, a freeze was imposed. It was to last for ten years, but was finally lifted in 1954, only lasting six months. CATV and commercial television were developed because they originally thought they would not have to be concerned with any competition from off-the-air signals due to the freeze. When the original concept of the freeze began, the metropolitan areas had a few stations while many areas further out in the suburbs and all the rural areas had no stations. Cable companies were ready and stepped in.

This gave CATV a very strong foothold. Even after the freeze was discontinued/lifted, what was implemented as a solution proved to be insufficient, so cable services continued to grow.

> *Fun fact: Overall, as of 1976, Pennsylvania had more municipalities served by cable service than all but one other state in the nation. Only California had more subscribers per total household than Pennsylvania.*

A few familiar franchises known to have serviced the township:

Cabelquities - In the 1970s ……….Their offices were in Rochester, PA.

Centre Video, Inc. - This cable service company was out of Leetsdale. The township had a new 15-year franchise with the company beginning 1982.

T C I Cable TV - became available as of 1986

Verizon

Comcast

> *Fun fact: In the mid 1980s, the basic cost for cable service in the area averaged $16.00 a month.*

Food Distributions Programs

Federal surplus food items have been distributed in various communities throughout the county through the years, including Center Township. Families would have to complete and sign a form, then were verified as qualifying. The distributions were done once a month and was a free public service. It was manned by volunteers of many public-spirited citizens who gave up at least four hours once a month to dispense the surplus food. Some specific information with the distributing of food in Center Township:

... Distribution of surplus food in 1955 was held at the CTFD #1.
... In 1958 and 1959, there were monthly distributions to nearly 100 persons. They used the Scout Building on Main Street by the CTFD #1 fire hall.
... In 1988 – butter, cheese and rice were distributed to eligible residents at the Center Grange Hall on Center Grange Road.

Land Fill Area

In 1978, the Center Township and Aliquippa Borough officials had a difference of views over an area along the boundaries of both communities. This all involved a landfill area along Monaca Road. Aliquippa was said to be allegedly operating this dump incorrectly. After a few meetings, they agreed to install better fencing at the landfill to curb windblown garbage and not to leave any dumped refuse to remain exposed at the end of a workday. Center officials, in turn accepted some responsibility for private residents reportedly dumping illegally near the upper entrance to the landfill. Center Township had an anti-dumping ordinance with a levy of a fine being only $100. The solicitor was going to prepare an amendment for the supervisors by the end of June in 1978 raising the levy to the legal maximum of $500.

Center Township currently offers exclusive free use to Center Township residents only. This yard waste recycling site is located on Vankirk Road, adjacent to the township's sanitary authority plant. It is not for use by private landscaping or lawn contractors and is open from mid-April through Thanksgiving. The township specifies - "Typical yard recycling and organic materials (grass clippings, hedge clippings, brush less than 7 inches in diameter) will be accepted. The site will be monitored and residents should be prepared to present identification."

~ ~ ~

Miscellaneous and General Facts for Potter Township

With the connections of Potter Township and Moon Township in the early years, I have included the following information to tie in some of the other information throughout this book that involves Potter Township. Potter Township, being formed from a part of Moon Township shortly prior to Center Township's erection means quite a few businesses, areas, schools, different associations, and families mentioned throughout this book just seem to cross over or blend with Center Township. This is in no way a history of Potter Township, there are other sources for information on its specific history and happenings, yet, with this in mind, I still thought it would be of interest to have just a bit of information on Potter Township.

Potter Township was once part of a 500,000-acre grant of land chartered to a group of men who formed the Ohio Company. The Ohio Company was organized in Virginia in 1748, through a petition which was approved by the King, this company only existed for four years. The Indians of the area were in control of the land for many years, but eventually were pushed west-ward as more and more land was settled. On one of his many surveying trips, George Washington made an entry regarding what is now Potter Township in his log. He wrote while making a stop at the mouth of the Raccoon Creek "...at its mouth and up, it is a good body of land." The Potter Township website states that Mrs. Nagy wrote a *History of Potter Township* and within her information, she stated that Wash. Potter, an attorney, arranged for a survey of the area (soon to become Potter Township). At the time of this survey, it was only necessary to have an area of not less than six square miles to organize a township. There were three square miles taken from the then Moon Township and three-square miles taken from Raccoon Township. In May 1912, a vote proved favor of a township being formed - "Potter."

During and soon after the Revolutionary War ended, settlers were coming to Moon Township, which included the area that would become Potter Township. Settling on the land was difficult with the hostile Indians still in the area. The Wallace family and Potter family were just a few of the early settlers in the 1780s. Mrs. Wallace and their infant son were scalped in 1782 when the Indians raided their farm. Not long after the raid on the Wallace farm, two brothers, Anderson and William Braden also came to settle on land (in the area which became known as Kobuta). Anderson survived an Indian attack, but the Indians killed his brother, William Braden. Anderson traveled back over the mountains and to avenge his brother's death, he returned with other members of the Braden family. One of the Bradens, James, purchased his land in the 1780s. Once he had cleared the land and built a home, he brought his future wife, Mary (Phillips) back to live. There was also a man named Douds with them. James and Mary had two daughters, Becky (who married James Potter) and Margaret (who married Robert Potter). These daughters and their husbands eventually inherited the Potter farms, all said to total 1200 acres. Members of the Braden and Potter families became owners of much acreage that spanned over the land from the Kobuta area onto the "Tank Farm" area. This land remained within the Braden and Potter families until around 1892 when portions were sold outside the families. On Nov 16, 1892, Theodore Hostetter purchased 196 acres of this land and purchased an additional 68 acres close to a year later. He built a country mansion on his estate in the 1890s. (See the Summer Homes section for much more Hostetter information and pictures.)

Eventually, William Braden became the owner of the land that was best known as the *Tank Farm*. The family eventually sold this property to Raymond Jefferies. This property contained a home known as the Old Stone House, often referred to as one of the oldest houses in Beaver County. Another home said to be owned by Mr. Jefferies was the Barclay house. He also had an area on his property along Raccoon Creek for picnicking and swimming known as Alum Rock Park. Many groups used this area for recreation including the 4-H clubs who used this area for county-wide picnics and events. Mr. Jefferies sold his property to the United States government just prior to WW II and it eventually became known as the Tank Farm. Robert "Bob" Braden became the owner of the land that became known as Kobuta. He sold it to Charles Weaver and John Bardall of West Virginia. For many years, of all the original families of the pre and Potter Township lands, the Dunns and the Douds were the only ones still living on original homesteads. To-date, the Douds-Floyd family homestead is the only original remaining homestead (for at least 120 years as of 2018).

~ ~ ~

MEDICAL

Beaver County Tuberculosis Sanatorium

The Beaver County Sanitarium was conceived for the care of tuberculosis patients. It was located along Old Brodhead Road (across from the Union Cemetery and currently part of the Penn State Beaver campus). It was sometimes referred to as the "Monaca Sanitarium" since Monaca was the closest town to its location. Again, as with the Poor Farm/County Home, this sanitarium was listed as one of the outstanding public institutions in Beaver County during its time. This sanitarium was built, owned, and operated entirely by county taxes with any additional income coming from patients' fees when applicable.

Prior to the existence of the sanitarium, the property and buildings were owned by Dr. Thomas Turnbull, Jr. and his wife Mabel. He was a prominent physician in Pittsburgh in the later 1800s/early 1900s. This farm/property was located further back off Brodhead Road, where the heart of the current Penn State Beaver campus sits. In 1896, the Turnbulls purchased the 93+ acres of property from Charles and Clara McLean (who purchased the acreage via a sheriff's sale in 1895). There was already some type of buildings on the property, but it is stated Dr. Turnbull built a 14-room building on the property hoping to establish a sanitarium for his patients. Unfortunately, due to financial difficulties, his plans of starting the sanitarium never developed to completion and after a few transactions, the Carnegie National Bank became the new owners of the building and 93+ acres in 1908.

This entire tract of land sat about 1200 feet above sea level and was well known for its clean air and the land held what was thought to be "healing" mineral springs. The view of the Ohio and Beaver Rivers from and/or adjacent to this property was also said to be quite grand. Note – in relation to the "view," one must remember that the current divided, multi lane highway leading into Monaca was not constructed at that time, and the land would have continued and been very easily accessible all the way to the river side of the current Sylvan Crest area.

Some back information on the property.

Between 1902 and 1919 the ownership and usage of the 93+ acres and any/all buildings along with a health resort becomes a bit sketchy and confusing. Some say that in 1905 another attempt to have the building and property become a country home or type of health resort for the people of Pittsburgh began. Folklore goes that Dr. Clemens Baelz (married to Amaline) came from Pittsburgh, PA and he leased the property. He treated patients and operated it very successfully for a few years. There was an attempt to incorporate under the laws of the State of Pennsylvania with the intentions of naming the business "Altamont Springs."

Dr. and Mabel Turnbull did not purchase the 93+ acres in Moon Township until 1896. I cannot say who owned the property prior to the Turnbulls other than the McLeans, but I do know the 93+ acre plot was a part of a larger tract that was sold by the County Sheriff in the sale to the McLeans (the Turnbull's deed only stated the Sheriff's name and not who had to surrender the property to the Sheriff). There was also a hospital/health resort run by Dr. Baelz in downtown Phillipsburg (Monaca), but.........the deed of the Moon Township property was dated in 1896, being well over 20 years after the dating of the allopathy and hydropathy hospital recorded to be in Phillipsburg. So, could there be any connection to these doctors, these health resorts, these happenings since the properties were basically adjacent to each other? Could the two campuses of these hospitals/ healing businesses/ resorts been shared or more common with each other? Could Dr. Baelz's business have been spread out and not been concentrated within a block or two of downtown Phillpsburg?

I personally find there to be a cloud of confusion which may come from the folklore, or it may possibly be actual happenings. The reason for my confusion stems from the fact even though the years found listed or recorded are quite different, there are still the same names and types of businesses involved. I found no deeds in Moon Township (or Phillipsburg for that matter) involving Dr. Baelz which may lend to him leasing his properties. Historic records state in the 1860s, Dr. Baelz was first involved with the popular and well-known health resort once located in Phillipsburg (Monaca) - the Water Cure Sanitarium. It was started by Dr. Edward Acker in the 1830s. He provided patients with forms of alternative treatments and medicine including allopathy and hydropathy. This "hospital"/health resort was credited as the first such hospital in Beaver County. Dr. Acker died at the age of 44 in 1853. All indications are that Dr. Baelz took over the sanitarium after Dr. Acker's death and it appears to have then become more of a "resort" than a hospital. Henry Cimiotti (also of Pittsburgh, PA) then purchased some of the property (probably including the buildings) and opened a hotel and summer resort in the early 1860s. Then there was also property and buildings purchased by Rev. William G. Taylor in 1865 who opened the Soldiers' Orphan School. I found that in the 1860s, Rev. Taylor also made many purchases of properties in both Phillipsburg (approximately 18 deeds) and in Moon Township (at least 6 deeds). The Moon Township deeds involved over a total of 176 acres, and all were in the area of parts of the current Sylvan Crest and adjacent to if not part of the current land of the Penn State campus. Regardless of all the ownerships, it is a fact that there was a large structure on the 93+ acre property during the time the Turnbulls were owners.

Some relayed the large structure that sat on the property was also possibly used as a night club, with no evidence found to substantiate this, it just may be a bit of embellishment as some folklore does evolve into. Some also state it was used as a hotel at some time in the early 1900s. This again was curious to me because it is also within the time span that Dr. Baelz was said to have been leasing the property. The folklore of the building being used as a hotel could stem from the fact Dr. Baelz had started a health "resort" where people paid to stay. The fact that people paid to stay there may have been what developed the thought of it being a "hotel." Visitors were not looking for mere lodging. Instead, it became increasing popular and used by persons who also wanted to immerse their bodies in the spring waters found on the property to take advantage of the said healing minerals. These guests were looking to rid their bodies of any disease and strengthen or restore their health. The business of the health resort began to decline when it was discovered that the once pure and sot after spring waters were said to have lost their healing properties after becoming contaminated with residue from coal mining in the immediate area.

Back to actual facts of the property...
The Carnegie National Bank became the owners of the 93+ acres of property via a sheriff's sale in 1908. The property was divided and sold --- 40+ acres in 1918 to Sydney Huffmyer (see further) and 53 acres in 1919 to H. T. Grimmell. Mr. Grimmell, a real estate agent in Monaca used a portion of this acreage and built a home for himself, he named his estate *Mona Manor*. Within a few years, Mr. Grimmell subdivided a large portion of his 53 acres into building lots (see Housing Areas section – Mona Manor). Sidney Huffmyer purchased the remaining 40+ acres of Dr. Turnbull's property. His acreage contained the former health resort building and Sidney turned the 14-room building into his home. (See Penn State information in the Education section for more details.) The house and property were then sold by the Huffmyers to Beaver County in the 1920s.

By 1923-1924, Drs. Fred and Ruth (Walker) Wilson had approval and started the Beaver County TB Sanitarium. Dr. Fred Wilson became fondly known simply as "Dr. Fred." He developed active tuberculosis in 1918 after the flu epidemic that year. He went to a sanitarium in New York for his treatment. When he returned home, he realized the need for such care in Beaver County and was responsible for taking the steps to have the Beaver County TB Sanitarium built. They opened their doors to care for TB patients and took in their first patient on Feb 14, 1923. That first patient admitted was determined not to have TB, but a lung infection contracted during the flu pandemic. There was almost a half dozen of other first persons admitted to the sanitarium that were found to not have active TB, but instead had rheumatic heart problems, severe flu symptoms or complications and other ailments. This did not only occur at the Beaver County TB Sanitarium but was occurring elsewhere in Pennsylvania at other hospitals and sanitariums. With these "false TB" situations happening so frequently, new guidelines were then followed, and prior to admission, new patients were accepted only if referred by the State Chest Clinic or if they had a positive lab test for TB.

As stated, the site of the sanitarium itself was on Sidney Huffmyer's former 40-acre piece of property with the previous health resort building/former Huffmyer home used to house the patients. It quickly became too small to meet the needs of the patients with expansion the only option. Plans were developed and the sanitarium was built. The new facility had a 50-bed capacity that was soon expanded to 60 beds. Even with the new guidelines for determining true TB cases, there was a waiting list of sometimes 30 or more persons to be admitted to the sanitarium. The building originally had sun porches and chat rooms, but they were converted to accommodate and expand the number of beds. Additionally, there was also a stone cottage which was converted as part of the sanitarium.

The treatment of TB prior to antibiotics and other methods consisted of rest, a good diet, and fresh air. The grounds of the sanitarium were planted and seeded and became a wonderful show place. Most of the produce was grown in the sanitarium gardens with the help of patients. As part of the program, patients would work in the gardens to help regain strength and keep the healing process going. The sanitarium also raised its own pigs, as well as chickens which meant there was always a supply of eggs. Milk for the patients was purchased from the neighboring farm of the Hartenbach family.

A new three storey hospital was constructed and contained a kitchen and had dining rooms on the first floor. On the second and third floors were quarters for the nurses and maids, an X-ray room, and a laboratory. It was said that when a TB patient would pass away, the body would first be taken to the lab, which would have been located where the old maintenance building used to be on the college campus. The pulmonary system was extracted and autopsied for further analysis. The organs of the deceased were then burned in the incinerator to prevent further spread of the disease. The bodies were then taken to the basement area of the caretaker's home/building (the area now called "the bunker" under the concrete slab) to be embalmed.

Drs. Fred and Ruth Wilson were instrumental in ridding Beaver County of TB. Dr. Fred and his wife dedicated their careers to treating TB, yet Dr. Fred died of the disease in 1955. After her husband's death, Dr. Ruth Wilson enrolled at New York Institute for Allergy and maintained a private practice in Beaver. She also ran the Department of Health's tuberculosis clinic in Bridgewater until 1984. Dr. John Boal relayed - "In an era when few women practiced medicine, Wilson was an advocate for working women. She also fought discrimination wherever she saw it." Dr. Ruth Wilson retired in 1984 after 65 years of practicing medicine, she died in Apr 1994 at the age of 97. While Drs. Fred and Ruth Wilson were at the sanitarium, they attended and care for an estimated 3,475 patients.

> Fun facts: Dr. Ruth Wilson was not only devoted and interested in medicine, but she also loved photography and travel. She was also interested in local history and donated thousands of dollars to historical groups such as Fort McIntosh Garrison and the Beaver Area Heritage Foundation where she was also a member. To show their appreciation for the many charitable gifts she made, it is said that once a year, members of the garrison would march past her house and fire their muskets, then give three cheers for "Dr. Ruth." She was also the President of the Beaver County Tuberculosis Association in 1956.

As a result of the drop in TB cases, the Beaver County sanitarium was no longer needed and soon ceased to be considered a TB sanitarium. The sanitarium was discontinued in Dec of 1956 and all patients were moved to Cresson or Mount Alto facilities. (Cresson, PA is adjacent to Altoona --- Mount Alto, PA is in the center of the state.) An editorial submitted by Dr. Ruth Wilson in 1956 stated that since the sanitarium would be closing, the Beaver County tax money would be used to maintain the then current sanitarium for elderly chronic patients and not for tuberculosis. She also said the public should be urged to purchase Christmas Seals to assure free monthly X-rays and the continued funding of work at state funded facilities.

Shortly after the sanitarium closed, the site became the Beaver County Hospital Annex and officially opened as such on Jan 1, 1957. It became home to wounded veterans and other patients from the Beaver County Hospital. It was sometimes referred to as the "old vet's hospital." Mrs. Zelma Lyons of Center Township was a registered nurse in the Annex and her husband and family lived in one of the apartment areas on the 2nd or 3rd floor of the hospital area. Mrs. Anne Fair was assistant head nurse. Dr. William Milliron was the staff doctor and was aided by 21 nurses and 15 other employees. They had charge of 66 patients as of 1958. Severely wounded veterans were welcomed there as they acclimated themselves to their injuries and worked their way back into society. Many of these veterans were considered disabled, missing limbs and some were blind when they returned from war. At that time in history, if you were unable to use your hands, walk, or see, then none of the industrial businesses considered you able to work. With the Poor Farm/County Home planning to close, many local elderlies were also given a home in the former sanitarium in 1958/early 60s. In 1963, the last of the severely wounded veterans and/or elderly residents were all moved from the former sanitarium site to the newly constructed Beaver County Geriatric Center. The former sanitarium buildings were left standing idle.

In 1965, just two years after the last patient was moved from the former sanitarium buildings, the buildings and property were donated to Pennsylvania State University by the Beaver County Commissioners. The main building of the former sanitarium became the original Administration Building for Penn State – Beaver Campus. It continued to be used for this purpose from 1965 until 2004 when the Ross Administration Building was built and opened, then all the former sanitarium buildings were razed. (See the Education section, under Penn State for more information and pictures.)

Former home.

These are original views of the buildings that once stood on the property that became that of the Beaver County TB Sanitarium. They were originally used for Turnbull's health resort, then the Huffmyer's family home. In various reports, there are differing details – some state the original 14 room building became incorporated into the structures of the expanded sanitarium hospital, while others indicate all were torn down when the newer sanitarium was erected. Regardless, the last standing sanitarium building was then used by the Penn State Beaver Campus for almost 50 years as their Administration Building. All the original buildings were razed in 2004.

Additional views of the main entrance to the Beaver County TB Sanitarium.

Photo courtesy Penn State

1953

~ ~ ~

Beaver County General Hospital   aka   Rochester General Hospital

Courtesy the BCHR & LF

This 1913 photo of the hospital was originally submitted by Fritz Blasche.   Two popular forms of transportation in 1913 are also illustrated in this photograph – Dr. Shugert's automobile and Dr. Cloak's horse and buggy.

The Beaver County General Hospital received its charter on Dec 13, 1894, and it was opened for work Jan 1, 1895, in the building that was formerly used as the Merchants' Hotel in Beaver Falls. It formed a Ladies' Auxiliary to the Board of Directors in 1898. Later the former Kenwood School for Boys in Kenwood was purchased, and this became the home of the hospital. It was determined by many of the local physicians that the lower Beaver Valley needed a hospital. After a considerable effort, the property at the corner of Pinney and Kentucky Streets in Rochester, PA was purchased, and the fourteen-roomed building on the lot then became the hospital.

A new building was erected and the Beaver County General Hospital located in Rochester was founded in the fall of 1899; it was a semi-private hospital / institution. The name was changed to Rochester General Hospital in Aug of 1900.   At first it was a semi-private hospital, but in 1902 it formed a Board of Directors and became public. The original Board of Directors was comprised of Drs. Rose, Allen, Gibson, Boal, Baker, Wickham, Scroggs, Jas. Gormley, Shugert, Marquis, Armstrong, and Ague. The next board was made up of Drs. Allen, Gormley, Shugert, Armstrong, Scroggs, Baker, Boal, Wickham, and Ague. Several of these doctors being associated with and/or based out of Monaca. Some other doctors to serve on the board included Drs. Shallenberger, McCaskey, Snodgrass, Peirsol, and Marcy.

Less than six months of being in operation, on Mar 11, 1901, the hospital's original building was partially destroyed by a fire. In 1902, the hospital was completely turned over to its board of directors. A modern building was then constructed with monies from a state appropriation and an equal amount being raised. In 1922, there was an annex built to the building. This hospital was regarded by the Pennsylvania Hospital Association as one of the leading and best-equipped hospitals in the state at that time. With the large growth in industry during the WWII era, there was a serious shortage of space in the hospital, so a 48-bed addition was completed in 1943 along with a complete lab and an X-ray department. In 1972, the Rochester General Hospital became a unit of the Medical Center of Beaver County. The hospital ceased to exist in the early 1980s, the result of local hospitals merging to become The Medical Center- Beaver, now Heritage Valley Beaver in Brighton Township.

The former hospital building in Rochester stood idle for several years before it was converted into and now serves as the Rochester Manor and Villa (Retirement Community) at 174 Virginia Avenue, Rochester, PA. In 1990, it was purchased by Robert Kopsack and his sons, Mark and Nathan assumed ownership.

Fun fact: In Feb 1921, the Rochester Hospital proudly announced that they had a new X-ray machine installed and it was ready for use. They stated the machine was "strictly modern and up-to-date in every particular and was one of the best in the country." They boasted the extra work that was being done in the large cities could now be done at the Rochester Hospital by Dr. F. H. McCaskey, Roentgenologist, who was in charge of the machine.

~ ~ ~

Aliquippa Hospital
1957 to Dec 2008

This hospital was located at 2500 Hospital Drive, Aliquippa, PA. It was built as a nonprofit institution. It was built in the "Cooper Heights" section of the Borough of Aliquippa. The campaign to raise monies to finance the more than two-million-dollar complex was initially funded by advances of $25,000 each by Local 1211, CIO-USW, and the Jones & Laughlin Steel Corporation. J & L pledged to match, dollar for dollar, gifts of employees and individuals in the area. Employees who would make contributions from their paychecks in turn would receive a health plan that afforded them care and/or treatment from the hospital once it was in operation. At the close of the campaign, J & L turned over a check for more than one million dollars! Many of the residents in Center Township were becoming employees of the J & L company and found the savings at this hospital to be quite welcomed.

Aliquippa hospital opened May 12, 1957. Although it will always be known and referred to as "Aliquippa Hospital", the hospital was renamed UPMC Beaver Valley in the late 1990s. It became known as the Commonwealth Medical Center (a for-profit enterprise) when they purchased the hospital for $23 million in 2007. The hospital originally had 100 beds, 24 private rooms, 30 semi-private, 4 four bed rooms, surgical unit with 53 beds, and two nurseries that each held ten bassinets. When built, there was room and plans for expansion of the facility. It was a 170-bed facility in the 1990s.

Original building in 1957.

Both photos taken from old postcards.

2007 photo with extension to front of the building.

The hospital lost $1.2 million dollars in the 1988-89 fiscal year. By Feb 1990, the Aliquippa Hospital was suffering greatly financially. The hospital's board of directors was considering one of two options to turn this problem around – hiring an outside management company or merging with one of the four hospitals in Pittsburgh. Gino Piroli, the newly elected president, stated that he preferred hiring a management team since a merger could mean the hospital might then cease to exist and possibly become a nursing facility. The latter being something the hospital board also did not want to happen. With the closing of J & L Steel and the loss of all benefits, including health coverage, so many former steelworkers and retirees had to seek their own medical insurance and this snowballed and greatly impacted the incoming operating funds for the hospital.

The hospital had been operating only a 96-bed facility late in 2008. In Nov of 2008, the state had banned the hospital from accepting new patients since the facility was violating licensing standards which included being in arrears of bills and they were short on essential supplies and equipment that ensured patient safety. The number of employees was reduced from 305 to only 189 also. There were still a few skilled nurses in the facility since they operate under a separate license and this portion of the facility would remain open until the remaining three residents were discharged or relocated.

The Aliquippa Commonwealth Hospital had filed for bankruptcy protection in 2002. This is what prompted the takeover and name change to Commonwealth Medical Center. The hemorrhaging of money continued with the hospital losing more than $12 million since 2004 prompting the Commonwealth Medical Center to also file for Chapter 11 bankruptcy restructuring the first of Dec 2008. One week later, on Dec 12, 2008, the hospital just closed rather abruptly. When the hospital notified the state Health Department that it had closed, the agency revoked its operating license and all "blue signs"* directing traffic to the facility had to be immediately removed or covered. *The blue colored signs along the highways with a big "H" on them and an arrow showing the direction of the hospital.

The chief executive officer and interim president of the hospital at that time, John O'Donnell, was quoted, "We want to express our heartfelt thanks to all steelworkers and the families of the steelworkers who unselfishly donated money to the hospital, the dedicated employees, physicians, volunteers and community members we have been privileged to serve these past 51 years."

The optimism that still flickered for the Commonwealth Medical Center reapplying for a new license or for anyone to come in and take over the hospital and starting from scratch was fully snuffed out by 2009. C. J. Betters bought the former hospital building and property for $250,000 and stated when he bought it there was "an opportunity to salvage it." Mr. Betters had contacted Global Links and Construction Junction to come in and remove medical equipment, furnishings, and building materials for recycling or reuse, they removed 10 truckloads. Global Links removed stretchers, waiting room furniture, medical supply cabinets, surgical supplies. Construction Junction took light fixtures, ceiling tiles, office furnishings. Asbestos removal was done in 2010.

After determining that since he bought the facility, Mr. Betters had spent more in maintaining it and guarding it all 24/7 than he had paid to purchase it. This prompted the decision for demolition of the entire building. By Mar of 2011, a half-dozen excavators had moved in and were dismantling the three-storey yellow brick facility that had once been the Aliquippa Hospital. Replacing the once proudly standing hospital facility were piles of metal, concrete blocks and bricks, and other materials. The demolition was expected to be completed by Apr or May of 2011, then the 29/30-acre piece of property would be prepared for its next usage.

An article in the Pittsburgh Business Times Dec 10, 2010, stated that a Cranberry-based Lutheran Senior Life, Heritage Valley Health System, and C. J. Betters Enterprises had formed a joint venture to develop the former Aliquippa Hospital property. There were plans from this jointure that included building what's known as a "greenhouse" model that affords elderly residents who need assistance to live in smaller groups in a facility designed as a private home instead of being more like traditional nursing homes.

So……………. Center Township residents now only had the new Heritage Valley Hospital in Beaver or in Sewickley as their closest medical facility.

~ ~ ~

Fact: Diphtheria was out of control in the mid/late 1910s. It was spread by the finest spray of spit coughed into the air of a room or while someone talked or laughed close to the face of another. It could also be transmitted from hand to hand by means of towels, common drinking cups or pencils, by a shared apple, common spoon, etc. Many of those who died were children. They reported sore throats, but parents first thought it simply "a sore throat" and the children were not treated soon enough. The body usually produces enough of its own antitoxin to destroy the germs, but when this does not occur, then an injection would be needed. A horse can manufacture a large quantity of diphtheria antitoxin when the diphtheria germs are injected into it. The fluid part of the horse's blood forms the antitoxin and can then be used and injected into an ill human. Once the disease was determined to be quite deadly, then anyone known to be exposed to diphtheria was given at least a thousand units of antitoxin which was proven to ward off catching the disease. This injection gave protection against diphtheria for three weeks. There were 17,717 cases of diphtheria in Pennsylvania in 1919, 1,833 died. Except for the antitoxin, more than 7,080 probably would have died.

Beaver County Home   aka   County Poor Farm

c between 1916 and 1921

Although the Beaver County Home and Hospital (aka County Poor Farm aka Beaver County Home for the Poor and Infirm) was located in Moon Township within the portion that became Potter Township, it was frequently associated with Monaca and Center because of the close proximity and the connection of roadways from the Home to those areas. The Poor House/Home was first established to accommodate poor and indigent persons, but over the course of its existence, it also gave refuge to the elderly, the infirm, the sick, and occasionally to the insane.

Fact: The first "inmate" of the home was 21-year-old John Murphy of New Brighton, being admitted in Apr 1853. He had a very intellectual mind, but a terribly deformed body. He was a very good influence on the lives of the other inmates who did associate with him. John spent almost his entire life in the Home. He died in Feb 1928 at 95 or 96 years of age.

Even before the vote to officially approve a county poor home was presented, the need for such a "home" was obvious. There was a small one-storey building used for providing a place for some of the people in the area that had no one to take them in or care for them. Prior to the vote in 1831 to build an official County Home, this very smaller, much less formal "home" was put into use, but being so small, it rapidly became overcrowded. In 1831, thirty-one years after Beaver County was founded, there was a meeting at the courthouse of the Beaver County Supervisors to discuss providing an official home for the poor. They called for a vote that year with the majority defeating the concept of a new home.

In 1842 it was reported the building being used as the poor house was located on the south side of the Ohio River about two and a half miles below Beaver, which places it in Moon Township. It was on a 138-acre plot of land that was formerly the Stone homestead, so this description places the first small poor house building on the same property as the next few larger poor-farm/houses. The residents of the home were required to do farm or other types of work at the home and/or on the property to earn their keep.

BCHR&LF
1842 view of the first building used to house the poor
– address was Bellowsville, Beaver County, PA

As previously stated, the need for more accommodations was quite evident and the idea of building a larger and more efficient home was presented to the voters for them to express their will regarding the establishment of such an institution in 1841 but it was defeated. In 1844, a vote was once again taken, but again the erection of a new county poorhouse was again defeated when the vote showed 1,533 were for the institution and 2,366 were against it.

At the general elections held on Oct 14, 1851, the county home project was put to the voters yet again, this time the vote, although very close, was 1,855 "for" and 1,738 "against." With this approval, the county purchased the 138-acre farm where the first structure was located. The stated price paid to George Stone for the property is reported in two different versions, but the end result is the same. One stated he was paid $6,900 while another stated the cost was $50 per acre (138 acres times $50 equals the $6,900). As previously mentioned, this land was located in what was called Moon Township, now Potter Township, on the property best known of Zinc Corp of America (the former St Joe Mineral property).

The county erected their first building in 1853 and it was described as sitting ½ mile from the main road (Frankfort Road), along the bank of the Ohio River, directly across from the Merrill Locks (No 6 – Industry, PA). This building was also a one-storey frame building, 16 x 32 feet. The original Stone house/home was used as the residence for the superintendents. This one-storey frame structure erected in 1853 ended up being torn down in 1855. The second home erected on the property was also a frame structure but a bit larger being a two-storey, 32 x 48 feet building and was completed in 1859. This newly erected home/hospital was described as one of the most modern and complete of its kind in the state.

Of the home's acreage, five were cultivated and one was used as a garden. "Inmates" reported very clean and first-class conditions. There was an average of twenty-five males and twenty-five females who resided at the home. These "inmates" of the house did the farming and much of the maintenance and chores of the home. Growing of crops was quite successful with tons of hay, bushels of potatoes and wheat, along with acres of corn and pumpkins crops. Along with chickens, there was also livestock, usually consisting of three horses, ten cows, one bull, and twenty-nine hogs.

Due to the continuing increase and demand for more space, there was another building added to the home. In 1868, work began on a main two-storey brick complex. 44 x 100 feet, was built for $18,000 and completed in 1870. By 1885 there were outbuildings and washhouses added to the property. The 1859 two-storey frame building was then used to house some of the residents and held the kitchen and dining room for everyone. The newest large brick structure was built for the use of the inmates. This new building was heated and lighted with gas, equipped with numerous fire escapes and fire extinguishers, as well as a 250-barrel water tank to be used in case of fire. In 1899, there were 32 large and airy sleeping rooms to accommodate 80 to 110 inmates, with the lower floor having separate parlors for males and females. There was always multiple and good literature provided for use by the inmates. There was a separate "pest house"* that was on the farm in an isolated area of the property.

> *Pest house – it was a common practice to have a separate building where any person with a terminal and contagious disease would have to reside to keep the disease from being spread to other healthy people. There were quite a few of these "houses" found in many of the townships/boroughs.
>
> Another pest house that is mentioned in the township was in a secluded area of the Mateer farm (corner of Brodhead and Marshall Roads).

The main home had evolved from just a place for elderly people (those whom had no one to take them in and care for them) to live out their lives, to then have elderly, physically challenged, and financially challenged adults and children living at the home. In 1899, the grounds and all the buildings were still reported as well kept and very clean. It was said that "The cellars and every out-of-the-way corner are scrupulously clean...." The greater part of the farm was used for growing produce that was prepared for all the residents. The only things brought in daily for use was flour and meat. There were over 500 fowls kept at the farm and were tended to by one man who would be placed in charge of the coops. There were approximately 1400 dozen eggs laid a year. One thousand eggs would be kept for setting and the remaining used for consumption.

Patients and residents of the home were frequently referred to as "inmates." They were well fed and even treated to special dinners on all holidays, as well as frequently different forms of entertainment provided for them, too. Not only were the inmates given the freedom to wonder the grounds, but they were also very useful in areas involving the laundry, bakery, kitchen, housekeeping, and elsewhere. All the children who became "inmates" of the home received instructions so eventually they could lead an independent life and be self-reliant. As soon as possible, they were placed into good homes, many becoming honored citizens.

> Fact: A newspaper article in The Daily Times on Jan 31, 1929 stated that the Beaver County Home was physically situated in Potter Township, the residents were not really considered a part of that township by the people there. This train of thought was because the residents of the home came from all over Beaver County and not just from Potter Township. The majority of census enumerators who did the listings of the home included it with the Moon/Center Township area censuses with only a couple years of enumerations included under Potter Township.

Many men served in the position of director of the institute. From 1852 through 1901 these included (those of Moon Township are underlined), 1852 - Joseph Douthett, Philip Cooper, David Shaner, 1853 - David Shaner, 1853-54 - Henry Engels of Industry, 1854-58 - Anthony Douthett/Dourthard of Darlington, 1853-63 - James Brittain of Chippewa, <u>1863-77 - Wm. Shrodes of Moon,</u> <u>1877-85 - Stephen Minor of Moon,</u> 1885-88 - J. W. Jack of Industry, 1888-92 - J. H. Ewing of Raccoon, <u>1892 -95 - George Engle of Moon,</u> 1895-98 - Wm. Thornburgh of Raccoon, and <u>1898-1901 - B. Elliott of Moon</u>.

After 1901, I also found the following from the census enumeration sheets (there were probably more persons before, after, or in between these persons, but I could not find listings), <u>1910 - John M. Shroads of Moon,</u> 1920 - Elizabeth Springer (possibly of Raccoon), and 1929 - Sherman Moore (his wife, (Mary) Marion Marshall Moore was Matron). In 1937, the home was under supervision of James L. Blair with Mrs. Blair in charge of all office work and the welfare and comfort of the women. In 1940, Frank Hart of New Brighton served, and his wife Edith was listed as "Asst. Supt.". As of Jan 1948, William H. Bickerstaff was superintendent of the county home. He was appointed by the commissioners with his wife and a registered nurse who supervised a staff of twenty-one nurses and four orderlies.

Other names included in a list of stewards or other heads in the County Home all serving for one or more terms were Robert Potter (1855), William Barnes (1856), James Sterling (1857), Henry Goehring (1858), Samuel Moorehead (1859), John White (1860), Samuel Wilson (1862), John K. Potter (1863), Samuel McManamy (1864), Samuel Gibson (1865), John Potter (1866), Samuel McManamy (1867), John Slentz (1868), Robert Cooper (1869), Hiram Reed (1870), Samuel Gibson (1871), John White (1872), Samuel McManamy (1873), Samuel E. Walton (1874), Samuel Boots (1875), Thomas Ramsey, William M. Reed (1875), Socrates A. Dickey, Joseph W. Appleton, Robert S. Newton, Philip V. Cooper, Thomas Reed, Richard Walton, Isaac Miner, Stephen Minor, John C. Christy, George H. Cleis, John S. Cunningham, James H. Springer, Joseph Carney, Andrew W. Tanner, James W. Mackall, J. Henry Shuster, Jacob A. Rose, and J. W. Carnegie.

Physicians who served at the Home were elected each January. These physicians included 1853-56 - Drs. George Allison of Beaver, 1855-58 - John Ramsey Miller of Raccoon, 1858-63 - Smith Cunningham of Beaver, <u>1863-69 - James S. Elliott of Moon,</u> 1869-82 - Presley M. Kerr of Raccoon, <u>1882-83 - John Bryan of Moon,</u> 1883-88 - J. H. Ramsey of Bridgewater, 1888-92 - James Scroggs, Jr. of Beaver, 1892-93 - G. A. Scroggs of Beaver, 1893-99 - James Scroggs, Jr. of Beaver, 1899-1902 - J. B. Armstrong of Beaver, 1901-1902 – J. R. Gormley of Monaca, and 1902-1903 - J. J. Allen of Monaca.

It is reported that while Mr. and Mrs. Stephen Minor were managing the home, they received $500 a year from the county for their services while working with a board of directors supervising the house. Mr. Minor supervised installing 140 rods (equals 770 yards) of board fencing being put up by the "inmates" who did this in exchange for a small quantity of tobacco. Mrs. Minor would make pies and cook for everyone. She was assisted often by Mrs. Margaret (Baker) Shrodes, the wife of the former manager.

Unfortunately, due to the low location of the site by the Ohio River, the almshouse property experienced frequent flooding. On Feb 7, 1884, the water rose 7 feet above the ground level.

c 1870s

Originally built with compassion and to aid and help by housing persons in need of assistance who had no one else to take care of them, the almshouse evolved to include care and housing for those, who no fault of their own, were elderly, infirm, blind, crippled, and some considered "unwanted" (all which caused severe need of income/money). It came to be a common view of people that it was considered a "black mark" against you if you ended up in the "county house." The "black mark" mind set came about because as is tradition, "taking care of family" is just consider to be the right thing to do. Therefore, many looked upon these residents as either being flat out broke and not having any family or friends who "wanted to" take care of them or who were willing to help. Once you review the individual situations, it is much clearer that many of the residents had deeper reasons for the home becoming their only choice for surviving.

As of 1884, the poor farm could accommodate 100 paupers.

Photo courtesy Richard "Bud" Temple
This is a photo of the Almshouse taken from across the river near Lock 6.

Fun fact: There was a group called Monaca Auxiliary to the Beaver County Home for the Aged that was started in 1913. It was made up mainly of women from Monaca, but also had a few members from Center and Potter Townships. Members helped raise funds for keeping up the room which they had furnished at the time of the opening of the home and other funds toward the general maintenance of the home. Mrs. Wilhelmina Lay held the group's meetings at her home (Atlantic Ave and Fifth Street in Monaca).

Just with the amount of constant usage, not to mention the multiple flooding events of the property, it is no wonder that the home was experiencing problems and beginning to rapidly show its age by 1913. It was obvious that a new facility was needed to replace the aged and worn structures. It was decided to erect a new home in a different area on the same property, an area which would not be affected by flooding. This new facility was completed in 1916. It had a central building with two 2-storey wings on either side. The central building sported a large, pillared portico/porch.

Photo courtesy Richard "Bud" Temple
1916 view of the then newer erected former Beaver County Home from across the river.

In 1920, officials provided a very detailed report on the Beaver County Home. The report stated that the county expended a little more than $71,370 to the care of the sick, aged, and helpless, as well as the homeless children and the few persons who were in need of temporary aid. The annual report was issued by Commissioners Frank D. Hart, Art W. Coombs, and Fred O. Javens. This report showed maintenance of the county home and farm for that year was $30,269.26, operation of the farm cost $9,878.63, and "indoor expenses" were $20,390.63. The indoor expenses included meat, groceries, clothes, shoes, fuel/gas, light/electric/power, medical supplies, newspapers, brooms, telephone, insurances, repairs, appliances. Also, in the expenses were the salaries of:

Dr. J. Scroggs, Jr.	S. E. Springer-Superintendent	Alma Young-Matron
Dr. D. C. Moore	Lucila Stark-Cook	Minnie Klump-Baker
Dan Hoisinger-Engineer	Elizabeth Lockhart-Cook	James Wallace-Attendant

Within the total expenses of the operation of the farm (the $9,878.63) were payments to other personnel. These included Farmers–James Springer, Elmer Johnston, Louis Groop; Gardener–Dominec Principatti; B. H. Dimit who sold pure bred Holstein to the farm; and miscellaneous supplies of stock feed, equipment repairs, seeds, fertilizer, new stock animals, horse shoeing, et cetera.

Also reported in 1920, were the expenses of $30,088.27 which included giving medical attendance and the necessities of life to all the worthy poor and those in need of temporary assistance. The care for the homeless children added $11,013.94 to that sun. The care and placement of the children involved several homes including the Beaver County Children's Home, home of Harriet E. Stewart, the Holy Family Children's Home, the Allegheny County Home, the Bethshan home, the Home of Good Shepherd, the home of Mary Beleyn, the home of Nettie Anderton, the home of N. P. Caughey, the home of Jennie Hollein, the home of J. L. Ripper, the H. M. Hays facility, and the Catholic Child Saving Bureau.

There were 200 beds by 1932 and still more were needed. In 1937, there were 219 residents – 186 men and 33 women. Within the home, there was a fully equipped hospital with two trained nurses on duty regularly. Also, in 1937, a W.P.A. project was assigned for repairing two porches and a passageway between the laundry and the main dormitory.

By 1940, the demand for more room continued to increase so a large 100 bed hospital was added/completed as a rear wing to the building – it was exactly the length of a football field. This remodeling not only added room for 100 beds but also a modern laundry in the basement, an auditorium, a chapel, a pharmacy, two solariums, rooms with outside exposure, living quarters for a medical staff of 12 persons, superintendent residents, a morgue, as well as several 9'x12' jail cells in the basement that would house "unruly" patients from time to time. There were also various farm outbuildings erected. The extensive remodel in the 1940s unfortunately bore no resemblance to the former home. After the "improvements" it was then known as the Beaver County Home and Hospital. It did however remain a working farm, complete with a dairy herd, sheep, pigs, and chickens.

Most of the patients in 1948 were quite elderly and/or their cases were incurable, meaning they really had come to the home to die, paying if they could or staying for free if they could not. Although records and census indicate that the residents were called "inmates," they were free to roam the grounds. All able-bodied inmates had to work on the grounds to earn their keep. Much of the food used in the home was still being grown there in 1952. There were gigantic gardens, and everything was canned for the winter. They still had cows, pigs, fresh milk, butter, buttermilk and eggs, hundreds of chickens, and butchering was done in the fall since there was also a smokehouse.

c1939/1940 aerial view. Date determined since this photo includes the newer addition that was added on the rear of the structure. The "front" of the building (with the giant pillars) faced the Ohio River.

The new home/hospital was making the news in 1940. Although this is a very poor grade picture, it is included to show what appeared in the Pittsburgh Press newspaper mid Apr 1940.

Beaver County Home Hospital to Make Public Debut

Beaver County's new $200,000 County Home Hospital of 91 beds, designed to care for the county's indigent, will be opened for public inspection Wednesday. Situated in Potter Twp., adjacent to the Home, the structure is shown above.

It features a chapel, pharmacy, two solariums and rooms with outside exposure, and living quarters for a medical staff of 12 persons.

Over a year in construction, the project was partially financed by a Public Works Administration grant of $87,000.

Sixty patients have already been removed from the County Home and installed in the hospital, which includes an administration division.

Beginning in the mid to late 1950s, the poor house turned its focus more toward the old and infirm rather than the poor and insane. At this time, the farm was no longer a "working farm;" patients/residents could simply enjoy the grounds and/or other residents' company. To alleviate overcrowding once again, in 1956, the infirm residents were moved to a former Beaver County Tuberculosis Sanitarium in Center Township (property that is currently that of the Penn State Beaver Campus). Approximately two hundred and twenty residents were still living in the home by Apr 1959. They were then moved into a new home/center the county had built above Beaver, the Beaver Valley Geriatric Center, now named Friendship Ridge.

Fact: For over 125 years, from the 1830s to Apr 1959, Beaver County had some form of a functioning "home" institute in Moon Township/Potter Township until the last residences were moved to the new building (now Friendship Ridge).

During WWII, a part of the Poorhouse property was sold. In 1955, the remaining property and the building were sold to St. Joseph Lead Co. for $750,000 for that plant's expansion. St. Joe then leased the former home to the county for $1 a year until the new structure in Brighton Township was completed. As of 2003 and for several years that followed, the 1940 addition portion of the Home served as Zinc Corporation's company corporate offices, then the entire building was closed and fenced off due to the majority of the entire building being in such severe disrepair. It all became the property of Horsehead Corp. Then the Shell business purchased all the land in the area, in came massive land moving equipment, and nothing remains of any of the former County Home except memories, a few records, and some older photographs.

Fact: John Wright had lived in the home since 1939 and in 1959 when other inmates of the home were moved to the new home, Wright refused to accompany them and remained around the old home for some time. Unfortunately, he was finally arrested and charged with vagrancy. After spending time in jail, Judge McCreary took compassion; he gave a very pleasing description of the new facilities to Mr. Wright, and he finally agreed to try it.

1921

Fact: The North Branch Church was closed beginning in Jul 1961 through the fall of 1962 while the educational wing of the building was completed as well as renovations to the sanctuary area. During this closing, church services were held in a portion of the Poor House. This location was used by the church since the Poor House had been abandoned in 1959.

These photos were taken by Richard Temple. Prior to all buildings being razed, in 2013, he was given a private tour and access to the buildings/grounds, to document information, and to take these photos.

Rear of the Poor Home before being razed

Front of the Poor Home before being razed

Front door and lobby area – anterooms on either side

View into the lobby

Stairs leading to the second floor

Door leading to inmate rooms from the lobby area

An individual inmate room

An Inmate Ward

Located in the basement of the main (center) building - two cells for any unruly inmates.

Fun fact: The cells were removed in the summer of 2014 when demolition was being done. They were originally stored/placed behind Potter Township municipal building to be available for display at the Potter Township Family Reunions.

~ ~ ~

Beaver Valley Geriatric Center   aka   Friendship Ridge

This facility is in Brighton Township. It was originally called Beaver Valley Geriatric Center, consisting of a five-storey main building & a west wing. The building was dedicated on Mar 13, 1959. Approximately two hundred and twenty residents from the County Home in Potter Township were moved into the new center in Apr 1959. In 1964, the remaining infirmed residents from the County Home in Potter, who had been moved to the tuberculosis sanitarium in Center Township, were also moved to this new center.

~ ~ ~

Gateway Rehabilitation Center   aka   Gateway Farms
1972 to current   Located on Moffett Run Road

Originally, though not receiving final approval, a two and half million-dollar center was proposed as a pilot project to rehabilitate alcoholics on a 10-acre site in Center Township in Jan 1970. It was to be a 150-bed center and was to be named Gateway Farms, Inc. Steve Petz owned the property where the center was planned to be built. This tract of land was in the Woodhaven Estates and Chapel Valley areas. Gateway Farms would have no facilities for withdrawing a patient from alcohol but was instead to be a facility to provide treatment, with focus on the resocialization of the "dried out" alcoholic. Therefore, it would not have housed any patients who were intoxicated. It was planned to take in both men and women who voluntarily committed themselves to 35-40 treatments beyond withdrawal and had certification by a physician. This facility never materialized at this Woodhaven Estates/Chapel Valley area location.

Approval was then given for a new site on Moffett Run Road, off Pleasant Drive, for the Gateway Farms with construction of the facility beginning Nov 1970, it opened in Jan of 1972. This facility was to include treatment and resocialization for patients. The first proposal for the Gateway Farms included a two-storey structure with the ground floor consisting of a large dining hall and multipurpose center, plus business offices and public area, with patient quarters to be on the upper level. The construction was going to be privately financed. As of 1980, it was a 28-day treatment center for persons addicted to alcohol and/or drugs.

In 1973, the center nearly closed. It was unable to provide funds to pay its employees, but a bookkeeper mortgaged his house to save it. This generous gesture was not made public until almost 15 years later. Dr. Abraham Twerski founded the Center, which was the first addiction treatment facility in the area. In 2001, Dr. Twerski, was officially retired but became Gateway's emeritus medical director.

1980

The campus of this facility has grown since it first opened in 1972. Currently there are 22 locations in Pennsylvania and Ohio, serving some 1,700 patients daily. In 2002, Gateway Rehabilitation Center had prevention and treatment programs for adults, youths, and families. It also publicized that it offered a network of services – three divisions, Gateway Genesis which has treatment and prevention programs, Gateway Corrections which has services for those in correction facilities, and the Ohio Division which includes Gateway's affiliation with Neil Kennedy Recovery Clinic in Youngstown. They also offered weeklong camp for teens, surrounding them with peers and adults who provided encouragement as they engaged in team building and leadership exercises. Originally, this center was for the rehabilitation of persons who suffered from the addiction of alcoholism. Today, it offers services for detox, inpatients, and outpatients for anyone who suffers from various substance abuse. Gateway Rehab is now listed as being the largest substance abuse and addiction recovery network serving the greater Pittsburgh region.

~ ~ ~

As of 2018, there was an active development project happening along the hillside, adjacent to the Beaver Valley Mall property, behind the former Sears Automotive Center. This land is part of both Potter and Center Townships. The developer was calling the area on this hillside "Bluffs at Glade Path." Included in this development are two medical facilities, as well as plans for two office buildings, a large climate-controlled storage facility, 180 apartments, and 80 condominiums.

Currently included in this development …

Allegheny Health Network Cancer Institute - Beaver
2019   Located behind the Beaver Valley Mall at 81 Wagner Road
May 13, 2019 was the official ribbon cutting to open the Allegheny Health Network Cancer Institute – Beaver. It is a 34,000 square foot, two-storey cancer center to provide "a wide array of clinical and support services, including state-of-the-art radiation oncology capabilities, medical oncology and infusion therapy, nutritional counseling, social services and access to cancer clinical trials." It is reported to provide employment for approximately 60 people.

Heritage Valley Health System
2019   Located behind the Beaver Valley Mall at 79 Wagner Road
They are to offer primary and specialty care for patients, as well as a walk-in clinic, diagnostic imaging and lab services, outpatient surgical services, physical therapy center, and a four-room ambulatory surgery center. The four-room ambulatory surgery center is considered to be state-of-the-art and offers outpatient surgical services in the specialties of orthopedics, ophthalmology, otolaryngology, general surgery, gynecology, podiatry, urology and pain management procedures. It has been described as "a new complex/medical neighborhood opened by HVMG Valley Internal Medicine." As of 2019, the doctors listed with suites in this complex included:

    Dr. Matthew Sniezek - Doctor of Osteopathic Medicine
    Dr. William Rust - Internal Medicine Specialist
    Stacy Stahl, CRNP - Nurse Practitioner, specializes in General Practice
    Dr. Gregg Zernich - family medicine
    Dr. Matthew Coombs - family medicine specialist
    Elizabeth Salyards, CRNP - Nurse Practitioner
    Dr. Lucas Heller - Internal Medicine and Endocrinology
    Karen May, CRNP - Nurse Practitioner

~ ~ ~

Fact: The end of Mar 1980, there was a newspaper article that stated Crossgates, a McMurry, PA firm, wanted to build a 120-bed convalescent center somewhere near the Beaver Valley Mall. It was to employ around 110 persons. Obviously, these plans never developed.

~ ~ ~

> The National Save-a-Life League, established in 1906 in New York, has as its object the dissuading of would-be suicides from taking their own lives.

Jun 1940 snippet in the local newspaper.

~ ~ ~

Earlier Physicians

Some of the very early physicians found to have lived in and/or served the people of Moon/Center Township are listed below.

    (Also see previous within the information of the County Home -- several of the early physicians in the township and county also served there.)

Samuel Adams – He was one of the earliest physicians in Beaver County, could have even been the earliest one. He came from Rowley, Massachusetts, and first settled along Chartiers Creek in Washington County, Pa. He removed to what is now Beaver County sometime before 1800 and settled at the Upper Falls of the Beaver. Dr. Adams and his eldest son, Milo Adams, were the only physicians in that day on this side of Pittsburgh. They were sent for professionally from sometimes thirty and forty miles away including residents of Moon Township. Mrs. Samuel Adams herself had acquired considerable knowledge of medicine and often compounded drugs for her husband and son, and in their absence she frequently even prescribe for patients and set fractured limbs.

George W. Allison – b 1803 in Washington, Pa. He was another very early physician who would be called upon by Moon Township residents. He studied medicine under Dr. Milo Adams. He was a member of the Beaver County Medical Society.

John Bryan – b 1828. He practiced medicine in Moon (Center) Township 1870s, 1880s, 1890, 1891. He practiced from his home which was along Brodhead Road. He served at the County Home in 1882 and 1883. (Also, see Homes and Families section the Bryan Family and see the Summer Homes section.)

Francis Flanegin Davis – b 1838; s/o John and Margaret (Flanegin) Davis, all became residents of Moon Township. In 1860 F. F. had just married, owned a home adjacent to his parents along Chapel Road and was listed as a student in medicine. Although when he first began to practice medicine, he lived in Moon/Center Township, he soon relocated in Independence/ Raccoon Township, but Dr. F. F. Davis still had patients from Moon/Center Township and made many home visits to his patients in the township. F. F. Davis was a surgeon of the 168th PA Infantry during the Civil War. He was admitted to the Beaver Co. PA Medical Society in 1865. After the war, he established a practice in Oil City, PA, where he became an honored physician and citizen. He remained a member of the Beaver County Medical Society. Two of his three children also practiced medicine – Dr. John F. Davis and Dr. Fannie Davis (she owned property in Center Township but established her main practiced in Pittsburgh, PA.).

Mayes Smith Davis – b 1860; s/o John and Margaret (Flanegin) Davis and brother to Dr. F. F. Davis. He was first a schoolteacher in Moon/Center Township in 1880. By 1882, he had become a doctor and began to practice medicine in Moon Township. He continued this practice a few years, but soon moved to Pittsburgh, Allegheny County where he continued his career of medicine/physician.

James S. Elliott – b 1825; s/o Wm. and Margaret Elliott. He attended school at Hookstown in 1850 and then read medicine with Dr. Cunningham of Beaver. After graduation he started his practice in Moon Township where he continued it for twenty years. He practiced from his home (in the Poor House Road/ Pleasant Drive area. His home was beside his parents in 1860. In 1869, he moved to Beaver Falls, where he practiced until his death in 1890. He also served at the County Home between 1863-1869.

James Scroggs, Jr. – b 1862. He came to live near the Maxwell and Flocker families in Bellowsville in 1894. In 1880, he was 18, living with his parents in Ohio Township, and was listed as a medical student. There is no indication of where he practiced medicine through the years except between 1893-1899 when he served at the County Home.

David Miller – b 1837. He was listed as an A P Physician in 1860 and lived near the William Shroades family. (I believe the "A P" was listed to indicate *advanced practitioner*.)

John Ramsey Miller – he was listed as being from Raccoon Township, but in the 1850s, this could have easily been parts of what became Potter or fluctuated into Moon Township. He served at the County Home between 1856-1858.

Presley M. Kerr – b 1838. He was listed as being from Raccoon Township, in the 1860s, this could have been parts of what became Potter or fluctuated into Moon Township. In 1860, Presley was listed as "physician & dentist." He served at the County Home between 1869-1882.

Joseph Baker – b 1895; s/o Joseph and Ada; became a dentist and had his own office (unknown location). Both father and son had homes off Brodhead Road on Ridge Road.

William Shroads – b 1853. Although he was not a physician, being a druggist, he would have been involved in the medical profession with others.

Sarah Springer – b 1870. She made her career of a nurse. In 1910 and 1920 she worked for private families, then in 1930 she was working in a hospital.

Elizabeth Springer – b 1865. She was the older sister of Sarah and was also a nurse. They were both daughters of James Springer.

John Wilson – b 1809. John and his family were only found listed on the Moon Township 1870 census. In 1860, they were living in Allegheny County and his real estate was listed at $25,000. It was evidently a well-to-do neighborhood with many of his neighbors having servants. Why Dr. Wilson came to live in Moon Township is unknown. By the 1880 census, they were once again back living in Allegheny County. All records of the county home indicate that Pressley Kerr (of Raccoon) was the physician in the county home from 1869 to 1882, so unless Dr. Wilson was unofficially substituting for Dr. Kerr or was needed as an assistant doctor, he would not have been servicing the county home while in Moon Township. John and family were listed immediately after all the residents of the county home which lends to their residency being in the Bellowsville area. The 1870 census had his occupation as *physician* and his real estate value that same census year was $27,600 and $1000 personal property (quite a sum for that date). The value of his real estate could possibly have been from his holdings in Allegheny County and just included in his assets while in Moon Township.

c1850

~ ~ ~

Physicians and other related medical facilities and businesses

Following is a loosely alphabetized list of medical professionals and/or medical/medical related businesses that were found to be in Center Township between 1930s and 2019.

As with all listings in this book, all dates listed under the names only indicate years that information was found and are included to give a guideline of years in business. These dates do not indicate opening or closing dates unless otherwise stated. Also, some individuals listed may be within an associate medical facility and not have private practices.

Note: Although a physician lived in Center Township, does not indicate they conducted their practice within Center Township, but he/she will still be listed just for being a known resident. Likewise, just because a physician conducts his/her practice within the township does not indicate they were a resident of the township.

Accuracy First – hearing aids – BV Mall

A.D.M.I.T – Brodhead Road
2019 Medical Testing – "The Drug & Alcohol Testing Professionals."

Aspen Dental – in open plaza - front area of BV Mall
current

Allcare Dental & Dentures – Lowe's plaza
2006

All About Smiles - Lowe's plaza
2019

American's Best Contacts & Eyeglasses Vision Store - Wagner Road
current

Dr. D. W. Baker – dentist –
1950s His practice was in Aliquippa.

Dr. Joseph H. Baker - physician / dentist – unknown office location
1910, 1920, 1930, 1940s

Beaver County Cancer & Heart Association – 1268, then renumbered 3582 Brodhead Road suite 104
2000, 2006 Opened in 1954.

Beaver Valley Center For Surgery – 3153 Brodhead Road
2011, 2019

Beaver Valley Crisis Pregnancy Center – Christy Drive
1986, 1994 Dawn Gibson was a director.

Beaver Valley Eye Center – 95 Golfview Drive
Opened in 1996–current Connected with the Sewickley Eye Group. Once located beside the site of former Woodworker Warehouse /currently Advanced Auto Parts.

Beaver Valley Orthopedic Associates – Brodhead Road
1996 Relocated from Beaver to this location early in 1996. Dr. John W. Lehman, M.D. and Bernard Hirsch, M.D.

Beaver Valley Professional Center
1988

Beltone Hearing Aid Center – 92 Pleasant Drive
1963, 1985 Also in Beaver and Zelienople – opened in 1963

Beltone Hearing Aid – BV Mall
1976, 1978

Dr. Julius J. Bergiel – Chiropractor - 92 Pleasant Drive
1988, 1992

Brighton Radiology Associates – 3572 Brodhead Road
current   Special service cardiology

Dr. Harry B. Burke, D.P.M. and Associates - 3578 Brodhead Road
1999, 2019

Brodhead Dental-Center, Inc. – 3544 Brodhead Road
1983 to current   Established in 1983 by Dr. Richard Gradisek.

Brodhead Health Center – 3428 Brodhead Road
1983, 1994   Opened in 1983 with Dr. Simmon Wilcox president of the center.   Closed.
   then………
Tristate Pulmonary Medical Practice
2019   Dr. Benjamin Laracuente, MD, FCCP – 3428 Brodhead Road

Dr. Martin Brotemarkle - dentist
1977

Dr. George E. Brummitt, D.M.D., P.C. – was 1169, renumbered 3489 Brodhead Road, Monaca
1977, 1990, 2019   General Dentistry

M. A. Callaghan – dentist - had his own dentistry business
1940

Center Medical Association, Inc. – 99 Autumn Street
1991   A group of Family Practice doctors - internal medicine & infectious disease, obstetrics & gynecology, and physical assistant in the offices.
   became………….
The Primary Health Network Plaza   aka   Autumn Street Health Center – 99 Autumn Street
current

Center Pediatric Complex – Brodhead Road
2019

Richard Covatto, D.M.D. – 3572 Brodhead Road
2019   Hi-tech family dentistry

Creative Medicine – D. Leo Plaza
2016, 2017

Dr. Sydney C. Davenport – Chiropractor – North Branch Road
1950s, 1960s   He had a patient/office room in the basement of their home, with the entry via a set of stairs located in the front of the home beside the porch. He also had an office in Rochester. Dr. S. C. and Ruth Davenport owned several acres, a barn, and had several horses. Dr. Davenport was also the chairman in 1966 of the township planning and zoning commission.

> *Fun fact: In 1936, Dr. Davenport was still living in Rochester. He was the co-operator of the Patterson Heights airport at that time. He owned an Irvin double parachute and would loan it out on display in different places. This Irvin chute was credited with saving the life of "Chilly" Thomas, a parachute tester. He carried the Irvin chute as a secondary when testing another chute that failed twice. Dr. Davenport also had an airplane service station and gasoline service station at the airport and added a lunch stand at the field in 1935.*

Dr. Felipe Chu – physician
1977

Dr. Matthew Coombs - family medicine specialist - 79 Wagner Road
current

Dalmo Optical – 131 Pleasant Drive
2000, 2019

Eger's Optometrist - BV Mall
1976   (Currently Optometric Care Inc. – see further)

Express Med Pharmacy Services – Walmart Plaza

Family & Cosmetic Dentistry – 3153 Brodhead Road
2019   Timothy A. Ungarean, D.M.D.   R.N. Fedorchak, D.M.D.

Frank Figley was the health officer for the South Side
1930s

Foot and Ankle Wellness Center – 3578 Brodhead Road
2019

James D. Harkins, D.M.D.
1988

Haczela Chiropractic – 111 Wagner Road
2003, 2019

Janes D. Harkins, D.M.D. – orthodontist - 3582 Brodhead Road

Heritage Valley Women's Health Center – 200 Pleasant Drive
2012, current   This facility offers a variety of diagnostic services for adult female patients.

Heritage Valley Medical Group – Village Shops – 3468 Brodhead Road
current

HVMG Primary Care Center – 3468 Brodhead Road
current

In Line Chiropractic / ILCC – Village Shops – 3468 Brodhead Road
1994, 1998, 2019   Founded in 1994.   Dr. Michele Askar

InSkin Laser & Body – 3572 Brodhead Road
2019

Donna L. Iannone, D.M.D., LLC – pediatric - 3582 Brodhead Road
2019

Nathan A. Johnson - radiologist - 3572 Brodhead Road
2019

Katsur Dental – Walmart Plaza
2019

Krishna K. Kasi, M.D. –1210 Brodhead Road, Monaca
1990   Pediatrician & Endocrinologist

Dr. Oscar Adolph Kratzert – dentist – res. Brodhead Road
1930s, 1940s, 1950s   They lived in a stone house that still stands today - the second home on the right after turning onto Oak Lane.   His practice was in Aliquippa.

Dr. Pau M. Kunzma – 1100 Brodhead Road
1988   Eye surgery.

Dr. Todd Henry Large – Chiropractic Specialist – 3572 Brodhead Road
2019

Lens Crafters -   BV Mall
Opened in 1996; took over the former Fine's Mens Shop space. Closed in 2006.

Dr. Jesse Mantel Optometrist Office – BV Mall
Opened in 1996 adjacent to Lens Crafters.   Independent optometrist Dr. Jesse Mantel opened an office in his own store front.

Med Express Urgent Care – Walmart Plaza

George F. Medich, M.D. – Bvr Cty Bone and Joint Clinic – 1252 N. Brodhead Road, Monaca
1990

John J. Michael, Jr. D.D.S. – Periodontist - 3582 Brodhead Road
2019

Dr. John F. Mitchell
1960s, 1972   Began his practice in the same location as former Dr. J. Gormley in Monaca.

Helen Morris – listed as a nurse in a private hospital on 1940 census

Dr. John A. Mitchell – Sanitorium Road (adjacent to Mona Manor, off lower entrance for Penn State)
1934, 1940s, 1953, 1958   He was a specialist in heart disease. (I do not know if he had a practice in Center Township.)   He started his business in Monaca on Aug 23, 1934. The building was razed when the area was needed for a parking lot in 1961. Dr. Mitchell was honored at a dinner at the PNA Club in Feb 1972 for his services to Monaca and Center Township area with many persons from the community in attendance.

Bryon E. Nastasi – radiology specialist - 3572 Brodhead Road
2019

Dr. Cinzia V. Newman, D.P.M. – 3600 Brodhead Road
2017, 2019

Robert G. Norkus, D.D.S. – Oral surgeon – 3578 Brodhead Road
2019

Nutra-Bolic – 1270 Brodhead Road
1986, 1987

Open MRI of Beaver Valley – Village Shops – 3468 Brodhead Road
2006, 2019

Optometric Eye Care – BV Mall
1977 to current   Originally known as Edger's Optometric Care.

Pain Control Center of Pittsburgh – 3624/27 Brodhead Road
current   This center is located adjacent to Snowy White cleaners.

Pearle Vision – to the front of parking lot of BV Mall
1985, 1991

Precision Endodontics – 113 Golfview Drive
current   Took over an office building that was built in the 1980s, adjacent to Wendy's.

Progressive Home Health, Inc – Walmart Plaza
2001, current   In the AAA Professional Center, behind Applebees.

Jay I. Reznik, D.M.D., M.D.S. – 1260 N. Brodhead Road, Monaca
1988, 1990   Pediatric Dentistry

Dr. Robert Serych, Jr. & Associates, P.C. – Optometrist – 3433 Brodhead Road
1989, 2019   Opened in 1989.

Sheffield Chiropractic Clinic – 3154 Brodhead Road
1987 to 2018   Dr. John L. Dishauzi originally opened his practice on Mill Street in Aliquippa, opened in Mar 1984. He built and opened his new office on Brodhead Road in 1987/88.

Skoff Dental Associates – Brodhead Road
1980s, 1990, current   Originally at 1256 N. Brodhead Road (renumbered #3578) with David M. Skoff, D.M.D. and Joseph J. Skoff, D.D.S.   The office was moved further on Brodhead Road and currently at 3532 Brodhead Road.

Kenneth B. Skolnick, M.D. – 3542 Brodhead Road
closed   Allergist / AAA Ear & Aid Specialists – affiliated with Kenneth Skolnick

Stay In Touch – Hearing Aid - 3578 Brodhead Road
2019

Tri-State Obstetrics & Gynecology – Center Place – Pleasant Drive
1990

Tri-State Pulmonary Medicine – 3428 Brodhead Road (corner Brodhead & Center Grange)
2019

Total Rehabilitation Systems LLC – Physical Therapy – 3572 Brodhead Road
current

Valley Neurological Associates offices – 1112 N Brodhead Road/ renumbered to 3452 Brodhead Road
Opened in 1985/89, 2019

Valley Vision Center – Village Shops – 3468 Brodhead Road
Opened in 1990   David Jaskiewicz, Optometrist and his wife Cynthia, owners.

Vision works – 118 Wagner Road
2019

J. A. Vogel – Center Grange Road
1956, 1958   He was also the doctor for the Jones and Laughlin Corporation.

Keith Wharton, M. D. – 1252/ now 3572 Brodhead Road
2019

Western Pennsylvania Incontinence Center For Woman – 3572 Brodhead Road
2001   Opened in spring of 2001.   Dr. Keith H. Wharton, Medical Director.

Dr. Gregg Zernich - family medicine - 79 Wagner Road
2019

Dr. Stephen Zernich, Jr – 104 N Brodhead Road
1950s

~ ~ ~

LIFE Beaver County – 131 Pleasant Drive
Current   Is located in the Center Place plaza. They assist and provide adult day services as an affordable option for seniors who wish to remain living at home.

~ ~ ~

Pharmacies

Gray Drugs – located in the BV Mall, main hallway, beside Orange Julius
1971 to 1987
    Was bought out and became…….
Rite Aid
1987 to 1995   This store closed in Aug 1995 when the lease expired. They put a note on their door that stated everyone should go to the Revco store in WalMart Plaza.
    Rite Aid closed and all became…..
Revco Drug Store – Beaver Valley Mall, then Gee Bee Plaza
1978, 1985, 1986, 1995   Was formerly the Gray Drug Store. When the Rite Aid at the mall closed in Aug 1995, a sign at the mall said prescriptions were transferred to this Revco (in the Walmart Plaza).   Revco was in the plaza when it was Gee Bees and remained while Walmart was being built.
    became ……
CVS Drug Store - Gee Bee Plaza
2003, closed   Was formerly a Gray Drug, then Revco Drug Store before becoming CVS.

Hoffman's Center Pharmacy – moved from Monaca to 1495 Brodhead Road, Center Square
                                          Shopping Center (next to former Loblaw's/now Center Stage)
1963, 1965, 1974, 1986   Opened in Center the first of Oct 1962. (See Shopping Center and Plaza section – Center Square Plaza for pictures of the store front.) Was found in Monaca as early as 1908, 1917.
    became….
Public Drug Store
1980s, 1988, 1989   The store front is currently Brew-ski's.

Med Fast – 3589 Brodhead Road
Opened prior to 2002.   Scott Angus and Mary Jo Russo were there in 2002.
    became….
Hometown Pharmacy
2017 to current   Jack Peffer, Pharmacist.

Rite Aid – 131 Pleasant Drive (See Shopping Center section - K-mart Plaza)
1980, 1985   Opened __; closed __.
    then became ……….
Public Drug Store
1988, closed
    then……….
Thrift Drug Store
closed

White Cross Drug Store – Gee Bee Plaza
1973

CVS – inside Target store
current

Walmart Pharmacy – inside Walmart store
current

Express Med Pharmacy Service – 3950 Brodhead Road
2019

~ ~ ~

While doing researching on any given subject or area, I always find what I consider interesting information that I just enjoy sharing. With the Beaver County TB Sanitorium being situated in Center Township during the earlier years, I thought this information would prove interesting. These may not specifically have originated in Center Township, but the residents were and may still be involved with purchasing and the usage of............

Christmas Seals

Tuberculosis was the leading cause of deaths in the United States in the early 1900s. Persons who contracted this disease were usually placed in one of the special hospitals, called sanitoriums. Doctors were finding that this was the most successful way of properly treating tuberculosis. (See previous information on Beaver County TB Sanitorium.) With so many persons being admitted to these sanitoriums, the facilities were experiencing tough times. One sanitorium in Delaware was about to close its doors if they could not raise $300. A volunteer and experienced fundraiser, Emily Bissell heard of this from her cousin who was a doctor. She designed and printed out a special holiday seal and sold them at the post office for a penny each on Dec 7, 1907. President Roosevelt heard of her campaign and gave his endorsement. By the end of that holiday season, Emily and her volunteers "had raised ten times the goal and the American Lung Association Christmas Seals were born."

The tradition of the Christmas Seals continued to grow each year, even through the years of World War I, The Great Depression, and World War II. The American Lung Association expanded their mission from not only fighting tuberculosis, but to include doing research for other respiratory diseases, including lung cancer. By the 1960s, they were also including the protection of children and families from air pollution and cigarette smoke. Even today, the American Lung Association receives much of their support through the purchases of Christmas Seals. This all shows that America in general, and surely the residents of Center Township, have and continue to purchase and seal holiday cards and packages with these all-important Christmas Seals.

> *Fact: The double-barred cross of the emblem was adopted by the National Association for the Study and Prevention of Tuberculosis (NASPT) in 1906 and they registered it as an official trademark in 1920. It is a modified version of the Cross of Lorraine, which is a variation of the Jerusalem or Patriarchal Cross. While attending a conference on tuberculosis in Berlin in 1902, Dr. Gilbert Sersiron of Paris proposed that this emblem become the symbol of the anti-TB crusade.*

Emily Bissell purchasing the very first Christmas Seal being in the Wilmington post office on Dec 7, 1907.

Samples of Christmas Seals sold over the years.

1908   1919   1920   1946

1985   2004   2017

~ ~ ~

Illnesses

Many illnesses listed throughout the earlier years are not commonly recognized nowadays or have new names attached to them............

Ill from brain fever (1904)   Brain fever was used to describe the medical condition for the inflammation of part of the brain, the condition also caused a fever. This was usually a life-threatening illness caused by a severe emotional upset.   Some other conditions that would have caused "brain fever" are Encephalitis – caused by a viral infection; Meningitis – the inflammation of the membranes that cover the brain and spinal cord; Cerebritis – inflammation of the cerebrum; and Scarlet fever - symptoms can include paranoia and hallucinations.

Grippe / Grip   This was the old fashion term attached to the condition commonly called "influenza" nowadays.   It is a viral disease.

Quinsy   Associated with tonsillitis. It occurs when an abscess forms between one of the tonsils and the wall of the throat.   It is a bacterial infection.

Dropsy   The old fashioned, less technical term, for edema – an excess of watery fluid collecting in the cavities or tissues of the body.

Consumption   This was the term often used for the various forms of tuberculosis, a condition brought on by the tubercle bacillus bacteria.   Often, pneumonia conditions were also associated with consumption.

Dyspepsia   This was often the name given to a common condition and described a group of symptoms from what is nowadays known as reflux or hiatal hernia, heartburn, belching, et cetera. It covered more of a group of symptoms than just one of the specific conditions.

Bealed jaw   This was generally caused by a cold settling on a decayed tooth.

Piles   Hemorrhoids

Imbibe/ Imbibed/ Imbibing   Drinking or consuming too much.   In one word…….. drunk. Many of the articles would simply say…… "They had imbibed far too many beers."

~ ~ ~

Old Time Cures

In 1921, there was a company that advertised Wyeth's Sage and Sulphur Compound for eliminating gray hair. Their ad said to put some of their solution on your comb or a soft brush and taking one strand at a time, run the comb/brush over the hair. By morning the gray hair was to have disappeared. It also boasted that besides beautifully darkening the hair after a few applications, it also produced a soft and lustrous appearance to the hair.

~ ~ ~

Article in The Daily Times – Jan 1941..........
"Before the Civil War the consumption of tobacco in the United States was less than four pounds per person in a year. Now it is more than eight and one-half pounds."

~ ~ ~

Fact: The Beaver County Medical Society was formed late in 1855. There was a call made through the county newspapers asking physicians to help form and join the society. This society prepared a constitution and conformed to the constitution of the State and the National Association.

~ ~ ~

Epidemics and/or Illnesses

An epidemic is when an infectious disease spreads within an area or community during a specific time period. The area of Moon/Center Township was considerably free from extremely serious epidemics of dangerous diseases when compared to other areas. With the advancement of medicines, there are fewer infectious disease outbreaks, or epidemics which occur. After reviewing many earlier records and death certificates, here is a listing of many of the diseases and illnesses that affected the people in Moon/Center Township, Beaver County, and even the United States through the years.

<u>Cholera</u> - is transmitted primarily by drinking water or eating food that has been contaminated by the cholera bacterium. The bacteria multiply in the small intestine. Through the feces of an infected person, including one with no noticeable symptoms, the disease can be passed on if it contacts the water supply by any means. The United States had three serious waves of cholera between 1832 and 1866. The pandemic began in India, and swiftly spread across the globe through trade routes. New York City was usually the first city to feel the impact of imported diseases.

Cholera became prevalent locally and throughout Beaver County, first appearing in Jul 1834 and there were even several fatalities from it. Cholera was another disease that became that of epidemic proportions several times in the area. Cholera was reported to first appear around 1834 in Kentucky with Samuel Hooper. He came on a steamboat (the Bryon) making it to Freedom, PA where he died. The next case in this area was of Captain Knowles, of the steamboat Eclipse, who came ashore at the mouth of the Big Beaver and died in five hours after being stricken. Cases of cholera subsided for a few years, but in 1849, cholera again became widespread in this valley.

Between 1866 and 1873, an estimated two to six Americans died per day with a total of outbreaks in North America killing some 50,000 Americans. Between 1881 and 1896, the fifth cholera pandemic cost at least another 50,000 lives. Immediate treatment for cholera is crucial since it can cause death. Treatment includes antibiotics, zinc supplementation, and rehydration.

It is unclear what actually ended the pandemic, perhaps the change in climates or quarantines, but it was most likely caused with the corrections and changes in the practices of disposing of human waste. Also, the change in water treatment has helped eradicated cholera in some countries, but the virus is still present elsewhere. Cholera is said to still causes nearly 130,000 deaths a year worldwide. People should get a vaccine for cholera if planning to travel to areas that are high-risk. The best way to prevent cholera is to wash hands regularly with soap and water and avoid drinking contaminated water.

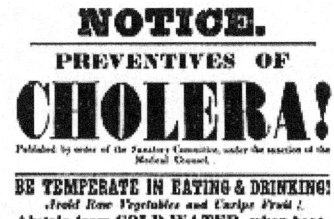

This handbill from 1832 stated to avoid raw vegetables and unripe fruit and to abstain from cold water and ardent spirits, but if indispensable, to take much less than usual. This shows how very little was known of the disease at that time. Between the 1810s and 1830s, the people in the United States were even led to believe that Cholera was being brought in by the Irish.

Typhoid Fever - was the cause of many deaths and serious illnesses in the mid 1800s and again in the very early 1900s. It was considered an epidemic in 1906 and was downgraded to "infection" by 1907. Being a strictly human-borne disease, Typhoid is carried in the bloodstream and intestinal tract. A person who has contracted the disease would have symptoms of high fever, stomach pains, and possible rashes. A secondary infection would come from contact with a carrier, or as was the case in most of Beaver County, and Moon Township, eating contaminated food or drinking polluted water. As the cause of the disease was determined and understood, the incidences of typhoid fever steadily declined due to vaccinations (starting in 1914) and the improvements in public sanitation, chlorination of water supplies, and hygiene. Being the most noted epidemic in Beaver County, it began in 1843, and by 1845, Typhoid fever was so severe and widespread through the Hookstown area and its neighborhood that it was often called the "Hookstown fever."

Scarlet Fever - a bacterial infection that can occur after strep throat. Like cholera, scarlet fever epidemics came in waves. During the 1858 epidemic, ninety-five percent of people who caught the virus were children. Older studies argue that scarlet fever declined due to improved nutrition, but research shows that improvements in public health were more likely the cause. There is no vaccine to prevent strep throat or scarlet fever. It is important for those with strep throat symptoms to seek treatment as quickly as possible. Your doctor will typically treat scarlet fever with antibiotics.

Tuberculosis - caused by bacteria that spreads person to person through microscopic droplets that are released into the air by an infected person. This happens when the infected person coughs, speaks, sneezes, spits, laughs, sings, et cetera. Although the disease of tuberculosis is contagious, it is not easy to catch since you have to spend quite a lot of time around someone who has it.
   Beginning in the late 1800s, through the earlier 1900s, tuberculosis became the leading cause of death for anyone from eight months old to eighty years old. Many times, the cause of death was simply listed as "consumption" rather than tuberculosis. Most lung diseases, such as pneumonia, and especially tuberculosis, were lumped with consumption as the cause of death since dying of tuberculosis seemed to have been a "dark" identification for the deceased. When a doctor would list the cause of death from true tuberculosis, he would use many different specifics such as "tuberculosis of the lungs," "Phthisis," "Pulmonalsis," or as stated above "Consumption."

Smallpox - North America first saw smallpox in the 1600s. Entire Native American tribes were wiped out from smallpox. The symptoms include a high fever, chills, severe back pain, and rashes. Edward Jenner developed a vaccine in 1770 from cow pox which helped peoples' bodies to be immune to the disease without actually contracting the disease.   Many people actively received this vaccination through the years, so by 1972, it was announced that smallpox was gone from the United States and vaccinations are no longer necessary.

Polio   -   a viral disease that affects the nervous system, causing paralysis. It spreads through direct contact with an infected person. The first major polio epidemic in the United States occurred in 1916 with the first occurring in New York and Boston. Polio outbreaks continued sporadically through the country for decades to come. By 1952, Polio had reached major epidemic levels in the United States.   Jonas E. Salk (U.S.) developed the first experimental safe dead-virus polio vaccine. Use in the U. S. for this dead-virus was started in 1955.   A few years later a live attenuated (weakened) oral polio vaccine (OPV) was developed by Dr. Albert Sabin and became available in 1961. It was administered by a few drops on a sugar cube.   This disease has had 57,628 reported cases, which includes 3,145 deaths. The vaccination to this disease proved successful for by 1962, the average number of cases dropped to 910. It is currently reported that the United States has been polio-free since 1979.

Getting vaccinated is very important before traveling. There's no cure for polio. Treatment involves increasing comfort levels and preventing complications.

Diphtheria   -   Between 1921 and 1925 was the Diphtheria epidemic.   In 1921, Diphtheria peaked with 206,000 cases reported. It causes swelling of the mucous membranes including the throat and can obstruct breathing and swallowing.   If the bacterial toxin enters the bloodstream, it can cause fatal heart and nerve damage.   By the end of the 1920s, there was a vaccination licensed for Diphtheria and was followed by a drastic drop in reported cases within the United States.   More than eighty percent of children in the United States are now vaccinated against Diphtheria, those who do contract it are treated with antibiotics.

Whooping Cough   -   Whooping Cough, also known as Pertussis, is a very contagious disease and one of the most commonly occurring in the U. S. Coughing attacks can last for months.   Whooping cough was also commonly known as "Chin cough."   The highest risk for life-threatening cases are infants too young for the vaccination.   Although prevalent in the United States since the earlier 1900s, between 2010 and 2014, cases were reported to increase. The health community now states that an increase in the number of cases will likely be the new normal due to the decline of those receiving the vaccination.   Many children in and around Center Township were on record as being stricken with Whooping Cough in the 1920s to 1930s.

Measles   -   a virus that causes a fever, runny nose, cough, red eyes, and sore throat, and later a rash that can spread over the whole body. It is a very contagious disease and spreads through the air.   In the early 1900s, most cases involved children who were inadequately vaccinated for the disease.   Doctors were even recommending a second vaccine for everyone. Since then, the disease has declined to fewer than 1,000 cases. Between 2014 and 2015, the United States once again experienced an outbreak of measles and was closely associated with the outbreak in the Philippines in 2014.   Vaccinations may still be currently recommended by doctors.

Meningitis   -   Meningitis spread throughout the U.S. in Oct of 2012.   This outbreak was linked to a contaminated steroid drug that was administered to patients as a spinal injection for back pain. The contaminated steroid was traced back to the New England Compounding Center in Framingham, Mass.   More than 30 people died in this outbreak.

West Nile Virus   -   By the end of Nov 2012, 48 states had reported West Nile virus infections in people, birds, or mosquitoes. There was a total of 5,245 cases of West Nile virus disease in people, including 236 deaths that occurred throughout the year.

Ebola   -   The first person to be diagnosed with Ebola from the United States was Thomas Eric Duncan. He died the first of Oct 2014.   Six days following Duncan's death, Nina Pham, a nurse who treated Duncan, became the first person to contract Ebola within the United States.

Flu - Different types of mutating influenza viruses have been reported throughout the years.

One particularly deadly flu, the "Spanish flu," was considered an epidemic beginning in 1918. The Spanish flu is sometimes considered the worst plague/pandemic in human history. Tradition is it received its name because of the particularly deadly outbreak in Spain that spring. Many publications list the Spanish flu as "the Great Dying, an apocalyptic pestilence that swept across the globe." It began to surface in the United States in Mar of 1918. By Sep of 1918, it was found quickly spreading through Beaver County. Most Moon/Center Township and other local residents were unaware of the impact of the Spanish flu until an article in the newspaper on Oct 3 which told of nine cases reported in Bridgewater. From there it quickly spread throughout the entire valley. The estimated deaths in Pennsylvania alone were set at 39,000 to 43,000. There were no specific numbers for Beaver County, but the newspapers reported hundreds died in the county. Soldiers of WWI were either carrying the disease with them to other areas of the world or they brought it back with them upon returning to their hometowns. Unlike many other pandemic events, the Spanish flu was just as deadly to healthy adults as it was to the elderly and very young. As quickly as the Spanish flu appeared, leaving an estimated twenty to fifty million (some even state one hundred million) dead world-wide, which included many, many children, this flu left just as suddenly. The deaths were either directly related to the flu or flu-related diseases. There were several persons who were said to have contracted tuberculosis after getting this Spanish flu during that time period.

Hospitals were overflowing with patience and many other venues were used as emergency clinics while treating persons who contracted the flu. There were times when so many people would be carried in only to be placed on the floor since there were not enough beds available. Sadly, there also became a shortage of caskets and families were resorting to making caskets themselves of scrap wood and even soap and fruit crates. Because there were so many deaths, funerals began to be limited to fifteen minutes and burials were also done by the families with the shortage of cemetery workers. Multiple burials with the death date of 1918 or 1919 can be found in all cemeteries. These individuals were most likely among the many victims of the Spanish flu. Cemeteries can reveal other dates of not only this 1918 flu outbreak, but that of many of the other pandemics where multiple burials with the same death year are found.

This Spanish flu, like many other variations, was spread by coughing, sneezing, or even speaking – spreading the virus into the air to be unsuspectedly inhaled by others. Suggestions for protection provided at the time were for people to wear gauze masks, not knowing that the virus could easily penetrate the gauze. Some suggested drinking coal oil as a home style preventative or cure but this proved to be ineffective. After the end of World War I, the reported cases of this flu began to decline. Sadly, with the many immigrants coming to America during this time period, people were pointing fingers at them for being the carriers and cause of the outbreak. These foreigners were soon proven innocent and not to be the cause of the flu when it was publicly known the Spanish flu was all over the world.

In 1957, the "Asian flu" was another variation of what is called the "flu." It was contracted by many people. The Asian flu is said to have caused nearly 70,000 deaths in the country before a vaccine became available. At the end of Apr in 2009, there were many confirmed cases of swine flu in the United States. The U.S. declared the outbreak a public health emergency. By the end of Oct in 2009, President Obama had declared the outbreak of the H1N1 flu virus, also called swine flu, a national emergency.

In 1976, an outbreak of the swine flu, (Influenza A virus - subtype H1N1) caused one death in Fort Dix, New Jersey and there were 13 others who were hospitalized. These incidents led to a mass immunization program. Evidence of the Swine Influenza A was related to the 1918 flu pandemic which killed twenty to fifty million people worldwide. This immunization program was ended after a large percent of the population of the United States had been administered the vaccine because after the program began, the vaccine was associated with an increase in reports of the Guillain-Barre Syndrome (which can cause paralysis, respiratory arrest, and death). Richard Krause, Director of the National Institute of Allergy and Infectious Diseases from 1975 to 1984, wrote "the government response to the swine flu outbreak was considered to be too fast and the response to the AIDS epidemic too slow." There were temporary clinics set up throughout the area for administering the vaccination to residents. One such clinic was held in the municipal building in downtown Monaca.

In mid-April 2009, there was a report of H1N1 flu (variation of swine flu) was a new strain of the influenza reported throughout the United States. It is still spreading from person-to-person in some parts all over of the world. Because this influenza mutates every year, it makes it essentially a new virus which people have little natural immunity to and can catch it more easily. Although it can be serious, most people who have become ill from H1N1 recover without hospitalization or medical treatment With the constant mutation of this flu, it makes the past or even the last year's vaccinations less effective, so it is important to get the current yearly vaccination to decrease your risk for contracting the flu.

The Round Scar Generation

Were you born prior to the 1970s? Check your upper left arm for a nice round scar. If you find one, then you belong to an exclusive group that is known as the "Round Scar Generation". This scar is a result of being punctured with a circle of needles in hopes of keeping you from catching smallpox. Your sacrifice of having a scarred arm for the remainder of your days enabled humanity to rid itself from this dreaded disease that claimed the lives of 30% of those it infected.

The disease had plagued humanity for a millennia, initially causing symptoms like the flu, however, these symptoms would quickly be followed by small reddish spots on the mouth, tongue, palate, and throat. Soon, the disease would attack the skin cells of a person, causing massive boils to develop on the body. So dreaded was this disease that finding a cure for it was a top priority for most of the world's healers. Even though there were repeated cases of Smallpox, it was never classified in epidemic form. The last natural case of Smallpox occurred in Somalia in 1977, and the disease was officially declared eradicated in 1980.

> *Fact: Another round scar that was left from a vaccination was that from a BCG vaccine. BCG stands for Bacillus Calmette-Guérin. This vaccine is used to protect people from human tuberculosis.*

~ ~ ~

It is reported that one of the largest hepatitis outbreaks in American history occurred in Center Township in Nov 2003. The outbreak occurred due to contaminated green onions at the now defunct Chi-Chi's Mexican restaurant that was located within the Beaver Valley Mall. There were over six hundred and sixty confirmed cases and four deaths.

~ ~ ~

Various other diseases, illnesses, causes of death

Many other diseases, illnesses, and/or causes of death were reported through the years in the Beaver County area, including Moon/Center Township. "It's important to remember that during the late 1800s and the early 1900s most of the terms used in death records were generic. The terms encompassed several meanings and generally described symptomology rather than a precise disease state --   what one person meant, wasn't necessarily what another meant."   There were also regional wordings and numerous variations in terminology……….. much like using the word "soda" in the northeast and "pop" in the Midwest ---- both meaning soft drink.

> *Fact: If you are interested in your ancestors, always try to find a cause of death for them. Illnesses may have caused an ancestor to be placed in a special home, a specific hospital, or even one of the local "pest houses." Having this information is a perfect example of opening up the past to help you define your ancestors. It may provide valuable clues to the life they lived and more importantly, may even reveal genetic diseases current generations should be aware of.*
>
> *Beginning in 1906, written copies of death certificates were required. There will be a written explanation or reason for death on a death certificate. If you look closely, there will*

also be a number handwritten (usually circled) somewhere in that same area on the certificate. "This often-overlooked number comes from the International Classification of Diseases (ICD), or the International Statistical Classification of Diseases and Related Health Problems as it is now known in full – and is currently maintained and updated by the World Health Organization. The ICD was originally developed in the late 1800s and was known as the Bertillon Classification of Causes of Death, after its developer Jacques Bertillon, and later the International List of Causes of Death. The coding system was designed, in part, to provide a unified way to communicate and track causes of death and was used by a variety of nations. The US began using it in about 1898."
(A list of these codes may be found at -- http://www.wolfbane.com/icd/index.html)

Many times in the early years, the verbiage used and/or the name of a diagnosis of an illness was very different from those currently used. Most are no longer used and may not be familiar to many. Following is a sampling of some of these diagnosis/illnesses that may be found listed during those earlier years.

Ablepsy – Blindness.

Apoplexy - Paralysis due to stroke.

Bright's Disease - Bright's Disease was a general term used to mean death caused by some form of kidney failure. Kidney diseases were defined by high concentrations of protein in the urine - uremia. This term is obsolete and no longer used.

Canine Madness - Rabies, contracted from being bitten by a rabid animal.

Canker - Ulceration of mouth or lips or herpes simplex.

Catalepsy - Seizures / trances.

Cerebritis - Inflammation of cerebrum or lead poisoning.

Chlorosis - Iron deficiency anemia.

Corruption – Infection.

Croup - Laryngitis, diphtheria, or strep throat.

Decrepitude - Feebleness due to old age.

Domestic Illness - Many times, this illness was a cause for a person to be isolated or quarantined in a hospital or institute or even to be placed in one of the local "pest houses." It was associated with mental breakdowns, depression, effects from a stroke, Alzheimer, even Parkinson. Any of these illnesses would have kept a person housebound and needing personal care.

Dropsy - Anasarca, ascites, water retention or eclampsia. Commonly known today as Congestive Heart Failure. The term generally referred to people who were swollen with water. They were prone to dropping things because the brain was also affected by the swelling causing neurological side effects. Common folk medicine treated dropsy with foxglove leaves (which are toxic).

Dry Bellyache - Lead poisoning.

Dyspepsia - Indigestion and heartburn. Heart attack symptoms.

Flux - An excessive flow or discharge of fluid like hemorrhage or diarrhea.

Green fever / sickness – Anemia.

Grippe/grip - Influenza like symptoms.

Grocer's itch - Skin disease caused by mites in sugar or flour.

Heat Stroke - Body temperature elevates because of surrounding environment temperature and body does not perspire to reduce temperature. Coma and death result if not reversed.

Jackson's March - was a common name given to the symptoms and illness now known as Epilepsy.

Lagrippe - Influenza.

Lock Jaw - Tetanus is an infection by a bacterium which is a cousin to that which causes gangrene and botulism. A person infected with this bacterium would first have neck and jaw stiffness, followed by difficulty opening or closing the jaw – thus the term "lock jaw."

Mania or Acute Mania - This was probably Alzheimer's Disease for which even today there is no known cure. It would have been associated with all forms of mental illness, senility, or dementia. It was also attached to symptoms of acute alcohol ingestion or the DT's. There are many different cultural definitions of mental illness. What is mentally ill in one culture may not be the same in another. Another familiar term associated with mental diseases was "softening of the brain."

Puerperal fever – also called child bed fever - Death was caused by bacterial infection during and after the process of giving birth. In the late 1800s, this was a common and dreaded consequence of motherhood. Most women gave birth at home with a midwife in attendance. In the 1800s, childbirth was second only to tuberculosis as the leading cause of death in women in their childbearing years. The infection may have been generated by the trauma of birth, the hand that examined/aided the woman giving birth, or exposure to an environment that was dirty or septic. Surgical intervention, when needed, for childbirth was generally performed by the barber surgeons of the time. Infant mortality for cesarean section was near 100%. The mother, if she survived, was often debilitated. Surgical intervention was also a leading cause of puerperal fever.
- Hemorrhage - Another danger to a woman during childbirth was the possibility for her to hemorrhage to death or to die from convulsions or "fits" following delivery of a baby.
- Milk Leg - Postpartum blood clots in the legs might also cause death. It often was listed on a death certificate as milk leg.

Quinsy - Was the general term associated with tonsillitis. Advances stages of this illness can be seen on the muscles of the neck near the jaw.

Rubeola - German measles.

Scirrhous - Cancerous tumors.

Screws – Rheumatism.

Teething - People may think this would be associated with infants, but prior to the actual discovery and use of antibiotics to treat infections and the practice of adequate dentistry, a person of any age who had teeth could easily have died from tooth infections.

Thrush or Aphtha - Childhood disease characterized by spots on mouth, lips and throat.

Worms or Worms Fit - Convulsions associated with teething, worms, elevated temperature, or diarrhea. It may have been a feeding problem or even associated with cystic fibrosis.

~ ~ ~

Fact: The Daily Times newspaper published an article the first of May 1935 stating there was a bill sponsored by Max Aaron, Philadelphia Republican, which would provide sterilization for mental defectives. It was reported to the floor of the Senate with an affirmative committee recommendation. It was felt that this would stop the reproduction of babies who would also have mentally defectives. I found no follow up to this bill.

~ ~ ~

2020 GLOBAL PANDEMIC – CORONAVIRUS / COVID-19

Throughout the writing of this book, I ended the majority of researching with 2019, leaving any happening, events, news, or information after 2019 to be recorded by another ambitious person. The only exception to this will be in this item regarding the pandemic of 2020 with the coronavirus aka COVID-19. There will be a needed conclusion to all that I do include further since technically, as I was proof reading and preparing my book for publication, we were still amid the coronavirus pandemic and numerous "stay-at-home" orders, along with many closings of business, and wearing masks remained mandated.

"A pandemic is a global outbreak of disease. Pandemics happen when a new virus emerges to infect people and can spread between people sustainably. Because there is little to no pre-existing immunity against the new virus, it spreads worldwide." "In the past century, there have been four pandemics caused by the emergence of new influenza viruses." As of Apr 2020, COVID-19 was reported in at least 185 countries and territories. The only countries that had not reported any cases of the coronavirus as of Apr 2020 were Comoros, Kiribati, Lesotho, Marshall Islands, Micronesia, Nauru, North Korea, Palau, Samoa, Sao Tome and Principe, Solomon Islands, Tajikistan, Tonga, Turkmenistan, Tuvalu, Vanuatu. Globally, a total of 3.1 million cases of the virus were reported as of the end of Apr 2020. A report dated Apr 29, 2020, stated that Beaver County had 392 cases known cases and 65 deaths.

Reports and news articles state the COVID-19 as a new disease, caused by a novel/new coronavirus that has not previously been seen in humans. Coronaviruses are a large family of viruses that are common in people and many different species of animals, including camels, cattle, cats, and bats. Rarely, animal coronaviruses can infect people and then spread between people such as with MERS-CoV, SARS-CoV, and now with this new virus, named SARS-CoV-2.

As of Dec 2019, the coronavirus was thought to be confined to China. But within just a few weeks, the virus, which causes the illness known as COVID-19, had become a global pandemic. This virus that causes COVID-19 is infecting people and spreading very easily from person to person supposedly being transmitted from droplets of bodily fluids - such as mucus and saliva. Persons can be infected by breathing in the virus if they are within close proximity of someone who has COVID-19, or by touching a contaminated surface and then touching their own eyes, nose or mouth. COVID-19 is reported particularly serious for all persons 65 years and older and/or anyone with an underlying medical condition. All persons falling into these categories were immediately told to take special precautions because they were at higher risk of developing severe COVID-19 illness.

Life in the United States (and many countries) changed overnight due to this COVID-19. At the very beginning of all the COVID-19 issues, everyone was advised to consistently wash their hands and not to touch their eyes or mouth. There was rapidly many more measures taken though --- State after state, county after county quickly began enforcing "stay-at-home" orders/regulations, schools were closed with students doing at home lessons, all "non-essential" businesses were ordered to close down, restaurants and churches were closed and many, many persons began to work from home if at all possible, no meetings or groups of over five people were to be held, doctors and hospitals were only tending to emergencies (no routine situations), "social distancing" with six foot distances between every person was required, plexiglass screens were installed overnight in many businesses, and all workers – in fact anyone who "had to" go out of their home were required to wear a proper face mask and gloves. It became necessary for most people to place an order online, letting the store do the shopping, then you either picked your order up at a designated "curb side" area or possibly could have it delivered to your home. <u>Any</u> item that came into your home was to be disinfected/wiped down. Again, life for everyone changed almost overnight and what was "normal" to everyone became a thing of the past! Sadly, thanks to this pandemic, it is predicted that we may never return to that "normal" ever again --- there will be new lifestyles, many small businesses may never open again, numerous jobs/positions will just disappear, there will be new shopping practices, new ways businesses are run, new work environments, et cetera. There were some easements starting by mid-May 2020 -- some easing of many of the social distancing, mask and glove wearing, types of businesses who may be open to the public………….but the results of these easements proved COVID-19 was still spreading at an alarming rate.

So, as I sit here and add this information to my book, if I do need to leave my home / property, I must be sure to wear my face mask. Following my doctor's advice, I personally have not been to church service, together with any friends, or in any store to shop for myself since Mar 13, 2020 (and it is the second week of Dec 2020). IF I would venture out of my home and encounter another person, I also MUST practice "social distancing" and keep six (6) feet away from them. I can personally relate that practicing "stay-at-home" is quite isolating! Hopefully, there is light at the end of the tunnel since a few companies have created vaccinations which are now being approved and will begin to be administered throughout the United States very soon.

~ ~ ~

For lack of a better section within this book to include this information...

Although not a "medical facility", I thought it important to include this information somewhere within the book. This facility served many youths who were found to have made quite poor choices in their young lives. It held youths from all areas within Beaver County, including Center Township.

Allencrest the Beaver County Juvenile Home – Dutch Ridge Road, Brighton Township
Dedicated in 1957 – closed 2009
This was a juvenile detention home. It was approved to be built in Aug 1955 and dedicated on Sep 28, 1957. It was originally a 25-bed facility and later years expanded to accommodate 37 residents. Once again, they dropped residency to 21 due to renovations being needed. Sadly, there were some youths from Center Township that spent periods of time in this facility, hopefully learning to make better future choices. All the juveniles that were still being retained at Allencrest were transferred to Jefferson County Detention Center in Steubenville, Ohio in Jul 2009. Allencrest officially closed in late 2009 but probation workers stayed in their offices in the facility, then moving to new quarters in the courthouse by early 2010. The buildings were demolished in Jul 2011.

Former Allencrest facility

~ ~ ~

ACTIVITIES and ORGANIZATIONS

Center Township has been home to and still has numerous organizations. Many of these are included in this section so readers may have an idea of how diverse interests were and are, but please know that this is just a sampling and by no means includes every one of them. I really did concentrate more on older and/or previous activities and organizations.

With Center Township originally being a true very rural area, it is no surprise that the Grange Hall was the first official "club" or organization to be officially formed in the township. Any Grange Hall was the hub of tightly knit communities in rural areas, and Center Township was no different. The original building is still standing (2019) and it is the hopes of many that it continues to be maintained and held to its historic nature since it is the only remaining business or community structure that represent the beginnings, unification, and characteristics of Center Township.

Many have the guidelines that a building must be at least 100 years old to be recognized as historic. The Grange Hall has almost met this guideline and as of Jan 2019 the building was 98 years old. Anyone and everyone who relates to Center Township should recognize and be very eager in keeping this Grange Hall building in its historic nature and preserved as the one and only existing piece of township and community history!

Being formed out of the much older Moon Township, Center Township is considered a quite young township in comparison to others, thus the reason the township is hard pressed to find many other business or community buildings with a 100-year-old history. Although the Grange Hall building is the only surviving community/business building still standing in the township, there are quite a few individual homes which are over 100 years old still standing. (See the section on Homes.)

For those who may not be familiar with the grange organization - The Pennsylvania State Grange is a family-oriented fraternal organization dedicated to the betterment of rural Pennsylvania through community service, education, legislation, and fellowship. Pennsylvania's first Grange was the Eagle Grange #001 which was officially organized Mar 4, 1871, two and a half years before the organization of the Pennsylvania State Grange on Sep 18, 1873. The Grange is the oldest American agricultural advocacy group. Granges are also credited to the establishment of rural free mail delivery.

Now, on to more information regarding Center Township's only remaining community structure...........

Center Grange Hall – NO. 1870
125 Center Grange Road, Monaca, PA 15061
CENTER JUNIOR GRANGE – NO. 123

The Center Grange was organized Jan 19, 1921 and held their first meetings in the Simon Field School house with Henry Hartenbach the first grange master. There were 51 charter members and immediately after organization, there were at least 10 additional people who wanted to unite with the new Grange.

The Center Grange Hall building was completed on Jul 4, 1922. This hall was built on land along Davis Lane (formerly of Henry Davis), the land was sold to Henry Hartenbach who donated a smaller plot of the land for use by the Grange. The building stands – at 125 Center Grange Road – currently used and last known to be owned by a religious institute.

The Grange #1870 purchased the former Grimmell Dairy barn and then constructed the new hall from the lumber of the former barn. Mr. Meany was the head of the committee that approved $275 for purchasing the barn. Volunteers worked Mondays and Thursdays of each week, as well as on holidays until the building was completed. The Grange held a picnic and square dance to celebrate the occasion but did not formerly dedicate the building until Aug 4, 1926. By 1931, a 'juvenile room' was added to the grange hall building. This addition was later also used for a kitchen and dining area until the completion of a basement where a kitchen was added.

The Center Grange #1870 fulfilled its destiny to the fullest being very dedicated to many, many township / community services and activities. One of the important services provided by The Grange was in assisting the farmers by pooling their orders for fertilizer, spray materials, seeds, and other products. By combining these normally smaller individual orders, it gave the farmers discounted prices since the Grange made large purchases in more of a bulk supply. In Feb 1921, Mr. Enoch S. W. Engle was selected the "purchasing agent" and handled all these orders.

A short sampling of some of the many activities to show how very active the Center Grange organization was in the township includes:

- Collected and sent gifts to members of the armed forces.
- Dedicated a club service flag and sent miniature service flags to those serving in the Army, Navy and Army Air Forces.
- Signed cards and sent them to service men.
- Made donations to the Center School's scholarship fund.
- Made donations to the Beaver County Easter Seal drives.
- Collected and distributed toys to children in the area.
- Collected used eyeglasses and hearing aid batteries for "Care and Ears to Hear."
- Held public farmers' markets during growing seasons.
- Held bake sales in conjunction with the markets.
- The Grange had a radio program in the 1940s that was broadcast over WBVP- Beaver Falls. They would not only provide informative and valuable information to all the farmers of the area, they would publicly announce events and happenings of the Grangers and and of all others occurring at the Hall.
- Held open public meetings to provide reports and information on community information on subjects such as……. insurance changes, political concerns, trends and concerns, health issues.
- Formed different leagues in various sports.
- Regularly had miscellaneous community events…
    (all early dances involved live orchestras)
    - square dances and other various dances, masquerade dances, bake sales, luncheons with homemade soups (with takeout available), spaghetti dinners, annual turkey dinner, prepared and served public roast beef dinners, rummage sales, fish fries, card parties.
- Held "old time song" fests.
- Had a Center Grange 4-H Sewing Club.
- Held talent shows for community residents.
- Supported a grange home economics committee and hosted state-wide home economic functions.
- Made and donated many cookies.
- The Grange did a traveling program depicting the history of the Grange organization.
- Entertained the State Grange and all the other local Grange organizations' members.
- Hosted County-wide Grange meetings and observances.
- Hosted the Western Jubilee events.
- Held Mother-Daughter banquets.
- Sponsored cover dish dinners.
- Held demonstrations of home canning for all interested residents. These were especially advertised and held during the Depression years or any years of recession to help all learn how to preserve and "put up" their own foods.
- Held bus trips to see various live performances, Pirate baseball games, and tours of many venues.
- Held women's activities.
- Sold Grange cookbooks, as well as Restaurant Coupon books.
- The Grange community services and activities also included assisting the state welfare office in aiding needed families during the depression, cooperating with the Beaver County Tuberculosis Association in conducting free X-ray clinics, assisted many other township and county organizations in civic betterment projects.

- They would also sponsor many different children's parties, various holiday based, costume parties, held general activities/contests with games and prizes, held many types of community dances.
- The Faith Lutheran Church congregation was started and met in the Center Grange Hall building in 1953 and 1958. (See section on Churches for more information on this church.)

Many of the adults from the township will remember the annual Township "Fair." This annual fair was first started and organized by The Grange organization. They sponsored their annual local fairs which were first known as the "Produce Show." These local fairs were events that were highly looked forward to each year by everyone in the township. First and foremost, all types of fruits and vegetables and flowers grown by the local residents were sold and/or on display and there were dances held. Unlike today, there were no mechanical rides, just simply games for the children and families. For obvious reasons, during the war time years, the Grange put these annual fairs on hold. They started the annual fairs back up in 1948 and I found the dates of Aug 18, 19 and 20 in 1949 when the Center Grange held their second annual Community Fair following WWII.

As with all events, things changed through the years. As the attractions for homegrown produce and flowers was diminishing, there were additional attractions added each year to keep the interest of township residents. While the number of families living in the township grew, the size of the annual fairs also grew considerably. With the increased number of people attending the events, the township volunteer fire department took over sponsoring the annual "fair." It was moved from the Grange Hall property to the grounds of the elementary school due to not only the size of the fair and its attractions, but for more available parking. (See Recreation and Entertainment section for more on the township fairs.)

Fun fact: Jun 6, 1995 – Center officials were considering an occupancy ordinance designed to specify the number of people in a building or room because of the Center Grange Hall, where officials said summer band concerts in 1994 "packed 'em in cheek to cheek".

The Center Grange Hall was not just a building where the Grangers held meetings and their own group and/or sponsored public activities, but the Center Grange Hall building itself actually served as a true township activity building, too. To help express how important the Grange Hall and organization was to Center Township over the years, I felt I should list just some of the many, many public activities, events, and uses involving the Grange Hall building itself. By relating many of these events and uses, it may help readers understand how influential this one group and this one building truly was to the township. The many uses and why the building itself, which housed so many various activities, lend to the previous statement of the historic importance the building has in the township. This list is in no way complete or limited to………

- The Grange was the only polling site of the residents for many years.
- The annual Township Fairs were first held at the Grange Hall and grounds for many years, then moved to another location due to the need for more parking. Concession stands were not only used by many of the township residents, but also were rented by Monaca, Pittsburgh, & many other local merchants and groups through the years.
- The Center Township Citizen Council held meetings at the Grange for residents and discussed Township issues.
- Center Township's PTA held public meetings in the grange hall.
- There were many sponsored round and square dances held in the hall by the Grange. These dances had many different live bands providing the music.
- Eighth Grade Commencement exercises of Center Township Schools for the first class of the new consolidated school was held for students to receive their diplomas in 1940.
- The Grange Hall was used as a museum for the Township's celebration during the nation's bicentennial with displays of antiques, photos, memorabilia, and handcrafted items.
- First Aid classes of Center Township were held in the hall.

- The hall was regularly rented out by individuals for celebrations, such as birthday parties, anniversaries, family reunions, baby showers/births, weddings, graduations, veterans home comings, honoring local athletes, group banquets, group and/or family picnics.
- Rented the hall to many various groups and organizations, including Pittsburgh Mercantile Company, Aliquippa Rotarians, Beaver Valley Schoolmen's Club, Monaca Lodge-No 1115 Independent Order of Odd Fellows, Faith Lutheran Church, Monaca Athletic Association, Young People's Forum of the Presbyterian Church, Monaca Junior Woman's Club held dinners and events in the Grange, Bell Telephone Company (to discuss extension of the company's rural telephone lines), Monaca Men's Club, Rural Woman's Club of Center Township, Monaca Junior Women's Club, Monaca Garden Club, Kiwanis Clubs, Mona Manor Farm and Garden 4H club, YMCA Retired Men's Club, Lower Beaver Valley Kiwanis Club, Beaver County Extension Office, Athletic Associations.
- County 4-H leaders and officers met (and held their regular group meetings) in the Grange Hall.

Miscellaneous information regarding Center Grange and its property.
- In 1972, the Center Grange, No. 1870 deeded property to Batchelor Brothers, Inc. This property was originally sold to the Grange in 1942 by J. Henry Forrest, evidently separate from the land that Henry and Rosa Hartenbach deeded to the Grange in 1922 and separate from other land from J. Henry Forrest in 1938. The Batchelor Brothers, Inc. turned around and sold this property in 1982, deeding it to Nora Lesha and Anna Petrella.
- In 1986, there was an Affidavit filed, stating per the National Grange Digest bylaws, section 15, the Pennsylvania State Grange could sell any property of a subordinate Grange (in this case - Center Grange No. 1870) if a subordinate Grange failed or ceased to function. So……in 1997, per that Affidavit, the Pennsylvania State Grange conveyed/deeded the property and building of the Center Grange to Beaver County Church.
- From all this information, it appears that the Center Grange No. 1870 was downsizing its assets by selling one of their properties in 1972, and that they had ceased to function by at least 1986 with the PA State Grange selling the remaining properties that were once of the Center Grange No. 1870. Trustees of Center Grange No. 1870 in 1987/1988 were James L. Lindey-Master, Ilda Weigle-Chairman of Exec. Committee, Dorothy R. McPherson, W. Reed McCartney.

Original Grange building 1930s

c1958   with youth room addition

2016

In viewing the three previous pictures, the original look of the Grange Hall has changed very little through the years. But since it was sold in 1997 – there was a metal roof added and the once familiar white exterior of the building was changed in color.

With the proven importance of this one building to the history of Center Township, many persons have expressed their concerns that the integrity of the interior and exterior of the building should never be changed. It is the strong hope that the current owners of the building recognize the importance of this building and it be preserved since it is among the few remaining early buildings of the Township. It needs repeating – this former Grange building is **the first and only** remaining public building of the township from the 1920s.

Center Grange Youth Club
Organized in Aug of 1939. The Junior Grange No. 123 was organized for children ages 5 to 14 while the regular Grange included members aged 14 or older. The Junior Grange was considered a social organization made up entirely of the younger children of Center Grange No. 1870 members. The Junior Grange meetings were held each month in the Grange Hall. (The No. 1870 group not only supported the Center Youth Club, but also several other various youth group activities.) Members of the Center Grange Youth Club attended Youth Camp and Juvenile Camp each year at the Raccoon State Park.

~ ~ ~

The Center Grangers and 4-H Clubs in Center Township did many activities and projects together. One of these was in Sep of 1934 -- Center Grange had a farm products and work display and the 4-H members were all invited to attend with friends and family members. 4-H Club members also displayed crops they had grown and garments and other articles they had made. Members of the local 4-H clubs participated in many of these same types of projects. They covered sewing, home making, capons, chickens, tomatoes, vegetable gardening, corn, livestock, horses, and other aspects of living in a rural community. Members of all the various Girls' and Boys' 4-H Clubs also participated in exhibitions at all the Grange Fairs. They also participated in the Hookstown Fair and several other fairs throughout the county.

4-H Clubs
Center Township

Some of the 4-H groups found associated with the township are listed further. Note – If an organizational start or disbandment date was found, it is included -- otherwise, the years listed beneath each group's name only indicate the year(s) information was found on that group to provide some type of a time frame of when the group was active.

Center Grange 4-H Sewing Club

The 4-H Girls' Club
Started in mid-1937 They held their meetings each week, many of them at the Center Township Grange Hall and occasionally in a different member's home. They learned how to make aprons and other items. There were quite a few news articles found on this group through the 1940s.

4-H Sew and Save Club
1950s Met in the Grange Hall.

4-H Agricultural Club
1950s Mrs. Henry Hartenbach was the leader in 1954.

4-H Home Economics Club
Started in 1927 and continued through at least 1950s
Mrs. Ralph Hartenbach was the leader in 1954.

Cook-If-You-Can Girls' 4-H Club
In 1941, Miss Vivian Hartenbach was the host of many of their meetings. These meetings were held at her home on Brodhead Road where the girls were taught to cook and serve breakfasts and other meals.

Center Farm and Sports 4-H Boys' Club
I did find in 1940 there was a Center Farm and Sports 4-H Boys' Club that had a mushball* team who played against other local mushball teams. One team they played was the Monaca Ramblers.

> *Mushball is a lot like softball, except the ball is so much softer and larger. There is no need for a glove, you catch it with your hands and because it is so soft, it is difficult to hit very far. Mushball originated in the Mushball Capital of the World, Chicago.

~ ~ ~

Potter Township 4-H Clubs

Potter Township also had a grange organization. It was instituted the end of Jan 1929 and was known as "Potter 4-H." No number was assigned to this group as of 1929. There were twenty-one members at the first meeting. The Potter School House No. 1 was used as a meeting place until some repairs were made at the No. 2 schoolhouse where they then met. The first officers were Master F. G. Anderson, Overseer-Antony Besch, Lecturer-Miss Ethel Anderson, Secretary-Mrs. Matilda Kennedy, Treasurer-Mr. Jeffreys, Steward-Albert Kennedy, Asst. Steward-John M. Phillis, Lady Asst. Steward-Mrs. Harvey Hayes, Chaplain- Mr. Hughes, Gate-Keeper- Gabrice Nusser, and Court-Mrs. E. G. Anderson, Mrs. Jeffreys, and Miss Janet Hughs. Potter Township's Grange organization was also involved with the 4-H groups. A few of these 4-H groups were:

4-H Boys' Club   Arthur F. Laughner was the club leader in 1939.

St. Joe 4-H Club   Membership included boys and girls in the 1940s.

4-H Girls' Club
1936 to the 1990s   The Potter Township 4-H Economics Club was organized in 1936. Mrs. Betty Krebs was the first President of this club. Miss Mary Jordan organized all the girls' clubs, and she was the leader in at least 1938, 1949, 1965. Mrs. Steven Ratey became a leader in March of 1969. They had various 4-H Club divisions, including Budle Pack Club and Field Club. Meetings were held in various locations, including Miss Jordan's home, school buildings, and the homes of the members. In 1949, they held parties and dances at the Kobuta Community Center.

~ ~ ~

Mr. and Mrs. L. H. Klingseisen, of Monaca, would offer their summer camp along Raccoon Creek in Potter Township for many groups and clubs to hold summer camps and other outings.

~ ~ ~

Various Organizations and Groups

Listed further is a strong sampling of some of the many other various Moon and Center Township groups and organizations whose names were found in archived publications. There may be simply just a name listed for some, while others will have some years the information was found for them listed below the name, and yet others will have more details if that information was available. I concentrated on the groups and organizations that existed in previous years and not those that are currently in existence. Again, please know that not all that existed or still exist are listed and none were omitted intentionally.

Acme Club
Organized in Sep 1901.   This group first met in the Morris Barnett building in Monaca which was built on corner of Ninth Street and Pennsylvania Avenue, then they moved their meetings to 711-713 Pennsylvania Avenue.   There were quite a few men from Moon/Center Township who were members of this club.

    1906 – changed the name to………….

Monaca Rod and Gun Club
The club maintained a summer camp in Oak Grove which was a designated area on the James Mateer farm in Center Township.   Each year, members would attend a summer camp in the Canadian woods.

Photo from Milestones magazine – BCHR&LF

An early photo of members of the Rod and Gun Club. Back row: Fritz Bechtel, Billy Meanor, Henry Miksch.   Front row: Joe Fisher, Joe Stein, Bill Bechtel, Carl Mattauch, Walter Buchholz.

Broadhead Road Homemakers Club
1962

Bunker Hill 4-H Club
Josephine Colaluca was president in 1957.

Business Men's Club (listed on Mercantile List in 1942 under Restaurants)

Center Grange Homemakers

Chapel Valley Swim Club
1974, 1976   Building was a polling site but then held at the Skyview Lounge in Oct 1976.

Center Township Boosters Club
1957, 1965

Center Baseball Boosters Club
1972   Proceeds from many fundraisers were used for township baseball summer programs.

Center Li'l Trojans' Booster Club
        Joseph Rossi – President - 1971

Center Li'l Trojans Football Mothers Auxiliary
1978

Center Civic Woman's Club
1962, 1965, 1971   Federated Sept 29, 1962.

Center Grange Homemakers
1975, 1982

Center Camping Coyotes
1975, 1978, 1979   They held their meetings in the Center VFW building.   Mrs. Marge Huffmyer, Mrs. Sharon Boring, Mrs. Carolyn Lucci worked with the children in 1975. Mr. and Mrs. Leroy Dunn were elected presidents in 1976. They held campouts at Trailerville, Unity, Ohio where they would participate in fishing, swimming, motorcycle riding and hiking.

Center Township Chemical Abuse Prevention Coalition
This coalition was formerly known as The Chemical People Task Force. They were a community group concerned with drug and alcohol abuse among young persons. This coalition would meet with other township groups, including churches and ministers to garner their support in their work.

Center Township Homemakers Club
1957   They met in various members' homes.

Center Township Ministerium
No date of its beginning or how long it existed was found, but this organization was in existence during at least the 1970s and 1980s. This ministerium would meet and discuss many issues with other ministeriums of surrounding towns and townships in Beaver County and even other counties. They provided scholarships to qualifying students of the district and worked with other community groups in many various matters, as well as had quite a few community worship services which were held in different churches through the years. Some of the churches who participated were – North Branch U. P., Faith and Vankirk Lutheran, University Baptist, St. Frances Cabrini R. C., Bunker Hill Community Church.

Center Township Riding Club
Organized in 1953   Held meetings at Dr. and Mrs. S. C/ Davenport's home on North Branch Road. They used a show ring and a ½ mile track made on the Evan Tilly property adjacent to the Davenports' property. The Davenports had a barn behind their home where they kept their own personal horses since their daughter competed and showed her horses for several years.

Center Township Veterans of Foreign Wars Post 1821   aka   **V.F.W.** - Bunker Hill Road
    The Center Township V.F.W. Post was organized on Sep 14, 1941. At that time there were 22 charter members. They were Chester Bell, Elmer Cochran, Earl Engle, George Figley, Curtis Gormley, Charles Grodis, Walter Huff (Walter was chosen as the first commander), John Kapitanich, Richard Leavitt, Walter Leavitt, Earl Leonard, Frank Maples, Herman Martin, William Patton, Goetonia Pelino, Raymond Plate, Frank Rushman, Ralph Shaffer, William Simpson, Harry Stout, Thomas Wilson, and Harry Wood.
    They purchased the old Bunker Hill School building and fashioned it into their meeting place. Then the entire building was remodeled and covered with brick. The front porch was made into a kitchen. There was an honor roll dedicated on the property in mid Jun 1958. This honor roll included names of WWI, WWII, and Korean veterans from Center Township. Post 1821 did many different community activities. Some of these were, in 1967, they offered free bicycle stickers, had dinners, and held bake sales. Members and its auxiliary also held annual picnics in the fall seasons at their post home on Bunker Hill Road.
    The Center Township V.F.W. Auxiliary of Post 1821 was organized on Jul 11, 1944. The first 30 charter members of this auxiliary included Josephine Cable, Jane Cochran, Jennie D'Alfonso, Rosa Engle, Helen Fronk, Catherine Gormley, Alice Hetzer, Lorraine Knox, Margaret Knox, Helena Leonard, Wilma Leonard, Ruth Martin, Agnes Merriman, Margaret Merriman, C. Ruth Malloy, Lettie Myers,

Anna Patton, Cathryn Patton, Josephine Pelino, Jean Pillar, Catherine Ruff (Catherine was elected the first Auxiliary president.), Irene Schwarz, Margaret Schwarz, Sara Schwarz, Mary Short, Ida Solkovy, Catherine Strickler, and Nora Swan.

Center Civic Women's Club
1962 to current   Held its first regular meeting in the Center Township Elementary School in Sep of 1962. It was hosted by Mrs. James McMasters, Mrs. John Shawger, Mrs. John Hodovanich, Mrs. Sidney Huffmyer, Mrs. Carl Vaughn, Mrs. Martin McCullough. The purpose of The Center Civic Women's Club was to develop the educational, civic, and social interest of its members, and to advance the welfare of the community.

Center Township 4-H Agriculture Club
1976

Center 4-H Crafty Stitchers

Center-Potter Senior Citizens
This group originally met in the VFW, Bunker Hill Road.

Centerettes
1950s   This was a singing group of eighth grade girls with Mrs. Harold Springer, music teacher and group's director. Donna Bowling was the president of the group. The group went to many various events to perform.

Center Township Boy Scouts
The Boy Scouts of America have always been a hard-working group of young men. They volunteer and help in many different areas. During war times they helped the United Service Organization Campaign by delivering posters and other promotional material. When there were tests run with black-out demonstrations, they helped in various towns and cities and other areas. During WWII times, many of the Boy Scouts members were trained and organized for service. They were recognized by national, state, and local government and public officials. They sold 2,350,977 Liberty Loan Bond subscriptions that totaled $354,859,262 and War Savings Stamps at $52,000,000. Collectively, during the same war time years, all the Scouts were credited with also collecting over 20,000,000 board feet of sot after walnut wood, collected a hundred carloads of fruit pits, and distributed over 30,000,000 pieces of government literature.

Rev. Henry Howells is listed to have organized the first Boy Scout Troup in Center Township - #454, and they were sponsored by the CTVFD #1 for over twenty-five years. Mr. Sterling Lewis of North Branch Road was also a Scoutmaster of Center Township Boy Scout Troup 454 in 1937. While he was employed at the Kobuta plant during WWII, he secured the former carpenters' building that was used while Kobuta was being built. The building was then moved to the CTVFD #1 property on Brodhead Road/Main Street. The Boy Scouts then began to hold their meetings in this building. The "Scout Hall" became the familiar name for the smaller building along Main Street, on property owned by the CTVFD #1. In 1954/55 the fire department decided to move the Scout Hall building to provide more parking for their events at the fire hall, so they moved the building from its original location (closer to the side entrance of the fire hall), reassembling it just a bit further down on their property on Main Street, where it still stands today (2019). This smaller building was used by the Boy Scout, Cub Scouts, Girls Scout, and Brownie troops of the township.

Updated former scout building on Main Street by the CTVFD #1 fire hall.

The Cub Scouts and Boy Scouts of Center Township had many notable Scout Masters over the years.
- Troup #434 had Mr. Galina as their scout leader in the 1960s. They would attend weekend camping trips to the Martin Galina camp in Tionesta.
- Cub Scout Pack 552 Den 4 – Mrs. Clara Roth, Den Mother in 1976…. Rocco DeMaiolo, Cubmaster.
- Mr. George Robbie was also one of the well-known and long-standing Scout Master of Troop 454 and post advisor and committee man for Troop 423. Mr. Robbie was also Scout Master of Troop 451 (Monaca Heights) and in 1958, there were five Cub Scout dens, one Boy Scout Troop - #454, and one Explorer Troop of #454. This Troop would hold their annual 3-day campout at the intersection of Brodhead Road and Center Grange Roads.
- Back to Sterling Lewis, the previously mentioned well-known leader within Troop #454. Mr. Lewis founded the *Fort McIntosh Indians Scout Organization* in 1978 and his wife, Louise, was a seamstress for the organization. This group was very known for their collection of Indian articles. The boys would dress in replicas of authentic Indian costumes and perform actual known dances of the Indians. They were very popular in parades and many other different events. I lived close to the Lewis family and looked forward to sneaking over to their house on the nights the group met and watched them while they practiced their dancing. These dances and movements always fascinated me since every movement or series of movements had specific symbolizations.

Monaca-Center Township Girl Scouts
1952, 1964, 1968, 1986   In 1958, there were six Girl Scout and Brownie Troops in Center Township. The Brownies and Girl Scouts of Center Township had many dedicated individuals as Troops Leaders over the years. I personally had Mrs. Brown and Mrs. Walton as leaders in the 1950s to 1970s.

The girls / troops would all look forward to the one week during the summer that would be spent attending Day-Camp, beginning at 9 or 9:30 a.m. each day until 2:00 or 3:00 p.m. In preparation for Day-Camp, girls would spend time during meetings for making a very popular item called "sit-upons" (see Fun fact further). Come "day-camp week" all would take a bag lunch for 4 of the 5 days. The last day all would get to use their sit-upons as they gathered around a big bond fire in the evening with songs, hot dogs, smores or just marshmallows. In the 1960s, the Girl Scouts' Day Camp was held at the Veterans of Foreign Wars Park, Center Township. At least by 1974, Day Camp was held on the Patton property, Bunker Hill Road. Another area used for Day-Camp was on what was known as the Good property, also known as the Old Log Cabin Inn Park. Camp Baker in Beaver Falls was another place the girls would meet in later years. (See more on this park area in the Homes and Family section under the Good Family information and see Parks information in the Entertainment and Recreation section.)

I do not think I even have to mention that the selling of Girl Scout Cookies has been and still is a long and popular tradition and fund-raising project for all Girl Scouts through the years. Who doesn't look forward to buying one or more boxes of these cookies?

> *Fun fact: A "sit-upon" was the Girl Scouts' version of a home-made seat cushion. It was something that each Girl Scout would make for herself. The troop provided each girl with one piece of oil cloth (approximately 24" x 30") and enough plastic cord to weave around the edges of this cloth. Making these seat cushions was a project for the girls for a few*

weeks at the troops' meetings. Girls would bring in old newspapers or even old magazines and the oil cloth would be folded in half to envelop the magazines/newspapers. Holes were then punched along the outer edges of the oil cloth and the plastic cord was woven through the holes to seal the edges of the oil cloth. Having your own sit-upon was a big deal!!!

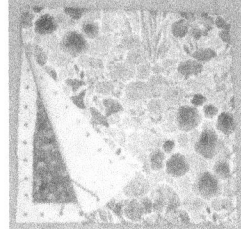 

Cadette Troop 267
1962   Meetings were held at the VFW, Bunker Hill Road. They were known to have camped at Camp Elliott, New Castle. Mrs. Veronica Holpek was leader in 1962.

Girl Scout Troop 67
1950s   Mrs. Wesley Pethick was leader, Miss Jane Brock was assistant in 1957.

GOP Club

Fisherman's Club of North Branch Church
1950s, 1960s

Knights of Columbus No 5825 – 3510 Brodhead Road
Ruling date – Nov 1940, current
The Knights of Columbus was founded in 1882. The needs of immigrants and families suffering from the death of a family's breadwinner led Father Michael J. McGivney to respond by founding this group. Their first principle is charity. They are made up of Catholic men of faith and men of charitable action.

LaCarte Club
1963   They would meet in alternating members' homes. Some members included Mary Patuc, Irene Vendemia, Mary Werling, Mimi Ryan, and Mary Swan.

Monaca-Center Lodge No. 791 Free and Accepted Masons – corner Pacific Ave and 14th Street
1961–current   This Lodge is not located in Center Township but is a combined Lodge of Center and Monaca members who hold their meetings in Monaca. Constituted on Mar 11, 1961. The Lodge purchased the old, dusty, abandoned station from the railroad in 1969. After over 10,000-man hours of labor donated by Lodge members, family, and friends, the new lodge became home of Monaca-Center Lodge No. 791. (This railroad station was built in the 1900s and in Apr 1910 it was moved from its original site at Colona (Monaca area) to this current location on the corner of Fourteenth Street and Pacific Avenue.)

Lodge No, 791 was holding its meetings in the Masonic Temple in Rochester before moving into the newly renovated railroad station in 1970/71. The furniture for this Lodge was donated by Grand Lodge. There are hand carved benches and chairs that date back 135 years and had been used in the "New Masonic Hall" in Philadelphia between 1855 – 1873. The upholstered furniture is of bright crimson and a rich blue carpeting adorn the 60 by 28-foot Lodge Room.

Monaca-Center Lions Club
1990

Monaca-Center Fraternity Club
1990   Organized and Chartered in 1963.   Their primary purpose was to acquire and maintain land and property wherein the members of the club and members of other lodges, clubs or associations could meet and engage in Fraternal, Social and Innocent past times.   They operated within the the Borough of Monaca and Center Township.   The board of directors included Calvin Swink-President, Geo. W. Rowse-Vice President, Fred T. Mawson-Secretary, Wm. J. Kiefer-Treasurer, and Members, James Sebastian, W. V. Aaron, Fred Aiken, Jr., V. I. Steed, John Kloos, Frank Lynch, Geo. McKeel, Carl Lutton, James Kovac, Frank Biskup, and Sam Prisuta.

Monaca Turn Verein (Turners)
Organized Apr 9, 1883 to current   This group started meeting in a small one-storey frame building at 819 Pennsylvania Avenue.   They moved to 699 Pacific Avenue (corner of former Seventh Street and Pacific Avenue.   Their first structure was a two-storey frame building which was completed and dedicated Nov 29, 1893.   The building was enlarged in 1901 with a 30 by 20-foot addition added on the back of the building.   In 1915 the building was again enlarged with a one-storey, 20 by 100-foot, brick structure on the front of the building.   This addition included two bowling alleys.   Another one-storey brick building, 50 by 100 feet, was added in 1938 and three more bowling alleys were added to the previous addition.   Turners occupied the building on Seventh Street and Pacific Avenue until 1980 when Phoenix Glass expanded and purchased all the properties in that area.   In Jan 1981, Turners purchased property and erected a modern new building at 1700 Brodhead Road, Center Township.   This new building includes a bar room, dining room, regulation size gymnasium, kitchen, banquet hall, racquetball courts, and six bowling lanes.

(See the Families and Homes section – Hartenbach Family -- the Activities and Organization section – and information on Grocery stores for more information on the property prior to it being purchased by Turners.)

Republican Club of Center Township
1971

Rural Women's Club
Organized Feb 1, 1938.   Met in the Center Grange Hall. They presented different programs to the community when solicited.   They also held many annual mother-daughter banquets.   First officers were Mrs. Arthur Laughner-President, Mrs. William Harper-Vice President, Miss Virginia Douds-Secretary, and Miss Louis McConnell-Treasurer.

Showstoppers

Suburban Women's Club of Center Township
1969, 1976   They use to have a Hallmark Art Contest where a high school student was selected as winner.   The club also had sewing contests and were known for providing needy families of the area with food, toys, clothing, and other assistance.

The Center Circle
1953   Met in members' homes.

Young Christian Homemakers Class of Bunker Hill Community Church
1957 to at least 1967   Mrs. Freda Ross – President in 1962. Held annual Christmas dinners and various events.

YMCA aka Beaver County Young Men's Christian Association
Previous to the opening of the Village Shops plaza on Brodhead Road, in 1978 the site was a consideration of the YMCA for building a center. The Beaver County Young Men's Christian Association purchased the property in 1978 from the Dorme Land Co. (previously owned by Mary Todora). After a consulting firm's survey showed the goal for this center could not be reached, the YMCA plans for their center did not further materialize. Instead of building their center in Center Township, they sold this property to C. J. Betters in 1984 and an open-air plaza was built. The YMCA then chose to locate their South Branch YMCA on Monaca Heights by Monaca's open-air water reservoirs. They opened this center on Dec 1, 1978. The YMCA center is currently located at 2236 Third Avenue, New Brighton, PA.

In the earlier years, Moon Township residents most likely joined the YMCA which was organized in 1901 and was located in Monaca. The YMCA closed this hall permanently Aug 31, 1907. This Monaca building was first at the corner of Eighth Street and Indiana Avenue and moved into the old skating rink on Pennsylvania Avenue. Although this group was only in Monaca from 1901 to 1907, they were a VERY active group and seemed to have multiple activities going on every week during this time period. They were always in the news, advertising one event or another with many Moon Township residents being involved.

~ ~ ~

Center Township P.T.A.
Organized in 1949.   The Center Township Parent-Teacher Association (P.T.A.) was originally started because of a group of women who gathered for a visit at the home of Mrs. James Aultman, Brodhead Road. These women began to discuss the need for such an organization as the P.T.A. After these women presented their concerns and thoughts to Mr. Alvin Elliott, the principal of the school, it was decided to hold an organizational meeting, elect officers, and officially have the Center Township P.T.A.

The Center Township Parent Teacher Association was officially organized in 1949. The first officers for this P.T.A. group were Mrs. James Ramsay-Pres., Mrs. Harold Broman-Vice Pres., Mrs. Rachel Shupe-Secy, and Stewart Lindsay-Treas.   They conducted their first official meeting in September of 1949.   Some of the other earlier Presidents of this P.T.A. also included Mrs. Alvin Albright, Mrs. D.W. Baker, Mrs. Stanley Brobeck, Mrs. John Dyrwal, Mrs. Lester Roosa, Mrs. George Sweitzer, Jr., Mrs. Henry Schier, Mrs. Daniel McPeek, and Mrs. Kenneth Wright.

This P.T.A. promoted an understanding and cooperation between the parents, the teachers, and the children, as well as providing many projects and programs for the schools. The Center P.T.A. always organized activities for the students of the Center Schools, too.   As early as 1963, they were sponsoring skating parties at the Aliquippa Roller Rink (now Kendrew Lounge). Additionally, at least in 1970, the Center PTA sponsored/supported a Savings Stamp sale.

The Center Township P.T.A. also had panel discussions which addressed the needs of the township, problems, concerns, and the township's future growth and then brought all these before the public.   In 1950, the Center Township P.T.A. was instrumental in the formation of the Center Township Citizens' Council (see further) which became known as the Center Township Citizens' Forum.

~ ~ ~

Center Township Citizens Council   aka   Center Township Citizens' Forum
Organized Jul 12, 1950   As previously mentioned, the P.T.A. was the main force behind creating this council. Mrs. James Ramsey, the first president of the Center Township P.T.A., appointed Mrs. Eric Garing to conduct a study to see if an organization could be formed in the township to help with school and township problems. The committee to be formed became known as the Center Township Citizens Council (aka Center Township Citizens' Forum). Mrs. Garing took her appointment seriously. After contacting all the organizations in the township, she held a meeting at her home on Center Grange Road.   The first persons to attend this meeting and be considered on the early "action team" were Mrs. William Dyke-Bunker Hill Community Church, Mr. Phillip Patton-Fire Co. #1, Mrs. Phillip Patton-Fire Co. #1 Auxiliary, Mrs. Joseph Zupsic-Fire Co. #2 Auxiliary, Mrs. Edwin Kalinoski-Fire Co. #1, W. F. Aaron-Center Grange, Clarence Bailes, L.A. Morris, and William Milne – all of Fire Co. #3, Fred Glasser-Center Township Supervisor, Alvin T. Albright-Center School Board, and from the P.T.A. - Stuart Lindsay, Fred Grine, Mrs. James Ramsey.

The committee was formed with the goal to furnish a non-partisan forum for creation of public opinion on matters of interest to township citizens. Gibson Brock was the first president of the council with Wesley Leonard-vice president, Fred Grine-secretary, and Woodrow Aaron-Treasurer. Each year, the Citizens Council held election of officers resulting in many new persons becoming the officers.   Paul Marthens was the president in 1952 and George Setters in 1953.   Eric Garing was another to serve as president in 1955 with James Korban-vice president and Mrs. Calvin McCon-secretary. Some other previous members included Mrs. Eric E. Garing, Charles Harper, Eugen Geist, Walter J. Cochran, Jr., John Egyud, and James Korban.   There was also a large turnover of members on the council throughout the years.

The first members of the "action team" decided to start things off with five meetings held within a week of their organization, all being at different locations throughout the township to accommodate as many residents as possible. The parents were all informed by ads in the newspaper and/or notices sent home by the school via the students. These notices made notes of the subject matters to be discussed on given dates with the location and times for the upcoming meetings.

from late May 1953

At each of the meetings held by the council, there was discussion of problems such as those of the fire departments, along with citizens using the council as a "sounding board for problems of roads, sewage disposal, and water."   Over the first few years of existence, this council was the driving force behind the establishment of the township's water system, establishing a planning commission, the improvement of street lighting, naming of streets, and highway safety. They also initiated action for various zoning areas in the township and helped raise funds for the fire department.   The council continued to work closely with the Center Township P.T.A. to solve problems within the schools.

Water System - The Citizens' Council started a drive for a water system in Center Township in Nov of 1951. A committee of residents was sent out to canvass the township regarding the need for a water system.   (for genealogy enthusiasts….)   This committee consisted of Mrs. John Edmond, Mrs. Logan Brubaker, Mrs. Bryon Collins, Mrs. Elbert O. Cone, Joseph Reinish, Clair T. Allison, John C. Kier, Eugene Geist, H. R. Dickson, Eric Garing, J. D. Baker, A. T. Albright, G. E. Brock, C. Jane Brock, Michael Mikula, Robert Bickerton, R.R. Morris, Louis D. Hibar, George Belich, Eli Uzelac, Steve Chunchick, Carmine Celeste, Andrew Minzak, Jr., L. A. Roosa, Paul Marthens, Woodrow Aaron, Howard Roosa, and Elmer Carlson.   Between mid-1952 and Jan 1953, more than 700 homeowners were contacted and agreed to the proposed water system plan.

What seemed like overnight, Center Township residents started to see major work occurring along Brodhead Road with trenches being dug along roadways and through lawns. There were mounds of the massive pipeline being created and waiting to be laid, too. Thanks to the persistence of the Citizens' Council, Center Township residents soon had public water......well, *almost* all residents.... the Stobo district of the township was not included in the water system as it was too far from the main water lines. In 1958, the water authority was petitioned by the Stobo residents to see if the lines could be extended so they could also have township water. Areas of Sylvan Crest were also excluded, they received their water from the Borough of Monaca for many years.

<u>Street Lighting</u> - Just as influential as the Center's Citizens Council was with many other township matters, they are credited with addressing the process for installation of streetlights throughout the township. The first project in this matter was done later in 1953 to very early in Jan of 1954 with the task of completing engineering and installation of streetlights on Brodhead Road and Center Grange Road by the Duquesne Light Company.

<u>Renaming of Roads</u> - At a Citizens' Council meeting held the end of Apr 1956, a committee was appointed to rename streets in the township. This street naming committee was comprised of Gibson Brock, Charles Whittingham, Woodrow Aaron, Eugene Geisy, I. Parsons, George Setters, and James Karbon. At the May 25, 1954 meeting of the Citizens' Council, Mike Chapes was named the chairman of a sub-committee that was responsible to prepare a particular petition that would be sent to Harrisburg. This petition was being made requesting a change in the name of "Poor House Run Road" to "Pleasant Drive." The petition had to be submitted to the state since this was a state highway at that time.

<u>Planning Commission</u> - The Center Township Citizens Council also was responsible for organizing the Center Township Planning Commission in the mid 1950s.

~ ~ ~

Citizens Council for Equity from Government
Another mention of a group in the township of residents was the Citizens Council for Equity from Government. They held an organizational meeting in early Aug 1992.

~ ~ ~

Center Township Progressive Democrats
Formed mid /end of 1962 - the first of 1963.
This group held meetings in the township building and all township residents were invited to attend. They had a slogan "Progress for Center." When they organized, they had a statement of purpose that said --- "is organized for the purpose of giving expression to political opinion and for electing officers to carry on the government of the township in a progressive manner." "It shall be the goal of this organization to promote a plan for township expansion that will hold the interest of all citizen voters and create a plan of long-range development with the best interest of all resident citizens and to educate all taxpayers of any plans and developments." In mid Feb 1963, the newly formed group elected William Frank-chairman, Robert Bickerton-vice chairman, Louise Rager-secy-treas, Stanley Brobeck-steering comm. chairman, and Edward Iorlido-publicity chairman. Some of the other members of this group included Robt. Rager, Sam'l. Colalella, Richard Giska, Wm. Frank, Joseph Zugay, Edward Miller, Steve Vuckovich, B. Rebich, Leonard Smith, Louis Hibar, Warren Hutchison, Wm. Bruce, Joseph Harper, B. Salasky, Helen Gillin, and Ortella Cowen.

~ ~ ~

POST OFFICES

Did you know that prior to Jul 1, 1845, envelopes were not used for small or simple letters? A sheet with the message was written and then just folded, the fold was sealed with wax, and the address added to the outside of the folded sheet. After regulations changed the rate being charged by the number of pieces of mail to being calculated by weight, the usage of envelopes became more frequent. Prior to the postal law of 1845 changing rates from number of pieces of mail, charges included delivery for up to thirty miles was 6.25 cents, thirty-one to eighty miles was 10 cents, eighty-one to one hundred and fifty miles was 12.5 cents, one hundred fifty one to four hundred miles was 18.75 cents, and over four hundred miles was 25 cents.

> *Fun fact: Spanish silver coin was still widely being used in America in the earlier 1800s. One piece was called a "penny bit" and was worth 6.14 cents in American money, another was an "eleven penny bit" and was worth 12.5 cents. The fractions of postal charges in the 1840s were established with the usage of these Spanish silver coins in mind.*

After the charges of postage was changed and determined according to weight, the charge was 3 cents for one half ounce and/or any fraction of up to one half ounce. Senders of all mail could choose to either pay in advance or they could leave this financial burden to be collected by the receiver of the mail. Prior to the adoption and usage of postage stamps in America in 1847, letters were marked or stamped with either "paid" or "cr" to designate how the postage charges were handled.

Beaver County had forty-four official post offices in 1903.

All the post offices listed further were officially opened by the U.S. Postal Service. The dates of appointment of all postmasters/postmistresses were also obtained from the Postal Service listings, as are many of the dates a post office was opened, discontinued, or consolidated. If known, the locations of these post offices will be listed, unfortunately, there were no e<u>xac</u>t addresses for any of the post offices within any of archived records of the USPS.

Shafer Post Office – corner of E. Shaffer and Brodhead Roads.
On Dec 24, 1880, there was an official post office approved and opened in Moon/Center Township named Shafer Post Office. Daniel Shafer was appointed the postmaster on that same date and the post office was located in Dan Shafer's home at the corner of E. Shafer and Brodhead Road.

Harry Gross was one of the men would deliver the mail from the Monaca Post Office to the Shafer Post Office on horseback. This post office only had two official post masters -- Dan Shafer followed by Ellen Shafer, appointed Jan 30, 1897. Shafer Post Office was discontinued Apr 4, 1901, with all mail from between this portion or section of Moon/Center Township including the New Sheffield area of Aliquppa then being service through the New Sheffield post office.

The Shafer family also had a small general store at this location. There was a nice log barn that was located on the property by the house, but it was torn down in the late 1950s or 1960s. The original home which was used as the post office was still standing as of 2014 but has since been razed, with a smaller apartment building built on the site. (Also see the Houses and Families section – Law Family; they operated the general store prior to leaving it to the Shafer family in a will.)

The Shaffer home once stood on the corner of E. Shaffer and Brodhead Road before being razed to make room for a small apartment complex building which is now located on the site.

Fun fact: With the Nov 25, 1914 decree officially forming Center Township from Moon Township, it was stated that the Shaffer's Post Office location would continue to be the fixed place for holding the township's elections. Once the Center Grange Hall was built, it became the township's voting site.

Baker's Landing – adjacent to the mouth of Moon Run along the Ohio River (by Elkhorn Run Road). This post office was located within an area of early Moon Township known as Baker's Landing. Baker's Landing area was located adjacent to the foot of the Elkhorn Run Hill, close to confluence of Moon Run and the Ohio River. Baker's Landing had a general store called the Baker Trading Post, the post office, and a docking area along the Ohio River. This area was most likely called a "landing" due to the access to the Ohio River. (See Housing Areas section for much more on this Baker's Landing area.)

Postmasters were Samuel Major, Jr. - May 22, 1878; Allen Brooks - Oct 28, 1878; William Lawson - Apr 20, 1883; Mrs. Janene (McGregor) Lawson - May 3, 1886; Anna McDonald - Oct 16, 1901. It was also written that Hannah Stewart operated this Post Office/Trading Post, too, but she was not recorded in the USPS files as being officially appointed a postmaster, so she may have just "helped" in the post office while working in the store.

The Baker's Landing Post Office was discontinued Jul 15, 1904 and mail then went through the Colona Post Office (see further).

Colona Post Office

The Baker's Landing Post Office was discontinued and on the same date (Jul 15, 1904) the post office for all in the area was then known as "Colona." The following served as postmasters/postmistresses: Anna McDonald - Jul 15, 1904; Raymond D. Carnahan - Aug 28, 1907; Lula C. Southward - Jan 29, 1914. The Colona Post Office was discontinued Mar 31, 1915, and all mail then was serviced through the Monaca Post Office (see further).

The next three post offices were all within reasonable walking distance of each other, all within about a one-mile area. The land area of the Bellowsville, Josephtown, and Kobuta Post Offices was originally Moon Township, eventually becoming part of Potter Township.

Bellowsville Post Office

The Bellowsville post office was in existence from 1874 until 1902. William Flocker was appointed postmaster Jan 12, 1874 and Mrs. Elizabeth S. Flocker was appointed postmistress, May 4, 1876. Mrs. Flocker is listed as receiving $66.24 and $30.67 payment in 1883.

The U.S. Postal Service discontinued Bellowsville post office on Oct 28, 1902, with all mail then being serviced in Monaca, PA. (See Bellowsville Ferry information – there is a map which indicates "W. Flockers Store & P. O.")

Josephtown Post Office

Not long after the whole area of Bellowsville seemed to disappear, the community/town of Josephtown appeared. Miss Ethel M. Anderson was appointed the postmistress Jul 3, 1931. The U.S. Postal Service discontinued this post office Aug 23, 1933, and as of Sep 15, 1933, all mail was serviced in Monaca.

Kobuta Post Office

This post office was <u>not</u> officially established by the U.S. Postal Service. It was more of a self-appointed postal office in the "community" that was known as Kobuta. Kobuta personnel handled and distributed the mail within the community themselves after a "blanket" delivery was made to a designated area within Kobuta (there was no indication of exactly who or which official post office made this "blanket" delivery). The mail was handled in this manner for the Kobuta residents from 1944 to 1955.

~ ~ ~

Satellite Post Offices in Center Township

Center Township has had a few satellite offices of the Monaca and/or Aliquippa post offices. None of these satellite locations made deliveries of mail but would offer limited services such as selling postage stamps and being a pickup/drop off location for mail/packages.

-- Hoffman's Center Pharmacy in the Center Square Plaza, Brodhead Road (currently Brew-Ski's).

-- Lindy's - Brodhead Road (currently Papa Dukes).

-- Staples - within the Walmart Plaza (sells basic postage stamps).

~ ~ ~

Monaca Post Office

As with many early post offices, Phillipsburg/Monaca's did not have an official post office building for many of the early years, but rather conducted business in the home of the current postmaster. Depending how centrally located one of these homes may have been, sometimes it was decided to use another designated building/location. Prior to Moon/Center Township having rural delivery, those serviced by the Water Cure (Monaca) post office would have had to gone into town to one of the designated locations of the post office to pick up their mail.

1856 – first post office of Phillipsburg was established under the name of *Water Cure*. The first location was at the Water Cure Sanitarium. Dr. Clement Baelz was the manager of the Sanitarium and Dec 6, 1956, he was appointed the first postmaster.

1858 to 1881– the post office location was in the Knapper Building. This building was once the Knapper home, then the Bechtel's home, and is now 111 Fourth Street.

Jul 20, 1892 – the post office name officially became Monaca / Borough of Monaca.

Oct 28, 1902 - the Bellowsville Post Office was discontinued. All mail was then serviced in Monaca.

Sep 1903 – petition was passed around requesting the removal of the local post office to be more centrally located in town.

Mar 31, 1915 – The Colona Post Office was discontinued, and all mail was then serviced through this Monaca Post Office. (See previously listed Baker's Landing and Colona Post Offices.)

1906 to 1934 - was located in the Keystone Building (still standing, adjacent to Municipal Building), then it was moved to a street level location in the then new Batchelor Building at 1026 Pennsylvania Avenue (still standing).

Jul 1, 1917 – city delivery was established. Prior to this, town residents had to go to the post office to pick up their mail, where each household/business had a "letter box" with a combination. Moon Township residents still had to go to Monaca to retrieve their mail.

Jan 16, 1928 – mounted delivery service was set up for Fourth and Fifth Wards (Monaca Heights).

Sep 8, 1928 – resolution asking the federal government to erect a modern post office was adopted since the post office was housed in a leased storeroom.

Sep 15, 1933 - The Josephtown Post Office was discontinued, then all mail was serviced in Monaca. There was no official date found of when mail began to be delivered to Center Township residents.

Apr 1961 – lot adjacent to the former George Washington School (now the fountain area) was determined as the site for the new post office building to be constructed. A local builder would construct the building and then lease it to the Post Office Department. This lease was done so taxes could still be collected on parcel since it wouldn't be owned by the government.

Apr 28, 1963 – New Post Office building was dedicated at 1015 Pennsylvania Avenue. It originally was beside the George Washington School building at that time. The former building used as the post office, as well as the school building were torn down and made into the current fountain/park area.

Aug 1998 through Feb 1999 – discussion was to build a new U.S. Postal Service Office building on property owned by the Monaca Volunteer Fire Department No. 1 along Pacific Avenue (adjacent to the railroad tracks, across from former Monaca Bowling Lanes).

Fun Fact: It is a rare sighting to currently find a free-standing metal mailbox. They were at one time plentifully located throughout all areas of Beaver County including Center Township.

The post offices in this area no longer use these boxes throughout communities and towns for the general public. They have removed almost every single one of them. The Monaca Post Office has a few of these mailboxes set up at the front of the post office building for "off hour" or more casual mail drop offs. Also, in the rear of the Monaca Post Office, there are two slightly modified versions of these boxes that the post office has set up for convenient drive-up drop off mail. If you have never noticed or seen one of these metal boxes up close, stop by and have a look.

~ ~ ~

Miscellaneous Post Offices adjacent to Moon/Center Township

Within Beaver County during the earlier years, township borders were still being adjusted and determined, including Moon Township's borders. Some of the borders involved those of Hopewell, Independence, and Raccoon. There were also other new townships being formed such as Potter Township from parts of Raccoon and Moon townships. All these factors caused residents along any one of the given sections of Moon Township that were adjacent or just close to that of other townships' borders may have been serviced by several different post offices. Some of the following post offices were listed within what eventually/actually became Sheffield, Aliquippa, Raccoon, Independence, Hopewell, and/or Potter Township. I have included some brief information on these various post offices since many of the families associated with Moon/Center Township could have been or were serviced by one of them. All the information/dates listed further were also obtained directly from records of the Postal Service early records. (See maps further.)

Note: Many of the surnames involved with these miscellaneous post offices relate to those of Moon/ Center Township residents. As you read through these, you may find some ancestors.

Parkison Post Office
This was a post office located within Raccoon/Potter Township area. Thomas Parkison was appointed postmaster Aug 18, 1841 (still postmaster in 1851); Henry Weygandt-May 15, 18__ (illegible); John R. Miller-Nov 20, 1855.

It then became the............

Potter Post Office
All mail was serviced at this post office as of Apr 15, 1859. James Potter became postmaster Apr 15, 1859.

In 1861, it once again changed and became the...................

Holt Post Office
As of Nov 2, 1861, the Holt Post Office was servicing the residents of its immediate area. The following were appointed postmasters: Samuel C. Gormely-Nov 2, 1861; John N. Dougherty-Mar 24, 18__; Jas. H. Christy-May 31, 1870; Mrs. Maria M. Christy-Dec 11, 1882 (In 1883 she is listed as receiving $52.09 salary.); Alonzo L. McMahon-Oct 25, 1888; Albert J. Lloyd-May 22, 1897; Irwin Baldwin-Apr 19, 1898; Homer J. Gormley-Aug 9, 1900. The Holt Post Office was discontinued Apr 4 or 13, 1901 with all mail then serviced through the New Sheffield Post Office. The community of Holt also had A. J. Lloyd who had a general merchandise store.

Green Garden Post Office
G. Forbes Todd was appointed postmaster Feb 25, 1863, then Michael Springer-Apr 25, 1867, who served in that position until it was discontinued. These are the only two postmasters I found who were officially appointed. The Green Garden Post Office was not discontinued until Apr 4/8, 1901, with all mail then being serviced through New Sheffield Post Office. (See Homes and Families section – Springer Family.) FYI -- In 1897, Green Garden community also had John G. Engle as Justice of the Peace and W.E. Harvey had a sawmill.

McCleary Post Office (within what became Raccoon Township)
Postmasters were David Ewing, May 27, 1858; Robert Hall, Mar 24, 1864; Robert Moore, Mar 28, 1896. This McCleary Post Office was discontinued on Apr 4 or 13, 1901, with all mail then being serviced through New Sheffield Post Office. FYI - In 1897, this small community also had W. D. Barnes/gen. blacksmith & wagon maker and Robert Moore/general merchandise store.

Service Post Office (within what became Raccoon Township)
This post office was first listed with David Reed as postmaster Aug 18, 1841. Other post masters were John Sterling-Apr 24, 1946; William Harrison-Jun 11, 1849; William Sterling in 1957; Daniel McCallister-Jun 5, 1862; James Shillito-Mar 24, 1865; John R. Littell-Mar 7, 1866; James Scott-Feb 9, 1875; Joseph Mchaffey-Apr 21, 1879; Stonewall Morgan-Nov 15, 1892; Robert L. Morgan-Apr 13, 1896; William McCague-Jun 24, 1897. This post office was closed, and all mail serviced at New Sheffield Post Office as of Apr 4, 1901. FYI - Service was a small community that also had two businesses in 1897 – W. McCague/general merchandise store and George Robinson/ undertaker.

New Sheffield Post Office
This post office had postmasters: John A Brown-Feb 15, 1849; John Wade-Jan 22, 1850; Thomas Bryan-Jul 22, 1851; John Scott-Dec 23, 1853; Samuel Boyd-Feb 2, 185_; William Calvert-Mar 17, 1864; Jno. T. Bruce-Mar 11, 1878; Wm. M. Calvert-Jan 9, 1879; Zachariah Hall-Sep 9 1885; Thomas S. Meaner-Dec 7, 1888; Wm. Calvert-Aug 13, 1889; Clarence Reed-Jul 17, 1893; Thomas Sterling-Sep 9, 1895; Wm. Calvert-Sep 23, 1897; Ellsworth Sweringen-May 5, 1902; Milton Bickett-Nov 25, 1907; John Orr-Nov 21, 1913; James M. Shaffer (Acting)-Mar 28, 1923; Mary J. Shaffer-Sep 10, 1923 (became Mrs. Kerr); Miss Jannett Orr (Acting)-Apr 1, 1925, Jannett Orr-Apr 3, 1925 (became Mrs. Todd); Wm. Bott (Acting)-Jul 10, 1934 and appointed Feb 5, 1935.
    The New Sheffield Post Office "absorbed" Seventy-Six, Service, Holt, Green Garden, McCleary, Duluth, Zeller, and Shafer Post Office when they were all discontinued in Apr 1901. The New Sheffield Post Office was discontinued Mar 18, 1938, and effective Mar 31, 1938, all mail was serviced at the Aliquippa Post Office.
    FYI - In 1897, New Sheffield also had a few familiar names as proprietors of businesses – Justice of the Peace/John Anderson; society/Ancient Order United Workmen; Dr. O.C. Engle/physician and surgeon; Erwin & Johnson/contractors & builders; Mark Maratta/dentist; Miller & Berry/merchant mills; George Sands/boot & shoemaker; D. Shafer/gen. blacksmith & wagon maker; Samuel Shafer/proprietor of hotel.

Woodlawn Post Office
I first found C. McDonald appointed a postmaster Nov 13, 1877. Other postmasters through the years were then R. W. Anderson-Oct 26, 1880; T. A. Torrence-Mar 10, 1882; Wm. Ritchie-Jun 8, 1886; James Ritchie-Jun 4, 1886; Thomas Torrence-Jul 13, 1889; John DeHaven-Apr 13, 1892; Anna Wilker-Sep 20, 1894; Mattie Ritchie-Jun 30, 1896; John Robinson-Jun 17, 1999; Jos. Irons-Jan 29, 1900; Fred Todd-Jun 11, 1902; Wm. Cochran-Jan 10, 1911; Christian Henderson-Mar 3, 1915; Robt. Simpson-Feb 7, 1922; Wilfred Troxel (Acting)-Mar 2, 1928. From 1928 through 1971, postmasters were Wilfred Troxel, Philip McNally, Mrs. Eleanor McNally (became Mrs. Hanna), Earl Cummings, Gina Piroli. Woodlawn Post Office was consolidated with and changed to Aliquippa Post Office Apr 16, 1928. FYI - In 1897, Woodlawn community had the Wilker Bros. General Merchandise Store.

Aliquippa Post Office
It appears that this Post Office first started later in 1892, with postmaster appointment of Joseph Stubert-Oct 12, 1892; followed by John Hall-Jun 11, 1897; Maggie Brown-Dec 11, 1900; Maggie Babb-May 14, 1902; Wm. Patton-Jan 10, 1903; Sarah Patton-Sep 28, 1907, Apr 29, 1908, and Apr 24, 1912; John C. Weigel-Apr 26, 1916 and Jun 5, 1920; Sarah Patton-Nov 1924. Aliquippa Post Office is still an active facility.

Duluth Post Office

This post office was in Independence Township and had appointed postmasters of John McCoy-Mar 3, 1892; John Harper-Sep 9, 1893; Thomas Nickols-Apr 4, 1894; J. M. McCoy-Jan 13, 1896; Michael Springer-Jun 24, 1897. Duluth Post Office was discontinued Apr 4, 1901, and all mail was then serviced by New Sheffield Post Office. FYI - In case you never heard of Duluth, it was a small community in the Aliquippa/Hopewell area recognized in a few directories and in 1897 had only a few businesses with proprietors -- Mrs. Mary Leech/groceries; Miller Bros./Gen. merchandise; Alexander White/Boot & Shoemaker; M.A. Springer/Gen. blacksmith & wagon maker; and White & McCully/millers of grain and feed.

Zeller Post Office

Zeller was a small community considered within Hopewell Township. It had its own post office for a few years with appointed postmasters Henry C. Zeller-Jul 29, 1891, and Mrs. Mary McCormick-Jul 20, 1892. As of Apr 4, 1901, all mail was then serviced by New Sheffield Post Office. FYI - In 1897, Zeller also had T. J. Bell as the Justice of the Peace and Clarence McCormack was proprietor of a general merchandise store.

Ethel Landing Post Office

The community of Ethel Landing was originally considered within Hopewell Township (Shipping Point, Shannopin). It had postmasters: Frank R. Morris-Jun 28, 1886; Minnie McCandlis-Aug 14, 1890; (she married) Mrs. Minnie B. Kohl-Jun 1, 1891; Miss Jennie Nye-Apr 16, 1892; Harry G. Bell-Aug 8, 189?; Hugh Wright-Oct 30, 1896; Hugh McCoy-Oct 10, 1899; Samuel Thompson-Apr 16, 1901. All mail was service through South Heights as of Feb 19, 1910.

FYI - Shannopin was an early community known for having a railroad station and a landing along the Ohio River. It was in what is currently the South Heights area. In 1897, this little-known community had organized societies, including, Independent Order of Odd Fellows and Knights of the Maccabees. There was a Justice of the Peace/E.E. Laughner, Columbus Powder Co., a hotel/D. E. Cusack, Laughner Bros./Dealers in general hardware, W. H. Musgrove & Bros/general merchandise, and W.S. Pugh/gen. blacksmith & wagon shop.

New Scottsville/Scottsville Post Office

New Scottsville was a community basically between the current Hopewell Junior High School and the Hopewell Shopping Center and included the area surrounding the current Ohio United Presbyterian Church. The appointed postmasters were George Downy-Mar 5, 1852; George Shannon–May 14, 1855; Michael Schade–Apr 24, 1856; Mrs. Elinor Green–Sep 15, 1863; James Wood–Nov 6, 1868; John McAfee–Feb 15, 1869; Samuel Shafer–Dec 1869; Daniel Shafer–Jan 25, 1870; Jno, Scott-Mar 10, 1874. This post office was discontinued on Jan 10, 1881.

Hookstown Post Office

I found a listing for this post office on Mar 20, 1818. The first postmaster listed was Joseph McGanen (no dates). Other postmasters were Jezekiel Carothers-Aug 24, 1839, Sam'l. McLaughlin-Jan 3, 1842; James Bryan-Jun 30, 194?; Edward Crail-May 15, 1849; Miss Jane Crail-Apr 7, 1852; Samuel Ferran-Dec 20, 1853; James Bryan–Feb 22, 1856; Thomas Moor-Jul 23, 1861; Mrs. Jennie Mercer–Jun 27, 1883; William Fuller-Jul 30, 1885; John Johnson-Sep 11, 1885; Robt Bryan-Feb 10, 1886; Jas Patterson-Aug 13, 1889; Robt Bryan -Mar 2, 1893; Frank Pugh-Jun 9, 1897; Frank Nelson-Feb 6, 1909; Joseph Bryan-Nov 2, 1914; Frank Nelson-Feb 26, 1919; Paul Lutton–acting 1940; Miss Olive K. Floyd-1940 and 1944. This post office also absorbed Frankfort Springs Post Office mail at the end of Nov 1900.

Seventy-Six Post Office

Postmasters included Dan'l McCallister–Jul 10, 1841; Aaron Bryan–Aug 21, 1852; David Reed-Mar 7, 1854; William Orr–Jan 28, 1862; W. F. Johnston-Feb 27, 1865; William Shannon–Jun 5, 1865; Joseph Davis-Feb 11, 1867; John S. Todd– Sep 6, 1872; G. W. Bruce–Mar 20, 1876; Wm. Shannon–Mar 4, 1878; Alexander McConnel–Jul 25, 1879. All mail was then serviced by New Sheffield as of 4 Apr 1901.

Mail Carriers

I only found a few persons who listed their occupations as mail carriers on the census. There was no indication which post office they worked with in making their deliveries. Likewise, it was not indicated "how" they made their deliveries – horse, horse and buggy, automobile.

    William Merriman – mail carrier - 1900
    Howard Anderson – mail carrier - 1910
    Melvin Cochran – mail carrier – 1920
    Harper Docktor – mail carrier – 1930, 1940
    Merle McConnell – mail carrier – 1940
    Albert Brown – mail carrier – 1940

There was also an article from 1906 in The Daily Times….
> "Ed. Meaney, Rural Free Delivery No. 3 carrier, had the rear axle of his buggy break while driving near Colona yesterday. Nothing daunted Ed, unhitched his horse and mounting the animal, finished his route."

This article did not specify exactly where or how large Ed's route was but I also found that he was known in the early 1900s as being a mail carrier in Moon Township -- remember, Monaca Heights area was considered part of Moon Township until the 1930s. (Also see Family Section for more on Ed. and the Meany family.)

~ ~ ~

Maps of early post offices.

Snippet from an 1895 Railroad map   Snippet of map showing some older post offices

These maps indicate quite a few of the previous mentioned post offices showing individual locations in proximity to each other……..Service, McCleary, Green Garden, Holt, New Sheffield, Seventy-Six, Woodlawn, Shannopin/Ethel Landing, Shafers, Bellowsville, Colona, Monaca. (Note: There is also listings for Aliquippa Park and Stobo on the 1895 RR map, but they were railroad station stops only and not Post Offices.) Neither of these above maps indicate any of the Baker's Landing post offices (see further regarding the various Baker's Landing areas).

> *Fun fact: Note on the left map above, listed below "South Monaca," there are two little known railroad stations listed. Each was developed and named by the P & LE Railroad – Kiasola and Stobo. Both stations were evidently discontinued in the very early 1900s because neither of these stations were listed on the railroad's timetables or maps after that time period.*
>
> *Kiasola was an early station on this railroad line; it was near the area where the railroad tracks cross by the confluent of Moon Run stream into the Ohio River and where Colona Avenue meets Route 51. This would place it having been within the current*

Monaca Borough. The Stobo station was located further outside Monaca, in current Center Township boundaries, in the area of where Elkhorn Run Road meets Route 51. There were originally two large tanks that were located along Route 51 and were said to be used by the trains at the Stobo Station as a water stop for their old steam engines. (See Housing Areas – Stobo/Vankirk.)

Another curious find regarding local post offices was that there were actually three being named "Baker's Landing." The only post office with the name Baker's Landing that I have information on would be the one that was located near the area of where the current Elkhorn Run Road comes out on Route 51, adjacent to Moon Run, just outside the boundaries of Monaca Borough. This Baker's Landing P.O. just outside Monaca was the only one with appointed postmasters by the U. S. Postal Service. The other two found on the next map, were not listed within any of the official postal service records.

I only found one map in an 1897 directory that had two of the three of the Baker's Landing Post Offices listed, indicating they most likely had quite short lives as post offices …

This is a section from an outline map of Beaver County, PA., by D. R. Watson, Publisher, 1898.
(I apologize for this map not being "clear" or easy to read.)

At first, I was confused in finding these additional Baker's post offices since there was a much more popular post office also called "Baker's Landing" at the opposite end of Monaca. The Baker's Landing Post Offices indicated above on the map must have only had a short history, yet were important enough or popular enough to very distinctly be marked on this older map. Neither of the two additional post offices were listed as an official post office by the U. S. Postal Service in their records from 1832 through the early 1900s. Since the map is from 1897, if these post offices would have had an officially appointed postmaster, it would have been listed in those early records.

The arrows on the previous 1898 map are indicating two of the three Baker's Landing post offices found to be within Moon Township...

- The upper left arrow (by the "M" of MOON) is pointing to a Baker's Landing P O which appears to have been located to the right of the confluence of Raccoon Creek and the Ohio River. This area would have been adjacent to or considered part of the Bellowsville area. Again, it was not listed as an official post office by the U. S. Postal Service in their records from 1832 through the early 1900s.

- The next Baker's Landing P O is indicated on the lower right side of the map, just above "CO." of ALLEGEHENY CO. This post office appears to be right on the early border line of Beaver and Allegheny counties. Just as with the above described Baker's Landing, this Baker's Landing post office was not listed as an official post office by the U. S. Postal Service in their records from 1832 through the early 1900s. As stated above, since the map is from 1897, the post office would have had an officially appointed postmaster or would have at least listed it in these early records.

- Curiously, the only Baker's Landing P O that actually was listed within the 1832 – 1900s records of the U. S. Postal Service and actually had officially approved postmasters is not indicated on this map, nor on either of the other two previous early maps. This Baker's Landing P.O. was in the area between the current Moon Run stream and Elkhorn Run Road, adjacent to the Ohio River. (See previous listed information on Baker's Landing Post Office, page 175.)

    Note: The other post offices also indicated on the previous map, include, the 76 P.O., Deluth P.O., Zellers P.O., New Scottsville P.O., Woodlawn P.O., Ethel Landing P.O (all below the word HOPEWELL); McCleary P.O., Holt P.O., and Green Garden P.O. (all above the word RACCOON).

~ ~ ~

FINANCAL INSTITUTES

Reminder – the dates below each name only indicate the dates that information was found, unless otherwise indicated, they do not represent the only dates of operation.

Colony Federal Savings & Loan Association aka **Colony Federal Savings Bank** -
1970, 1972, 1977, 1991   139 Golfview Drive
A colonial style building was constructed the first of Oct 1970, opening to the public Oct 18, 1971. Before the building was razed, it was situated on the patch of open land between the main entrance roadway to the Beaver Valley Mall and the current tall signage of "Center Point Shopping Center." This location became the main office of the institute in Jan 1984.

This institute originated from the former *Phillipsburg Building and Loan* started by 19 local businessmen in 1889 with its office in Monaca. The name was officially changed Aug 7, 1937, to *Monaca Federal Savings and Loan Association* (1937 to 1971). As of 1971 (a span of 82 years), there had only been five presidents, Felix Lay, Martin W. Carey, Paul Mattach, Alex Bucsko, and then John W. Figley. On Sep 14, 1971, the name changed again to *Colony Federal Savings and Loan Association* (1971 to 1982). The Monaca office remained at 1299 Pennsylvania Ave. from 1971 to 1982. By Jan 1984 a new building was erected in Center Township and they had moved their main offices to this new building. They merged once again with *First Federal of Erie* early in 1982 and again changed the name............*Colony First Federal Savings and Loan Association* (1982 to 1990) aka First Federal Savings and Loan Association.   By May 1990 once again the name was changed to Colony Federal Savings Bank aka Colony Savings Bank F.S.B.   Beaver Trust Company acquired Colony Savings on Oct 11, 1991 (see further).

1971

then operated as...

Beaver Trust Company – 139 Golfview Drive
Oct 11, 1991 to 1993
    changed name and became ...

First Western Bank – 139 Golfview Drive
Sep 10, 1993, 1997
    merged into and became...

Sky Bank
Aug 7, 1999 to 2007   They also had drive-in building in the BV Mall parking lot area.
    merged into and became...

Huntington National Bank
Sep 21, 2007 to current   There is an office inside the mall and a satellite/drive-to in the outer parking lot area.   (They closed their downtown Monaca Branch Office on Pennsylvania office in 2012 and sold that building.)

Century National – Beaver Valley Mall
pre-1989

Citizens Bank in 1997 - Milne Drive
current   They have a drive-in location at the Wal-Mart plaza.

C.M.P.E.A. Federal Credit Union
Opened in 1966
Was originally run from the Treasurer's home, then there was an office on Monaca Heights – both locations only had the Treasurer as the main employee. Lastly the office was moved to the Lucci Plaza on Brodhead Road. CMPEA stood for Center, Monaca, Potter, Education Association and was originally only open to these school districts' employees and their family members.
   then became…

Freedom United Federal Credit Union – was 1271, now 3589 Brodhead Road
current
This credit union was originally chartered in the fall of 1939 by the employees of the Freedom Oil Company, Freedom, PA. In Jan of 1987 the name was changed to Freedom United FCU and C.M.P.E.A. merged into the organization.

Peoples Bank of Western PA
1970 to 1995
   Was the 2nd oldest unit in the Beaver Valley Mall in 1985. Peoples was planning on opening a new office in late spring 2001 at 101 Golfview Drive. The institution itself was started Feb 26, 1934. The name changed over the years, and it became known as Peoples Home Savings.
   On Nov 13, 1995, they changed name again and became…

First Commonwealth Bank
   became…

ESB Bank
   Built an office at 3531 Brodhead Road.
   then became…

WesBanco – 3531 Brodhead Road
current

Lendmark Financial Services LLC – Walmart Plaza
current

New Alliance Federal Credit Union – 101 Golfview Drive
2006, current

Ambridge Savings and Loan Association – Beaver Valley Mall
1971, 1972

Economy Savings Association
1985

Fortune Financial Services – 3582 Brodhead Road
2019   A national financial advisory

Clearview Federal Credit Union – 210 Golfview Drive
current

The First National Bank of Monaca – 1491 Old Brodhead Road - Center Square Plaza
1965, 1967, 1970s
      The main office in Monaca opened this branch office in the Center Square plaza in the 1960s after they had erected a new building (1954) at the corner of Pennsylvania Avenue and Tenth Street. This bank office was located on the end of the building adjacent to the former Loblaw store. They also had a drive-thru added to the side of the building.
    on Sep 1, 1974 – the First National Bank of Monaca became...

The National Bank of Beaver County
1974 to 1985
    then Jul 23, 1985, was approved and merged with Century National Bank and Trust Company, Rochester, PA and became...

Century National Bank, Center Square Office
1999 to ?   They started in 1999. After this bank office closed, the space became that of Sweet Supplies.

~ ~ ~

EDUCATION

The Constitution of 1776 and that of 1790 gave cause to establish "a school or schools in every county." In Mar of 1802 and a similar law passed on Apr 4, 1809, provided for obtaining all the names of children between the ages of five and twelve years whose parents could not pay for their child's (children's) schooling. These parents were to be informed that they were at liberty to send their child (children) to the most convenient school free of any expenses. It was not until the Act of the General Assembly in Apr 1, 1834, for free common schools of the State was passed and approved, it stated that children were to be taught in English. This law also stated that the expenses of having said school(s) would be paid by having a tax apportion. The household school tax was set at $104.61 with Center Township having 232 taxable residents.

Education has always been of value to the residents of Moon/Center Township. As early as in the 1800s, Moon/Center Township had designated or built school buildings to educate the children. When these early schools were first being used, they consisted of only one large room, therefore becoming fondly known as "one-room schoolhouses". This means that all the children who qualified for first through eighth grade would be taught by one teacher, all together, in what was usually the one and only room of the school. Depending on the population of an area, there could be as few as 6 students to as many as 40 or more attending just one school.

> *Fact:* "By 1828, over half of the estimated 400,000 children between the ages of five and fifteen throughout Pennsylvania were not enrolled in any school at all."

Within a typical one-room school, the youngest children would be seated in the front of the classroom, with the oldest students sitting in the back. Reading, writing/penmanship, spelling, arithmetic, history, and geography were the subjects taught to all the students. Some teachers also taught classes called elocution which taught the students how to stand tall and use their voices effectively. These teachers felt that public speaking was an essential skill, so it was just as important for the children to receive these lessons, too. The teachers' desks were most likely at the front of the classroom, sometimes being placed on a raised platform. There would be a wood or coal burning stove located in the room for providing heat in the cold weather.

> *Fun fact:* During the one-room schoolhouse days, the Beaver County teachers' organization recommend textbooks to be used in the classrooms (1845). These included Peter Parley's *Common School History*, Mitchell's *Geographies*, Roswell C. Smith's *Grammar*, Davies' *Arithmetic*, Cobb's New Speller, and Willard's *United States History*.

The schoolhouse buildings were quite simple in their construction and the inside was furnished just as straightforward. Student desks varied greatly from just simple benches to possibly a tad fancier pieces of furniture with actual writing areas. Blackboards in most of the earlier schools were exactly as the word implies, boards painted black. They progressed in style to be made of larger, smooth, thin sheets of black or dark grey slate stone. Students in the very early years would have probably used pieces of soft limestone to write on the blackboards and a piece of sheepskin would have been used as the eraser. Calcium carbonate was also used for chalk, once it was mixed with water (and sometimes even clay) and formed into smaller sticks, then dried. Specific textbooks were not required for many of the very early schools. They used whatever books were available and those books which were shared by multiple students.

> *Fun fact:* James Pillans, headmaster and teacher in Edinburgh, Scotland is credited with inventing the first slate blackboard in 1801.

A typical school day was usually divided into many short periods. Assignments would be given to the students to keep them busy and then the teacher would call students up to her desk for them to recite different material they were to have learned. The teacher usually called the students up by their grade level – all the third graders at one time or all the sixth graders, et cetera, depending on the blend and number of students in attendance. Some teachers thought it a good idea to assure the students were actually working and would have them all read their assignment more or less to themselves, but yet slightly aloud while she worked with a specific grade level of students at her desk. Can you image how noisy this would have made that one room with so many students reading aloud?

A typical rural one room classroom. Note the stove to the left of this picture.

There was no "indoor plumbing" during the early, first schools. Everyone had to go outside and use the outhouse for their bathroom needs. Some schools only had one outhouse while others had a separate one for the girls and one for the boys. Water would be drawn from a well by using a hand pump if a school was lucky enough to have one.

The site of a school building would be decided so it would be as centrally located to a more populated area since most of the children had to walk to and from. Prior to it being approved and required to provide transportation, walking to school was the norm. Some children were lucky enough to be able to ride a horse or may get a ride in more of a taxi type horse and buggy or wagon when a neighbor could provide such a luxury for surrounding families.

A school year was similar as nowadays with students attending classes during the fall, winter, and spring. But, during the 1800s, most children (including those in Moon Township) attended school for only four or five months out of the year because the older boys (and sometimes girls) were usually needed to work on the family farms in the spring, summer, and fall, therefore only attending school during the winter months. The teacher was in charge of all the daily chores in the upkeep, cleaning, and essentials of that school. He/she would delegate students to help with these chores. Typically, an older boy would usually pump water and bring it in to be used as needed while the younger children would be assigned tasks such as cleaning the blackboards. The teacher needed to arrive early in the cold weather to start a fire in the stove.

Most of the lessons and schooling for the children involved memorization. Knowing facts and how to use them were the principal goals. A popular event in the early schools was the spelling bee. The students would line up along the wall and the teacher would give the student at the head of the line a word to spell. If the student spelled it correctly, he/she remained standing, if not the student had to sit down. This would continue through the lined-up of students until there was only one student still standing – the winner. Some teachers would have a special spelling bee at the end of the year with the families of the students being invited to attend and watch.

There were not many high schools in the majority of areas prior to WWI. Once a child 'graduated' from the one-room schoolhouse, which was fairly equivalent to eighth grade, they simply stopped attending school. There were children who wanted to continue learning, so there was a county test these children would take to see if they were ready or would qualify for more schooling. Most students that did pursue to further their education were found to qualify which confirmed that the former one-room schoolhouse teachers were doing an excellent job at molding the minds of those young people. For those students that did qualify, the task would begin to not only find a higher education school they could attend, but also finding a means of getting to and from the school along with the actual time away from home chores to attend the classes. Remember, most children were depended upon in helping maintain the homestead and/or farm.

~ ~ ~

- Prior to 1863, the school term consisted of 5 months of classes for all students.
- By 1863, the school term was increased to 6 months of classes.
- Between 1863 and 1867, the school term was increased from 6 to 7 months of classes.
- Between 1867 and 1921, the school term was increased to 7 ½ months of classes.
- For the 1922 school term, there was another increase to 8 months of classes.
- Currently there are a required amount of 180 days with at least 5 hours of classes for all school age children in Pennsylvania (900 total hours for full day classes, 450 total hours for ½ day classes). Accrued student absences may not exceed 10 total days during any school year for students attending all day classes. A school district is required to have a full school term consist of 180 total days with the additional days for teacher in-service instruction, and Act 80 Days as approved by the State.

~ ~ ~

Continuing to increase schools to accommodate an increasing population, in reviewing the results of the act of 1834, there were records found of the establishing of schools in Moon Township. Then in minute records of Apr 25, 1836, for the entire Beaver County, there were five sub-districts -- Phillipsburg, Weigle, Irons, Vankirk, and Rainbow's (but no designation of a location for any of these as far as where or which township – just Beaver County). There was also mention of a contract included in the minutes for building a new schoolhouse, just that it was within Beaver County, no district mentioned. Two more districts were recorded as being added, as well as two schoolhouses being built by the end of 1846. This report also stated that within these schools of Beaver County, both German and English languages were often taught, with two teachers frequently employed at the same school when one teacher could not teach both languages.

Moon Township definitely had their own school houses by 1843 as witnessed by finding a lengthy will and the statement………."In 1843, Joseph Alcorn, a wealthy farmer of Moon Township willed a valuable farm to the public schools of the township, the proceeds to be equally divided among the schools. The farm, by neglect, decreased so in value, that the directors sold it in 1869 for $10,000, which by judicious management brought an income of $800 per annum to the township" for the schools. (See Alcorn Family in Homes and Family section.)

Sometime in 1868, there were additional large schools built in Moon Township and there was also a tax levied for three years to cover the cost of building those schools. By 1877/1878, the report stated, "the township can boast five excellent houses, that are a credit to the county, and the schools are in a healthy condition." On Caldwell's 1876 map, there are five schools indicated throughout Moon/Center Township area. They were marked as *School House-No. 1* (Alcorn), *School House-No. 2* (Simon Field), *Bunker Hill School House* (no number), *Mount Pleasant School House-No. 4* (aka better known as the *Davis School*), and *School House* (no number listed or name, but it was in the Vankirk area).

The original school district for the township was listed either as simply *Moon School District*, but more commonly found to be *Moon Township School District*. The school district made numerous purchases of land. The first purchases were for properties and school buildings, the additional purchases appear to have been to just add some property adjacent to each of the schools. Included with each of the one room schools listed further will be the details of dates, prices paid, and from whom the properties were purchased.

~ ~ ~

MOON / CENTER TOWNSHIP SCHOOLS

One-Room School Houses

The one-room schoolhouses of Moon/Center Township serviced children as early as 1840s and into the 1940s. As previously stated, there were five of these one-room schools. In 1919, there were directives in place through the School Code that directly affected the one-room schoolhouse system. This law required school districts to begin to close any one-room school that had an annual enrollment of ten students or less, and then a district was to consolidate schools to better serve the students. Additionally, if a student had to travel more than one and a half miles to attend any consolidated school, the district was to provide free transportation.

To justify after Center Township was erected from Moon Township, all the deeds found during the selling of the five former one-room school houses in Moon/Center Township had the same statement on them --- *"The said Moon Township was subdivided in the year 1914, and that part of the said Township in which said above described land is located, became part of Center Township."*

> *Fun fact: Many of the early one room schoolhouses were built with two front doors, side by side. The Alcorn School House had such two door entrances. This provided a separate entrance for the boys and one for the girls to enter through. Also, many of the schools also followed the practice of the boys sitting on one side of the room and the girls sitting on the other.*

The one-room schoolhouses of Moon/Center Township found to exist...

Alcorn School House – corner of Brodhead Road and Marshall Road
It received its name for the Robert and Martha Alcorn family who received $5.00 in 1849 for a one-fourth acre (40 perches) lot. The original building of this school was torn down. It is tradition that the bricks from it were used to make a summer kitchen for a nearby farmhouse. The next school building was on the same one-fourth acre of land located along a lot on the corner of Brodhead and Marshall Roads. This school was one room in a frame building and then had a one room portable school building that sat adjacent to it. In May 1941, Center Township Board of Education approved to add one additional room on to the Alcorn school building and one on to the Bunker Hill School building due to increased enrollments. In 1875, the school district purchased an additional one acre and 93 perches lot from George and Eve Elizabeth Docktor for $106 to add to the quarter-acre lot of the school.

1940s/50s

2019

With the constant growth and increase in students, the Board once again had a change in their plans and instead of the proposed additions to the Alcorn School, the Board voted to begin closing the one-room schoolhouses and to move forward with the expansion of the "Consolidated Elementary" school to accommodate all students. Alcorn school had classes in the 1920s and 1930s and in 1941 there were still children grade 1 through 3 attending classes in this school. In Aug 1941, the School District advertised for accepting bids to sell off several of their one room schoolhouses, the Alcorn School and its two lots were among these schools. In Oct 1941, both lots and school building went to the highest bid of $1600, made by George and Freda Mateer.

Melvern Mackall was the teacher at Alcorn school in 1905-1906 with 55 students (see further). Mrs. Gray was one of the teachers at Alcorn School in 1927 and there were 40 students in her charge. Hope Stevenson was one of the teachers in 1938, with 61 students.

Melvern Mackall

The school was officially closed at the end of the school year in 1941. The former school building is still standing (2019) and currently houses a private family (families).

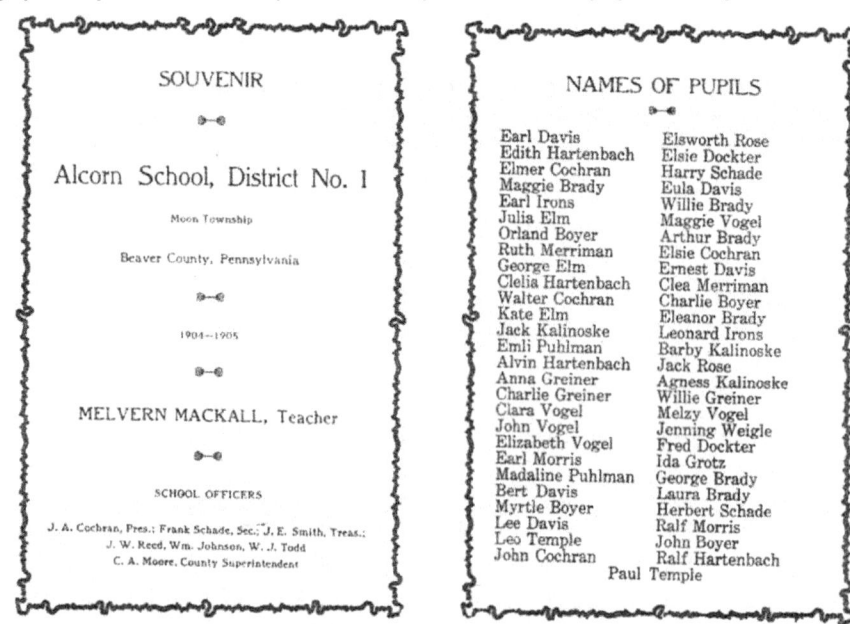

Fun fact: There is (was) a Beaver County One Room School House Association. This group of former one room schoolhouse students continued to hold reunions for many years. There are many persons alive today who attended these former one room schools in the township, but it appears that the actual Association has disbanded since I could find nothing further on it as of 2016. Alcorn School house previously held its own reunions, too.

Fun fact: It was a tradition of not only Moon/Center Township's schools, but in all rural schools, to hold a picnic the last day of school each year. Students were also allowed to take their younger brothers and sisters to school on the last day.

Simon Field School House – Brodhead Road (across from current 2 large water storage tanks).

1911 photo with bell tower still in place

c1940 photo

The Simon Field School House was built on a lot along Brodhead Road, between Snowy White Cleaners and Gentile Professional Building. The 143+ perches (.9 acres) lot was purchased from John and Elizabeth Bryan in 1876 for $80. Tradition passed down through the years states this school was built on the edge of a field that is said to have been owned by a man named Simon _?_ or _?_ Simon (thus the name of the school). I did not find anyone with a first name or surname of Simon on any early documents as living in that area, so I cannot verify this tradition. I did uncover information of the first patent on the property being of Jacob Bauseman, who sold the property to Daniel Weigel, then it went to the Bickerstaff family, then became that of Dr. Bryan (followed by McCormick/ Coombs/Smith). The only deed found with the Moon Township School District was that of the one with John Bryan being the person to deed the property for the school in Mar of 1876. Facts regarding this school that were also found included it did sit at the location as described above, it was a true one room school, and was indeed called "Simon Field School House."

Due to overcrowding in the schools, Simon Field School started half day sessions in Sep 1931. The building was still in use in 1936. Shortly after 1936, the school building and property were sold. In 1941, the lot that Dr. Bryan originally sold to the school district (143+ perches) and school building were sold to W. H. Hayes for $760. Mr. Hayes then sold all to the Coombs family in 1943. Again, there is tradition handed down that the school building itself was then sold to Jennings Weigel. The tradition continues that after most of the township schools were consolidated in 1939, Mr. Weigel began to tear down the school building, using all supplies for his own use. With there being a connection between the Coombs and Weigel families, it gives some merit to Mr. Weigel coming in possession of the school building and not the property. None the less, as of the late 1940s to the 1950s, the former school building no longer stands.

There were 21 pupils listed in the school in 1905. Ada Staub McCleary was the teacher in 1911 and C. E. Douds has been listed for being a teacher in this school at some point through the years, too.

Vankirk School House - Vankirk Road

Former VanKirk School House with the vestibule added and being used as a church.

In 1852, the Moon Township School District purchased 40 perches (1/4 acre) of property from James and Margaret McCullough for $5.00. The one room, frame Vankirk School House was erected on this property. Family lore is that the five school directors (Noble McDonald, John Stewart, Thomas Morrison, Amos Ewing, and Zack Figley) could not decide on a name for this school, but they finally decided to name it after Stephen Vankirk, the first teacher in the school. (It would also be a good guess that the whole area being known as Vankirk came from the same Vankirk family who lived in the area.)

Later, in 1871, James and Margaret McCullough also sold the school district an additional one-acre of land for $115 to be used with the schoolhouse. In this transaction it was stated that there was also free use of the "old Steedman Spring" which was close to the Vankirk School. D. D. Eberle was found to be one of the teachers of this school. The Vankirk School House had students attending Grade 1 through 8 through the years.

The school was officially closed in 1941 when the school district accepted the bid of $405.00 submitted for both properties and the former schoolhouse in Oct 1941 from the Vankirk Lutheran Church of Center Township. The residents of the Vankirk/Stobo area were starting their own

Lutheran Church and ask Rev. Charles E. Read, pastor of Monaca Redeemer Lutheran Church, if he would be interested in helping start this church. After all the details were worked out, Rev. Read was granted permission by the Center Township School Board to also use the Vankirk School. So, as of Mar 10, 1929, the church was already using the school for their services in addition to the regularly held school classes. (See Church section.) In 1939/40, the Batchelor family donated a piece of ground to the church and the congregation had planned to erect a concrete block building, but with the discussions of the one room schools possibly closing, they then decided to wait and purchase the school building they had been using. After the school closed, it was moved across the road to the donated church lot and a basement was added. A vestibule for the church was built to the front of the former school building and an addition to the original building was erected in 1970. The original, good bones of the school are still standing within the church at 106 Vankirk Road.

Bunker Hill School House – Bunker Hill Road

c 1890s

This school was built on a one-quarter acre lot. John and Mary Douds were paid $5.00 for the property in 1855. It was situated on the site of the current V.F.W. Post along Bunker Hill Road. The school district then added to the school's property by purchasing 99 ½ perches (.62 acre) from Samuel and Agnes Shaffer for $65.00 in 1874.

The first schoolhouse was destroyed by fire in the winter of 1917 but was replaced by a more modern brick building "of neat appearance and pleasant arrangement." The newer building was still a one room schoolhouse that sat on a one-fourth acre of land. In May 1941, Center Township Board of Education approved to add one room on to both the Alcorn school building and one on to this Bunker Hill School building due to increased enrollments. However, the Board changed their plans and instead of the proposed additions to either school, the Board voted to close the one room schoolhouses and move forward with the expansion of the "Consolidated Elementary" school to accommodate all students.

The Bunker Hill School House was closed and the property and former schoolhouse were sold to James A. Cochran and Thomas F. Mateer for $700. It appears Mr. Cochran and Mr. Mateer may have been representatives of the V.F.W. because the Center Township Veterans of Foreign War (V.F.W.) Post #1821 bought the brick school building and its property in 1941. The school building was then remodeled into a social hall, then it was completely torn down when the V.F.W. erected their current social hall.

Davis School House   aka   Mount Pleasant School House – on Chapel Road
John and Margaret Davis sold one-fourth acre of land to the school district for $5.00 in 1855 and the one-room, frame Davis School House was erected. The school and property originally were situated on the west side of Chapel Road, but the road was straightened, and this changed the location of the

school to be on the east side of the road. The school district then purchased an additional one acre of land for $80.00 from James Warnock in 1875 to add to the Davis School House property.

Davis School building

The school closed in 1939. The school district put both properties and the former schoolhouse up for sale. A bid in 1945 of $325.00 from the Thomas family was accepted for the one-acre lot and the bid in 1947 of $100 from T. Haffey for the quarter acre and schoolhouse was accepted. The former schoolhouse is still standing along Chapel Road and is a private resident.

The Davis School was referenced to as Mount Pleasant School House-No. 4 on Caldwell's map for some unknown reason. When the school building was referenced as Mount Pleasant by Caldwell in 1876, it was located on Chapel Road, adjacent to the Davis family farms and the William Bruce and James Forsthye properties. Mr. Caldwell's drawings show what he labeled as Mount Pleasant School, to be situated where the Davis School was located. The fact that the Davis School was NOT included anywhere else on this 1876 map, it is obvious that the Davis School and Mount Pleasant School House-No. 4 were one in the same. With these facts, it still provides no explanation as to the name "Mount Pleasant" or why/where that name would have originated. Some publications state the name of the schoolhouse was simply changed, but there are no official records of this name change. Also, with many historical records stating that in 1876 there were only 5 schools within the borders of what was to become Center Township, it reinforces there were no additional schools, so, it was either Mt Pleasant or Davis School, but not both. Another fact -- there are records stating various persons as being a teacher in the Davis School, but none state Mount Pleasant. Caldwell was only human and therefore capable of error. He may have placed or was given the incorrect name for this schoolhouse when doing this 1876 atlas. With that being said, I also cannot see such a mistake occurring since Caldwell seemed to have taken great pains to mark his maps very carefully, so.... Until there is other proof found, let's just say it may have been known as the Mt. Pleasant School, but best known as the Davis School House.

~ ~ ~

Schools located on current Monaca Heights

There were properties and at least two schools erected in this former area of Moon Township with all transactions being done by the "Moon Township School District." The current area of Monaca Heights was formerly included within Moon Township prior to being annexed to the Monaca Borough in the 1930s, therefore, the whole area would have been under that of the Moon Township School District. In mid-May of 1903, a petition was circulated among the residents of this area (now Monaca Heights) and presented to the Moon Township School District's school board asking that a new schoolhouse be erected for the children in their area. The petition stated that this school would better accommodate the children in that particular area of the growing community. The Moon Township school directors decided to open a school at that new community, then also known as Colona.

Note: Although both of the following schools were erected under the Moon Township School District in 1903 and after the annex to Monaca Boro, both eventually became part of the Monaca School District.

I will start with what became best known in later years as the Fifth Ward School.........

The old Jackson residence was in the area of what later became designated as the Fifth Ward on Monaca Heights. It was remodeled and made suitable for school purposes for the winter of 1902 and was also used in 1903 while a new school building was to be erected.

Original Colona School House
of Moon Township School District

...became the Monaca Fifth Ward School in the
Monaca School District - built in c1955/56

In 1903, this new school was built and originally called the Colona School House. It was a four-room wooden structure located by Jackson Avenue and Ridge Street (now Ridge Road) and was to originally house children in grades one and two of the area. The original property was bought for $3.00 from the Allaire Land Co. Once the area was no longer considered part of Moon or Center Township but that of Monaca Borough, this first school building was then considered that of the Monaca School District. The original school building was replaced with a new school structure shortly after 1955. This new school had two floors and eight classrooms and became known as the Fifth Ward School. Once this new building was completed, the first frame school was razed.

> *Fact: In 1912, due to a case of scarlet fever at Colona – the school was closed one Thursday and Friday to be fumigated. School / classes were resumed the following Monday.*

Now information on what became the Fourth Ward School.......

Also, in 1903, the Moon Township School District's school board purchased property in a laid-out plan of lots for $1.00 from James and Julia Welch, the land was originally owned by George Docktor. This property was in what was the Welch plan of houses. Between 1916 and the 1920s, the Moon Township School District purchased several additional adjacent lots from the Welch estate to increase the school's property. All lots were along Walnut Street and adjacent to Allen Avenue in the current Monaca Heights (then part of Moon Township). This area of the current Monaca Heights became known as the Fourth Ward.

This schoolhouse was erected in c1908
and housed students in this area of
the then Moon Township.

New Fourth Ward School building being erected,
the original school is in background.

After being annexed to Monaca and becoming part of the Monaca School District in the 1930s, it was decided to build a new Fourth Ward School on Monaca Heights in 1956 - a six-room elementary school. Monaca School District erected the new school building on the same site, behind the existing first school building, and the original schoolhouse was then razed. The new school was closed in 1992, then sold, and in 2013 was converted into and remains an apartment complex.

View of former Fourth Ward School in 2015 after conversion to an apartment complex in 2013.

Back to true Center Township schools…………

Center School aka **Central School** – Brodhead Road
This school was built in the mid 1930s, a few years prior to the *Consolidated School* being built. It served students in grades seven and eight. After the Central School was closed, it was sold and became a private home of the George Cain family. Extensive remodeling was done to the former building once it became a private home.

Fun fact: A May 1935 article in The Daily Times announced the following teachers were "elected" at the monthly meeting of the Center Township Board of Education.
*   Central School—Seventh Grade…Hazel Baumgartel of Vanport and*
*   Eighth Grade…Thomas Mansell of Hookstown*
*   Simon Field School---Mary Fischer of Beaver*
*   Bunker Hill School---Mary Rarick of New Brighton*
*   Davis School---Anna Meany of Center Township*
*   Vankirk School---Dolores Sheets of New Brighton*
*   Alcorn School- 1--Martha Sochor of Center Township*
*   Alcorn 2 --- Jessie Warden of Bridgewater.*

As the One-Room Schools were being phased out………..

Dealing with all the existing former one-room schoolhouses into the 1930's it was apparent, to comply with rulings of the State, there was a need for consolidation of the educational services in Center Township. With a local bond issue and assistance from W.P.A., Center Township was going to be constructing an eight-room building on a lot on Center Grange Road…

With the Davis School having closed earlier, the Board of Education was proposing to close the remaining four one-room schools and put the school buildings up for sale. They requested sealed bids for the four school buildings in Jan 1941. These bids must have been rejected, no acceptable bids were received, or the Board simply changed their minds because…………… In May 1941, to accommodate the increased enrollments, Center Township Board of Education approved to add an additional room on to the Alcorn school building and one additional room on to the Bunker Hill School building instead of selling. Yet, there was again a legal ad for sealed bids put in the paper in Aug 1941. With the rapid growth and constant increase in students, the Board once again made a change in their plans and instead of the proposed additions, the Board voted to close the Bunker Hill and Alcorn one-room schoolhouses and to move forward with the expansion of the "Consolidated Elementary" school to accommodate all students.

The enrollment had made a large jump of 70 more students, from 455 in 1941 to 525 in 1942, so the Board approved to hold half day sessions to accommodate all the students when the school session opened Aug 31, 1942. These half day sessions were held until steel could be purchased to complete the construction of the additional four rooms to the consolidated building. (Steel was at a premium due the demand and restrictions of the War Production Board at Washington D.C.) In the 1949-50 school term, enrollment was still climbing and was at approximately 610 students, so the half day sessions were continued for grades one, two, and three. Full day schedules were held for students in grades four through eight.

The Consolidated School – 225 Center Grange Road
(This school was later named *Center Grange Elementary* (see further).)
Jun 22, 1937 – The Center Township Board of Education held a special meeting to purchase bonds to erect a new Consolidated Elementary School on Center Grange Road. In Jul of 1937, the Center Township School District purchased four acres along Center Grange Road from the Billigen family. The Board of Directors advertised for proposals/bids in mid Sep 1938, they then met in the Simon Field School building to open said bids. Plans continued and the school was completed and opened in Oct 1939. The school building was built on the four-acre lot. E. J. Carlisle and H. P. Sharer were the architects, and the general contractors were Cook-Anderson Company of Beaver. This school was going to accommodate the students from the Bunker Hill, Simon Field, former Davis, and Central schools, with the Alcorn and Vankirk schools remaining open. During 1950 to 1954, the district also purchased other properties which brought this school's property to around thirty acres.

As of 1940, there were three school buildings in use………..The Consolidated Elementary located on Center Grange Road which housed primary to eighth grade students inclusive in its eight rooms, the one-room Vankirk School building, and the one-room Alcorn School building. By 1941, only students in grades one through seven were attending the Consolidated Elementary (there was no mention where the eighth-grade students attended.) The population of the township was in fast forward as far as growth and within a few years, the Consolidated School was overcrowded, and the eight classrooms were accommodating twice the number of students originally planned for.

In 1941/1942, an addition of classrooms to the Consolidated School on Center Grange Road was approved to be made due to the ever-increasing number of students. This decision brought an end of an era in the township's one-room schoolhouses because with this addition of classrooms, the last two one-room schoolhouses in use - Alcorn and Vankirk - were going to be closed and all students in grades one through eight would be housed in the Consolidated School. Shortly after construction began on the addition to the Consolidated School, it was hindered by the continuing shortage of needed materials caused by the war efforts. The school directors had no choice, but to go to half-day classes so all students could attend the required school sessions within the currently available classrooms. The construction supplies were not the only complications during this time period. Transportation for all students was doubled by the necessity of half-day sessions and gas usage placed providing this transportation in danger due to the gasoline shortages from the war efforts.

There was still no secondary grade level school in the township so all students at the ninth through twelfth grade levels had to choose to attended classes in Monaca or Aliquippa or another secondary school in the area until into the 1960s, provided they passed the required annual test prior to admission.

Fun Fact: Just a side note – Oct 10, 1955 - The Center Township School Board passed a resolution banning all girls attending the Center Township Consolidated School from wearing slacks and blue jeans to school.

The members of the School Board in 1939 were Richard Weigle-Pres., John H. Coombs-Vice Pres., Harry Biskup, David W. Lewis, John M. Anderson, and J. Henry Forrest. Mr. Alvin Elliott was the first principal in The Consolidated School. He maintained this position until he resigned in 1956 when he accepted a position as principal of the Kales County schools in Ohio. The former principal of the Jones School in Aliquippa, Mr. John Montini, became the principal of The Consolidated School in Oct of 1956. Mr. Montini was living in Beaver Falls at that time but had been raised in Aliquippa.

In 1958/59, John Montini was still the supervising principal, there were thirty-one teachers in the school, Mrs. Henry Antkiewica was the school nurse, Mrs. Leroy Boyer was the secretary, Mr. Thomas Haffey was the custodian and had Mrs. Mark Postlewaite and Mrs. Mary Ventresca as his assistants. Also, the school had nineteen rooms and plans were being made to add another ten classrooms. About this same time period, the School Board members consisted of Mrs. Alvin Albright-Pres., Dr. James Dorn-Vice Pres., Mrs. Charles Davies, Alvin Harper, Daniel McPeek, and Mrs. Lester Rosa-School Board Secretary.

Fun fact: The Center Township Parent Teacher Association (P.T.A.) was organized in 1949. Mrs. James Ramsey was the first president of the organization.

Fun fact: Kindergarten instruction was first discussed by school board directors in Mar 1965. It was not initiated at that time due to lack of space, and was tabled until at least 1966.

Center Grange Elementary – 225 Center Grange Road (formerly the *Consolidated Elementary*) By 1961, following the dissolution of the very short jointure/merger with Monaca Schools (see further), there was yet another ten-room addition made to this schoolhouse, formerly known as the Consolidated School. The name of the building had become Center Grange Elementary School. After the Todd Lane Elementary School was built, only kindergarten and grade one students attended classes in this elementary school.

The Center Grange building closed as a township schoolhouse at the end of the 1986/87 school year and was used by the Beaver Valley Intermediate Unit (BVIU) and other organizations for many years before the entire building was finally torn down after the new primary school was built in 2007.

Photo courtesy John Bickerton
This is a view of the front of the original Consolidate School. (An addition to this school can be seen to the extreme right of the picture.) There was also an additional wing to this school extending out from the back of the building.

This picture depicts the new front which was part of the addition to the original building. A portion of the original two-storey brick building can be seen in the upper left of this picture.

Center and Potter Schools had merged in 1971 and then known as the Center Area School District. Edward Elder, Principal of the Center Grange Elementary School at the time, presented a plan to bus approximately thirty-five students to Potter Township Elementary School beginning in

September which would help alleviate some over crowdedness. These Center students would be picked up on stops between Bechtel Street and close to the Wilhelm stops. Also, within his plan, two fourth-grade classes (estimate of fifty-four students) would attend their classes in the new Todd Lane School, while the other four fourth grade classes would stay at the Center Grange building. By using Mr. Elder's plan, it would also open a music room and a library in the Center Grange building. I could not find anything further on the acceptance or date for execution of this plan.

Mid Mar 1976, the Center Area School Board was considering "shifting" students from The Consolidate School building/Center Grange Elementary School to other buildings to help alleviate the still growing enrollment of students. The Sherwood Plan of homes was under construction in 1976 and another forty homes were being built in other existing plans which meant the estimated student enrollments would be greatly increasing once again.

Senior High School – 160 Baker Road Extension

Photo courtesy John Bickerton
View of the Junior (foreground) and Senior High Building (background) in the 1980s.

View of front entrance of Central Valley High School – 2018

With the failure of the jointure with Monaca Schools in the 1950s and the jointure's dissolution, it was decided and approved to hire architects Campbell and Green to design a new junior-senior high school building in Center Township. (See further for information on this first jointure.) As of 1960, there were approximately three hundred seventy-five secondary students from Center Township who were attending classes in Monaca, Aliquippa, Beaver, Hopewell, or Rochester. At that time, students were encouraged to choose any of these schools except Monaca only due to their already over-crowded conditions.

The State granted approval for the construction of a junior-senior high school building in the fall of 1961. The Rea Construction Company of Pittsburgh started work in early spring of 1962. This new school would be home to students in grades seven through twelve. The original plot of land totaled close to 50 ½ acres of land deeded to the school district by widow Grace Stepp in Sep 1960. This same property was conveyed to Jacob Stepp by deed of Jacob Vogel in 1946. The school district's only other larger purchase of land for the campus was in 1997, with about 11.5 acres. This acreage was adjacent to the tennis court area and purchased from John and Thelma Caputo, previously being part of the former Jacob Vogel farm. The new school was constructed in a "U" shape with the bulk of the basic classrooms being in the two wing extensions.

The first graduating class of this new school was in 1965. I did not research the date when the first graduating ceremony was held in the CCBC Dome, but by c1976 they were being held at CCBC instead of in the high school's auditorium.

Following the latest merger with Monaca School District, the entire former senior and junior high school complex currently houses students nine through twelve and is considered the Central Valley High School, part of Central Valley School District.

Junior High School - adjoined with the former Senior High building by a long hallway.

By 1965, it was apparent that there was a need for even more classrooms to accommodate the very quickly growing number of school age students in the township. It was approved by the Center School Board and the State to construct an addition to the fairly new secondary building. This addition was under construction in 1967 and completed by 1968. It was not only adjacent to the current junior-senior high school but was built to mimic the "U" shape. The addition of the two full wings and other facilities was connected to the original junior-senior high school by a long, enclosed hallway. One full wing of the addition was completed and open for classes the beginning of the 1967-68 school year and the second wing and other areas were completed by the following year. Once completed, this addition, as stated, consisted of matching double wings to that of the secondary school building, excepting one wing consisted of just one level and the second wing was two-storey.

With this addition to the then current junior-senior high school building, realignment of students would be --- Center Grange Elementary would house grades one through three, the new addition adjacent to the secondary school building would house grades four through six, and the current junior-senior high school would house grades seven through twelve.

This addition to the secondary building soon officially became the Center Junior High School and home to students in grades six through eighth grade with the name eventually being changed to Center Middle School. It continued to house these grade levels of students until the latest merger of the Monaca and Center school districts. The building now serves as part of / an extension to the Central Valley Senior High School building for students in grades nine through twelve.

Todd Lane Elementary – 113 Todd Lane

Photo courtesy John Bickerton
The Todd Lane School from 1971 through 2017

Renovated look of 2018/19

This school building was constructed in 1971. Also, in 1971, the Center Schools and Potter Schools had a merger (see further). This new elementary building was to accommodate students in grades four through six, but instead only housed students up to the fifth-grade level with the sixth graders being housed in the newer junior/middle school building. The land and campus for this school was purchased through a few transactions in 1969 and 1970, consisting of former properties of a few families – Preece, Huffmyer, and Brobeck.

Since this elementary school was built to accommodate the "pod concept" there were very large classroom areas throughout the building, each having sliding, accordion type doors to sub divide if needed. As this concept was phased out, the school went through several renovations to eliminate the large classrooms' areas and create more traditional sized classrooms. The school had another renovation and updates done in 1995. The latest updates and major renovations were done in 2018 which included changing the look of the outside of the building, too. The school is now part of Central Valley School District and retained the name Todd Lane Elementary School. It currently houses grades three through five children.

Center Grange Primary School – Center Grange Road

Once again, it was determined that the increase in the number of school age students in the township facilitated another school to be built. The site for this new primary/elementary school was decided upon - located adjacent to the site of the older Center Grange Elementary building. This new primary school was erected in 2007. Within a few years of its completion came the latest merger of the Monaca and Center Area school district. This school is currently used as the Primary Building of Central Valley Schools for students in Kindergarten through Grade 2.

~ ~ ~

Fun fact: Center School District began formulating plans of adding kindergarten classes to the curriculum in 1965. These plans were not carried out at that time due to the limitation on classroom space, but kept in the planning stages with hopes of implimenting by the 1966 school year.

~ ~ ~

Fun photo:

This is a 1944/45 (during war times) picture of the teachers and principal in front of The Consolidated School (later renamed Center Elementary School). There were ½ day sessions at this time.
Left to right.....BACK ROW: unidentified; unidentified; Miss Charolette Cain (?); James Lindey; Alvin Elliott-Principal; John Paine; Mrs. Louise (Mercer) Wright; Mrs. Margaret Davis; Mrs. Alice Gordon Peterson.
FRONT ROW: Mrs. Nancy (Jarrett) Est; Mrs. Elizabeth Strother; Mrs. Nancy (Coombs) Lyons; Mrs. Rachel (Cauffe) Shupe; Mrs. Isabel Overholt(?); Mrs. Katherine Hallman; Mrs. Virginia (Douds) Floyd-Secty; unidentified

Jointures / Mergers

There was a little known or forgotten jointure between Center Area and Monaca school districts prior to the most recent 2009 Central Valley School District being formed. That first jointure occurred in 1957 (see further). Even earlier than the 1957 jointure, almost one hundred years earlier, there was a form of a jointure, well more of a "sharing" of schools, between the Moon Township School District and the Phillipsburg School District.......

In 1864, a school that had been built on a triangular lot in Phillipsburg located between Lacock Street (now Sixth Street), Third Street (now Washington Avenue), and Garden Street (now Fifth Street) was to be shared by Phillipsburg and Moon Township school districts. The lot was to be known as "the school lot" where English and German would be taught. The building that was built in Phillipsburg on this triangle shaped lot was known as "The Ark." The Moon Township School District School Directors paid $1.00 and were represented by Robert Nevin, John Hood, David Mesner, Jos. Kronk, Morton Baker, and Wm. Baker. The representatives for the Phillipsburg School District were Jacob Schaffer, Jacob Strawbacker, and Augustus Smith.

> *Fun facts regarding "The Ark":*
> *Prior to the school building known as "The Ark"..........When the New Philadelphia Society was still in Phillipsburg, there was a little red brick school house built to educate the children. It was erected on the above described triangular shaped lot. It was built in 1840 and had been torn down in 1884. Then there was another frame building erected on this lot between 1840 and 1850 and it was known through the years as "The Ark." Records indicate it was painted white with green shutters on the windows. The curriculum taught in The Ark consisted of instruction in reading, writing, and arithmetic, along with English and German. Although the other red brick building was torn down in 1884, The Ark survived much longer. When the First Ward School was built, The Ark was purchased by Rev. W. G. Taylor and was moved to property on the low 900s on Pennsylvania Avenue where it was set up and used as the public hall. After the first brick building was torn down and The Ark was moved, there was a beautiful large gazebo built on the triangular "school lot." Through the years, The Ark building was used as a school, once it was moved to Pennsylvania Avenue it was used as the town hall, then used by the Presbyterian Church, and then used as a restaurant and residency. It was purchased along with an adjacent vacant lot by Louis Stoll and was torn down for him to build a new theatre building in 1926.*

The little known or forgotten Jointure of 1957

As stated, the most recent 2009 jointure of the former Monaca and the Center Area school districts was not the first to occur between these two districts....

In the early 1950s, the Pennsylvania Department of Public Instruction gave direction to the various counties to begin making plans to reorganize their districts with mergers and/or jointures where possible. In 1953, the Beaver County Board chose the plan for Center Township and Potter Township school districts to form a jointure. The state was dissatisfied with this plan of action so instead, a new plan was developed for Center Township, Potter Township, and Monaca school districts to form one district (Administrative Unit Number XII). This newest plan was calling for one elementary school in Potter Township, four elementary schools in Monaca, and two elementary schools in Center Township. There was to be only one secondary grade school for students in grades seven through twelve, with the location of this school to be decided upon and agreed upon by all three former districts. The location of this secondary school had to be centrally located to all students and had to be agreed upon by all three districts, which eventually became the downfall of this jointure.

Center's School Board voted to include and form the school jointure with Monaca on May 5, 1956. In Jul 1958 the jointure was formed with the newly formed district being known as Monaca

Area School District and some references stated it as Monaca Area Joint Schools. The name of "Monaca" being in the name did not designate the former school district of Monaca but was instead the chosen name since all three districts had the post office address of "Monaca." Almost immediately after the approval was given for this jointure, plans began to be ironed out and specifics and details were being discussed, especially regarding the site of where the new jointure's secondary school was going to be built.

Here is how this first jointure played out.

1957 – The Monaca, Center, and Potter school districts formed a jointure in compliance with the State Department of Public Instructions promotion of overall reduction in the number of school districts in the Commonwealth.

The 1957 jointure was fair. The agreement provided that each community paid for every student in the jointure according to enrollment. This meant, if Center Township had more students in the schools, it paid more, if Monaca had more, it paid more, and the same with Potter. Dr. Harry Fink was the supervising principal during this jointure. Again, some information stated it was known as the Monaca Area School District while others state it as being named Monaca Area Joint Schools. If for some reason this combining of schools would have been a *merger*, it would have been the fifth union school district and would be governed by one school board and financed under one tax structure, **but** with no official merger approved, it continued to operate under the present *jointure* system set up. This meant that each district was represented accordingly on the governing School Board.

1957 - The new six-room Fourth Ward Elementary Building was completed (to house 180 students).

1958 – At the polls in November, the voters of Monaca rejected changing the merger to a jointure by a vote of 1799 to 1119, while on the other hand, the voters in Center Township voted 1180 to 453 to approve accepting a jointure to a merger. Members of the joint board formed by this merger all favored the union district proposal, two of the members opposed holding referendum on the issue in Oct 1958. It was still a *jointure* at that time.

Integration of Center Township elementary students into Monaca elementary schools was started in 1958 for the first time. This allowed Center Township students to have a full day of classes for the first time in many years. There were at least three elementary schools in Monaca that the Center students were attending.

The newly formed Monaca Area School District/Monaca Area Joint Schools chose an architect for the new secondary level school, the next task was to choose a suitable and agreed upon site for the building. There were several choices proposed:

- 42 acres on the property owned by the Stone Quarry Club in Monaca. It was located a little over 1 ½ miles from the center of the new district's population. The cost was $130,000.
- 50.12 acres – the Stepp farm in Center Township. It was located 6/10 of a mile from the center of the new district's population. The cost was to be $93,000.
- 94.5 acres of property owned by the Mancini family in Center Township. This property was also 6/10 of a mile from the center of the new district's population. The cost was to be $79,000.
- 101.29 acres on property owned by St. Joseph Lead Company in Center Township. It was located 1.3 miles from the center of the new district's population. The cost - $65,000.
- The site of the current Stephen Philips Homes on Monaca Heights.

1959 – The new Monaca Area School District/Monaca Area Joint Schools's board voted and approved to choose the 94.5-acre Mancini property as the site of the new secondary school. With this site being located in Center Township, it meant that Monaca's secondary grade level children would have to be bussed each day to the school. Many of the Monaca residents did not approve of their children being bussed out of Monaca to Center Township.

The oppositions continued and the newly formed district decided to totally reject all plans and properties and presented a new plan of action. The new plan was to erect a senior high school (for grades nine to twelve) on an 8-acre plot of Mateer property which was located just outside the Monaca Borough limits in Center Township (along Marshal Road). A junior high school would then be created in Monaca by possibly renovating the George Washington school or to renovate and use the former senior high school, both these buildings being in downtown Monaca.

The members of the new board of the Monaca Area Joint Schools / Monaca Area School District were finding it increasingly difficult to work together to resolve issues with the jointure. The discord between the members of this board was leading all to consider dissolution of the jointure entirely.

1960 – There were fifteen total members of the joint board from Monaca and Center. I only found fourteen names of these members which included Alvin Harper, Francis Duvall, David Figley, Daniel McPeek, Dr. S. James Dorn, L. S. Patton, Mrs. Velma Albright, Mrs. Helen Davies, Ralph Viola, Dr. David C. Benninghof, Robert J. Pritchard, Fred Geusen, Dr. William G. Milliron, and Mitchel Thomas.

The 8-acre Mateer site was not approved by the State due to its size (they recommended at least 40 acres for a suburban setting) and the fact that there were gas utility lines that crossed through the property. The board's most current plans at that time called for construction of a senior high school adequate to house 900 students in grades 10-12. The architects, however, disagreed with the State, and felt the Mateer site was quite adequate for the type of school needed to fill these needs.

As of Apr 1960, the joint district was also now expecting and discussing building a junior high school on the Steppe farm property in Center Township for 590 students. There would also be renovations done to the then senior high school building in downtown Monaca to accommodate 450 junior high students which would allow the present junior high building in Monaca to be used for elementary classes.

Also, in Apr 1960, a letter was submitted to the Bureau of School Buildings stating that it was feared by all concerned that if an agreement was not reached on a site acceptable to all the recognized school districts of the jointure, that the jointure itself would be in jeopardy. The letter went on to state "Our schools are becoming overcrowded and soon we will have to go on half-day sessions or tuition a large number of students at a much higher cost than under local education and receive a correspondingly less amount of state aid." It also stated that "it could be argued that the site (Mateer) is not a suburban site—but urban, since its general location is well within the center of population of the joint district."

One last attempt to save the jointure was made in May of 1960 when it was proposed to put the choosing of the site of where to build the high school on the ballot for the public to vote. This motion did not pass at the joint board's meeting. As a result of all the conflicts and discord, this jointure only lasted officially until Jun 30, 1960, when it was voted on by the joint board to dissolve it because neither side could agree on the site for a new high school and the state had rejected other sites. Therefore, all three districts went back to being separate districts and Monaca chose a site and built their own high school building with Center Township taking the same action. Although Monaca was left to stand alone once out of the jointure, Center still had the possibility of merging with Potter and becoming partners (see further).

In Mar of 1965, there was still referencing and discussion of a decree by the State Board of Education for another possible merger involving Monaca and Potter Township, obviously this forced merger never matured.

Merger - 1971
In 1971, Potter Township Schools merged with Center Township Schools. With this merger, the Potter Township School District and Center Township School District became known as the Center Area School District. Even before this 1971 merger, the Potter Township Elementary School at 612 Frankfort Road, had been used to provide classes for some of the Center Township students up to grade six. The designated Center students were bussed to the Potter Elementary School in the late 1950s and early 1960s for classes.

Because of this 1971 merger, all Potter Township students were then part of the Center Area School District and were automatically included in the latest, voluntary merger between Monaca and Center Schools in 2009.

Most recent Merger - 2009

Once again, the Monaca and Center schools engaged in joining up to form a new school district. This time it was a voluntary merger and the State gave its seal of approval. Working out all the details of this voluntary merger seemed to progress very much smoother than the first attempt to join the two districts. Center Area School District and Monaca Area School District are now known as...

Central Valley School District

2007 – In the fall of 2007, the Center Area and Monaca school boards both approved resolutions to complete a historic and voluntary merger of their districts. It is the first voluntary merger of school districts in Pennsylvania.

2009 - The Monaca Area School District and Center Area School Districts voluntary merger was complete and the new name of the school district became Central Valley School District.

As of 2019, the merger proves to have gone smoothing and continues to do very well.

The current Central Valley School District's school buildings (2019) are:
- The former Center High and Middle School complex at 160 Baker Road Extension is now the **Central Valley Senior High School** with students in grades nine through twelve.
- The former Monaca High School building at 1500 Allen Avenue is now the **Central Valley Middle School** for students in grades six, seven, and eight.
- The Todd Lane Elementary School building at 113 Todd Lane is now still named **Todd Lane Elementary** with students in grades three, four, and five.
- The **Center Grange Primary School** at 225 Center Grange Road retained its name and is for students in kindergarten, first, and second grade.

Mascots

Prior to the 2009 jointure,

    Monaca Schools were known as the Indians.
    The former school colors were red and blue.

A full colored mosaic tile Indian portrait formerly appeared on the Monaca Junior High School building.

Center Township School District was formerly known as the Trojans.
The former school colors were Royal Blue and Silver Grey.

Following the merger in 2009,
    The new mascot for the Central Valley Schools became the Warriors.
    The new school colors are Carolina Blue and Navy Blue.

~ ~ ~

CENTER ALUMNI HALL OF FAME
Center Area School District
2002 - 2015

Center Alumni Hall of Fame and its original committee began in 2002 with the goal "to honor the many graduates who have distinguished themselves in their workplace and communities, while upholding their standards of character." Though not listed, let it be known that there is an endless list of CHS graduates who have given back quite a bit to their community, have made grand achievements, and have had success and been outstanding in his or her chosen field of endeavors.

2003
- Julie Bologna (1990)
- Alvin J. Harper (1976)
- Dr. Gianni (Nan) DeVincent Hayes (1967)
- Reverend Philip Kanfush, OSB (1980)
- Major John W. Macroglou (1967)
- Mark Vlasic (1982)
- Dr. Suzanne Vogel-Scibilia (1977)
- Millicent White (1988)

2004
- Daniel M. D'Antonio (1973)
- Edward DeChellis (1977)
- Bill Gentile (1969)
- Alex J. Gladis (1970)
- Richard J. Gradisek (1973)
- Joseph Letteri (1975)
- Sandra Reigel (1978)
- Bob Trimble (1975)

2005
- Dr. Eugene A. Bonaroti (1982)
- Glenda M. (Swink) Christy (1966)
- Lauren Lynn Miller (1988)
- Daniel Radakovich (1976)
- Dr. Vincent J. Taormina (1970)
- John E. Tate (1973)
- Reverend Steven F. Vesolich (1965)
- Dr. Kristen Zvonar (1988)

2006
- Jeffrey G. Druzak (1979)
- David J. Dzumba (1977)
- Colonel Scott E. Gilson (1980)
- Pamela L. Hart (1982)
- Colonel Edward Lucci, M.D. (1979)
- Corporal Joseph R. Pokorny, Jr. (1978)
- Joan E. Yasolsky (1981)
- Captain Ronald W. Zaperach (1970)

2007
- Carla Bianco (1987)
- Elena Gutierrez-Farewik, Ph.D. (1991)
- Jack D. Hayes, Lt.Col. USAF (1976)
- Meghan Majorowski (1993)
- Karen Michael (1979)
- Nicholas Pesut, V.M.D. (1969)
- Phillip E. Savage, Ph.D. (1978)
- Walter "Skip" Sylvester (1977)

2008
- Albert (Rich) DeFilippi (1974)
- Donna Leasha George (1974)
- David L. Hodge (1978)
- Joseph J. Klimchak III (1987)
- Tai H. Park (1979)
- Linda Hayes Tischler (1966)
- Rade B. Vukmir, MD, JD (1977)
- Kiesha Lalama-White (1991)

2009
- Andrea Mackowick Bartko, Esq. (1980)
- Michele Bendekovic (1986)
- Charles J. Betters (1967)
- Edward Currie, Ph.D. (1967)
- Daniel DiCola, M.D. (1970)
- Larry D. Lucci (1976)
- Dr. Michael Sisk (1979)
- Michael G. Zeglinski (1984)

2010
- Keith A. Christenson (1973)
- Joseph D'Alessandris (1972)
- Michael Funk (1989)
- Richard M. Lipscomb, Jr., D.D.S. (1985)
- Mark D. Miller (1975)
- Stephen Morris, Ph.D. (1979)
- Michael Sirko (1971)
- Beverly L. Szedny Pietrandrea (1978)

2011
- Dan Girata (1975)
- Tom Hays (1976)
- Donna Manojlovich Belich (1965)
- Michael Nalli, Esq. (1991)
- Joseph O'Neill (1967)
- Carl Sestito, M.D. (1983)
- Jan Ujevich Bellhy (1979)
- George "Butch" Zatezalo (1966)

2012
- Tony Amadio (1969)
- Nicole A. Ceravolo Begg (1990)
- Stephen D. Colafella (1988)
- William J. Greer (1990)
- Cynthia Kotun (1973)
- Eric R. Lechman (1987)
- Darrin Taormina (1983)
- Daniel C. Young (1984)

2013
- Alexander Andres (1982)
- Nicola A. Francalancia, MD (1974)
- LeeAnn Kutzko Ranieri, DNP (1972)
- Larry Milosh (1972)
- Jeffrey Paladina (1990)
- Donna Prosper DeFilippi (1974)
- Joseph Stiefel, PhD (1990)

2014
- Dr. Daniel Castagna (1994)
- Stephen Christian (1974)
- Brent Darroch (1995)
- Kristi DeMaiolo Harper (1986)
- David Dudo (1988)
- David McClintic (1994)
- Charles Richardson, Ph.D. (1969)
- Dr. Janet Todorczuk (1973)

2015
- Meagan Aaron (1994)
- James Cochran (1977)
- Jonathan Dohanich, DVM (1996)
- Mike Rossi (1977)
- Michael Siget (1994)
- Deborah Speer Hess (1968)
- Rev. Alyce Weaver Dunn (1980)

Miscellaneous educational information...

The General Assembly developed and passed an act in 1854. This established the office of County Superintendent of Common Schools and required a central administrative officer be in place in each county. There was a succession of well chosen men who filled the position of County Superintendent of all the schools in Beaver County. This officer was required to also administer high school examinations to any and all students who chose to further their education once they finished their one-room school learning. In 1923, there were places in Aliquippa and Monaca where students would be administered this test. This same year, nineteen Moon Township students took this test and all passed.

Each of these Beaver County Superintendents had to submit a report that was published in the *"Report of the Superintendent of Common Schools of the Commonwealth of Pennsylvania, Department of Public Instruction."* I did not secure any one publications that listed all the past County Superintendents but I did come across some of their names in my research. Although this list is not exclusively of residents of Moon/Center Township, I chose to list those names that were found for general interest. (This is only a partial list.)

1855 - Thomas Nicholson of Frankfort Springs - he was the first county superintendent for Beaver County; he died in 1872.

1855-1856 – George Cope – he was appointed to fill the unexpired term of Thomas Nicholson.

1856-1857 – Scudder Hart Piersol of West Bridgewater

1857-1858 – R. N. Avery

1858-1863 – Thomas Carothers – he was appointed in 1858 to fill the unexpired term of R. N. Avery

1863-1867 – J. I. Reed - In his reports to the Superintendent of Common Schools of the Commonwealth of Pennsylvania, he reported 5 schools in Moon Township, average number of months school was taught – 4, there were 4 male teachers and 1 female teacher- all with an average salary of $37, and there were 154 male students and 107 females. During his term, the schools listed as providing auxiliaries in furthering education to students of Moon Township were Beaver Academy, Beaver Female seminary, Prof. A. H. Calvert's select schools at Hookstown and New Sheffield, the Union schools of New Brighton, Rochester, Bridgewater, Beaver, Freedom, and the North-Western Normal school at Edinboro. He also made the suggestions of 1) further increase of the State appropriation, 2) the minimum school term be increased to six or seven months, 3) the number of school directors be reduced to three and they should be paid for their labor.

1867-1869 – James Whitham of Murdocksville – was appointed to fill the unexpired portion of J. I Reed's second term

1869-1872 – G. M. Fields

1872-1875 – M. L. Knight – In his 1874 report, he stated there were two new and substantial houses built in Moon Township. There were 5 schools with an average of 5 months of school taught. There were 5 male teachers with average salaries of $40 and 140 male students, 101 female students. Beaver County was also stated as one of the wealthiest in the State within the total report, not just Mr. Knight's information.

1875-1881 – Benjamin Franklin of Industry, PA – served six years total

1881-1884 – J. S. Briggs – re-elected in May 1884, but resigned Sept 1, 1884

1884 - James M. Reed of Beaver – filled Briggs's vacancy, served two years and nine months (He made it his rule to visit every school in the county at least once a year.)

1887-1890 – James M. Reed – he resigned, effective Jan 1, 1890

1890-1896 - John G. Hillman, first he finished J. M. Reed's term, then was elected in May 1890 and re-elected in 1893

1896-1905 – Chester A. Moore – elected 1896, re-elected 1899 and 1902

1909-1921 – D. C. Locke

1966 - Dr. H. C. Elder

Though not included on any of the official lists I did find, there was mention of H. N. W. Hoyt of New Brighton (unknown term) and of E. D. Davidson of Center in at least 1939.

Fun fact: The adopted early 1800 school law provided for the election of directors in each school district within Beaver County. Robert Nevin of Moon Township was one of the persons, he was elected to this position in 1834.

Supervisory Positions

Though not an inclusive list, some of the supervisory positions held in the Moon Township schools through the earlier years included...

School Directors

1851/52	Moon Township School District.....Wilson Uselton, Daniel Springer, Jacob Noss, Daniel Short, Thomas McCoy, Andrew McCullough, William Elliott, Thomas Ayres
1864	Moon Township School District .....Robert Nevin, John Hood, David Mesner, Joseph Kronk, Morton Baker, William Baker
1876	Moon Township School District .....Geo. Shroades, John Wilhelm, Geo. Fath, Daniel C. Bruce, John McCullough, John Shafer
1897	Moon Township School District .....Pres.-James S. Calvert, Secy-Henry Davis, Members-Noble McDonald, Frederick Erb, D. B. Short, and J. P. Cooper
1897	Independent School District (Bellowsville).....Pres.-Walter S. Dunn, Secy-John C. Dunn, Jr., and members F. J. Flocker and George Wallace.
1898	Moon Independent School District.....Pres.-Walter S. Dunn, Sec'y-John C. Dunn, Jr., F. J. Flocker, George Wallace, Bellowsville
1903	Moon Township School District .....James Cochran, John P. Cooper, Frank S. Schade, James Todd, George Mateer, John Barto
1904-1905	Moon Township school board included A.A. Cochran-Pres., Frank Schade-Secy, J. E. Smith-Treas, J. W. Reed, William Johnson, and T. J. Todd

In the early 1900s, John P. Cooper was listed as serving as a member of the school board for nine years. James Davis was listed as a member of the school board for five years.

In Nov of 1914, when Judge Holt decreed the erection of Center Township from Moon Township, Center was to have its own school district, separate from the schools located on the portion of Moon that is now known as Monaca Heights. Center's school district was designated to be of the fourth class and the following school directors were appointed, Anderson Davidson, Armstrong Gorsuch, William Kugel, John Cooper, J. A. Patterson.

Fun fact: The Beaver County School Directors' Association was started in 1904.

Fun fact: Woodrow Aaron served as a School Director for at least 10 years.

Some other and/or more recent Center School District administrators
- Alvin Elliot – School Principal beginning in 1940s and 1950s
- John W. Montini – 1960-1967 - Elementary Supervisor and Elementary Principal
- Dr. Harry E. Fink – prior to 1967-Supervising Principal; beginning 1967/68-Superintendent of Center Schools
- Donald Bradshaw – beginning 1967 – Director of Elementary Education and then Superintendent
- Rudy Gradisek – beginning 1969 –High School Principal, also served as Secondary Director of Education, and then Superintendent
- Dr. Victory Morrone – beginning 1984 – Superintendent
- Edward Elder – beginning 1969 – Elementary Principal and later, Superintendent
- John Zigerelli – beginning 1967 – Elementary Principal
- Philip M. Kanfush, Jr. – beginning 1969 – High School Principal
- Ronald DeBacco – Assistant High School Principal
- Samuel Gagliardi – Assistant High School Principal and then Middle/Junior High School Principal
- Michael McCullough – became Assistant High School Principal; then Assistant Superintendent; in 2002 he was assigned a dual duty of Assistant Superintendent and of Middle School Principal.

As of 2017/18, the Central Valley School District Administration consists of Dr. Nicholas Perry-Superintendent, Shawn McCreary-High School Principal, Mark Vukovcan-High School Assistant Principal, Brian Dolph-Middle School Principal, Christina Feragotti-Middle School Assistant Principal, Kelly Sherbondy-Todd Lane Elem. School Principal, and Carla Kosanovich-Center Grange Principal.

The 2017/18 Central Valley School District School Board: Thomas Mowad-Board President, George Zaritski-Board Vice-President, Thomas King-Board Treasurer, and Board members, David Ambrose, Donna Belcastro, Dennis Bloom, Joseph O'Neill, Nicholas Unis, Dante Ross.

~ ~ ~

Fact: As with most Beaver County schools, student enrollments of Center Schools also showed a decline starting with the 1970s.

Fact: The Daily Times – Jun 1940 stated, "The states of Pennsylvania and Utah have protective legislature safeguarding public school teachers from dismissal for religious or political views.

~ ~ ~

Teachers

Prior to 1820, Thomas Murray and David Blair taught in New Sheffield and vicinity; Thomas Bryan taught near Service; John Murray, Robert Moffit, and Miss Mary Davis taught in the central and eastern sections of the south side of the county. On the west side of the south-side section were Alexander McCollough, George McCollough, Elizabeth McCollough, Paden Moore, John P. Hudson, Aaron Eaton, Matthew Anderson, Hon. John H. Reddick, and Samuel Pollock.

Fact: Records from the mid 1920s show that the annual average salary of a teacher in Moon Township was estimated to be $723.

Between 1840 and 1940, there were several individuals listed in various records and/or on the census enumerations as being a teacher. Some have a general time period of when they were teaching. All that were found on the census sheets have the year of the census listed. If known, their ages are included in parenthesis.

- James McCormick – 1840s, 1850s
- John McCormick – 1860s
- John R. Alcorn – 1850 (22)
- Samuel Burneson – 1860 (33)
- Alice Elder – 1870 (21)
- Jacob Blume – 1880 (20)
- George Douds – 1880 (22)
- George McDonald – 1880 (24)
- Blanche LeGoullon – late 1800s, 1900s
- James M. "J M" Phillis – 1800s
- John R. Mateer – 1900 (23)
- James Springer – 1900 (25)
- Ada Staub – 1910 (22)
- Dorothy Irwin – 1920 (19)
- Ada Staub – 1920 (31)
- Loualine Preece – 1930 (26), 1940 (36)
- Charity Goll – 1940
- Lori Wilt – 1940
- Charity Black – 1940 – art teacher
- James Mateer – 1940
- Samuel McCormick – 1860s
- William VanKirk – 1850 (29)
- Henry Zimmerly – 1860 (22)
- John Zimmerly – 1870 (29)
- Homer Bryan – 1870 (teacher, then became a doctor)
- Oliver Engle – 1880 (22)
- Homer Bryan – 1880 (22)
- Margaret Davis – late 1800s
- John R. Mateer – late 1800s
- James M. Shafer – late 1800s-1900s
- John Springer – 1900 (31)
- Herbert Glasser – 1910 (19)
- Marie Irwin – 1920 (21)
- Alta Weigle – 1920 (19)
- Mary Cooper – 1930 (22)
- Virginia Reed – 1940
- Dorothy Herbeck – 1940
- Iris Wilt – 1940
- Stanley Berkman – 1940
- Esther (Brown) Mateer – 1900s

~ ~ ~

As mentioned quite a few times, many aspects of Potter and Moon/Center Township have meshed during the course of time, add to the mix that when Potter was formed from a portion of Moon Township, the original boundaries of these townships were sometimes quite "gray." In fact, even nowadays, when you travel between Center and Potter on the many secondary roads, it is still difficult to sometimes distinguish exactly where the boundaries of each township may be. Another connection between these two townships was with the schools, so.........

With all that being said, this is why I chose to also include a brief history of the schoolhouses of Potter Township. Some of the one room school buildings may have never had any Moon/Center students in attendance, while others absolutely did service some of these children.

Potter Township Schools

Schools in Potter Township were organized long before Potter Township itself was formed in 1912. Unfortunately, it has been found that there is not too much written history of the schools until after Potter Township was incorporated. In addition to being listed as Moon Township School District in the 1800s, some very early references to the schools in the Bellowsville Area of Potter Township were either as "Independent School District of Moon Township" or "Common Schools, Moon Township."

Shortly after the erection of Potter Township and prior to the merger with Center Schools, Potter had its own School Board and a Potter Township PTA. The Potter Township Parent-Teacher Association was organized Aug 15, 1949. This group was instrumental in many functions of the schools over the years. During their first year of organization, mothers volunteered and worked in the Potter Township and Kobuta schools to serve hot soup each day. When the new twelve classroom Potter School opened a cafeteria within the school, the P.T.A. purchased the juice glasses, water glasses, sherbet maker, and salad maker. They also purchased and planted the trees and shrubbery around the new school.

Potter #1 or Independent School – along Frankfort Road

Courtesy Richard Temple

This picture was taken on Oct 2, 1901, at the Independent School, Bellowsville.
Pictured: Miss Mary McKoan-teacher, Rebecca Douds, Gula Baker, and Thomas Flocker.
Miss Clara Frank also taught in the Independent School. She had her home in Monaca.
Note the two doors – one for the boys to use, one for the girls.

Prior to 1852, the Common Schools, Moon Township District had erected a schoolhouse on land belonging to William Irwin. In 1852, for $5.00, William Irwin's widow, Sarah, and her children officially deeded the one-quarter lot to the Common Schools, Moon Township District. In this deed of 1852, it states the schoolhouse was already erected and made of brick. The lot was deeded to the St. Joseph Lead Company in Dec 1939 by the Potter Township School District. In this 1939 deed, instead of "brick," it stated that the school was a one-storey "frame" schoolhouse.

In 1875, George Dobbs of Bellowsville deeded one-half acre of his property to the Independent School District, Moon Township. There was no mention of a school building either erected or to be erected on this property. Curiously, the description of the property did not state it was adjacent to any other school property though – just adjacent to the Frankfort Road, James L. Deens' property, and the County Poor House property. In the mid 1870s, the districts were adding more property to all the schools in the area, so this land purchase from George Dobbs may have been just to give more land to an existing school property.

An 1877/78 report by the Commonwealth of Pennsylvania stated that in 1871, the northwest sub-district of Moon Township petitioned the Legislature for an independent district – it was granted, and the district was formed. This was in the time frame for the formation of Bellowsville. As stated in another section, the village immediately addressed starting a schoolhouse which was fashioned from one of the old buildings. They remodeled the building, enlarged a playground area, and enclosed the property with a nice fence. As with a few other township schools, this school received an annual income from the Alcorn estate which averaged around $133. This report went on to state "The school is now advanced to the front of enterprising, efficient schools, and will give a good account of itself."

This school building was located on property of the St. Joe Lead Co. that became owned by the Zinc Corporation of America (ZCA), along Frankfort Road in what was the Bellowsville area which became Potter Township. To add to the confusion of early schools, there was another school located in Raccoon Township that was called Potter School, the two schools should not be confused. The Independent School also served many of the residents in Moon Township who lived in the encircling/immediate area. This Independent School/Potter School #1 was used as a school until 1939, and then classes were held in the new brick building donated by the St. Joseph Lead Co. (See further.)

Potter #2 or Badlam Place School – Mowry Road
This school was located on a portion of the roadway formerly known as Mowry Road, passing Bauer, continuing straight and not turning right - there was a ZCA gate blocking anyone from continuing on the road. It was closed as a schoolhouse in 1920 due to a lack of pupils. The building was used for many years as a meeting place for Grange members. It was then sold and remained standing for many years simply known as the *Badlam Place*. This schoolhouse was built on a section of 248 acres that belonged to James and Ethel Potter who deeded it to Stephen and Helen Badlam in 1929. Mrs. Badlam, then a widow, sold the property to the St. Joseph Lead Company in Dec 1963 recognizing any rights/consideration of the property and school building (see St. Joseph School).

St. Joe School Building – on property of former St. Joseph Lead Company, along Frankfort Road.
In about 1937, the State Department of Education was strongly suggesting that Potter Township join with a neighboring school district, most likely due to the size of its enrollments. Rather than this jointure, Mr. George Weaton, a resident of Potter Township and connected with St. Joseph Lead Company, became involved in this matter and with his help and influence, it was decided that one school be built, be equipped, and turned over to the Potter School District. With Mr. Weaton's involvement, the St. Joseph Lead Co. deeded 2 acres to the Potter Township School on Dec 28, 1939. This gives more validation that The School District of Potter Township was definitely in existence prior to 1940. The St. Joseph Lead Company conveyed/deeded the two-acre lot which already contained a one-storey brick building "suitable for a public school." This property and building were sold to the school district with the specific statement included in the deed "for school

purposes, and school purposes only, and upon the said School District or any other successor school district ceasing to use the same for the purpose of the School District, the said premises shall revert to the grantor herein, its successors and assigns."

This new brick building, now a school, replaced the original Potter #1/Independent School which was a farm structure (see Potter #1 previous). This new one-storey brick school building had two classrooms, a small kitchen, a storage room, heater room, and water well. There was also an outdoor play area. When the new Potter Elementary School was erected and opened in Sep of 1950 on Frankfort Road/Route 18, this small school was closed but the building was used as a community center for several more years. In Jul 1961, the Potter Township School District deeded the 2 acres of land and the one-storey brick building back to the St. Joseph Co. as required by the original deed. About that same time, the former school building also became the site used by Beaver County for Special Education classes.

Kobuta School – Montgomery Dam Road

Photo courtesy Joann Bishop (used in Beaver County Yearbook)

This school was in the area of the construction gate of Nova, down Montgomery Dam Road. It was built shortly after the Kobuta Plant was erected. With all the homes and families moving in to the Kobuta community, there was insufficient room in the existing St. Joe School Building for all the children of the Kobuta families. By the beginning of the 1943 school year there were over one hundred pupils attending classes in the Kobuta community building and the kitchen area had to be turned into an additional classroom. It was obvious that this new community of Kobuta needed a separate school building, so the Kobuta School was erected.

There were four rooms in the Kobuta School that were used for classes, along with one room at the St. Joe School Building. Even with these classrooms, overcrowding still became a problem, so the seventh and eighth grade pupils were sent to Center Township and later to Monaca. In about 1947, it was once again decided to build additional buildings. Due to many limitations, the plan to just enlarge the St. Joe School Building was cancelled and a location for a completely new and larger school was persued. It was decided to move the schools away from the industrial area of Potter Township, so a site at the top of the hill along Frankfort Road, toward the western end of Potter Township was decided upon. A total of approximately 80 acres of property was purchased and the Potter School was built.

Potter School – 612 Frankfort Road

1970s

Potter School – 612 Frankfort Road

This twelve-room "U" shaped school was a one-storey brick building, erected on approximately 21 acres of land at 612 Frankfort Road, Potter Township. There was a recreation center (combination gymnasium and auditorium) to be located between the two wings of classroom but due to the cost and insufficient funds, this recreation center was removed from the plans for this school and left an open area which then gave the building its "U" shape.

Potter Township School District originally purchased the land for this school from J. Clair Potts in Oct 1948. In the spring of 1949 construction was started on the new Potter School building. It was completed and ready for use by the start of the school term in Sep of 1950. With the opening of this new school, there was no need for the St. Joe School Building, so it was closed as a school building and became a community center for several years. Water had to be hauled from the St. Joe Lead company due to major difficulties in supplying the school building with an adequate water supply, but finally, a good well was drilled, and water was then readily available.

This new Potter School had excess classroom space over the years and began to help service elementary students from Raccoon Township, South Beaver County School District, and Center Township for several years. Center Area School District became the title holders when the Center Township and Potter Township school districts were consolidated by adjudication of the Pennsylvania State Board of Education and became one administrative unit in 1969. As of 1971, the two districts merged to form the Center Area School District. The school still operated as an elementary school until the building was closed as a school in 1978/79.

After the closing, portions of the building were rented to various businesses until the Center Township School District sold the former Potter Township property to Teddy and Evelyn Telesz of Aliquippa, PA in 1986. The building and property were sold in 2007 by the Telesz family to PNE Realty, LLC. The PNE Realty, LLC then became landlords of the former school with agreements made to Tiny Treasurers Daycare Center, then Somewhere Over the Rainbow child care business, the Keystone Simulation and Education Center (KSEC), and the Pocket Nurse Enterprises, LLC (supplier of nursing/medical supplies).

There was a playground area on the right side of the original school building that became a paved parking lot. By 2011, there was a concrete and steel building under construction on this portion of the property. There is now the multi-storey building that is home of Pocket Nurse – 610 Frankfort Road. As of 2014, the former school building was listed for lease, then in mid 2016, the former Potter School building and 3.886 acres were listed "for sale."

Known Potter School Principals were Thomas Malloy (1953), John Drobbs (1966), and Joseph Skoff (unknown years).

former Potter School   Poket Nurse building erected adjacent to the former school
2018 view of the former Potter School and adjacent property.

~ ~ ~

Did you know…

In Jun of 1968 when Center Township was in need of building a new elementary school, that the Center Township School Board had to have authorization and approval from both the Monaca School Board and Potter Township Board before they could proceed with construction plans?

Why…… well……. The authorization to create any type of debt by any of these school districts was necessary from the other two districts' boards because at that time, the three districts were placed in the same administrative district by the County Board. This meant that if there would be any merger between Potter, Center, and/or Monaca school districts – then the other school districts would also be responsible for the financial obligation(s) generated if and when a merger may occur. Potter and Monaca boards eventually did give their approval, and the new elementary building was erected in Center Township. This is just more proof that Monaca and Center and Potter areas, residents, and schools seem to keep being tied together even without, or prior to formal jointures or mergers.

Student Transportation

1920s

1956

Providing transportation to the students stemmed from a law in 1919 which stated the children would receive transportation to the school if they lived more than one and a half miles from the school. Secondary grade level students were also to receive transportation to one of the local high schools since the township still did not have a secondary grade school of its own. With this legislation in place, transportation of the students to the Center Township schools was in full force. This was close to the same time the first one-room schoolhouses were being closed and the students were attending the new consolidated township school in 1939. Not only did the township have to provide busing to its secondary school students prior to having its own secondary school, but in 1965, a new law was in the process of being passed which required the school districts to also provide transportation to any student within the township that chose to attend a private or parochial school.

Some of the first bus transportation was provided by James Mitchell. (J. H. Mitchel started a draying and transferring business in Monaca in Mar 1903.)

I do not know if this was the very first year of a contract or possibly being a renewal, but in 1934, George Huffmyer was awarded a contract for transporting the students to the schools. Mr. Huffmyer provided this service to the students and schools for at least twenty years. He owned his own busses, and they were parked/kept at their home and garage along Chapel Road. Mr. Huffmyer retired as a bus contractor in 1966.

John Hineman and Simon Hineman were contracted in 1954 to operate nine busses to transport students to and from The Consolidated School. It did not state if this was a new contract or a renewal of a previous contract. In the 1970s, the Ferguson Bus Co. had purchased the buses owned by brothers John and Simon Hineman, along with a building for the bus company. The McCarter Coach and Tour also was involved in transporting school students. As of 2016, Ferguson Bus Company (Blair Ferguson) had been providing bus services throughout Beaver County for eighty-nine years, forty of those in Beaver County.

Rhodes Transit (James Rhodes) was also a past and most current provider of bus services for Center Township Schools.

School bus drivers are more than just a driver -- 99% of them have and still go out of their way to know the names of their regular riders, who all the parents are, and which student(s) loads or unloads at each designated stop. School bus drivers are required to be able to navigate through snow and sleet and the dead of night with their precious "cargo;" said cargo just happens to be the future of tomorrow. Many men and women have taken on the occupation of being a bus driver – not a job for the faint of heart.

Does anyone remember the iconic Jean Morris who transported countless numbers of township students via school bus for many years? Jean also became one of the main coordinators of all the bus route scheduling for the district for many years.

Another familiar face among the district's drivers was John Bender who drove a bus for Center Area Schools for over 20 years.

~ ~ ~

Universities and Colleges

Many of the younger residents of Beaver County and especially Center Township may not realize that the college campuses in the area today are all fairly new in comparison with the age of the township. It wasn't until the early 1960s that all the campuses in Center Township started in the area. Within an estimated five-year span, Penn State-Beaver and Community College of Beaver County joined other higher education institutes of the surrounding areas in helping residents further their educations and prepare for careers. Many, many years before any of the colleges actually made their home in Center Township, residents of Moon/ Center were pursuing to further their education and could have attended classes at the other local colleges or academies of the area.

These are the college campuses previously found or currently within Center Township.

Pennsylvania State University aka **Penn State Beaver Campus** - Brodhead Road
1965 to current

Beginning in the 1800s, the Hartenbach, Trumbull, and/or Huffmyer families owned the properties that now makes up the campus of Penn State - Beaver. From the entrance on the right of the campus with the two stone pillars, to the area on the left side of the campus by the baseball fields was all a part of these former farmlands. The Hartenbach's barn once stood where the Giusti amphitheater was built (see pictures further). The current pond by the amphitheater is the only remaining pond of several originally existing on the former farm. The 1880s Hartenbach home and farm were purchased by Penn State with a contingency that Mr. and Mrs. Hartenbach could live in their home until their deaths. (See the Families and Homes section for more on the Hartenbachs and this farm.)

    The acreage that surrounds and now contains the Ross Administration Building was not only part of the former TB Sanitarium but was originally owned by Dr. Turnbull, a prominent physician in Pittsburgh in the late 1800s/early 1900s. He purchased 93+ acres and had a very large fourteen room building/home erected. He planned to start a sanitarium, but financial difficulties occurred, and the Carnegie National Bank became the next owners of the building and farm land. Dr. Baelz leased the property in 1905, attempting to have a county home and health resort for the people of Pittsburgh. Dr. Baelz took advantage of using the once valued mineral springs on the property which were sought after for the suspected healing qualities of the waters. Some folklore and even Penn State state that in the early 1900s, the building was used as a small hotel, but it seems this belief may be more of an embellishment. Though it may have appeared as a hotel since people payed to stay there, it was actually considered a health resort started by Dr. Baelz. (See TB Sanitarium in the Medical section for more information.)

    A few years after 1905, the former Turnbull property was divided into two parcels. Sidney Huffmyer purchased 40 acres of the Turnbull property which included the large 14 room building which the Huffmyers turned into their home. Shortly after Mr. Huffmyer's purchase, Mr. Grimmell obtained the remaining 54 acres on the far side of the property (currently Mona Manor area). (See the Housing Area section.) The Huffmyer house and property were sold to Beaver County in the early 1920s. By 1923-1924, Drs. Fred and Ruth (Walker) Wilson were turning the former home into a sanitarium and were opening their doors to care for TB patients. The Wilsons began taking the steps to expand and have a proper Beaver County TB Sanitarium built. The sanitarium was discontinued in Dec 1956 and patients were moved to Cresson or Mount Alto facilities. The Beaver County Hospital Annex then occupied the facilities as of Jan 1, 1957. All patients of the Annex were transferred to the Beaver County Geriatric Center by 1963. The larger home/health resort was used by the sanitorium but as the need increased to house the sick, so did the need for more/larger buildings of the asylum. (See Medical Section for more information regarding the sanitarium and former ownerships of the land and pictures of the Beaver County TB Sanitarium.)

    All the former buildings of the sanitorium that had been erected on this portion of the current college campus were fitted to become facilities of the new Penn State Beaver Campus. There have been a few sources that state the campus sits on a little over 100 acres, another states 105 acres, and yet another states 90 acres. Regardless of what the true actual amount of land is, the campus is now on a beautifully landscaped piece of property that once was open wilderness, then turned into homesteads and farmlands, and further tamed with the addition of buildings and activity related to healing.

Pennsylvania State University saw a need for a campus in Beaver County and the Beaver County Commissioners were looking for someone to take over the former Huffmyer/sanitarium property they now owned. In 1964, Penn State accepted the offer to purchase this parcel of property. The land was purchased from Beaver County and construction began of some new structures along with the updating of existing buildings. The Beaver Campus of Pennsylvania State University opened in 1965. The college admitted 97 students for its first semester using the former sanitarium buildings for some classrooms and the campus's offices. On Apr 3, 1968, the school acquired the nearby Hartenbach farm from Ralph and Margaret Hartenbach. The deed indicates all the land was truthfully donated to the college since the agreed price was $1.00. This sale was contingent on the Hartenbach's retaining possession of and being allowed to live in their house for the rest of their lives, then it would also become property of the school.

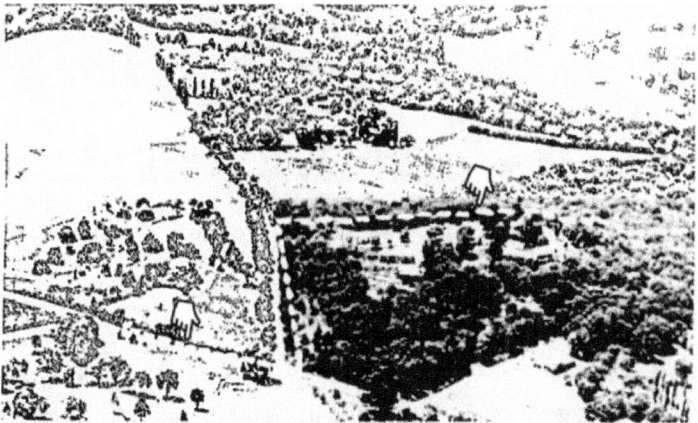

I apologize for the very poor quality of this photograph, nevertheless, I wanted to include it to show how the area of and around the current Penn State Beaver Campus previously appeared when it was still farmland. This is a 1965 aerial view of the land prior to the campus being developed. The pointer on the bottom left indicates Brodhead Road. The pointer in the middle of the photograph is to indicate the dotted line on the photo outlining the present area of the campus.   Note how undeveloped all the surrounding area was in 1965.

This is a 1972 aerial view of the campus as it was being developed into the campus. The small pointer on the right in this photo indicates Harmony Hall. Brodhead Road is along the bottom of the photo. The Ohio River is along the top of the photograph.

Campus officials were busy for a few years as they transformed the former site of the sanitarium and farmlands into a safe environment as a college campus.   Several cisterns were discovered which were used by farmers to store water during dry times.   As these were discovered, maintenance workers would have to fill in these ditches so people did not fall into them. There was a multi-stall garage that was used by the campus for storing vehicles, equipment, and for a workshop. The small cottage that was formerly used by the caretaker of the sanitarium remained on campus for many years, too. A large portion of the original sanitarium buildings continued to be used by the university until 2004 when the former sanitarium buildings were demolished and the Ross Administration Building was completed. All that remains of the previous sanitarium today is under a concrete slab over a basement area.

c1967-1969   Photo courtesy Penn State
This photo shows the original buildings of the sanitarium (top left) and some of the new construction taking place on the campus as they are erecting what is now Baker Engineering & Science Building. (See Medical section for more pictures of the previous sanitarium.

The university went through a building spurt between 1967 and 1969 when the addition of The Baker Engineering and Science Building, the library, a general classroom building, the campus food service building, and a residency for students (Harmony Hall) were all erected. In 1971, the college also built a multipurpose building and a gymnasium as well as beginning the student union building.

The expansion of the campus continued into 1991 with the building of three Lions Court apartment buildings for townhouse-style residence halls. In 1994 the student union tripled in size and was turned into the Study Learning Center. From 1994 until present, the campus has continued to grow and be updated including improvements made to existing buildings --- the enlargement of the food service building to create a food court, the demolition of all former sanitarium buildings and construction of the new Ross Administration Building. In 1999/2000, the campus offered its first four-year degree -- a bachelor's degree in information sciences and technology experience.

Photo from Dec 2012 "Roar" publication distributed by Penn State
The last of the original sanitarium as it was being razed in 2004.

1976 was also a busy year for the university when they added a 700-seat amphitheater. In conjunction with the addition of the Brodhead Cultural Center and Giusti Amphitheater, an existing farm pond was converted into an attraction. Adjacent to this pond was a smaller former Hartenbach home which was converted into the Baker-Dugan Museum. It was once filled with many artifacts and treasurers of the 1800 and 1900s but within the past several years, the museum was closed and many of the articles that could once be viewed inside have been removed. This former museum building was located above the parking lot of the Cultural Center but has been razed.

Performance at the amphitheater

The photograph on the left is a view of a portion of the former Hartenbach farm that is now the pond and Giusti Amphitheater. Not included in the photograph is Brodhead Road which would be a bit further off to the left of this photo. This photograph shows the former "drive" which led from Brodhead Road, past the barn and up to the house that sat on the hillside where Chapel Road meets Brodhead Road. (The photograph on the left would have been taken from approximately where the house once stood.) The barn was razed by the university shortly after the purchase of the property and the original home became unoccupied and was left standing until a few years ago when it was also razed.

View of the duck pond with amphitheater in background.

The campus has two entrances within a few hundred feet of each other. One is off Brodhead Road and located adjacent to the amphitheater, the other has two large stone pillars at its entrance, also off Brodhead Road.

College Drive entrance off Brodhead Road

Marquee at University Drive entrance off Brodhead Road

View of improved campus.

Fun fact: Just like in most communities, Center is not without its tales of ghosts. This tale is centered on the campus of Penn State Beaver. With Penn State Beaver on the property once being the site of a TB sanitarium and then a site where the elderly were housed and severely wounded veterans made their adjustments back into civilian lives, it should not be a surprise that reports of paranormal activity take place. Many students over the years have claimed to have seen "the lady in white." She has been spotted in the old, original sanitarium building that was used as the first Administration Building on campus. Many have claimed it is the ghost of a young girl who most likely died while being treated in the sanitarium. Others have also reported that although not actually viewed, they have "felt" a spirit in what had been used as the old maintenance building (located between the Ross Administration building parking lot and the Laboratory Classroom building). The "feeling" of sadness and malicious dread was reported to wash over those who would be by the former fireplace located in the building.

There were other areas on campus that could make the hairs on the back of the neck stand up, too. On the other side of the campus in Harmony Hall, there were reports of something rustling through things in students' rooms, lights would mysteriously turn on and off, voices have been heard, and one report of hearing a man's voice say "oh my gosh" - but no one was there.

Fun fact: The Concrete Slab……. The former sanitarium building that once stood on this site is nothing more than a 'concrete slab' today. The former building was considered to be in the worse condition of all the original sanitarium buildings. The old building was razed and replaced with the new Ross Administration building in 2004. The campus was using the basement area under this old sanitarium building as their information technology hub. To move this IT hub would have been at an exorbitant cost, so the university chose to keep it where it was and instead "seal it" with the concrete slab. Students and personnel now refer to this area as "the bunker" because it is said that when you are in the hub, it feels like a bomb shelter. The campus now uses the surface of the slab area to host outdoor activities.

Photo from Dec 2012 "Roar" publication distributed by Penn State.

Community College of Beaver County   aka   **CCBC** – 1 Campus Drive, off Poplar Drive
(1963) 1973 to current

Community College of Beaver County was conceived as a means for individuals who were unable to seek a college education right out of high school or to further education coming out of another college. This concept has expanded and now also includes persons who are established in careers or the work force and want to enhance their jobs or careers. Many educators and employers will agree that today, two years spent at CCBC is equivalent to two years of any four-year institute. For many years, various colleges would not transfer credits earned from CCBC, but that has changed over the years. Business and education have always been a natural merger and CCBC can fulfill any gap between the two. It continues to be a very affordable alternative in any pursuit of higher education.

The Community College of Beaver County was originally formed and located in Freedom, PA in about 1963. The college used several of the former buildings located in downtown Freedom as classrooms and administration offices. In 1966, they were leasing a few floors of the Freedom National Bank building, along with seventeen vacant storefronts. The college originally chose the location of Freedom due to the county's bus routes at that time. When the construction of the four-lane Route 65 began, it forced the school to look for another location.

CCBC purchased 94.772 acres of property in Center Township in 1967 from the Mancini family and began to create its own campus. Many times, the Mancini family is the only one mentioned when referencing the history of CCBC, but……………some recognition should also go to Brown Irwin, Corbin Profader, George Eichman, and then Jappy Patterson. Brown Irwin became the owner of 124 acres of the property in 1835. He turned around and sold it to Corbin Profader in 1835. The Profader family then deeded Corbin's property to George Eichman in 1901 who in turn sold the same 124 acres to Jappy (Joshua A.) Patterson's wife, Jennie R. in 1906. Jappy started his own farm and had his Pleasant Valley Dairy business on the property until he sold 94+ acres of his farm to Peter Mancini in 1947. Peter then entered a Declaration of Trust for the property to include his brothers Favion and Frank as owners in 1959 and the 94.772 acres was sold to CCBC in 1967. (Also see Patterson Family information.)

So, from the once fertile farmland of the former owners, development, and construction of the CCBC campus began. They constructed five buildings on a 75-acre portion of the property before moving the classes officially from Freedom and into Center Township. The first new building of CCBC was the Allied Health Building which was completed in 1973. The college began operating an air traffic control tower at the Beaver County Airport in 1984, and as the interest for continued education grew, the college built their Aviation Sciences Center on the county airport's property in 1990. The Library Resource Center and a renovation of the Applied Arts building occurred in 1997, along with a welding and auto service facilities being converted into a high-tech communications, computer, and art laboratory. Margaret Williams-Bethlyn was the CCBC President from 1971 until she retired in 1999.

Originally the only entrance to the campus was off Poplar Drive. Today, there are three means of accessing the college campus by vehicle --- from Route 18/Brodhead Road onto Community College Drive -- from Center Grange Road onto Poplar Drive (extension) -- from Baker Road onto the original Poplar Avenue/Drive. As of 2015/16, a fourth, non-vehicular means to access to the CCBC campus was developed. With the aid of current grant monies being applied, there is a lighted walking path connecting from the Central Valley High School campus to the Community College campus and the pathway continues to the Center Primary School on Center Grange Road.

Through the years, the Beaver County Area Vocational Technical School has leased acreage from the CCBC for their facilities. (See further.)

One of the most notable landmarks in Center Township is the "Golden Dome." It was constructed in 1976 even though, to many of the current residents in Center Township, the site of the CCBC Dome may seem to have always existed. Until this athletic complex was completed, all sporting events were held off-campus.

"The Dome"

A view of the campus – for orientation, Poplar Drive is the roadway at the bottom of the picture.

The college made renovations which were completed in late spring of 2017. There were campus walkways widened and landscaping (including trees added) to make the whole campus look more user friendly and give a more "park like" environment. The renovation project was expected to come in slightly under the budgeted $8 million. The renovations also included a variety of other projects -- new heating/air conditioning and roofing, repaved parking lots, repaired parking lot storm-water systems, new exterior signage, a gazebo, a patio area outside the Student Services Center, and a new pedestrian bridge in front of the Learning Resource Center. In addition, several aspects of the renovations included new magnetic locking systems in all campus buildings and brighter LED lights outside to help improve campus safety and security. There was even a new logo that was unveiled in 2009 featuring "CCBC" in blue letters crossed by a white swoosh trimmed in a copper penny color. Accompanying the logo is the tagline "Your road to your future!" As mentioned previously, the college also worked with Center Township to build a walkway that runs from Center Grange Primary School through the CCBC campus to the Central Valley High School. This walkway is for public use and available to all interested in exercise. CCBC celebrated their 50th anniversary in May 2017.

Community College of Beaver County debuted the arched, skid-resistant pedestrian bridge.

Fact: Updates to the college's Aviation Sciences Center at the Beaver County Airport in Chippewa Township were made to accompany those done on the main campus. Changes such as repaving, new signage and revamped landscaping created continuity between the two facilities.

Beaver County Career and Technology Center aka
1978 to current   **Beaver County Vocational Technical School**

The current Beaver County Area Vocational Technical School opened its doors in the fall of 1978 but is now known as the Beaver County Career and Technology Center. This school is currently located at 145 Poplar Drive, adjacent to the CCBC campus. They are funded through citizens' and businesses' taxes and offer a tuition-free education to high school students from all the current fourteen Beaver County School Districts.

In 1975, plans were being developed and specifications for the proposed current buildings to be located and erected on 25 acres leased/donated by the Community College of Beaver County. The final proposed Vo-Tech campus plans were contingent on all the then fifteen area school districts in Beaver County -- now fourteen with merger of Monaca and Center -- committing themselves to the building project. By committing to the project, each school was agreeing to pay its share of the 6% architectural fee. The schools in Beaver County found the courses to be offered through Vo-Tech would be very beneficial to their high school students since as of 1975 only Ambridge and Aliquippa schools offered their own auto mechanics, electric and machine shop classes. Aliquippa had an additional auto body course, too. The BC Vo-Tech offered twenty proposed courses at their school and eight vo-tech courses in facilities at CCBC. With a new campus of their own, the twenty-eight proposed courses would all be offered within their own buildings and campus area.

The transfer of the land from CCBC, along with all plans, development, and specifications were completed by the first of Mar 1977. Work had begun on grading and then building the current BC Vo-Tech School along Poplar Drive.

1977
Developing the land for the new Vo-Tech campus.

The following information was taken directly from their web page since I felt their wording gave such a wonderful and clear explanation of what they do and offer.

"The Beaver County Career & Technology Center is a full-time career and technology center that serves the youth of Beaver County in Pennsylvania."

"The Beaver County CTC is dedicated to providing programs consisting of high quality, cutting-edge technical training integrated with a strong academic education and an emphasis on critical thinking, problem-solving, decision-making, and team-building skills. The curriculum is closely tied to the needs of business and industry. Through twice-yearly Craft Committee meetings, advisors guide program development to assure that the curriculum and equipment match the needs and standards of employers. Employers tell us what skills are needed for success in their fields and those are the skills we teach. Instructors align course curriculums with the skills employers need for employees to be successful."

Nowadays, the Beaver County Career and Technology Center and the Community College of Beaver County established a cooperative educational program. Students who have completed any one of the seventeen approved programs at the Career and Technology Center are eligible to receive twenty-four credits toward an Associate Degree in Applied Technology from CCBC. They may enroll at CCBC and receive their degree after they complete the appropriate requirements.

Beaver Valley Intermediate Unit #27 aka Beaver County Intermediate Unit –
147 Poplar Drive (adjacent to the Beaver County Vo-Tech/Career and Technology Center)
1970 to current

The BVIU / BCIU is just one of Pennsylvania's twenty-nine Intermediate Units that were created in 1970. Their operations are conducted by an Advisory Council comprised of the current fourteen local district superintendents in Beaver County who meet monthly to review programs and services. The BCIU was first located at 1256 Brodhead Road which became 3578 Brodhead Road after renumbering of Brodhead Road.

former Brodhead Road location

The Beaver Valley Intermediate Unit planned to complete an 8500 sq. foot facility on N. Brodhead Road in the A & R Complex building (adjacent to the former A & R Restaurant building). It was set to open Jul 1, 1973, but actually had the official opening May 21, 1974, with open house held May 20 through May 24, 1974. The building they were going to be moving into was built and owned by Anthony DelTurco (who also owned the restaurant) and the BVIU would be paying a yearly rental of $24,000 on a five-year contract. Mar 14, 1974 was "Moving Day" for the BVIU and their facilities were set up. On Monday, May 20, 1974, the newly appointed Beaver County school officials and nineteen reappointed administrators took the oath of office at a mass swearing-in ceremony at the new centrally located facility on North Brodhead Road in Center Township.

Judge John N. Sawyer administering the oath of office to the county officials at a mass swearing-in ceremony in the new N. Brodhead Road location.

The following were on the 1974 BVIU administrative board:
   Frank Mastalski – BVIU Board President
   Dr. Melvin Miller-Superintendent - Blackhawk School District
   Dr. Francis Matika – BVIU Assistant Executive Director
   John Milanovich, BVIU Executive Director
   Lawrence Maravich –Superintendent, Aliquippa
   Dominic Carifo – Asst Supt – Aliquippa
   Dr. Douglas Lehman – Asst Supt – Aliquippa
   Dr. Paul Vochko – Supt – Ambridge
   Dr. Stanley Duplaga – Asst Supt – Ambridge
   Dr. Dale McDonald – Supt – Beaver
   Dr. J. Richard Fruth - Supt – Big Beaver Falls
   Stanley Brobeck – Asst Supt – Big Beaver Falls
   Dr. Harry Fink – Supt – Center Area
   Robert Cercone – Supt – Freedom
   Camillo Bonomi – Supt – Hopewell
   Steven Mulik – Asst Supt – Hopewell
   Dr. Charles Henderson – Supt – Midland
   Christy Mangin – Supt – Monaca
   Dr. William Zeffiro – Supt – New Brighton
   Kenneth Yonkee – Supt – Northeastern Bvr County
   Matthew Hosie – Supt – Rochester
   Albert Troiano – Supt – Western Beaver

Over time, the staff of the BVIU came to use 3 separate buildings -- in Beaver (on Corporation Street), in Monaca (Third Ward School), and in Rochester (Pinney Street School). Following the closure of the former Center Grange Elementary Building at 225 Center Grange Road, the BVIU moved from their Brodhead Road location to occupy the school building. They occupied this former school building until 2005. The Beaver County Area Vocational-Technical School Authority is currently leasing approximately 8 2/3 acres of property to the this intermediate unit. All the buildings were erected and owned by the BVIU #27. It was a 99-year lease of the property, beginning Sep 2005.

The following information was taken directly from the BVIU web page since once again, I felt their wording gave such a clear explanation of what they do/offer. "Intermediate units are regional educational service agencies and provide programs and resources to Commonwealth schools. Through cooperation and collaboration among school districts and community agencies, intermediate units work to provide innovative, responsive and cost-effective programs."

"The Beaver Valley Intermediate Unit (BVIU) is comprised of the fourteen local school districts, the New Horizon School for students with disabilities and the Beaver County Career and Technology Center. We serve four area charter schools and 11 non-public schools."

The BVIU also provided county wide availability and delivery for audio visual materials to the schools for many years. The Beaver Valley Intermediate Unit continues its importance to the educational institutes within Beaver County. They award contracts to merchants for supplies based on the needs expressed by the schools. These supplies, being purchased in bulk afford a substantial savings to the school districts.

Mountain State University - Brodhead Road
2004 to 2011

This school was founded in 1933 as Beckley College with the name changed to Mountain State University about 2001. Berkley College was nearly bankrupt when Dr. Charles H. Polk was named president in 1991. School officials revitalized the school and added four-year degree programs, on line classes, and began to open branch campuses.

In 2003, the Pennsylvania Department of Education approved Mountain State (W.VA) University to operate a branch campus to offer undergraduate and graduate programs in Beaver County. MSU chose Center Township for this campus. They had programs designed for working adults and offered a degree in eighteen months. For a bachelor's degree, students had to have close to two-thirds of their college credits completed elsewhere. Mountain State University's main campus was in southern West Virginia in the town of Beckley. The school also had branch campuses in Orlando, Fla.; Martinsburg, W.VA.; Mooresville, N.C.; Hickory, N.C.; and Washington, D.C.

In Aug 2004, the school leased the former Andiamo's Restaurant space in the Village Shoppe Plaza on Brodhead Road. They renovated it into two classrooms, a computer lab, offices, and a lunchroom. MSU held their first commencement on Jun 30, 2006, at Community College for the first fifteen graduates of their Center Township Campus. In Jan 2011, MSU announced that they were moving this campus to the CCBC's campus by Mar or Apr. They would be leasing six classrooms, nine offices, a computer lab, and a large reception area. This move afforded students at CCBC the chance to earn a four-year college degree, or graduate degree without leaving home. At the time of the move the school had one hundred and ten students enrolled at this Center Township/Beaver County campus.

Mountain State University ceased to operate effective Jan 2013 but all degrees conferred on or before Dec 31, 2012 were valid and issued by an accredited institution.

~ ~ ~

Not a college or educational institute, but rather a business associated with learning………
Sylvan Learning Center – 115 Wagner Road (beside Lowe's Plaza)
This center closed at this location in 2002. It offered tutoring and services to all who needed guidance in learning skills for better studying, therefore affording an opportunity for further education.

~ ~ ~

Other colleges and higher education institutes

One interesting article from an 1878 publication of *Common Schools of Pennsylvania*…………

COLLEGES, ACADEMIES, AND SEMINARIES
"Of the several colleges, academies, and seminaries, established in Beaver County, Beaver County Institute of Sciences, Darlington Academy, Frankfort Academy, Phillipsburg Soldiers' Orphan School, Greenwood Seminary, the Kenwood Boarding School for Boys, and other private schools have been discontinued."

"Beaver College and Musical Institute, established in 1853; Beaver Female Seminary, opened in 1854; Frankfort Academy and Normal School, founded in 1871; North Sewickley Academy, and the Young Men's Library Association, of New Brighton, still exist, to aid in the cause of general education."

Although the following were/are physically located outside the current township's boundaries, all were/are very popular colleges and higher education institutes. It is a fact that many current township residents have attended one of the following listed colleges. It is also very likely many of the earlier Moon/Center Township residents would have attended one of these institutes.

Geneva College
1848 to current
Even though Geneva College is definitely not within the boundaries of Center Township, it played a large role with Moon/Center Township residents who wanted to obtain a degree at a college closer to home in the late 1800s and well into the 1900s. This was especially true with any of the women who pursued a career of teaching. Geneva College was started in 1848 in Northwood Ohio. It was founded within the Reformed Presbyterian Church in that community. Geneva soon outgrew these facilities and in 1880, an offer by the church was accepted for 10 acres of land and $20,000 for a building from the Harmony Society in an area the Harmonists had settled by Beaver Falls. Once in the Beaver Falls area, while completing the first building, *Old Main*, Geneva used another building to hold classes; that building became home to Holy Spirit Fellowship Church.

> *Fun fact: The Harmonists were a 19th Century communal religious group. They fled their Lutheran Church in their homeland of Germany, coming to America and finally settling in what is now Old Economy in Ambridge. The group dissolved in 1905. The last member died in 1920. (I have much more detailed information on the Harmonites in my book Monaca aka Phillipsburg.)*

Geneva College continued to grow and *North Hall* was the second building constructed on campus in 1888. It was used as a female student dormitory and dining hall. This building was razed in 1952, *Memorial Hall* replaced it and became a male dormitory. In 1890, growth continued with a small gymnasium being built. This small gym was demolished in 1910 and replaced with the Johnson Gymnasium. The 33rd Street Field was put into use for athletic events, then moved to the Reeves Stadium which was built in 1925. The Merriman Athletic Complex now sits on property that was once the Armstrong Cork Co facility. The company turned the property over to the college in 1969 and 1974. Geneva College's campus has undergone numerous renovations through the years, and it continues to be an excellent institute of further education.

> *Fun fact: Geneva's small gymnasium was built in 1890. It gained fame while holding a now historical event which was the first college basketball game in the United States and played in this gymnasium. Geneva defeated the New Brighton YMCA at this game.*

Thiel Hall at Phillipsburg - 129 Fourth Street (originally called Hanover Street), Monaca, PA
Dec 1865 - a Lutheran Institution of higher learning of the Pittsburgh Synod was established. It became known as Thiel College in 1866. It was founded as a co-educational institution in 1869 at Greensburg, PA as the result of a meeting at the Lutheran Church Pittsburgh Synod convention between Dr. William Passavant and A. Louis Thiel. It became a college to serve western Pennsylvania. A. Louis and Barbara Thiel gave $4,000 to their pastor, Rev. G. A. Wenzel, D.D. to start the school. The Thiel's made their gift because they wanted to "give back" and share their profits made from investments in the oil region in western Pennsylvania. (Their $4,000 in 1869 would be equivalent to a little over $75,300 nowadays.)

Reverend Dr. William Passavant was chosen because he campaigned for organizing a Lutheran college in the region for many years. With this passion, he was more than willing to become involved. In the spring of 1866, a former Water Cure building / Hotel of Cimiotti was purchased, later an adjoining house and lot were also bought. Thiel College was officially incorporated and opened in Monaca on Sep 1, 1870. It was located approximately where the current Monacatootha Apartments now stand (2019). The former hotel and ballroom were set aside for religious services, to the sacred purpose of Christian education with the building receiving the title of *Thiel Hall*.

Professor (Rev.) Giese, of Milwaukee, was the first instructor and there were five students attending the school. Rev. W. Kopp was added to the staff by the close of the first year. Rev. H. E. Jacobs D.D., L.L.D., assisted by Prof J. F. Feltshans of PA College, Gettysburg were hired when Rev. Giese accepted a call to NY.

The presence of Theil College in Monaca was short lived, and it was moved to the Academy Building in Greensville, PA Sep 1871.

courtesy of the BCHR&LF
The former Cimiotti and Central Hotel, then became the Theil Hall of Thiel College, in Phillipsburg (Monaca) in 1866.

Soldiers' Orphan School - Pennsylvania Avenue Extension and Fourth Street
(these were formerly Factory Street and Hanover Street)
As of Dec 1865, this was the first soldiers' orphan school in Pennsylvania. The need for this school was a direct result of the Civil War. The organizer and supervisor for the proposed school became the Rev. William G. Taylor, D.D.   Rev. Taylor bought the former Water Cure building (which had been a summer/health resort, but had closed), repairs were made, it was enlarged, and then furnished appropriately. There was a four-storey dwelling added (34 x 44 feet), an additional school room, a chapel, a boys' hall, a girls' hall, and 41 acres of property were also bought. In 1870 and 1873 more acreage was bought to make a total of 210 acres. The facility also included a laundry, bakery, and additional cook room.

It is difficult to determine if any of the children enrolled in this school would have been from Moon/Township with just their names being listed and no former parent or homestead location, but I would imagine that there would have been at least a few from this area in attendance or possibly even some township residents working within the school. The yearly average number of students in attendance at the school was estimated to be 140.   Six hundred and seventeen orphans were cared for with over 200 of whom required medical attention upon arrival.

Dr. Taylor not only bore the expenses of $48,000 to purchase the property/buildings, but he also used his own monies and tastefully decorated all the buildings – old and new. The girls' parlors and music rooms were furnished with Brussels carpets, chairs, piano, and an organ in the chapel. It was felt that "taste" was essential to instill culture in the girls and boys. The cost for providing the housing and education to the students was…. $115 per student under 10 years and $150 per student over 10 to 16 years old. The state prescribed eight grades as the extent of the educational courses. Dr. Taylor provided four grade levels of mathematical and scientific courses, and one-fourth of the orphans were able to finish all these courses.   No student was promoted unless his standing was at least 75%, and in 1874, the state inspectors found that the average standing of students in the school to be 93%. All the laws of health were carried out also, including proper food for physical and mental growth, as well as all clothing fitted and adapted, including well-fitting shoes. The children-maintained cleanliness of body, house, school rooms, wash and out houses. The buildings were very well lit, had excellent ventilation, and the children were permitted nine hours of regular sleep. The boys received one-hour regular military drilling, play time in the morning, noon, evening, and recess in addition to their classroom time and daily duties. The girls also received daily classroom time and under the guidance of Dr. Taylor's wife, each girl acquired a systematic and practical knowledge of domestic work, including classes in scrubbing, washing, ironing, housecleaning, dining-room work, dishwashing, cooking, all kinds of baking, mending, darning, plain family sewing, dressmaking, bonnet trimming, housekeeping, sweeping, bed making, arranging rooms and parlors. Every room, the kitchens, and the washrooms were open for the inspection of visitors all days except Sunday from 8 am until 5 pm.

On Aug 22, 1876, the main building accidentally caught fire and was totally destroyed. It was a loss of $25,000, but the insurance would only pay $10,300. This loss caused the school to close after ten and a half years of successful business. Thus, the Soldiers' Orphan School ceased forever.

Note - This is an actual photograph of the school, not a drawing.   Little Beaver Historical Society

The building on the left was located on the same area where the current Sewage Plant of Monaca is located, this building burned down in 1876. The larger building on the right of the picture was still standing when they were constructing the RR tunnel coming into Monaca. Also, on the building to the right, you can see quite a few of the children on the porch roof, some on the lower porch, and a few standing infront of the porch.

Some other interesting historical information to note in this picture.........
...All the former buildings on the hillside behind the school. They were all torn down when the railroad tracks were laid in that area. The Welsh Brick Company was in the area behind these buildings and the current Beaver Valley Alloy Company is still located in that same area.

For orientation.... the railroad tracks are currently laid through the area of the buildings at the top of the picture and the beginning of current RR bridge would be in the upper right of the picture. The current railroad viaduct was not yet constructed when this picture was taken, but would be to the left, just out of the picture.

...The roadway that is running horizonal in front of the school buildings was originally named Factory Street and is now Pennsylvania Avenue Extension. The road along the bottom of the picture was originally named First Street and is now Pennsylvania Avenue.

Beaver County Commercial College – opened in around 1902

BEAVER COUNTY COMMERCIAL COLLEGE, Beaver, Pa.

We teach Bookkeeping, Shorthand and Typewriting, and all other commercial branches practically. Business men recognize the merits of our school and apply to us for office help. Fall term opens August 30th. Write for catalogue. **W. P. POLLOCK, Principal.**

1909 ad

Garfield Business Institute –2590 Ridge Road
Originally known as *Butcher's Business College* in Beaver Falls in 1895. It became known as Garfield College aka Garfield Business Institute. It was in the Reno Building at 170 Madison Street in Rochester by 1917. They were next located in the Reeves Building in Beaver Falls and opened for classes in Aug 1977 in Monaca on Marshall Road. In May 1985, they moved to the former Fifth Ward School building on Monaca Heights at 2590 Ridge Road where it was located as of Aug 1990. Garfield Business Institute was then located in New Brighton and in 2006 I found – "ADVANTAGE TRAINING, INC. (formerly GARFIELD BUSINESS INSTITUTE) 430 Corporation Drive Aliquippa, PA 15001."

Info-Age Computer School of Beaver County – 2590 Ridge Road (the old Fifth Ward Elementary building)
Founded in 1984 by Dr. Anthony J. Meta and several associates. It was privately owned and considered a sister school to Garfield Business Institute.

~ ~ ~

There were several other very early colleges, academies, and seminaries throughout Beaver County that Moon Township residents/young adults could have also attended to pursue their interests and education. One would imagine that coming from humble rural homesteads, there would not have been many Moon Township young people who could be afforded the opportunity to attend school past the eighth grade, let alone an institute of higher education beyond a secondary school. Some were fortune enough to do just that, which is evident when you look at the occupations of these early township young people once they became adults. Just to name a few of these other very early institutes.

Beaver County Institute of Sciences
Beaver County Commercial College
Beaver County Institute, of New Brighton (Organized in 1837)
Greenwood Seminary
the Kenwood Boarding School for Boys (Est. 1855)
New Brighton Female Seminary (Est. in 1833)
Beaver College (Est. in 1853)
Beaver Musical Institute (Est. in 1868)
Beaver Female Seminary (opened in 1854)
North Sewickley Academy
Greersburg Academy (Est. in 1802)
Darlington Academy
Frankfort Academy and Normal School (founded in 1871)
the Young Men's Library Association, of New Brighton
Duff's College, a Business College,7th Ave. and 10th St., Beaver Falls (1800s)
Westminster College, New Wilmington, PA (founded in 1852)

~ ~ ~

CHURCHES and CEMETERIES

[8]"Then have them make a sanctuary for me, and I will dwell among them." [9]"Make this tabernacle and all its furnishings exactly like the pattern I will show you." – Exodus 25:8-9

Worship was always of great significance in Moon/Center Township. Whether a formal church building, a private home, a barn, a garage, or simply gathered outside, people found a way to regularly meet and hold services. There were and still are many places of worship within the township.

CHURCHES

McGuire Chapel - Chapel Road
Tradition says that as of 1854 there was not a Methodist Society on Moon Township's side of the river. Daniel Carey, having a great enthusiasm for promoting this form of evangelical Christianity, started to hold prayer meetings in his own home. This Methodist Society was organized in 1857, holding their first meetings in the Davis School House on Chapel Road. Daniel Carey was granted a license and placed in charge of this new Society as its class leader. As often as a preacher could be obtained, there were services held. Meantime Mr. Carey would hold prayer and class meetings every Sunday.

Rev. Latshaw McGuire and the Rev. T. N. Boyle were appointed as preachers in charge and the construction of the McGuire Chapel building began on the two acres of land Corbin Profader had donated of his farm for the chapel's usage. The new church building was completed early 1859. McGuire Chapel was a Methodist Episcopal Church and was named after the first pastor. In addition to Rev. McGuire, the church was serviced by John Wright and Keegle, then J. J. Farrell. In 1864, Eaton and N. P. Kerr were appointed and succeeded by J. V. Yarnall and James Jones.

Some families and individuals who united with the McGuire Chapel were Corban Profader, Philip Cooper, Henry Landis, Wilson Uselton, Wash. Grimm, Samuel Moore, Squire Elliott, James Davis, Braden, John Mohler, Joseph Craig, Angeline Minor, Mary Minor, George Winkle, Mary Winkle, Moses Winkle, Henry Raff, Sarah Baker, Christian Merriman, Samuel Bickerstaff, Hannah Bickerstaff, and Nancy Markee. With these first members of this chapel being residents of Moon Township and of Phillipsburg, it was soon decided to build a separate church in Phillipsburg, too, for those families. A building was purchased in Phillipsburg and a Sunday School was organized. Daniel Carey was the first Superintendent, serving in this position for eleven consecutive years. The Phillipsburg church building was erected in 1865. (This was named the Methodist Episcopal Church of Phillipsburg and is now known as Monaca Methodist Church – 813 Indiana Avenue, Monaca.)

In March of 1866, the McGuire Chapel was dropped by the Circuit and the congregation became attached to the church in Phillipsburg. There were still activities and festivals being held at the McGuire Chapel building in 1908, but with the church no longer being regularly attended and maintained, it became very run down and soon fell into disrepair, the furnishings were removed, and the building was eventually torn down. Family tradition is a house along Chapel Road was built from lumber that was once part of the McGuire Chapel. (It was related to me, Virginia and Robert Glasser lived in this home.)

McGuire Chapel

North Branch Presbyterian Church

The North Branch Church was started in 1833 as a branch of Mount Carmel U.P. Church (see further). Many of the residents of Moon Township attended services at Mount Carmel Church. Due to the great distance they had to travel, at that time using ruff roads and horses and buggies, the need for a church closer to the Moon Township homes was recognized. In 1833, Rev. J. D. Ray was visiting in the area when Daniel Weigle approached him and offered the use of his barn as a temporary location to hold services, and Daniel's house would be available when the weather turned cold. Rev. J. D. Ray was also guaranteed the sum of $100 for preaching every three weeks. Rev. Ray accepted Mr. Weigle's offer, and the North Branch of Mount Carmel Church was formed. It did not take long before the Bethlehem church began to object to the North Branch of Mount Carmel Church, stating it was encroaching on their territory, but Presbytery defined the boundaries, thus settling the matter.

> *Fact: The original name of the church was North Branch Old School Presbyterian Church. This name was officially changed to North Branch United Presbyterian Church on Jan 18, 1960.*

The attendance at Mr. Weigle's barn and home was so great that it was decided by 1834 to build a new house of worship for the congregation. Mr. Weigle donated the land for the church and the men began almost at once to fell all the necessary trees for the wood, building a 35 x 45 feet house of worship. William Irwin and John Hood used their teams of horses and traveled to Fallston to get the needed wooden slabs for seats. Once there were leg holes bored in the undersides, the church then had sufficient seating in the church. These bench type seats were used for many years, being replaced by solid oak pews.

The first mention of a meeting of session at North Branch was on Sep 17, 1835, this occurred in the house of Daniel Weigle, Sr. The first statistical report of this pastorate was in Apr 1837 with 130 persons reported by Rev. Ray in attendance. North Branch church secured a separation from Mount Carmel in 1843. There were 56 members on record at North Branch in 1844 and the first Elders at that time being James N. Douds, James R. Lafferty, and William Shroades. Between 1844 and 1870, other Elders included J. W. Taylor, Henry Phillis, James Stewart, Samuel Thompson, Andrew McDonald, Henry Alcorn, William Elliott, William Douds, James Johnston, and Stephen Meaner. Some of the early surnames of members and their families included Carey, Baker, Braden, Davis, Douds, Elliott, Irwin, Hood, Jackson, Landis, McBriar, Stewart, Shroad, Weigle, Zimmerly. In 1865, it was legally chartered by the state of Pennsylvania as the *North Branch Old School Presbyterian Church*.

Due to the very rapid growth of the congregation, it was necessary close to 1850, to build an addition of 10 feet on to the church which made the building 35' x 55'. From 1833 to 1928 the church building was of simple wood construction built by the members. The continued growth of the congregation warranted improvements and changes to be made to the church between 1850 and 1928. On Sep 22, 1929, there was a dedication to the church building which just had a total remodeling and was once again expanded and updated, making the church building from 1927/28 to 1962/63 of red brick, with multiple stained-glass windows. The church sanctuary area still has most of the original stained-glass windows that were given in memory of early members/families of the church. There were some of the original stained-glass windows removed as remodeling projects were done. Rev. J. R. Thomson became the pastor of the church at the time of the 1927 remodeling and served as the pastor at North Branch for 30 years.

> *Fact: There was a corner stone of the new church laid Nov 4, 1928.*

In 1957-the church chose to break all ties with their mother church, Mount Carmel. Jul 1, 1958, Rev. Harold W. Bowman became the Pastor. In Nov 1958, a Manse was completed on property donated from Art Coombs. This property was located on North Branch Road, a short distance from the church and Rev. Bowman and his family were the first occupants of the Manse. In Jan 1959, the congregation voted and changed the name to *The North Branch United Presbyterian Church*.

Fact: Members of the congregation were expelled for more than one reason. To be reinstated, a person had to appear at church service and have his restoration publicly announced by the pastor who also would state the reason for the suspension.

A new addition, a two-storey wing, was added to the side of the brick church building in 1962 to accommodate the needed space for Sunday School classrooms. The additions of a choir room, furnace room, Pastor's Office, and Library-Lounge area were also included within the new two-storey wing addition. Other additions/improvements in 1962 included enlargement of the sanctuary area and a new, expanded narthex area. Church membership as of Dec 31, 1982 was 470.

Fact: The first woman Elder of North Branch Church was Eleanor Lehman in 1966. The first woman Clerk of Session was Beth Speer in Feb of 1967.

1834

1840

1960s

2019

Fun fact: North Branch Church always had a very active and well attended program of classes for the children each week on Sunday mornings. Along with these classes, they offered an incentive to the children and would give an award each year to all children who had achieved perfect attendance. The first award you would receive was a decorative and colorful round pin to wear. The second year's award was a gold leaf circle that clipped on around the pin. The third award was a bar to attach to the bottom of the round pin and gold leaf circle. Likewise, each year of perfect attendance, you would receive another bar with the goal to see how many bars you could add and proudly wear to church each Sunday. Being a life-long member of North Branch Church, earning the pin, wreath, and bars was something you looked forward to. (I still have my pin and bars. ☺) Not until my own children began to attend Sunday School did the realization hit me that my parents should have received the same awards each year since they were the ones making sure I had the back ground and encouragement to attend so many years of weekly Sunday School even on those Sunday mornings I am sure I was not as inclined to 'rise and shine'.

The following Reverends and Pastors served at North Branch Church through the years: J. D. Ray 1833-1842, Joseph Raif, Samuel Hain 1844-1847, Joseph Hazlett 1847-1851, James Henderson 1851-1853, Albert C. Rockwell 1853-1856, James M. Smith 1856-1865, P. J. Cummings 1866-1873, J. R. Pomroy 1873-1875, George W. Shaffer 1875-1879, Rev. Earseman 1885-1886, Matthew Rutherford 1887-1888, John Jay Shroades 1890-1897, John T. Hackett 1897-1903, P. J. Cummings 1904-1907, Charles R. McCracken 1909-1912, Ralph E. Thurston 1915-1918, S. L./R. Johnston 1918-1920, W. J. Engle 1921-1926, J. R. Thomson 1927-1957 (30 years), Harold Bowman 1958-1967, Vance Yarnelle (Interim) 1967-1968, William J. Green 1968-1983, Joseph Hill (Interim) 1983-1984, Gregory Seckman 1984-1993, Joseph Hill (Interim) 1993-1994, Marvin Barney 1994-2009, James Steiner (Interim) 2009-2011, Kimberly Merrill (Interim) 2011-2011, A. Beery 2012-2015, Deborah Huffmyer (Interim) 2016-2019, and Rev. Don Snyder (temporary) 2019-2020s.
(Also see Mt. Carmel Church further.)

Free Methodist Church of Sylvan Crest   aka   **Sylvan Crest Free Methodist Church**
This church was built on Wagner Road in the Sylvan Crest area of the township by a small group of people in that area who felt the need of a Sunday School and church building close to their homes. They started by meeting in the fire department building. In 1943, a lot was donated by Mr. and Mrs. Ray Johnson to be used for the building site of the church building and interested residents completed the basement of the church. They then met in it until the church building was completed in 1956. Rev. Donald Rosenbaum was the first pastor.
  This church and the Free Methodist Church (which was organized in Jan 1904) in Monaca merged/joined in 1971/1972 and became the current Monacrest Free Methodist Church now located on the corner of Elmira and Walnut Street in Monaca Heights. The former Sylvan Crest Free Methodist Church building was sold after the merger and was converted into a private home and is still used as such nowadays.

Bunker Hill Community Church – 170 Pleasant Drive
A group of spiritual persons met in Sep of 1942 at the home of Mr. and Mrs. Harold Swogger on Moffett Run Road* (*now a section of Pleasant Drive). They discussed starting a non-denominational Sunday School for the Bunker Hill area residents. It was decided to hold the first

Sunday School in the V.F.W. Post which was formerly the Bunker Hill School building. Attendance quickly grew and averaged as high as 100. Mr. and Mrs. Pearl Lowery donated a piece of ground along Moffett Run Road*. The property was cleared, and excavation began, the footer was completed and thanks to a generous donation, the members and their friends erected a large 36' x 50' basement. A regular Sunday School was then started. As of 1949, the church began to collect for a fund to complete the actual church building.

The Bunker Hill Community Church was officially organized Jun 6, 1951 and chartered in 1955. At this time, the congregation still did not have a church building erected since they had decided not to erect this church on the current basement structure. Instead, an acre of ground was purchased from Mr. and Mrs. Harold Swogger on Pleasant Drive and a new church basement was built. By 1957, the first services were held in the upstairs of the new building which had not yet quite been completed. Through multiple donations, the church building received stain glass windows and other needed windows. There was a copper bell in the bell tower which was donated by the Jones & Laughlin Steel Corporation through Mr. R. A. Wilsoncroft. This bell came from a J & L steamboat.

The exterior of the church still looks as it did in the late 1950s and is also still well attended. A few familiar family names of this church were Rev. Alexander, Rev. Howells, Parsons, Dyke, Myers, Schwarz, McKeel, Wickham, Lowery, Jones, Rambo, Good, McCartney, Blair, Rev. Alexander, and Mason.

The Vankirk Lutheran Church aka **Vankirk Mission** – 106 Vankirk Road
The residents in the Vankirk aka Stobo area recognized the need for a church near their homes. Rev. Charles E. Read was pastor of Monaca Redeemer Lutheran Church and became interested in starting a church for the Vankirk area. He was given permission from the church in Monaca to do so if it did not interfere with his work at the Monaca church. Rev. Read also was granted permission by the Center Township School Board to use the one-room Vankirk School building for holding services. The first Sunday School service was held on Mar 10, 1929. Teachers included Mrs. Herman Weigle, Mrs. Fred Shively, Mrs. A. C. Fath, Mrs. Henry Shepard, and the Pastor. Preaching services began on May 5, 1929, with fifty-two people present; Rev. Read was Superintendent, Elma Shively was the Secretary, and Edward Erickson, Treasurer.

The Batchelor family donated a piece of ground in the area to the church in 1939/40. A charter was received and recorded on Mar 2, 1940, for the church under the name of the Vankirk Lutheran Church. There was a groundbreaking event held on Sep 22, 1940, and by May of 1941 a small building was to be erected. The congregation had planned to erect a concrete block building, but then decided to purchase the recently closed school building they had been using, move it across the road to the new church lot and put a basement under it. The school building was moved, the cornerstone was laid in Jul 1942, and in Mar 1943, a vestibule was built to the front of the church and electrical wiring was added to the basement. There was an addition erected to the church building in 1970. (See Vankirk School House information in the Education section for another photograph of earlier building.)

 c 1980    2019

St Frances Cabrini Catholic Church – 115 Trinity Drive
This Parish was established on May 24, 1961, with the Most Reverend John J. Wright, Bishop of the Pittsburgh Dioceses. The church building was officially dedicated Jul 19, 1964. The property included about ten and one-half acres of the former Hall family farm along Chapel Road. This land was given to the Dioceses of Pittsburgh on Aug 2, 1960 by Mrs. Mary Hall. (Ebenezer and Mary Hall purchased the property from Pankraz and Cecilia Finzel in 1927 - see Dusold Family information in Houses and Family section.)   The first Mass was held in the William Leasha home on Hall Road Jun 4, 1961, then daily Masses were held in the Center Bowling Lanes while the church building was being erected. Work was completed on the part of the building area that was to be the gymnasium area for the church. It was furnished and the first mass was celebrated in this new building on Dec 22, 1963. A social hall and seven classrooms were also constructed and completed in Feb 1971. Rev. Thomas O'Connell was appointed pastor in 1969, he retired in 1996. Rev. Joseph Kleppner was appointed pastor in 1996. He retired in 2014. As of 2019, there was a parish grouping of St. John the Baptist (Monaca), St. Titus (Aliquippa), Our Lady of Fatima (Hopewell), and this St. Frances Cabrini with masses being held at various times in each of the churches.

Faith Lutheran Church – 100 Center Grange Road
After a very promising survey was taken in Center Township by the Board of American Missions of the United Lutheran Church of America, a seminary student, Mr. LeRoy Dobbe decided to take a year's internship and organize the interested people into a congregation in the area. Sunday School services were started late in Aug of 1953 and worship services began in Oct of the same year, all held in the Center Grange Hall building. With sixty-six people, the charter was signed on Jan 17, 1954 for the Faith Lutheran Church. Two lots on the corner of Brodhead Road and Center Grange Road were purchased in Mar 1954. By the fall of 1954, plans for the church building were completed and work had started. In 1956, the church purchased additional property from Andrew and Ann Miller (owners of Babe's custard stand). The first service was held in the new church building on Jul 20, 1958. There were three hundred and twelve baptized members, two hundred and two confirmed, and one hundred seventy-six communing members.

University Baptist Church, SBC (Southern Baptist Church)
I did not find much of the earlier history of this church regarding when it was first formed and/or organized in Center Township. By Aug 1971, they had purchased land that was formerly and/or at least adjacent to Frank Kalinoski's former property along Brodhead Road (before the renumbering of Brodhead Road, the address was 1251). This property extended from Brodhead Road back to Joshua Patterson's former property (currently CCBC). At the time the University Baptist Church made this purchase, the owners of the property were William and Agnes Fezell. The Fezells had acquired different portions of the land from various individuals. In the 1940s, they had land from Joseph and Mary Normann, Daryl Coe, Michael Uyak, Jr., with only the 3.04 acres on the corner of Poplar Drive and Community College Drive (that now faces CCBC) being named for the church, and erection of the church building began. While the new church was under construction, the congregation held services in the building along Brodhead Road, currently 3571 Brodhead Road (this building was previously Meiter's Garage, then Pelino's Bar, Colony Center Bar, and Beaver Valley Office Equipment, currently The Healing Place). In 1976, Rev. Fred Jolly was the pastor and the University Baptist Church (Southern Baptist Council) and they still had their principal office address as being on Brodhead Road.

The church changed their name and became..........

Open Door Baptist Church - 118 Community College Drive
The Open Door Baptist Church sold the building and property along Poplar Drive in 1992 to the Trinity Evangelical Free Church.

Beginning in 1992............

Trinity Evangelical Free Church - 118 Community College Drive
This church was known as Trinity Community Church of Center Township, f/k/a Trinity Evangelical Free Church of Center Township, a/k/a Trinity Evangelical Free Church. In Sep 2015, there was yet another deed of the property and building to the Centerpoint Community Church of Center Township due to a name change. The pastor of this church is Stephen Vesolich.

The church changed the name in 2015 and became..........

Centerpoint Community Church of Center Township – 118 Community College Drive
This is the name of the current church. Stephen Vesolich, Pastor.

Christian House Chapel /Southern Baptist Council
This church was started in Apr 28, 1991. It was once located in the area by the Montgomery Dam. In the 1990s, the congregation moved to the former Mount Pleasant Presbyterian Church site at 811 Frankfort Road in Raccoon Township. Mount Pleasant purchased 39 acres a short distance further along Route 18 (Frankfort Road) and erected a new church building. Both churches currently are in Raccoon Township.

Church of Jesus Christ of Latter Day Saints (Mormon) – 114 Church Drive
Mormon missionaries served in this area for many years. In 1966, the church purchased a portion of the property that was originally part of the Kalinoski farm. They erected their church building in 1968/71 and the chapel was added 1978.

Aliquippa Christian Assembly – off W. Shaffer Road
In 1991, Theodore Rebich, Jr. sold/deeded 10 acres of property to this assembly and in 1994 additional property for a right of way/drive was also obtained. The organization also purchased an additional 1.71 acres in 1996 from another individual. This assembly is still active.

City Reach Church Central Valley – Center Grange Road
Living Water Fellowship began to use the former Center Grange No. 1870 building and property. This building and property were purchased by the Beaver County Church in 1997.

Jehovah's Witnesses Kingdom Hall – 108 Spruce Drive
The Rochester Congregation of Jehovah's Witnesses purchased many individual lots of property on Cedar Drive, off Spruce Drive in 1987. The building is said to have been erected by volunteers in just 3 days in Oct 1988, dedicated in 1989. In 2007/08, the Monaca Congregation of Jehovah's Witnesses were deeded the property and building from the Rochester Congregation. This deed was actually only to legally/officially make a name change.

Mt. Carmel Church - Brodhead Road – Sheffield, Aliquippa
The original building of this congregation was in Moon Township (now Center Township). The current Mt. Carmel Church building is now situated in the Borough of Aliquippa's New Sheffield area. Mt. Carmel Church was first known by the name of White Oaks Flats Church. The first church building stood on a portion of the property that is currently the Mount Carmel Cemetery, located at the end of Mount Carmel Lane, off Brodhead Road. There are said to still be some bricks of the earlier church's structure that remains within the cemetery's grounds.

The exact date of the founding of Mount Carmel is unknown but the first written records begin on Oct 22, 1793 in the minutes of Presbytery of Ohio when supplies (request for a pastor) were requested for White Oak Flats, Mill Creek, Mouth of Raccoon, and Kings Creek. From these minutes, it is written that the Mount Carmel congregation was first formed in 1793. As stated, the original name of the church was the White Oak Flats Church, with this name seemingly chosen because of the large primeval white oak trees that then covered the area. Application was made and permission of Presbytery was granted to change the name of the church to Mount Carmel in Oct 1829.

The first meeting house established by the congregation in the 1700s was referred to as a *'tent'*, which stood in the general area of the current church building, which during that period was considered a part of Hopewell Township. The word "tent" may not have meant the same as one envisions nowadays but instead would have been more of a gazebo type structure with no formal walls, doors, or windows. The membership gathered and worshipped in the 'tent' from about 1794 until 1814. The latter date of 1814 is used because there are minutes existing of two session meetings held on Jun 22 and Jul 7, 1812, that stated the meetings were "held at the tent."

The first official church structure was built of hewed logs on the property in what is now Center Township and part of the current Mt. Carmel Cemetery. A few years later, a frame structure was added to one end of the log structure. Then in 1835, a *branch* was established, which later became known as the North Branch Church. Both the addition and the formation of North Branch Church were the result of the growth in the church population and/or to make the church more accessible to its members that lived some miles to the north. (See North Branch Church previous.) On Sabbath morning of Apr 16, 1837, the entire 1814 church was destroyed by a fire. The congregation erected another church building on the same property. It was larger and made more comfortable than the old building. It was built entirely of brick, measured fifty by forty feet, and fifteen feet high from foundation to eves at a cost of $2,000. Unfortunately, I found no surviving pictures of these early church buildings at this site in Center Township. This brick church officially opened in 1838 and served the congregation until the 1870s when a much larger structure was needed. Some writings have related the first church building was built on the same site as the original "tent" (which was in New Sheffield), but in a 1934 address delivered by Rev. J. R. Thomson, he stated that in 1813/1814, a house of worship was erected on the same property they were currently using -- meaning the church building was built at the location of the current cemetery. His statement disproves the believe that the very first church building was erected on the current property of the Mount Carmel church.

With the need to expand not only the growing congregation, but the expanding need for more burial ground in the cemetery, the congregation elected to place the new church back where it had all begun almost a hundred years earlier in New Sheffield, along Brodhead Road, most likely on or near the very place where the earlier "tent" had stood. Dr. J. F. Cooper donated the land for this new 1870s church. The new church was dedicated in 1874. Shortly thereafter, the brick church at the cemetery was dismantled, and since then newer graves have taken over the spot where the church once stood. Some of the foundation stones of the 1838 church can still be seen among the graves in the center of the cemetery. The new 1870s church building cost $8,000 and was still standing in the mid/late 1900s, with the name being changed to Mount Carmel Presbyterian Church. There was an educational wing added to the rear of this original frame building. The frame portion of the church was torn down and a new sanctuary was erected. There were many small wooden crosses made from the dismantled frame church and sold to raise funds to supplement construction of the new structure.

Mt. Carmel Church building built in the 1870s at its current location at the intersection of Brodhead Road, Kennedy Blvd, and Mill Street in Sheffield, Aliquippa.

The old frame with addition attached just prior to demolition.

Current look of the church building.

Some of the first members of White Oak Flats included Henry and Esther (Patton) Bryan, their daughters – Jane and Margaret, members of the Douds family (including John and Mary (Hutchison) Douds and his parents). Membership for the most part steadily grew, having some periods of fluctuation when larger number of transfers occurred, including 1810 – 39, 1815 - 100, 1822 – 124, 1842 - 163, 1882 - 185, and 1934 - 481.

The list of actual Pastors to the church is quite lengthy. On Aug 21, 1810, Rev. Andrew McDonald became the pastor. He held this position until Oct 22, 1823. Rev. McDonald is buried in the Mount Carmel cemetery. Other pastors of the church after Rev. McDonald included Rev. W. J. Fraser 1825-1826, Rev. Robt. Rutherford 1827-1828, Rev. James D. Ray 1829-1843, Rev. David McKinney (a supply) 1860-1862, Rev. W. G. Taylor 1862-1865, Rev. P. J. Cummings 1866-1882, he came back in 1886 to 1898, Dr. B. B. Luther 1902-1903 (the minutes reflect his days were few and evil), Rev. J. D. Campbell 1904-1907, Rev G. S. Macauley (Supply and Pastor) 1908-1913, Rev. R. E. Thurston 1915-1917, Rev. S. L. Johnston 1918-1920, Rev W. J. Engle 1921-1926, and Rev. J. R. Thomson 1927-1958.

Through the years of 1794 to 1902, there were also quite a few missionaries and supplies of the church who filled in the gaps when there was no true Pastor of the church. Many of those found included: Revs. John R. Agnew, J. F. Andrews, Dr. J. J. Beacon, S. S. Bergen, J. F. Boyd, Mr. Bracken, John Brice, Mr. Cochran, Robert Dilworth, Mr. Eastman, William Eaton, Mr. Edwards, Samuel Hare, John Hazlett, Samuel Henderson, Mr. R. Hill, Samuel Jennings, Keiling, Lee, Mr. McClain, Alexander McCandless, McCully, David McKinney, Dr. John McMillen, Robert McPhearson, Boyd Mercer, J. N. Mercer, Mr. Neely, William Nesbitt, A.B. Quay, Mr. Ralstone, H. H. Ryland, Abraham Scott, William Scott, G. W. Shaffer, Thomas Stevenson, J. J. Wells, John Wood.

~ ~ ~

Miscellaneous other Early Local Churches

Prior to official churches being established in Moon Townships, early residents may have attended services at any one of the churches listed further. Even though it was quite a trip to have made for attending church services at one of these churches with horse and buggy being the early means of transportation, this indicates how strong these early residents' faith was for them to make these long trips to attend a church of their choice. Family ties to churches and tradition were also strong draws for Moon Township residents to continue to attend a church so many miles away from their homestead. There is some information further on a few of these early churches for those who may be interested or had ancestors who may have attended one of these churches.

Mill Creek Church   aka   Mill Creek United Presbyterian Church of Hookstown   and
currently   Mill Creek Evangelical Presbyterian Church of Hookstown

Mill Creek church's history lists the year 1784 for being the accepted date of its beginning as a church, this places Mill Creek among one of the oldest Presbyterian congregations in the region. (Mill Creek was once said to be the oldest of any denomination in Beaver County, but it was discovered that the Service Church was operating at least by 1779.) Application for supplies was made to the Presbytery of Redstone in 1785.

The first meeting places, even in winter, were out in the forests using a pulpit of logs with the people sitting on logs conveniently arranged. The first actual meeting house was an 18 x 20-foot log structure located on the property where the old portion of the current cemetery is located. This church had neither doors nor windows and was lighted from the roof. The entrance into the church was by underground passage. Why you might ask, well, these measures were taken for protection from the Indians who sometimes were in a killing mood. The second church building was built across the road from the cemetery, constructed of double hewn logs, 30 x 60 feet. This church had no floor or door at first, but both were added, as were a pulpit, pews, and stoves. In 1832 the log church was replaced by a 50 x 60-foot brick edifice with a raised platform. In 1869, this church was replaced with a 70 x 48-foot brick church. Once again in 1882, a 70 x 38-foot church building was constructed. The church building of the Mill Creek Church was expanded and now includes a large sanctuary, fellowship hall, and many classrooms. The church is now located along 5005 PA-151, Hookstown, PA.

"In Aug 2015 the congregation voted for dismissal from the Presbyterian Church U.S.A. to seek a denominational home more in line with its historic Presbyterian roots and orthodox Christian faith. In Sep 2016, the Presbytery of the Alleghenies of the Evangelical Presbyterian Church received Mill Creek into its membership, and the name was subsequently changed to Mill Creek Evangelical Presbyterian of Hookstown." The Old Mill Creek Church Cemetery is located off Old Mill Creek Road, which is off Routes 30 and/or 168, Hookstown.

As families grew and members reach maturity, moving further away from their parents' homesteads, many moved their place of worships to those of closer proximity, including Mt. Carmel Church and/or North Branch Church to name a few.

Photo by Andrew Buda / from the church web page.   Plaque at the site of the cemetery.

Mill Creek Church – was a mother church to many other congregations including:
- 1830 – Bethlehem   1849 – Glasgow   Frankfort (U.P.)
- 1835 – Frankfort   1854 – Hookstown   Hanover
- 1840 – Liverpool, Ohio   Tomlinson Run (U.P.)   Hookstown (U.P.)

Service Creek Church aka **Service Church** – 491 Service Church Road, Aliquippa
This church is located along the banks of the Ambridge reservoir. It was organized in the 1700's and is one of the oldest, even reported the oldest church of any denomination in the county. In 1792, the Rev. John Anderson, D.D. was installed as its pastor. In 1794 – Service Creek Church is reported as a great influence of the merger with the first seminary established west of the Alleghenies by the Rev. Anderson who was elected by the Associate Presbytery of Pennsylvania as its teacher in divinity in Apr 1794. They gave him the option to locate the seminary and he chose a site about one mile west of Service Church on the road from Beaver to Frankfort Springs.

Books were a very valuable asset in the early years and this seminary formed a library which consisted of about eight hundred such valuable books. The first church building is said to have been a log cabin that was replaced by a 50 x 60-foot brick structure. In addition to Rev. Anderson, other early pastors of the church were Rev. William Meek McElwee, D.D., Rev. David Carson, D.D., Rev. John Roe, Rev W. J. Golden, Rev. A. P. Gibson, and K. W. McFarland. Some of the early members included the Nelsons, Shillitos, Craigs, Shanes, Haneys, Ewings, Robertsons, Littells, Campbells, McKibbens, Smiths families.

Service Creek Church cemetery is now known as John Anderson Memorial Cemetery, named for Dr. John Anderson, the pastor from 1788-1810.

Bethlehem Presbyterian Church – 183 New Bethlehem Church Road, Aliquippa
William Rambo and John Potter were among the group of men who wanted to start a church in the region of Raccoon Creek. Many members of the Mt. Carmel and Mill Creek churches were looking for a church closer to their homes. Mr. Potter began to hold a Sabbath school in the early fall of 1830 and first met in the home of Edward Crail. This Sabbath school was held in many various private homes until the church was erected. Some of these homes were of William Conner, John Potter, and Abraham Vaughn. Rev. John K. Cunningham was appointed to preach and organize the church in 1832, but he was not assigned as the pastor of the church. William Rambo and Jonathan Cross were ordained and installed as a few of the early elders. The church had no regular pastor for 11 years and seven months, but sill grew to a membership of one hundred fifty. Rev. Samuel Hair was the first regular pastor of Bethlehem. He started in the fall of 1844. Other early pastors after Rev. Hair were John Hazlett, Rev. A. O. Rockwell, Rev. James M. Smith, Rev. William White, Rev. J. S. Pomeroy, Rev. George Shaffer, Rev. D. L. Dickey, Rev. M. Cummings, Rev. J. H. Hunter, Mrev. T. P. Potts, M. M. Rogers. Some early members of Bethlehem were the Kerr, Gormley, Tucker, Cross, Wilson, Rambo, Potter, Engle, Elliott, Hood, and Christy families. From Rev. Hair to Rev. Smith (1844 until about 1877), Bethlehem was connected with the North Branch Church. Bethlehem then became connected with Hookstown. William Rambo donated the land for the church building and graveyard. He is also credited with building the church in 1832 with funds raised by the people.

> *Fun fact: It was written in one of the history books (referring to the church....) "This was the first building of any kind that was erected in that neighborhood without the use of whisky by the workers."*

Mouth of Raccoon Church
There has never been any previous mention of this church in local history to my knowledge, yet it is proven to have existed when you review the minutes of Redstone Presbytery and Presbytery of Ohio. These minutes and records do indeed state that the *Mouth of Raccoon Church* was sufficiently organized and trails back to at least Oct 1788. The Mouth of Raccoon Church made a request for a pastor in Oct of 1793 according to the minutes of the Presbytery of Ohio. By the name of the

church, it would seem this church was in the area of the mouth of Raccoon Creek which would have been in the original Moon Township boundaries during the 1700s.

Exerpt from 1793-1819 minutes of the Ohio Presbytery in the 1889 publication of *History of the Presbytery of Washington, including a brief account*................

> Applications for supplies were made from Mill Creek, King's Creek, White Oak Flats, and the Mouth of Raccoon.

* * * * * *

With the time frame of the above excerpt being prior to 1823, it indicates the Mouth of Raccoon, Bethlehem Church, and Raccoon U. P. Church were definitely three separate churches or perhaps the recorded organization date of Bethlehem Church and/or Raccoon U. P. Church in the early 1820s is incorrect and was actually much earlier. I have no additional information at this time for the Mouth of Raccoon Church.

Raccoon Church aka **Raccoon U. P. Church** – Crissman Drive, Aliquippa

The New Life Presbyterian Church of Hopewell Township states that Raccoon Associate Reformed Church was organized in about 1823. The congregation first met in homes and/or barns, including the barn of William McCune. It is estimated that they erected their new frame church in 1837 on the west edge of the same property as the current cemetery, along Mill Street, Aliquippa, PA. The old foundation of this first building was discovered in the digging of a grave. The current Raccoon Church is much further in on Raccoon Creek from the mouth of the creek, so whether that designates it a completely separate church of the Mouth of Raccoon Church (see previous) or not is unknown. By 1867, they had erected a second church building on the site of the current church on Crissman Drive, off Patterson Drive and Golf Course Road, Aliquippa, PA.

The first elders of this congregation were James McCormick and William McCune. Some of the early ministers in the 1800s included James Prestly, Robert Armstrong, William Wilson, James Witherspoon, James Sharp, Hugh Millin, M. D. Telford. With the second church building being erected c1867 on the same site as the current New Life Presbyterian Church of Hopewell Township, the New Life church states it has common history with the Raccoon United Presbyterian Church. The New Life church currently has their building adjacent to the current Raccoon Church Cemetery along Mill Street, Aliquippa, Pa. and Raccoon U. P. Church currently sits further off Mill Street, on Crissman Drive.

Kings Creek Church

Kings Creek Presbyterian Church was organized in 1785. It was located approximately four miles from Florence, Washington County (in Hanover Township). The congregation moved to Florence PA and from that location, it was renamed Cross Roads Presbyterian Church because it was near the intersection of Pittsburgh-Steubenville Pike and Washington-Georgetown Road. It was renamed again later to Florence Presbyterian Church. The cemetery is located in Raccoon Creek State Park grounds. I included the information on this church since there were several mentions of it attached to families that settled in this area of the former Moon Township. The trip to and from this church would surely have been an all-day venture in those very early years for anyone living in what became Center Township.

Mt. Pleasant Church – 846 State Route 18, Aliquippa

This church came from a merger in 1876 of the members of the United Presbyterian Church of Hookstown and the Service United Presbyterian Church of Raccoon Township. They built a new church on J. A. Ingles' farm. Rev D. W. Carson was asked to serve the new group. The congregation approved naming the new church Mt. Pleasant Congregation in 1877. This first building was destroyed by fire in the summer of 1900, but the pulpit furniture and many of the pews survived the fire. The congregation quickly rebuilt the burned church. Prior to 2001, 39 acres of new property was purchased and mid 1997 construction began on a new church building.

~ ~ ~

Miscellaneous information.....
1848 – two original congregations of Beaver County merged (The Associate (Seceders) and The Associated Reform) and resulted in The United Presbyterian Church of North America.

~ ~ ~

A very well-known pastor in Beaver County was Rev. John R. Thomson. When he died Sep 19, 1966, there was a special article in the local newspaper stating his death.......

Retired Minister
Is Taken by Death

Rev. John R. Thomson, North Branch Road, Center Township, retired United Presbyterian minister, died Monday at 12:50 p.m. in Aliquippa Hospital following an illness of several days. He was 75.

Rev. Thomson had been serving as supply pastor for Service UP Church, Raccoon Township and Frankfort Springs UP Church.

He had been pastor of North Branch Church, Center Township, and Mt. Carmel Church, Aliquippa, for 31 years until his retirement in 1958.

Survivors include his widow Mary McCready Thomson, his son, Richard, and daughter, Mary Lee (both still living at home), and his brother, Harry.

There was a private funeral service held for Rev. Thomson in the Welch Funeral Home, Hookstown officiated by Rev. James W. St. Clair who was the pastor at First UP Church in Bridgewater.

Rev. Thompson was born in Nov 1890, son of David and Margaret (Crooks) Thompson of Pulaski Township. Rev. and Mary had been living on Brodhead Road, Aliquippa, PA at the time of his death. They are buried in the Beaver Cemetery.

~ ~ ~

Cemeteries

Fact: Typically, the difference between a cemetery and a graveyard is...a cemetery does not adjoin or is not adjacent to a church whereas a graveyard refers to a burial ground within a churchyard.

Following is a condensed list of cemeteries and graveyards of the township. There is more detailed information included further for many of these.

The immediate Center, Potter, and Monaca area has several larger, more public cemeteries:
    Beaver County Memorial Park Cemetery
    Union Cemetery
    Fairview Cemetery   aka   McLaughlin Cemetery
    Vankirk Cemetery   aka   McCollough (McCullough) Cemetery
    McGuire Chapel Cemetery
    Baker   aka   Baldwin Monaca Cemetery
    Mt. Carmel Cemetery
    North Branch Cemetery
    Monaca German Lutheran Cemetery   aka   St. Peter's Evangelical Lutheran
    St. John's Catholic Cemetery
    St. Joseph's Cemetery

The cemeteries listed below were not very large cemeteries and most likely burials were done specifically for family members on their farm property. These are all lesser known or cemeteries which no longer exist (many exact locations are unknown), therefore, there is not much information on many of these except the fact they do/did exist.

- Baker Cemetery aka Figley Farm Cemetery
- Otto Farm Burial –Temple Road
- Smega Farm Burial –Elkhorn Road
- Weigel Private Cemetery
- Stone Cemetery – Potter Township
- Weaton Cemetery – Potter Township
- Beaver County Poor Home Cemetery
- Laubscher Farm Burial –on Chapel Road
- Braden/Potter Cemetery
- Douds Cemetery
- Fath Burial –on Elkhorn Road
- Fath Farm Burials
- Kozar's Burial
- Beaver County Memorial Park

~ ~ ~

McGuire Chapel Cemetery aka **Chapel Valley Cemetery**

This cemetery is located on Chapel Road heading toward Monaca, a short distance from the intersection of Chapel and Center Grange Roads. It was established at the time of the McGuire Chapel in 1859. The cemetery was adjacent to the chapel building which was built in 1858/59 on 2 acres of farmland donated land from Corban Prophader. The name of the church and cemetery came from the first pastor, Latchall McGuire.

As his project to earn the ranking of Eagle Scout, Anthony Kinest took on the task of cleaning up the cemetery. He also researched many old documents, as well as contacting many people to properly locate and identify as many of the burials/grave sites as possible. Some of the surnames from this cemetery include Baker, Coleman, Cooper, Craig, Ewing, Fath, Glasser, Hamilton, Irwin, Johnston, Landis, Moffett, Shivler, Stewart, Uselton, and Weigel.

North Branch Cemetery - adjacent to the church building on North Branch Road

The church and cemetery are visible from the intersection of Routes 18 and Brodhead Road (formerly 18 & 51). This is considered to be first used beginning when the church was built in 1833 and indeed, is among the very old cemeteries. In 2002/2003, over one hundred seventy years later it was closed off to any additional lots being sold. A few of the oldest burials I found on record were Samuel Baily–d. Dec 1826, William Shroads–d. Feb 1842, Nancy Jane Shroads–b. Jan 1847–d. Apr 1847, Brown Irwin–d. Dec 1849, and Susannah Bickerstaff–d. Aug 1847. Some of the other names of family members buried in this cemetery include Alcorn, Badders, Bailey, Baker, Barto, Bickerstaff, Black, Blair, Bruce, Campbell, Cochran, Davis, Douds, Dunn, Engle, Figley, Grinder, Hicks, Huffmyer, Irwin, Johnston, Jordan, Landis, Manor, McCullough, McDonald, Meaner, Minor, Raw, Shroads, Smith, Stewart, Todd, Weigel, White, Winkle, Zimmerly.

Mount Carmel Cemetery   -   Located in Center Township, off Brodhead Road on Orchard Street. This cemetery was the original cemetery first used for members of the White Oak Presbyterian Church congregation (the original name of Mount Carmel Church). It is situated on former Cooper and Baker properties. The original church building was first located within the current cemetery property prior to a new structure being built at the present location of the Mount Carmel Church on Brodhead Road in New Sheffield.

This cemetery contains over four hundred fifty burials. Burials are still held in this cemetery. The church owned the property at this site by at least 1822 since records indicate Daniel McDonald was buried here in 1822. His stone is no longer visible, but others show dates in the late 1820s and early 1830s. One of the oldest legible stones in this cemetery is of Nancy Cross, who died in 1834 in the 6th year of her age. The oldest deed found of this land for this cemetery was of 1 ½ acres. A deed dated Jun 7, 1837, shows John and Elizabeth Cooper selling 4 acres of land to the church for $10.00 and stipulated on the deed for "use as a place of worship and a burying ground." Also, within this same deed, it shows this acreage being adjacent to land previously purchased by the church from William Cooley (nothing further was found regarding this purchase).

Some surnames of burials include Anderson, Baker, Barry, Blair, Boyd, Brotherton, Bruce, Chamberlain, Champion, Cross, Cummings, Davidson, Davis, Douds, Elder, Engle, Erwin, Figley, Haffey, Hutchinson, Irons, Irwin, Johnston, Kronk, Long, Maratta, McClintock, McDonald, Moore, Oliver, Reed, Riddle, Ritchie, Riter, Schrodes, Shrodes, Scott, Springer, Steen, Stewart, Tate, Temple, Todd, Uselton, Wallace, White, and Zimmerly.

St. Joseph's Cemetery   aka   **St. Titus Cemetery**   - Temple Road
It is located off Elkhorn Road, on Temple Road, one to two miles in on the left (near the area referred to as Plan 11 of Aliquippa).   There are 2 entrances to this cemetery. St. Joseph's was started in 1906 and was used for burying parishioners from St. Joseph's Catholic Church in West Aliquippa.   When this church was closed, the parishioners began to attend St. Titus Church in Aliquippa and they took care for the cemetery at that time. Although there have been some more recent burials here, the majority are now interned in Hopewell Township at the Roman Catholic Cemetery.   Information has been held by the St. Titus Rectory in Aliquippa but are said to be very poor records.

St. John the Baptist Parish Cemetery – Chapel Road
This cemetery is located along Chapel Road, a short distance from the corner of Brodhead and Chapel Roads, and a short distance past the Monaca Turn Verein parking lot. The cemetery consists of 11 acres. An above ground columbarium was added in the 2000s. There are quite a few more than six hundred burials in this cemetery.

Fath Farm Burial
This cemetery is located on the former Fath's farmland on Elkhorn Road.

Laubscher Farm Burials
The Laubscher family owned many acres of land along Chapel Road.   Family tradition, death certificates, and other historical records have provided information and stated there were indeed burials done on the family's farm. Exactly where the burials were located is unknown.

Fairview Cemetery
This cemetery is now within/part of the Union Cemetery property. It is on the upper left portion at the very top of the hill. At the onset, Mr. Schlosser owned the Fairview Cemetery. The road to this cemetery originally began on Marshall Road, just opposite the former Mateer barn, and extended to the top of the hill. This former roadway would have been approximately where the current roadway is still used by the owners of the garage/car business across from the former Mateer's car sales.

A Nov 1933 article provides definite proof of the Fairview Cemetery's existence. These are some snippets from this article.   *...A Monaca cemetery, in Center Township, formerly Moon Township....*

...On the north by Marshall Road Extension....   ...On the east by lands of Frederick Docktor & now or formerly of William Temple heirs....   ...On the west by the Union Cemetery....   ...Total - containing 10 acres and 71 perches....

There were also numerous mentions of veterans of WWI that were said to be buried in the Fairview Cemetery. From visiting my own parents' gravesites in the Union Cemetery, I can verify that there are indeed numerous veterans buried in this portion of the cemetery. Fairview Cemetery was blended/incorporated into Union Cemetery and is now called the *Fairview Section of the Union Cemetery*.

Union Cemetery - Located on corner of Brodhead and Chapel Road

From c. late 1800s to 1900
This picture includes the "tent" or gazebo that was used within the Fairview / Union Cemetery.

Union Cemetery is listed among the oldest and most historic cemeteries in Beaver County. It is also know for the many war veterans and distinguished community leaders buried in the cemetery. The original property of this cemetery was purchased from George Docker in 1890 and consisted of 35 to 40 acres. It was originally started by Edward Kaye and Herman Speyer, later owned by the Bachelor Brothers until the early 2000s. Today it is under other ownership. Union Cemetery had an office located at 1020 Pennsylvania Avenue in at least 1956. Fairview Cemetery was the original cemetery and became incorporated into the Union Cemetery.

Leaf Bros., Civil Engineers, laid out the lots in Union Cemetery in 1890 and entered the plat map in Dec 1893. This plat map showed the cemetery was basically laid out in a circular shape. In the center of the cemetery was a large circle of ground that simply had the large letters of G.A.R., with no plots for graves within this circle. There were two main roadways that appeared on the map. Each of these made a complete circle around/through the cemetery. Carfield Avenue went left and right from the main entrance and Lincoln Avenue was the inner circle roadway. There were smaller roadways or possibly just walking paths listed throughout the entire cemetery also. These included Ridge Avenue, Honeysuckle Path, Hillside Path, Pansy Path, Evergreen Path, Lily Path, Carp Path, Oak Leaf Path, Laurel Path, Locust Path, Cedar Walk, Magnola Walk, Pennsylvania Walk, and two others whose names could not be read.

From c. late 1800s to 1900

Former look of the entrance for Union Cemetery.

Current view of the entrance for Union Cemetery 2014

Until more recently, there was a stone and metal fencing that enclosed a lily pond at the front of the cemetery property along Brodhead Road. This was originally built under a beautiful weeping willow tree. The 1893 plat map listed this pond as Carp Pond. A separate small roadway that appears to have come off Brodhead Road right by the pond and circled around the pond, was also on this original plat map. The willow tree has long since been removed, and more recently, all the stone border and railing around the pond, too. The pond now simply has a natural border and appearance.

Vankirk Cemetery   aka   **McCollough (McCullough) Cemetery**
The Vankirk Cemetery is located in the woods at the end of Vankirk Road which is off Monaca Road. The 1876 atlas shows Andy McCullough owned 47 acres, Jas. McCullough owned 48 acres, and William Vankirk owned 28 acres – all surrounding the area of the cemetery. The American Legion of Monaca use to maintain this cemetery, but current caregivers are unknown. Unfortunately, it was terribly overgrown when I last visited the area.

There are only about sixteen stones still visible. From these stones, it is evident that this cemetery existed at least by the 1830s, however, there are even records that indicate there were burials here prior to 1785. None of the very early stones exist now. The earliest stone still visible is of Catharine Winkler who died 10/3/1837 aged 73 years. A few other burials indicate John Winkler, d. 12/30/1848, aged 98 years and Elizabeth Hicks, daughter of William and Abigail, b. 10/4/1836-d. 2/20/1851. Names of family members known to be buried in this cemetery are Vankirk, McCullough, Black, Carson, Cassiday, Craig, Ewing, Graham, Hicks, Huffmyer, McCollough, Red, Winkler.

Kozar's Burials
Records indicate only one burial is located here. This burial is reported to be only ten yards from the front porch of the over 140-year-old, large, two storey, wood frame home that sits in a cool, damp hollow off East Shaffer Road. It marks the location of the ashes of Joseph Kozar. In 1922, Karl Hanel and his wife purchased this home in a tax sale. Karl's wife became a widow in 1940, with records indicating he was found hanging in the barn, an apparent suicide at the age of 61. The barn has been torn down. Close to 1945, Joseph and Margaret (Hanel) Kozar moved in and were living with Margaret's widowed mother, Mrs. Karl Hanel. The actual known burial at this site is of Joseph Kozar, s/o Mr. and Mrs. Stefan Kozar. As 2005, the gravestone was said to still be in place. (See family section for more on this older farmhouse – Hanel/Kozar.)

Otto Farm Burial – This family's farm was located on Temple Road.

Smega Farm Burial – This family's farm was located on Elkhorn Road.

Moffett Family Cemetery aka **Center Cemetery**
This cemetery's location is listed on the Moffett Mill Road. The Moffett farmland once extended from the Center Exit of the Beaver Valley expressway down to Raccoon Creek. The Moffett Mill was in the valley along Raccoon Creek not far from the cemetery. In the mid 1960s there were but a dozen stones that were visible, only 4 of those were readable, but most of the stones are missing.

Moffett Cemetery is an almost forgotten Beaver County Cemetery and terribly overgrown. It was once called Center Cemetery and was owned by the Center Church, which no longer exists. It received its name of Moffett Cemetery, most likely because it is actually situated along Moffett Mill

Road. (Moffett Mill Road begins in Center Township by the current bus station and eventually comes out by Gum's Run Road and then Holt Road. The road is very, very narrow, unpaved for great portions, and has no guard rails.)

Baker Cemetery aka **Figley Farm Cemetery** - Located off Pleasant Drive.
This cemetery was situated atop a high knoll along Pleasant Drive. There were approximately 40 Baker family members who were known to be buried here between the frontier days and shortly after the Civil War. It was established in 1800 by George Baker on his land as a family cemetery for his family and heirs. His family was one of the first permanent families to settle in Beaver County. Since the cemetery was not being regularly maintained, it became quickly overgrown and needed cleaned up. Instead of it being maintained, it is said a local resident took it upon himself to just pull and remove the old sandstone tombstones once he had purchased the property. When some family members discovered what had happened, the man was apprehended for the crime, and he returned the stones. BUT, when he returned them, he simply dumped them in one pile. After this act of vandalism, with no official mapping of this cemetery, properly marking all the grave sites with the correct tombstones was impossible. There is said to be only one original stone in the burial ground, that of Elizabeth Short. As of 2018, this cemetery is said to be "for sale."

Under this newspaper photograph (by Terrance Salav) was printed, "Slag, put on last week, now covers this road which was cut through the center of the old Baker Cemetery on Pleasant Dr., Center Twp., three weeks ago by Duquesne Light subcontractors. The road goes toward the former Zon farm which is now a Duquesne Light transformer and distribution center. Only those two tombstones, dated 1852 and 1873, can be seen now at the cemetery. No one seems to know what happened to dozens of other tombstones on this site."

 Current memorial at the site of former cemetery.

Denver Walton did some research on this cemetery and within his findings was the following information (exactly as he had entered the information on his page):
    Baker, Margaret   *w/o Daniel*   *d. (not leg.)*
    Coleman, Kezia   *w/o J. C.*   *d. 1-9-1852 66 yr.*
    Rambo, Mary M.   *w/o P. M.*   *d. 10-31-1851 In 19th yr. of marriage*
    Rambo, Michael   *d. 8-31-1862 72yr 9m 8d*
    Reed, Samuel   *d. 9-9-1863 80yr 3m 13d*
   (an inscription on stone)
"The days of years are three score years and ten: and if by reason of strength they be fourscore years, yet is their strength labour and sorrow: for it is soon cut off and we fly away."
    Short, Elizabeth   *w/o*   *d. 12-9-1867 66yr 10m 29d*

Mr. Walton's notes also stated, "Severely vandalized over the years. Only six stones left upon my visit, Oct 30, 1971–none in proper position." "George Baker, pioneer settler of Beaver County, is buried here." "This is no. 35 on the 1936 W.P.A. list. (called Figley Farm Cemetery)"

Weigel Private Cemetery
For unknown reasons, the location of these graves and their markers were disrespected and ignored even though there were tombstones marking the burials and even reports of a fence around the area. One can only speculate that owning property, erecting buildings, and making money was more important than respecting the resting places of interred bodies.

The property of this cemetery was located between Stone Quarry Road and Brodhead Road on the former John Weigel farm. It was just above and/or part of the hillside that was removed to put in the Center Square Shopping Center along Brodhead Road. Additionally, several homes were also erected just above the shopping center and most recently, a new hotel building was erected. To the best of my knowledge, no stones were recovered, or bodies relocated. The last known burial at this cemetery was in Apr 1915. This was of Nancy Weigel, d/o John and Margaret (Baker) Weigel.

Beaver County Memorial Park
This 8-acre lot was once land of Melvin Cochran. Several local men are said to have started this cemetery. It is located along Baker Road – just before the stop sign at Engle Street - the cemetery is set back off the road a short distance on the right. Sadly, this cemetery has been vandalized and even disrespectfully used as a recreational vehicle site with little support of law enforcement agencies. At last report, there were only three stones that remain, two are of the Abee family and one of an Anderson. Family tradition indicates there are more graves on this property and there is documentation of at least eleven indigents from the Beaver County Poor Home who were recorded to be buried in this cemetery. Records also indicate that at least four plots were purchased in 1930 by the Abee family. A former owner of the cemetery took off with the money for future burial plots which had been been pre-paid. With this prepaid money, this former owner also took all the information of how many, the locations, and the names of all persons who had already been buried in this cemetery.

I do not understand the negligence of this cemetery because it became the property of Beaver County in 1986 yet it has not been properly maintained to any degree since that same time! Why is Beaver County not stepping up to the plate?

Beaver County Poor Home Cemetery – Potter Township
The cemetery/burials plots that were located on the property of the Poor Home no longer exist. No official records or documentation of a specific plot of land at the home being designated for burial of the deceased inmates of this home has been found. However, there have been unofficial references, family histories, and mentions of over three hundred bodies being interred on the property of the Home through the years. Jonas Potts and his wife Mary Heckathorn Potts were originally buried on Phillis Island, on the Ohio River (the Shippingport/Georgetown area), and although I found no date, it was reported that they were later reinterred in the *Beaver County Poor Home Cemetery*. (James died at a very advanced age in 1814, his wife died in 1812/1813.) The specific mention of this cemetery in various documents tends to indicate there was actually a formal burial ground for the Home. There is also some information of eleven residents of the Poor Home who were buried in the Beaver County Memorial Park Cemetery on Baker Road in Center Township (see previous).

With so many indications of burials on the grounds of the County Home, it amazes me that all were so disrespected and ignored through the years. The former Poor Home property was not accessible to the public once it became private property of the ZCA plant. Not only was the land disturbed with erection of industrial businesses, but it was also dug up during the construction of the Beaver Valley Expressway and bridge. Then this former property becoming totally unrecognizable with all the land moving that has occurred due to the Shell company Surely, within those years, someone had to have uncovered or discovered some evidence of those many burials. It is obvious that the vast majority of the gravesites at the County Home met a very disrespectful fate with all the industrial construction and/or land moving equipment through the years.
(See Stone Cemetery and Bellowsville Burials further.)

Stone Cemetery – Potter Township
This cemetery was located on the hillside on the opposite side of the road from the former St. Joseph Lead company along Frankfort Road. Members of the Stone family were buried in the cemetery in the mid to later 1800s. There were even headstones to mark the graves, yet their resting places were not maintained or even respected until unearthed by land moving equipment in 2015. Through all the deeds of property, it is puzzling to me as to why this cemetery was not sought out since it was absolutely mentioned in earlier land deeds and other legal paperwork. If I can read and decipher this information in former deeds, then why was it not read, communicated, and respected by others with all the writing of deeds related to the purchases of the property?

I will say, that unlike when the Beaver Valley Expressway was being constructed, ignoring trepidation, in Aug 2015, the Shell company did report finding burials in the area along the Potter and Center Townships lines while using all their massive machines. Crews that were excavating at the site for Shell in the area of the old Horsehead Corp. found a headstone marked "Adam Stone" along with two skulls, vertebrae, long bones, and coffin nails. A relative of the Stone family was located and the bones were moved and interred in the Beaver Cemetery next to grandchildren of Adam Stone. What a shame none of the other burials received the same respect or outcome.

Researching done by Ed Lackner shows a partial listing of those who were buried in this cemetery: Adam Stone–d. Aug 6, 1849, David Stone–d. Jun 13, 1872, Elizabeth Stone–d. Apr 15, 1850, Jacob Stone, and Eliza Ann Stone-wife of Jacob. Mr. Lackner also had a note within his research papers that stated Adam Stone had acquired his land from John Anderson Braden. (See Braden/Potter Cemetery further.)

Prior to the Shell "land moving" beginning, it was last report that visible in this cemetery was a ½ headstone, 2 bases, and 1 complete headstone that read "Elizabeth, daughter of Adam A. Stone - Died Apr 15, 1850, aged 19 years."

Fact: George Stone had sold 138 acres of his land at $50 per acre for the site of the Beaver County Poor Home. This indicates how much of this acreage was formerly the Stone farm. (See more details in the Medical section on the Poor Home.)

Bellowsville Burials
Associated with the burials of the Poor Home would be those that occurred with the adjacent area of Bellowsville. This small town or village existed between approximately the 1860s into the earlier 1900s. It has been estimated that there were residents in Bellowsville numbering between two hundred to three hundred during these years. Records also indicate this small community was well established and even had its own post office until 1902, they had several different businesses, and more specifically, there was a cemetery for the Bellowsville residents. A proper assumption would be this cemetery would have been located somewhere in the boundaries of the village proper. Historical records indeed indicate there have been numerous burials in and around this entire area between the Ohio River and quite a distance inland. Unfortunately, many were evidently interned in what was never recorded or designated as "official" burial grounds or over the years was plainly a long since forgotten area, therefore making it impossible to include in topographical mapping.

In my opinion, there was probably no attention given in the area when the construction of the Beaver Valley Expressway was underway. If there were any burials uncovered in the Bellowsville area, in the Poor Home cemetery, and even the now known Indian Mounds, they either were unintentionally disregarded or were never disseminated due to red tape and delays that would have occurred by reporting them. It would be a fair guess to say that many more forgotten grave sites were additionally disturbed with all the current land moving going on by the Shell company.

Braden/Potter Cemetery (Potter Township)
This cemetery was located off Raccoon Creek Road, sadly, it no longer exits. The burials were located up on the top of the steep hill on the side of the road about a quarter of a mile from the bridge on Route 18 on Raccoon Creek Road. The cemetery once contained remains of at least James Braden and his wife Margaret (Irwin) Braden. They owned 400 acres named *Naiad's Delight*,

adjacent to the mouth of Raccoon Creek. James died in 1806 and Margaret in 1834, both were buried (along with others) on their farm in this family cemetery. Unfortunately, the burial sites became overgrown and then the land was sold outside the family. Not until about 1960 did the owner of the property at that time stumbled upon the tombstones. With the practice of burials occurring on private property being long since forbidden, this owner did not imagine or realize that these stones were marking the actual burial sites. Not wanting any further weathering of or damage of the tombstones to occur, he pulled the two stones and took them to his barn, leaning them against the barn where they remained for years. In 1970, Frank R. Braden, Jr. (G-G-G-Grandchild of James and Margaret) was in search of his family's roots and decided to go back to the former family's farm to look around. That owner of the former Braden farm was glad to meet Frank and gave the tombstones to Frank who then took them to his home in Coraopolis for safe keeping. There were more than just James and Margaret buried in this cemetery. It was found that Potter family members were also buried in this cemetery along with the Braden family since the two families were intertwined through marriages. In 1900, the Potter family reinterred all the Bradens and Potters who were buried there and reburied their remains in the Mill Creek Hill Cemetery in Hookstown, PA. All these reburied remains are marked with smaller stones containing the names of those reinterred and lined up on each side of a large headstone -- the Braden name on one side and the Potter name on the other.

Douds Cemetery - reported to be located on one of the Douds family's farms.

Weaton Cemetery – Potter Township - This cemetery was located on Weaton Drive which is just before the intersection of Route 18 and Mowry Road and the former Weaton farm sat at the end of this drive. There were two known Weaton burials here – George F Weaton, Sr.-d. Dec 1959 and Gertrude (Cornell) Weaton–d. Mar 1950. For whatever reason to this disrespectful action, the headstones were removed and were being stored in an old garage at the end of the Weaton Drive in 2005. The remains were moved from the back of the former Weaton Home to Sylvania Hill Cemetery.

Indian Burial Mounds
When Nova and ZCA moved to Potter Township, they found many Indian burial mounds along the riverbanks between the two companies. They had to have permission from the Indian Nation heads before moving them. Unearthing these Indian burial mounds did have one glimmer of positivity. It prompted finding, publishing, and developing a map of all archeology digs known to be in Beaver County. The Beaver County Historical Research and Landmarks Foundation can supply information to locating these burials. With this information now on record for all known Indian burial sites, it should prevent such violations of these sites from hopefully occurring again.

Baldwin Cemetery aka **Baker Cemetery** - Monaca Borough
Located on a portion of the original Baker lands and afterwards sold to the Baldwins, about 100 yards south of Twenty-first Street (between the overhead pass by Beaver Street and the private entrance of the former Colonial Steel Company). In 1901/02, the property on and around this cemetery was purchased for the building of a railroad spur to service the local factories. The Baldwin family, being the current owners of the property petitioned and was granted an injunction for the area of the cemetery to remain undisturbed. This cemetery has remained in its original condition since that time and is still accessible to the public. In 1799, Anthony Baker received his patent to this property. He set aside this plot for the family's private burying ground. There are up to fifty graves, including Anthony Baker, Revolutionary War soldier. Almost all members of the first two or three generations of this Baker family are buried here including other soldiers. The first person to be buried in this cemetery was said to be in 1819 - Hannah Baker, daughter of Anthony. Martha Baker was the last to be buried in 1868. Other surnames found in this cemetery include Shrodes, Alcorn, Hoisinger, and Rambo. This cemetery is often associated with the former site known as Baker's Landing of Moon Township.

Monaca German Lutheran Cemetery   aka   St. Peter's Church Cemetery
This cemetery is located at the lower end of Monaca, at the entrance to Monaca from Route 18. It once belonged to St. Peter's Evangelical Lutheran Church of Monaca, but in Jul 1944, the St. Peter's Church transferred the church cemetery, commonly known then as "the old Monaca Cemetery," to the Borough of Monaca. The borough accepted the transfer and promised to preserve the cemetery as a historic landmark of the community and to keep the same in a dignified and clean condition. Most of the church members were from Germany, so many of the tombstones are in German.

Geboren = born   Gestorben = died   Hefrau von = wife of

This is a section of a 1903 picture of the railroad bridge being constructed as you enter Monaca. I included this because it also gave a view of the Lutheran Church's cemetery. If you look behind the puffs of steam on the right side of the picture, you can see the original gazebo structure that once stood in the cemetery. Note the steeple in the top, middle of the picture – this is of the old Lutheran Church. If you look really closely, you can see one of the tops of the Monaca-Rochester former suspension bridge in the top right corner and a portion of the LeGoullon's coal tipple in the bottom right corner.

~ ~ ~

ENTERTAINMENT and RECREATION

Early on, entertainment in Moon Township / Center Township was usually very local and simple. Dancing was the biggest form of entertainment. Before Center Township was officially named as such from Moon Township, the residents held their dances in various areas of the township. Many community dances and events were held on residents' properties, utilizing the larger barns of the farmers. Holding picnics was another well-known event for residents. Corn roasts, impromptu gatherings, and even sled riding parties were also held by the local farmers and landowners in the township.

Many local family gatherings (reunions, birthday parties, anniversaries, et cetera) were held at one or more of the popular locations listed further, as were even more community affairs. The Center Grange Hall became a very popular venue. There were also annual township wide Community / School Picnics held at the Center Grange Hall. Most often though, families would just make a day of spending time along a stream/creek on their own property, at one of the beaches along the Ohio River in Monaca, or somewhere along Raccoon Creek where all would enjoy swimming, lounging, and picnicking. Beginning in the mid 1900s, larger, designated recreational picnic parks and amusement parks became more easily accessible, so residents were then holding many more gatherings and events at these locales. Going to a trolley or amusement park was a special treat once those became more numerous. Presque Isle on Lake Erie and Geneva-on-the-Lake, Ohio were also two other places mentioned where local residents would frequent for family fun. Beginning around the mid 1900s, there were school picnics held at Idora Park, Youngstown, Ohio (1960s, 1970s). After Idora closed, the school picnics were held at Kennywood Park, West Mifflin. There is much more information on specific areas and the amusement parks further on in this section.

Dancing

--One of the first popular public spots in 1908 or 1909 for local entertainment was the open-air dance pavilion on the Davis property. There were two known Davis pavilions. One pavilion was closer to the intersection of Center Grange Road (first known as Davis Lane). This pavilion was along Davis Lane in the area adjacent to the former Center Grange Hall building. The other one was on Chapel Road and sat down in behind the current houses at 277 and 273 Center Grange Road. The remnants of this pavilion were still visible not too many years ago, but I don't know if that's still currently true. (See Homes and Family section for more on the Davis family.)

--The Streit family also had an open-air dance hall which was located on Chapel Road, not far from the current intersection of East Shaffer and Chapel Roads. It was discontinued about 1917.

--Jennings Weigle's barn was very popular for several different types of events.

--There were also several mentions of round and square dancing and polkas that were held at the Craig Farm in Center-Monaca area. I have no confirmation of this, but I suspect this may have been the Hiram Craig farm which was located in the Baker's Landing/Vankirk/Stobo area.

Blue Bird Dance Hall aka **Golden Chain** – Brodhead Road
There was the well-known dance hall on or adjacent to the Mike Meiter property on Brodhead Road called the *Blue Bird*. I have mentioned the *Blue Bird* in various sections throughout this book since different activities and organizations held events in or near it. It was built in 1930 by Harry and Andy Biskup with the first dance being held there on Decoration Day in 1930. The Biskup brothers would play and furnish the music especially for round and square dancing. Roy Miller was another musician to provide live entertainment in the *Blue Bird*. There were dances held every Saturday night and from an ad found in 1933, the building was of fair size being able to hold up to 300 "dancing" people (see further). It was not only a popular venue for the Center Township residents, but other local communities/towns people came to enjoy the merriment.

The Blue Bird building was used for public meetings during the 1930s and 1940s. The first Center Township Fire Department was organized in this dance hall in 1930. The dance hall building was still standing until at least mid 1958 but no longer used as a dance hall because I found information in May of 1958 with it then referenced as "the old Bluebird Dance Hall." To the best of my estimation, this building was located adjacent to where the Golden Dawn Supermarket was built in 1962 (currently home to Beaver County Beverage and Fastenal).

Dancing—Bus service to Blue Bird dance hall. Leaves corner Ninth street and Pennsylvania avenue, Monaca, at 8:30, Saturday night. 3.14	WANTED: 300 persons to attend dances Monday, Wednesday and Saturday at the Golden Chain on Brodhead road, formerly the Bluebird Dance Hall. Good orchestra each night. No cover charge 4 20
1931 ad	1933 ad

Between 1931 and 1933, the Blue Bird dance hall became known as the *Golden Chain*. The building was reportedly then occupied by Lyle McCon sometime after the 1940s. Lyle is listed as using it as an auto repair shop which was run by McCon and Mike Meiter (See Automotive section). The building was again sold, and then torn down sometime after 1958. The land was then subdivided into building lots and Lincolnshire Drive was added (now known as Lincoln Drive). (See Housing Plans section.)

~ ~ ~

Music was always a very big part of the activities of the earlier families and residents in Moon/Center Township. One popular band for events and dancing was the Martin Mild Band. Martin was a resident of the township, born in the earlier 1880s. He was a glass worker in 1910, and then in 1920 and 1930 had a dairy farm. From approximately 1910 on, he lived on River Road / Frankfort Road and by 1942, Martin and Sarah (Gref) were living in Columbiana, Ohio.

This photograph was forwarded to me anonymously, with no mention as to who took the picture or where it was taken, just that it is of Martin Mild's Band of Monaca in 1912-1916. I do like to have origins of such pictures, but this was such a wonderful picture that I still chose to share it. This was a very popular group that played at many events and affairs in Monaca and Moon/Center Township. There were only a few names of members listed along with this picture, many were related............
Back Row: Martin is in the middle, Samuel Gref (Martin's brother-in-law) is to the left of him, and Michael Weiss (his sister-in-law's husband) to the right of him. Front Row: John Gref (Martin's brother-in-law) is by the small drum.

~ ~ ~

Fun fact: These were a few of the other more popular "night spots" outside the Center Township area also mentioned within the researched material that were frequented for a special night out by township residents. In addition to the many venues in downtown Monaca, a few others included:

        The Carlton – 1098 Duss Avenue, Ambridge (1938)
        Eva's Tavern – 412 Hopewell Ave, Aliquippa (1959)
        Mim's Place – 345 Maplewood Ave, Ambridge (1959)
        Northern Lounge – Northern Lights Shoppers City (1959)

Fishing

If relaxing and fishing was what someone was looking for, then the Moon/Center Township residents had locations for that. By nature, there are many areas in Center Township that have naturally formed ponds, big and small -- some marshy areas were given a bit of help from residents to formed ponds and small lakes, too. Research only uncovered a few that were used more publicly.

Lyon's Lake - The Lyon's not only owned properties in the Todd Lane and Edgewater Drive area, but there was also a Lyon's family who lived on Brodhead Road and their property went over the hill and met up with properties along the current Edgewater Drive. The area of the current lake was a marshy area and could not be used for anything very constructive, so it was decided to form a large pond or what came to be called a "lake." There was an earthen retaining wall formed and a small concrete over-flow dam constructed to one side of this wall, all at the far end of the soon to be lake area. The area "pooled" nicely to form the lake, being mainly fed by Moon Run creek and from then on it was simply known as *Lyon's Lake*. In the 1960s and 1970s, there was a small dock that had been built and a cable was strung across the lake which was used to ride a suspended tire or rope allowing swimmers to drop into the water. It was a gathering place for swimming on the hot summer days and for ice skating during the winters. There were forms of aquatic life within this lake by the blue heron that made regular visits, but whether it was used by any anglers is unknown. This former watering hole has lost its defined shorelines and has become much more "natural" in its appearance nowadays with the shorelines no longer defined. It is still there and continues to be a valuable asset to the wildlife of the area.

McCracken's Lakes – located off Cochran Drive. These lakes were a popular, ideal local spot for some quiet, relaxing time and great fishing. These lakes were actually stocked with fish, and for a small fee, anglers could go to McCracken's lakes from the 1940s through at least 1967. There were two very nice sized adjacent lakes on the property, both were operated by James and Alice (Miller) McCracken of Center Township. The end of Dec in 1967 is the last mention of McCracken's Lakes I could find but this does not mean they didn't permit fishing there any longer, it just means I found no further advertisements or listings regarding these lakes. James and Alice purchased this property from the widow Anna Williams in 1932. James died in 1971, and Alice soon sold the property to her son.

1967 ad

Hall's Lake -- owned by the Hall family and located on Hall Road (off Chapel Road). In the 1950s it was known as "an excellent fishing sight." Currently, there is a small fence enclosing the pond making it more private.

Unnamed small lake/large pond – behind the house adjacent to McGuire Cemetery on Chapel Road.

Unnamed small pond – behind one of the homes in the 700s along Chapel Road

~ ~ ~

Fun information............
Although not a true activity, site, or location, I could not write the history of Center Township and not mention one very familiar summer time activity....I am referring to Snow Cones.

John Bickerton is an icon to the kids of Center Township. Not only was he one of their favorite teachers, active in almost any activity or event at the school, and the Director of Student Activities at the school for many years, but he was and is still a welcome site on any given day every summer. He drives through the entire Center Township area and sells snow cones, previously out the back of his station wagon and nowadays, his famous red truck. Mr. Bickerton had a knack for remembering names and could always easily converse with all those who flagged him down for a snow cone. Kids wait to hear the jingle of the bells and then run out to buy either a regular sized snow cone or one of his *iceberg* sized cones. Many remember as a bonus, if you were the lucky one, you got a free cone because every 25th snow cone was a free one. Mr. Bickerton is still quite active in the township and is also still entertaining all with his snow cones as of Jul 2019. ☺

~ ~ ~

> *Fun Fact: Did you know that Center Township was almost the home of the Beaver County Ice Rink that is now located at Bradys Run Park? The Beaver County Commissioners proposed a plan to purchase property and construct a multi-million dollar recreation complex on a 50-acre site off North Brodhead Road that went back toward Community College. The county wanted to build an ice rink and multi-purpose recreation building on ten acres and sell the remaining unneeded portion of the property to the community college. Mary Todora was the owner the property at the time. Center Township had many concerns with this proposal. One being that the township first heard of the project in the newspaper and not from the county, in other words, none of the county's officials had contacted the township's planning and zoning commission first. Needless to say, the project never developed in Center, but instead the ice rink was moved and completed at the Bradys Run Park.*

Golf

When ask what activities are available in Center Township, 9 or 18 holes of "golf" is not one that can be included nowadays. But back in the 1930s through the 1960s, it was a well-known business and activity that many local and even celebrity golfers would have absolutely included on their lists.

Raccoon Golf Course   aka   Pettibon's Golf Course
If enjoying a round of golf was the choice of relaxation or one's favorite competition sport, then that could be done between 1937 and 1965 at Raccoon Golf Course   aka   Pettibon's Golf Course. The Beaver Valley Mall in Center Township now sits upon the majority of the area of the former golf course. Raccoon Golf Course was a very nice, yet challenging course and was played regularly by township golfers, the leading golfers of the area, as well as weekend golfers and other well-known golfers from outside the townships and area.

Some say Arthur Pettibon was persuaded by his friend from Beaver, Bob Baker (a car salesman) to start the golf course. They reportedly went in together to begin turning the land into a golf course. Mitchell Lewis of Ohio, a veteran golf pro and designer of several courses was hired as the manager of the new course. Mr. Pettibon was building the 9-hole golf course for "the poor working man" and he did indeed prove that with the very reasonable green fees he charged.

Prior to 1937, the property, now occupied by the Beaver Valley Mall and its environs, was farm land, as was the majority of Center Township at that time. This made it quite pliable for Pettibon to turn the land into a plush golf course in no time. The complete 18-hole golf course was built in two stages. Mr. Pettibon also donated some of his first land purchase to the township's water department which built a tank at the south end of the golf course. Some commented this was a smart move for Pettibon since obviously it was a source of water that was much needed if the grass conditions were going to be improved. (There was once a single, smaller water tank that sat adjacent to the authority's building, but it has since been torn down.)

The actual land of the entire golf course involved a few major purchases for Arthur and Hazel Pettibon. They eventually purchased a total of 174 acres of land to complete the 18-hole golf course. Per a deed dated Jun 7, 1937, a 76.05-acre portion of the land was purchased from Thomas Schmoutz, William J./Antonia Schmoutz, and Bertha/Paul Aussprung. It was the last of the former Henry G. Schmoutz farmland that Henry left to his children. There was a Miss Bernice Orpelli, a young lady from Beaver Falls who was a clerk in a private office who became involved in this transaction by 1938 when Mr. and Mrs. Pettibon transferred the property to her for $1.00, but within minutes, another deed transferred it right back to the Pettibons – evidently some form of legal action for clarity of the original deed (?). (See the Schmoutz Family information for more details on the original farmland.) Mr. Pettibon then developed the first 9 holes of the golf course. The Raccoon Golf Course was advertising for memberships to the golf course in 1937 and the local newspapers stated he had the "grand opening" on Jul 3rd, 1937.

By 1941, Mr. Pettibon's 9-hole course was proving to be quite successful, and he then wanted to expand and complete a full 18-hole course. James Mateer had owned the adjacent, desired, and needed property for the additional 9-holes. Mr. Mateer had purchased this acreage in about 1926, and there was a barn, out buildings, and a very nice farmhouse on the property. Despite the fact neither James Mateer nor his family actually lived on the property, he did maintain the land and the many, many fruit trees on the property. I found no information for who, if anyone, did occupy or possibly rented the farmhouse at the time Mr. Pettibon made the purchase. In 1941, James Mateer, whose health was failing, was not properly attending to this farmland that was adjacent to the then 9-hole golf course, so James made the decision to sell his 98-acre farm to Mr. Pettibon and the deed was entered Aug 11, 1941. This acreage is the right side/portion of the land area of the current BV Mall (Boscov area and former Sears Auto area). This farm then gave Arthur and Hazel Pettibon 174 total acres. (See Houses and Families section for more information on these families.)

> *Fun fact: This may be of interest to all the genealogists reading this book....*
> *The first purchase made by Mr. Pettibon involved land that had quite a few previous deed transactions......*
> *John Wilhelm purchased five separate parcels between 1850 and 1866 and sold all to Henry G. Schmoutz in 1886 for a total of $6,500...*
> > *1850 – 57+ acres – John Stewart to John Wilhelm, then to Henry G. Schmoutz*
> > *1857 – (2) 30 acres and almost ½ acre – Wm. Shroads to John Wilhelm, then to Henry G. Schmoutz*
> > *1863 – 7 acres – Washington Weigle to John Wilhelm, then to Henry G. Schmoutz*
> > *1866 – 15 acres – Thomas Reed to John Wilhelm, then to Henry G. Schmoutz*
>
> *Henry G. Schmoutz left all his land to his children via his will. They, in turn, sold 76+ acres of their father's former farm for $9,886.50 to Mr. Pettibon in Apr 1937.*
>
> *The second purchase made by Mr. Pettibon for the 98-acre plot of land had also seen quite a few previous owners. The deeds involved with Arthur's second purchase were:*
> > *1866 – 98 acres - Thomas Reed to George Docktor, Sr. - $5,500*
> > *1872 – 28 acres - Jacob Vogt to George Docktor, Sr. - $? (this gave George 126 acres)*
> > *1895 – 126 acres – George Docktor, Sr. to George Docktor, Jr. - $10,000*
> > *1926 – 98 acres – George Docktor, Jr. to James Mateer - $7,000*
> > *1937 – 98 acres – James Mateer to Arthur W. Pettibon - $7,000*

Back to the golf course...

Shortly after Arthur W. Pettibon opened the first 9-hole course for business in 1937, A. W. began to clear and ready his second purchase of 1941. He added and then completed 9 more holes by 1943, making Raccoon Golf Course a 72 par, beautiful 18-hole course. One site stated there were ten par 4s, four par 3s, and four par 5s. The "front 9" were flatter, while the back nine were located on rolling ground and more treacherous. One article stated the distance on the front 9 was 2,929 yards and the back 9 measured 3,020. The first hole on the course was a 340-yard par 4. (I have no idea how accurate these figures are, but I've reported them as they were found.)

The original 9-hole course also had a club house and a "The Professional's Shop" which were both erected by Jun 1937. The original club house was a beautiful structure and well maintained, it was a two-storey frame structure. It had a very large main ball room that could hold up to 13 couches, miscellaneous chairs, and other furniture and still have room for "live entertainment" along with the whole center of the room open for couples to dance. Beside the main ball room was another area almost the same size as the ball room. Both the ball room and one of the larger rooms adjacent to it had very large and ornate fireplaces. The area adjacent to the ball room was sectioned off, the larger portion was more of an extension of the ball room and used for dining. When needed the whole ball room would be used for bigger events and dining could be set up in both these areas. In the remaining area of this second section, there was a kitchen area and office area. The second floor of the club house had restrooms, along with areas used as reading and smoking rooms. For the golfers and club members use, the basement area was fitted up with showers, lockers, additional rest rooms, and a laundry room.

Along with the first club house, Mr. Pettibon included tennis courts and even a grove of trees was turned into a picnic ground to cater to valley churches and other social groups. The Pettibons also erected a very nice two-storey brick home for themselves at the front edge of the property. This two-storey brick home formerly sat approximately where the current Silo business is located. When the multi-lane highway was built, it divided the property of the golf course from that of their private house. The house and its property were eventually sold in the late 1980s or earlier 1990s and the house was moved a short distance on Brodhead Road. It is still a private resident, and sits off Wilhelm Drive, behind the Center Car Wash. (See Houses on the Move section.)

By 1945, Mr. Pettibon had erected the second club house and pro shop for the newly expanded golf course. Once the new club house was completed, he sold some of the acreage of the front corner of the original 9-hole area of the course and the 1st club house to Elton and Elsie Tate. This acreage and former club house were purchased by the Tates in Nov 1946, all was located closest to the current large intersection and current site of Hampton Hotel. Elton and Elsie Tate were my grandparents, so I can relate quite a bit of information on the former club house since it was converted into their home. (I have included all this information of their home and the former club house in the Houses and Families section – Tate Family.)

The former location of the first club house, originally sat a short distance from the first location of the then Route 18 roadway. The intersection was redesigned to become the large intersection of 18 & 51 (today known as Rt. 18 and Brodhead Road). That corner/section of the golf course, which included the site of the first club house, would have sat on higher property that was greatly altered and "cut into" to become the current intersection. Past articles on the golf course state the club house was located close to where the current Boscov's sits. Although this carries some truth since a club house was located there, they fail to mention this was the placement of the "second" club house. I can assure you, the location of the "first" club house was between the still standing red brick building and the Hampton Hotel, on the former Macy's side of the mall. Many may remember the former home being that of a bridal shop that was razed for the Hampton Hotel.

The second Club House was located in the area just to the right of the main entrance drive to the BV Mall, between the area of the former Best Buy store and the current Boscov's store. Since it is tradition for golf courses to keep the club house close to the first and last tees, the second /new club house was needed due to the shifting of the course's layout with the additional 9 holes. I have included pictures of both club houses (see further). Within the immediate area of the 1st club house picture would have been the 1st and 9th holes for the original course at that time, in the area of the second club house would have been the relocated 1st, 9th, and 18th holes.

To help orient the entire location of both the original 9 holes and additional 9 holes, the picnic pavilion area, the 1st and 2nd club houses, and pro shops of the golf course…..start with the land that currently extends from almost the middle of the current intersection of Route 18 and Brodhead Road, then down to the lower entrance roadway of the BV Mall (by former ToysRUs), then follow behind the current satellite buildings of the mall (former Tropical Zone location) and go past the current BV Auto Mall and Ollie's store. Continue over the hillside (past the current end of the mall's parking lot), continuing and parallel to the river, the properties of the newest health facility buildings, and on toward almost the current Cinemark Center. Then past the former Steak n' Shake and onto the multi-lane highway, and finally on down into the current intersection to the point of start. That may seem like a lot of property, but one must remember there was over 170 acres and it was a proper 18-hole golf course.

Up until 2017, if you could have looked over the hill along the parking lot right behind the former Sears Automotive Center building, it was still possible to make out traces of a few former greens of the old golf course. All this land is currently "moved" and there are multiple businesses and/or condo buildings erected on the property.

Golf enthusiast may recognize some of the once more well-known golfers of the area including the likes of Vasile Daniel of Monaca, Stan Namola of Chippewa Township, Pete Vuckson of Beaver, and Bill Gabal of Baden (Aliquippa). A pro-golfer, Ken Sumner of Erie also played there in the summer of 1954 and became the resident pro-advisor succeeding Mitch Lewis, Bob Dawson, Bert Whitehead, and Glen Welsch. Russ Franks, a 16-year-old junior at Monaca High School in 1954, was serving his apprenticeship at Raccoon Golf Course as Mr. Sumner's assistant. Mr. Sumner continued to work there until it closed in 1965.

Following are two maps related to the former golf course. It appears these maps were merely drawn to give orientation and perspectives of the lands and development of them into the golf course. Neither map is drawn to scale or absolutely accurate or proportionally correct. They do help considerably in showing and orienting where and how the former golf course would have appeared.

This first map shows the combined layout of all property that was purchased for the entire 18-hole golf course. Although not indicated, the Ohio River would run parallel to the left of this map.

The current Golfview Road is really just a portion of the original Golf View Drive (see on the right of the next map, by the wording "Fox Farm"). Compare with the second map to see how the current Golfview Road still connects on to Stone Quarry Road.

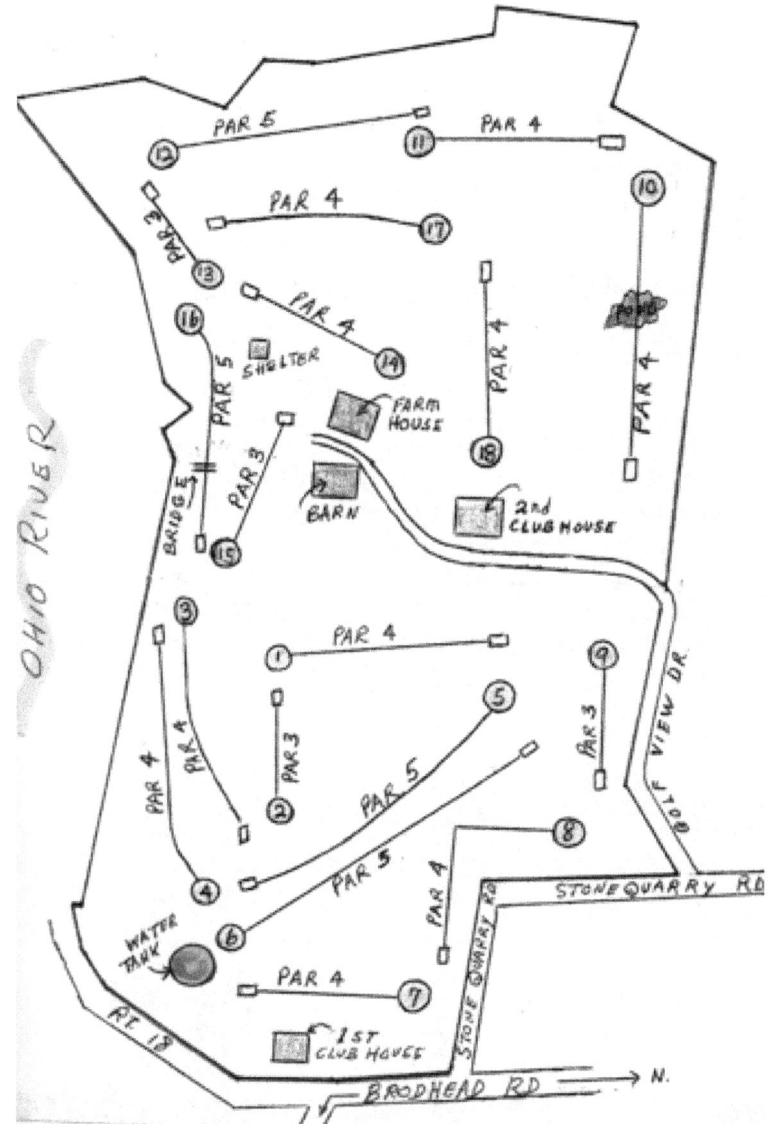

This map to the left is a bit more defined and shows how both properties were blended and laid out into the 18-hole golf course. It also shows locations of the first Club House (bottom of map), the second Club House (middle of map), and where the original farmhouse and barn from the second purchase of land would have been located. Also, on this map is indicated the entire former *Golf View Drive* which led off Stone Quarry Road, past the second Club House, and into the golf course. This "lane" was also the drive/ lane that led into the former Docktor / Mateer farm.)

If the current multi-lane highway would be sketched on this map, it would pass through the words "View Dr" and then go straight toward the right side of the first Club House at the bottom of the map. The current Hampton Hotel sits just to the left of where the "1st Club House" is indicated.

Fun fact: One of the ads for a "tourney" at the golf course included a layout of the course and then had hints to entice golfers....... "the scenic No. 8 fairway, a dog-leg layout of 300 yards which can be shortened by driving over the trees...." "... The green is .....just in front of a row of poplar trees." It did make the course sound interesting☺

Between 1937 and 1965, Raccoon Golf Course held many tournaments and would advertise for amateurs, whether from Beaver County or elsewhere, to enter. Each tournament offered refreshments in the clubhouse throughout the day and a buffet dinner served in the late afternoon or early evening followed by the presentation of trophies and awards. Tee off for a tournament was usually eight a.m. on Saturday mornings.

View of the first Club House

This is a personal photograph of the first club house in later 1940s. Elton Tate is pictured in front of the former first club house which became the Tate's home. Entrance to the basement area with the showers and lockers was on the right side of the building. The ball room and dining area took up the entire first floor area. The kitchen area and office area were on the right side (the white extension). The second floor consisted of restrooms, smoking rooms, and reading rooms.

For orientation --- all the property was cut into and removed from the left of the photograph and close to almost where Mr. Tate is standing. This was done for the formation and enlarging the intersection. The current Hampton's parking lot would begin somewhere just behind the house in this picture. The current intersection would be to the left of this photograph. (See Roads section for more on the intersection of Brodhead and Route 18; see Homes and Families section – Tate Family.)

Second Club House

I am not certain if the building to the left side of this photograph is a newer structure, but is probably the original barn from the Docktor / Mateer property. It was used to store equipment and supplies for the maintenance of the golf course.

This picture shows the tee for the first hole with a sand trap to the left. To the right of the sand trap is the green of the ninth hole. If you look very carefully, you can make out the Club House hidden behind all the trees in the middle of the picture. This second Club House was also a very large frame building to accommodate all the club's activities.

For orientation – the back of this second club house would have been about where the parking areas and/or current open air plaza where the UPS Store is located. The current Boscov's location would begin on the left of the picture not too far past the rear of the pictured barn/outbuilding. The current multi-lane highway would be along the right side of this photograph. The main entrance drive to the BV Mall was laid through the area of the former first and ninth holes and the sand trap (in front of the pictured club house).

Fun fact: Although A. W. Pettibon did indeed have a passion for his golf course, it is said he never actually played golf.

The top-left pointer is to indicate the view of the golf course prior to the BV Mall being built. To give bearings of this picture – starting on the bottom left of the picture is Brodhead Road. It continues in front of some of the homes (as it still does). The pointer on the right shows the area where York Way comes out of St. James Park onto North Branch Road and where North Branch Road comes out on to Brodhead Road. You can also see a small glimpse of Brodhead Road leading toward the current intersection below the pointer on the right. (The current housing plan known as St. James Park is along the bottom of the photograph. There is a full view of this picture showing more of St. James Park in the Housing Areas section.)

It was noted at the time of sale that Raccoon Golf Course had been considered the most appealing public course in the county. By Feb 1967, the Pettibon Raccoon Golf Course was disappearing as grading was being done for the new mall.

> **For Rent**
> Why clutter up your house with parties? The club room at Pettibon Raccoon Golf Course is an ideal spot. Rent it and see. You may bring your own lunch and refreshments. Phone Roch. 2008.
> 10 3-9 Inc
> 1941

> FOR THE MAN IN YOUR LIFE — All kinds of golf merchandise or a 1964 Season Ticket Phone Ken Sumner, Pettibon's Raccoon Golf Course, Monaca, 774-9775 or 775-3987.
> 1963 ad

The dining area of the Club House on the golf course was known as Raccoon Country Club. Although owned by Mr. Pettibon, it was managed separately.

> **RACCOON COUNTRY CLUB**
> (Pettibon's Place)
> Brodhead Road, Route 51,
> R. F. D., Monaca
> Under new management—
> E. J. Spahr, Pittsburgh, Pa.
> (Formerly with Joyce Catering Co. of Pittsburgh)
> **DINE and DANCE**
> 1940

Fun Fact: Edward Gallagher, Monaca Heights was the first to get a hole in one on the 185-yard sixth hole at the Pettibon's Raccoon Golf Course in Jul 1938. He was playing with Earl Cookson, Bud Pettibon, and Paul Vollmer.

In 1965, excluding the Tate's property and home and the Water Authority's property, the acreage of the 18-hole golf course was sold to Herbert and William Sullivan of McKeesport, who were known for developing shopping centers in the Pittsburgh area. Although A. W. Pettibon never fully disclosed the selling price of his golf course property, the deed for the sale stated $500,000 dollars. This may seem like quite a tidy profit from the less than $20,000 of his original purchase costs but remember, his original cost does not include all involved with developing such a noted golf course, two club houses, other buildings, salaries, and upkeep through the years, et cetera. The majority of the property sold to the Sullivans became the site of the Beaver Valley Mall. Beaver County residents got their first look at the new Beaver Valley Mall in Nov 1969, with the opening of the first anchor store, Gimbels. The official grand opening of the mall was Sept 23, 1970, and the once popular and frequently used Pettibon's Raccoon Golf Course was but a memory. (See Shopping Centers and Plaza section for more on the BV Mall.)

The picture below is looking south into Center Township. The top left pointer indicates current Golf View Drive and what was to become the main entrance to to the BV Mall.

The pointer in the top right shows the location of the original/first club house that became the home of Mr. and Mrs. Tate. The main intersection in Center Township is also seen in this picture adjacent to that same pointer. The lower-left arrow shows the approximate location of the former second club house. The pointer at the bottom right of the picture shows a few of the sand traps that were located in the area just past the Sears Auto Center building. These went undisturbed for over 50 years, but all of these have been eliminated with the new construction along that hillside (2018).

Even though this picture was taken from almost the completely opposite direction of the previous picture, you can still see how the mall property consumed the former golf course land. I have inserted pointers for orientations between the two pictures........the top pointer is showing the sand traps just past the Sears Auto building and the pointer on the right would be an approximate location of the former second Club House. The location of the first club house and the main township intersection are not in this picture, but would have been a bit further from the left corner area of the picture.

1937

I found the information on this 1937 ad interesting, so I decided to include what it said below.

"Located at the intersection of Routes 51 and i8, South of Monaca, will be open for play in a short time. All those desiring a season ticket of the coming season will please fill out the attached coupon and mail to: A. W. Pettibon 387 Connecticut Ave., Rochester, Pa.
All individual season tickets will be twenty-five dollars ($25.00) and family tickets which shall include husband, wife and children under 19 years of age, will be $30.00.
We have completed the grading and preliminary work on the course, and the remaining work will be rushed to completion soon as the weather permits.
We expect to begin construction of a club house with showers and lockers as soon as it is possible and have same completed for use in the early summer."

The coupon at the bottom of the ad stated……

"I wish to apply for a season ticket for the Spring and Summer of 1937 on the new PETTIBON GOLF COURSE. I understand that all applications will be filed in the order of arrival and that the right is reserved by A. W. PETTIBON to fill only those which he feels can be well taken care of, so to not over-crowd the course. I agree to pay half the fee when billed for the same, and the balance within ten days after the course is opened. I further understand that by signing my application before February 15th, that an individual ticket is to cost me $20.00 in place of $25.00 and a family ticket is to cost $25.00 in place of $30.00 and that all those holding 1937 tickets shall have preference for succeeding years."

Information on Mr. Pettibon
Arthur W. and Hazel (Sutherland) Pettibon lived in Ambridge in 1920 and then Rochester in 1930, 1940. Along with other relatives, his main interest was the Pettibon Dairy company in Rochester and the Drinkmore Dairy in Aliquippa from 1922 until 1953, which is when he sold the main dairy farm. His family came from Washington County/Jefferson Twp. and were farmers. A. W. died of a heart attack in his home in 1967 at the age of 68, his wife Hazel was still alive in 1992 at age 96. The large two-storey brick home for the Pettibons was built in 1946. It stood on the site of the Aaron's/Silo store (beside King's Restaurant) when it was sold, and as previously stated, it was then moved in the late 1980s/early 1990s to its current location along Wilhelm Drive/behind the Center Car Wash.

Ironwood Golf – 660/ renumbered to 3036 Brodhead Road
Ironwood was established in 1995. It started as a golf practice facility/driving range that also has a pro shop and offers a full line of services from custom club fitting to golf equipment for expert and novice golfers alike. Most recently, it has added a miniature golf course with waterfalls, wooden bridges, and a picnic area. In 2001 they added a short game area with chipping and putting greens and covered, heated tees for year-round practice. As of 2016 it was owned by Larry Milosh.

~ ~ ~

Township Fairs

As previously mentioned, Township fairs were another long-standing event for Center residents. The first fairs were sponsored and held on the property of the Center Grange Hall on Center Grange Road. These early fairs did not have mechanical rides but were centered on displays and selling farm grown produce and homemade items, games were available for the young and old alike for pure fun. There was always live music and dances held, too.

The Fire Department No. 1 had been sponsoring an "indoor fair" from the 1910s. These early fairs were first held in the Firemen's Hall on Brodhead Road.

> **INDOOR FAIR**
> Firemen's Hall Brodhead Rd.,
> Monaca
> Every Thursday Evening
> 8:30 sharp
> Special Awards
> Sponsored by Center Township
> Fire Department No. 1

Aug 1916

The Center Grange then began to sponsor and organize the Center Township Fair for many years before they were once again taken over by the Center Township Volunteer Fire Department with all profits benefiting the fire department. I am not sure exactly when the Center Grange handed the reins back over to the Fire Department, but I found where the Ladies Auxiliary to Fire Department No. 1 were sponsoring the "street fair" in Jul 1949. Listed as the 42nd Fireman's Fair on Jul 1989, would mean they started in 1947. The proceeds from the 42nd fair were to be used for the payment of a new fire truck.

The practice of organizing and holding a very nice parade on Center Grange Road to kick off the week of each annual fair also became a local and popular event once the fire department took over organizing the fair events. Eventually, after many years of the annual fairs being held, companies were being hired to provide many of the games and mechanical rides for the fairs.

Along with the need for more room to accommodate the size of the fairgrounds, more space was also needed for the crowds and for much more parking areas, so the yearly event just had to be moved from the Grange Hall property and were then held on the Center Grange School's property. I could not locate an exact year for when the fair events were moved to Center Grange School grounds, but the earliest mention I found was in the 1960s. Just like being unable to find an exact date for the beginning of the township fairs being sponsored by the fire department, I could not find any information regarding the final year of a township fair. There were still notices in the newspaper in 1991, but no proof this was the last year for the event. The parades are still held each year with all the township's recreational softball and baseball teams participating, the township and other local fire departments with their trucks, the school bands, and other attractions.

In addition to the township's annual fairs, the CTVF Dept #3 at Vankirk would hold their own firemen's fair at the Vankirk Playground on Vankirk Road on the fire hall property. I found no beginning or ending dates other than some information of these fairs in 1970, 1972, 1977. There was a tragedy at one of their fairs when the motor on the Ferris wheel malfunctioned. The operator of the Ferris wheel was credited with saving many from injury but very sadly, the malfunction caused one of the seats to fall from the wheel fatally injuring an 11-year-old son of a Center Township family.

~ ~ ~

Center Township also began to hold what they called "Community Picnics." Beginning in the mid 1900s, they were held annually mid-June at the now defunct Idora Park, Youngstown, Ohio. Busses would typically leave for the park at 10 am and then leave the park for the return trip at 6 pm. Even the Township offices were closed on the day of these community picnics. These picnics eventually became known as "School Picnics" through later years and as of 2018 are still designated one day in June as the "School Picnic". Sometime after the 1970s they were being held at Kennywood Park, West Mifflin, PA.) (See further for information on both these amusement parks.)

~ ~ ~

Park Areas

Using archived newspaper articles, it is apparent that many of the following parks would have been used by a wide variety of groups, communities of people, and families of the township, and many of surrounding areas.

Unnamed park areas

---I found information printed during the 1930s/1940s on the Michaluk family which stated there was a park area on or adjacent to the former O.C. Cluss lumber business site. This was an area used for many various gatherings. There was special note of events for those of the Polish community. The articles told of Polish orchestras being there and Polish foods that were served during the events. Articles stated that anyone who owned a truck would load up a neighborhood's Polish community and take them to these events, but all nationalities and races were welcomed.

---There was another park on Green Garden Road used for all types of celebrations. No absolute location or name was found, just several articles. These articles mentioned various families of the township attending some type of event or reunion "in the park area on Green Garden Road."

Old Log Cabin Inn Park – off Brodhead Road by or formerly the O'Brien / Cooper property

In c1925/1930, John Gross and Mr. Ewing purchased part of the O'Brian/Cooper family farm and built a dance hall called the LOG CABIN. The structure/building and property was then purchased by Mr. and Mrs. William Stevens in 1946 and was still a popular picnic spot for organizations for many years. The Boy Scouts and Girl Scouts also had their campgrounds adjacent to or at the former Log Cabin Inn Park area.

    Tradition has it that the name for this park area was inspired from the log house that was still standing in that area at that time and did so up until the earlier or mid 1940s. This log house and the surrounding property belonged first to the Baker family. The tract of land and the log home was then sold to the Shively family, and lastly to the Good family. This tract of land was received from William Penn and granted to the Baker family. (See the Homes and Families section - Good Family.)

    I ascertained it was adjacent to the Bunker Hill area in the area surrounding Milne Drive/Gross Drive from findings in several mentions and articles of the Old Log Cabin Park/ Old Log Cabin Inn Park being the location of a family gathering, a picnic, or other events. I found no pictures, maps, or absolute directions as to exactly where the location would have been, nor why the word "Inn" was often included in the name. There can still be seen traces of a roadway along Brodhead, across from Ziggy's Tux Shop, that leads down into the wooded area where this park most likely would have been. The deed of John Gross to Mr. and Mrs. Stevens in 1946 stated the property contained 14.85 acres. Down into the valley in this area was a section that was used by the boy and girl scout troops as a camping site in the 1950s and 1960s. I strongly suspect that close to or even this very area is what was once the Old Log Cabin Inn site. The Cooper family farms were formerly all over this area and the Gross family came to own some of those former properties, but again, no pictures, maps, or absolute proof, just general information.

Alum Rock Park

This was a picnic and swimming type area that was developed by Mr. William R. Jeffreys on his property above the Potter Bridge on acreage along Raccoon Creek. It was once part of the Braden family farm. There were many county-wide girls' and boys' 4-H club events held at this park. The park area was located adjacent to Raccoon Creek which also provided swimming for all those who attended these events. (See War Time section for more on how this park was absorbed in the acreage sold by Mr. Jeffreys to the U.S. government who developed the "tank farm.")

Speaking of Raccoon Creek........

Many area residents, including Moon/Center Township residents and even Monaca residents, had camping areas and "summer camps" all along Raccoon Creek. The owners of these properties would always welcome groups, clubs, and other families to use their properties for various activities, including hunting trips. There were numerous articles regarding this or of a family spending a weekend or sometimes a full week or two at someone's "camp" along Raccoon Creek. It may not have been some fancy summer resort, but the peace and quiet and the fact that many just got away from everyday work for a few days, made visits to these "camps" quite a treat for everyone.

1911 newspaper article – *"Mr. and Mrs. H. J. Skelton, H. J. Taylor and family, Fred Bechtel and brother William, William Stoops, W. Bucholtz Frank Lockhart, Phylis Faust, Bert Carver and Miss Laura Glenn were guest of Mr. and Mrs. Carl Miksch, at their camp in Fishpot Hollow, Raccoon Creek, yesterday."*

Even sections of individual farms in Moon/Center Township were used for recreation. Throughout the newspapers were snippets of events and happenings with many mentions of various individual families or a club, organization, group of people, or church groups spending a day, weekend, or sometimes an entire week on someone's farm. There were quite large barns on various farms that were used for holding dances and other events. I presume these farm owners probably also had some areas of their farms that were very suitable for a camping area. Many would have had some type of stream or creek on the property, too. In the wintertime, there was always a listing of a sleigh riding event and parties held on township families' properties, too. In 1907 alone, there were newspaper articles stating............

    Henry Miller (Moon Township) held many family sleigh riding events on his property.
    James Trotter (Bellowsville) – hosted several sleigh riding parties.
    Mr. and Mrs. Samuel Calhoun (Moon Township) held multiple sleigh riding events.
    The Mateer Family held many sleigh riding events also.

Two articles from a 1911 newspaper
... *"About twelve students of Beaver College.... left to-day for camp on Israel Wagner's farm in Moon Township, to be gone a week or ten days."*

..."*The Turners (club) who have been camping on the Douds farm, will break camp and return home Wednesday."*

Ravine Park
This park is being included in this section since many Center Township families held their reunions and other events at this park. This was a picnic park situated close to the Center Township border but was actually within the Hopewell/Aliquippa area. It was located in an area along the present-day Kennedy Boulevard. Ravine Park was also very often referred to as Elk Park and/or Beaver Park. The Mount Vernon School in Hopewell Township, which operated along Monaca Road above Plan 11 from 1862 until 1910, also held many of their annual picnics/reunions in Ravine Park. The first such annual picnic of the school was held in 1920.

~ ~ ~

Township Recreation

Over the years, there have been many areas throughout the township that were designated and used for recreational activities (and/or social activities). In 1962 there were six recreational facilities available in the township, by 1971 there were seven facilities. Starting in or close to 1978, until recently, there were at least twenty-five facilities considered active. These facilities fall into three categories, Public, Semi-public, Private. Some of the facilities I have listed below have closed or "disappeared" over the years while there are other areas that have been added within the township and may not be listed.

Before I go into descriptions and specifics of each of the three categories of township recreational/park facilities, let me say……… All the areas listed under "Public" were also open for usage outside the specific times they were used by the township's Recreation Programs. During these "outside the Recreation Program times," children and others could freely go to use these playgrounds and areas. Sylvan Crest, Sherwood, Vankirk, and others were among these areas. In the summer months, on designated dates and times, is when the township would schedule, organized, and supervise structured Recreation Programs with activities. These were usually held over a six to eight-week period when the schools were not in session.

These Recreation Programs would have many activities to accommodate children of all ages, including games of pick-up baseball, football, basketball, wheelbarrow races, all different lengths of foot races, horseshoe-pitching, practices for the Community Night talent show, acrobatics, physical fitness classes, hikes in the vicinities of each recreation site, finger painting, watercolor painting, and others limited only to the imagination of the kids or supervisors. There were puppet shows presented thanks to the arts and crafts done over the summer by the children and there was always some form of dancing most years also. There was a golf program and even tournaments (started in 1961) held each year at Pettibon's Raccoon Golf Course. In the 1960s, the youngsters would even be treated to afternoon swim sessions at Monaca Pool in downtown Monaca.

Almost all the earlier summer programs would end with a Community Night. All township families were invited and there would be a "wiener roast" served by the supervisors and volunteers. Adults were always invited to participate in the Community Night activities including the one-legged and three-legged races. The adults also had their own contests which might include such activities as baby bottle drinking race and egg tosses.

The summer recreation programs in the 1960s and 1970s were listed as financed by Center Township School Board, Center Township Supervisors, and various civic groups and business firms. They used several different areas to accommodate as many township children as possible. I do not have exact starting years or ending years of all these playground/recreation sites in Center Township but have included dates when there was information provided or found. (The playground areas that were in existence in the earlier years (1960s, 1970s) are marked with double asterisks **.)

Some of the personnel and supervisors were hired and paid for their positions, others were strictly volunteering at a site. Just to name a few of the past supervisors and instructors included with these earlier playgrounds and summer recreation programs …. Charles Sirko, Jr. (supervisor - 1962), Howard (Sarge) Alberts was one of the well-known tennis instructors as of the 1960s, and by 1966, many of the Center Area teachers were filling their summer days by becoming instructors and playground supervisors. Just to name a few of these teachers - James D'Antonio, Ossie Signore, Sandy Grossi, Marlene Farris/Greer, Ron DeBacco, Sarge Alberts, George Avdellas, Irene Petuc/Hoover, Maureen Cregan, Joann Benedict, and the list goes on and on.

Center Township now boasts of over 100 acres of public and semi-public land within the township, all donated to recreation or pleasure services. These public owned recreational areas meet the current minimum size and location standards recommended by the National Parks and Recreation Association. The school district facilities and adult education, sports and cultural facilities of the post-secondary educational institutions in the township, are also reported to contribute significantly to leisure-time opportunities for township residents.

Public –available to all residents of the township

**Golden Dawn Playground – Brodhead Road – (now defunct)
   3.35 acres with play equipment, basketball hoop, picnic pavilion.
   It was one of the Center Township Summer Recreation sites.
   This playground was located behind the former Golden Dawn Supermarket (former Fastnal and current Beaver County Beverage) – programs were held at least into the 1970s.
   This playground area was eliminated in 1978.

**Sylvan Crest Playground – Grandview Avenue
   1.7 acres with play equipment, basketball court, ballfield, picnic pavilion.
   It was one of the early Center Township Summer Recreation sites.
   This recreational area is considered a neighborhood park and is still maintained.

**Vankirk Playground – started a summer program in 1960
   7 acres – play equipment, playfields, ballfield, basketball courts, pavilion. This playground started in 1960; programs continued into at least the 1970s; it was one of the Center Township Summer Recreation sites.
   The playground equipment was removed in the fall of each year (at least during the 1960s) and stored in the township building during the winter months.

**Xenos Playground   aka   Emanuel Xenos Memorial   aka   Ulysses M. Xenos Memorial Park
   Earlier records indicate it was along Columbia Drive but later records state Bainbridge Drive.
   4 acres– play equipment, pavilion. It was one of the Center Township Summer Recreation sites. In 1966, Eugene R. Thomas of Stone Quarry Road offered the supervisors a lease of 29 acres for recreational use at the park in Chapel Valley for $1 per year. Programs were held here at least into the 1970s. Center Township Supervisors were involved in the bidding of purchasing the property in 2015 – nothing further.

**Central Valley High School – Baker Road Extension
   Formerly known as   Center Area Senior High   and   Center Area Middle-Sr. High
   30 acres with ballfields, fitness trail, playfields, tennis courts, gymnasium, auditorium, stadium, track/football field. Center Township Summer Recreation programs were started in 1964 and held at the schools until at least into the 1970s. Installation of outdoor basketball backstops was underway in 1964.
   Residents may now use the newer Wellness Center facility that is located at the rear of the senior high building -- requires a membership fee, there are also other restrictions that must be met to use this facility.

**Todd Lane Elementary School Playground – there is a playground area for public use; several ballfields are also located on this school's property.
   It is currently listed as the Central Valley Elementary Playground–Todd Lane – with 2 acres.

**Central Valley Primary Center Playground – Center Grange Road
   Formerly known as Center Grange Elementary Playground
   1.5 acres with play equipment, and 4 soccer fields.
   The CT Recreation Board received authorization in Sep 1962 to purchase steel fencing to be erected along Center Grange Road at the Center Township Elementary School, where a small playground was to be opened in the fall of 1962. The fence would enclose a playground that included a 16-foot sliding board and an eight-swing set that had been purchased for the area. There were plans to purchase an additional horizontal ladder, too.   This playground opened in 1963 and had programs at least into the 1970s. In 1962 they sponsored the basketball summer programs. The original school building was demolished and a new Primary Center was erected.

**Memorial Park – I found nothing else on this park/playground or its location, just the name and that it was included in the earlier recreational programs. It was first used in 1966 and continued until at least into the 1970s.

Sherwood Acres Playground – Kings/Sherwood Drives
    0.75 acres with play equipment.   Neighborhood playground area.

Fred Taddeo Township Park – Center Grange Road with 2nd access off Chapel Road
    14 acres, playground area, picnic pavilions, tot lots, ballfields, playfields, basketball courts, tennis courts   (See further for more on this park and Center Township's current Recreation Program.)

~ ~ ~

Semi-public – not publicly owned, but available to the public
with restrictions (fees and/or membership).

For these next listings, they were not the same type of "recreation site" as previously listed, but still used to provide a form of recreation. They were open to the public for use with the owners' prior knowledge, reservations, and/or a fee.

Unnamed
    In 1978, there were plans for the Young Families Christian Association facility proposed for 6.5 acres at the current intersection of Brodhead Road and Sherwood Drive. This facility was to house an indoor swimming pool, handball courts, outdoor tennis courts, and meeting rooms. This facility never materialized, and no buildings were constructed. There was also another separate proposal to use this same site for developing an ice-skating facility, but those plans also never materialized.

PSU Brodhead Cultural Center – Brodhead Road
    7.9 acres with amphitheater, refreshment area, exhibit areas, natural areas, parking.

PSU Campus – off Brodhead Road
    25 acres with 3 playing fields, 6 basketball courts, 4 tennis courts, gymnasium, student union.

CCBC / Community College of Beaver County – Poplar Drive
    25 acres with classrooms, gymnasium, ballfield, playfield, basketball, walking trail.

CTVFD – Fire Station No. 1 – corner of Brodhead Road/Main Street
    0.5 acres with social hall.

CTVFD – Fire Station No. 2 – Grandview Avenue
    1 acre with social hall.

CTVFD – Fire Station No. 3 – Vankirk Road
    1 acre with social hall.

VFW / Veterans of Foreign Wars – Bunker Hill Road
    5 acres with meeting hall, ballfield.

Center Township Grange Hall – Center Grange Hall (now defunct for usage)
    2 acres with social hall

St. Francis Cabrini – Chapel Road
    1 acre with social hall.

Monaca Turner's Club – corner of Brodhead Road/Chapel Road
    1.5 acres with indoor racquetball courts, bowling alley, social hall, gymnasium.

Boy Scout Hall – Patterson/Main Street
    0.5 acres with meeting facilities.

McCracken's Lakes – see Private
Lyon's Lake – see Private
Hall's Lake – see Private

Raccoon Golf Course – defunct (see Golfing category in this section for much more information)
    1937 to 1960s   It was used for some of the township's recreation programs, but otherwise patrons had to pay to use the facilities.

~ ~ ~

Private – privately owned facilities - not available to the general public.

Beaver Lakes Apartments – formerly Canterbury Manor
    2 acres with tennis court, swimming pool, playfield, social room.

Brodhead North Condos
    1 acre with swimming pool.

Chapel Valley Swim Club
    3 acres with swimming pool.

McCracken's Lake – Cochran Drive (now defunct for public usages)
    10 acres with fishing, waterfowl. (see previous Fishing section.)

Lyons Lake – Edgewater Drive (now defunct for public usages)
    2 acres with fishing, swimming, waterfowl. (See previous Fishing section.)

Hall's Lake – Hall Road (now defunct for public usages)
    1.5 acres with fish, waterfowl.   (See previous Fishing section.)

~ ~ ~

CTR – Center Township Recreation

The Center Township Recreation Board has maintained a program in the township for well over fifty years. It was an organization created by the Center Township Supervisors. Charles Sirko was elected the recreation director in 1962. Mr. Sirko and Thomas Mohr were elected the board's representatives to the Beaver County Health and Welfare Council the same year. In Sep 1962, Mr. Sirko reported that several additional play sites were being considered for 1963, but none of the new sites were listed at that time.   Mr. Sirko was authorized to prepare the necessary forms once again for application for United Fund financial assistance for the 1963 year.

Currently (2018), there is still the Center Township Recreation (CTR) which is a non-profit organization and was created by the Center Township Supervisors. Nowadays they help to organize many family and children activities such as Easter Egg Hunt, T-Ball, Flag Football, Movies in the Park, Fall Fest, Breakfast/Lunch with Santa, Mother/Son Spring Fling, food truck rally & car cruise in August, a Fall Fest in October, Center Light up Night (Christmas in the Park) and a holiday formal (father/daughter dance) in December.   Like those in the past, the CTR also sponsors Summer Camp Programs which include "Tennis, Basketball, Volleyball and Arts & Crafts for all children in kindergarten through fifth grade with some programs offered to older youths when applicable."

The current CTR organizes events that are held in the park each month and posts these on their on-line newsletter. The most current CTR members and volunteers (2019): Lesa Mastrofrancesco (President), Lorraine DiCioccio-Johns (Vice President), Rene' Kostosky (Secretary), Keith Kostosky, Melissa Borello, Darin Smoot, Jonathan Dugan, Vicki Colalella-Dugan, and Kirk Johns.

Center Municipal Park   /   Fred Taddeo Municipal Park

As early as 1974 plans were being made for a recreation complex project – the Center Municipal Park. It was decided to develop 12.4 acres behind and adjacent to the municipal building property on Center Grange Road. It was to have access roads from both Center Grange and Chapel Roads and would have tennis and basketball courts, baseball fields, picnic areas and shelters, playground area, an all-purpose field, and parking areas.

In November of 1976, the plans were formulated into results and the construction for a new baseball complex was underway. It was sponsored by the Center Township Baseball Boosters and the 475 Quarter-master Company. At one time, when this area was first developed as a public park area, there used to be a very large mound of dirt that had a few huge, shorter sections of very large concrete piping you could crawl through – they have since been removed.

This 1974 recreational area was all renamed the "Fred Taddeo Municipal Park" and is currently described as an outdoor picnic type setting that is open for public usage including schedule usage of the pavilion areas. This park includes five recreational fields used for T-ball, baseball, and softball leagues. It also has two batting cages, two tennis courts, two basketball courts, a sand volleyball court, a playground area, three picnic pavilions, a stage area, restrooms, and large open field areas for outside events. There are two entrances to access all areas of the park, one is from Center Grange Road and one from Chapel Road. There are parking lots available for vehicles at each of the two entrances.

~ ~ ~

Before I leave the subject of "recreation" I must make mention of a few much less "approved' recreational areas in the township. ☺

---Many of the kids from especially the Woodhaven and Chapel Valley area used the area that is now the Brookhaven Estates as a "gathering place," most likely engaging in what parents and officials would consider less than "approved" activities. It was known to those who frequented it as the "Mutes." I have no firm answer to the origin of the name, but one friend suggested that it could have developed from the fact that whoever attended events here had to be "mute" about what took place. ☺

---Another area the underage kids would hang out at was Grimm's Field. This gathering place was in the area behind the old Rebich Beer Distributer / Cabinet World. The Grimm family lived in the area, so I deduce that's how this hangout area obtained its name.

---I found two areas that had to do with the name "sewage."
    One was told to me to be "the sewage plant;" a popular "party site" for kids and will surely be familiar to many former and/or current residents ☺ Just for the record, I was also told there is no type of "sewage plant" in the area so no one could give a reason for the name. This meeting area was in a wooded area near Trinity Drive and Whitehall Avenue by Sunshine Valley Plan and St. Francis Cabrini Church.
    "There's going to be a sewage." was a very familiar phrase or statement to mean there would be a party was planned. This reference was made to the area of what is traditionally known as "Seven Bridges" – between Elkhorn Run Road and Shades Hollow Road. Unlike the previous site, the township had a designated sewage plant within the area, so the name was fitting.

~ ~ ~

Swimming

Swimming pools were definitely not of great popularity in the 1910s/1920s when Center Township was formed and not for many years later. People were using the local creeks, ponds, and/or the beaches located along the Ohio River. (Yes, I said swimming in the Ohio River – see further.) Of the local creeks, Raccoon and Elkhorn Run Creeks were most popularly utilized because of "swimming holes" which were formed when people would construct crude, make-shift dams from rogue logs/branches and the many sandstone rocks found in the beds of the creeks. These dams would cause an area of the creek to pool into deeper water. These pools could be from knee-deep to extended depths for actual swimming and even diving. Regardless of how big one of the streams or creeks, just having access to any cool, running water on a hot summer day was enjoyable --- cooling off is cooling off when it is hot out. (See Creeks, Waterways, River section for more details on each of the following listings.)

Elkhorn Run - Elkhorn Run Creek was a popular and great place to cool off. There were areas that were even used for running grist and sawmills, so there were definite areas with an amount of "flow" associated with this creek.

Raccoon Creek - portions wind through both Center and Potter Townships
Beginning in the 1800s, there were several locations along Raccoon Creek that were popular "swimming holes." There were places like Hober's Beach and Lubert's Beach which were used frequently for public picnics and outings. The creek provided excellent swimming and plenty of space along either of its banks for various activities. Many people owned or rented property along the creek and would camp there at various times all year round. Hunting in the area was also a frequent activity. In the earlier to mid 1900s, Mr. Bittner of Monaca made his sot-after turtle soup from turtles he would take from Raccoon Creek.

c   1900 - Raccoon Creek

Later in the 1900s a very popular location on Raccoon Creek for swimmers and families to gather was called *Sandy Beach*. Waters of the creek in this area were deep enough that a person could even enjoy doing some diving from the ledges above the shoreline of the creek.

Not only did Raccoon Creek become such a popular place for people to frequent for swimming and fishing, but many would engage in washing vehicles. As the popularity of using Raccoon Creek became more widespread, many of the residents who owned property along the creek had to begin to monitor people who venture into the creek and would be found walking up or down the creek banks while fishing, turtle hunting, et cetera. To help start monitoring who would be found "in the creek" by any given resident's home (the areas along the Raccoon Creek Road, Fishpot Run, et cetera), there was a group formed, *Raccoon Creek Canoe Club and Preservation League*. This group began to issue "cards" to those who expressed interest in frequenting the creek on a more regular basis as a means to help control trespassing onto their properties.

~ ~ ~

Chapel Valley Swimming Pool
The homes in Chapel Valley originally had a pool built to privately accommodate the residents who lived within Chapel Valley homes. In 2016 the information obtained from the Chapel Valley Pool site states that it was founded in 1970. Passes could be purchased which gave access to use the pool. It goes on to state that it is still a private, non-profit swim club and now includes a 25-meter heated pool, a diving board, baby pool, basketball court, and concession stand. From its early beginning, it has definitely gone through many improvements.

Canterbury Manor Pool   aka   **Beaver Creek Apartments Pool**
This housing complex also had a pool and limited non-residents were permitted to obtain permission (for a fee) to use their pool and facilities after it was establish in the 1970s.

~ ~ ~

Monaca Swimming Pool – 16th Street and Indiana Avenue
1953 to 1991
Center Township has never had a township pool. Residents did have the opportunity to either go on random days or to obtain swimming passes to use others' community pools including the Monaca Swimming pool. Monaca's pool was a quite popular place in its time. As the Ohio River began to prove to be a less desirable place to swim, discussions for a swimming pool in Monaca began as early as 1937 but was not approved until 1953. Monaca Borough chose a tract of land between Washington and Indiana Avenues and between Fifteenth and Sixteenth Street for the location of the

pool. Aug 1954 the pool was nearing completion – consisted of the pool, bath houses, concession stand and surrounding grounds for other recreational activities. The swimming pool itself was an L-shaped construction with the deeper diving area in the smaller portion of the "L." It had a lower diving board and a high diving board. It opened in the summer 1955.

In 1982, the pool had extensive repairs approved. Since the pool was originally built on land that was filled at one time, the settling was taking its toll on the property and the pool itself. There were extensive repairs needed to keep the pool in operating and most of all in safe condition. The Monaca council found it not feasible to make any further repair the pool and unfortunately approved the closing of the only public pool in the borough. The pool was closed in 1991. Jul 7, 1995, a bid was awarded to have the L-shaped cement pool filled in and grass planted over the site. The concession stand was left standing and is still used nowadays for various activities, the remaining property is an open grassy area.

Fun fact – Mr. Nichol would give lifeguard lessons and certify lifeguards at the Monaca pool. I took lifeguard lessons at this pool from Mr. Nichol and worked as a lifeguard there for three summers in the earlier 1970s. It was a fun job and the pool was always full of swimmers, even on the cloudy days.

High dive   Regular dive   Bath houses

For orientation – you can see Indiana Avenue on the right of this picture. The football stadium is on the other side of Indiana Avenue, directly across from the former bath house building.

DiMatia Pool / Daniel DiMatia Recreation Center Pool – Aliquippa
c1960 to official closing in 2013

For some of the families who lived closer to the New Sheffield side of the township, there was also the DiMatia Pool they may have used through the years. The concept of the pool was started with some residents (including Mr. Chamovitz), all were living in the DiMatia housing plan. The concept grew to form an organization with officers, bylaws, and all. The pool was a rectangular shape and had both low and high diving boards. There was also a kiddy pool and a pool club house/bathhouse. The pool site was in the area between Chapel Road and Christine Drive, adjacent to the DiMatia plan of homes, access to the pool area was via Grant Street. It was constructed on a parcel of land donated by the DiMatias who were also the builders of all the houses in the neighborhood. They gifted the parcel on the condition the pool be named for their son, Daniel, who had been killed in an accident not long before. It was a private pool and required approval of the organization to become a member. Members could invite guests to accompany them for a swim. The usual substitute precondition for consideration of membership included residing within walking distance of the pool. There was a reunion for members of the DiMatia Pool held in 2018 with approximately 75 people in attendance.

~ ~ ~

Ohio River beaches............
As previously mentioned, even with the various creeks and streams in the township, in the earlier years, many Moon/Center Township residents could also enjoy cooling off in the Ohio River. There were said to be quite nice beaches along the area known as Bellowsville and a few others along the stretch of the former Narrows Road.

For the most part, Center residents may have found the ride into Monaca well worth it for a day "at the beach;" many of the residents had relatives and close friends living in Monaca so it became a nice family day. One must remember that the Ohio River had no real depth to it in the early years. In fact, during hot, dry summers, the riverbanks grew, the center of the river shrank, and the total average depth of the river might only be a foot or two.

Heavy pollution of the river was the demise of these river beaches and swimming areas, all prior to the dams increasing the depth of the river. Once the river was deemed unsafe and too "dirty" to swim in, the beach areas in Monaca naturally became much less desirable to use. The creeks and streams in Center and Potter Townships were still quite unpolluted, so I am sure the tides turned and instead of Center residents going to Monaca, Monaca residents were seeking out the creeks and streams in Moon/Center and Potter Townships for those refreshing dips. Even before the water in the Ohio River was proven to be quite polluted and considered unsafe, many articles state how various Monaca residents were spending a vacation or weekend on Raccoon Creek in either Moon/Center Township or Potter Township.

With all that being said, here is some information on what the Moon/Center residents would have found in Monaca for recreational swimming.

Monaca Beaches
Monaca once had two separate municipal beaches with bath houses. One was located where the current pump house is and referenced as "Monaca Beach." The second beach area was a little further upriver by the end of Twelfth Street and appropriately called "Twelfth Street Beach."

Again, I will remind you that the river was not as deep and dangerous back in the late 1800s and earlier 1900s as it is nowadays. In those earlier years, at best, the deepest part of the river by Monaca was probably 10 feet and that would be in the middle of the river where the large boats would travel. Along the shorelines, the Ohio River was much shallower as seen in the pictures further. In 1916, a citizen committee raised money to put the Monaca beaches in good condition. Money was even raised, and an offer was received for a concession stand to provide refreshments.

All the beach and swimming areas that were accessible for people to use as bathing/swimming beaches also had areas for picnicking, corn roasts, campfires, camping out, storing canoes and row boats, and even beach houses. Local bands and musicians would come and provide added entertainment. During the 1910s, the entire community and friends would join in a corn roast and have beach parties. The bath houses and bathing beaches were used daily during the hot summer days into the 1920s.

> *Fun fact: Edward Mahan of Pittsburgh leased the municipal bathing beach at Twelfth Street and had the area cleaned up and put in shape for the 1917 summer season. The bath houses were remodeled, other improvements were made, and new equipment was added. Mr. Mahan expected to make the beach the most popular resort in Monaca's section of the county with it opening on May 26, 1917.*

By 1926, the beach houses had already been abandoned which indicates that residents were no longer so fond of using the polluted Ohio River as a place to swim. In the spring of 1926, council was approached and asked approval for use of the currently abandoned beach houses to be used by the Monaca Aquatic Club. But only a few months after this request was made, there was a petition by the Monaca citizens presented to the town council asking for once again, a permanent park and bathing beach to be available to them. This petition also made the claim that in previous years, Monaca was the first to have a bathing beach in the county and they wanted their bathing beaches restored.

> *Fun fact: Another activity in the 1930s, the local Boy Scouts would hold events on the Ohio, starting from the Monaca beach, going by row boats across the river to the Beaver beach area and then rowing back to Monaca.*

The popularity of swimming in the river dropped drastically when it was again exposed and absolutely proven how unhealthy it was to be swimming in the heavily polluted waters of the Ohio River. The waters were increasingly polluted due to the growing industrial and mine pollutions, also remember that in the earlier days of the 1900s, it was a common practice for sewage lines of <u>all</u> communities to be drained into the Ohio without being processed or cleaned as is required today. With so many communities, including Pittsburgh, all "dumping" those pollutants into the rivers, they mixed with the water and flowed down stream. This seriously affected the quality of the river water by the time it reached the Monaca and Center Township areas. With that last statement being said --- *yuk*....one can only imagine how polluted the rivers and streams were back then!

The next few pictures show many people enjoying the beaches of Monaca Borough. Note how far from the shore line many of the people have gone. These pictures clearly indicate how much shallower the Ohio River was in those earlier years. The depth reflected in these pictures was more of the "norm" of the river.

BCHR&LF

The swimsuits and caps are just adorable. It was evidently uneventful to see the steam boat passing up or down the river since no one seems too concerned with it.

BCHR&LF

Monaca Aquatic Bathing Beach (by Monaca Water Works)   (Note the trolley on the bridge.)

In this picture, if you look very closely (top right side), you can see the bridge across the mouth of the Beaver River on the opposite side of the river. Also, again note how far out on the river that people could comfortably walk and still only be mid-body deep in the water.

1920s   Photo from Monaca Borough

~ ~ ~

Roller Skating

Vintage post card of Melody Lane Roller Rink, Hookstown, PA) - a typical roller skating rink in the 1950s

For many years, roller skating was one of the most popular recreations along with dancing. In the late 1800s and early/mid 1900s many buildings were multi-purposed and those with large wooden floors were not just used for the business, athletics, and/or dances, but also used for roller skating whenever possible. I did not find any rinks or buildings used for roller skating in Moon/Center Township, but then there were not larger buildings in the township during those early years except barns which traditionally had dirt floors. I did find two men, D. J. Mitchell and George V. Mullen who recognized the need for a permanent roller rink. They formed a partnership and started a roller-skating rink in Monaca in 1907.

Prior to any exclusive or official skating rinks, there were many occasions of roller skating in the gymnasium of the Young Men's Christian Association in Monaca prior to 1907. The association's gymnasium was located somewhere on Pennsylvania Avenue and was called *Association Hall*. The YMCA was closing its door for good in Monaca. An article in the Aug 31, 1907 newspaper stated that the association would keep the hall open that evening "to give those who desire to have a farewell skate the opportunity." Another building being used for roller skating in Monaca was the Bank Hall (currently Ball Furniture) where skating parties were held in 1907 with it being stated that large crowds would be in attendance. In late Feb 1907, the Eagles in Monaca fitted up a rink on the first floor, under the social rooms of their building, for roller skating. There was live music provided at many of the roller-skating events, most orchestra's being local. There were numerous snippets of information in the local newspaper listings stating some residents of Moon and early Center Township attended these various skating parties. This all indicates that the Moon/Center residents also enjoyed and participated in roller skating whenever possible.

A few of the local and very popular skating rinks in the area were:

Monaca Roller Skating Rink aka **Silver Slipper Roller Rink** - 823 Pennsylvania Avenue
and the **Monaca Roller Skating Rink** – 1752 Pennsylvania Avenue

1907 to the 1950s
The first official skating rink in Monaca was in the building at 823 Pennsylvania Avenue. It was also known as The Monaca Silver Slipper Roller Rink. During non-skating times/days, the rink was used for other activities such as boxing matches of various levels.

There was a new skating rink built, named The Monaca Roller Skating Rink at 1752 Pennsylvania Avenue. It then became the site of the now demolished Polish Club. This rink was still being used as of 1948, evidenced by advertisement of skating parties and events on those dates. An unexpected heavy snowfall of between 40 and 48 inches on Nov 24, 1950, caused the roof of the skating rink to collapse. Fortunately, there was no one in the structure when the collapse occurred. No further mention of the skating rink can be found after this roof collapse.

Fun ads

To Race For Championship.
For the roller skating championship of the Valley, Raymon Wubbeler, of Beaver Falls, and Hubert Wagner, of Monaca, will meet this evening in a mile race at the Monaca roller skating rink. Both men are trained to the minute for the event and the rivalry is intense.

1909

Hallowe'en Masquerade Party
AT
MONACA SILVER SLIPPER SKATING RINK
TONIGHT – 8 to 11
Door Prizes   Costume Prizes   Noise Makers
Skating Every Tues. Thru Sun. 8 to 11
Sunday Afternoon 2 to 4

Oct 1948

Aliquippa Roller Rink – was 1410 / now 2590 Brodhead Road, Aliquippa

The rink was built in 1949. It was owned by Mr. and Mrs. Anton Krancevic in 1960. They sold multiple properties including the rink to Marilyn Kendrew in Apr 1986. The building is no longer a skating rink; it is currently now known as "Kendrews," a bar and grill. Center Township groups were known to sponsor many skating parties at the Aliquippa Roller Rink, Center's P.T.A. in particular did so at least in the 1960s.

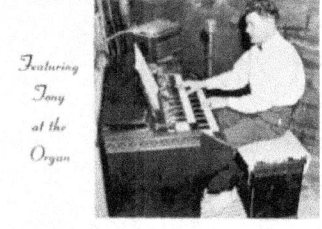

1956

Melody Lane Roller Skating Rink – Hookstown

Opened in 1955; closed in 1995.

This was a very popular skating rink for many of the Center Township clubs, church groups, and individual residents, it was the "go to" rink for my family and church for many years. ☺ Myrle K. "Bud" Berger, Jr. and Patricia his wife were the owners and operators of the Melody Lanes Skating Rink.

The Bergers often related that roller skating was a "cheap activity" for people when compared to the cost of admission to a movie, plus, they reminded everyone that it was an excellent family activity and great exercise. By 1978, after a slump in the popularity of roller skating, the Bergers truly felt that skating was going to become popular again. Although it made no giant leaps and bounds in making a come-back, it still held its own. This may have been due to the fact it was one of only four skating rinks that was still open in Beaver County and still played only organ music (which became a tradition through the years and of all older rinks). Early in Feb 1995, there was a fire that destroyed the 40-year-old skating rink. (Patricia died at 76 in 2012, Bud died at 80 in 2014.)

(Also see the picture at the beginning of this section for the inside view of Melody Lane.)

Booth where the organist sat.

 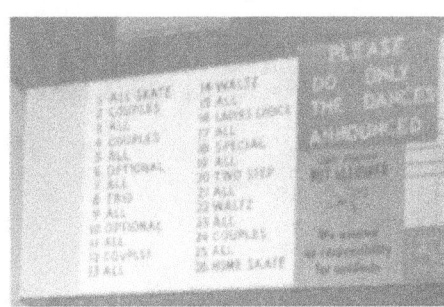

~ ~ ~

Bowling

Center Lanes – 708/709 - renumbered 3084 Brodhead Road
1959 to current
Center Lanes opened Jan 22, 1959. During the earlier years of the lanes, there used to be a nursery, snack bar, and a 400 car parking lot. The Colonial Lounge also became attached to front of the building. In the earlier 1960s, the bowling alley was used by St. Francis parish as a church while their building was being erected. The bowling lanes property consists of multiple prior lots. Martin Lytle was the president of the business in 1958 and signed the mortgage. Ronald Sokol was the president of the Center Bowling Inc. in 1984 when the property was sold to Mr. and Mrs. Dawson, Mr. and Mrs. Garvey, and Nedbat Bowling, Inc. in 1984. Center Lanes was next purchased by current owners James & Donna Manganello at a sheriff's sale in 1990.

1974

1975

~ ~ ~

Brodhead Cultural Center – Penn State Beaver Campus, Center Township
1976, Current   See pictures and more information in the Education section.

~ ~ ~

Car Racing

In the 1950s, there was racing in the adjacent area for those township residents that enjoyed the cars.

Valley Speedway aka **Marshall's Speedway** – Kane Road, Aliquippa
1950s   Was an oval track – dirt.

1950s ad

Clearview Speedway – off Green Garden Road
1950s   Was an oval track – dirt.

~ ~ ~

MOVIE THEATERS
TOWNSHIP THEATERS

Cinemark Center Township Marketplace aka **Cinemark Theater** - 99 Wagner Road
2004 to current   This movie center was built in 2004.   Dustin Whitlock - Manager (2015).   It has twelve screens and 2,000 seats. It was operated by Piano, TX based Cinemark USA (as of 2015).   Considered to be located in the Township Market Place Plaza.

Beaver Valley Mall Cinema aka   **Mall Cinema** aka **Cinema World I II III**
Opened in 1970 - closed 1992.
Formerly located to the right and in front of the small, open-air satellite mall, all situated to the left of the main BV Mall complex and parking lot.   Opened in 1970 as a two-screen theater. By Jun 1974, the building was remodeled --- Theater 1 had been briefly closed and split into two theaters, it was then billed as Cinema I   II   III.   In 1975, Carl Fisk was the Manager. The theater was owned by General Cinema Corp, Boston.   The theater housed three screens.   The average cost of a ticket was $2.50 to $3.00.   In Jun 1981, it opened to a four-screen theatre, having split Theater 2 this time.   Owners of Cinema in Apr 1983 until Dec 1988 was General Cinema.   Cinema World Inc. purchased the theater in the fall of 1989. Bob Sutton was the Manager until 1992. Bob started as a doorman in 1976 and worked his way up to manager.   The newest movie in mid Apr 1991 was *Mortal Thoughts*.
   Cinema World Inc. made the decision to close the theater as of the end of Sep 1992.   The building had been empty and was being torn down by 1995. The site was replaced with a Circuit City store (currently the Beaver County Auto business).

Aug 11, 1971

Jaws – *Pink Panther* - *Rollerball*
were the movies playing mid Sep, 1975

Movie Theater at the GeeBee Plaza aka **Movie World**   aka **Carmike Cinema Movie World**
Opened late in 1974 - closed 2004
This theater building was in the GeeBee Shopping Center/Walmart Plaza.   Cinemette Corp of America leased 15,000 sq. feet in the GeeBee Shopping Center plaza area to build the theatre in 1973. The lease was for 20 years from Robert A. Kathery & Assoc. Ltd of the GeeBee Shopping Center. It had four screens in Sep 1975. Owners of the Cinema in Apr 1983 was General Cinema. In the summer of 1985, it expanded to seven screens, a 2000 seat theatre.   Dave Duffy was the manager in 1988.   Cinema World Inc. became owner of the theater in 1989.   It was called "Movie World at GeeBee Plaza" until 1992. Dave Duffy was still the manager in 1991, 1992. By 2000 it was owned by Carmike Cinema.   Bob LaCava was the manager in 2001 and Chad Ours was manager in 2003.   Movie World was there in 1975 to 1992 ---- in 1994 to 2002, it was called "Cinema World" but still was often referenced as "Movie World at Wal-Mart."   The entire theater closed in or close to 2004. Plans to tear down the building were in place for Jul 2005.   The building was demolished, and Applebee's Restaurant is now located on that site.

Apr 1983

~ ~ ~

Early Theaters from surrounding areas

Knowing that many of the Moon/Center Township's earlier residents would have been patrons of other theaters in the surrounding areas prior to any theaters being built within the township, I chose to include the following information.

Those listed further are a run of various other theatres that were not in Center Township, but all would have most likely been attended by some of the early township residents while they were open for business. My grandparents and several of my aunts and uncles spoke of going to movies or other shows and events in many of these various theatres and I even went to many movies at a few of these theatres when I was much younger. I did not want to make this a "history of local theatres," but rather wanted to include these theatres to refresh anyone's memory who may have heard of some of these or like me, even frequented a few of them. (The dates under the names indicate what years information was found on them and does not indicate years of operation unless otherwise indicated.)

Ed Harvey was known as one of the moving picture pioneers within Beaver County. He opened the Grand Theater in New Brighton in 1906 and then opened the first theater in Aliquippa in 1911......

The Grand Theatre – Franklin Street, Aliquippa
1911 to ___

Ed Harvey executed a long-term lease of his Aliquippa movie house property to Anthony Jim in 1928, but within this documentation, there was no name of the movie house. Shortly thereafter Mr. Jim sublet the theatre and gave an option for its purchase to Samuel Hyman and H. Rosenthal, who went into possession and operated it. They formed the Aliquippa Amusement Company, a corporation which had been organized by them to operate the theatre.

Other early theaters most likely visited by township residents and credited with being in Aliquippa ....

Queen Theatre – Aliquippa – 540 Franklin Street (became "Avenue")
    Renamed in 1936 to the..........
New Harvey Theatre – 540 to 560 Franklin Avenue, Aliquippa
Located across from the Steelworkers building which became the First National Bank in Aliquippa. Ed Harvey, owner. It sat next to the Harvey bowling alleys with a door connecting the two buildings. An old ad in a 1919 Condor publication had it listed as Harvey Amusements, 502 Franklin Avenue. It was advertised as having a Grand Theater, bowling, and pocket billiards. Then, a 1924 Condor listing had the "New Harvey Theater" being at 558 Franklin Avenue. The 1928 and 1929 mercantile tax lists had this theater simply listed as the "Harvey" with 560 Franklin Avenue as the address.

All this information is confusing since the State Theater (see further) was located at 540/560 Franklin Avenue in 1921.........perhaps this building was demolished or most likely total remodeled for the State Theater?

State Theater - 540/560 Franklin Avenue
Constructed in 1921 - closed 1975 - demolished sometime after Apr 1993
In Dec of 1921, the Woodlawn News had a dedication article for the State Theater – "Modern Moving Picture House Opens Doors." Ed Harvey was the original owner. It was classified as having thematic architecture which was popular in the "golden age" of the moving pictures. It was designed by the architectural firm of Carlisle & Sharrer, Pittsburgh, PA; Earl E. Shaffer of Aliquippa was the general contractor; Klein Electric of Aliquippa installed the electrical work and lighting system; and Bert Dinsmore of Aliquippa completed the interior decorating.

There was an article in the Beaver County Times Dec 24, 1964, that stated the theater had been closed for a period of time due to smoke damage from an adjacent building's (Villa's Lounge) fire in October and would be reopening on Dec 25th. The $50,000 remodeling after the smoke damage included removing the balcony area, providing 700 seats on the main floor, adding new pink and red wall to wall carpeting, and new stage curtains. Earnest Stern was the president of Associated Theaters who were the owners and Peter Loschiavo was the manager. Peter also served as the projectionist from 1958 to 1975. Mr. C or J Lund served as a manager before 1964 (he also managed the Temple and Strand theatres). The article also stated that the theater was fifty years old at that time which would make the original date of 1914. I found this 1914 date confusing/conflicting since 1921 is the date given for the construction of the building. The building stood idle from 1975 and fell into horrible disrepair. Although the interior had remodeling done in 1964, the outside of the building remained as it was when built in 1921. Due to the architect and the use of terra cotta décor on the exterior, the building itself was classified as a historical building, so the state required Aliquippa to compile a historical study of the structure prior to them tearing down the building.

from the 1920s

1930 post card (see pointer)

Prior to being razed.

Temple Theatre – 471 Franklin Avenue, Aliquippa (30s & 40s)
Opened Nov 25, 1936   It was a three-storey building that housed the Aliquippa Elks Lodge and seated 668 to 750. There was a contest to choose a name for the theatre which was won by Marion Schwarts. J. C. Lund – manager (also managed the Strand and State theatres). The keystone on the building has "1918" on it. There is no found official closing date.

2015 view of former theatre's building

Rialto – lower Franklin Ave, Aliquippa (near corner of Cochran Street)
Opened 1926 (by same company that owned the Strand).   Closed by the end of the 1930s. Later became the Red Fox theater showing only adult movies.

Strand Theatre – 276 Franklin Avenue, Aliquippa
1928 to 1950s/1960s   J. C. Lund was a manager (also managed the State and Temple theatres).   Existed in the 1930s – seated 550.   The building appeared empty but was still standing in Aug 2016.

former view

current view

For those early Center Township residents who wanted to venture across the river for a movie or show………..

West Theatre –   I found mention of this theatre but have no further information.

The Royce Theatre - had an ad in Beaver County Times - Nov 1978…….There was a tour of Beaver County sights in the fall of 1984 and the Royce was on the list as "the Royce Theater, the smallest theater in the world, in Rochester."

The Home Theatre – Rochester, PA   (1914)

People's Family Theatre – Brighton Avenue, Rochester, PA   (1908…)

Colonial Theatre – New York Avenue, Rochester
This theater was popular in the silent screen era and the WWI era.   There were movies and events held in this theatre in 1911 and 1914.   A description of the theatre in a 1911 theatrical guide states there is a highway that runs through what used to be the theater property.   This theatre was included on the 1928 mercantile tax list.

Grand Opera House - Rochester
In a Julius Cahn's Official Theatrical Guide from 1901/1902 and 1906/1907, this opera house was described as having W. D. Campbell as the lessee and manager and then Geo. S. Challis was the manager.   It had illumination from gas and electric, footlights, 28 x 28-foot stage opening, curtains, theatre section on the second floor, rigging loft, and 5 trap doors.

The Majestic Theater   aka   **New Majestic Theater** – Main Street, Rochester
Opened in 1908 on Brighton Avenue. According to the Beaver County Mercantile Appraiser's List of Jun 20, 1930, the Majestic was the only theater in Rochester.   In 1909, they showed four pictures a night and they advertised "new pictures daily of four reels" and "Friday is always amateur night, and it is great."   In 1914 adult admission was 15 cents and children 10 cents.   In 1919 the Majestic underwent improvements with a new pipe organ, increased the seating with new upholstered seats, added paneling, and changed the lighting system.   In 1920 had a Seeburg-Smith theatre pipe organ installed.   In 1921 admission was 28 cents for the main floor, 22 cents for balcony and 11 cents for children ---- all prices included "war tax."   From 1921, the admission kept going up, and by 1926, matinee was adult 40 cents / children 15 cents with evenings higher, main floor 50 cents, balcony 40 cents, and children 15 cents.   In 1927 they announced the beginning of the Vaudeville Season.

 vintage post card of th Majestic Theater

The Oriental Theater –121 Hinds Street
Opened Labor Day weekend in 1931 and was closed in 1972. It was built by the Winograd family with the architect being Michael DeAngelis (who was 25 years old when he designed the Oriental). In Jun 1940, main floor admission was 30 cents, balcony was 25 cents and children were 10 cents. In Mar 1954 the first 3D movie was shown. It was owned and operated by Associated Theaters, Pittsburgh in 1968. During a severe storm in Sep 1972, lightning struck the theater and bricks were blown from the chimney, but no fire was reported. It was demolished early in Aug of 2001.

The Family Theater – Hinds Street, Rochester, PA
Grand Opening was on Sept 2, 1949. It was built by the same Winograd brothers who built the Oriental. Built exclusively for the exhibition of sound motion pictures. It has been said that like many theater owners, the Family would show the "B" movies. Theater owners who were forced to buy "package" deals from studios, they would show the feature movies in their larger theater and the lesser movies in the 2nd theater. It was owned and operated by Associated Theaters, Pittsburgh, in 1968. It closed by 1982. The building is still standing, there is now a curb cut in front of the theater and a pair of garage doors where the entrance used to be, but there are still two poster cases out front and some decorative tile work at the entrance. You can see the patch of concrete where the box office once stood.

former   current

So, after reviewing all these available theaters, it is evident that if a Moon/Center Township resident wanted to see a good movie, they did have quite a selection of venues to pick from.

~ ~ ~

And what would entertainment for the Center Township residents be without including ...

Drive-In Theaters

A favorite pass time of many Center Township residents was for a family, even with some of the neighborhood kids, to all get in a car or truck and head to a drive-in theater. This would be just one of the fun events for a special and "big" night out. Drive-in theaters were considered quite a popular form of entertainment during the 1950s and 1960s, and they actually held their popularity for many decades.

Drive-in theaters in general are a part of Americana. As of 2015, there were as few as 300 drive-in theaters still in business when there was once over 4,000 of them. Each time another drive-in theater closes and is torn down, it is another symbol and a piece of America gone by the wayside.

Fun fact: Pennsylvania alone had numerous drive-in theaters. The number of drive-in theaters fluctuated over the years... 59 in 1948, 165 in 1954, 181 in 1958, 166 in 1963, 170 in 1967, 126 in 1972, 141 in 1977, 115 in 1982, 75 in 1987, and 36 in 1999.

Center Township did not have any drive-in theaters of its own, but some of the local favorite drive-ins township residents visited were:

Kane Road Drive-In Theater

Opened in 1954 and operated by the Gray family until it closed in Sep 2013. Steve Gray, Jr. made it his life's work with the Kane Road Drive-In. He ran the projector himself and remembred when the films were transitioning to digital. The upgrade to accommodate this transitition cost him more than $100,000 to implement, a cost he found very hard to endure, yet still remained in business. Many reflected back at the years this drive-in was open and stated that Steve Gray, Jr. ran the theater "with his heart." It has been said that he never made a fortune from the business and some years he even lost money. "He just did it because that was him." The giant screen structure stood as a reminder of the many years of entertainment and fun the theater provided. After the drive in closed, all the buildings were finally demolished in Oct 2015. The former site is now home to a 220+ unit apartment complex. Many people were very sad to see yet another drive-in theater disappear.

(All of the following drive-in theaters became members of the "Beaver Valley Drive-In Assn.")

ABC Drive-In Theater – was on Route 88 (off State Street by Northern Lights Shopping Center) Opened Aug 20, 1948. It was often listed as being located "between Rochester and Ambridge." They added their playground area in 1949. It was owned in the 1950s by Co-Op Circuit, then by General Drive-In/General Cinema Corp. until well into the 1960s. The first movie was *Without Reservations. It* started as a one screen theater and in 1981, it became a larger drive-in with between 600 and 750 parking spaces and two screens. It closed the end of the 1982 (possibly 1983) season. All was demolished and now a housing development called Villas of Economy is on the site.

1953

Green Garden Drive-In Theater – was off Green Garden Road on Todd Road, near Raccoon Creek. Opened in Jul 31, 1948 with one screen theater and 350 car parking spaces. The actual name of the drive-in was "Green Gardens" and their marquee had "Green Gardens Open Air Theatre" on it. The first movie was *Tarzan and the Leopard Woman* starring Johnny Weissmuller. It was owned and operated by Joseph Kulik. It closed the end of the 1967 season for construction of the Beaver Valley Expressway which was going to run right through the property.

1953

Brook Side Drive-In Theater – at the Allegheny/Beaver County line
Opened Jul 25, 1947 as a one screen theater with 400 car parking. It was operated by R.W. Thompson, Jr and Searn-Hana Co-Operative Theatre Services. It closed after their movies on Sep 6, 1987. The Sewickley Creek Greenhouse (formerly Brookside Country Market) is now on the site.

1953

Spot Light 88 Drive-In Theater – was Route 88, Beaver Falls (Mercer Road)
Opened Jun 17, 1948 with one screen and added a second screen in 1981 providing 608 car parking. A third screen was added in 1983 and they were designated as Red, Yellow, and Green screens. It was owned by Hanna Theatre Services. On May 31, 1985, a severe tornado took a path over the area of the theater and within twenty minutes the drive-in (and many homes and other businesses) were completely destroyed. The site was then used for the Spotlight 88 Flea Market.

1953

Tusca Drive-In Theater – Tuscarawas Road (by intersection of Dutch Ridge Road), Beaver
Opened Sep 27, 1950 with one screen theater and 500 car spaces. Dr. Lering was the owner in 1956. The first movie was *Buck Privates* (trial opening) and *American Guerilla In The Philippines* (grand opening night). The last newspaper listing was Sep 1, 1991. Beaver Meadows assisted living facility is currently on the site now.

1953

Hi-Way 51 Drive-In Theater aka **Super 51 Drive-In** –on Route 51 (Darlington Road)
Opened May 1, 1948 with one screen and provided 500 car parking. It was owned by John Wincek (Wincek and Tate). Newspaper listings indicated the last night of operations was Aug 28 1967, then it was completely renovated, renamed Super 51 Drive-In, and reopened Jun 26 1969. It is now the site of the Chippewa Township Municipal Building.

1953

AMUSEMENT and PICNIC PARKS

Many of the early Moon / Center Township residents, as with other areas' residents, would scrimp and save and do what was then a splurge by making a day of it at one of the trolley traction parks.

Aside from swimming and other activities, many of the early residents and even residents on through the later years, easily found pleasure in spending a day at an amusement park, having a picnic, and were especially known for holding family reunions at many of these parks. When I delved into researching for this book, so many interesting bits of information kept surfacing or were shared with me on how Moon/ Center residents would take excursion trips and picnics to many of the more local parks and picnicking areas. Therefore, in this particular section, I decided to include a condensed amount of information on the parks since they were reasonably close enough to be visited by many of the Moon/Center Township residents if so desired. Also, through the years, many businesses sponsored a yearly special family day for their employees and families at some of the venues I have listed further.

As you will see, there was no shortage of attractions to take a person's mind off the hard work and worries of daily life. Although through the earlier years the main occupation of residents was farming, that does not rule out that these people could not save up and occasionally afford a special day or weekend elsewhere than on their farms. Imagine the excitement of everyone as they boarded a trolley, maybe a train, or even an excursion steamboat, to a go on a well-earned day of fun, a vacation, picnic, or reunion. Into the 1940s and 1950s, almost every household had a family car and many times everyone would load into the car and take a fun road trip for a day away from it all, too. So, all that being said, indulge my desire to share this information.

Not all the following information relates to just amusement parks which had mechanical rides, some of the "parks" strictly offered picnic groves, theaters, boats, and the most popular draw was the dancing in some quite elaborate dance pavilions. Later, some of these parks built or expanded and included amusement rides and areas for swimming, with both these attractions becoming more numerous and more of the popular draws as the forerunning activities began to fade in popularity.

Almost any records or information found on most of these amusement parks stated one common fact -- they were started either by a railroad company or by one of the trolley companies. The railroads had already developed a solid business transporting both material items and humans but found adding a park area(s) along their routes was a boost to increase business. The trolley companies relied solely on transporting humans from place to place daily and found a less consistent clientele. Therefore, the trolley companies rapidly began to develop their own amusement parks along already established routes so they could be assured to increase their businesses during evening hours and on weekends when normal usage of the trolleys was low. Because of this fact, the trolley companies seemed to be the first to do the most building of entertainment parks and areas, rather than the railroad companies. The trolley companies would advertise special trip values and discounts when using their trollies. This transportation of people to and from their parks thus boosted their trolley businesses, not to mention the profits from what was spent within the parks, since the park also belonged to the company.

Approximately by 1890, the first trolley lines were up and running and by 1900 to 1910, local people were beginning to enjoy the pleasure of visiting some of the amusement parks. This became a quite popular activity and between 1895 and 1905, Pennsylvania's trolley companies seemed to be the front runner in the number of amusement parks that were being developed. Again, none of these parks and areas were actually "in" Moon/Center Township, but they were accessible by either the local trolley run, by train, by automobiles, and even steamboats. With limited township households having the ability to own a car to just drive around for pleasure trips, the alternate forms of transportation provided direct route to and from their sponsored park(s). All three alternate forms would also provide additional entertainment on the rides to and from the parks, especially on the steamboats. Even though I found no park owned or built by a steamboat company, some steamboat companies saw the opportunity to increase passenger usage and made their boat business strictly on excursion trips to and from these different amusement parks. The train companies owned their own stations/depots, along their routes, so even if they did not own a specific park, they partnered with the parks and areas close to these stations for very affordable package deals. With the area and room to provide dancing and entertainment to the passengers while in route, trains and/or steamboats became a popular means of traveling to and from many of the parks.

As the popularity of amusement parks grew through the years, many more were started and soon there were numerous parks available to choose from. The ones I have chosen to list were located within reasonable driving distance for Moon/Center Township residents who wanted to hold a reunion or make a special "vacation day." They could have chosen to load up the car and drive there themselves. But, again, with cars being more of a luxury in the early 1900s for most, it was more sensible to travel to Monaca, Rochester, or Aliquippa and take an excursion steamboat, train, or trolley to one of the many parks.

Even with the parks that were closest to Moon/Center Township in the early 1900s, it would still have been an all-day excursion when a family did make the journey. Sometimes whole communities made a day of going to one of the accessible parks. A whole town or community just "shut down" to afford as many people as possible the opportunity to be able to attend that day's entertainment. Large picnic baskets of food were prepared, swimming suits were packed, "comfortable clothes" were put on, and off the family would go. (I will mention here that in the early 1900s, I am positive not all the clothes were as "comfortable" as one might think -- see the older pictures and post cards I have included further.) The style of clothing worn in those early 1900s consisted of men in suits, ties, and hats and the women were in long dresses and hats, too. They may have thought this "comfortable" or "park attire," but I cannot help but think how uncomfortable and hot all must have been while spending a full day out in the sun and heat, not to mention participating in any dancing. I would bet the ride home in closer quarters would have been a "ripe" experience to say the least. ☺

As quickly as the trolley parks began to spring up, it seems the same companies began to sell off their parks. They just seemed uninterested in putting their money into these business ventures any longer. The Pittsburgh Railways Company was one of the earlier companies to sell off their parks – Oakmont, Southern, Calhoun, and Kennywood were sold. All four of the parks were sold to one new owner who closed Calhoun and Oakwood almost before the ink was dry on the papers. The new owner did continue to maintain Southern Park until 1910, then making all their investments into Kennywood. Even with no new amusement parks being built, and many of the smaller ones closing, there were still a little over seventy parks up and running in Pennsylvania alone.

Many of the once more-simple amusement parks began to convert into what one would call exposition parks. Luna Park was in Pittsburgh as of 1905. Where most parks were simpler and built in more "open" areas, *Luna* was built right in the heart of Pittsburgh and had over sixty thousand electric lights and quite intricate and ornate architect on the buildings. It also reached out to people for their business by offering live entertainment, animal acts, concert bands, and a water chute ride.

The Depression years took a major toll on many of the existing parks, as it did with all factors in the lives of the American people. Between weather events, including flooding, financial difficulty, and people not having the means to use their precious funds for going to parks, there were probably over one-third of the parks that closed in Pennsylvania alone. Then came WWII, another blow to the park industries. With materials being used for the war efforts, not to mention the gasoline and food rationing …. it just seemed amusement parks were not a priority from the industrial side of things right down to the available finances of families of any given area.

> *Noteworthy fact: Sadly, many of the trolley parks and for that matter businesses and other establishments were still practicing segregation in the earlier years and were considered "whites-only". This terrible action prompted a group of African-American churches in the Pittsburgh area to come together in the 1940s to provide the same amusement park experiences for those not welcomed elsewhere. This prompted the opening of Fairview Park in Westmoreland County, PA.*

With America still healing from WWII, the 1950s and 1960s proved more prosperous for the amusement industry with the postwar baby boom and parks updating their rides to cater to the "kids." There were even newer parks added to the agenda during these times. Unfortunately, the 1960s also were the last years of most of the trolley services in the area. Increasing insurance costs and competition from other amusement parks added to the failure of many of the former trolley car amusement parks.

By the 1970s, the parks were back to being on the decline. Most were showing their age and having all wood structures, many were forced to close after severe fires or devastating storms – neither were friendly to the aging wooden structures of the older parks. Factories were closing and putting a strain on family incomes. Highways were being expanded and changed the access to many of the parks or engulfed the park areas for their own construction and/or expansion.

I wanted to include the following information on some of the accessible parks to the Moon/Center township families because many persons may have either memory of going to some of these parks, family photographs of times spent at one of the parks or would have listened to their parents or other relatives who shared stories of going to one or more of these parks. Several of the parks I have listed were open for business in the 1800s and earlier 1900s, several others were open well into the 1900s, and a few are still open to the public nowadays. Have a look at some of these parks and see if you remember hearing details of any of them or even visiting some of them. I personally can check off more than I care to admit. These were parks my parents and other family members would frequent with me when I was growing up. Many of those visits were generated by a company's family day, a school picnic, or one of the many family reunions. (Again, remember, the dates below the names will only indicate years that information was found on that park unless otherwise stated.)

Aliquippa Park – Aliquippa, PA
Open Jul 1, 1880 to 1909
On Jul 1, 1880, the Pittsburgh and Lake Erie Railroad developed an amusement park in Aliquippa – Woodlawn/West Aliquippa. (In the earlier years, West Aliquippa was known as just Aliquippa and Aliquippa proper was referred to as Woodlawn.)

Although at first there was not much information available on this park, further "digging" did help more to surface. First of all, the new information gives me cause to correct my error in reporting that this park was located on Crow's Island. It was not! It was developed on the mainland adjacent to the railroad tracks. I apologize for reporting the incorrect information in my book *Monaca aka Phillipsburg*. The P&LE Railroad made the practice to assign names for all their stations/depots using popular and local names of native Indians. They named their depot stop at Woodlawn, "*Aliquippa.*" It is reported they chose this name from the famous folklore of the Indian queen from the Pittsburgh area. When it was decided by the P&LE RR to help increase their income and passenger usage and develop this amusement area near their Aliquippa depot, Jacob Henrici, president of the P&LE RR at the time, named the park – *Aliquippa Park*.

Aliquippa Park was situated on approximately 100 acres and not only provided areas for picnicking, a beautiful dance pavilion, and other events, the park also offered boating on the Ohio River, had ball parks, a pony track, tennis courts, a restaurant, a roller coaster, souvenir stands, a merry-go-round, and a photographic gallery. There were many baseball and football games played at the park's fields. The park itself was easily accessible by train but there was some information of steamboats providing transportation, too. The park hired local boys to work in the park to operate the rides, sell the tickets, work at concession stands, and do clean up maintenance. It is said that the boys could be seen leading the ponies to the riverbank to receive a bath.

Even after the Aliquippa Park closed, the docking area was still used by the excursion riverboats as a place to embark and disembark people of the area. The boats would tie up to a dock along the river shoreline where many times they would play their calliope as the passengers were boarding. Many of these excursion steamboats were heading to places like Rock Springs Park in Chester, West Virginia and other closer parks, which were located closer to the river.

As with most parks, Aliquippa Park also became defunct prior to 1918.   What once was a place of fun and relaxation, along with gardens, became industrial land.

The Dance Hall* and Dining Room in the Aliquippa Park.   c 1907

*See information on J & L Steel under the Businesses section. There are several pictures of this Dance Hall after it was moved, placed upon a two-storey building, and then used as one J & L's office and drafting buildings.

Entrance to the park area.   Milestones / BCHR&LF

Merry-go-round   Milestones / BCHR&LF

Fun fact: It is often written Aliquippa was named for Queen Aliquippa, and that she was an Iroquois leader who, in the mid-18th century is said to have ruled over much of what is now the Greater Pittsburgh area.   Amid this information, it is also often said that the Indian Queen lived in the Aliquippa area.   Historical records state these beliefs are not altogether accurate.

While it is true Aliquippa was an Indian – she was a Seneca Indian – the history records indicate one of the places she lived was near the mouth of the Chartiers Creek and no evidence of her ever living even near the city of Aliquippa.   The city of Aliquippa actually extracted its name from the depot/station name that was chosen and assigned by the Pittsburgh and Lake Erie Railroad which was built in 1880 on the land that is now West Aliquippa. The railroad company, in accordance with their practice, assigned the name of the depot/station after the Indian personality Aliquippa.

The area of the community of West Aliquippa started off in the mid 1700s being called "Logstown" by the British after Logstown Run that runs through the area. This Logstown area was sparsely populated but was then being called "Aliquippa" by the late 1800s due to the location of the RR depot/station and their amusement park. There was the smaller steel works - Aliquippa Steel Works Co. – which started their mill in 1892 in the area now known as West Aliquippa. In the very first years of the 1900s, Jones and Laughlin was moving in and the then called Woodlawn area (currently Aliquippa) was rapidly developing. (See Industrial section for more on the mills.) Very soon after, Woodlawn became known as "Aliquippa" and what was original "Aliquippa" portion of the area then became known as "West Aliquippa."

~ ~ ~

Junction Stretch aka Junction Park
1901 to 1941

Junction Park was considered a "trolley park." It was built by the Beaver Valley Traction Company. Junction Park, located between Rochester and New Brighton, was full of entertainment ventures for persons of any age. The 25-acre site of the park was originally known as Marquis Swamp. In Jan 1901, the Beaver Valley Traction Company announced they would be improving the property and building an amusement park. They filled in, leveled the entire area, and completed the park by May 1901. The first concert held at the park was by the Pittsburgh Philharmonic Orchestra. This entertainment area had it all, roller coasters, carousel, fun house, toboggan slide, automatic swings, dance hall, dinner theater, athletic fields, picnic areas, swimming pool, and most of all easy access for local people. Many old timers used to recall and tell the story of how in 1909 Ringling Brothers Circus came to town. They unloaded 26 elephants from the train and paraded them down the street. This was done to announce the circus's arrival and to promote attendance to the circus that was being held at Junction Park. Junction Park area was even used as a training camp for WWII soldiers.

1904 ad

The park advertised as having the largest dancing pavilion in Western Pennsylvania with floor space for 400 couples, a ladies' retiring and dressing rooms, gentlemen's smoking rooms, card rooms, a kitchen and dining rooms, along with bowling alleys and shooting gallery in the basement area.

Dance pavilion – Junction Park

Junction Park had open athletic grounds and several other enclosed dining rooms with water, gas, electric, lights, and free usage of tables, all giving opportunities for picnics and family events. There was a year-round roller-skating rink that provided an electric band organ and Chicago skates*. The carousal was advertised as the "biggest 5-cent ride going." The theater had a seating capacity of nearly 1,000 people. Many up-to-date vaudeville acts made their presence there. Organizations and fraternal groups could arrange group picnics, as well as Home Coming Events and patriotic events were welcomed. The pavilion rental was available for private parties, too. If horse racing was your interest, there was a half-mile racetrack added in 1912 with the stables equipped with gas, electric lights, and running water. County fairs were held in the Junction Stretch including all the displays and animals. Junction Park let it be known that they had their standards since no paddle wheels, crooked games or gambling was allowed, immoral shows were taboo, and persons bringing intoxicants upon the grounds were liable to arrest. All intoxicated persons were promptly ejected.

 * Chicago Skates is among one of the oldest roller skate brands still in activity. It was founded in 1905 by Elisha Clark Ware, and then managed by his three sons Ralph, Walter and Robert. Chicago Roller Skates Company soon became one of the greatest brands of the 20th century.

In 1904, the park added a toboggan slide and automatic swings. The Olympic size swimming pool was added to the park in 1929. In the 1920s, during prohibition, the dance pavilion became the *Greystone Garden* speakeasy purveying illegal whiskey, wine, and beer. On Mar 19, 1945 a fire destroyed the original wooden Greystone Garden's building in just one hour. They rebuilt it and the dance bands once again began to perform. Sometime in the 1960s Jim Grogg and Anthony Reda partnered and took over the operations of the Greystone Gardens. They remodeled and renamed it the *Speakeasy*. Once again tragedy struck when a faulty air conditioner in the Speakeasy caught fire in Sep of 1971. The ballroom, the kitchen, and the office were destroyed, but the front bar room was undamaged. Shortly after this fire the building was sold and once again restoration took place. The Speakeasy building was sold in 1984 and it changed hands three more times, finally closing in the mid 2000s. Last known, the building and property sat empty. If you are a hometown *Beaver Countian* and over 50 years old, you may remember the nightclub called *Morry's Speakeasy* which became known as *Chameleon Junction* (closed in early 2000). This building was part of the original dance pavilion of Junction Park's *Greystone Gardens* building of the 1930s. Within it were the memories of many big bands, entertainers, musicians, and singers performing in the establishment for over eighty years.

Due to damages from several floods affecting the park, less interest in the park area, and the fact that busses were replacing the trolleys, the amusement portion of the park closed in 1941. The amusement rides were sold and soon all were gone. Although the go cart track, trampoline center, miniature golf course, and roller rink still attracted some families, for the most part, the Junction Stretch heydays were a thing of the past. The swimming pool was still used until 1964 when it was closed. It became the location of the former Fisher's Big Wheel and Shop n' Save stores. In 1963, the new highway, Route 65, was under construction and was built through the heart of what once was Junction Park. The entire park was closed in 1964, but despite fires, floods, and many changes in styles of music, the former diner theater/speakeasy endured the longest.

1945 ad

1940 ad

1937 ad

~ ~ ~

Morado Springs Park – Beaver Falls, PA
1891 to 1937
This park sat on thirty-two acres. As of 2017, this would be the area where a defunct small open mall sits, by Caputo Insurance Agency, Inc, and across the road from C. J. Rombold Engine Builders – all along the Big Beaver Blvd/Rt 18. It was considered a getaway place for many people in the surrounding areas. The Beaver County Traction Company opened Morado Park in 1891. They would run open-air summer cars to and from the park, especially during the 1920s. It was always thought of as primarily a picnic ground, but there is an ad stating it had at least a carousel. The park was also known for its mineral springs and waters. It is said that there was a swimming area in the Beaver River even though the river would have been heavily polluted at that time. No park would be complete without a dance hall, and Morado had one. The park closed in 1937. After Morado closed, the dance hall stayed open and was turned into a skating rink in about 1942. The building burned to the ground on Oct 23, 1945, in a suspicious fire. In doing my research, there were many articles regarding reunions and larger community events held at the park. It was quite a small park as far as the trolley/train parks go and nothing can be found but mention of the one ride, the carousel. It is worth mentioning that even without all the mechanical attractions, it survived longer than Junction Park.

1911 Post Card   "Dancing Pavilion and Lilly Pond, Morado Park, Beaver Falls, Pa"

~ ~ ~

Conneaut Lake   aka   **Exposition Park**
1892 to   current
Many summer days were enjoyed at Conneaut Lake and the Conneaut Lake Park. In Aug of 1892 the park was opened as *Exposition Park.* Col. Frank Mantor opened the park as a permanent fairground and exposition for livestock, machinery, and industrial products from Western Pennsylvania. It was previously land used as a boat landing evolving into a combination of a small town and a fairground, many hotels and other exhibition halls began to spring up along with small businesses, and many cottages were also built hoping to take advantage of the flow of people to *Exposition Park*. *Exposition Park* also included a dance hall, a convention hall, and a bathhouse. The park's first mechanical ride was a carousel which opened in 1899. In 1901 the Pittsburgh & Shenango Valley Railroad became the owners. They built several hotels on the property and in 1907 added trolley service to the means of accessing the park since boat or train had been the only ways previously. The park was renamed *Conneaut Lake Park* in 1920. There was a midway added along with other rides, including in 1922, the *Figure Eight* rollercoaster which was modernized and renamed the *Jack Rabbit.* In 1923, a bumper car ride and in 1925, the *Tumble Bug were added*.

Fire has been the biggest enemy of this park. There was a horrible fire in 1908 which destroyed many of the park's original buildings. They were then replaced with new concrete block construction including the Dreamland Ballroom. In 1943, a large portion of the Hotel Conneaut was destroyed in a fire that was sparked when it was struck by lightning. Legend still exists stating the ghost of Elizabeth, a bride who was staying at the hotel, supposedly died in the fire, and is said to still haunt the hotel. In 2008, a fire once again destroyed the beautiful Dreamland Ballroom. The most recent fire in Aug 2013 destroyed the dockside restaurant, the historic beach front building.

To add to the troubles of the park, the trolley service to Conneaut Lake Park ended in 1927, which was the same occurrence at other bigger amusement parks. New owners took over the park the end of Sep 1929, but things didn't improve, mostly due to the Depression years. The park was heading for liquidation by late 1932. The Depression years affected everyone, therefore a decision by the two controlling banks of the park had to face foreclosure on the park. The one bank, Crawford County Trust Company, was in agreement with the foreclosure, but the other bank, People's Pittsburgh Trust wanted to give the park one more year, but this extension proved fruitless.

In Nov 1933, Conneaut Lake Park was auctioned off and People's Pittsburgh Trust purchased it for $35,000. People's was not interested in running an amusement park, nor did they want to lose their investment, so the bank continued to do upgrades to the park. In 1935, the bathhouse was replaced by the Beach Club. In 1936, a 600-foot-long boardwalk was added between the club and the hotel. In 1937, the wooden roller coaster, the Blue Streak, was built*. The Jack Rabbit was torn down in 1938 and five new rides were added. In 1943, the portion of the former 300 room hotel that was not destroyed in the fire was again being used and was then a 133-room hotel. By 1944 Conneaut Lake Park was out of bankruptcy and purchased by an investor group led by Dr. Harry Winslow, a local surgeon. This group added the Tilt-A-Whirl and a Ferris wheel in 1949, the Castle of Fun and Crazy Maze in 1950. A kiddie ride section was completed in 1954. By the 1990s, the park saw many owners and changes. Park rides were auctioned off, bankruptcy was filed, and interest in the park declined.

> *Fun fact: The Blue Streak roller coast, built in 1937, is the 17th oldest wooden roller coaster in the United States. Additionally, the park states it is ranked 5th in America and 50th in the world as roller coaster rides go. It is also one of two shallow coasters designed by Ed Vettel, of Pittsburgh, that is still operating. It contains a 77-foot-high section and is a 2,900-foot-long ride. Blue Streak was one of the first rides to be named an ACE Coaster Classic, which designates those rare coasters that operate in a traditional manner.

A nonprofit corporation was last overseeing the amusement park. They filed for federal bankruptcy protection in Dec 2014 to reorganize its finances, including close to $1.03 million owed in overdue real estate taxes going back as far as 2007. Although the park has changed dramatically over the years, it is still stands today providing amusement entertainment to visitors, as well as the beach accommodations to the lake. The park marked its 125th anniversary in 2016.

Blue Streak roller coaster

Carousel –*Exposition Park*

The former beach, boat house and restaurant in the 1940s.

Idlewild Park – Ligonier Valley
1878 to current
Founded in 1878 by Thomas Mellon along the Ligonier Valley Railroad line. I found several places that stated this was the first trolley park in Pittsburgh. Additional information also states that it is one of the very few that is still open today, as well as the oldest in Pennsylvania and the third oldest in America. It was originally a campground and picnic area where people could not only enjoy all the scenic views, but also fishing, boating, dancing, and picnicking. By 1900, Idlewild had expanded and added a steam powered carousel they located in the middle of the park area. It contains 48 hand-carved horses and two chariots. In 1920, the merry-go-round was added, as was the wooden Rollo Coaster* in 1938 (children's roller coaster), the Whip in 1939, and the canopy covered Caterpillar in 1947. One of the most popular additions occurred in 1956 with the Story Book Forrest. It is one of the last, largest, and best-preserved versions of these type of roadside attractions in America. In 1956 they also added one of the last operating Tumble Bug rides. Changes and updates have continued to occur within the park keeping it current and fresh.

> *Fun fact: The wood used to build the Rollo Coaster was from trees on the park property and cut using a sawmill that was built on site.

Among the many fun memories I have while growing up, when my parents loaded us in the car and went for a day to Idlewild, especially Story Book Forest is at the top of the list. My favorite "live" characters were Snow White and the Old Woman Who Lived In The Shoe. Both these characters were just so nice, but that giant book at the entrance was pretty impressive, too.

Nowadays, the park has added a section known as the SoakZone, but it is still listed as one of the best children's parks and a great family park.

~ ~ ~

Idora Park – Youngstown, Ohio
1899 to 1984
This park was built by the Youngstown Park and Falls Street Railway Company and opened May 30, 1899 with the original name of *Terminal Park*. The park included a bandstand, theater, dance pavilion, a roller coaster, a circle swing, and concession stands. By the end of 1899, it was renamed *Idora Park*. The Idora Park Ballroom opened Jun 30, 1910. It was an open-air ballroom being constructed similar to the one in Coney Island, NY. With a beautiful hardwood floor, it was eventually enclosed making it usable year-round. Guests could enjoy music by many famous bands and musicians, including the Glenn Miller Orchestra, the Tommy Dorsey Orchestra, the Eagles, Ray Charles, Maynard Ferguson, Blue Oyster Cult and The Monkees. With larger state and national amusement parks taking over in the years to follow, Idora soon met with decline in popularity. By the early 1980s, the park was considered "a relic." Then a devastating fire on Apr 26, 1984, caused millions of dollars' worth of damage and destroyed many concessions stands, the park office, and many of the historic wooden rides. This fire was reportedly started by a welder's torch. After this fire, the park was abandoned. Up until the 1984 fire causing its closure, Idora Park was one of the nation's few remaining urban or trolley amusement parks. The ballroom escaped the 1984 fire, but on Mar 5, 2001, a suspicious fire starting in the basement of the building also destroyed that historic and landmark building.

In the 1950s and 1960s, Center Township held their one-day Community Picnics each June at Idora Park.

Original dance hall of Idora Park.

The water had colored lights behind it.

last dance pavilion   Entrance area   (picture taken from parking lot area)

Fun fact: The original carousel of Idora Park was created in 1922 by the Philadelphia Toboggan Company, Designated as PTC No. 61. It is a classic 3-row carousel with forty-eight carved horses and two chariots, being a thirty "jumpers," eighteen "standers," with the band organ façade. It was sold to NY residents David and Jane Walentas. They restored the merry go round and it was renamed Jane's Carousel and was donated to the Brooklyn Bridge Park Development Corporation in NY. It is housed in a plexiglass "jewel box" structure.

~ ~ ~

Rock Point Park – Ellwood City
c1885 to 1912
The park is said to have opened in 1885 and officially closed in 1912. The site the park was located on is now the Rock Point Nature Area and is open to the public. Rock Point Park was like so many others, built as a "trolley/railroad park." People were known to dress up, take the New Brighton & New Castle Railroad (or later the Beaver & Ellwood Railroad) train and spend the day at the park. The life of this park was short lived due to a spark from the train's engine starting a fire that destroyed most of the park. Rock Point Park was also known as *Felician Park* for a short period of time.

Dance Pavilion   vintage post card

~ ~ ~

Rock Springs Park – Chester, West Virginia
1857 (1897) to 1970

The location of this park was once thought of as a sacred hunting ground by the Archaic Indians. George Washington's journals stated that in Oct 1770 he reportedly camped near the park entrance and drank from the mineral waters of Rock Springs. In 1857, the property was known as Rock Springs Grove and was donated by the Marks Farm for church picnics. It consisted of hiking trails, picnic pavilions, and a small dancing platform. As time went on, a lunch room, baseball diamond, roller rink, and merry-go-round were added. In 1893, a new bridge over the Ohio River opened a streetcar line and turned Rock Springs into a full-blown amusement park. Construction was underway in 1896 and this park officially opened in 1897. The Beaver Valley Traction Company purchased Rock Springs Park in 1900, Charles "C. A." Smith took over managing the park. Many new attractions and rides were added, including forming a three and half acre lake. The park also became accessible by train and waterway. Rock Springs had a popular dining hall called the Green Lantern Inn where many groups, including those of Moon Township, would hold events and gather for meals. There were three major fires in the park occurring in 1914, 1915, and 1917. Even with a third dance hall being opened in 1918, the park's business continued to decline. Mr. Smith sold the park to C. C. and Grace Macdonald at the end of the 1925 season.

The Macdonald family made improvements to the park including a carousel in 1927 and the Cyclone roller coaster in 1928. The Macdonalds also erected a log cabin in 1927 and used this as their home. In 1934/35, Mr. and Mrs. Macdonald gave ownership of the park to their daughter and husband, Virginia and Robert Hand. The Hands then lived in the log house and raised their sons in this home. They spent their entire married life operating Rock Springs Park. The park remained in family possession until 1970 when the Hands were looking forward to retiring from the business. Unfortunately, Robert Hand died in the fall of 1970 and the park never reopened. Most of the rides were soon sold. On Jun 26, 1974, the last dance at *Virginia Gardens* (the dance hall) was held as the final event at Rock Springs Park before the project of rerouting US Route 30 began. The remaining rides and structures were auctioned off, the site was cleared, the lake was drained, and all traces of the park were soon gone. The log house survived and was moved to a new location where it still stands today.

In going through my own family's reunion pictures, I found that many of our reunions were held at this park.

Vintage post cards from Rock Springs Park

Entrance of Rock Springs Park

The main street through Rock Springs Park

Dancing Pavilion, Rock Springs Park

~ ~ ~

White Swan Park – 1 ½ miles from Pittsburgh Airport
1955 to 1989

White Swan Park was a very small park compared to many others in the area. It opened in 1955 and had seven rides and three lakes and operated for thirty-four seasons. It was operated by brother and sister Roy Todd and Margaret Kleeman, Margaret's husband also helped build it. The name was given to the park because they intended to bring white swans to the park's original lakes, but due to the swans being prey to wildlife, the swan idea never materialized. It sat on 40 acres and eventually featured a kiddie park and fifteen rides including a merry-go-round, a Ferris wheel, a tilt a whirl, a small rollercoaster, a giant slide, a Scrambler ride, and a full-sized train that went around the perimeter of the park. There were also midway games and six picnic shelters, a refreshment stand, a skeet ball building, and a miniature golf course. The baby boom after WWII proved to supply the park with more than enough families and children to keep it prospering.

After the park's 1989 season, the Pennsylvania Department of Transportation bought the park to make improvements on the roadway (Route 60 to the airport). PennDOT paid the family four million dollars for the property. All the amusements and other artifacts were sold at auction and White Swan Park joined the ranks of being defunct. Roy Todd and Margaret Kleeman held a reunion in Aug of 1991 at Kennywood Park for all the former White Swan employees. Everyone talked of the former days when it was called a family park, how people met at White Swan Park and ended up getting married, and of all the help/employees being local people.

~ ~ ~

Kennywood Park – Pittsburgh, PA
1898 to current

Kennywood Park became a popular attraction for the residents of Moon Township and is still that of those in not only Center Township but of surrounding area residents. It was originally considered one of the small trolley parks when it was founded in 1898 on a 40-acre plot of land in Allegheny County, PA. This land was first part of a farm owned by Anthony Kenny and even in the 1860s had already became a popular place for picnics with all the wooded area and trees on the property – thus the name Kennywood. The Monongahela Street Railway Company, controlled by Andrew Mellon, leased the land from the Kenny family and built the park. Mr. Mellon was not really interested in providing a park, but more so to increase the business of the trolley company. Two of the park's original buildings still stand – the carousel pavilion and the restaurant (originally called the Casino). In the early 1900s, like many of the other trolley parks, Kennywood was fighting to survive. The Monongahela Street Railway Company wanted to get out of the amusement park business so in 1902 they subleased the park to a Boston company and later to a group from Aspinwall. By 1906 the trolley company had leased the park to A.S. McSwigan, Frederick W. Henninger, and A. F. Meghan. These three men started the Kennywood Park Limited in 1906. The same time Kennywood was changing hands, three other parks were under the same contract – Calhoun Park, Southern Park, and Oakwood Park. Immediately after the transaction was complete, Calhoun and Oakwood Parks were closed but Kennywood and Southern Park were left open. Eventually, by 1910, Southern Park was also closed, and all the attention was centered on Kennywood Park.

Between 1900 and 1930 there were many changes made to the park. They built 3 roller coasters and added a huge swimming pool. Dancing became a popular past time during the Great Depression and was probably what truly kept the park from closing. From 1930 to 1950 the park had great dance bands in the park and following the depression era, more rides were being added again. The old Victorian Windmill was once located in the middle of the lagoon area. It is one of the oldest structures in the park being built in 1921. It was copied from a similar attraction in Coney Island, Ohio. It was moved in 1940 to the front of the park to make room for the Traver circle swing aka Rocketships. Some of the rides included the Noah's Ark, a used Ferris wheel, and a miniature train.

School picnics started to become quite popular in the 1950s and again many rides were added, especially to Kiddieland. In 1995, Lost Kennywood was situated on a portion of the area where the park's former swimming pool had been located. They used a one-third scale of the original Luna Park entrance to mark the entrance to the area. From the 1950s through today (2019), there have been expansions made to the park and many rides have been removed and/or added. Kennywood remains one of the best amusement parks in America. It was entered as a designated national historic landmark in 1987.

Center Township was just one of many schools that enjoyed celebrating their annual community and/or school picnics beginning in the later 1930s and into the 2010s. Some of the first township's picnics were held at Idora Park, this continued at least into the mid 1960s, then these "school/community picnics" were held at Kennywood. The Center High School Bands participated in many of Kennywood Festivals over the years.

Noah's Ark

~ ~ ~

Non-amusement ride parks……

As previously stated, there are still many "recreational" areas in Center Township, but the Fred Taddeo Park is the only one with any acreage attached to it and the one considered the township's main community park/recreational area.   See previous Recreation information.

Some other local non-amusement ride parks in the area used by Moon/Center Township residents:

Allaire Park   aka   John A. Antoline Park
1930s to current   Property on Jackson Street (directly behind the Fifth Ward School) was donated to the Borough of Monaca in 1936 by the Allaire Land Co. It was donated to the Borough with the stipulation that it would not be used for anything other than recreation or park use. The first work on the area was done in 1936 by the W.P.A. and the help of some interested citizens. It was partially cleared and used as a park with improvements made in Apr 1964. There were waterslides added which opened in 1984, these had a thirty-four-foot vertical drop into a landing pool. The slides were built by a Coraopolis based Water Adventure, Inc. who were also the beginning operators of the slides. The borough then maintained ownership of the property until Water Slides of Monaca, Inc. took over the lease of the slides in 1999. The waterslides at Allaire Park aka John A. Antoline Park were closed in 2002 and dismantled in Aug 2005.   They fell victim to 1) a property dispute between the borough and the owner of the adjoining property, 2) the abandonment by the most recent operator, the Aliquippa based Water Slides of Monaca, Inc., owned by James Giammaria.

Bradys Run Park – off Route 51, Brighton Township
1947 to current   This nature park area was established in 1947. It is in Brighton Township and is a county-owned park open to the public. Bradys Run Park is currently considered one of Beaver County's largest parks consisting of almost 2000 acres. The park opened with just usage of the grounds and pavilions, then additions of swimming, fishing, walking and jogging trails, a lodge building, playground area, horse arena, 5 softball fields, 2 basketball courts, ice arena, electricity, charcoal grills, and restrooms. In recent years, this is home to the annual Maple Syrup Festivals and Festival of Trees, too. Another annual event at Bradys Run Park is the stocking of the lake with fish for new fishing seasons' opening days. The lake in the park now encompasses 28 acres. It is a man-made lake which was built by Beaver County in 1948. It had an average depth of 7 to 10 feet with a few areas being up to 21 feet. After it was drained again in 2011 and more silt removed, the depths increased. The park has "cleaned up" the lake several times over the years. This involves having to remove several feet of silt from the bottom of the lake which tends to choke off aquatic life. They added small improvements over the years such as boat docks, a bath house, fresh sand for the swimming beach area, paving once dirt roads, upgrading the pavilions, adding charcoal grills, wiring the park with electricity to the pavilions, et cetera. In 1976, construction of the enclosed ice-skating arena was started and was completed in 1977.

Raccoon State Park
1935 to current   The property of the park was initially planned to be a 14,000-acre national park. The property was once farmlands. The federal government bought the property for two main reasons. The first was to provide inexpensive recreational facilities for people of the entire Pittsburgh area. The second reason was to provide the farmers who originally owned the land to turn over their "sub marginal areas" and be given new land where they could have much more productive farms to earn a decent living. The park was turned over to the state in 1945.

During the great depression, Raccoon Park was established as a Recreational Demonstration Area with the Civilian Conservation Corps (C.C.C.) constructing its earliest buildings in 1935. The C.C.C. announced in May of 1935 that Raccoon Creek and Clinton, PA would be two locations in Beaver County for additional C.C.C. camps in Western Pennsylvania. These two areas became part of the ninety-eight total camps in Western Pennsylvania. The park area and buildings were added to the National Register of Historic Places in 1987 for their distinctive architecture, their role as parts of a recreational area, and reflecting the federal government's attempts to resolve the poverty of the Depression. The park offers many activities, including hiking on forty-two miles of trails to choose from, swimming and beach area, enjoying the lake by kayak, canoe, rowboat, or hydro bike, the Wildflower Reserve, camping, environmental education programs, fishing, visiting the Frankfort Mineral Springs, staying in a cabin or the Lakeside Lodge, and/or hunting for small game, deer, and turkey.

Frankfort Mineral Springs   and   Raccoon Park – Hookstown, PA -Route 18
1800s to current   The very small borough of Frankfort Springs grew out of the Mineral Springs Resort that once was present in the area. It was advertised in 1843 as a small village near a cool, romantic glen, thickly studded with forest trees and a mineral spring. The actual springs are located by the entrance to Raccoon State Park. The land included in the current park area has a history of its own with Levi Dugan owning the first property in 1772, including the mineral springs. Isaac Stevens then purchased the acreage in 1788, followed by Edward McGinnis in 1827. The area developed into a Victorian era health resort, Mineral Springs Resort. This resort soon became known as Frankfort Mineral Springs. With the mineral spring water containing fifteen different minerals, it was believed to have had curative powers, curing everything from kidney ailments to indigestion. Edward McGinnis discovered the springs and to capitalize on his investment, built his resort atop a hill in what is now part of the Raccoon Creek State Park.

Other than the resort being known for its healing powers, it was also visited by mostly the wealthy as a social gathering place. It was not uncommon to find guests spending a month or more at the resort. There would be as many as 200 guests at one time staying at the resort. It was a very prosperous resort in its day and featured a three-storey hotel with double-decker porches, dance hall, livery stable, and numerous guest cottages.

James Bigger was the next to own the mineral springs, making his purchasing in 1884 at the height of the Victorian era. He had to make many renovations to the time worn buildings of the resort. This period was the heyday of the resort with two dirt tennis courts being added. Besides a resident doctor, there were farmers on staff who raised much of the food needed. 1912 showed the decline of interest in the resort and the hotel became more popularly used for travelers and long-term renters. Frankfort Mineral Springs closed in 1912. Between 1927 and 1928 the hotel was destroyed by fire with the unofficial blame going to one of the resident's wood stoves. The dance hall remained in use in the 1930s and 1940s. In 1960, Raccoon Creek State Park purchased the mineral springs area. There was one remaining building from the mineral springs resort that remained, a guest cottage, which was turned into a museum in 1972. Unfortunately, it was broken into, and all the artifacts were stolen or destroyed.

The state park is considered to have opened in the early 1930s. The park is part of an area that consists of 7,572 acres of land with the lake at Raccoon State Park covering 101 acres, having a five-hundred-foot sand/turf beach.

by Patrick Adams   from libraries.PSU.edu
Artist drawing of the way the Frankfort Mineral Springs resort would have looked.

Buttermilk Falls   aka   **Homewood Falls** – Beaver Falls (Homewood)
1800s to current   This nature park is sometimes referred to as a hidden oasis. It obtained its name from the Homewood Sandstone Quarry near the waterfall in the park. Stones were quarried to be used in nearby tunnels, roadways, and the Western Penitentiary in Pittsburgh. The quarry can still be seen if you make your way to the bottom of the waterfall. Although known most recently as the Buttermilk Falls, it was referred to by locals in the area as Homewood Falls and even earlier was known as Smiddy's Falls. The name Buttermilk is said to have begun in 1870, by reason of a group of Civil War veterans who enjoyed picnicking in the area while enjoying their choice of beverages – buttermilk.

The area has been landmarked for its historic value being the site of the headquarters of General Israel Putnam, Commander in the Highlands in 1779. Homewood Junction (simply called *Homewood* and sometimes *Racine*) was settled in 1831 and grew quickly with the Ohio & Pennsylvania Railroad's arrival in 1852. The hard-gray stone began to be quarried about 1852 and employed up to one hundred or so men. Work declined in the 1870s, but once again started up in early 1902. The water way that feeds the falls is Clark's Run. The 40-foot waterfall cascades adjacent to the site of the old railroad tracks. Many residents from all the local towns and areas would have come to the site to enjoy hiking, swimming, and summer picnics.

Fun fact: There are two other waterfalls located very close to this location that also go by the name Buttermilk – one near the southern end of 5th Ave in Koppel and the other along Wampum Run in Wampum.

~ ~ ~

HOTELS

With Moon/Center Township being such a rural area for many years, there were no formal hotels needed in the immediate area. The surrounding towns of Phillipsburg/Monaca, Rochester, Beaver Falls, New Brighton, and others did have such businesses when needed. Most "out of town" people would find the generous hospitality of township family members or one of the local residents when there was a place needed to stay. Eventually there were a few hotels closer to and even within Center Township and Potter Township, but this did not occur until after at least 1940. In Mar of 1980, a McMurray, PA firm, Crossgates, wanted to build a "first-class" hotel-motel that would have employed two hundred persons, but these plans obviously never developed. However, for some reason, recent Center Township officials are making up for this and have found it an ongoing marathon for giving approval to hotel establishment after hotel establishment to erect their buildings in the township. Additionally, and sadly, they are all concentrated in one very small area of the township, most within view of each other!

Valley View Hotel – Sylvan Crest
1953 to 1970s
This once very stately yellow brick building was first erected as the Welsh family mansion and then became a summer mansion to the Tenor and Garland families. By the 19140s, this fourteen-room home went through some renovations and became the Valley View Hotel. E. M. and Flora Love mortgaged the property and mansion through Eliza B. (and John W.) Garland in Jul 1918. The Loves sold the house and almost 5 acres of land to Frederick J. and Mable Shue in Sep 1944. I could find no evidence to prove or disprove that the Loves actually occupied the home but the deed to the Shues stated it was still considered a fourteen-room dwelling. The Shues appear to have converted the former mansion into a hotel. They owned this property and the former mansion/then hotel until late in Jul 1972 when they sold all to Louis Pappan. Mr. Pappan did not continue to use the building as a hotel business, but instead used the entire building for storing his restaurant equipment and files. The former mansion/hotel caught fire in 1981 and was totally destroyed. Mr. Pappan had the entire structure razed and then sold the property along with other surrounding properties he had purchased and multiple private homes have since been erected. (See Summer Homes section in Volume II for pictures of the former mansion when owned by the Welch and/or Garland families.)

Photos courtesy BCHR&LF

c1970s views of the former mansion after it had been converted to a hotel and sold to Mr. Pappan. Although it was still a very large, impressive building, the elegancy, massive wrap around porch, and general patina of the former mansion were no longer present. (See Summer Homes section in Volume II for pictures of the building in its heyday.)

Valley View Hotel
Sylvan Crest, Monaca
Round and Square Dancing
Every Friday and Saturday Night
Sandwiches and Drinks
Phone Roch. 1014

Jun 1953 ad

This was all that was left of a once beautiful three-storey, fourteen-room, brick, mansion shortly after the fire.   This remaining scorched portion of the structure was torn down.

In 1972, Lou Pappan was acquiring multiple properties adjacent to the former mansion/then hotel. He eventually also purchased the other Garland property and mansion located within the Sylvan Crest area.   Mr. Pappan simply used both the former mansions for storage of various restaurant supplies and files.   After Mr. Pappan became the owner, the buildings began to fall into disarray and sadly, neither stands today.

> *Fun fact: Beginning Nov 1965 through 1966, while being used as a hotel, it housed many members of the crew of men doing the construction of creating the new highway coming from the mall area into Monaca which may give some perspective to the size of this once private mansion. Once this stately home was converted into a hotel, there was a bar room created which also included a pool table.   I am certain that there would have also been several very nice fireplaces throughout the home evidenced by the multiple chimneys on the original building.   Whether they remained and were still used once it was converted to a hotel is unknown. Also unknown is the actual number of hotel rooms which were available.*

Kobuta Hotel – 427 Frankfort Road, Potter Township
Opened in c1949.
This building had a bar, kitchen, and dining room area on the first floor with hotel type rooms for rent on the upper level.   It was built during the years that the small community of Kobuta was also established. (See Housing Plans and Areas for much more on the Kobuta community.)   The Kobuta Hotel building was not used as a true hotel for many of the years after the community of Kobuta ceased to exist, but instead the second-floor rooms were rented/leased out for specific extended periods of time. There was also an area of property to the right of and behind the Kobuta Hotel that was designated for people to rent a space to "park" their mobile homes and live there.

In the earlier years, all the land had formerly been that of or adjacent to a few others including McCulloughs, Potters, Barnes, and Phillis families.   The Kobuta Hotel was located on a ten-acre lot and sold to the Lattanzios in 1943 by R. Ross Barnes. By 1942, Antonio and Marie Lattanzio had made a few purchases of properties adjacent to the Kobuta Hotel prior to purchasing the property and actual Kobuta Hotel building. In 1972, Miss Nena Skoff leased the Kobuta Hotel from the widow Marie Lattanzio. It was a five-year lease with the option to renew for another five years (taking it to 1982).   In 1974, Miss Skoff was no longer leasing, but became the owner of all of the former Lattanzio properties, including the Kobuta Hotel building.   Josephine Lang was the widow of Robert D. Lang. In 1994, she purchased the hotel and property along with all the adjacent property from Miss Skoff.   "Josie" continued to operate the business until 2011.   In 2011 the Three Center Independent Oil Real Estate, L.P. purchased all the properties from the Lang family at a <u>very</u> moderate price.   Then this company turned around and sold all to Shell in 2016 for $2,500,000, making a very sizeable profit over what they paid the Lang family!   (See Restaurant and Taverns section in Volume II.)

The last day of business for the Kobuta bar and second floor apartments was the end of Apr 2011.   Ironically, on that Friday evening, a fire broke out in a vacant apartment located on the second floor.   Even though there were still tenants in many of the other rooms/apartments, there were no injuries from the fire.   With many disgruntled tenants being told they had to evacuate by Apr 30th, the fire came as no surprise to Mrs. Lang's family who were trying to help her close the business down. The cause of the fire was under investigation.

2011 – the building has since been razed

Bay's Motel – 848 Monaca Road
This property was part of a 26-acre parcel located partially in Center Township and part in Aliquippa Boro, all formerly owned by John and Lillian Baird.   Ulysses "Bay" and Jennie Blocker purchased 7.79 acres of the property from the widow Lillian Baird in 1956. There was a one-storey brick home with a separate building of motel units behind it on the property.   Ulysses "Bay" and Jennie (Law) Blocker named the business Bay's Motel.   They also had a Bay's Motel in Chippewa Township and owned and operated the Bay's Lounge in Aliquippa.

~ ~ ~

More recently, the Center Township Supervisors began approving what many residents related to me as the "invasion of hotels."   Beginning in 2002 to 2019, there have been nine (yes NINE) hotels erected and all concentrated in one small area of Center Township encircling the Beaver Valley Mall. I was also told there is rumor of yet another unit expected to be completed in the area behind the former Sears Auto Center at the BV Mall.

The current nine hotels include:

Holiday Inn Express Hotel & Suites – 105 Stone Quarry Road
Opened later in Oct 2002.   Three-storey, sixty rooms and suites, heated indoor pool, exercise room.

Hampton Inn Pit Beaver Valley –Fairview Drive
Opened in 2005.   Four floors, fifty-seven rooms, heated indoor pool, exercise room.

Comfort Suites – 1523 Old Brodhead Road
Opened Jul 2007.   Three floors, forty rooms.

The Inn aka **Inns of America** – 1525 Old Brodhead Road
Opened in 2007

Fairfield Inn & Suites by Marriott – 1438 Brodhead Road
Built in 2015.   Four floors, seventy-two rooms, ten suites, heated indoor swimming pool, exercise room.

View of property before the hotel.

Current view of property.

Beaver Valley My Place – 138 Stone Quarry Road
Built in 2016.   The land was formerly that of Leroy Hudson.   William Jacober sold all to the Hudson family in 1950. Monold, Inc purchased the land from the Hudsons in 1961. Edwin Becker was the last owner and in 2014 he sold to Beaver Valley My Place.

View of property before the hotel.

Current view

Home2 Suites - 1000 Wagner Road Extension South (extension of Stoney Ridge Drive, off Beaver Valley Mall Blvd. Opened in 2018.
This hotel is officially listed as *Home2 Suites by Hilton Pittsburgh Beaver Valley*.

Hilton Garden Inn – 2000 Wagner Road Extension South (extension of Stoney Ridge Drive, off Beaver Valley Mall Blvd. Opened in 2019

Suburban Extended Stay Hotel – 1528 Old Brodhead Road (adjacent to Comfort Suite)
2018   Was under construction May/Apr 2017.   Opened earlier in 2018.

~ ~ ~

The entire following section is also not meant to be a "history lesson," but will provide quite a bit of information on the early and current newspapers of the area. While talking with several older residents of the township, many of these newspapers were mentioned. As all the information is perused, readers will find there is miscellaneous information intertwined in all the information that makes connections to the Moon/Center Township area and/or residents.

Fun fact: In the early years, a very popular usage of old newspapers was as padding under the larger area rugs in homes. Placing these newspapers under the rugs not only provided comfort, but also added much needed installation to a room. Outdated newspapers would also be sold for a very reasonable price by the merchants and/or newspaper businesses to all interested persons.

NEWSPAPERS - NEWS STANDS - PRINTING

"Back in the day" most people kept up on the news of their area by just mere talking and gossiping to each other when they would gather for an event, attend church, or be working together. Families made a regular event of eating together daily, actually sitting, talking, and sharing with each other. Friends and neighbors also met regularly just to check on each other and offer any assistance they could to each other, so sharing news was easily accomplished. Contrary to popular belief, men were considered the biggest "gossipers," especially during those earlier years. They would meet up in small groups and have regular chat sessions with each other at a local blacksmith shop, a general store, other businesses, or a tavern/"watering hole." All this would keep everyone in an area up to date on who was doing what, who was ill, who moved in or out of an area, who was either out of town visiting or had others come to visit them, who had new livestock, what crops were being grown, how everyone was doing, who was selling something, et cetera.

Prior to more established businesses being present in Moon/Center Township, the local towns were selling newspapers in general stores, pharmacies, and other businesses. Some papers offered a mail delivery service with subscriptions, too. This was most appealing to the rural residents. The practice of being hired as a delivery boy for a local newspaper was one of the staple jobs for younger boys in towns and in country settings.

In the very early years of local newspapers, there was a mixture of news events that covered all areas of Beaver County in any given newspaper. Each paper was more of a "general" newspaper including smaller columns for many of the individual community's news/happenings. They also had news items from all of Pennsylvania, other states, government items, weather events, farm news, and even a few ads. With the increase of area households purchasing local newspapers, it became necessary to provide more pertinent than widespread news to the readers. To boost the sale of newspapers to the more rural areas, many would have articles with important details for those in agriculture, livestock, and general farming. Typically, a local newspaper would provide varying points of interest with politics and editorials which were always of interest. It also did not take long for local merchant highlights and multiple ads to soon became popular.

There were numerous newspapers being published in the area surrounding Moon Township but beginning just after Center Township was formed from Moon Township, many of the events and happenings of the area were included primarily in two different newspapers. These two newspapers each covered events and happenings of different areas of Moon/Center Township. One side was included with the Woodlawn, Aliquippa, and Hopewell side of the township. The other side of the township was usually included with the Monaca, Rochester, Freedom, Baden, Beaver Falls, New Brighton areas. For many years, much of the news for a large portion of Moon/Center Township was just added into the column of news reported of Phillipsburg/Monaca. This even continued well past the time Center Township was officially formed.

Before I give a brief listing of many of the newspapers that the township residents would have been likely to read, I will delve into some information found on those persons who did the collecting of information and reporting for the newspapers.

Reporters

What successful newspaper did not have dedicated reporters seeking out and providing the information to be published? I wanted to include information on just some of the early reporters who covered the happenings in and adjacent to Moon/Center Township.

These early reporters consisted of people who would go around and gather or be provided with "happenings" of all these local areas and would then submit them to be published in the newspapers. Some of this information would include trivial bits of information, some information was of a serious nature, while other tidbits and happenings were more humorous. Throwing "privacy" to the wind, many local residents would regularly provide the reporters of the area with quite a variety of news which would then be included in the reporters' columns. Examples of the regularly reported items included all local church events or services, deaths, marriages, recent births, who and where a person was relocating to, who went on a vacation or visited someone, who was selling or buying a new house or farm, any opening or closing or relocation of a business, and anyone who may be sick, on the mend, or in the hospital.

Some of the reporters found ……………

---Harry Palmer and Charles R. Frank of Monaca were the first reporters found in the 1800s.
---Charles R. Frank first became a reporter on the Daily Argus and in 1886 he accepted the position of reporter on the Daily News which he held until his death in mid Jan 1889.
   ---Charles' wife, Mrs. ? Frank, then did the reporting for a few months.
---Harvey J. Taylor took over after Mrs. Frank.
---H. Dwight Anderson accepted a position as reporter on the Daily Times in 1899. He first covered the Beaver Falls – New Brighton districts, and later Rochester – Monaca – Moon areas.
---Frank L. Anderson became a reporter for various areas, and eventually for the Rochester and Monaca (including Moon Township) areas in the early 1900s.
---Charles O. Dentzer succeeded Mr. Anderson and covered these areas in the early 1900s.
---Thomas Beaver of Monaca was covering Monaca and Moon Township during the early 1900s for the *Star* newspaper (possibly the *Daily Star*).
---Marshall R. Hall of Monaca was listed as the sporting editor of the Daily Times at least in 1911 and 1912.
---Mrs. Mae Perdew Gaertner
   Through the years, although women were not placed very high on the "food chain" for many years, I did find it fun to find a local woman, Mrs. Gaertner, who stepped forward to become a reporter. She regularly contributed much information to the newspapers (*The Daily Times* in particular). She was considered a veteran local newspaper woman with more than a quarter of a century of service as of 1937, beginning her newspaper activity back in 1910 as a reporter for the old Beaver "*Star.*" She then became an employee of the "*Tribune*" in Beaver Falls. In 1916, Miss Mae Perdew married Elmer Gaertner of Monaca and became the mother of two daughters. Mae took a brief break from reporting but re-entered the newspaper field and was employed by *The Times*. Her husband died in 1936 and she not only tended to her family, but continued her work, publishing "the happenings" in the area. In 1935, Mae worked out of the Time Offices located in the Oriental Theater Building, Rochester (the *Times* also still had their main office in Beaver on Third Street).
---Mrs. Mildred Ross Dyke
   In the 1950s and 1960s, Mrs. Dyke was a familiar name to most in Beaver Valley, especially in Center Township. Mildred Ross Dyke was the first exclusive Center Township correspondent for *The Beaver Valley Times* (now *Beaver County Times*). *The Beaver Valley Times* printed two editions that were delivered within the township – the Beaver edition and the Aliquippa edition (this newspaper's predecessor was the *Aliquippa Gazette*). She provided

all the information for the section of the *Beaver Valley Times* under the Town and Local News sections. She gathered all available information from Center Township, still including general events, birthdates, prayer services, Grange news, scouting and 4-H happenings/events, as well as those in the hospitals, illnesses, birth and death information. If there was anything going on in Center Township, Mildred Ross Dyke knew about it and shared it with readers.

---Mrs. Mildred (W. Reed) McCartney

Mrs. McCartney was another very popular reporter. By 1970, she was published and doing the reporting of the happenings throughout the township.

---Mrs. Joseph Molnar   -   Mrs. Molnar was one of the contacts and columnists for Potter Township.

There is no doubt in my mind that there were many other reporters over the years, male and female, who should be mentioned, but I could not obtain a complete "list" and did not find any others noted in publications or archived newspapers for reporting local township information.

Following is a condensed amount of information on newspapers that were most likely available to or subscribed to by the residents of the Moon / Center Township area from the 1800s to the present. As readers will see, it is evident there were quite a few different newspapers available for subscription to Moon Township and surrounding residents through the years. The current *Beaver County Times* comes from the evolution of several of these previous newspapers.

Newspapers

Available in Beaver County and
Moon / Center Township

I do not have all the names of publications or publishers/editors' names, nor personally reviewed many of the available surviving copies of most of these newspapers. But it is a fact there were newspapers published between Nov 4, 1807 to Sep 1, 1818 that supplied news worthy items and information to people of all classes, the politicians, the tradesmen, office holders, and even the farmers and other hard-working people of the township and the county.

It was definitely more an act of "love" for the majority for all early newspapers to be published. The first publishers/editors of these newspapers were not "ignorant upstarts" who just tried to have political gains, but rather were intellectual men with strength and culture. The majority of each of these early publishers/editors personally carried much of the expense in printing and providing the newspapers to interested people, many also did most of the labor involved, too. It was not for the lack of that intelligence, or hard work and determination that caused many of the newspapers to fail, owners to give up, or any of them to sell out, but rather the conditions did not afford these newspapers a clear path for success. What I mean by this is, in the earlier years, there was just absolutely a limited audience to any specific publication in Beaver County.

During the times of these very early newspapers, profit was typically very low because there were still limited inhabitants living in any of the current familiar towns, townships, and areas. In the early 1800s Fallston only had a flouring mill, Beaver Falls (then Brighton) only had a few lots laid out, New Brighton did not even have a name yet (only Wolf's flouring mill), and Bridgewater (then Sharon) had Burr's boat building business. Phillipsburg (now Monaca) was also just developing. Almost everywhere else in the valley, including Moon Township, was still basically dense forests and wilderness and slowly being settled. This all meant there was such a limited purchasing audience to any specific publication in these rural areas. As stated, with the burden of expenses in most cases being carried solely by the owners of these newspapers, it explains the frequent changes in ownerships. History shows that without a profitable income from the sale of said newspapers, no one individual was usually capable to carry those expenses for any period of time.

Also, note, those that did live in the valley in the 1800s, particularly in the rural areas, would sometimes not get current news from the "outside world" for a few months. This occurred since not every early household in Moon Township, and other areas, could afford to purchase the available newspapers. Many times, one family would purchase the latest available copy and then it was shared or passed on to neighbors and other family households. By the time some received these shared copies, the news was quite outdated.

When it came to the equipment these early editors used, it was very simple and crude. Each word was formed by laboriously picking from pieces in the printer's case of type and each letter set individually. Also, the early presses only printed one page at a time. The first presses were most likely a Ramage press, followed by a Franklin press, and then came the Washington hand press (well known to many printer enthusiasts).

In listing the following newspapers, readers will notice that many of the newspapers were specifically related to either a republic or a democratic political party. For this reason, depending on which political party a household favored would also depend on which newspaper they were willing to commit to reading.

Monaca Herald
The *Monaca Herald* was one of the most popular local newspaper available for the Moon/Center Township residents found in the early 1900s. Since this was a newspaper started for the express purpose of publishing news of the Monaca and Moon Township areas, I thought I would include all of Mr. Jones' initial editorial to show the objective in his starting this paper................

"Upon entering the field of journalism, done after a long consideration, we are determined to give to Monaca, Aliquippa and the six townships south of the Ohio river, in Beaver county, the prominence and the opportunities that can only be secured through the influence and use of the press. We do not want to advance the idea that the county papers have ignored, or forgotten us, but the fact that north of the river is a territory very thickly populated, and closely connected by a network of railroads, naturally unites their sympathies through social and business intercourse, resulting in the practical isolation, in many respects, of this district. We do not want to infer that this is intentional, but occasioned because most of this territory is composed of a farming district and cannot be reached without great difficulty and expense. These conditions we hope to be able to overcome to some extent, by devoting our time and talent to the interest of this district, and with this thought in view, we send out the first number of the "Monaca Herald" which we hope the citizens will help us in making the representative of our interests and advancement."

Monaca Herald
--Known dates – Nov 13, 1903 to ?.
--It was a seven column, four-page paper that had a $1 per year subscription.
--The office of the *Monaca Herald* was on Pennsylvania Avenue, Monaca.
--This new weekly paper was originally called "*Monaca News*" – but the name was changed by
 Nov 16, 1903, to "*Monaca Herald*" because of a possible conflict that might occur between it
 and the *Beaver Valley News* which was published at New Brighton.
--The cylinder press arrived, was set up, and the paper was ready to be printed on Nov 19, 1903.
--George A. Jones – editor and manager at least in Nov 1903, 1904. Cornelius Wurzel also worked
 here in 1903.
--Oliver Boyd entered the *Monaca Herald* office as an apprentice and Harry Patton was on the
 Monaca Herald's force in Mar 1904.

Residents that lived closer to the Woodlawn/Aliquippa side of the township may have found the following newspapers of interest to them.

The Aliquippa Standard
The Aliquippa Standard was published beginning Aug 17, 1907 by the Aliquippa Print. Co. It was a weekly publication and continued at least to the end of Aug 1909. It was said to have been an independent Republican newspaper.

Woodlawn Gazette
This newspaper was published by the Franklin Publishing Co. between May 19, 1922 and 1928. It was distributed semi-weekly in the Woodlawn/Aliquippa area.
    It was succeeded by…………………

Aliquippa Gazette
The Aliquippa Gazette was in publication between 1928 and 1941. It was published by the Franklin Publishing Co. on a daily basis except on Sundays. The editorial, advertising, and circulation employees of the Aliquippa Gazette were all members of the American Newspaper Guild (C.I.O.) and all went out on strike on Wednesday, November 5, 1942. The strike was said to have developed due to demands which "the management refused after once accepting them in substance."
    It was succeeded by ………………………..

The Aliquippa News
This paper was published semi-weekly by the Aliquippa Unit of the Newspaper Guild of Pittsburgh between Nov 19, 1941 and 1942. The Chronicling America Historic American Newspapers included this with their information of The Aliquippa News -- "Local residents lost the only medium for learning community news when the Aliquippa gazette ceased operations because of a strike. The Aliquippa news will publish as often as possible, but will be discontinued when the strike is settled."
    Then…………….

Aliquippa News-Gazette
Published daily (except Saturday and Sunday) by the Aliquippa Pub. Co. in c1942 to ????
    Then……………

The Aliquippa News Herald
This was a weekly newspaper published by the Citizens Print. and Pub. Co. beginning in 1943 to ????
    This newspaper was short lived because……………

The Aliquippa Times
Was published daily, except Saturdays, Sundays, and holidays, by the Times Pub. Co. It appears to have only survived a few weeks in 1943.
    Became………………

The Evening Times
This paper was published beginning in 1943. It was also a daily publication (except Saturdays, Sundays, and holidays). The Times Pub. Co. was the publisher.

there were also……..

The Union Press
This paper was published beginning Aug 11, 1937 on a weekly frequency. The publisher was Lodge 1211 of the Amalgamated Assoc. of Iron, Steel and Tin Workers of North America (considered an "official organ of Lodge 1211…..").

Star News
This was another newspaper published in Aliquippa by R.A. Palket, Co. in 1987/1988. It covered happenings in Sewickley, Leetsdale, Moon (Allegheny County), Coraopolis, Neville Island.

~ ~ ~

Next, is a listing of the cluster of newspapers started in the 1800s. These publications were available to all interested in the valley. These newspapers may not have been consistently found within the township during the earlier years since not all households would have been afforded the luxury to purchase them or even found any other persons who would have shared them between households. That being said, I still felt it important to include them since a few copies of these papers have been known to be found in very old attics and other buildings, which means they did actually make their way into the hands of township residents.

Minerva
-- this is said to be the first/earliest paper; it is noted as the first paper published in Beaver County which any copy is known to be in existence.
-- Known dates – Nov 4, 1807 to as late as Jan 9, 1811.
-- Published in Beavertown (Beaver) every Saturday by John Berry.
-- Four-page sheet; ten and a half by seventeen inches in size.
-- $2.00 per year (and if sent by post, $2.50/year).
--Notes: The *Minerva* was devoted to the Republican party. The writings of the *Minerva* are said to have been of "a high character, and evidences ability and candor, with literary excellence." The head line was evidently a wood cut, near the center was a representation of the goddess "Minerva," with a plumed helmet on her head, on the left was "The," and on the right "Minerva," (the lettering was about 1" in height). Below the headline – "This folio of four pages * * * * happy work! What is it but a map of busy life, its fluctuations and its vast concerns", then came the volume #, issue #, day, month, day, year. Close to one third of the first column contained the terms of subscription and some advertising.

It is not known how long this paper was actually published, but it was the same in type, size, and general format as the *Wester Cabinet*, so it is said with a change in publisher, came the change in name, too. Joseph W. White followed John Berry and next to be published……….

Western Cabinet
--Known dates – Jul 4, 1812 to about Feb/Mar 1813 (no official end date)
--Published in Beavertown (Beaver) every Saturday by Joseph W. White.
--$2.00 per year.
--Notes: It was the same size as the *Minerva,* same style and type, same general appearance except Mr. White changed the name. Its motto – "The basis of our political system is the right of the people to make and to alter the constitution of Government – Washington." Mr. White's successors were J. and A. Logan. It is not known how long this paper was published, but as it appears to have ended, the *Crisis* seemed to begin.

The water gets a little muddy between the next two papers - the *Crisis* and the *Beaver Gazette*. They both began within three weeks of each other. There is a theory that these two newspapers consolidated and then named the *Crisis and Beaver Gazette.*

Crisis   Beaver Gazette   Crisis and Beaver Gazette
The *Crisis*……
--Known dates – May 22, 1813 to cApr 30, 1814 (the Logans were editors), but evidence shows even with no editor listed, it was still existing as of Nov 10, 1815.
--Published in Beaver every Saturday morning by J. (James) & A. (Andrew) Logan.
--Notes: Again, the same size as the *Minerva* and same general style. They had their printing office adjoining the Court House.
   and……
The *Beaver Gazette*……
--Known dates – Jun 8, 1813 to cMar 15, 1817 (or possibly later -?-)
--It was the same size as the *Crisis.* A. Logan was publisher.
--Published every Saturday at $2.00 per year.
--Notes: Motto – "Free but not Licentious." A copy of the paper dated Apr 4, 1818 still had A. Logan as the publisher with the same motto from 1813.
   then…
The Crisis and Beaver Gazette
--Known dates – started Jun 10, 1813.
--All were published by A. Logan and had the same motto as the *Gazette.*
--Even with the copies of this newspaper being found, there are records also found in the same time period for both the other two individual papers (*Crisis* and *Beaver Gazette*) for two or more years later than 1813, which appears to discount that these two papers were consolidated.
-- The Volume 3, No. 45 issue had the same motto as the *Beaver Gazette* –"Free but not Licentious."
-- The last issue found for the *Crisis and Beaver Gazette* is No. 45 on Apr 18, 1816, with A. Logan as publisher. Being "No. 45", indicates there were quite a few issues of this newspaper.

One theory for the three names of the newspaper lapsing over the years would be -– With such a high fever heat of politics during this time, the seemingly consolidated *Crisis and Beaver Gazette* may have just been an outlet of expression to other political enemies. Another theory to the three names (*Crisis*, *Beaver Gazette*, and *Crisis and Beaver Gazette*) would be that "it is possible that the names were applied randomly at different times, as it suited them, without regard to continuity of the name." Whether or not the consolidation indeed occurred, it is a fact that all three were published by one or both Logan brothers. There are three known copies of the "consolidated" paper known to be in existence. All three had their own Volume 3 listed.

So, regardless of the actual true name…….After approximately five years of partial success, on Sep 1, 1818, James Logan began what was considered the successor of all three papers and he named this new publication the ………

Western Argus
--Known dates – Sep 1, 1818 to Dec 1859.
--Published in Beaver.
--James Logan had sole control until Jan of 1825 when he sold it to Thomas Henry who retained the name of the paper. In 1830, the names of the printers and publishers were of T. & W. Henry. Thomas Henry retired and sold the paper to his son William the end of Jan 1831 who retained the name of the paper until 1843 (see further). Wm. Henry remained editor until 1851.
--Notes: Following the ownership going to Thomas Henry, a true controversy occurred between him and the Logans who had begun to publish the *Republican* (see further). This feud became quite heated at times and editorials were VERY expressive. The feud was sparked by the fact that with the sale in 1925 to Mr. Henry. It was understood that the Logans promised to keep out of the newspaper business, yet the Logans began the *Republican* in 1926.

The name of the paper was changed on Aug 2, 1843 to…….

Beaver Argus
--Known dates – 1843 to 1853.
--It was enlarged and included seven columns to a page.
--William Henry took in his brother, Albert G. as a partner the end of Jun 1850. Mid Nov, 1851, William sold his interest to Michael Weyand. This meant that A. G. Henry and Michael Weyand were now the editors.

With Mr. Weyand and A. G. Henry as partners, the name of the paper was once again changed on Jul 27, 1853 to……

Beaver County Argus   aka   The Beaver Weekly Argus
--Known dates – 1853 to 1859
--It was a weekly publication.
--Jun 28, 1854, Jacob Weyand, brother of Michael bought A. G. Henry's interest in the paper. Jacob wasn't in the picture for very long and retired from the *Argus* on Dec 16, 1857 and sold all his interest to his brother Michael. Michael Weyand retired in Dec 1859 and sold all interest to Samuel Davenport.

 Wed, May 30, 1860

Mr. Davenport made yet another name change, going back to …...

Beaver Argus
--Included in the head line was "Established 1818" which dates it back to the Western Argus. Mr. Davenport sold his interest to Thomas C. Nicholson the end of Dec 1861 and Mr. Nicholson assumed charge. T. C. Nicholson & Co. became the publisher of the Argus on Jan 1, 1862.
--A string of editors then occurred for the paper...
- On Sep 17, 1862, Mr. Nicholson and his two acting editors were enlisted in the Civil War and an editorial asked the readers to bear with them for a short time until they returned.
- Feb 11, 1863, De Lorma Imbrie assumed control of the *Argus* as editor and proprietor. Mr. Imbrie retired Nov 2, 1864.

- D. W. Scott, Jr. took over the business within a week and was editor and manager. (Mr. Scott was a resident of Hopewell Township.)

Due to ill health, Mr. Scott sold his interest in the paper…

- M. S. Quay and J. S. Rutan bought the paper on Jan 4, 1865. Mr. Rutan purchased M. S. Quay's interest Oct 18, 1865 and was then sole editor.
- J. S. Rutan & Co. then had J. L. Anderson become another member of the company.
- Jul 11, 1866, Jacob Weyand purchased the newspaper and business and took charge as editor and proprietor.
- Mr. Weyand sold his interest to Robert L. Treiber Jan 8, 1873.

 Wednesday, Apr 30, 1862

Fact: Daily Argus – May 1883 to 1896. It was the second daily newspaper in the county. Owned by W. F. Bliss and his brother Howard Bliss who bought out W. I. Reed's interest in Sep 1885 (W.I. Reed was of Moon Township). Howard was also listed as editor of the Beaver "Star" in 1910.

Another newspaper thrown into the mix…

Radical aka **Beaver Radical**
--Know dates: Dec 11, 1868 to Sep 17, 1873.
--Matthew S. Quay established the Radical in Nov of 1868 in opposition to the Argus.
--There were no regular lists of subscribers to the paper when James S. Rutan, manager of the *Radical*, bought the paper from Mr. Quay in 1872.
--The Beaver Radical then consolidated with the *Argus* in 1873 with Mr. Rutan as editor and Jacob Weyand as business manager (see *Argus* previous.). It became an authority in Republican politics of the State.

 Friday, Jan 3, 1873

This rival papers of the *Argus* and the *Radical* (see further) continued separately from Nov 1868 until Sep 17, 1873, at which time the two papers were consolidated and became the………….

The Argus and Radical
--Known dates – Sep 17, 1873 to May, 1903.
--Published by the Beaver Printing Company; James S. Rutan, editor; Jacob Weyand, business mgr.
--The office burned Mar 17, 1874, but publications resumed the first of Apr 1874.
--In Dec of 1879, Smith Curtis bought out James S. Rutan's interest and became editor. Then William Irwin Reed (of Moon Township (s/o Thomas and Francis (Irwin) Reed), bought Jacob Weyand's interest, becoming business manager.

Fun fact: Wm. I. Reed was noted as a "well-equipped and thorough journalist." He was involved in starting the Daily Argus *in May 1883, the second daily paper in the county, which ran for a few years and then was discontinued (see previous).*

--Mr. Reed sold his interest in the *Argus and Radical* on Sep 1, 1885 to W. F. Bliss. W. F. Bliss's brother, Howard also became involved with the paper. In 1890, the Bliss brothers sold their interest in the *Argus and Radical* to Capt. John E. Smith (of Georgetown). Capt. Smith sold his holdings to his partner Smith Curtis who then conducted all the business of the paper, issuing it on a weekly basis.

 Wednesday, Sep 24, 1873

The Radical Printing Company of Beaver was granted a charter which absorbed the *Argus and Radical*. It included buying the plant, name and "good will."

And guess what – another name change. A daily paper was started…………

The Daily X-Ray
--Started as a daily paper on May 4, 1903.
--It became a morning paper (except Sundays) on Jun 29, 1903.
--It was short lived and ceased publications as of Jul 13, 1903.
--F. L. Parker was editor and business manager.
--Mar 26, 1904, the paper was sold at public auction and bought by Joseph L. Holmes.
--May 1904, Smith Curtis bought the plant from Mr. Homes.
--Notes: Their first issue stated – "In one sense it is a new paper, being under a new management and new name, but in another, it is an evolution from the weekly *Argus and Radical* whose lineal descent reaches, in unbroken succession, to the old "*Western Argus*', published in Beaver in 1818."

Mr. Curtis set the name back to….

Argus and Radical
--Smith Curtis made it a weekly publication again.
   (This paper resulted in a merger of the *Beaver Argus* and the *Beaver Radical* in 1862.)

The Beaver Times   aka **The Times**
--Established Apr 1, 1874.
   This places the beginning of this paper back to the *Argus and Radical* after the office burned Mar 17, 1874 and its publications resuming the first of April.
--This publication started in the spring after the consolidation of the *Argus and the Radical* with Michael Weyand, editor. Mr. Weyand came out of a long retirement to once again follow journalism. He did not particularly like the aims and purposes of the *Argus and Radical* politically, so he took the opportunity to start this new paper. In the first edition, Mr. Weyand didn't make grand promises, but rather included in his statement – "without volunteering any very specific pledges as to what we propose to do, or promise not to do, we simply say that we embark in the present undertaking with no private schemes to work out, and no personal animosities to gratify…."
--The paper began as a nine column, four-page paper. It sold for six cents a week.
--In Feb 1898, Michael Weyand was retained as editor until Jan 1, 1900 at which time he became the postmaster in Beaver.
--*The Times* continued as a weekly publication until Apr 27, 1900, when a daily edition was also started. It was an eight column, four-page paper; Beaver Publishing Company; T. S. Laughlin was General Manager and Michael Weyand was the Editor.
--Mr. Weyand was succeeded by Ellis N. Bigger, Esq. Mr. Bigger wrote the editorials until his death in Jul 1902. Robert La Ross was then in editorial charge until his death in Jan 1903.

Tuesday evening, Jan 1, 1901

Fact: Mr. Weyand held one of the longest careers in newspaper work of anyone in Western Pennsylvania. He was also the oldest in service as an editor in Beaver County in his time. He served 8 years on the Argus and at least twenty-six years on the Times. His chief assistant was his son Henry S. Weyand.

--Both *The Beaver Times* and *The Daily Times* had within their headlines "Est. April 2, 1874." This date indicates both these newspapers evolved down through *The Argus and Radical*. *The Argus and Radical* was actually started in Sep 17, 1873, but I repeat, the office burned in mid Mar 1874 and publications were resumed in a new office the first of Apr, 1874. This is the date they are using as the start or establishment for whatever reason.

It remained *The Beaver Times* until between Jul 13 & 14, 1906, then became known as…………

The Daily Times   aka   Rochester and Beaver   The Daily Times
--Below the headline was a box with the following information:
   The Daily Times – Established Apr 2, 1874.   The Beaver Argus – Established Nov 4, 1808.
--Consolidated Jul 1, 1930.   Had a Rochester Office–Oriental Theatre Bldg. and the main Beaver office–Third Street.   The Daily Times Company, Inc – publisher.
--Published every evening except Sunday.   Cost – 50 cents/month, 15 cents/week by carrier.
--In the early 1920s, the headline had *THE DAILY TIMES* and centered beneath this was
   A CLEAN NEWSY NEWSPAPER FOR THE HOME.
--E. L. Freeland was owner and general manager in 1925 and Jack Malone, the managing editor.

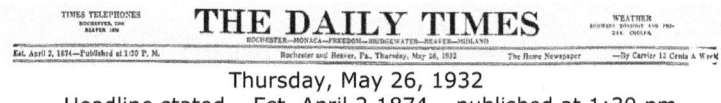

Thursday, May 26, 1932
Headline stated – Est. April 2 1874 – published at 1:30 pm

Following *The Daily Times*, the name once again changed several times …

Beaver Valley Times
--Headline stated established Oct 16, 1946.   In 1946, it stated the Daily Times and Western Argus preceded it.   In 1946, B. W. Calkins-President, E. J. Harn-Secy/Treas, C. H. Wood-General Manager, and Jack Malone-Managing Editor.   By 1960, S. W. Calkins-President, Michael M. Pennock-General Manager, Ralph Temples-managing editor, and Jack Malone-Editor.   They still had a Beaver Office and a Rochester Office in 1946.   By at least 1958, offices were in Beaver, Rochester, Aliquippa, and Ambridge.
--Subscriptions were $6.00/year in 1946 and at $18.00/year by 1960.   It was published every evening except Sunday by the Beaver Newspaper, Inc.

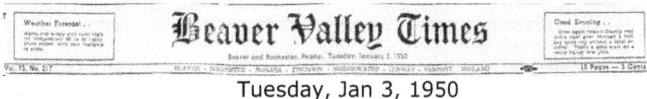

Tuesday, Jan 3, 1950

It continued as *Beaver Valley Times* until the end of 1959 or first of 1960, then………………

Beaver County Times
As of Feb 1, 1960, the head line was *Beaver County Times* and had "*Beaver County's HOMETOWN Daily Newspaper*" under it.   It was still published each evening except Sunday by Beaver Newspaper, Inc.   1 year subscription was $21.00.   Feb 1, 1960, S. W. Calkins-President, Michael Pennock-General Manager, Jack Malone-Editor, Ralph Temples-Managing Editor.   They still had offices in Beaver, Rochester, Aliquippa, and Ambridge.   By the end of Dec, 2000, they only had offices listed in Beaver and Moon Township (of Allegheny County).   They were publishing newspapers Monday through Friday and Sunday mornings.   A one year subscription was $140.40.   Rich Wasko was Managing Editor, Jim Pane-Chief Copy Editor, Alan Buncher-Exec. Editor, and Tom Bickert-Assoc. Editor.

 Thursday, Jul 9, 1998

The Times

𝕿𝖍𝖊 𝕿𝖎𝖒𝖊𝖘 Current

   Also………………………………..

By 1985/86, the *Times* had started a section within the newspaper specifically for the Moon Township and Coraopolis areas (both of Allegheny County).

**MOON TOWNSHIP –
CORAOPOLIS AREA TIMES**

   Then…………………………….

.... by the end of Dec 1986, it was a separate newspaper and called "An edition of the *Beaver County Times*." As of 2007, it was $152.10/year subscription and published by Beaver Newspaper, Inc. with Managing Editor, Tom Bickert.

 Wednesday, Dec 3, 1986

~ ~ ~

Now to add more newspapers to the mix from those previously mentioned...(These publications interested all those strongly involved in politics through those early years, and may still interest all involved in politics.)

As stated, political parties seemed to be the driving forces with many of the earlier newspapers. The following are being mentioned only because the Logans were involved and connected with a "feud" with Mr. Henry. Although not immediately "local," to Moon/Center Township, here are some of the other more local newspapers that surely made it into the hands of the township residents that enjoyed reading of rivalries and conflicts or who were strong supporters of either the Republican party or Democratic party.

Republican aka Beaver Republican – said to have been the first Democratic paper published in the county. It was a four-page, five column sheet. (The Whig party existed 1836, then in 1856 by the Republican party.)
--Known dates – Jun, 1826 to May 6, 1835. Published in Beaver by Logan & English, then in 1828 by A. & J. Logan, Feb 26, 1829 by James Logan and James Sharp, and by May 5, 1831 just Andrew Logan is named as editor and proprietor. Jun 20, 1834, Andrew Logan retired as editor and was succeeded by his brother James. James only held the editor position until Sep 1834 when Andrew once again took over. There was yet another new editor in Nov 1834, J. & E. Beeson (of Ohio).

Then, due to the "hot political times" and "of two separate and widely distinct political parties," came a new paper established to replace the *Republican* called the ....

Democratic Watchman
--Known dates – Jun 19, 1835 to almost mid Dec 1835. Published by J. Beeson.
   Then...

The Aurora
--Known dates: Mar 1836 to Mar 1, 1839. Started by Alexander R. Niblo.
   Then....

Beaver River Gazette
--Known dates: Feb 13, 1834 to May 3, 1834. Started by Dr. R. B. Barker and Reese C. Fleeson.
--Published every Thursday; six-column, four-page paper.
   The next known paper was...

Western Star aka Star
--Known dates – Dec 15, 1843. Started by Washington Bigler and William Denlinger.
--Mr. Bigler retired from the firm in Jan 1846. Mr. Denlinger temporarily retired and was succeeded by Major John Irons who only remained for a few months on the paper. When Major Irons left, Mr. Denlinger returned to the *Star*. Mr. Denlinger once again left the paper Sep 8, 1852. Mr. Connelly and R. G. McGregor took over management. About 1857/58, N. C. Barker and his son A.C. were in full control of the paper.
--Notes: With Thomas Henry connected to this newspaper, the *Western Star* was most likely "handled" by the *Argus*. This paper changed hands quite a few times. Dr. R. B. Barker also wrote many editorials for this publication. The writing abilities of Dr. Barker and William Henry of the Argus were said to show they were the "ablest of the editors of the county, and have not been excelled by any others in their style..." Someone broke into the *Star* office on

Jun 30, 1861, and the press was taken apart, the arms carried away with several cases of type, and all dumped into the Ohio River.   Almost all was recovered within a few weeks. Shortly after, the Barclays disposed of their interests in the paper.

Barkers disposed of their interest to O.S. Long on Jul 10, 1861 who then sold to James H. Odell in 1865. Mr. Odell changed the name to the…

Local   aka   Beaver Local

--J. H. Odell sold this paper to T. Burton in Dec 1868. Mr. Burton then sold to W. H. Schwartz. Mr. Schwartz did not have the paper for any length of time before it was discontinued and sold at constable's sale.

E. B. Williams purchased the paper on May 10, 1871 and the name was changed to….

Conservative

--Mr. Williams ran the publication alone until Jan 1873.   John Bigger bought half interest and by Aug 1873 Mr. Williams had retired, and Mr. Bigger was sole owner.   The *Conservative* was discontinued in Jan 1874.

Robert L. Treiber and M. J. White bought all the material of the former *Conservative* and started the paper back up under the name of the *Democrat*…

Democrat

--Mr. Treiber became sole owner within a few months after Mr. White retired.   In Oct 1876, the plant was sold at Sheriff's sale and bought by John J. Wickham.   Mr. Wickham sold all the material to John S. Hoopes.

The Beaver County Democrat.
The Only Democratic Newspaper in Beaver County.

As happened many times…. the name was changed once again…

Beaver County Post

--On Oct 5, 1877, there was a new publisher, Dr. R. S. Kennedy who…………yep, changed the name to the…

Commoner

(There was another publication named the *Commoner* started in May 1897 by the Rochester Publishing Company with R. W. Stiffey editor.)

--Known dates – Oct 1877 to 1879. Published in Beaver, PA.   Editor – R. S. Kennedy.

Dr. Kennedy never cared for the name *Commoner,* so, in 1879 he changed the name back to….

Star

--Known dates – 1879 to 1887.

--It was a weekly newspaper. Mr. R. S. Kennedy enlarged the office, added new type, a press was added.   He joined in a partnership with Charles F. Whisler in Oct 1884. After six months, Mr. Whisler was full owner, but within months, Lewis W. Reed joined with Mr. Whisler in the publication.   They soon sold their interests back to Mr. Kennedy by Oct 1885 and retired from the paper. Mr. Kennedy sold the *Star* to Mr. Mellon in Sep 1887 and retired.   Mr. Mellon consolidated the *Star* and his paper in Beaver Falls, the *Globe* and it became known as the *Glove-Star*.

--Mr. Mellon joined up with William Porter, M. D. and Richard Stiffey in Sep 1891.

Guess what happened………they not only moved the publication to Beaver, but changed the name back to the….

Star and also started the Daily Star
Daily Star

--In Jan 1894, the plant was sold to a stock company. In Feb 1895, the "Star Publishing Company" was chartered.

--There was a fire on Mar 25, 1897 that totally destroyed the entire outfit. They had a new building by Jul 1898 and completely new outfit installed.

--Mr. Porter resigned in Feb 1899 and his successor was David L. McNees.

--This *Star* was published weekly until 1900 when it was changed to a semi-weekly publication.

Note: It had local writers on the paper including Thomas Beaver of Monaca for covering Moon Township and the Boro of Monaca.

Beaver River Gazette

--Know dates -   Feb 11, 1834 to latter part of 1834/early in 1835.   Published in Beaver every Thursday and sold for $2.00 per year.
--Its motto read – "In proportion as the structure of a Government gives force to public opinion, it is essential that public opinion should be enlightened."
--Started by Dr. R. B. Barker (of Pittsburgh) and Reece C. Fleeson.
--Notes: These two men started this newspaper and played upon the controversy going on between the *Western Star*, *Republican*, and sometimes the *Argus*.   Their first copy stated they would be impartial politically and went on to say "But in so doing we will endeavor to avoid that rancor and personal invective so justly offensive to decency and good sense." Even with this statement, a newspaper war broke out between Dr. Barker of the *Gazette* and Mr. Logan of the *Republican*.   The *Gazette* tried to purchase the *Republican*, but Mr. Logan backed out of the deal.   With both papers in the same political field, it likely is the reason both soon failed.

Fun fact: Dr. Barker's wife, Eliza (Hunter) Barker contributed many poetic writings to her husband's paper.   With a "brilliancy of intellect," she met and tutored many people – one of her pupils was Stephen C. Foster.

~ ~ ~

WEATHER
Tornados

Photo of a tornado in Beaver County in 1985.

Listed below are a number of reported tornado events that occurred in Beaver County, PA through the years. Although many of the tornados did not touch down within the borders of Moon/Center Township, all township residents would have been included in the warnings and threats would have definitely been realistic. Rather than trying to determine exactly where a tornado actually touched down, all known and reported tornados are included further. This is done since even without an official tornado forming, the winds and storms that move in and/or accompany one typically cause quite severe weather to all other areas adjacent to it.

Jun 4, 1907 - On Tuesday evening, Jun 4, 1907, around 8:00 pm, there was a horrible wind and rainstorm that passed over the lower Beaver Valley and did many thousands of dollars' worth of damage. It was never classified as a tornado, yet the winds that came in with this storm did damages equal to those of a tornado. It was compared to being more of a cyclone as far as the correspondences from damage claims made because of the storm.

Jun 28, 1924 - On Saturday, Jun 28, 1924, the whole Beaver Valley was hit with what they called a cyclone. The Daily Times newspaper stated, "Worst Cyclone in History of Beaver Valley…." The storm brought in pounding rains, hail, winds, leaving damage and destruction where it hit. One article stated that it looked like France after all the bombings. All the area towns and communities sustained severe damages from this cyclone and Center Township was among the areas hit hardest by this storm. There were porches and roofs blown off many homes as well as numerous windows being shattered, and trees uprooted. Although there were thousands of dollars in damages done, there was only one casualty reported which was in Monaca, George Kane, a night engineer at the water works plant. He was badly bruised by falling bricks as a brick wall caved in when the roof was blown off. With the electric power being compromised, telephone service didn't work and there were no electric lights. Though it was not common nor allowed by law in 1924, hardware store merchants opened their stores on Sunday to give people access to purchase window glass and other supplies needed to make repairs on their homes.

Jun 10, 1954 – F2 Tornado in Beaver County – 0 fatalities, 3 injuries.

May 12, 1956 – F2 Tornado in Beaver County (lower portion of Center Township, upper portion of Aliquippa Borough) – 0 fatalities, 0 injuries.

Apr 23, 1966 – F1 Tornado in Beaver County – 0 fatalities, 0 injuries.

Jul 23, 1970 – There was an unofficial report of a F1 Tornado in Beaver County.

Sep 3, 1970 - Tornado hit the Center Township and Monaca area at a little after 7 pm on Saturday evening the third of Sep 1970. It was quite fast moving and basically traveled along the Ohio River, bouncing in and out of areas of Center Township. Then it passed over some of Monaca Heights, and traveled down 14th Street Hill, and on into Monaca. It destroyed the majority of Marcello Block and Mecklem Lumber companies (both in Monaca) and damages were reported to more than 50 homes. It may have only lasted an estimated 3 minutes. It appeared to develop just before the Vanport expressway bridge and basically followed the path of the river. Then it traveled over a two-mile track and was 100 yards wide in some spots as it caused most of its destruction in Monaca. There were 5 reported injuries and 0 fatalities.

Damages to the grounds of Marcello Block Co.

Mar 24, 1975 and Jun 4, 1975 – F1 and F2 (respectively) Tornados in Beaver County (Freedom area); 0 fatalities, 0 injuries.

Jul 11, 1976 – No offical "F" scale assigned to this Tornado in Beaver County; 0 fatalities, 0 injuries.

Jun 16, 1978 – An unofficial F1 Tornado was reported in Beaver County.

Jun 20/21, 1981 – F1 Tornado in Beaver County; 0 fatalities, 0 injuries.

Jul 4 and Jul 19, 1983 – F1 Tornado in Beaver County; 0 fatalities, 1 injury.

May 31, 1985 - There was what was considered a "tornado outbreak" that passed through eastern Ohio and northwestern Pennsylvania on May 31, 1985. There was not just one tornado on this day in 1985, but one report stating twenty-three tornadoes swept through the area. Some fizzled out as quickly as they developed, others caused much damage before dissolving. The storms that developed only ripened throughout the day and by evening the tornado warnings were up and active for all in the valley. "The storm killed three in Beaver County and injured dozens, staying on the ground for 55 minutes and traveling 39 miles from Big Beaver to just north of Cranberry Township. It destroyed more than 200 homes and the Big Beaver Shopping Plaza in mere minutes."

At some points during these storms, one was classified as a F5. This monster storm was nearly a half-mile wide. Center and Potter townships and the Borough of Monaca, escaped damages from F3 to F5 tornados that began near Erie, PA and spanned to Beaver, PA. When all was said and done, there were 9 fatalities and 120 injured in Beaver and Butler counties, and a total of 65 people were reported to have died in PA.

Jul 22, 1990 – F1 Tornado in Beaver County; 0 fatalities, 0 injuries.

Jul 29, 1994 – Unofficial F1 Tornado in Beaver County.

Apr 9, 1998 and Jun 2, 1998 – F1 Tornados in Beaver County; 0 fatalities, 0 injuries. On Jun 2nd, there were several confirmed tornados not only in Beaver County, but throughout the surrounding counties including...5:30 pm (Raccoon area) and another at 7:30 pm (south of the Raccoon area).

Apr 28 and Nov, 2002 - Tornadoes struck a number of states from Louisiana to Pennsylvania, including Beaver County (F1) on Veterans Day. There was a total of 36 people killed as a result of these storms.

July 10, 2017 - There was a tornado reported to have hit the upper right corner of Beaver County area at 1:57 pm.

Fact: The Fujita Tornado Damage Scale is the benchmark by which tornado severity were gauged between 1971 and 2007. Using this scale, it meant a tornado of F3 would have had a minimum wind speed of 158 mph and caused severe damage. An F3 storm is capable of being responsible for roofs and walls being torn off well-constructed houses, trains being overturned, trees in a forest being uprooted, and heavy cars being lifted and thrown.

~ ~ ~

Major Snow Falls of the Area

There have been countless cases of heavy snow fall in and around Center and Potter townships through the years. I have listed a few.

<u>1944</u> - During the winter of 1944 there was 15+ inches of snow that fell quite rapidly in the area. It paralyzed all the surrounding areas.

<u>Nov 24, 1950</u> - Depending exactly where you lived, a totally unpredicted snowstorm caused 40 to 48 inches of snow to fall all throughout Beaver County. During the early morning hours on that day after Thanksgiving, the heavy, wet snow began to fall and 48 hours later, with high winds and frigid temperatures thrown into the mix, there was damage, death, and distress. Businesses were forced to close with workers not able to get to work. Cars and trucks were abandoned on roads and main streets in towns alike.

Milestones/BCHR&LF
This is a photo of Kobuta homes in Potter Township after the snow storm.

In Jan 1977, the Ohio River completely froze over, as did many of the creeks and streams including those in the township. The pictures below show what a frozen Ohio River looks like. Note in the picture to the left, there are many people who were brave enough (or should we say lacking common sense) to venture far out onto the ice and toward the middle of the river.

<u>Jan 1978</u> - At least 25 inches of snow fell over 3 days crippling the area.

<u>Mar 12-14, 1993</u> - This storm was labeled "Superstorm". The weathermen were predicting FEET of snow from this front as it moved through the area. When the snow first started to fall, it was a much slower rate and many thought the weather people were making a bigger deal of it all than was necessary, but by midday, things began to get serious. The snow fall quickly turned into assaulting, heavy, wind-driven snow. Some places received so much snow by the time it did stop that people were sequestered to their homes and other places for up to three days while roads and parking lots were being cleared. The severe winds had caused massive drifting which only added to the incredible amount of snow, some drifts were up to 15 feet high. Then on top of all the inches of snow, a layer of over an inch of sleet/ice formed, and yet more snow came down on top of the layer of ice. This

storm yielded 25.3 inches of snow. This snow was considered lighter as opposed to the possibility of that much snow being considered wetter. A wetter snow would have made it much heavier which would have done even more damage by the additional weight to all those inches of snow.

Jan 1994 - The first few days of Jan in 1994 were definitely "snow days." There was more than ten inches of snow dumped on the region and several days of threats of freezing rain, too. There were closures everywhere and even cancellations at the airport. There was more snow and freezing rain predictions on Jan 7th.

Feb 6, 2010 - This weekend snowstorm paralyzed many areas. The official accumulation at Pittsburgh International Airport was 21.1 inches, but many areas received even more. This storm laid a very heavy and wet snow that felled trees and limbs and snapped electrical wires leaving over 130,000 customers without electricity for many days. To add to the already troubling situation, the temperatures were only in the single digits. This storm was persistent in that throughout its duration, an average of one inch of snow fell per hour, something that many meteorologists found most interesting from a scientific standpoint.

Mar 2017 – Center Township and many adjacent areas prepared for a predicted significant snow fall event, as did most of Pennsylvania. Many school districts and business made the call to postpone opening or announced closures ahead of the predicted storm. Fortunately, there was barely more than a few snowflakes that were seen by residents. Meteorologists reported this was due to a "midlevel dry spot" (an area of dry air that takes the moisture out of the snow formation zone). Even though western Pennsylvania did not suffer from this front, the eastern part of the state did not escape the predicted snow fall where snowfall exceeded 20 inches.

~ ~ ~

Drought and Flooding

Moon/Center Township does not have the amount of river front property as other areas, nor has or is it consistently affected by the swelling of the Ohio River with the majority of the township's land situated either a safe distance from or above the river. But this does not mean that the township itself has not been affected by major flooding events with all the streams and creeks that do travel throughout the township since all have been known for overflowing their banks. Also, as the lands were being cleared and more and more trees and vegetation eliminated, this contributed greatly to many landslides effecting the area, too. Even though the Pennsylvania Governors began to approve millions of dollars to complete dams along the rivers and for work to be done on some of the large main streams to help control the flows of those waters, especially during flooding, this did not help control the amount of water flowing in the smaller streams and creeks. If the main rivers were reaching proportional flood levels, remember, the rivers are fed by all the many smaller streams. Therefore, it goes without saying, there would also have been noted high-water within the township along all the streams and creeks. The flooding from these streams and creeks means there was suffering and damages for numerous residents of Moon/Center Township. If a township resident's actual home was not affected by a period of flooding, this does not mean that the actual land escaped the excessive water. During the early years when farming was the main occupation, fields could have easily been submerged in water which would have destroyed many acres of crops.

It is important to remember many times the angry waters of a flooding condition destroyed, or at the very least, threatened many people and/or their properties. But there were just as many times when the lack of rain and/or snow through a winter would cause low water levels which posed many problems of a whole different matter. Low water levels caused problems in the river communities and businesses who relied on the river, causing just as many heartaches for the township farmers and households. They would have also suffered with low water levels of the township creeks and streams. Lack of rain meant that all wells could also run dry which could affect personal and household usage and also for providing water to the crops or livestock.

> *Fun fact: During the very early years, the waters of rivers and streams were not only considered normally shallower, but also the water was quite unpolluted and very clear, you could easily see to the bottom of the river or a larger creek.*

One recorded event of the lack of water was in 1881 when the river traffic was halted in the Rochester and Monaca and other river community areas due to the fact the Ohio River had reached its lowest level on record – 1 foot, 9 inches. This low of a river level would have indicated that all the creeks and streams of Moon Township would have had their driest times also, thus affecting crops and livestock.

There were many periods of time through the years where lack of rain caused drought watches, drought warnings, or full out droughts throughout Beaver County. I did not locate any specific chart of these for any of the early years, but it is inevitable that many of the farmers and residents of the township endured periods of hardships due to very dry conditions. Even if the surface ground did not show signs of lack of water, there were many times everyone would have been affected by "an invisible drought." An invisible drought would follow a very dry period of weather and the groundwater supplies were seriously compromised. Many people don't think about or have much concern during an invisible drought because they can not see groundwater, but there are serious ramifications none the less. The last and most noted period considered a drought within the township and Beaver County was in Aug of 1999. 2016 started off and was a very dry year until mid-August when a series of rainstorms raised the rainfall deficits more than 6 inches for the year.

Throughout this book, it has been stated to note the importance of remembering in the earlier years, the Ohio River was never as deep as it is nowadays. There were even times during dry periods of weather when people could easily walk through the waters of the Ohio River from one side to the other. In the 1700s, the soldiers or those providing supplies readily crossed the river back and forth to Fort McIntosh. In later years there were times when steamboats could not travel the Ohio River due to lack of depth with the water. In the 1800s and earlier 1900s, the Ohio River would be considered "deep" if it was even 9 feet deep. Except for homesteaders or businesses located directly adjacent to the river's banks, it took a lot of rain or melting snow to cause the river to do serious flooding.

Monaca-Rochester bridge   Little Beaver Historical Society

This picture shows just one of the shallower stages of the Ohio River in the early 1900s. The pointer on the right is indicating how much of the shore is exposed from the normal water mark. (Rochester is to the left of the picture, Monaca is on the right side.)

There are a few more pictures of the river in the Entertainment and Recreation section under the Swimming category. These pictures will show how naturally shallow the water once was on the Ohio River in the earlier years and how far out into the river swimmers could comfortably venture.

Fun fact: During the periods of very low water levels on the Ohio River, the steamboats and other boats could have possibly still made it up or down the river using the very middle of the river if all they were doing was passing through. If ships were laden with cargo to be delivered, the shallower water did not permit the ships to get close enough to docks/wharfs, so the cargo had to be carried from the boat (positioned in the middle of the river) to the wharf area or normal shoreline. For people who wanted to board or disembark a steamer or other larger boat during low water levels would have been an exhausting venture also. Passengers boarding or arriving would have definitely had to do some walking over and through the sandy, gravely, dirt/mud of the exposed riverbed and most likely some wading through a bit of shallow water to reach their boat. Nowadays, those who did not come from a river town or area that greatly centered around a river/waterway for support, business, and transportation, or those who have never been involved in any type of farming or depended on well water just cannot appreciate what low water levels could mean.

Finding information on flooding events was a bit easier than information on droughts. There is an extraction from the *History of Beaver County* which will give an indication of how many times the Ohio River's levels were compromised. Even though this listing states "the Ohio River at Pittsburgh," the inevitable flooding or high waters would have eventually traveled further down river. All the creeks and streams, including those in the township itself, would have also been swollen, during these same periods of time, remembering they all feed into the river which increases the river's levels.

Homesteads along the township's creeks and streams would have surely suffered substantial damages to their homes and/or properties during periods of actual flooding or at the very least, excessive rain or rapid snow melts. Even those who did not live directly along a creek/stream or the river would most likely have suffered from all the excessive rain or quick thawing of the snow. Even without direct contact to a stream or creek, pooling of excessive water in various areas of a homestead would have easily damaged personal property, homes, stored supplies, fruit cellars, fields, roadways, equipment, affected livestock, et cetera.

(Extracted information from History of Beaver County..................)

"*anything above 22 feet was considered a flood stage on the Ohio River...."

Former high-water marks in the Ohio River at Pittsburg:

Year	Month	Feet	Year	Month	Feet	Year	Month	Feet
1810	Nov 10	32	1874	Jan 8	22.4	1886	Apr 7	22.6
1832	Feb 10	35	1875	Aug	25	1888	Jul 11	22
1840	"	26.9	1875	Dec 28	21.6	1888	Aug 22	26
1847	"	26.9	1876	Jun	26	1889	Jun 1	24
1852	Apr 19	31.9	1876	Sep 19	23	1890	Mar 23	24.3
1860	" 12	29.7	1877	Jan 17	23.9	1891	Jan 3	23
1861	Sep 20	30.9	1877	Jul	25.6	1891	Feb 18	31.3
1862	Jan 20	28.7	1878	Dec 11	23.2	1892	Jan 15	22.9
1862	Apr 23	25	1879	Mar	20	1895	Jan 8	25.8
1865	Mar 4	24	1880	Feb	21.6	1895	Feb 7	24
1865	Mar 18	31.4	1881	" 11	23.4	1896	Jul 26	21.8
1865	Apr 1	21.6	1881	Jun 10	27.1	1897	Feb 24	28.9
1865	May 12	21.6	1882	Jan 28	21	1898	Mar 24	28.5
1866	Feb 10	32	1883	Feb 3	28	1900	Nov 27	27.8
1868	Mar	22.6	1884	Feb 6	33.3	1901	Apr 21	27.4
1873	Dec 14	25.6	1885	Jan 17	23			

Following are some findings on the times of great flooding in the area. Very few of the publications or newspapers specifically centered or mentioned Moon/Center Township, but there were a few articles.

1810 – Known as the "Pumpkin Flood." Water was measured at thirty-two feet in Pittsburgh. The local streams and areas along the shores of the Ohio River in Moon Township experienced flooding situations due to the excessive rain. This flood received its nickname name due to the fact it is said there many pumpkins washed from farmers' fields and were floating around in the high water.

Feb, 1832 - The flooding that occurred at this time was the first to be found recorded in local papers. The *Beaver Argus* stated, "Such a scene has never before occurred in our neighborhood........" It went on to say that "many light buildings were carried away with hay and grain stacks and fences. The loss in the range where the water rose is incalculable." This tells me that many of the homesteads that were located lower or close to the Ohio River banks, as well as those along such streams as Raccoon Creek and other streams within Moon Township, would have also suffered substantial damages to crops, buildings, and homes due to the excessive rains that occurred.

Mar 18, 1852 - Pittsburgh once again measured thirty-one feet and nine inches of flood waters. They blamed this flood on the rapidly melting of snow from rains. The creeks and streams also overflowed their banks with the excessive water from the melting snow.

Aug 12, 1861 - These flood waters swept away several bridges. A rise in Big Beaver (Beaver River) swept away the C. & P. railroad bridge at Rochester, even destroying the piers.

Feb 5, 6, and 7, 1884 - This flood was considered one of the greatest, with rains causing snow to melt rapidly were again stated as the source for all the flooding. Jesse Smith kept a record in his hotel register at Smith's Ferry. He stated on *Feb 5 the water was nine feet; Feb 6, rained all night, water twenty-five feet and rising twelve inches per hour; Feb 7, river four feet in the house and three feet and ten inches higher than in 1852, fifteen inches higher than in 1832, and five feet higher than in 1810.* The reports stated rushing waters in Big Beaver (Beaver River) swept away the Fallston bridge. The bridge then lodged against the old wooden bridge at Bridgewater and both bridges were then swept against the C. & P. railroad bridge. The three bridges were then carried out into the Ohio River and crashed against the P & LE railroad bridge, tearing out many of the iron spans. (See picture further.)

Mar 15, 1907 - Extreme and rapid rain fall caused many of the local smaller creeks and streams to overflow their banks unexpectedly. Once these creeks and streams emptied into the rivers, they in turn began to overflow their banks at an alarming rate.

Sep 16, 1911 - The quickness of the rising waters due to the storm caused five empty barges belonging to the Ohio River Combine to break loose upriver but were caught by the Exporter and Voyager tow boats at dam No 5. The higher waters in the Beaver Falls area caused the Beaver River to also flood. Over a forty feet section of the woodwork at the Tenth street bridge in the Beaver River went down with a crash due to the volumes of water pressing against it. The middle section of the dam gave way also, and the entire dam was weakened.

Jan and Apr 1913 - 1913 had a particularly wet start due to rains and melting snow. There were several occasions of localized flooding events.

Mar 23, 1913 - There were multiple periods of rain in the area, but on Easter Sunday, Mar 23, 1913, devastating rains hit the area. Threats of flooding were feared since for two weeks before the rains on this day, the area had been victim to intense storms. With the rains that hit on that March day, the streams and soon, the rivers were all spilling out over their banks at an alarming rate. Bridges were once again threatened, many roadways, railroad tracks, and properties were all underwater before anyone realized what was happening.

Nov/Dec 1921 - On Nov 29, 1921, it was announced that for the first time in many years a November flood was threatening the lowlands of Beaver County as the Ohio River had passed the flood stage. It was expected to reach a crest of 34 or 35 feet by that evening at Merrill Dam in Vanport. With the river rising, that meant that all secondary streams and creeks had been cresting and exceeding their banks also.

Fall, 1932 - As with many of the other periods of flooding, excessive rain caused the creeks and streams to quickly rise, resulting in multiple claims of basements flooding, fields and crops being destroyed, and many other personal properties being destroyed by water damage.

May 1935 - The first day of May in 1935, *The Daily Times* was warning Beaver County residents that due to the current heavy rains, the Allegheny and Monongahela Rivers were feeding excessive water into the Ohio River. The Ohio River was rising at an alarming rate of .25 feet an hour. It was reported that a 16-foot stage was existing at the U.S. Lock No. 6 near Vanport, with a 25-foot crest expected. They stated that if the flood stage was reached, it would be the first of the season and the first in recent years. The biggest concern was that it would be sufficient to flood the coffer style dam at the construction site of the new Montgomery Island Dam.

St Patrick's Day Flood – 1936 - When elderly local people refer to a flood, it usually goes back to the "Great St. Patrick Day Flood" that occurred in 1936. No one alive today can relay the tales of previous flooding events to the local communities. So, the 1936 flood is the only one where tales can still be shared from personal experiences or from children of those who related the information to them. This flood is included in one of the worse to have occurred in Beaver County.

After a horrible winter freeze that still left the ground frozen solid, heavy March rains moved in and continued relentlessly. All the rainwater along with the melting rushed into the creeks, then into the rivers, both causing the flooding of local residents. This flood caused millions of dollars in damages and many deaths. More than 60 people died in Pittsburgh, 25 died in Johnston, and Beaver County reported a 17-year boy died in Aliquippa. Monaca's Water Works building also took another hit from this flood. Unfortunately, the Montgomery Dam was still not completed (not until Aug 1936) and therefore was not able to provide the planned defensive measures to help with this great flood.

Jan 1952 - The flooding in Jan 1952 was reported to have inundated 1,000,000 acres of farmland in five states, including Pennsylvania, Ohio, and West Virginia. Along with the flooding, there was also a weather front that moved in and brought snow and icy winds to add to the area residents' problems. One report stated that the property damage "would remain absolutely incalculable" until actual evaluations could be made with manual inspections.

The Ohio River crested at Montgomery Island Dam at 27.8 feet in the upper pool and 39.4 in the lower pool (25 feet was considered flood stage). Many of the major roads had to close either due to high water or numerous landslides. Two barges in the Ohio River broke loose in the high water also, as well as one at Kobuta. Raccoon Creek overflowed its banks causing damage to dozens of homes along the creek and in other low-lying areas. The local newspaper reported many farm residents were isolated for a time after Raccoon Creek spilled over its banks, submerging, if not washing away roadways.

1952
Flood waters from Raccoon Creek flooded not only roads, but many homes and properties.
Just goes to show that owning a horse in the mid 1900s was still definitely beneficial.

Oct 1954 - In mid Oct 1954, it was reported in the Beaver Valley Times that the heaviest rains of the year caused the rivers and streams to flow over their banks. The flooding was causing disruption in telephone and electric power, flooded highways, cellars to be flooded, and quite a bit of widespread damage to all the low-lying areas. Some roadways were even washed out or blocked by mud. There were many land sides and many reports of crop damage.

In addition to the heavy rains, there were high winds that also broke off and/or uprooted numerous trees which in turn caused road blockage and damages to homes and other structures. Montgomery Dam moved machinery to higher ground. This was to be the first time that buildings at the dam had been flooded since Jan 1952. 3.36 inches of rain fell between 7 am Friday and 7 am Saturday (Oct 15 & 16, 1954). The river crested at 28 feet – 2 feet above flood stage by evening on Oct 16.

Mar 3, 1955 - Due to high waters and strong currents in the river, 6 barges, each loaded with 900 tons of coal, broke loose from the Colona Dock at Monaca. They were carried about three miles down the Ohio before five of them were caught within a short time and returned to their moorings. The crew of the diesel boat, Gateway, owned by Bill Grimm Company of Pittsburgh was in the vicinity and caught the barges. The crew of the LaBelle, a Wheeling Steel Corporation diesel also helped. One of the six barges hit a pier of the Monaca-Rochester highway bridge and sank near the P & L E railroad bridge. Roads along the creeks and streams in the township were impassable due to high water, others because of deep mud.

Mar 6, 1963 - Creeks and streams in the township once again spilled over their banks and many properties were damaged. The creeks and streams fed into the Ohio and caused it to exceed its depth. High waters once again caused a barge loaded with coal to break loose from docks at the Conway Yards and was carried down the Ohio River crashing into a pier of the Monaca-East Rochester Toll bridge.

Jan 19 and 20, 1996 - A blizzard just a week prior put down an average of thirty inches of snow that blanketed most of Pennsylvania, then a freak weather condition occurred. The temperatures warmed almost overnight and with this weather front, in a matter of hours on Friday, Jan 19, a cloud burst dumped between two and five inches of rain over almost all of Pennsylvania. The rain melted the snow so rapidly that flooding was the only logical outcome. Ice jams were common with large, car sized, frozen chunks of ice acting as battering rams, smashing anything in their path. By Saturday, Jan 20th, the rains had stopped. The Ohio River's levels actually dropped a little giving all the false security of relief. Ice jams in all the local streams had only begun to break up, letting them stop spilling over their banks and start to flow freely. Once again, their excessive waters reached the Ohio, and the second flood began, and the waters rose so rapidly that even old-time river officials were amazed. Flooding and ice jams not only caused damage in Center Township, but also in Beaver County towns and other townships all along the Ohio River, as well as in downtown Pittsburgh.

Nov 30, 2003 - Heavy rains were once again the cause for numerous properties to be flooded throughout the township, including flooding of numerous roads. The Ohio River waters rose and caused damages in the path of its rushing waters. There were 20 runaway barges that broke loose close to Ambridge that made their way down the river hurtling past several bridges and smashing boat docks. Immediately, the police and firefighters were told to close the Ambridge-Aliquippa Bridge, the East Rochester-Monaca Bridge, and the Rochester-Monaca Bridge while the sand and gravel filled barges tore down river past the bridges. None of the barges struck the three bridges, but one barge bumped into the CSX Railroad Bridge but caused no damage. The Vanport Bridge was also closed as the barges continued down the river. The barges were finally rounded up by towboats in the Potter Township area. None of these barges reached the Montgomery Dam.

Sep 19, 2004 – Over 6 inches of rain fell due to the remnants of Hurricane Ivan and caused swollen creeks in the township to spill their banks.

May 5, 2011
There were widespread heavy rains that caused flooding in the Ohio River Valley.

Other than the one photograph of flooding from the Raccoon Creek (see previous), I found no early photographs specifically of Moon/Center Township with flooding results from the very early years. The County Home which was situated along the banks of the Ohio River and records state the Home suffered many flooding events.

The following several photographs will reflect how severe and damaging flooding of the Ohio River could be. They show the aftermath from flooding, including damages to the P&LE railroad bridge in Monaca. Even though this bridge may not have been in the township, the pictures help reflect how distructive these waters would have been to lowly homes and barns, not to mention properties and crops in the township further down river if <u>metal</u> bridges could be destroyed.

Photo from Monaca Borough
There was no date attached to this photo, but it shows how high the flood water was on the Monaca Water Works building during one of the numerous flooding events over the years.

The next pictures are of what was left of the original Monaca-Beaver P & LE railroad bridge after the flood in 1884 destroyed it, along with 3 other local bridges. This photo was taken after the flood waters receded some and was taken looking from the Beaver side of the river toward Monaca. Note the men standing on the tracks in the lower left of the photo, no doubt evaluating and inspecting the damage. Also note the house(s)/buildings in the upper right of the photograph, along with all the other debris that appear to have been swept down by the flood waters.   Remember, this was not a wooden bridge, but instead a wrought iron bridge, built in 1878. (It was the first railroad bridge from Monaca to Beaver, and the P & LE railroad referenced the repaired/ replacement bridge as the "second" with the current railroad bridge being considered the "third" bridge between Beaver and Monaca.)

Courtesy Beaver County Genealogy Center

Photo from History of Beaver County, Pennsylvania and Its Centennial Celebration
View of damages to the 1878 railroad bridge before flood waters totally receded.

Photo from Transactions of the American Society of Civil Engineers
(Left) 1890 single track bridge that replaced the wrought iron bridge built in 1878 which was destroyed by the flood in 1884.
(Right) The new 1910 double track cantilever railroad bridge.

Fun fact: Just for those interested, in conjunction with the above bridge information…….
The photograph above was taken from the Sylvan Crest area showing all three of the railroad bridges that have existed through the years. All these bridges were built to cross the Ohio River between Monaca and Beaver. This photograph shows the still exposed original piers of the bridge destroyed by the 1884 flood (look just to the right of the smaller bridge), then the "second" bridge that was built to replace the damaged bridge (the smaller of the two bridges), along with the current, larger railroad bridge. The piers of the first 1878 bridge (flooded/damaged) and then the entire structure and piers of the "second" single track bridge built in 1890 were eventually all removed shortly after the current railroad bridge (larger one - on the right) was completed in 1910.

~ ~ ~

WAR TIMES

When it comes to listing persons who served in any given conflict, it is not a simple task to just say "the following persons served from Center Township." One must remember that in the earlier years, residency was most often simply listed as *South Side* in Beaver County which included not just Moon/Center Township, but also known to include Hanover, Greene, Raccoon, Potter, Hopewell, and Independence. Even when information is provided for Moon Township, remembering the vast area the original Moon Township once covered, it leaves the door open to include persons from Raccoon, Potter, Hopewell, and Monaca, and again, not just the current Center Township area. Then, even after the time of the formal establishment of Center Township through to current years, there is still difficulty in determining a residency with there being two post offices that service the township - Aliquippa and Monaca. Seldom can a search for information be made simply by entering "Center Township." I am stating all this to clarify how difficult it was to obtain names of just township residents who served in all the military conflicts through the years. It may also help readers realize why many times throughout this book I may have included a wide range of areas when providing various information.

Revolutionary War

The Revolutionary War was fought between 1775 and 1783. It was initiated with the growing tensions between the thirteen North American colonies who were still under Great Britain rule and that of the colonial government (represented the British crown). The British government was trying to raise revenue and was taxing the colonies (the Stamp Act of 1765, the Townshend Tariffs of 1767, and the Tea Act of 1773). The colonists began to protest these taxes because they did not have representation in Parliament or other rights of other British subjects who were also being taxed. Then British soldiers killed five men when they opened fire on a mob of colonists (the Boston Massacre) in 1770. This prompted a group of Bostonians, dressed as Mohawk Indians, to board some British ships and dump 352 chests of tea into the Boston Harbor. Great Britain then tried to reassert imperial authority by passing a series of measures (the Intolerable, or Coercive Acts).

A group of colonial delegates (including George Washington, Samuel Adams, Patrick Henry, John Jay) met in Sep 1774 which led to the First Continental Congress. This Congress did not demand independence from Britain but instead denounced taxation without representation. They declared the rights due every American citizen, including "life, liberty, property, assembly, and trial by jury." This Continental Congress took a vote to meet once again in May 1775 to make decisions on further actions, violence had already begun and in essence the war was starting.

Apr 1775 is the date most associated with when the Revolutionary War was started. It began as essentially a civil war, then France entered into the conflict, aiding the colonist in 1778. This made it an international war. The Americans won their independence when the British surrendered at Yorktown, Virginia in 1781, yet the fighting did not officially end until 1783.

It is an almost impossible task to obtain a complete list of all the soldiers of this Revolutionary War who already had established a homestead or would later have made their homes in Moon Township or even Beaver County. Some have been identified and verified as becoming township residents, but this list is very short in comparison to the many that served in the war. There are a few names found in the *The History of Beaver County, Pennsylvania - 1888*, that were known to have settled in Moon Township. Robert Agnew, George Bruce, William Cassidy, Michael Chrisler, Zachariah Figley, and David Scott to name a few. There are many others that can be identified with generally settling throughout Beaver County, but none of those names specifically state "Moon Township." Thankfully, many of these soldiers are now personally honored by members of various groups who have traced their lineage back to these patriots.

Fun fact: Did you know...............
….. Paul Revere did not make his famous "ride" on Apr 18, 1775 alone. William Dawes and Samuel Prescott rode along with him, as well as an estimated forty more men who joined in along the way.

Fun fact: Did you know…………
….. Women, African Americans, and Native Americans all also fought for the Revolutionary War cause. It is reported that thousands of women traveled with the Continental army working as laundresses, cooks, nurses, and even spies or couriers. Some even took over for wounded husbands on the battlefields.

War of 1812 (1812 – 1815)

Prior to the erection of Center Township, many residents of Beaver County participated in the early conflicts. Beaver County as a whole was a strong supporter of General Abner Lacock in the War of 1812. The residents actively supported his beliefs for the maintenance of American rights and honor. There were no troops called out from Beaver County during the first two years of this war, but still county men came forward to serve in the militia when the Erie lake frontier was threatened in 1814.

There were two regiments of militia represented - the 138th and the 26th. *The History of Beaver County, Pennsylvania – 1888*, had the following listed as the men of these regiments, but remember, these names include men from all the areas of the "South Side" and not specifically from Moon/Center Township.

Captain Robert Lieper's company, 138th regiment. It was recruited on the "South Side." Captain, Robert Lieper; lieutenant, John Warnick; ensign, Joseph Calhoun; sergeants, David Wilson, Henry Davis, Noah Potts, Erastus Rudd; corporals, Joseph Brown, Aaron Sutton, Thomas Barnes, Thomas Potts; privates, Allen, Solomon; Applegate, David; Brunton, Thomas; Barnes, Thomas; Brown, George; Butler, George; Beals, William; Creegthon, John; Crain, Adonijah; Douglas, Nathaniel; Ferguson, Hans; Grimes, James; Gilliland, John; Hamilton, James; Hannah, Alex.; Hovington, Zenas; Henry, Hays; Hamilton, James; Latter, William; Lewis, John; Liper, William; McElheny, Robert; McCray, James; McHenry, Charles; McCune, William; Moore, Robert; McCure, Thomas; Nelson, John; Odell, John; Parkinson, James; Patterson, Guy; Reed, William; Reed, Alex.; Richmond, John; Seeley, Samuel; Stone, Jackson; Smith, Jr. John; Smith, John; Shane, Cornelius; Santel, Alpha; Smith, James; Shively, Jacob; Thomasburg, John; Veasey, Elisha; Vincent, Thomas; Withrow, Thomas; Wood, Silas; Wilson, James.

The roll of this company is certified by William McCune, lieutenant; and yet no record exists of his promotion from private to lieutenant. In the receipt roll for the period from February 23 to March 23, he is reported as lieutenant.

Captain William Calhoun's company, 138th regiment. Recruited on the "South Side": Captain, William Calhoun; lieutenant, Thomas Hartford; ensign, Benjamin Laughlin; sergeants, Thomas Sevaney, Daniel Heckathorn, Adam Gibb, Robt. Neilson, Patrick Caughey; corporals, Jonathan Grimståw, Andrew Hayes, William McCullough, James Allison; privates, Allison, James; Bear, Charles; Butler, Abiah; Baker, George; Carson, William; Clear, George; Cunnington, Clifford; Caughey, Patrick; Douglass, John; Decker, Daniel; Farrat, William; Foush, Michael; Ford, Eli; Hodge, William; Hall, James; Hartford, Thomas; Hight, Aaron; Hamilton, John; Jamison, William; Justice, Joseph; Kinners, James; Lockhart, Hiram; Lockhart, Allen; Laughlin, Wilson; Laird, William; Laird, John; Laughlin, Benjamin; Langfit, James; Mercer, Nottingham; McCauley, Hugh; Miller, Samuel; McCullough, Wm.; Myers, George; Neilson, Robert; Neilson, William; Patten, Robert; Patten, James; Patten, William; Skillen, Hugh; Sevaney, John; Snyder, Jacob S; Shafer, Anthony; Sands, Andrew; Swaney, Thomas; Swany, Thomas; Thompson, Benj.; Thompson, James; Woods, William; Weitzell, Henry; Willoughby, Charles; Wilson, Wm.

It will be seen that Thomas Hartford was promoted from private to be lieutenant; Patrick Caughey to be sergeant, and James Allison to be corporal, after the first month's service.

Captain Robert Imbrie's company, being 2d Company, 1st Battalion, 26th regiment, Pennsylvania Militia; commanded by Major Andrew Jenkins; served at Erie from 15 February to 23 March, 1814: Captain, Robert Imbrie; lieutenant, James Henry; ensign, James Veasey; sergeants; A. M'Kinnon, William Moore, John M'Cormick: corporals, William Roland, James Ferrel, John M'Coy, William Hammond; privates, Anderson, Thomas; Bottomfelt, Samuel; Bolliner, Simon; Bell, John, Jr.; Bell, John; Bower, Samuel; Boyd, William; Boyd, Andrew; Brown, John; Cristler, George; Caston, William; Caldoo, James; Clark, James; Cochran, James; Cyphey, David; Dermon, John; Daugherty, Richard; Daugherty, George; Eckles, Thomas; Eckles, John; Fisner, John; Fowler, Archibald; Fegans, John; Holmes, Joseph; Hutchinson, William; Hickey, John; Harvey, James; Hawk, John; Hawk, Jonathan; Hawk, Benjamin; Hinds, John; Harper, David; Imbrie, James; Irvin, James; Junkins, Samuel; Johnson, John; Jack, Thomas; Laughlin, Samuel; Little, William; Little, James; Leonard, Hull; Madison, Samuel; Matthews, Duncan; McDowell, John; McDevit, Henry; Miller, Joseph; Manon, James; McMurray, James; Miller, Moses; Moore, James; McNeal, James; McBride, Samuel; McGowan, Ebenezer; Melony, Henry; Newton, John; Naymen, Daniel; Parks, Thomas; Park, David; Pollock, James; Pollock, Samuel; Roger, Jacob; Reed, Matthew; Scott, Thomas; Semple, Robert; Sharp, John; Shaffer, Jacob; Summerwell, John; Smith, Andrew; Simpson, William; Shaffer, Peter; Scott, George; Smith, Benjamin; Slater, Jacob; Vancokle, Richard; White, Samuel.

Fact: During this war, monthly pay to soldiers was quite modest, Captain-$40, Lieutenant-$30, Ensign-$20, Sergeant-$12, Corporal-$11, and Private-$10.

Also found in *The History of Beaver County, Pennsylvania – 1888*, was a copy of the original handbill that at the time was in the possession of Carnegie Library, Pittsburgh. This is just further evidence of how the local men did support the efforts in 1812.

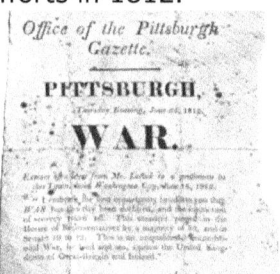

The small print on this handbill included,
PITTSBURGH,
Thursday Evening, June 25, 1812
WAR.
Extract of a letter from Mr. Lacock to a gentleman in
this Town, dated Washington City, June 18, 1812.

"I embrace the first opportunity to inform you that WAR has this day been declared, and the injunction of secrecy taken off. This measure passed in the House of Representatives by a majority of 30, and in Senate 19 to 13. This is an unqualified, unconditional War, by land and sea, against the United Kingdoms of Great-Britain and Ireland."

Mexican-American War (1846-1848)

Very soon after his election as President, James Polk made an offer to purchase much of the land that is currently the U.S. Southwest. His offer to purchase this land was rejected. Between 1844 and 1845, he then instigated a fight by moving troops into the disputed area between the Rio Grande and Nueces River (at that time, part of Mexico). This started the conflicts between Mexico, Texas, and the United States. As the hostilities continued between Mexico, Texas, and the United States, and with U. S. casualties occurring, on May 13, 1847, Congress declared that "by act of the

Republic of Mexico, a state of war exists between that government and the United States." On that date, President Polk was then authorized to accept fifty thousand volunteers and was appropriated ten million dollars.

Beaver County was largely made up of Whigs who were opposed to the necessity of the war, while the Democrats, as a rule, were in favor of it. There were no companies or other organizations who went to Mexico directly listed as being from Beaver County however, a few individuals did go through Pittsburgh to join and give their support. A soldier of the Mexican War, William Thomas of Philadelphia, is buried in the old graveyard in Beaver. Donations were collected for the erection of a tombstone for Mr. Thomas. The top of the tombstone is broken off obliquely, to indicate the premature death of the soldier. William had been a member of Captain Joseph Hill's company (D), 1st Pennsylvania volunteers.

This was the first armed conflict that was mainly fought on foreign soil. At the conclusion of this war, Mexico had lost close to one-third of its territory which includes all present-day California, Utah, Nevada, Arizona, and New Mexico.

Fact: Gold was discovered in California just days before Mexico ceded the land to the United States in the Treaty of Guadalupe Hidalgo (signed Feb 2, 1848).

Civil War   aka   The War of the Rebellion (1861 - 1865)

This war saw more than five million soldiers come forward to serve within the United States, half a million lost their lives. On Feb 4, 1861, there was a convention, "The People's Meeting," held at the courthouse in Beaver. This convention was held to determine the sentiment of the Beaver County people as to the development of this war. Following are snippets taken directly from *The History of Beaver County, Pennsylvania – 1888*.

> Great activity was manifested by the advocates of the two parties to secure a large attendance of their adherents. The Democrats had the advantage in that they secured the organization of the meeting, they having had the president, all the vice-presidents but two, and both the secretaries. Hon. Joseph Irwin was chairman; James Wallace, Henry Alcorn, Thomas Conway, Boston Grove, Ephraim Jones, Levi Barnes, Jacob Wagner, John Graham, William Leaf, William F. Lafferty, Robert Russell, Elwood Thomas and David Stanton—the last two Republicans—were vice-presidents, and Robert Potter and N. C. Barclay were secretaries.
>
> Lewis Taylor and N. P. Fetterman, both Democrats, had been selected to address the meeting. These being both absent, S. B. Wilson, Esq., was chosen to perform that duty, which he did in his usual forcible manner.
>
> The Republicans having meantime assembled in vast numbers, Richard P. Roberts, one of their number, was loudly called to make a speech, and responded in an address of an hour and a half.
>
> A series of resolutions was read by S. B. Wilson, Esq., and voted upon, against the protests of the Republicans. They were anti coercion anti-abolition, anti-war, etc. After they were passed the Democratic officials withdrew, leaving the Republicans to reorganize, and pass a series of resolutions, which are thus reported in the *Argus:*
>
> *Resolved,* That it is the duty of the Federal government to protect the Federal property, and execute the Federal laws, and for these purposes to employ all means at its disposal.
>
> *Resolved,* That the imposition of the institution of slavery upon the people of a territory against their will, or without consent, whether by congressional legislation, or constitutional enactment, is in direct conflict with the spirit and purpose of a republican form of government.

Resolved, That any statute of any state which conflicts with the constitution or laws of the United States should be repealed.

Resolved, That we are opposed to any interference with the institution of slavery in the states where it now exists, or by which it may hereafter be legalized, either by the federal congress or by the free states, or by illegal individual enterprise, such as was exemplified in the murderous fray of John Brown against Virginia.

Resolved, That the thanks of the nation are due to our President, James Buchanan, for the promptness with which he extricated himself from the ruinous policy into which he had been misled by traitors; for purging his cabinet of their presence, and for surrounding himself by such patriotic and competent advisers as Holt, Scott, Dix and Stanton, in whose statesmanship and fidelity to the Union all parties can confide.

Resolved, That, since the purchase of Florida and Louisiana territories by the government of the United States was to secure unmolested commerce in the Gulf, and the free navigation of the Mississippi and its tributaries as transits to the ocean, and since their maintenance as territories and states has been secured only by the lavish expenditure of the blood and treasure of the whole nation, the recent revolutionary acts of levying war, and by coercion seizing and holding the forts and arsenals, hospitals and treasury of the United States, forcibly driving the United States troops from the other property of the United States, dishonoring the national flag in the eyes of the world, is treasonable in character and in violation of the equality, fraternity and common rights of all the states, and thus imposes the patriotic duty of the people of all the states, as citizens of the United States, to rally to the common defense of our common Union and the constitution.

The records of the period are not complete; but in the *Western Star* of April 26, 1861, thirteen days after the firing on Fort Sumter, we find an account of the great meeting held at Beaver, on the 22d of April, to meet the imperative demands of the hour. The meeting was organized by electing the following officers:

President—Hon. Daniel Agnew. *Vice presidents*—Hon. Joseph Irvin, Hon. William Cairns, Major Thomas McCreery, Moses Doak, Dr. John McCarroll, Archibald Robertson, Isaac Covert, Daniel Dawson, Robert Douthett, Moses Hendrickson, Hon. John Scott, Andrew Watterson, B Wilde, Dr. M. Lawrence, John Graebing, Robert Wallace, William D. Eakin, Major R. Darragh, Major David Warnock, Thomas McClure, Thornton Shinn, Dr. Parmer. *Secretaries*—Henry Hice, P. L. Grim, W. B. Lemon, S. Davenport, J. Trimble.

A committee of seven, namely, B. B. Chamberlin, Jno. Allison, Thos. McClure, R. P. Roberts, S. B. Wilson, Archibald Robertson and P. L. Grim, was appointed to prepare business for the meeting, and then adjourned. On reassembling, David Critchlow sang that patriotic and soul-stirring song, the Marseillaise hymn, after which the committee submitted the following report, which was unanimously adopted:

WHEREAS, The government under which we live, and which has secured to our fathers and to us the rights guaranteed by the constitution adopted by the patriots of the revolution, under the genial protection of which the American people have enjoyed a greater amount of happiness and a higher degree of personal liberty and prosperity than has ever been vouchsafed to any nation upon earth, is now assailed by an organized band of traitors, who threaten its destruction and the subversion of the constitution; and whereas, an army of rebels from the Southern states is now marching upon the national capital for the purpose of usurping the powers of government, it therefore becomes the duty of every citizen who loves his country, and whose heart beats with patriotic emotion, to manifest his patriotism by promptly uniting with our fellow-citizens of other states and communities, in sustaining the constitution and laws of our country, and in every legal and constitutional manner vindicate the authority and majesty of the government, either by taking up arms in its defense, or by aiding such of our patriotic citizens who may volunteer to serve in the armies of the Republic; therefore

>   *Resolved,* That a general county committee of safety composed of one hundred men be appointed, for the purpose of considering the duties devolving upon all loyal citizens, in any emergency that may arise during the civil war now raging between the constituted authorities of the nation and the aggressive and rebellious states; and that also the organization of local committees be recommended in different localities of the county.
>
>   *Resolved,* That a home military organization be recommended in every locality of the county, and that in view of the emergencies now arising, all encouragement be extended to the formation of volunteer corps, to act on requisition of the general and state authorities.
>
>   *Resolved,* That a committee of six persons be appointed in each election district of the county to see that the families of our noble, brave and patriotic citizens who may volunteer to serve our common country be properly cared for and protected during the absence of their natural protectors, and that we unitedly pledge our sacred honors and fortunes to enable said committee to carry this resolution into effect.
>
>   *Resolved,* That the president of this meeting appoint and announce the above committees at his earliest convenience.

There was a District Committee appointed by the chairman in pursuance with one of the resolutions (listed above). A few of the names on that committee appear familiar within known Moon Township residents. Remember that during this time period, the boundaries of the townships were still "floating" quite a bit so I have included all the names listed not only in Moon Township, but also from a few of the surrounding townships. (Names are spelled as found.)

> D. B. Short, John Davis, Daniel Figley, Milo Reed, Hill Douds, Robert Cooper, Harry Alcorn, William McBriar (all of Moon Township); Robert Moffit, James Smith, R.R. Gamble, Alexander Ewing, Samuel Kennedy, and James Hall (all of Raccoon Township); James Sterling, Henry Reed, Dr. A. R. Thomson, William Reed, Alexander Gibb, Benjamin Butler, William Butler, William McCoy, Thomas Standish (all of Independence Township); Robert Duncan, Robert C. Scott, James Irons, G. K. Shannon, Thomas McKee, John R. McCune, William A. Thomson, James Jordan (all of Hopewell Township); and Francis LeGoullon, G. Trompeter, John M. Shrodes, Lawrence F. Schaffer, Joseph Bentel, Peter Markay (all of Phillipsburg).

This District Committee of safety was instrumental in helping with enlistments and aiding in the caring of the families of those who did enlist in service. Each member of this committee took an oath or affirmation – "You and each of you do swear by Almighty God, the searcher of all hearts (or affirm) that you will support the constitution of the United States, and the constitution of Pennsylvania, and that you will maintain, support and defend the government of the United States against treason and rebellion." May 17, 1861, among the area men, the following companies were reported. From Phillipsburg, was Capt. Andrew Simon with 60 men, and from Raccoon, Capt. James Smith with 45 men. Most of these men, however, were without arms.

Again, no single list of the men who enlisted specifically from Moon Township was available. All listings found were those of individual Companies and Regiments of all the Pennsylvania Volunteers and each very lengthy, therefore I have not included them in this book. The regiments all seemed to be represented by Beaver County men, all blended with other counties and even other states and therefore were difficult to impossible to correctly distinguish. I recommend that if you have an ancestor from the county who served in this war, that you obtain a copy of the *The History of Beaver County, Pennsylvania including Its Early Settlement - 1888* or one of many other publications to peruse.

This is a copy of a handbill as printed in *The History of Beaver County* for a meeting that was held in the Court House. Since the statement on this handbill was very interesting, a transcription of the very small print on the handbill is included further.

Fellow Citizens, arouse! The rest of Peace is broken. War's alarms are upon us. We are threatened with immediate invasion by the South. The news of the last twenty-four hours is exciting, and informs us that following speedily upon the fall of Sumter, by the hands of the insurgents, Virginia has seceded. The armory at Harper's Ferry has been seized, and an army is about moving to invade the Capital of the Nation. In a few hours Washington may be in the hands of the enemy. Immediate action is necessary for the protection of our homes and the soil of our country. At a large meeting held in the Court House, the undersigned were appointed a Committee to call a Public Meeting of the citizens of the county at the

COURT HOUSE,

on MONDAY, April 22nd, 1861, at 11 o'clock, A. M. to take immediate measures for a thorough organization of the Military of the County.

COME ONE. COME ALL:

the danger is imminent. Immediate action is imperative.

THOMAS CUNNINGHAM, DANIEL AGNEW, THOMAS McCREERY, R. P. ROBERTS, WM. B. CLARKE, JOS. C. WILSON, JAMES DARRAGH, S. B. WILSON, SAMUEL DAVENPORT, B. B. CHAMBERLIN.

A Company of Riflemen for immediate service is now being organized. Persons desirous of joining will report themselves at the Prothonotary's Office.

BRIGHTON TIMES PRINT

World War I
(Jul 28, 1914 until Nov 11, 1918)

World War I, also known as the *First World War* and/or the *Great War,* involved the Allies which included most of the nations of Europe along with Russia, the United States, the Middle East, and other regions against the Central Powers. The Central Powers included mainly Germany, Austria-Hungary, and Turkey. In WWI, the United States' allies in Europe, as well as the U.S. soldiers were facing starvation. The allies' farmers were participating in the war, or most farmlands had been turned into battlefields. Herbert Hoover was appointed to be head of a newly developed U.S. Food Administration by President Woodrow Wilson. Mr. Hoover was to develop a plan to manage wartime, distribute, and transport supplies. He developed the voluntary program which relied on Americans to show their compassion and their sense of patriotism to make the program work. His plan included having Americans voluntarily conserving food and other supplies.

Center Township was a little over three years from being formed when WWI began. All United States citizens were urged to participate in the war efforts and local newspapers and publications seemed to be the major form of spreading the word and providing the information to the general public. Moon Township (Center and Potter Township) residents proved to be just as patriotic and supportive during all the military conflicts of the nations as all other adjacent towns and communities and all-American citizens. They participated in the rationing programs and the War Bond programs and even those few residents without farmland or acreage participated with Victory Gardens. For anyone who does not know about the rationing programs, there is a shortened portion on them further on in this section, as well as some examples of the advertising and actual rationing materials.

Church services encouraged members of congregations to donate blood which would be used in saving the lives of thousands of wounded service men. Savings and loan associations were authorized to act as agents in the distribution of Defense Bonds. Entertainment establishments in the township and other areas would coordinate admissions through war bond purchases to help do their part in support of the war. There were rallies and residents encouraged to attend and purchase Defense Bonds /War Bonds and Stamps. All citizens were encouraged to postpone spending and refrain from the buying of goods which demanded materials and labor from all businesses who should be concentrating on supporting the war effort. Although not officially enforced, the U.S. government repeatedly reminded citizens to voluntarily conserve and/or save in general as their part of the war effort. Rationing was not actually enforced until the WWII years.

World War I Service Men

The Beaver County History Research and Landmark Foundation was fortunate enough to have received a copy of the book *Beaver Valley Towns in the World War*. This book listed residents from the following towns who served during WW I: *Beaver Falls, New Brighton, Rochester, Beaver, Monaca, Freedom, Conway, Ambridge, Woodlawn,* and *Other Nearby Places*. I felt it important to include a portion of this information in this section of the book. Unfortunately, I do not know of any similar publication for all those who served in the Korea, WW II, Vietnam, or any other wars or conflicts or I would have absolutely included them in this section also. More than 4.7 million Americans served during WWI. There were 116,516 Americans who died in WWI and more than 204,000 Americans who returned home wounded.

Please note – I have only copied and included pages from Chapter V of the above-mentioned book because this section had all the combined names (alphabetically) of all the service men from the Moon/Center Township, Monaca, Monaca Heights, Colona, Georgetown, Hookstown, and Ohioville areas. I am certain you will agree that when this book was published, it was an effort of love and respect for the War History Society to accumulate all this information and publish it to share and honor these service men.

Anyone interested in genealogy will find the following pages quite interesting with not only the names listed, but also some individual information for those listed. Some of the men listed have specifically where they were living, others have no location, thus the reason I simply included all the pages rather than try to extract names. On Page 2 in this book there is no date of publication, author, nor publishing company. It simply stated:

> "Compilers' Note
>
> *We present here with "Beaver Valley Towns in the World War."*
>
> *This work is to commemorate the part of local towns in the winning of the Great War, and we trust it will meet with the approval of all who may review its pages.*
>
> *Authentic war records, such as appear in this book, will form the most valuable data concerning the history of the days of 1917 and 1918. the canvass was made by an experienced force of representatives and no expense was spared to make the work as complete and accurate as possible. Whatever may be lacking comes not from want of honest endeavor on our part.*
>
> *No attempt has been made to glorify one name at the expense of another. By design, all have been treated as nearly as possible in the same way, a fact that may possibly be appreciated more sincerely by the service men themselves than by any others. We trust that this history will be loved by children in the days to come because it records fathers and brothers, uncles or cousins who gave their services to our country in the time of need.*
>
> *We extend our sincere thanks to the citizens of the communities, represented in this work who have shown their appreciation of the work by their patronage, also to those who so courteously assisted our representatives in collecting the information.*
>
> *We offer our book believing it serves a useful purpose. We trust it will be received in the same spirit in which it was compiled.*
>
> WAR HISTORY SOCIETY.
>   *Publishers*"

CHAPTER V

The following records are those of the service men of Monaca, Monaca Heights, Colona, Georgetown, Hookstown and Ohioville

ADAMS, JOSEPH A.—Born December 28, 1898. Son of Mr. Joseph Adams. Entered service April, 1917. Assigned to Columbus Barracks, Fort Wayne, Detroit and Camp Merritt. Attached to Medical Department. Went overseas in March, 1918. Returned in May, 1919. Honorably discharged June, 1919.

ALEXANDER, GEORGE McKINLEY—Born August 20, 1895. Son of Mr. William Alexander. Entered service in the United States Navy March, 1915. Assigned to Newport, R. I. Attached to U. S. S. Delaware. Saw service in France and England. December 1, 1919, still in service at Scotland.

ALLISON, HOMER M.—Born May 5, 1893. Son of Henry and Ada Allison of Georgetown, Pa. Entered service October 5, 1917. Assigned to Camp Sherman, Camp Mills, Camp Merritt and Camp Dix. Attached to Supply Company, 323rd Field Artillery, 83rd Division. Saw service at Grand Montagne, Argonne Forest. Honorably discharged May 27, 1919.

BARNETT, MAX H.—Born January 1889. Son of Mr. Morris Barnett. Entered service April 2, 1918. Assigned to Camp Lee. Attached to Company A, 319th Infantry, 80th Division. Went overseas May 17, 1918. Saw service at Meuse-Argonne. Wounded. Honorably discharged June 9, 1919, with the rank of Sergeant.

BARNETT, WILLIAM—Born March 1, 1891. Son of Mr. Morris Barnett. Entered service April 2, 1918. Assigned to Camp Lee and Newport News. Attached to Company D, 315th Machine Gun Battalion, 80th Division. Honorably discharged November 29, 1918.

BEAL, ERNEST D.—Born April 4, 1894. Son of Levi S. and Eva B. Beal, of Hookstown, Pa. Entered service June 26, 1918. Assigned to Camp Sherman and Camp Dix. Attached to Headquarters Company, 333rd Field Artillery, 79th Division. Went overseas September, 1918. Returned May 28, 1919. Honorably discharged June 4, 1919.

BEESON, HERBERT HAMPTON—Born August 12, 1892. Son of Mrs. Eva Hampton Beeson, of Cleveland, O. Assigned to Camp Hancock. Attached to Quartermaster Motor Transport Corps. Went overseas September 28, 1918. Returned February, 1919. Honorably discharged February 18, 1919, with rank of Second Lieutenant.

BEHARKA, JOHN—Born February 6, 1896. Son of Eva Beharka of Monaca. Entered the service October 7, 1917. Assigned to Camp Sherman, Camp Forrest and Camp Gordon. Attached to Company B, 17th Infantry. Honorably discharged January 22, 1919.

BELL, WILLIAM R.—Born October 18, 1888. Son of Mrs. J. A. Scott of Woodlawn, Pa. Entered service February 5, 1918. Assigned to Camp Sherman. Attached to Company F, 332nd Infantry, 83rd Division. Left for overseas June 8, 1918. Saw service in France and Italy. Returned April 14, 1919. Honorably discharged April 24, 1919.

BRANNON, JAMES CHARLES — Born October 21, 1900. Son of Mr. David Brannon of Monaca. Entered service April, 1919, in the United States Navy. Assigned to Newport, R. I. Attached to U. S. S. San Francisco. December 1, 1919, still in service.

BRECKENRIDGE, CLEMENS EHRENFELD—Born March 17, 1897. Son of Mr. and Mrs. William Breckenridge of Monaca. Entered service August 15, 1918. Assigned to University of Pittsburgh, Camp Jackson and Camp Meade. Attached to Battery E, 11th Field Artillery. Honorably discharged on January 6, 1919.

BROBECK, JAMES M.—Born February 28, 1890. Son of Mr. David Brobeck of Monaca. Entered the service February, 1917. Assigned to Camp Sherman and Camp Merritt. Attached to Central Record Office. Honorably discharged in June, 1919, holding the rank of Sergeant.

BROOKS, GEORGE—Born May 14, 1893. Entered the service April 25, 1918. Assigned to Camp Sherman, Camp Mills and Camp Upton. Attached to Company C, 308th Ammunition Train, 83rd Division. Left for overseas June 13, 1918. Saw service West of Meuse, Grand Montagne and East of the Meuse. Returned home April 27, 1919. Honorably discharged May 14, 1919.

BRYAN, WALLACE—Born May 10, 1882. Son of Robert M. and Belle S. Bryan of Hookstown, Pa. Entered the service June 23, 1917. Attached to Company G, 4th Infantry, 3rd Division. Participated in the battles at Marne Offensive, Chateau Thierry, St. Mihiel, Argonne and Verdun. Wounded. Honorably discharged.

BURNS, RALPH L.—Son of Mr. and Mrs. W. R. Burns of Colona, Pa. Entered the service September 18, 1917. Assigned to Camp Sherman. Attached to 304th Quartermaster Corps. Honorably discharged May 14, 1919.

BURNS, WILLIAM L.—Son of Mr. and Mrs. W. R. Burns, of Colona, Pa. Entered the service December 13, 1917. Assigned to Camp Sherman. Attached to Headquarters Company, 323rd Light Field Artillery, 32nd Division. Went overseas June 10, 1918. Saw service at Argonne, Grand Montagne and Meuse. Honorably discharged from the service May 27, 1919.

BUSANG, DAVID ALLEN—Born December 23, 1898. Son of Mr. Frank Busang. Entered service in July, 1917. Assigned to Gettysburg, Camp Greene, Camp Johnson and Newport News. Attached to Quartermaster Corps. Went overseas September, 1918. Returned July, 1919. Honorably discharged July, 1919, with rank of Corporal.

BUSANG, GEORGE WALTER — Born June 30, 1894. Son of Mr. William J. Busang of Cleveland, O. Entered the service April, 1918. Assigned to Camp Lee. Attached to Company A, 319th Infantry, 80th Division. Went overseas in May, 1918. Saw service at St. Mihiel and Meuse-Argonne. Wounded in action. Honorably discharged in June, 1919.

CLARKE, JAMES ALBERT — Born March 10, 1897. Son of Mr. and Mrs. James E. Clarke of Monaca. Entered service May, 1918. Assigned to Columbus Barracks and Camp Lee. Attached to Officers' Training School. Honorably discharged December, 1918.

CLARKE, RALPH GRAHAM—Born June 13, 1894. Son of Mr. and Mrs. James Clarke, Monaca, Pa. Entered service September 26, 1917. Assigned to Gettysburg, Camp Green and Camp Merritt. Attached to Company I, 60th Infantry, 3rd Division. Went overseas April 14, 1918. Wounded in the Argonne. Honorably discharged February 14, 1919, with rank of Sergeant.

CLOUGHLEY, ROBERT J.—Born September 1, 1899. Son of Robert and Mary Cloughley of Colona, Pa. Entered service May 6, 1918. Assigned to Fort Rodman. Attached to Battery E, 73rd Artillery. Went overseas September 25, 1918. Returned December 23, 1918. Honorably discharged December 30, 1918.

COENE, WADE M.—Born October 1, 1895. Son of Mr. Julius Coene of Monaca, Pa. Entered the service July, 1917. Assigned to Columbus, O., Kelly Field, Dayton and Wilbur Wright Field. Attached to Aviation. Honorably discharged March, 1919, holding the rank of Second Lieutenant.

COLLIGAN, JOHN J.—Born November 26, 1892. Son of James and Theresa Colligan, of Ironton, O. Entered service October 18, 1917. Assigned to Camp Hicks. Attached to 148th Aero Squadron. Went overseas February 26, 1918. Saw service at Somme. Returned March 24, 1919. Honorably discharged April 3, 1919.

CORNELIUS, FRANK H.—Born on July 4, 1898. Son of Mr. Vincent Cornelius of Monaca. Entered the service October, 1918. Assigned to University of Pittsburgh. Attached to Motor Transport, S. A. T. C. Honorably discharged December 10, 1918.

CREDE, LLOYD S.—Born May 5, 1893. Son of B. B. W. and Emma Crede of New Brighton, Pa Entered service November 21, 1917. Assigned to Princeton, N. J., Houston, Texas, San Leon, Texas. Attached to 96th Aero Squadron. Went overseas September 13, 1918. Returned February 6, 1919. Honorably discharged February 8, 1919, with rank of Second Lieutenant.

CURTIS, HARRISON—Born January 13, 1890. Son of Mrs. Harriet Curtis, of Monaca, Pa. Entered service April, 1918. Assigned to Camp Sherman, Camp Upton and Camp Dix. Attached to Company F, 802nd Pioneer Infantry. Went overseas August, 1918. Saw service at Verdun and Argonne Forest. Wounded. Honorably discharged April 15, 1919.

DALZELL, CLINTON, GEORGE — Born May 2, 1900. Son of Mr. William Dalzell, of Monaca. Entered service October 1, 1918. Assigned to University of Pittsburgh. Attached to S. A. T. C. Honorably discharged December 14, 1918.

DAVIS, EARL B.—Born December 17, 1892. Son of Mr. Frank Davis, Monaca, Pa. Entered service August 29, 1918. Assigned to Camp Lee and Camp Dix. Attached to 54th Guard Company, A. S. C. Went overseas October 14, 1918. Returned July 13, 1919. Honorably discharged July 18, 1919.

DELP, RONALD OTTO — Born March 22, 1896. Son of Mr. Turl Delp of Monaca. Entered service February 5, 1918. Assigned to Camp Sherman, Newark, N. J., and Camp Dix. Attached to Company G, 332nd Infantry. Honorably discharged May 14, 1919.

DINDINGER, FRANKLIN T.—Born February 13, 1890. Son of Mrs. Elizabeth Dindinger of Wampum, Pa. Entered the service August, 1918. Assigned to Fort Benjamin Harrison. Attached to Company A, 138th Engineers. Honorably discharged from the service December 18, 1918, with rank of Sergeant.

EBERHARDT, WILLIAM F.—Born January 9, 1894. Son of Mr. and Mrs. George Eberhardt, of Monaca, Pa. Entered the service December 14, 1917. Assigned to Camp Sherman. Attached to Company C, 158th Depot Brigade. Honorably discharged from the service December 10, 1918, with rank of Sergeant.

ELSTNER, RICHARD A.—Born on January 24, 1897. Son of Mr. and Mrs. Richard Elstner, Monaca, Pa. Entered the service August 29, 1918. Assigned to Camp Lee. Attached to Quartermaster Corps, Utilities Branch. Honorably discharged February 15, 1919, with rank of Sergeant.

ERB, GEORGE F.—Born May 13, 1891. Son of C. and Elizabeth Erb, of Monaca. Entered the service December 14, 1917. Assigned to Camps Sherman, Mills and Dix. Attached to Battery B, 323rd Field Artillery, 32nd Division. Went overseas June 10, 1918. Saw service at Meuse-Argonne and other battles. Honorably discharged May 27, 1919.

FANACCIA, JOSEPH—Born February, 1894. Son of Mr. and Mrs. Angelo Fanaccia, of Italy. Entered service February 6, 1918. Assigned to Camp Sherman and Camp Dix. Attached to 166th Ammunition Train, 41st Division. Went overseas March, 1918. Returned February, 1919. Honorably discharged March 4, 1919.

FAUST, GORDON LEE—Born June 23, 1893. Son of Mr. Phillip Faust, of Monaca. Entered service June 5, 1917. Assigned to Oakmont, Pittsburgh. Attached to Company F, 15th Engineers. Went overseas July 9, 1917. Saw service at St. Mihiel and Meuse-Argonne. Honorably discharged May 15, 1919 with rank of Corporal.

FAUST, HENRY LAIS—Born September, 1899. Son of Mr. Phillip Faust, of Monaca. Entered the service October 2, 1918. Assigned to Plattsburg, Pa. Attached to S. A. T. C. Honorably discharged December 23, 1918.

FINN, ROBERT—Born December 23, 1895. Son of Mr. Henry Finn, of Monaca, Pa. Entered the service May, 1917. Assigned to Camp Hancock. Attached to Company A, 18th Infantry. Honorably discharged November, 1918.

FLEISCHER, MICHAEL E. — Born March, 1897. Son of Mrs. Katherine Fleischer, of Monaca. Entered the service June 27, 1917. Assigned to Camp Hancock and Camp Dix. Attached to Headquarters Company, 108th Machine Gun Battalion. Went overseas May 3, 1918. In active service. Returned May 16, 1919. Honorably discharged May 26, 1919, with rank of Wagoner.

FOLLAND, WILLIAM B.—Born on June 1, 1890. Son of Mrs. Margaret Folland, of Monaca. Entered the service August, 1918. Assigned to Camp Lee and Camp Dix. Attached to Company A, 705th Regiment, 51st Guard. Left for overseas October, 1918. Returned July, 1919. Honorably discharged July, 1919.

GLASSER, JOHN—Born 1898. Son of Mr. Harry C. Glasser, of Monaca, Pa. Entered the service in July, 1917. Assigned to Kelly Field, Dayton, and Wilbur Wright Field. Went overseas in the Summer of 1918. Returned April, 1919. Honorably discharged in the Spring of 1919.

GOSS, GEORGE—Born April 29, 1900. Son of Mr. John Goss, of Monaca, Pa. Entered the service April 29, 1918. Assigned to Columbus, Ohio. Attached to Field Artillery. December 1, 1919, still in service.

HANSHEW, EARL—Born June 9, 1895. Son of Mr. W. A. Hanshew, of Monaca, Pa. Entered the service July, 1917. Assigned to Camp Hancock, Camp Upton and Schenley Park, Pittsburgh. Attached to Company A, 111th Infantry, 28th Division. Went overseas May, 1918. Wounded in action and died August 12, 1919. Buried in France.

HASLETT, ELLSWORTH—Born on July 4, 1899. Son of Mr. John Haslett, of Monaca, Pa. Entered service August 3, 1917. Assigned to Camp Sheridan and Camp Sherman. Attached to Company B, 135th Machine Gun Battalion. Went overseas June 15, 1918. Saw active service. Returned March 15, 1919. Honorably discharged April 9, 1919 with rank of Corporal.

HASLETT, ROBERT—Born November, 1894. Son of Mr. John Haslett, of Monaca. Entered service August 3, 1917. Assigned to Camp Sheridan and Camp Sherman. Attached to Company B, 135th Machine Gun Battalion. Went overseas June 15, 1918. Saw active service. Honorably discharged on April 9, 1919.

HAYS, EDSON M.—Born September 1, 1895. Son of Mr. and Mrs. F. M. Hays of Monaca. Entered the service December 5, 1917. Assigned to Columbus Barracks. Attached to Medical Corps. Honorably discharged June 27, 1919, with rank of Corporal.

HAZLETT, JAMES ROY—Born January 10, 1896. Son of Mr. James Roy Hazlett, Sr., of Monaca. Entered the service May, 1917. Assigned to Camp Humphreys and Camp Mills. Attached to Company N, 21st Engineers. Went overseas November, 1917. Returned July, 1919. Honorably discharged July, 1919.

HECKERMAN, WILLIAM H.—Born October 1, 1889. Son of William J. and Louisa Heckerman, Monaca, Pa. Entered the service April 1, 1918. Assigned to Camp Lee. Attached to Company 8, 2nd Battalion, 155th Depot Brigade. Honorably discharged February 21, 1919, with rank of Sergeant.

HENRY, DALBERT R.—Born October 28, 1896. Son of Mr. James Henry, Monaca. Entered the service September, 1918. Assigned to Camp Forrest. Attached to Company L, Engineers. Honorably discharged in February, 1919.

HICKS, JAMES D.—Born October 21, 1888. Son of Mrs. Anna G. Hicks of Monaca. Entered service, April, 1917. Assigned to Camp Lee. Attached to 32nd Company, 8th Training Battalion. Honorably discharged December 16, 1918, with rank of Sergeant.

HILL, MARK—Born Feb. 27, 1896. Son of Mr. Mary Hill, of Monaca. Entered service September 5, 1917. Assigned to Camp Sherman and Camp Mills. Attached to Battery F, 323rd Field Artillery, 32nd Division. Went overseas June 10, 1918. Saw service at Meuse-Argonne and other battles. Returned May 13, 1919. Honorably discharged May 26, 1919.

HOOD, JOSEPH B.—Born August 15, 1897. Son of Mr. William Hood of Monaca. Entered service August, 1918. Assigned to University of Pittsburgh. Attached to S. A. T. C. Honorably discharged December 15, 1918, with rank of Corporal.

HOUSER, RALPH DAVID—Born May 11, 1895. Son of Harry and Elizabeth Houser of Colona, Pa. Entered service February 5, 1918. Assigned to Camp Sherman. Attached to Battery C, 323rd Light Field Artillery, 32nd Division. Went overseas June 10, 1918. Saw service at Argonne, Grand Montagne and East of Meuse. Honorably discharged May 27, 1919, with rank of Corporal.

HUNTER, ROBERT F.—Born July 22, 1895. Son of Mr. and Mrs. James E. Hunter of Monaca. Entered service February 6, 1918. Assigned to Camp Sherman and Camp Merritt. Attached to Company F, 125th Infantry, 32nd Division. Went overseas March, 1918. Saw service at Alsace, Chateau Thierry, Meuse-Argonne. Wounded. Honorably discharged May 25, 1919.

JOHNSON, ELMER E.—Born September, 1897. Son of Mr. John H. Johnson of Monaca, Entered the service July, 1917. Assigned to Fort Benjamin Harrison and Camp Sherman. Attached to Field Hospital No. 15, 2nd Division. Went overseas December, 1918. Saw service at Aisne Sector, Chateau Thierry, Marne and St. Mihiel. Honorably discharged August 14, 1919.

JOHNSTON, MILO G.—Born August 17, 1897. Son of Mr. and Mrs. Alexander Johnston, of Monaca. Entered service June 7, 1918. Assigned to Camp Greenleaf. Attached to Base Hospital No. 55, Medical Corps. Went overseas on August 30, 1918. Gassed in action. Honorably discharged June 12, 1919.

KELLY, GEORGE THOMAS—Born January 1, 1899. Son of Mrs. Margaret A. Kelly of Monaca. Entered service Spring of 1917. Assigned to Pittsburgh, Pa., and Camp Hancock. Attached to Company A, 109th Infantry. Went overseas September 8, 1918. Saw service at St. Mihiel, Meuse-Argonne and Vesle. Honorably discharged May 16, 1919.

KINDELL, NOLON M.—Born 1895. Son of Mr. William M. Kindell, of Bradford, O. Entered the service May, 1917, in the United States Navy. Assigned to Newport, Pensacola and Fort Worth. Attached to Naval Aviation. Went overseas Spring of 1918. Returned Spring of 1919. Honorably discharged in August, 1919, with rank of Lieutenant.

KOEHLER, EDWARD C.—Born on February 21, 1898. Son of Mr. Paulus E. Koehler, of Monaca. Entered service Spring of 1917. Assigned to Camp Taylor. Attached to Officers' Training School. Honorably discharged June, 1919, with rank of Second Lieutenant.

KOEHLER, HOWARD R.—Born on May 31, 1889. Son of Mr. Paulus E. Koehler of Monaca. Entered service Spring of 1917. Assigned to Camp Sherman and Camp Mills. Attached to Company F, 323rd Field Artillery, 32nd Division. Went overseas June 10, 1918. Saw service at Meuse-Argonne. Honorably discharged May 27, 1919, with rank of Sergeant.

KOPCAK, JOSEPH—Son of Mr. Stephen Kopcak, of Monaca. Entered service January, 1919. Assigned to Washington, D. C., and Hawaiian Islands. Attached to Cavalry. November 29, 1919, still in the service.

LAIS, GEORGE JAMES—Born May 5, 1898. Son of Mr. and Mrs. George H. Lais, of Monaca. Entered the United States Navy October 1, 1918. Assigned to Pitt University. Attached to Naval Reserves. Released from service but subject to call.

LAIS, ROLLO V.—Born September 19, 1896. Son of Mr. and Mrs. George H. Lais, Monaca, Pa. Entered service June 30, 1918. Assigned to Naval Training Station, Cleveland. Attached to Naval Reserve. Released from service, but subject to call.

LAUGHLIN, ROBERT P.—Born in March, 1896. Son of James and Rose Laughlin, of Georgetown, Pa. Entered the service December, 1917. Assigned to Camp Sherman. Attached to Battery B, 323rd Field Artillery. Honorably discharged April 28, 1918.

LOTZ, CHESTER—Born January 9, 1895. Son of Mr. Nickolos Lotz, Rochester. Entered the service in September, 1917. Assigned to Camps Sherman, Mills and Dix. Attached to Battery E, 323rd Light Field Artillery, 32nd Division. Went overseas in June, 1918. Participated in several battles. Returned May, 1919. Honorably discharged May 28, 1919.

LAUGHLIN, HOMER—Born November 28, 1892. Son of Mr. R. L. Laughlin, of Georgetown. Entered service July 27, 1918. Assigned to Camp Lee, Newport News, Camp Mills and Camp Dix. Attached to Company L, 61st Infantry, 51st Division. Went overseas September 15, 1918. In the battle of Meuse-Argonne. Returned July 19, 1919. Honorably discharged July 26, 1919.

LISTON, THOMAS GEORGE—Born April 7, 1896. Son of Mr. and Mrs. M. M. Liston, of Monaca. Entered service October 7, 1917. Assigned to Camp Sherman. Attached to Battery F, 323rd Field Artillery, 32nd Division. Went overseas June 10, 1918. Participated in battles at Argonne, Grand Montague, Marne. Honorably discharged May 27, 1919.

McCARTHY, MOLLY A.—Born on March 22, 1884. Entered service March 1, 1917. Assigned to Belview Hospital, N. Y. Attached to Belview Unit. Went overseas in March, 1917. Honorably discharged June, 1919.

McCLURG, MILO J.—Born August 22, 1887. Son of J. R. and Martha McClurg, of Monaca. Entered service September 4, 1918. Assigned to Camp Forrest. Attached to Second Provisional Regimental Company. Honorably discharged December 20, 1918.

McCREARY, JOHN CHARLES—Born January 29, 1899. Son of Mr. and Mrs. T. W. McCreary, of Monaca. Entered service September, 1918. Assigned to Allegheny College, Meadville, Pa. Attached to S. A. T. C. Honorably discharged December, 1918.

McCREARY, ROBERT EMMETT—Born August 24, 1898. Son of Mr. and Mrs. T. W. McCreary, of Monaca. Entered service August 30, 1918, in the United States Navy. Assigned to Cleveland, Chicago and Palm Bay. Attached to Navy. Released May 10, 1919, subject to call.

McELWEE, JOHN—Born April 23, 1891. Son of Mrs. Hanna McElwee of Ireland. Entered the service November 17, 1917. Assigned to Camp Hamilton, Canada. Attached to 58th Canadian Infantry Battalion. Went overseas January, 1918. Participated in several battles. Honorbly discharged March 23, 1919.

McELWEE, THOMAS—Son of Mr. and Mrs. James McElwee, of Monaca, Pa. Entered service August 17, 1917. Assigned to Syracuse. N. Y., and Camp Greene. Attached to Company M, 38th Infantry. Participated in the battles of the Meuse-Argonne. Died from wounds received in action October 10, 1918. Buried in France.

MACKALL, GAIL—Born May 12, 1896. Son of Mrs. Harriet Mackall of Georgetown. Entered the service February 21, 1918. Asigned to Camp Travis, Camp Merritt. Attached to Company N, 19th Engineers. Went overseas April 22, 1918. Saw service at Chateau Thierry. Honorably discharged in May, 1919.

MACKALL, JOHN EDWARD—Born August 7, 1887. Son of Mrs. Jennie B. Mackall, of Georgetown. Entered service December 13, 1917. Assigned to Camp Sherman, Fort Niagara, Newport News and Camp Dix. Attached to Company B, 45th Battalion. Honorably discharged January 21, 1919.

MARKEY, EWING H.—Born in 1893. Son of Mr. James Markey, of Monaca. Entered service April 1, 1918. Assigned to Camps Lee, Dix and Sherman. Attached to Company E, 319 Infantry, 80th Division. Went overseas May 18, 1918. Saw service at St. Mihiel and Meuse Argonne. Honorably discharged June 12, 1919.

MATTAUCH, CARL—Born January 17, 1889. Son of Mrs. Annie Mattauch, of Australia. Entered the service April 1, 1918. Assigned to Camps Lee, Dix and Sherman. Attached to Company E, 319th Infantry, 80th Division. Went overseas May 18, 1918. Saw service at the Meuse-Argonne and St. Mihiel. Honorably discharged June 12, 1919.

MIKSCH, CARLTON ARNOLD—Born October 11, 1899. Son of Mr. and Mrs. Miksch, of Monaca. Entered the service October 23, 1918. Assigned to Allegheny College, Meadville, Pa. Attached to Company A, S. A. T. C. Honorably discharged December 11, 1918.

MIKSCH, HARRY NORTHWOOD—Born November 1, 1897. Son of Mr. and Mrs. Carl Miksch, of Monaca, Pa. Entered the service October 23, 1918. Assigned to Allegheny College, Meadville, Pa. Attached to Company A, S. A. T. C. Honorably discharged December 11, 1918.

MILLER, JAMES A. JR.—Born January 20, 1899. Son of Mr. and Mrs. James A. Miller, of Monaca. Entered service September, 1918. Assigned to University of Pittsburgh. Attached to S. A. T. C. Honorably discharged December, 1918, with rank of Corporal.

MILLER, PAUL JAMES—Born September 26, 1892. Son of Mr. and Mrs. J. A. Miller, of Monaca. Entered service February 6, 1918. Assigned to Camp Sherman. Attached to 20th Engineers. Went overseas March 27, 1918. Returned on June 1, 1919. Honorably discharged June 12, 1919.

MILLER, ROY M.—Born July 28, 1894. Son of Mr. and Mrs. Fred Miller, of Monaca. Entered service September 18, 1917. Assigned to Camp Sherman and Camp Dix. Attached to Headquarters Company, 323rd Field Artillery. Left for overses June 10, 1918. Saw service at Meuse-Argonne, Montagne. Honorably discharged May 27, 1919, with rank of Corporal.

MILLER, WILLIAM J.—Born September 6, 1894. Son of Mr. and Mrs. J. A. Miller, of Monaca. Entered service September 6, 1917. Assigned to Camp Sherman. Attached to Battery C, 323rd Light Field Artillery, 32nd Division. Went overseas June 10, 1918. Saw service at Argonne, Grand Montague, East of Meuse. Honorably dischrged May 27, 1919, with the rank of Sergeant.

MOOREHOUSE, JAMES H.—Born July 7, 1893. Son of Mr. and Mrs. J. W. Moorehouse, of Monaca. Entered service January 15, 1918. Assigned to New York. Attached to Army Field Clerk. Went overseas February 8, 1918. Awarded citation from General Pershing. Honorably discharged September 19, 1919.

MURPHY, PATRICK—Born June 30, 1891. Entered service July, 1918. Assigned to Camp Merritt and Camp Gordon. Attached to General Pershing Guards. Went overseas August, 1918. Returned June, 1919. Honorably discharged June, 1919.

MURPHY, WILLIAM—Born April 13, 1895. Entered service September, 1918. Assigned to Camp Humphreys. Attached to Engineers. Honorably discharged December, 1918.

MYERS, ROBERT—Born March 4, 1892. Son of James and Alice Myers of Monaca. Entered service July 11, 1917. Assigned to Gettysburg and Camp Greene. Attached to Company C, 7th Infantry. 3rd Division. Went overseas April 6, 1918. Participated in several battles. Honorably discharged on August 27, 1918.

MYERS, GEORGE WALTER—Born August 1, 1889. Son of James and Alice Myers of Monaca. Assigned to Camp Sherman. Attached to Headquarters Company, 112th Infantry, 28th Division. Went overseas May, 1918. Saw service at Meuse-Argonne, Chateu Thierry and St. Mihiel. Returned May, 1919. Honorably discharged May 12, 1919.

MYERS, JAMES W.—Born March 15, 1887. Son of James and Alice Myers of Monaca. Entered service September 19, 1917. Assigned to Camp Sherman, Waco, Texas, and Camp Upton. Attached to Battery F, 323rd Light Field Artillery, 32nd Division. Went overseas May 7, 1918. Saw service at St. Die. Honorably discharged August 8, 1919.

NELSON, HAROLD M.—Born February 27, 1895. Son of Frank E. and Maud E. Nelson, Hookstown, Pa. Entered the service December 11, 1917. Assigned to Columbus Barracks, Kelly Field and Hempstead, L. I. Attached to 258th Aero Squadron. Went overseas May 2, 1918. Returned May, 1919. Honorably discharged May 12, 1919, with rank of Sergeant.

BEAVER VALLEY TOWNS IN THE WORLD WAR

NICKLE, CHARLES LEROY—Born October 6, 1894. Son of Henry S. and Lorena M. Nickle, Hookstown, Pa. Entered the service April 25, 1918. Assigned to Camp Sherman and Camp Mills. Attached to Company B, 112th Infantry, 28th Division. Went overseas June, 1918. Participated in the battles at St. Mihiel, Verdun and Argonne Forest. Killed in action. Buried in American Cemetery at Exermont, France.

ORR, SAMUEL J.—Born January 13, 1897. Son of Mrs. J. A. Scott, of Colona, Pa. Entered service on August 17, 1917. Assigned to Columbus Barracks. Attached to 102nd Aero Squadron. Went overseas on November 23, 1917. Saw service in England and France. Honorably discharged in May, 1919.

POTTER, JOHN B.—Born December 29, 1894. Son of Mr. John P. Potter, of Monaca. Entered service October 7, 1917. Assigned to Camps Sherman, Mills and Dix. Attached to Company F, 323rd Field Artillery, 32nd Division. Went overseas June, 1918. Saw service at Meuse-Argonne, Grand Montague. Returned May 13, 1919. Honorably discharged May 27, 1919, with rank of Sergeant.

POTTER, ZACHARY F.—Born July 15, 1892. Son of Mr. John P. Potter of Monaca. Entered service on October 3, 1917. Assigned to Camp Sherman and Camp Mills. Attached to Battery E, 323rd Field Artillery, 32nd Division. Went overseas June 10, 1918. Saw service at Meuse-Argonne and other battles. Honorably discharged on May 27, 1919, with rank of Saddler.

PROVENCE, DAVID L.—Born December 1, 1889. Entered service in January, 1917. Assigned to Camp Sherman and Camp Lee. Attached to Company E, 323rd Artillery, 32nd Division. Went overseas June 10, 1919. Saw service at Meuse-Argonne and Chateau Thierry. Honorably discharged May 29, 1919, with rank of Corporal.

REINEHR, ALBERT—Son of Andrew Reinehr, of Monaca, Pa. Entered service June, 1918. Assigned to Camps Merritt and Sherman. Attached to Company H, 332nd Infantry, 83rd Division. Participated in several engagements in Italy. Honorably discharged April, 1919.

SCHACHERN, LELAND J.—Born March 1, 1900. Son of Joseph Schachern of Monaca, Pa. Entered service October 1, 1918. Attached to Company A, S. A. T. C., at Allegheny College, Meadville, Pa. Honorably discharged December 13, 1918.

SCHATZINGER, EDWARD J.—Born October 7, 1887. Son of John and Mary Schatzinger, of Colona, Pa. Entered service April 2, 1918. Assigned to Camp Lee. Attached to Company F, 319th Infantry, 80th Division. Went overseas May 18, 1918. Saw service at Meuse-Argonne, and St. Mihiel. Honorably discharged June 12, 1919.

SCHATZINGER, JOSEPH J.—Born September 13, 1887. Son of John and Mary Schatzinger, of Colona, Pa. Entered service September 22, 1917. Assigned to Camp Sherman. Attached to Company C, 26th Infantry, 1st Division. Went overseas June 28, 1918. Saw service at St. Mihiel, Meuse-Argonne and Sarzerais. Honorably discharged September 24, 1919, holding rank of Corporal.

SCHUPAY, STEVEN JACOB—Born July 18, 1897. Son of Mrs. John Schupay of Monaca, Pa. Entered service September 21, 1918. Assigned to Camp Greenleaf and Camp Upton. Attached to Base Hospital No. 110. Went overseas November 12, 1918. Honorably discharged July 10, 1919.

SCHMIDT, FRED W.—Born April 27, 1897. Son of Mrs. M. Kirchner of Monaca, Pa. Entered service September 5, 1918. Assigned to Camp Lee. Attached to Quartermaster Corps, U. S. Army. Honorably discharged May 14, 1919, holding rank of Corporal.

SCHWARTZ, WILLIAM ROSS—Born January 22, 1891. Son of Mrs. F. R. Schwartz of Monaca, Pa. Entered service September 5, 1917. Assigned to Camp Sherman. Attached to Battery C, 323rd Light Field Artillery. Went overseas on June 10, 1918. Saw service at Argonne Sector, Grande Montague. Honorably discharged May 27, 1919, holding rank of Sergeant.

SEPHTON, FRANK—Born August 7, 1887. Son of John T. Sephton of Monaca, Pa. Entered service April 1, 1918. Assigned to Camps Lee and Sherman. Attached to Company G, 320th Infantry, 80th Division. Went overseas May 18, 1918. Saw service at Meuse-Argonne and St. Mihiel. Awarded Victory Medal. Honorably discharged June 9, 1919.

SERGEANT, CHARLES E.—Born April 19, 1889. Son of Harry and Matilda Sergeant, of Colona, Pa. Entered service February 6, 1918. Assigned to Camp Sherman. Attached to Company G, 332nd Infantry. Went overseas June 8, 1918. Saw service at Vittoio Venteo, Tagliamento River, Pont della Delizia and on the Italian front. Honorably discharged April 24, 1919.

SERGEANT, KENNETH J.—Born June 15, 1896. Son of Harry and Matilda Sergeant, of Colona, Pa. Entered service September 6, 1913. Assigned to Camp Greenleaf. Attached to Medical Department. Honorably discharged March 3, 1919.

SHEMONE, JOSEPH CHARLES—Born March 1, 1897. Son of Mrs. Anna Shemone of Monaca, Pa. Entered service September 4, 1918. Assigned to Camp Forrest and Camp Sherman. Attached to Company B, 124th Engineers. Honorably discharged December, 1918.

SIMMONS, LAWRENCE F.—Born December 10, 1897. Son of John and Anna Simmons of Colona, Pa. Entered service August 17, 1917. Assigned to Columbus Barracks and San Antonio, Texas. Went overseas November 23, 1917. Served in England and France. Honorably discharged May 1, 1919, holding rank of Corporal.

SKOOG, WILLIAM F.—Born May 5, 1895. Son of Mrs. L. F. Skoog, of Monaca, Pa. Entered service December 14, 1917. Assigned to Camp Sherman. Attached to Battery B, 323rd Artillery. Honorably discharged January 23, 1918.

SOMMERS, FREDERICK FRANK—Born April 13, 1895. Son of Mrs. Frederick Sommers, of Monaca, Pa. Entered service October 7, 1917. Assigned to Camp Sherman. Attached to Battery F, 323rd Field Artillery, 32nd Division. Went overseas June 10, 1918. Saw service at Meuse-Argonne. Honorably discharged May 27, 1919.

SOWASH, CLARE R.—Born January 17, 1898. Son of Charles B. Sowash of Monaca, Pa. Entered service July 21, 1917. Assigned to Camp Greene. Attached to Company A, 58th Infantry, 4th Division. Went overseas May 7, 1918. Saw service at Meuse-Argonne, Champagne and Aisne. Honorably discharged August 2, 1919.

STEINER, THEODORE ARNOLD—Born May 20, 1900. Son of E. B. and Florence M. Steiner. Enteerd service October 1, 1918. Assigned to Thiel College. Attached to S. A. T. C. Honorably discharged December 11, 1918.

STJERNQUIST, CARL F.—Born August 1, 1889. Son of Mrs. Josephine Stjernquist, of Monaca, Pa. Entered service April, 1917. Assigned to Camp Upton. Attached to 106th Infantry. Honorably discharged March, 1919.

STJERNQUIST, GUST E.—Born May 12, 1895. Son of Mrs. Josephine Stjernquist, of Monaca, Pa. Entered service October 5, 1917. Assigned to Camp Sherman. Attached to Battery F, 323rd Light Field Artillery. Went overseas on June 10, 1919. Saw service at Argonne St. Mihiel, Grande Montague and Meuse. Honorably discharged May 27, 1919.

SWEARINGEN, CHARLES R.—Born November 12, 1892. Son of Jackson and Lillian B. Swearingen, of Georgetown, Pa. Entered the service October 2, 1917. Assigned to Camp Funston, Camp Kearney, Camp Mills and Camp Merritt. Attached to Headquarters Company, 160th Infantry, 40th Division. Went overseas August 8, 1918. Gassed. Honorably discharged July 10, 1919, with rank of Corporal.

TAYLOR, HAROLD A.—Born November 7, 1897. Son of Herby J. Taylor, of Monaca, Pa. Entered service November, 1918. Assigned to Paris Island, S. C. Attached to U. S. S. M. C. Honorably discharged April, 1919.

TINPANO, ANGELO—Born April 13, 1891. Son of Fernando Tinpano, of Monaca, Pa. Entered the service December 13, 1917. Assigned to Camp Sherman. Attached to Company B, 323rd Light Field Artillery, 32nd Division. Honorably discharged October 29, 1918.

TODD, FRANCIS O.—Born January 16, 1887. Entered the service July 29, 1918. Assigned to Camps Merritt and Dix. Attached to Quartermaster's Corps. Honorably discharged February 3, 1919.

TODD, THOMAS D.—Born November 18, 1889. Entered service February 4, 1918. Assigned to Camp Sherman. Attached to Company G, 332nd Infantry, 83rd Division. Honorably discharged March 13, 1919.

TRUMPETER, WILLIAM CLIFTON—Born November 26, 1898. Son of Mr. and Mrs. W. M. Trumpeter, of Monaca, Pa. Entered service October 2, 1918. Assigned to Carnegie Tech. Attached to S. A. T. C. Honorably discharged December 17, 1918.

TURNECK, RALPH J.—Born March 17, 1896. Entered service May 23, 1917. Attached to Company D, 5th Engineers, 5th Division. Went overseas July 9, 1917. Saw service at Chateau Thierry, Verdun, Soissons and Belleau Woods. Returned May, 1919. Honorably discharged May 14, 1919, with the rank of Sergeant.

WEIGHEL, WALKER JENNINGS—Born March 7, 1897. Son of Henry Weighel, of Monaca, Pa. Entered service September, 1918. Assigned to Great Lakes. Attached to Naval Reserve. Honorably discharged January, 1919.

WEINMAN, ROBERT B.—Born January 29, 1894. Son of Mr. and Mrs. George Weinman of Monaca, Pa. Entered service September 1918. Assigned to Washington, D. C. Attached to Medical Department. Honorably discharged June, 1919.

WINKLE, GEORGE A.—Born August 23, 1895. Son of George W. Winkle of Monaca, Pa. Entered service September 5, 1917. Assigned to Camp Sherman. Attached to Battery F, 323rd Light Field Artillery, 32nd Division. Died, April 21, 1918, at Camp Sherman, Ohio.

WOODFIELD, CHARLES — Born April 20, 1892. Son of James and Louisa S. Woodfield of Colona, Pa. Entered service September 18, 1917. Assigned to Camp Sherman. Attached to Battery F, 323rd Field Artillery. Went overseas June 10, 1918. Saw service at Argonne, Bois-de-Grande. Honorably discharged May 27, 1919, with rank of Corporal.

WRIGHT, WILLIAM ROY—Born July 2, 1895. Son of Charles S. and Julia V. Wright. Entered the service September 19, 1918. Assigned to Camps Sherman, Mills and Dix. Attached to Supply Company, 323rd Artillery, 83rd Division. Went overseas June 10, 1918. Saw service at Meuse-Argonne. Slightly gassed. Honorably discharged July 15, 1919.

ZIGERELLI, JAMES—Born April, 1896. Son of Mr. Joseph Zigerelli, of Monaca. Entered service in January, 1918. Assigned to Camp Sherman and Camp Dix. Attached to Company M, 16th Infantry. Went overseas April, 1918. Was wounded in action twice. Honorably discharged October, 1919.

ZIGERELLI, JOHN F.—Born January 29, 1897. Son of Mr. Frank Zigerelli, of Monaca. Entered the service September 4, 1918. Assigned to Camp Forrest and Camp Sherman. Attached to Engineers. Honorably discharged December 20, 1918.

ZIGERELLI, OTTO—Born July 4, 1891. Son of Mr. Joseph Zigerelli, of Monaca. Entered the service September, 1917. Assigned to Camp Sherman and Camp Dix. Attached to Company F, 323rd Field Artillery, 32nd Division. Honorably discharged December, 1918.

ZINKE, FRANK H.—Born August 24, 1899. Son of Mr. and Mrs. Frank Zinke, of Monaca, Pa. Entered the service in September, 1918. Assigned to Geneva College. Attached to S. A. T. C. Honorably discharged December, 1918.

World War II (WWII)
multiple dates are referenced with WWII
Jul 7, 1937/Sep 1, 1939 until Aug 15, 1945/Sep 2, 1945.

The first date on records for Japan invading China and initiating WWII in the Pacific is Jul 7, 1937. The date of Sep 1, 1939 is used to indicate the German invasion of Poland, with Britain and France declaring war on Germany two days later. The war is listed as ending in Europe on May 8, 1945. Japan surrendered on Aug 15, 1945. The atomic bombing of Hiroshima and Nagasaki led to the emperor Hirohito agreeing to the final surrender of Japan on Sep 2, 1945.

World War II was perhaps the most significant period of the 20th century. It brought about major advancements in technology and also laid the groundwork permitting post-war social changes including the end of European colonialism, the civil rights movement in the United States, and the modern women's rights movement. The programs for exploring outer space also occurred in the years following WWII. Center Township has no designated memorial sites to honor the men of WWII, but many of the township men's families had their names added to a memorial site in one of the surrounding communities, so these do have names of the township's residents listed on them.

See further in this section for more information on enforced rationings and procedures of WWII.

Korean War
Jun 25, 1950 until Jul 27, 1953.

As with other major wars involving the United Sates, this war not only resulted in the lose of many American lives, but also definitely affected rural America in several ways.   There was a temporary increase in farm incomes with the increased demand for food to support the troops.   Farming families found themselves short-handed as many of the young people were pulled off the farms to serve their country.   This war was one of the leading reasons for the increase of the government's commodity support payments to farmers, but it also reduced the excessively abundant supply of over-produced farm products that had been stockpiled by the Commodity Credit Corporations (C.C.C.)* in the late 1940s.   Unfortunately, after the war, although the farmers were finally seemingly making headway, farm prices came under pressure by consumers demanding lower food prices.   *This C.C.C. "should not be confused with the first C.C.C. - Civil Conservation Corp which was in affect between 1933-1942.   This C.C.C./Commodity Credit Corporations was a "government-owned and operated entity that was created to stabilize, support, and protect farm income and prices. This C.C.C. also helps maintain balanced and adequate supplies of agricultural commodities and aids in their orderly distribution."

Vietnam War (1955 – 1973)

Direct U.S. military involvement with the Vietnam War began in 1955 with the arrival of the first advisers.   The first combat troops arrived Mar 8, 1965. War was never actually declared, yet it is recorded that the Vietnam War was the longest war that America had gone through.   This war was also a costly armed conflict that had the communist regime of North Vietnam and its southern allies (Viet Cong) pitted against South Vietnam and the United States (its principal ally).   A cease-fire occurred in Jan 1973 and Aug 15, 1973 is listed as the official last date for U.S. involvement. (Apr 1975 marks the finishing date of the end of the conflict). The U.S. troops withdrew in 1973, the unification of Vietnam under Communist control occurred two years later.   Once again employment levels were greatly affected with the demand for Americans to enlist and serve their country. Many of the young men of Center Township came forth and were enlisted in this war.   It has been reported there were more than three million people (58,000 Americans) killed during this conflict.

Stamp Sale Totals Are Announced

By MILDRED ROSS DYKE

A total of $253.92 in United States Savings Stamps was sold at a recent "Stamp Day" sale in Center Township Elementary School.

Mrs. Mabel Focks, savings stamps sale chairman for the Center School Parent-Teacher Association, announced 857 ten-cent stamps and 713 25-cent stamps were purchased by students.

Mrs. Beulah Marickovich, PTA president, and Mrs. George Gary, a member, attended the recent Boy Scout recognition dinner in Monaca American Legion Hall. They also represented the PTA at a recent meeting of the Beaver County Council of PTA's in Beaver.

Dec 1962

Pupils Help Nation By School Savings Plan

AS THE WAR in Vietnam drags on, with no end to it in sight, more and more money is needed by the U.S. government to support our troops in the combat zone. At the same time, disloyalty to our nation is rampant across the country.

This has made the Treasury Department's School Savings Program more important than ever. Under this program, now in its 27th year, school pupils buy U.S. Savings Stamps on a given day each week. When enough stamps are accumulated, they may be converted into U.S. Savings Bonds. (Savings Stamps also may be purchased at post offices in denominations of 10 cents to $5.)

The School Savings Program gives Beaver County youngsters the opportunity to support the American troops in Vietnam and at the same time show their loyalty to their country. Many local boys and girls have fathers or older brothers fighting in Vietnam and to them the war is real — and sometimes tragic.

Young people who participate in the program, and it should be conducted in every local school, are learning a lesson in Americanism. They are developing the habit of thrift and learning about the responsibilities of good citizenship, both of which will stand them in good stead in later life. Equally important, they are helping to defend freedom and sharing in the nation's war effort.

Dec 1967

And lastly, the United States is still involved in...

Gulf War   Iraq   Afghanistan   War of Terror

~ ~ ~

Veterans Memorials

There were many different groups formed to aid soldiers and the families of the soldiers during war time conflicts. One local group during WWII was the Prisoner of War committee that worked with the *Prisoner of War Program of the International Red Cross*. This group worked untiringly in the prison camps and distributed standard food packages and assisted with medical supplies and recreational equipment. In Jul 1944, the local Chairman was Mrs. Elsie Tate of Center Township (my grandmother). They assisted the families of the men held as prisoners of war (one was my father) with interpretation regarding regulations and with personal packages. The 1944 War Fund, Chairman, Robert E McCreary, of Monaca, collected and distributed the funds for the Red Cross. With committees and funds such as these, it saved duplications and confusions and permitted other groups and/or individuals with necessary information regarding actual needs at the military posts and requests made by commanding officers.

As previously stated, Center Township does not have their own memorial for veterans of the wars. Yet, numerous individuals who were born and bred or lived in Center Township did indeed serve. Many sustained injuries and many even lost their lives in the conflicts that involved the United States. Names of veterans who became residents of Center Township may be found listed on one of these memorials, particularly in either Monaca or Aliquippa. Aliquippa's Veterans' Memorial is located on Main Street in Plan 12. Monaca's Veterans' Memorial plaques are in front of the Monaca Post Office and at Memorial Park located on the triangular lot between Fifth and Sixth Streets. As I tried to explain previously, it is difficult to identify the numerous township residents within publicized listings of veterans. I truly believe this is due to the township having both an Aliquippa or a Monaca mailing address, and the "hometown" being listed for a veteran was one of these post offices rather than Center Township itself. Another reason may be because many listings categorize these men too generally, being either simply as from "Beaver County" or even more generally as just "Pennsylvania" and not specifically Center Township. Though these names are not on a designated plaque in Center Township, this does not mean that these veterans should be thought of with any less respect of any other veteran during any of the wars. A Center Township Veterans' Memorial would be a great project for an up-and-coming Eagle Scout or any person who may want to undertake such a project, wouldn't it?

Each year, Veterans Day is an opportunity not only to honor and thank all who fought for freedom throughout our nation's history, but to reaffirm our support for those who currently wear a uniform and are still serving. Their efforts and sacrifices make a real difference. Thank you to all these persons, our country is stronger, and the world is a better place because of your dedication.

~ ~ ~

Beaver County's First Total Blackout during WW II - Jun 11, 1942
The federal government sponsored public service announcements to promote everyone's participation in all drills and to assure people knew what to do during WW II. The whole concept of these actions was that enemy planes could not target what they could not see. Any light that was visible from above could attract bombs and gunfire. At the sound of alarms, people in cars were to pull over, turn off lights, and find shelter in the nearest building. People who were in their homes were to pull down the blinds on the windows and keep the light inside to a minimum. Businesses were to do the same.

All citizens were also told to keep 50 feet of garden hose with a spray nozzle, 100 pounds of sand separated into four containers, 3 three-gallon metal buckets (one with sand and two with water), a long-handled shovel with a square edge, a hoe or rake, an ax or hatchet, a ladder, leather gloves, and dark glasses. This was quite a demand of articles for some lower income people. Technically, anyone who didn't comply with the blackout orders and keep these required supplies on hand could have been arrested. It was found that such arrests were very rare, though.

It was 9:15 pm on Jun 11, 1942, as sirens, factory whistles, and church bells signaled the start of the first total blackout trial run in the history of Beaver County. It was an eerie sight to see streetlamps rapidly going out, section by section, town by town, community by community. Then it seemed like an intense hush also settled over the entire area, as if all signs of life just ceased. The Beaver and Ohio valleys turned from a bustling group of communities to a vast black mass. There was only the light of the moon illuminating an occasional roof top.

There was total cooperation with not even a match flared in the darkness. No light was visible, except some in plants engaged in war production. Lights were faintly visible at the war plants in Monaca, but Conway Yard was in almost complete darkness. A light did blaze at the site of Koppers, the new synthetic rubber plant. There was even a completely blacked-out passenger train which sped across the Beaver-Monaca bridge. There was a dull, red glow above the J & L plant, lights twinkled at the Colona river-rail terminal, and a towboat pilot making a landing briefly swept the shore with a searchlight.   Had this been a "true blackout" and not just a drill, even the war plants would have blackened out their lights to hide their locations.

Suddenly, the sirens began again, sounding the "all clear" signal. Section by section, town by town, area by area, the streetlights came back on and homes became illuminated once again. Automobile headlamps could be seen starting to move along streets and roadways again.   Beaver County's first total blackout was over.   Center Township, in fact, the entire Beaver Valley reported a successful blackout that evening and said there was 100% cooperation from the citizens, persons passing through areas, and businesses.   No violations of the blackout rules were reported.

During the blackout, many areas also practiced simulated fires with the fire departments responding. Simulated injury cases with first aid treatment and preparation for being taken to a hospital were all practiced. A guard on the Rochester-Monaca bridge reportedly stopped a car and demanded to see credentials from the occupants. One of the occupants reportedly held up a machine gun and said to the guard "How will this do?" It was said these two occupants of the car were U.S. Army officers who were observing the result of the blackout in the county.

 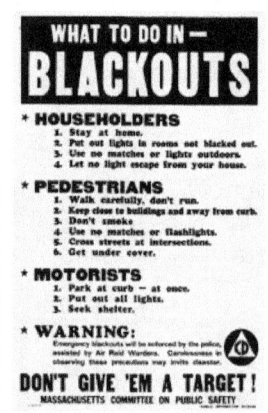 

Day Air Raid Test
During WWII, with the many concerns and worries of Japan conducting air raids on random parts of the United States. The government did their best to make all citizens aware of the procedures and what they should do in case of a daytime air raid. To give people practice of these procedures, there were various, sometimes weekly, air raid drills conducted in all areas. With the frequency of these tests, many people became complacent to these drills, and some even chose to ignore them. As a result, some communities and counties began conducting "surprise" drills. By holding unscheduled drills, it was thought the American people would be kept much more on their toes and more apt to respond appropriately.

Wednesday, Aug 26, 1942, was one of the specific/planned dates nine Western Pennsylvania counties were to be involved in the staging of a daylight air raid drill. It was to begin at 1:45 PM and last for 15 minutes. Very shortly prior to this scheduled air raid drill, there were plans for a "surprise raid." The surprise air raid was abandoned even though many local officials and defense councils truly felt, some even stipulated, the test be unexpected by the general public. Rather than causing complete panic among the many residents of Western Pennsylvania, it was decided to distribute complete rules for the drill so the general public had sufficient time to know what to do before the actual date of a test. The general procedures included that all traffic stop and streets be cleared of pedestrians.

★ ★ ★ AIR RAID RULES ★ ★ ★

YOU WILL BE WARNED
When enemy planes are spotted moving in your direction, watchers, many miles away will set in motion the machinery of protection. You will hear the warning signal. When danger is past, the "all clear" will be signaled.

YOUR BIGGEST JOB
There are many things you can do to protect your family if an air raid comes. Nothing is so important as to keep calm. Make certain every member of your family knows the air raid rules.

KNOW YOUR AIR RAID WARDENS
You should know by sight and by name the Air Raid Wardens in your block at home, and in the building where you work. Every member of your family should be prepared to carry out your warden's instructions. He has been trained to help you protect your family.

BLACKOUTS
Select the safest place in your house for general air raid and blackout purposes. Be prepared to blanket the windows or cover the glass with opaque protective material. Be sure

IF YOU ARE AT HOME . . . Get your family together in the safest room in the house, and stay there. Turn off your gas stove but not the pilot light. Turn out the lights in rooms not blacked out. Stay away from windows. Don't go outdoors and don't use your telephone.

★ ★ ★

IF YOU ARE ON THE STREET . . . Obey the orders of the Air Raid Wardens. Go home if you can walk there in a few minutes. Otherwise, get off the street and into the best shelter you can find. Get into or close to a large building. Avoid large windows, particularly show windows. Don't join crowd. If it is dark, don't light matches and don't smoke.

★ ★ ★

IF YOU ARE AT SCHOOL . . . Do exactly what your teacher tells you to do.

★ ★ ★

IF YOU ARE IN A STREET CAR OR BUS . . . The operator will try to stop near a good shelter; go into it and stay there until the all clear sounds.

★ ★ ★

IF YOU ARE IN AN AUTOMOBILE . . . Drive to curb and park immediately. Shut off lights and ignition and seek shelter.

★ ★ ★

IF YOU ARE IN A CHURCH, THEATER OR OTHER PUBLIC GATHERING . . . Stay seated, remain calm, obey orders. Panic can be as dangerous as bombs.

★ ★ ★

IF YOU ARE NOT NEAR SHELTER AND HEAR BOMBS FALLING . . . Get off the street and lie face down on the ground, preferably in a low spot.

that no lights can be seen from the outside. Keep your blackout material ready for instant use.

THINGS TO CHECK:
Have you removed inflammable material from your attic?
Have you followed your wardens' advice about equipment for fire protection?
Have you selected the refuge room for your family?
Are blankets available for first aid?
Do you have simple first aid supplies on hand?
Has a member of your family had first aid training?

IN GENERAL
Use your Common Sense. Keep Calm. Locate a safe place wherever your daily routine takes you. Remember that direct hits are few. The greatest danger is from shattered glass, flying debris and fire.

YOUR AIR RAID WARDEN IS

NAME

ADDRESS

PHONE No.

KEEP CALM
Panic hurts more people than bombs.

DON'T make telephone calls during a raid. All lines are needed for vital messages.

FOLLOW these rules of conduct for yourself and family. They are based on experience.

DON'T shut off main gas supply unless house is damaged or gas supply fails.

FOLLOW your warden's advice for protection against fire.

CONTROLLING INCENDIARY BOMBS

If an incendiary bomb comes through your roof, it is your job to control it. Prompt action on your part will control the fire.
Bring your fire fighting equipment to the scene at once.
Shoot a jet of water directly at the bomb without delay, to put it out of action quickly.
Then use the jet, quickly, to quench fragments and the remains of the bomb, and any fires that might have been started.
Be absolutely sure the fire is out before you leave the scene.
Use a coarse spray only where scattering of metal must be avoided.
Use sand only if a bomb falls where it is not likely to start a fire, or if water is not available.

Check carefully for smoldering fires.
CONSULT YOUR AIR RAID WARDEN for detailed advice and instructions.
COOPERATE WITH YOUR AIR RAID WARDEN.

CINCINNATI METROPOLITAN REGION
CITIZENS DEFENSE CORPS

Dana T. Merrill
Dana T. Merrill, Brig. Gen., U. S. A., Ret.
REGIONAL COORDINATOR

~ ~ ~

Late in 1941, schools were beginning to introduce pupils to some of the activities associated with war. Depending on the locations of a particular school(s), specific procedures and practices were followed. For most schools in the cities or that had rural schools where students could walk to school, the procedures were quite similar. Here is an example of the procedures for an air raid drill that was held in Beaver.

> "Pupils were dismissed from classes and instructed to go home as promptly and in as orderly a manner as possible. Pupils living outside Beaver were to go to the home of friends. Forms were sent to the parents of all pupils, to be returned to the schools this afternoon, on which the time of the arrival of each pupil at home was to be recorded. Further air raid warning drills will be held, perhaps once each month, near the close of the school day."

~ ~ ~

Rationing Programs

During WWI, there was no official or required rationing plan, Americans were to voluntarily conserve food and other supplies to show their compassion and their sense of patriotism to make the program work. Throughout WWI and WWII, there were posters found everywhere and propaganda distributed that strongly encouraged and/or reminded American citizens to greatly reduce and conserve their usage and consumption of meats, wheat, sugar, and fats. They were asked not to waste groceries and to eat more fresh fruits and vegetables since these were too difficult to properly transport overseas. There was advertising of "meatless Tuesdays" and "wheatless Wednesdays" to also encourage Americans to curtail their eating habits so more could be shipped to the soldiers. The citizens did not disappoint Mr. Hoover. All the conservation and support provided by the American citizens allowed the food shipments to Europe to be doubled within a year.

Most of the rural homemakers in Center Township had experience at "putting up" (canning / preserving) foods with this being part of the area's lifestyle. For those that just may not have had the knowledge, there were canning demonstrations at the Center Grange Hall and other Beaver County community Grange buildings so all households had the comprehension for preserving multiple items as crops matured. Recipes were published and distributed that had substitutions for all the limited or rationed provisions.

> *Fact: Mr. Hoover saw to it that shipments of foods continued to the millions of people in central Europe even after the war ended. As head of the American Relief Administration, coupled with his continued concern to help these people to receive such much-needed food, earned Mr. Hoover the nickname of the "Great Humanitarian."*

Center Township was completely different from surrounding towns and cities in that it did not have even near as many businesses or industrial areas and was still being considered a rural area. The citizens of the township were the same as all others, though, and treated the happenings and programs during all the conflicts with the upmost seriousness. In other words, the township residents and families participated and adhered to any restrictions just as other citizens of the United States. The very small print on this pay bill included:

To meet the needs of our armed forces and fighting allies, a Government order limits the amount of meat delivered to stores and restaurants.
To share the supply fairly, all civilians are asked to limit their consumption of beef, veal, lamb, mutton and pork to 2 ½ lbs. per person per week.
(then it listed "Your Fair Weekly Share")
You can add these foods to your share: liver, sweetbreads, kidneys, brains and other variety meats, also poultry and fish.

Published by FOODS REQUIREMENT COMMITTEE –
War Production Board – Claude R. Wickard, Chairman

Fact: Residents were also told to save all their peach and apricot pits. They were collected in barrels in various locations throughout areas and were given to the government who used the pits to make a war gas. (1914-1918 – WW I)

Not long after America entered WWII, the U.S. government found that voluntary conservation was just not proving as effective as it was in WWI. Food shortages began almost immediately with the economy shifting to war production seemingly overnight. The U.S. government made the decision to officially enforce rationing of certain essential items and on Jan 30, 1942, the Emergency Price Control Act granted the Office of Price Administration (OPA) approval to set price limits and ration food to discourage hoarding. They also felt that this would be the fair way for equal distribution of the scarce items. What did this mean for the American citizens and township residents? It meant that even if you could afford more, you could not simply walk into a store and buy sugar, butter, meat, and other items in whatever quantity or whenever you wanted. Nor could you pull into a gasoline station and just fill up your car's gas tank whenever or as often as you wanted to. The government only allowed you to purchase a small amount of the items they labelled as being rationed.

With the government's rationing system in place, Americans were finding many restrictions placed on their daily lives. By the spring of 1942, there were restrictions on imported foods and transportation of goods was curtailed due to the shortage of rubber tires. You could not purchase sugar without government issued food coupons. In Nov 1942, vouchers for coffee were introduced. By Mar 1943, meats, cheese, fats, canned fished, canned milk, other processed foods, silk, nylon, shoes, household appliances, and many other items were added to the rationed list.

Every American citizen was entitled to the war ration books. The OPA would accept the ration book applications. Once an application was processed, then they would issue ration books. Each book contained stamps that could be torn out to purchase restricted foods and other supplies. Each rationed item was given a number of points based on its availability. You could use 48 "blue points" to buy canned, bottled, or dried foods and 64 "red points" to buy meat, fish, and dairy items each month (that is IF the items were in stock at the market).

from local 1917 newspaper

   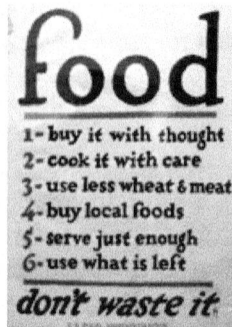

Along with the rationing books being in place, citizens were asked to turn in old tires, raincoats, gloves, garden hoses, and rubber shoes and boots for recycling. To save rubber, Americans were also asked to cut back on their driving and to save gas, by driving slower and/or to share rides whenever possible. Rationing of gasoline was enforced nationwide in Dec 1942. Anything using metal was rationed (which affected construction projects) and Americans were urged to turn in scrap metal for recycling. Women were urged to save waste fat and greases and turn them into the butchers who would pay for the fat and then sell it to rendering plants so it could be processed into explosives. Paper was needed for packing weapons and equipment to be shipped overseas, so all scrap and used paper was also collected.

Just like with any other program, with this tight rationing system, it didn't take long for misuse to crop up. The "black market" developed all over the country with forged ration stamps and stolen items being illegally resold. This upheld the old saying "the rich get richer;" common persons were at the mercy of what was doled out to them while others didn't seem to feel the strain quite the same.

Nov 1944 ads

Take your KITCHEN FATS to your meat dealer. They will help win the war

GOOD WASTE PAPER is needed in our war effort. Save it.

SAVE MORE USED FATS GET EXTRA RED POINTS.

Feb 1945

~ ~ ~

A condensed list of rationed items during WWII.

Rationed Items	Rationing Duration	Rationed Items	Rationing Duration
Tires	January 1942 to December 1945	Sugar	May 1942 to 1947
Cars	February 1942 to October 1945	Coffee	November 1942 to July 1943
Bicycles	July 1942 to September 1945	Processed Foods	March 1943 to August 1945
Gasoline	May 1942 to August 1945	Meats, canned fish	March 1943 to November 1945
Fuel Oil & Kerosene	October 1942 to August 1945	Cheese, canned milk, fats	March 1943 to November 1945
Solid Fuels	September 1943 to August 1945		
Stoves	December 1942 to August 1945	Typewriters	March 1942 to April 1944
Rubber Footwear	October 1942 to September 1945		
Shoes	February 1943 to October 1945		

~ ~ ~

When a person applied for rationing shares, at the bottom of the application was the following.

READ BEFORE SIGNING
In accepting this book, I recognize that it remains the property of the United States Government.
I will use it only in the manner and for the purposes authorized by the Office of Price Administration.

~ ~ ~

"Types of rationing included:
UNIFORM COUPON RATIONING - provided equal shares of a single commodity to all consumers
 (example-sugar);
POINT RATIONING - provided equivalent shares of commodities by coupons issued for points which
 could be spent for any combination of items in the group (processed foods, meats, fats,
 cheese);
DIFFERENTIAL COUPON RATIONING - provided shares of a single product according to varying needs
 (gasoline, fuel oil); and
CERTIFICATE RATIONING - allowed individuals products only after an application demonstrated need
 (tires, cars, stoves, typewriters)."

Major purchases such as automobiles, bicycles, and kitchen appliances required special certificates and proof of need. Also, the government and military needed so many typewriters for communications, thus the need for their rationing.

~ ~ ~

There were five separate rationing books that were produced. Book One series, Book Two series, Book Three series, and Book Four series were issued over the periods of 1942 and 1943. A fifth book was prepared and ready, but none were needed or issued.

Every member of a family, including children, were eligible to apply for a separate ration book. It has been recorded that by the end of WWII, there were over one hundred million of each of the ration books printed. Rationing ended when supplies were sufficient to meet demands. Most of the ration restrictions didn't end until Aug 1945. The restrictions and rationing on processed foods and other items like gasoline and fuel oil were removed, but the rationing of sugar* was in place in some parts of the country until 1947.   *Sugar was the first item to be rationed since Japan caused our nation's supply of sugar to quickly be reduced by more than one third.

    <u>Book One</u> was issued five months after the U.S. entered the WWII in 1942.
When this book was issued, the registrar would ask you, or the person who applied for your book, how much sugar you owned on that date. If you had any sugar, you were allowed to keep it, but stamps representing this quantity were torn from your group (except for a small amount which you were allowed to keep without losing any stamps).   If your War Ration Book One was issued to you on application by a member of your family, the number of stamps torn from the books of the family was based on the amount of sugar owned by the family, divided as equally as possible among all the books issued to that family.

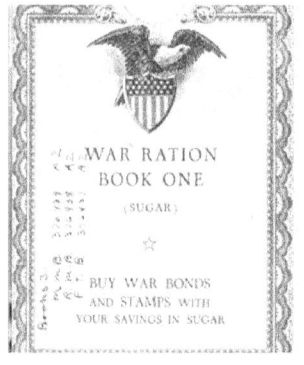

~ ~ ~

    <u>Book Two</u> series was issued in Jan 1943.
Instructions with this book stated, "This book is the property of the United States Government. It is unlawful to sell or give it to any other person or to use it or permit anyone else to use it, except to

obtain rationed goods for the person to whom it was issued. Persons who violate Rationing Regulations are subject to $10,000 fine or imprisonment, or both."

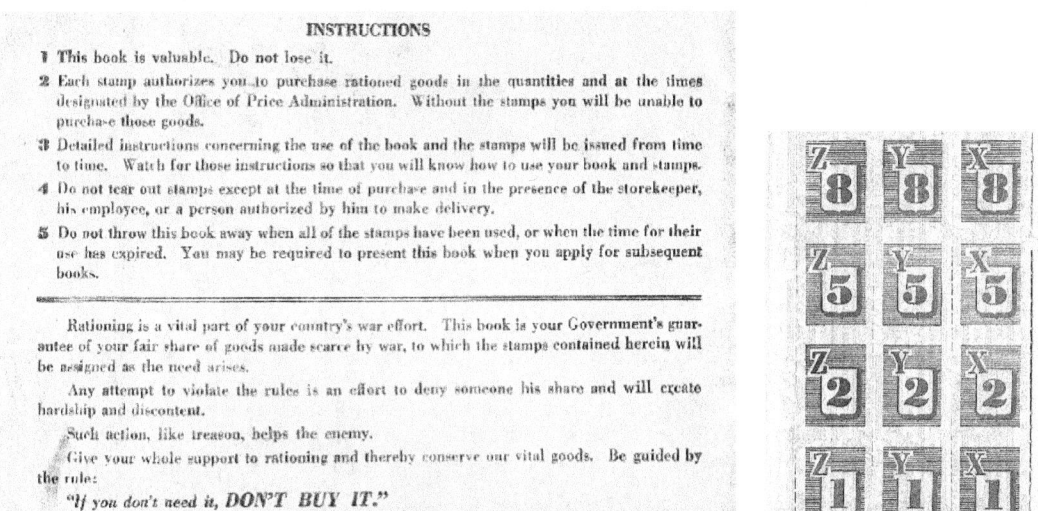

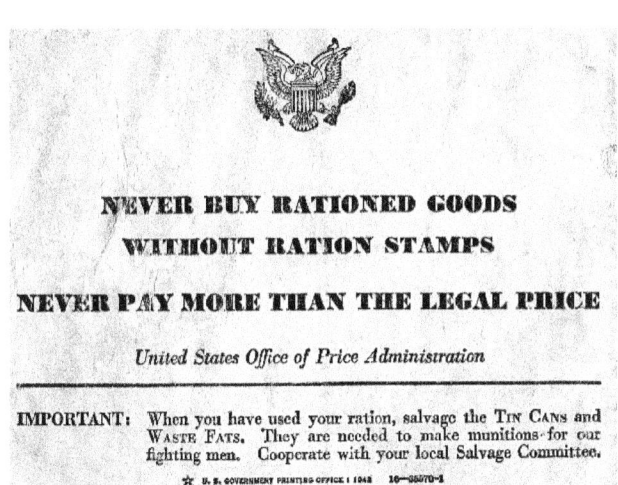

~ ~ ~

Book Three series was issued in Oct 1943.

Book Four series was issued toward the end of 1943.

~ ~ ~

Book Five

The government had a fifth book prepared and ready for distribution, but none were needed nor issued.

~ ~ ~

HOW TO USE YOUR WAR RATION BOOK

IMPORTANT.—Before the stamps of the War Ration Book may be used, the person for whom it was issued must sign it as indicated in the book. The name of a person under 18 years of age may be signed either by such person or by his father, mother, or guardian.

For future reference, make and keep a record of the serial number of your book and the number of your issuing Ration Board, as indicated in your book.

Your first War Ration Book has been issued to you, originally containing 28 War Ration Stamps. Other books may be issued at later dates. The following instructions apply to your first book and will apply to any later books, unless otherwise ordered by the Office of Price Administration. In order to obtain a later book, the first book must be turned in. You should preserve War Ration Books with the greatest possible care.

1. From time to time the Office of Price Administration may issue Orders rationing certain products. After the dates indicated by such Orders, these products can be purchased only through the use of War Ration Books containing valid War Ration Stamps.

2. The Orders of the Office of Price Administration will designate the stamps to be used for the purchase of a particular rationed product, the period during which each of these stamps may be used, and the amounts which may be bought with each stamp.

3. Stamps become valid for use only when and as directed by the Orders of the Office of Price Administration.

4. Unless otherwise announced, the Ration Week is from Saturday midnight to the following Saturday midnight.

5. War Ration Stamps may be used in any retail store in the United States.

6. War Ration Stamps may be used only by or for the person named and described in the War Ration Book.

7. Every person must see that his War Ration Book is kept in a safe place and properly used. Parents are responsible for the safekeeping and use of their children's War Ration Books.

8. When you buy any rationed product, the proper stamp must be detached in the presence of the storekeeper, his employee, or the person making delivery on his behalf. If a stamp is torn out of the War Ration Book in any other way than above indicated, it becomes void. If a stamp is partly torn or mutilated and more than one-half of it remains in the book, it is valid. Otherwise it becomes void.

9. If your War Ration Book is lost, destroyed, stolen, or mutilated, you should report that fact to the local Ration Board.

10. If you enter a hospital, or other institution, and expect to be there for more than 10 days, you must turn your War Ration Book over to the person in charge. It will be returned to you upon your request when you leave.

11. When a person dies, his War Ration Book must be returned to the local Ration Board, in accordance with the Regulations.

12. If you have any complaints, questions, or difficulties regarding your War Ration Book, consult your local Ration Board.

NOTE

The first stamps in War Ration Book One will be used for the purchase of sugar. When this book was issued, the registrar asked you, or the person who applied for your book, how much sugar you owned on that date. If you had any sugar, you were allowed to keep it, but stamps representing this quantity were torn from your book (except for a small amount which you were allowed to keep without losing any stamps). If your War Ration Book One was issued to you on application by a member of your family, the number of stamps torn from the books of the family was based on the amount of sugar owned by the family, and was divided as equally as possible among all these books.

Points

Each cut of meat was assigned a point value per pound, based not on price or quality, but on scarcity. These point values varied throughout the war depending on supply and demand. "Variety meats" such as kidney, liver, brain, and tongue had little use for the military, so their point values were low. On May 3, 1944, thanks to a good supply, all meats except steak and choice cuts of beef were removed from rationing—temporarily.

✳✳✳   ✳✳✳   ✳✳✳   ✳✳✳   ✳✳✳

Ration coins (introduced in 1944) allowed retailers to give change back for food bought with ration stamps.

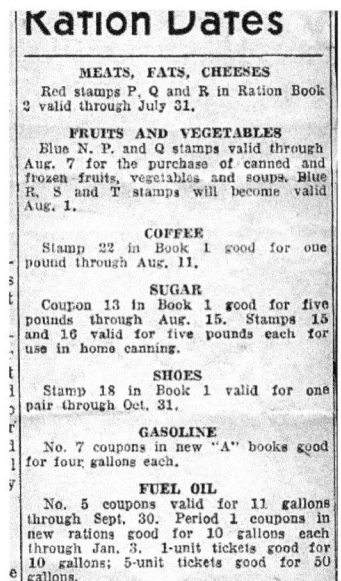

~ ~ ~

Mileage Ration - Fuel Oil Ration

"Dealers in fuel oil or their representatives are hereby authorized to deliver fuel oil to the above person or his agent for use at the above address and are required to detach from this sheet coupons having a gallonage value equal to the quantity of oil delivered, in accordance with the rules and regulations of the Office of Price Administration in effect at the time of such delivery. At the time of delivery, the dealer or his agent must fill in the delivery record below."

These booklets or sheets with the "Mileage Ration" and "Fuel Oil Ration Coupons" had the following instructions, as well as a small form to be filled in by the dealer.

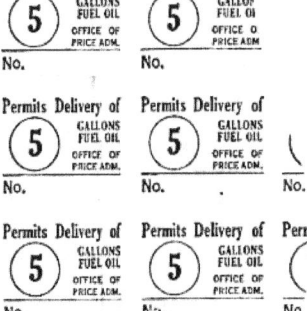

Fuel Oil Ration Coupons

~ ~ ~

The 1943 Sears, Roebuck and Co. catalog assured Americans that they could buy rationed shoes from Sears by mail. *"Simply detach War Ration Stamp No. 17 from your War Ration Book No. 1 (sugar and coffee book) and pin it to your order."*   (Even though the War Ration book stated "void if detached," under the shoe rationing order, the government permitted holders of War Rationing Book No. 1 to tear out War Ration Stamp No. 17 in order to attach it to orders when buying rationed shoes by mail.)

Yes, You Can Buy Rationed Shoes from Sears by Mail

Simply detach War Ration Stamp No. 17 from your War Ration Book No. 1 (sugar and coffee book) and pin it to your order.

NO RATION COUPON IS NEEDED FOR THESE: Soft and hard-soled house slippers, infants' soft-soled shoes, and rubber footwear such as arctics, gaiters, work, dress and toe rubbers.

Question: Can I buy Rationed Shoes by mail?
Answer: Yes.

Question: How?
Answer: Tear out War Ration Stamp No. 17 from your War Ration Book No. 1 (sugar and coffee book). Pin it to your order and send order in the regular way.

Question: Am I allowed to tear War Ration Stamp No. 17 out of War Ration Book No. 1?
Answer: Yes. Even though the War Ration Book states "void if detached." Under the shoe rationing order, the government permits holders of War Rationing Book No. 1 to tear out War Ration Stamp No. 17 in order to attach it to your order when buying rationed shoes by mail.

Question: Must I send money as well as War Ration Stamp?
Answer: Of course War Ration Stamp No. 17 merely permits you to buy shoes under the Rationing order. Handle all other details of your mail order in the usual way.

Question: If you cannot fill my order, will I get back my War Ration Stamp?
Answer: Yes, your War Ration Stamp and your money will be returned to you.

Question: Do I need to send in a War Ration Stamp on an even exchange?
Answer: No.

Question: Is War Ration Stamp No. 17 transferable?
Answer: Yes, among members of the same household. For example, mothers and fathers can use their War Ration Stamps to provide extra shoes for their children.

Question: Should I send in my complete War Ration Book with my mail order?
Answer: No. Send in War Ration Stamp No. 17 only when ordering shoes.

Question: How long may I use War Ration Stamp No. 17 in ordering shoes?
Answer: Until June 15th, 1943.

Question: What happens after June 15, 1943?
Answer: The government will issue instructions as to the proper War Ration Stamp to use after that date. You will be advised through the newspapers and by radio.

Question: What if I do not have a War Ration Book No. 1?
Answer: Apply to your local War Price and Rationing board.

Question: What if I have used all my No. 17 War Ration Stamps?
Answer: Apply to your local War Price and Rationing board for a shoe purchase certificate. Attach this certificate to your mail order.

~ ~ ~

There was a growing problem of transportation facilities diminishing due to the drastic rubber shortage and lack of new equipment. Within the War Transportation Committee was a Traffic Committee that investigated the possibility of installing a passenger ferry to haul workers from possibly Monaca, Beaver and Vanport to the St. Joseph Lead Company plant, as well as the new synthetic rubber plant.   By using a ferry system, it would eliminate a daily roundtrip in many individual vehicles being done by a large volume of the current workers.

~ ~ ~

Some other instructions regarding rationing ....

Feb. 1, 1944
SPECIAL NOTE:
Token program begins Feb. 27. One-point red tokens will be given in change for Red Stamps and one-point Blue Tokens for Blue Stamps. Stamps will be worth 10 points each. Tear Stamps out across Ration Book instead of up and down. Following Stamps become valid Feb. 27:

MEATS AND FATS
Red Stamps A8, B8 and C8 (Book Four) good for 10 points each, Feb. 27 through May 20.

PROCESSED FOODS
Blue Stamps A8, B8, C8, D8 (Book Four) good for 10 points each, Feb. 27 through May 20. Following Stamps remain at present point values.

PROCESSED FOODS
Green Stamps G, H and J (Book Four) good Jan. 1 through Feb. 20.
Green Stamps K, L and M (Book Four) good Feb. 1 through Mar. 20

MEATS AND FATS
Brown Stamps V (Book Three) good Jan. 23 through Feb. 26.
Brown Stamps W good Jan. 30 through Feb. 26.
Brown Stamps X good Feb. 6 through Feb. 26.
Brown Stamps Y good Feb. 13 through Mar. 20.
Brown Stamps Z good Feb. 20 through Mar 20.

SUGAR
Stamp No. 30 (Book Four) good for five pounds Jan. 16 through Mar. 31.

SHOES
Stamp No. 18 (Book One) good for one pair indefinitely. Airplane Stamp No. 1 (Book Three) good for one pair indefinitely.

FUEL OIL
Period No. 2 coupons good for ten gallons per unit through Feb. 7.
Period No. 3 coupons good for ten gallons per unit through Mar. 13.
Period No. 4 coupons and Period No. 5 coupons good for ten gallons per unit Feb. 8 through Sept. 30.

GASOLINE
No. 10 coupons in A book good for three gallons each Jan. 22 through Mar. 21.
B2 and C2 supplemental ration coupons good for five gallons each B1 and C1 coupons remain good for two gallons each. All coupons

Instructions with this listing also stated:
  Tear stamps out across Ration Book instead of up and down.
  Sugar: Stamp No. 30 (Book Four) good for five pounds Jan 16 through Mar 31.
  Fuel Oil: Period No. 2 coupons good for ten gallons per unit through Mar. 13.
  Shoes: Airplane Stamp No. 1 (Book Three) good for one pair indefinitely.

~ ~ ~

War time advertising that was included with numerous want ads for employment were for boys 16 and 17 years old since the men were no longer as available being off and fighting in the war. Women were definitely encouraged and did step in for the men. Women proved their importance as they filled in where the shortfall of male workers occurred. Many women were considered as "doing a man's work" as these pictures portray.

This lady is on top of a tank car, loading finished product for shipment.   Part of the Kobuta plant can be seen behind her.

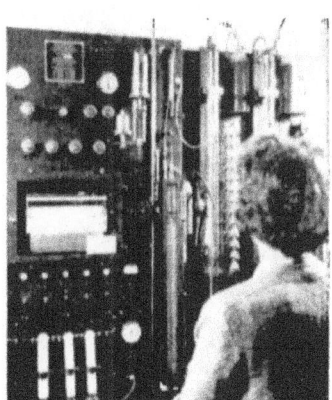

This woman is running a styrene into the apparatus used for distillation tests; a part of the product control procedure at Kobuta.

~ ~ ~

Many ads from various companies and plants would have basically the same statements on their want ads in the employment section of local newspapers. The following were found in 1943 to 1945, at the beginning of want ads section in the newspapers.

Help Wanted—Male

"The War Manpower Commission has ruled that all males in this area may be hired solely upon referral of the United States Employment Service or designated agencies."

Help Wanted--Female

"The War Manpower Commission has ruled that all women in this area now employed in essential activity may be hired only by other essential employers and must have a Statement of Availability." 1944

Miscellaneous ads..................

WAR PLANT CAFETERIA
Experienced:
Bus Girls   Bakers   Cashiers   Salad Girl
Head Sandwich Girl   Female Truck Drivers
The Brandt & Brandt Industrial Cafeteria Operators.
KOPPERS SYNTHETIC RUBBER PLANT
Camp Beaver, Monaca, Pa.

Apr 1943 in The Pittsburgh Press

ALL DAYLIGHT WORK FOR MEN AND WOMEN
WE WILL DEFINITELY EMPLOY WOMEN AFTER THE WAR IS TOTALLY WON
MEN AND WOMEN NEEDED FOR LABORING, OPERATORS OF PIPE CUTTING MACHINES AND TAPPING MACHINE OPERATORS
Regular Work Week — 48 hours — 5½ days
GOOD WAGES — PIECE WORK — BONUS
PITTSBURGH SCREW and BOLT CORP.
COLONA DIVISION, MONACA
Apply U. S. E. S. or our office   Statement of availability required.

May 1945

WANTED MEN and WOMEN
To Work on Army and Navy Ordnance Materiel, No Experience Required.
ALSO BOYS 16 AND 17 WHO ARE ABLE TO PROCURE WORKING CERTIFICATES
Women, here's your opportunity to help your husband, brother, sweetheart, or friend in the service and make excellent wages while doing so!
We also need the following experi... Electricians, Lathe Operator...
APPLY...

WANTED MEN and WOMEN
Mechanics — Semi-Skilled — Laborers
to Produce
SLAB ZINC - ZINC OXIDE - SULPHURIC ACID
Slab Zinc for Catridge and Shell Brass, Ship Propeller Bronze, Bomb Parts, etc. Zinc Oxide for Natural and Synthetic Rubber, Chemical Warfare, Electrical Insulation, etc. Sulphuric Acid for Munitions and Steel Manufacture.
All of these products are raw materials for the manufacture of material of offense
ST. JOSEPH LEAD COMPANY
Of Pennsylvania, Josephtown, Pa.
Telephone for appointment, Roch. 3281
If now employed in Essential Industry, statement of availability is required

(Note the address above – "*Josephtown, Pa*")
The last sentence on this 1943 ad may be too small to read, but states *"If now employed in Essential Industry, a statement of availability is required"*

The need for this statement was almost always included in all want ads. But even if not actually printed, the requirement of the statement was strictly enforced.

~ ~ ~

Boy Scouts were very active in doing their part during war times. Scouts helped the United Service Organization campaign by delivering over 30,000,000 pieces of government literature, posters, and other promotional material. They also participated in the blackout test demonstrations that were held in some of the areas, cities, and towns. During war times, Boy Scouts received special training and organized for service, they were given responsible assignments. Many of their efforts were recognized by national, state, and local public officials. Scouts also were credited with selling 2,350,977 Liberty Loan Bond subscriptions which totaled $354,859,262 and War Savings Stamps at over $52,000,000.

All the general public was encouraged to save scrap black walnut wood, paper, and fruit pits. The Scouts collected over 20,000,000 board feet of the sorely needed walnut wood*. They also collected a hundred carloads of fruit pits.   *The black walnut wood was used to make airplane propellers during WWI. The U.S. government continued to encourage people to give their black walnut trees (and/or wood) to the military to support the war effort during WWII.

~ ~ ~

BUY U. S. DEFENSE BONDS AND STAMPS   1941

War Bonds

In early 1941, a Defense Savings staff was established within the Office of the Secretary and was responsible for promoting savings bond sales to the general public. War Propaganda, Marketing, and Bond Promotion War stamps and bonds played a critical role in selling "the idea of war" to a divided American people. The Treasury used the selling and buying of bonds as a central part of a dedicated propaganda campaign. Obligations to one's family, children, parents, friends, and to the "American Way of Life" were strongly invoked in this campaign to organize Americans on the home front and abroad during World War II. Hollywood, advertising firms, corporations, and small businesses were also key players in the marketing of stamps and bonds.

In addition to targeting special market categories like women, immigrants, and African Americans, the Treasury Department's campaign targeted children. They were considered a vital part of the home front war bond market. Children were one of the special market segments in the Treasury's campaign, they were also exposed to an overwhelming amount of advertising and war propaganda targeted at the general public. Children enjoyed much of the same media entertainment, movies, and radio shows as adults during the war, especially in comic strips and comic books. Therefore, children were constantly urged to purchase stamps and bonds through advertisements in comic books, posters, radio shows, popular songs, and movies with war stamp and bond themes.

Apr 1945

It doesn't take any spade work to cultivate this kind of Victory Garden!

All it takes is common sense.

If you plant a War Bond that costs you $37.50 you get a yield of $50.00. The wisest financiers will tell you there's no better investment in the world. An investment free from every kind of risk—every future disaster! An investment that offers you, in the uncertain years to come, tangible security guaranteed by the United States Government.

Rich or poor—you cannot afford to ignore the rich return your country offers for the loan of your money, or the wisdom of this, the shrewdest investment you can make!

Buy Bonds now when your country needs your dollars to help win the war.

And once your money is safe and sound in War Bonds—don't be tempted to cash them in. Wait for the golden harvest you're entitled to—wait till they're fully matured!

Keep Faith with our Fighters—buy War Bonds for keeps!

THIS ADVERTISEMENT IS A WEEKLY CONTRIBUTION TO AMERICA'S ALL-OUT WAR EFFORT BY THE FOLLOWING BUSINESS INSTITUTIONS:

Barnett's Booterie	Farmers Bldg. & Loan Ass'n	Gordon Camp	Reich's	G. W. Walton Hdwe. Co.
Beaver Lunch	The First National Bank of Monaca	Hartzel Furniture Co.	Rowse's Drug Store	White Front Super Market
Beaver Theatre	The Fort McIntosh Nat'l Bank	Guthrie's Restaurant	Henry Camp, Cleaner	The Phoenix Glass Company
Beaver Trust Company	G. E. McNees, Jeweler & Watchmaker	P. W. Hetzel, Druggist	Miller's Cleaning Shoppe	Sahli Motor Co.
Bruehl's News	Beaver Valley Motor Coach Co.	Jordan's	Mills Radio Co.	Shane Bros.
Robt. F. Garvin	Freedom Federal Savings & Loan Ass'n	Mecklem Brothers	C. H. Niedergal Co.	Beaver Cash Market
Levine Bros. Hdwe.	Impervious Varnish Company	Farmers & Producers	Penn-Beaver	L. D. Sheets, Funeral Home
J. A. Allan, Jeweler	Michel-Meier Glass Company	Dietz Bakery	Pettibon Dairy Co.	Bob Stout
J. T. Anderson	Carraise Home Construction Co.	The Freedom Casket Co.	Schweiger Service	St. Joseph Lead Co.
Balamut Electric Shop	The James W. Doncaster Agency, Inc.			

Many citizens also met with the propaganda via war stamp and bond advertisements placed in newspapers, magazines, posters, billboards, bus and trolley cars, menus, milk cartons, greeting cards, utility bill inserts, and even matchbook covers. Once the United States entered WWII, following the bombing of Pearl Harbor on Dec 7, 1941, everything labeled "Defense" became labeled "War" --- "defense stamps and bonds" became "war stamps and bonds." Sales of the stamps and bonds were moderate before WWII, but during World War II, eighty-five million Americans purchased bonds worth 185.7 billion dollars.

WAR NEEDS MONEY!

"...will cost money to defeat Japan. Your government calls on YOU to help NOW.

"Buy Defense Bonds and Stamps today. Buy them every day, if you can. But buy them on a regular basis.

"Bonds cost as little as $18.75, Stamps come as low as 10 cents. Defense Bonds and Stamps can be bought at all banks and post offices, and Stamps can also be purchased at retail stores and from your newspaper carrier boy.

"This newspaper urges all Americans to support your government with your dollars."

~ ~ ~

During war times, there were many sacrifices that had to be made. The following articles were all found in local newspapers.

Shortage Of Tennis, Golf Balls Feared

NEW YORK, Dec 19—Better not swear at your golf ball when it trickles into a trap. Treat it well. It may be a long time before you get another. Likewise refrain from whamming your tennis ball in anger over the fence.

Both pastimes face an unprecedented shortage in pellets because of the record-breaking rush on sports goods stores that followed publication of drastic rubber conserving orders which go into effect on January 4.

Officials of the United States Golf Association and the U.S. Lawn Tennis Association are optimistic that the shortage will not be as acute as threatened. But their optimism is not shared by leading sports goods manufacturers.

1941

Amusement Prices To Be Taxed Soon

It was reported today that amusement admission prices will be taxed automatically July 1 when the new Federal tax becomes effective.

The increase to cover the tax will be: 3 cents on 25 and 30 cents; 4 cents on 35 and 40 cents, and 5 cents on 45 and 50 cents.

The tax is being imposed by the Federal Government to help finance the national defense program and would not profit the amusement operator.

Jun 1940

Suspension Of Foil Ban Is Announced

By the United Press
WASHINGTON, Nov. 29—The 30-day suspension of an order restricting use of lead and tin foil in packaging, announced by Priorities Director Donald M. Nelson, will make possible a further study of the imminent metal shortages prompting the move.

Nelson's division began an immediate survey of causes underlying the order so that "a final reckoning may be reached as to whether the order should be revoked, modified or put into effect unchanged.

As originally planned, the restrictions would have prohibited after March 15 the use of tin or lead composition foil in manufacture of packaging for tobacco products, all beverages, confections, ribbons for typewriters and other business machines, friction tape and photographic film.

Nov 1941

National Daylight Time Is Proposed

WASHINGTON, Dec. 19.—A nation-wide daylight savings plan to offset wartime blackouts was demanded in the Senate today by Senators Downey, Democrat, California, and Brewster, Republican, Maine.

The California senator presented a petition from San Francisco urging Congress to enact such a system so that workers and the public might reach home before nightfall. In Los Angeles, Downey said, blackouts had caused a five-fold increase in automobile accidents.

Brewster said he was informed that more persons in England had been killed during blackouts and by action of home guards than had died in Nazi bombings.

Dec 1941

~ ~ ~

There was also a War Tax accessed on certain things and activities, including movie theaters who charge 25 cents/adults and 15 cents/children (these prices included the *War Tax*).

~ ~ ~

NEW DRAFT REGISTRANTS TO BE ENROLLED HERE TUESDAY

Every man in Pennsylvania who has attained the 21st anniversary of the day of his birth subsequent to October 16, 1940, and before midnight July 1, 1941—with a few specific exceptions made by Congress—must register with his local Selective Service board on July 1, Dr. William Mather Lewis, state director, said today.

Aliens, as well as American citizens, who have reached 21 years of age by July 1 must be registered, Dr. Lewis emphasized. He also pointed out that aliens between the ages of 21 and 36 years, who have come to the United States since the first registration on October 16, 1940, and have not been registered, must appear before local boards on July 1 to register.

Special registrars will be provided to register men who cannot appear before the local boards because of illness or other incapacity.

Every man subject to registration who is an inmate of an asylum, jail, penitentiary, reformatory, or similar institution on July 1 is required to register on the day he leaves the institution.

PENALTY CITED

Dr. Lewis pointed out today that the penalty for failing to comply with the Selective Training and Service Act is five years' imprisonment and a fine of $10,000.

Approximately 65,000 Pennsylvanians are expected to register tomorrow. Registrations will be taken by the local boards between 7 a.m. and 9 p.m., Eastern Standard Time.

Dr Lewis urged all men who are not certain of their responsibilities, or who desire information, to check with the local boards in their communities.

Jun 1941

~ ~ ~

1970s..............
WWI and WWII were not the only times the government solicited Americans to buy, buy, buy. In the 1960s and 1970s they were once again asking all citizens to show their support and buy U. S. Savings Bonds. Americans were very supportive during WWI, but not quite as enthusiastic with WWII. They were still showing support to the government by the 1960s and 1970s and buying their share of U. S. Savings Bonds.

Often it was said that it was a measure of their lack of business acumen that Americans would be buying approximately $6 million worth of U.S. Savings Bonds in 1973, even though they could have received a much higher rate of interest at banks. It was a fact that Savings Bonds had come a long way since the bond rallies of the 1940s, when they were being sold to finance a world war and also to curb the domestic consumption. School children bought them up in the 1940s, saving up little red stamps with minutemen on them, even though the Treasury was only paying 2.9 per cent interest on them.

Some facts of the Savings Bonds being purchased in the 1970s:
- Under many circumstances compared to bank rates, Savings Bonds were a terrible buy.

- Savings Bonds were safer than bank accounts only if one could conceive of Congress letting the Federal Deposit Insurance Corp. go down the drain.
- There were many advantages to Savings Bonds including the fact that with some simple planning, you could get out of paying any federal income tax on the interest on Series E Bonds, the most common type of Savings Bond.
- There were many advantages to holding the Savings Bonds beyond their maturity dates, something that wasn't available with time deposits in banks and other institutions.
- People could convert Series E Bonds into Series H Bonds – one way of providing retirement income and escaping income taxes.
- During most of the years between 1964 and 1973, Savings Bonds had not contributed a penny toward financing federal deficits because more was paid out on bonds that had been cashed in when compared to the amount when they had been purchased. There were campaigns in 1970 to get people to cash in their bonds on the grounds that bonds were a poor investment and as a protest against the Vietnam War. It was thought that Bonds were marketed primarily to those at the lower end of the economic scale, unlike other government securities that could pay higher interest and were marketed in higher denominations that only the rich could afford. In fact, between 1964 and 1970, the Treasury had to actually borrow $7 billion elsewhere just to pay off people who were cashing in their bonds.
- Interest rates were increased after 1972, from 5.5 per cent to 6 per cent, to encourage people to keep buying them. The public was subjected to a massive and continued selling job to encourage buying more Savings Bonds. Even the military strongly urged soldiers by Company Bond Officers to buy bonds. The propaganda to buy Savings Bonds was working because many, many people continued to buy the bonds which yielded almost two per cent less than banks (which were between 7.25 and 7.5 per cent on certificates of deposit and some savings accounts).

10 cent Savings Bond stamp album school students would purchase.

Sample bonds

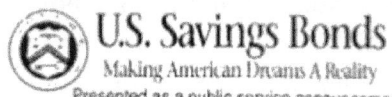

Feb 1966

~ ~ ~

A key "war plant"..................
The Koppers Company in Kobuta, Potter Township, was built during World War II for the manufacturing of synthetic rubber. It was built by the government in 1943, at a cost of $61 million. Koppers continued to operate the plant on lease even after the war. (See pictures and additional information in the Industries section on Koppers Company and in the Housing section on the Kobuta community.)

~ ~ ~

Tank Farm – Potter Township
As well known, ships, aircraft, and other military equipment require massive amounts of fuel. In their preparation for the war in 1942, the U.S. Government established strategic fuel facilities near key locations and ports. One was the tank farm project located in Potter Township on Mowry Road. The government felt these facilities were needed to hide and protect the storage of aviation fuel from possible air attacks by the enemy.

An article in The Daily Times earlier in 1941, stated rumors were persisting that the U.S. Army Engineers were interested in a large track of land near the mouth of Raccoon Creek on the south side of the Ohio River. The government engineers had been making surveys for weeks and there were test holes being drilled. Surveys had also been made of other adjacent properties, including the nearby former Hostetter farm, which had a 4,000-foot frontage on the Ohio River. These properties were all being well suited for manufacturing sites.

At that particular time, the 300-acres of land above the Potter Bridge on Route 18 belonged to Mr. and Mrs. William R. Jeffreys of Beaver. The Jeffreys had purchased this former Braden family property in Aug of 1930. This specific parcel was only a portion of the acreage originally purchased/patented by James Braden from the Commonwealth of Pennsylvania on Oct 11, 1788, when it was still Raccoon Township. There was originally an estimated 1,000 acres of south side real estate, but massive acreage had been sold to the St. Joseph Lead Company along the Ohio River. The Jeffreys' property was surveyed by the U.S. Engineers and determined to contain 293.04 acres. This land included Alum Rock Park along Raccoon Creek and other farmland, much of which was under cultivation. Mr. Jeffreys was said to have been engaged in raising beef steer, cattle, and Belgian horses. The property already contained a two-storey stone farmhouse, a frame barn, and a 40'x40' wagon shed.

The federal government did indeed purchase the almost 300-acres of the former Braden farm in Potter Township in 1941, from Mr. and Mrs. Jeffreys. This purchase also included the house, stable, and wagon shed on the property. While this parcel was owned by the government, they used the property as a "tank farm" which was classified as a secret project with the government. They made the decision to build the massive "tank farm" on this acreage to hold over 10-million gallons of high-octane aviation fuel in six huge underground tanks. This was such a secretive operation that the local residents were sworn to absolute secrecy. The acreage was disguised as a farm and contained what simply appeared to be a farm with a house and two large barns, along with a few pieces of farm equipment strategically placed. The farmhouse was converted to a changing and generator house and the barns were used for ethyl blending. Pump houses were also erected and cleverly disguised as residential homes elsewhere on nearby properties between the "tank farm" and the river.

The former farm was converted by trucking in the needed steel components to build the sunken storage tanks. Each tank was riveted together on-site. Once the tanks were all completed, the area was filled in with dirt to cover and hid the assembled tanks, making them officially known as "underground storage tanks" (UST). As the tanks were being completed, the former farm's buildings were also converted, and the miscellaneous houses/pump stations were erected. Along with the tanks, and buildings, there was also an estimated 8 miles of pipeline which led from the "tank farm" to a barge area and railroad car and truck loading area. The pump houses, which were disguised as smaller farmhouses, aided in the moving of the fuel as needed.

Throughout the years when the property was actively being used by the government, the entire parcel was enclosed with inconspicuous security fencing. The "locals" took their sworn secrecy seriously and would ward off any trespassers or curious persons. They surprisingly kept quite tight lipped regarding the actual usage of the property. By the mid 1960s it was no longer a secret project area, yet the folk lore continued to spread. There were many tales of mystery and fabrications of why this property had chain link and barb wire fencing around it and what the literal usage of it was. Some of the tales included it had hidden missile launching pads. Through the years following the end of the war, eventually bits and pieces of the truth began to emerge. From the mid 1960s until 1975, my family's Sunday rides would almost always include going past the property at least once a month to see if there was any activity or if you could spot anything other than one of the barns and a small building.

In 1963, the government sold the land as a surplus to Beaver County, who then resold the property to St. Joe Lead Company (became Zinc Corp. of America). The property was subdivided, and the six huge underground fuel tanks remained, along with several of the buildings which were still standing on one of the lots. All consisting of almost 63 ½ acres.

The tanks themselves were no longer being used by 1963. They had been drained, yet the empty tanks remained in place along with all the piping, all buried underground. The actual ownership of the property changed hands over the years. From 1941 to 1963, the Air Force owned the property. Then 1964 to 1984, St. Joe Mineral were the owners, and 1985 to 2004, Horsehead Industries owned the property. With a Chapter 11 bankruptcy proceeding, Horsehead Industries abandoned the "tank farm" and Potter Township eventually became the owners by eminent domain. Under the Formerly Used Defense Sites (FUDS) program, the U.S. Army Corps of Engineers Baltimore District began the process of assessing and finding a solution to cleaning up the properties. Many studies and assessments were done over the years to evaluate the environmental impact of the entire site. Explosive Ordnance Technologies, Inc (EOTI) was awarded the project portion of it all, this was awarded through the US Army Engineering Support Center Huntsville Worldwide Remediation Services (WERS) contract.

Finally, the "remediation project" was started, as was the chore to expose and remove the underground piping and all the tanks, all to be properly taken apart for off-site recycling.

Photos from Milestone s BCHR&LF

This is a photo of one of the underground hi-octane aircraft fuel tanks in the process of being removed by the US Army Corp of Engineers. This was a 1.74-million-gallon tank. The Air Force Petroleum, Oil and Lubricant Facility was located along Mowry Road in Potter Township, Monaca during WWII. These underground tanks on the "fuel tank farm" were finally removed in 2012.

This picture reflects the massive size of these tanks, this is a photo of a person inside one of the 1.74-million-gallon tanks.

This photo is showing a huge pile of the scraps from the tanks. The building was the former stone farmhouse which was converted to a generator and changing station.

~ ~ ~

Information which was made available to the public in 1956.........

IN CASE OF ATOMIC ATTACK

Remember this Special Radio Frequency: 640 k. c. or 1240 k. c.

Under the CONELRAD System, in case of enemy attack, all radios will go off the air and certain stations will begin broadcasting at 640 kilocycles and 1240 kilocycles. Turn your radio to 64 or 124 for messages from federal, state and local Civilian Defense agencies.

KNOW THESE OFFICIAL AIR RAID SIGNALS:
ALERT: 3 Minutes of wailing sirens or horns.
ALL CLEAR: 3 One Minute blasts. Two minutes of silence between blasts.

FOLLOW THESE AIR RAID INSTRUCTIONS:
FIRE is an air raid's most horrible result. Take sensible precautions against causes of unnecessary fires—faulty electrical circuits and fixtures, accumulated junk and trash. Keep your home clear of fire hazards.

ATOMIC ATTACK PROTECTION

ALWAYS Put First Things First And NEVER Lose Your Head And —

1. **TRY TO GET SHIELDED**
   If you have time, get down in a basement or subway. Should you unexpectedly be caught out-of-doors, seek shelter alongside a building, or jump in any handy ditch or gutter.

2. **DROP FLAT ON GROUND OR FLOOR**
   To keep from being tossed about and to lessen the chances of being struck by falling and flying objects, flatten out at the base of a wall, or at the bottom of a bank.

3. **BURY YOUR FACE IN YOUR HANDS**
   When you drop flat, hide your eyes in the crook of your elbow. That will protect your face from flash burns, prevent temporary blindness and keep flying objects out of your eyes.

4. **DON'T RUSH OUTSIDE RIGHT AFTER A BOMBING**
   After an air burst, wait a few minutes, then go help to fight fires. After other kinds of bursts, wait at least one hour to give lingering radiation some chance to die down.

5. **DON'T TAKE CHANCES WITH FOOD OR WATER IN OPEN CONTAINERS**
   To prevent radioactive poisoning or disease, select your food and water with care. When there is reason to believe they may be contaminated, stick to canned and bottled things if possible.

6. **DON'T START RUMORS**
   In the confusion that follows a bombing, a single rumor might touch off a panic that could cost your life.

KEYS TO HOUSEHOLD SAFETY

1. **STRIVE FOR "FIREPROOF HOUSEKEEPING"**
   Don't let trash pile up, and keep waste paper in covered containers. When an alert sounds, do all you can to eliminate sparks by shutting off the oil burner and covering all open flames.

2. **KNOW YOUR OWN HOME**
   Know which is the safest part of your cellar, learn how to turn off your oil burner and what to do about utilities.

3. **HAVE EMERGENCY EQUIPMENT AND SUPPLIES HANDY**
   Always have a good flashlight, a radio, first-aid equipment and a supply of canned goods in the house.

4. **CLOSE ALL WINDOWS AND DOORS AND DRAW THE BLINDS**
   If you have time when an alert sounds, close the house up tight in order to keep out fire sparks and radioactive dusts and to lessen the chances of being cut by flying glass. Keep the house closed until all danger is past.

5. **USE THE TELEPHONE ONLY FOR TRUE EMERGENCIES**
   Do not use the phone unless absolutely necessary. Leave the lines open for real emergency traffic.

~ ~ ~

GREAT DEPRESSION

W.P.A.   C.C.C.   New Deal

Between 1929 and 1939, Center Township residents suffered along with all other Americans in the worst economic downturn in the history of the industrialized world known as *The Great Depression*. Through these years spending and investments dropped which caused a drastic decline in industrial output. There were massive layoffs as company after company began to close. It all started after the stock market crashed in Oct 1929, which wiped out millions of investors and caused panic on Wall Street. 1933 was considered the peak of Great Depression. This is when most reached their lowest point. Also, by this time, almost half of the banks in America had failed. There were approximately fifteen million Americans who were unemployed. Franklin D. Roosevelt was president, and he began addressing the public over the radio in a series of talks that became known as "fireside chats." The public reacted very favorably to these broadcasts and confidence slowly began to be restored.

Rather than just provide relief in the form of checks and/or food, Harry Hopkins (the relief administrator) thought it better for the government to provide jobs. Thus, the government took many other actions to address the troubles. Congress was to pass reform legislation and therefore reopen any banks still determined to be sound. There were programs and institutions to aid in recovery from the Great Depression under Roosevelts "New Deal" plan. This plan included the Works Progress Administration (W.P.A.) which provided people a position in a permanent job program from 1935 to 1943. Even though all these actions did produce signs of some recovery, there was another recession that hit in 1937. This was caused partly by the Federal Reserve's new requirements for money in reserve. This second recession reversed many of the steps that had been taken forward in the economy, production, and employment. It proved to extend the effects of the Great Depressions.

The New Deal agency

It was started by an executive order signed by President Franklin D. Roosevelt on May 6, 1933. It was one of many Great Depression relief programs created under the auspices of the Emergency Relief Appropriations Act signed by Roosevelt in Apr 1933. The American New Deal agency employed millions of unemployed people to carry out public works projects.

Between 1935 and 1943 the W.P.A. provided almost eight and a half million jobs to Americans who would have otherwise been on relief rolls. The W.P.A. spent an estimated 10.5 billion dollars (would be equal to over 192 billion dollars nowadays). Some of the various agencies which were started consisted of: 1933 – Civilian Conservation Corps (C.C.C.)
        1933 – 1934 – Civil Works Administration (C.W.A.)
        1933 – 1938 – Federal Emergency Relief Administration (F.E.R.A.)
        1935 – 1939 – Works Progress Administration (W.P.A.)
Effective Jul 1, 1939, the Federal Works Agency (F.W.A.) was also established.

C.C.C. - Civilian Conservation Corps.

The C.C.C. was a part of the New Deal plan. It was a public work relief program that operated between 1933 and 1942 for men who were unemployed, unmarried, and 18 to 25 years of age. The ages were then expanded to include 17 to 28. It was started to provide jobs for these young single men and to relieve their families whose members had difficulty finding jobs during the Great Depression. Many young men of the township (and entire area) left their homes and headed off to join the C.C.C. These young men were watching their families suffering to provide food. Many felt if they left, it was one less mouth to feed at home. They were guaranteed three meals a day if in the C.C.C. and they would also have monies to share with their families. C.C.C. workers often commented on how good the food was at the C.C.C. camps. As a testament to this, it was reported that on an average, each worker gained eleven pounds during their C.C.C. service time.

C.C.C. camps were supervised by the military; therefore, the camp life closely resembled a military regimen. Many had the men up and starting their day at 6:30 am, then some type of physical exercise which was followed by a breakfast, then roll call. The men typically worked from 8 a.m. until 4 p.m. and had to be back at camp with lights out by 10 p.m. They each were paid $30 per month with $25 of that being sent back home to their families. Many of the men also took advantage of classes that were offered on Saturdays. They could earn educational certificates after completing 156 hours of training. These hours were combined and covered many various programs.

Records indicate that the C.C.C. workers planted nearly three billion trees, built over 125,000 miles of roads, strung thousands of miles of telephone lines, built 800 new parks in 47 states, and cleaned/improved thousands of beaches. Local workers were also used to combat forest fires and gave assistance and aid to families in the area affected by the 1936's St. Patrick's Day flood.

There was no specific listing with individual township names, but Beaver County had more than 600 estimated young people in the C.C.C. There were at least two known of the many camps which were associated with the current Raccoon Park area. The actual camp buildings no longer exist but the projects completed by the workers of the C.C.C. are still being used, many in Raccoon Park itself.

W.P.A. – Works Progress Administration / renamed to Works Projects Administration
This program was part of and considered the most successful of the New Deal plans. It was started in 1935 by President Roosevelt. It was renamed in 1939 to Works Projects Administration. W.P.A. was designed to provide relief for any unemployed person by providing jobs and income to millions of Americans. Only one member of any given household could hold a W.P.A. position and any person seeking to apply for any W.P.A. work had to prove they were on welfare to get a job. This program was said to have provided dignity to those who had been begging for handouts.

The W.P.A. was responsible for building structures, airports, seaports, bridges, paving roads, and creating parks. It also funded humanities programs, including Federal Arts Project, Federal Writers Project, Federal Theatre Project, National Health Survey, and the Historical Records Survey (H.R.S.). The H.R.S. was organized in 1935 and responsible for documenting resources for research into American history. The H.R.S. was responsible for creating soundex indexes of the federal census, compiled indexes of vital statistics, cemetery interments, school records, military records, maps, newspapers, and the list goes on and on. These indexes have been placed on microfilms by many other organizations. Genealogists, really anyone, who has or will be conducting researching should be aware of the W.P.A. publications in the area(s) of researching because many historical records survey programs were established as a branch or division of the federal W.P.A.

There were many township residents who were employed by the W.P.A. programs. There were numerous projects done across Beaver County --- paving of roads, inventory of all school properties, and the recording of inscriptions from tombstone in county cemeteries. I did not find specific details of many major projects performed exclusively in Center Township through the W.P.A. One project known to be done in the township was the Baker Cemetery (also known as Figley Farm Cemetery) off Pleasant Drive. It was listed as No. 35 on the 1936 W.P.A. list. The closest infrastructure type project found was in 1936 was the W.P.A. spending $10,000 in painting and repairing the Beaver County Home in Potter Township. It was done by forty men over a four-month period.

Several other projects were also done adjacent to Center and Potter townships, some are even still standing. These included, the 1889 wharf in Monaca (now defunct, formerly along the shoreline by the current Water Works building) was enlarged, the Monaca Water Works building and almost all the retaining walls and block work surrounding/adjacent to the Water Works were erected, a fountain area not far from the Water Works building (fountain no longer operates but the round structure still stands) was built, and repairs were done to various athletic fields in the Monaca borough. Allaire Park on Monaca Heights was developed/built as one of the projects. They also worked with the C.C.C. to build many retaining walls, including the lengthy one on 14th Street Hill and the former retaining wall of the German Lutheran cemetery. The W.P.A. assisted the C.C.C. in developing and establishing Raccoon Park as a Recreational Demonstration Area, constructing its earliest buildings in 1935. (See Recreation section.) They constructed the former Gypsy Glenn Park (now Shaw Park) in Beaver, and a picnic pavilion, the borough pool, and the high school football stadium.

Additionally, the U.S. Treasury Department's Section of Fine Arts commissioned artists to create works for public display in postal buildings across the country during the Great Depression. There were several of these done in Beaver County. One was completed by Niles Spencer, titled *Western Pennsylvania*. It was a 15 feet 4 inches wide by 5 feet 7 inches high canvas mural done in oil and was pasted to the wall of the Aliquippa Post Office in Jan 1938. The mural hung for three decades before it was necessary to remove it during the renovation of the post office in the 1960s. Unfortunately, the contractors literally took no care and just ripped it off the wall, causing massive and what some say unrepairable damage. The remnants of this mural were moved to the Smithsonian American Art Museum in Washington, D.C., and it remains in storage there.

There are only a few other known art works remaining in the immediate area. A wood relief sculpture, *Steel Workers*, by Humbert Albrizio is in the Midland Post Office. An oil on canvas mural by Eugene Higgins (born in Missouri), *The Armistice Letter*, is in the Beaver Falls Post Office. Richard Hay Kenah (native of New Brighton) completed an oil on canvas mural for the auditorium of the old Ambridge High School. It is a depiction of the Harmony Society. It was donated to Old Economy in Ambridge. The mural was carefully removed, taken to Harrisburg for restoration, and may be viewed today at the Old Economy Village Visitor's Center. There was also a three-piece wood relief sculpture, *Racoon, Deer, and Fox,* completed by Nena de Brennecke (born in Argentina) that once hung in the Coraopolis Post Office. It disappeared when the post office was sold in c1980 and currently remains missing.

All inclusive, it is reported between 1935 and 1943, W.P.A. workers and/or the C.C.C. built:
- 650,000 miles of roads
- 78,000 bridges
- 700 miles of airport runway
- 125,000 civilian and military buildings
- 800 airports (built, improved or enlarged)

Not just manual work was utilized through the Great Depression because of these programs, many other projects were done, and as mentioned previous, even artists and authors were put to work. In general, many of these workers were also responsible for:
- 900 million hot lunches served to school children
- 1,500 nursery schools operated
- 225,000 musical concerts presented to 150 million people
- 475,000 works of art, 276 books, and 701 pamphlets created
- delivered library books (sometimes on horseback) to rural outposts
- provided disaster relief for hurricane and flood victims (including in Western Pennsylvania with the 1936 St. Patrick's Day flood)
- sewed clothing and bed sheets for those in need
- cleared slums, repaired toys, helped the sick and provided electricity to places that never before had even seen an electric light

During the years of the Great Depression, not only America and Americans suffered; it also aided the rise of extremist political movements in Europe. Adolf Hitler's Nazi regime in Germany was one of the most notable of these. In 1939, war broke out in Europe largely due to the German aggression. With this, the United States was remaining neutral, but the W.P.A. then centered more of their attention in aiding the military infrastructure of the United States. Then the Japanese attack Pearl Harbor in Dec 1941. Although the Great Depression was ending, America was then entering into WWII and the nation's factories were put back in full production mode; this greatly reduced the unemployment rate to even below the pre-Depression levels.

(Anyone who may have an interest in learning more on the W.P.A. should purchase Nick Taylor's 2008 book "*American Made: The Enduring Legacy of the W.P.A.: When FDR Put the Nation to Work*;" it is very informative.)

On the 1940 census enumeration, the following township persons were found to have been employed by and working on projects of the W.P.A. or C.C.C. These persons had either W.P.A. or C.C.C. actually listed on the census sheet as their employer.

- Harry Adamson – hospital
- John Anderson – stone mason
- John Buchazk -
- Judson Campbell – laborer
- Raymond Doak – supervisor
- Hugo Eder – laborer
- Howard Equanlauf – laborer
- John Esherr – laborer
- George Fath – laborer - construction project
- Howard Gillian – laborer
- William Grimes - laborer
- Carl Irons – foreman
- John Jolley – laborer – state highway
- Charles Kugel – stone mason – water works
- Bennie Lutcha – laborer
- Charles Laughhead – Manager – water works
- Fred Mateer – foreman
- Lawrence Multans – laborer
- Josef Mamula – laborer
- Jacob Parsons – stone quarry
- Ray Patterson – laborer – state highway
- Evertt Patterson – truck driver – state highway
- Steve Perun - laborer
- David Rambo – carpentry
- Eli Rebich – laborer
- Henry Shephard - laborer
- Alvin Speary – stone mason
- Melvin Sutton – driver
- Andy Tedic
- Rudy Tedic
- Frank Tepole – stone cutter – water works
- Delbert Weigle - laborer - construction project
- Erwin Winkle – stone mason
- Thomas Winkle
- Anna Zimmerman – sewing

~ ~ ~

Fun fact: Congress also passed the Social Security Act in 1935 since America was the only country in the world at that time without some form of unemployment insurance or social security. This Act provided Americans with unemployment, disability, and pensions for their old age for the first time.

ADS and INTERESTING ARTICLES

Big fashion sales, whatever the newest trend, and even automobiles may not have been the top priority for many of the early Moon/Center Township residents through the years. Instead, they would probably open a local newspaper, like *The Daily Times*, one of the predecessors to the *Beaver County Times*, and search for weather forecasts, the Farm Bureau Notes, and other farming and gardening news.

From the 1920s:

THRESH WHEAT NOW AND AVOID HEAVY LOSSES.

There is urgent need of threshing the wheat at once, placing it in air-tight bins in the granary and fumigating with carbon bisulphide to prevent further damage from the Angoumois grain moth. This insect is infesting the wheat crop in some 13 counties in the southeast corner of Pennsylvania and causes an estimated annual loss of one million dollars. The longer the wheat stays in the straw the more damage will be done, so thresh the grain at once.

For complete instructions on eradicating this pest, write to the Bureau of Plant Industry, Pennsylvania Department of Agriculture, Harrisburg, Pa.

DAIRY HINTS.

The size of the herd should determine the size of the new silo. A tall narrow silo is better for a small herd than a short one of large diameter. From two to three inches should be fed from the top of the silage each day in order to avoid any possibility of the silage molding from the surface.

A good judge of bottled milk will look at the bottom of the bottle rather than the cream line. Clean milk is of vital importance at all times, but especially during the summer months. In buying milk consider therefore the amount of sediment in the bottom of the bottles and the possibility of germ contamination, as well as the cream line. Not all rich milk is safe milk.

FARM BUREAU NOTES

GARDEN HINTS

If celery plants start slowly, encourage them by better cultivation, watering if possible, or perhaps a dash of nitrate of soda along the row. The nitrate may be mixed with the water at the rate of one teaspoonful of nitrate crystals in one gallon of water. The nitrate will produce quick growth, which is desired since slow growing celery is never of high quality and may run to seed.

About one week after celery plants have been set out into the field they should be sprayed with Bordeaux mixture 4-4-50 to prevent blight.

FARMERS ADVERTISING

Advertisers Should Notify This Office When They Want Their Ads Discontinued.

WANTED—Coon, skunk or hunting dog. Address George E. Negley, O.

FOR SALE—Two Guernsey cows fresh with calf at side, one bred three months; good milkers and cows; will sell reasonable. Sproat, R. F. D. Conway, Pa.

FOR SALE — Four-year-old horse. Address George Burson, Ohio.

FOR SALE—Two registered Friesian cows, young bull calf. Freed, Racine, Pa., Homewood Ju...

FOR SALE — Registered white sows and pigs. Registration J. A. Boak & Sons, New Castle, R. D No. 4.   7|14-21-28—8

LATE BLIGHT

STATE COLLEGE, Pa., Aug. 18.— Pennsylvania potato growers are facing an enormous loss this year as a result of an epidemic of late blight and only quick action on their part will prevent the destruction of a large part of the crop. Coming as early as it has, this dreaded disease of the potato will cut the yield 50 per cent or more in the important potato growing sections of the state.

The unusual amount of rainfall accompanied by cool nights has furnished such ideal conditions for the development and spread of the blight that already hundreds of fields have been destroyed and with the continuation of rainy weather growers may look for an epidemic of blight such as Pennsylvania has not seen in years.

Growers whose plants are still alive their vines are protected against blight by thoroughly spraying them with Bordeaux Mixture every ten to 14 days. If blight has already entered the field the spraying will help very materially in checking the spread of the disease.

County farm bureau agents can give complete details as to the mixing and applying of Bordeaux.

~ ~ ~

The following notice found in a local newspaper was not limited to Center Township, but the subject matter would have been of great interest to many of the farmers in the township. I found it quite concerning since I did not know that TB could be transmitted this way.....

> The herd of Arnold Brothers, Beaver Falls, R. D. 4, was recently tested by the Federal and State authorities under the Accredited Herd Plan. This makes a total of 20 herds in Beaver county which have passed the first test showing that they are free from tuberculosis.

~ ~ ~

1912 "Poultry Notes" -

"Collect eggs every day shortly before noon, or preferably twice daily, at noon and at dusk. A chick, like a baby, will get good or bad habits according to the way it is started in this world. To keep chicks growing and thriving they must be fed well and often, and their crops kept clean. Separate the chicks as soon as sex can be distinguished, because one will retard the growth of the other."

~ ~ ~

> Agriculture is the backbone of the nation. History has proven this. Every nation since the beginning of time that has forgotten God and neglected agriculture has failed.

Mar 1921

~ ~ ~

Snippets of additional local news items:

> **Remedy for Sprains.**
> Bruise thoroughly one handful of green sage leaves, boil them in a gill of vinegar for ten minutes, apply to the sprained joint as a poultice between folded muslin. Rest the joint as much as possible.

from 1911

AN OLD RECIPE TO DARKEN HAIR

Sage Tea and Sulphur Turns Gray, Faded Hair Dark and Glossy

Almost everyone knows that Sage Tea and Sulphur, properly compounded, brings back the natural color and lustre to the hair when faded, streaked or gray. Years ago the only way to get this mixture was to make it at home, which is mussy and troublesome.

Nowadays we simply ask at any drug store for "Wyeth's Sage and Sulphur Compound." You will get a large bottle of this old-time recipe improved by the addition of other ingredients, at very little cost. Everybody uses this preparation now, because no one can possibly tell that you darkened your hair, as it does it so naturally and evenly. You dampen a sponge or soft brush with it and draw this through your hair, taking one small strand at a time; by morning the gray hair disappears, and after another application or two, your hair becomes beautifully dark, thick and glossy and you look years younger. Adv.

from 1924

~ ~ ~

A small article in The Daily Times in Jul 1925 made me smile.   This article was title "The Good Old Days."   Even in 1925, they had "good old days" ☺

THE GOOD OLD DAYS.

Newspapers often speak of the good old days. But were they any better than they are today? In the so-called good old days the world never enjoyed the exercise of dodging automobiles; there was no static to exercise one's vocal chords; a bootlegger was just a plain bum instead of a financier, and if a man ever dreamed of an airpplane he took a big dose of castor oil the next day for a bilious attack. There is a mistake. These are the good old days."

~ ~ ~

In the earlier years, most Center residents had a true need to own some type of firearm. The area was quite rural, and many aided a hunter to provide auxiliary meat for the family tables. I am sure that many of these residents were not pleased with this action.

Act Requiring Arms Registration Sought

By the United Press

WASHINGTON, Jan. 2—A Justice Department official today said Congress would be asked to enact legislation requiring the registration of all firearms as a defense measure.

The measure will be urged, he said, as a protective step against efforts of fifth column elements to build up secret arsenals which might endanger internal security. Fingerprinting of the owners of all types of firearms also will be recommended.

The administration has made several attempts to obtain legislation requiring registration of firearms, but each has failed in the House. Prior proposals would have required a license fee. The fee proposal has been eliminated from the new measure.

The Daily Times – Jan of 1941

~ ~ ~

Where is "Lonely-Land" on the Map?

"Lonely-Land" is the home without a Beaver County Telephone

Beaver County Telephone Company

Contract Department 5222

1917 ad

~ ~ ~

Identity problems………………
   With all the advertising, computer apps, and guidelines to protect your identity nowadays, I found this 1986 contest very interesting………….

Note – you were to enter your social security number in the blank box above and submit it to be eligible for a prize.   Talk about handing out private information on a silver spoon !!!!

~ ~ ~

Fun Fact: Do you remember this cartoon strip?

Beaver County Times - Jan 1963

'Beetle Baily' To Start Monday

The popular cartoon strip "Beetle Baily" will start in the comic pages of the TIMES Monday.

Mort Walker, creator cartoonist of the strip about the Army's worst private, has found out that not only if you laugh the world laughs with you, but pays good money for the privilege as well.

In eleven years the Kansas-born artist has skyrocketed to the very peak of the cartoon world with his strip about the gawky, permanent yardbird of the Army which has become one of the two most popular comic strips in the world today.

But being on top isn't anything new for the quiet-spoken Walker. At the tender age of 26, before he created Beetle and began his daily strip, he was the number one magazine gag cartoonist in the country in the amount of sales.

His first cartoon sale was at the age of eleven. By the age of 14 he was selling gag cartoons regularly to "Child Life," "Inside Detective" and "Flying Aces" magazine. At 15 he was a comic strip artist for a daily metropolitan newspaper; by 16 more than 300 of his cartoons had been published.

Mort is one of four children and was born Addison Morton Walker in Eldorado, Kansas, Sept. 3, 1923. The family later moved to Kansas City where he attended high school. It was there he began drawing a strip called "The Lime-Juicers" for the now-defunct Kansas City Journal. When the paper folded, Mort went to work after school in the stockroom of the Hallmark greeting card company. Within three years he became its chief designer. He was just 18.

* * *

THEN he enrolled at the University of Missouri but shortly after he was drafted and became a rifleman in an infantry company. Thus Beetle was born but nobody knew it yet. He later attended infantry OCS and then served in Italy as an intelligence and investigating officer. He was discharged in 1946 as a first lieutenant.

In New York, after graduation from the University of Missouri, he had a hard time of it for awhile. His first 200 cartoons were rejected but his persistent pounding on editors' doors paid off eventually. Within a short time after his first sale there, he became one of the top 10 magazine cartoonists in the country. In 1949 he married the girl back home, Jean Suffill, an artist from Kansas City. They now live in Greenwich, Conn., with their six children, four boys and two girls.

Walker rates exceptionally high with other artists as well as the public. In 1953 he won the Billy DeBeck Memorial Award of the National Cartoonists Society — the "Oscar" of the cartoon profession. This is an honor which in the past has gone only to long-established artists in this field such as Chic Young, Milton Caniff and Roy Crane, all of whom have had features going for 20 years or more.

Then in 1955 the Banshees, famous New York luncheon club of artists, writers, editors and others in the creative fields, presented its "Silver Lady" award to him, naming him the "outstanding newspaper cartoonist of 1955." Conspicuous in the audience of nearly a thousand were 19 generals, four admirals and 21 winners of the Congressional Medal of Honor — all avowed Beetle fans.

THE ARMY loves Beetle now but back in 1954 someone — never fully identified — decided to eliminate him from the Tokyo edition of the "Stars and Stripes" because the strip allegedly poked too much fun at the brass. This "breaking" of Beetle was the making of him.

After the news services and news magazines had spread it around the globe, the brass announced that it was dropped because of "lack of interest." About this time, mail started arriving from Korea and other points asking what happened to Beetle and the Pentagon hurriedly disclaimed any connection with the deed. Meantime, back at the office, clients were fighting to sign Beetle up as their paper's exclusive property. He now appears in 640 newspapers throughout the world.

~ ~ ~

Fun fact: In 1800, prices for items were:

Sugar – 35 cents/lb.   Salt - $13.75/bushel   Whiskey - $1.85/gallon

~ ~ ~

The Daily Times would often put in little "statements" as fillers to balance columns.

1941 – The odds in shooting craps are 351 to 344 against the caster.

1950s - tip for farmers: A rusty knife can be cleaned very satisfactorily by dipping a damp cloth in ashes and rubbing the blade thoroughly until the rust disappears.

~ ~ ~

An ad from Dec in 1925

"Give a RADIO.....For the tot who delights in bed-time stories; to the woman who wants household helps; to the miss or matron who loves music and song; to grandma who wants to live again in the days of Annie Laurie and the stately minuet; to the man of affairs who wants immediate touch with the world news and stock market; to those who want jazz, jest or jollity—a radio is a welcome gift."

~ ~ ~

As stated in the Newspaper section, homeowners would use old newspapers under carpets in the home to provide padding and extra warmth.   This statement was found in a 1909 issue of The Daily Times.

"Old papers for sale at this office, one hundred in a bundle, suitable for placing under carpets. Ten cents a bundle."

~ ~ ~

In Jul 1917, the local newspaper, The Daily Times, had ads for these two items.   Personally, I never heard of either, but they were evidently in stores of the area since they were being locally advertised.

Fun facts:
I did not find which exact stores carried these two products, but..........
   The Battle Creek Breakfast Food Co. was the originator of Washington Crisps, but the name of the company was changed in 1910.
   Ridgways Tea was from Ridgways Incorporated, New York, N.Y. and Chicago, Ill.   They had filed for a patent for the name of Ridgways Tea for their packages in 1916.

~ ~ ~

It is apparent for numerous years, many residents within Center Township have been displeased with decisions being made by the local officials.   When will our local officials begin to listen?

from 1989
> If the Board votes for the commercial zoning of Brodhead, they may think they are voting for "progress." But that "progress" was exactly what I was trying to get away from when I moved here. Please, let's keep Center the residential community that it is, not build it into a congested traffic jam.

~ ~ ~

Fun Facts: Although not specific to Moon/Center Township, but rather the entire United States, I found the following listing.   Some of the information is interesting because as of May 1, 1908, there were "legal holidays" in some states, yet not others.

LEGAL HOLIDAYS IN THE UNITED STATES
(Revised to May 1, 1908)

Jan 1 - New Year's Day –In all the States except Colorado, Kentucky, Massachusetts, New Hampshire, and Rhode Island.
Jan 8 - Anniversary of the Battle of New Orleans –In Louisiana.
Jan 19- Lee's Birthday –In Florida, Georgia, North Carolina, South Carolina, and Virginia.
Feb 12- Lincoln's Birthday –In Connecticut, Illinois, Minnesota, New Jersey, New York, North Dakota, Pennsylvania, and Washington.
Feb 14- Mardi Gras –In Alabama and Louisiana.
Feb 22- Washington's Birthday –In all the States except Colorado, Iowa, Mississippi, New Mexico.
Feb 24 to Apr 10 – Lent begins Feb 24; Lent ends Apr 10.
Mar 2 – Anniversary of Texan Independence –In Texas.
Mar 4 – Firemen's Anniversary –In New Orleans, La.
Mar 4 – (In every fourth year) – Inauguration Day – In Washington, D. C.
Apr   - First Wednesday in, State Election Day – In Rhode Island.
Apr 9 - Good Friday –In Alabama, Louisiana, Maryland, Minnesota, Pennsylvania, Tennessee, and Connecticut.
Apr 15- Arbor Day –In Utah.
Apr 18- Fast Day –In New Hampshire.
Apr 20- Patriots' Day –In Massachusetts and Maine.
Apr 21- Anniversary of the Battle of San Jacinto –In Texas.
Apr 26- Memorial Day –In Alabama, Florida, and Georgia.
May 10-Memorial Day –In North Carolina and South Carolina
May 20-Anniversary of the Signing of the Mecklenburg Declaration of Independence – In North Carolina.
May 30-Decoration Day –In Arizona, California, Connecticut, Delaware, District of Columbia, Iowa, Illinois, Indiana, Kansas, Kentucky, Maine, Maryland, Massachusetts, Michigan, Minnesota, Missouri, Montana, Nebraska, Nevada, New Hampshire, New Jersey, New York, North Dakota, Ohio, Oklahoma, Oregon, Pennsylvania, Rhode Island, Tennessee, Utah, Vermont, Wisconsin, Washington, and Wyoming.
Jun 3 - Jefferson Davis' Birthday –In Florida.
Jul 4 - Independence Day –In all the States except Colorado.   (See further)
Jul 24 – Pioneers' Day –In Utah.
Aug 16- Bennington Battle Day –In Vermont.
Sep   - First Monday in, Labor Day – In Alabama, Colorado, California, Connecticut, Delaware, District of Columbia, Florida, Georgia, Illinois, Indiana, Iowa, Kansas, Maine, Maryland, Massachusetts, Michigan, Minnesota, Missouri, Montana, Nebraska, New Hampshire, New Jersey, New York, Ohio, Oregon, Pennsylvania, Rhode Island, North Carolina, South Dakota, Tennessee, Texas, Utah, Virginia, and Washington.   In Wisconsin the Governor is authorized to set apart a day each year, to be observed as Labor Day.
Sep 9 – Admission Day –In California.
Oct 31- Admission in the Union Day –In Nevada.

Nov - First Tuesday after First Monday, General Election Day – In Arizona, California, Florida, Idaho, Indiana, Kansas, Maryland, Minnesota, Missouri, Montana, Nevada, New Hampshire, New Jersey, New York, North Dakota, Oklahoma, Oregon, Pennsylvania, Rhode Island, South Carolina, South Dakota, Tennessee, Texas, Washington, West Virginia, Wisconsin, and Wyoming.

Nov 25- Labor Day –In Louisiana.

Nov - Last Thursday in, Thanksgiving Day –Is observed in all the States, though in some it is not a statutory holiday.

Dec 25- Christmas Day –In all States except Colorado.

Sundays and Fast Days – whenever appointed, are legal holidays in nearly all the States.

Arbor Day - a legal holiday in Kansas, North Dakota, Rhode Island, and Wyoming, the day being set by the Governors. In Nebraska, Apr 22; California, Sep 9; Colorado, on the third Friday in Apr; and Idaho, Friday after May 1.

Every Saturday after 12 o'clock noon is a legal holiday in Connecticut, Florida, Maine, New York; and New Jersey, the District of Columbia, Massachusetts, Michigan, Pennsylvania, Rhode Island, Virginia, Washington, Annapolis-Md., Charleston County-S.C., Wilmington-Del., and the County of Newcast, (except St. George's Hundred), every city in Missouri with 100,000 inhabitants, and every city or municipality in Ohio having 50,000 or more inhabitants. Pennsylvania, Maryland, and City of New Orleans, Jun 1 to Sep 30. Saturday afternoon is a holiday during Jun, Jul, and Aug in every city of Colorado having a population of 100,000 or over. The afternoon of Nov 23 is a half-holiday in Frederick County-Md. Congress has at various times appointed Special Holidays and has recognized the existence of certain days as holidays for commercial purposes in such legislation as the Bankruptcy Act, but there is no general statute on the subject. The proclamation of the President designating a day of thanksgiving makes it a holiday only in those States which provided it by law.

~ ~ ~

Fun fact: The last Monday of May is when we now celebrate Memorial Day.   Did you know that this holiday was originally only known as DECLARATION DAY*?*

This is an American holiday to honor men and women who died while serving in the U.S. military. With the Civil War claiming more lives than any other conflict in U.S. History, it had been found that by the late 1860s, people throughout America were holding springtime tribute to all these fallen soldiers. They would decorate their graves and have prayers spoken. On May 5, 1868, a leader of an organization for Northern Civil War veterans, General John A. Logan, called for a nationwide day of remembrance to occur the end of each May. By 1890, each of the northern states had made the day an official state holiday. The southern states continued to honor their dead-on separate dates until after WWI. Following WWI, not just fallen veterans of the Civil War were honored, but all fallen veterans were honored.

In 1968, Congress passed the Uniform Monday Holiday Act, which established Memorial Day as the last Monday in May. This it went into effect in 1971 and it also declared it as a federal holiday.

1912

Fun fact: Armistice Day was the original title given to the day to recognize and honor all those who participated in World War I. On the 11th hour of the 11th day of the 11th month of 1918, a temporary end of fighting was declared between the Allied nations and Germany in World War I (then called "the Great War"). Many areas would hold parades and public gatherings as well as pausing business activities at 11 am each Nov 11th to honor all those who participated in "the Great War." On Jun 4, 1926, Congress passed a resolution that the anniversary of Nov 11, 1918, should be commemorated and they called it Armistice Day. An act approved on May 13, 1938, made Nov 11 a legal federal holiday in the United States. When Congress passed the Uniform Holidays Bill, they set the original observation of Veterans' Day to occur on the fourth Monday in October. This new date caused too much confusion! President Gerald R. Ford signed a new law that changed the observation of Veterans Day to Nov 11th beginning in 1978. This is how Armistice Day became known as Memorial Day.

1918   1928

Armistice Day

Remember the day, ten years ago. When the bells rang, the whistles shrieked, telling the world that the war was over, and that the boys—those who had not already paid the supreme sacrifice— would soon be back with us.

1928 ad in The Daily Times

~ ~ ~

THIS AND THAT..............

Center Township was known for many additional "Firsts". Here are a few examples:
- In 1921, Mrs. Everett Patterson was the first woman to have her name drawn for jury duty in the Beaver County Court House.
- The first automobile in the township was owed by a resident on Chapel Road, David Mitchell.
- The first Rochester Motor Coach to run through the township was started on Aug 27, 1937. It operated over Brodhead Road to Aliquippa. Bill Yoder and his drivers made many runs from early morning until after midnight on an hourly schedule with hundreds of passengers daily. During the WWII times, there was standing room only on these busses. Following the war years, the service was extended onto River Road and to Ambridge, but work was more sluggish, and more people were once again driving their own automobiles. This meant there was no longer the need for as many frequent runs. By the 1950s, the high-volume bus service was no longer needed, so in 1958, the company cut the usage of busses traveling Brodhead Road to just four runs a day, yet each still only had a few passengers on each run. The reduced usage of busses and the increased personal automobile usage was not exclusive to Center Township. It was a plague that spread all over the country. Even with the driving force and backing of the township's Citizens Council, the number of passengers from Center Township never increased and the bus company was struggling to stay in business. Mr. Yoder expanded his interests and started a charter service, as well as school and church busses usage. Even to this day, there are still efforts and interests in having the bus services throughout Center Township.
- Pleasant Drive was the first to receive streetlights in the township. The lights were installed by Duquesne Light Company from Brodhead Road to the Potter Township line. (There are portions of the current Pleasant Drive that were known by various names over the years – Poor House Run Road, Moffett Mill Road, Moffett Mill Run Road. See Roads sections for more information on these various names.)
- Center Township residents were always known to take care of family, neighbors, and anyone who chose the township as their home. To this day, there are still programs and places for anyone who needs assistance to find it. To offer help, did you know that in about 1955, the first surplus food distribution occurred in Center Township? Mrs. Burton McPherson was the first to take charge of this distribution. She was assisted by Mrs. Walter Davis, Mrs. Louis Depner, Mrs. Antonio Infantozzi, and Mrs. Leo Parrish. Mrs. Depner took over the distribution after Mrs. McPherson died. Many families received the surplus food thanks to the efforts of these women.

~ ~ ~

Even in the 1920s, health was a very important concern and smoking was being recognized as unhealthy. There were many ways for those interested to stop, including this advertisement.

QUIT TOBACCO
So easy to drop Cigarette, Cigar, or Chewing habit

No-To-Bac has helped thousands to break the costly, nerve-shattering tobacco habit. Whenever you have a longing for a smoke or chew, just place a harmless No-To-Bac tablet in your mouth instead. All desire stops. Shortly the habit is completely broken, and you are better off mentally, physically, financially. It's so easy, so simple. Get a box of No-To-Bac and if it doesn't release you from all craving for tobacco in any form, your druggist will refund your money without question. No-To-Bac is made by the owners of Cascarets, therefore is thoroughly reliable.—Adv.

Aug 1920

~ ~ ~

An important day for all women is Aug 21, 1920. For the first time in their lives, Grandmas, Aunties, Mothers, Daughters, and Sisters could place their names on the registry list of eligible voters in Beaver County, **but** they had to be properly assessed.

All females in the township who wished to vote had to be at least 21 years of age, a resident of PA for at least one year, and of the district at least two months before Nov 2. Foreign-born women were permitted to vote on naturalization papers of their husbands or fathers. The women had to pay a ninety cent tax at the time of registering and secure a tax receipt order on or before Oct 2, in order to qualify to vote in Nov. Whether sole or joint owner of the property, women had to produce a tax receipt of the property, and women between ages 21 and 22, had to show proof of age. (Either classification of these women meant they did not have to be assessed, but could simply register to vote.)

How Women, Who Are Eligible to Vote, May Be Properly Assessed

Today and Wednesday women may be assessed in any one of the polling places throughout the county. One polling place is ituated in eac election district. Information as to a person's polling place may easil; be obtained by inquiring of some male voter. The polling places will b open on the two days named from 10 o'clock in the morning until o'clock in the afternoon and from 6 to 9 o'clock at night. Women wishin to be assessed should appear in person, though one adult may assess al eligible members of his or her family.

Those appearing for assessment will be required to give their names street addresses, voting districts, wards, borough or township The; must be at least 21 years of age., residents of Pennsylvania for at leas one year, and of the district at least two months before November Foreign-born women may vote on naturalization papers of their husb and or fathers.

Women may pay taxes, 90 cents, at the time of registering and so cure a tax receipt order. It costsnothing to be assessed, but taxes mus be paid on or before October 2 in order to be qualified to vote Novem ber 2.

Women holding property tax receipts, whether they are sole or join owners of the property, and women between the ages of 21 and 22 need no be assessed,. The former may register and vote on the presentation o the tax receipt and the latter on age. Women of both classes shoul register in order to vote.

Mrs. Cummings Weigle (Mary) was the first woman to vote in the township. She cast her vote in 1921 at the first voting place, which was at the home of Mr. and Mrs. Sidney Huffmyer when their home was on the soon to be TB Sanitarium/Beaver County Hospital Annex (and was situated on part of the property that is now the Beaver Campus of Penn State).

In the later 1950s, it was necessary to have two polling locations in the township – one was in the Center Grange Hall building (on Chapel Road) and the second was in the Scout Hall on Main Street (small building by the CTVFD #1).

~ ~ ~

(1920s) There was an organization formed called American Committee for Relief in Ireland. This American Committee for Relief in Ireland was a non-sectarian, non-political committee, formed to meet the needs of suffering humanity in that distressed land. It had a fixed budget of $10,240,000 to meet the needs of the Irish people. To support this American Committee, Center Township, Colona, Monaca Heights, and Monaca all formed a local organization they named *American Relief in Ireland*. These four communities began a house-to-house canvas in a drive under the auspices of the local organization. The first canvas of this organization was held on Mar 29, 1921. They held their meetings in the municipal building where they would make reports of their work. Newspaper articles all reported that the work was progressing well and was very encouraging.

~ ~ ~

Events/happenings between 1914 and 2017

Through time, there have been innumerable discoveries, inventions, and advancements. Following is a list of just a few of the happenings through the past 103 years from the formation of Center Township beginning in 1914 to 2017. This span of years has provided many first, historic, and memorial happenings. See how many of these events you may have heard older persons discuss or how many have occurred within your life time…..

1914
- World War I began; Austria declared war on Serbia; Germany on Russia and France; Britain on Germany.
- The world's first red and green traffic lights were installed in Cleveland.
- Cost of a first-class stamp: $0.02
- Winsor McCay unleashed *Gertie the Dinosaur*, the first animated cartoon.

1915
- Ford rolled their one millionth automobile off the assembly line.
- Audrey Munson was the first actress to shed her clothes on screen while playing a model for a sculptor in the film *Inspiration*.
- Association for the Prevention and Relief of Heart Disease was founded; renamed the American Heart Association.

1916
- Charlie Chaplin earned an unprecedented $10,000 a week when he signed on with Mutual Studios.
- The final form of general relativity was published; included gravity.
- New York and Boston had epidemic break outs of polio; outbreaks continued for many following decades.

1917
- U.S. declared war with Germany on Apr 6; the first U.S. combat troops arrived in France.
- There was a world-wide influenza pandemic; nearly 20 million died from this influenza by 1920, with 500,000 in the U.S. alone. This influenza killed many more than the number of American soldiers killed in World War I. (Called the Spanish flu; see 1918.)
- Cost of a first-class stamp: $0.02
- Solar Eclipse made headlines.

1918
- One dollar in 1918 equaled more than $16.75 in 2018 based on inflation.
- President Woodrow Wilson became the first president to travel to Europe while serving as president; he attended the Versailles Peace Conference in France.
- Kansas had the first case of Spanish flu in the United States; 675,000 Americans died from this flu.
- A total solar eclipse covered the United States in a similar path to the one in 2017, the last time totality crossed the nation from Pacific to Atlantic. (See 1979, 2017.)
- The armistice was signed, signaling an end to the First World War; Yugoslavia was formed.
- Grocery bags with handles were invented; not patented until 1929.
- "Tarzan of the Apes" was released; the first of the Tarzan films.

1919
- The 18th Amendment (Prohibition) was adopted; it prohibited the sale of alcoholic beverages anywhere in the U.S. It was ratified on Jan 16.
- American Telephone and Telegraph Company introduced the first dial telephones.
- The Royal Astronomical Society saw the predicted effect during a solar eclipse and confirmed Albert Einstein's theory of general relativity.

1920
- The 19th amendment (Women's suffrage) was ratified.
- The first commercial radio broadcast was transmitted by KDKA, a Pittsburgh Westinghouse station.
- Speakeasies replaced saloons as the center of social activity.
- Robert Goddard's work with rockets was announced at the Smithsonian Institution.
- Electric cars were in existence for many years, but during the 1920s the electric car ceased to be a viable commercial product. The electric car's downfall was attributable to a number of factors, including the desire for longer distance vehicles, their lack of horsepower, and the ready availability of gasoline.

1921
- The first burial was held on Nov 11 at the Tomb of the Unknown Soldier in Arlington National Cemetery.
- Babe Ruth, New York Yankee pitcher hit his 138th homerun; this broke the career home-run record that had been held by Roger Connor for 23 years.
- Vitamin D was discovered; shown to prevent rickets.   Vitamin E was discovered.
- Insulin was first used to treat diabetes by Frederick Banting and Herbert Best.
- The polygraph ("lie detector") machine was developed by John Larson.

1922
- The Lincoln Memorial was dedicated in Washington, D.C. on May 30.
- *Reader's Digest* debuts. Started by Dewitt and Lila Wallace out of a basement in Manhattan. The couple published their first issue in Feb with an initial run of 1,500 copies.
- A primitive, two-color process was first used.

1923
- A whooping cough (pertussis) vaccine was developed (see 1926).
- First vaccine for diphtheria.
- German Shepherd Rin Tin Tin became film's first canine star.
- *Time, The Weekly News-Magazine* (aka Time Magazine) was started by Briton Hadden and Henry Luce. It was first called *Facts*. They made it so a busy person could read it in an hour; name was changed to *Time* with the slogan "Take Time–It's Brief".   The first issue featured Joseph G. Cannon, the retired Speaker of the House of Representatives on the cover.

1924
- The first Macy's Thanksgiving Day parade was held.
- George and Gladys Dick demonstrated that the cause of scarlet fever was streptococcus.
- The first Pasteurized Milk Ordinance (PMO) was passed in 1924; milk products once accounted for approximately 25% of all foodborne illness -- since they account for less than 1% of foodborne illness.

1925
- The silent movie version of *Ben-Hur* was released; it cost a record-setting $3.95 million to produce.
- Vitamin A deficiency is shown to cause night blindness.
- The first television image was transmitted in London by John Baird.

1926
- RCA, General Electric, and Westinghouse establish NBC, which operates two national radio networks.
- The first liquid fuel rocket was fired by Robert Goddard.
- Automobile antifreeze was used; it allowed people to use cars year-round.
- The first use of the vaccine for pertussis (whooping cough).

1927
- The first all-electronic television was demonstrated by Philo T. Farnsworth. (See 1934.)
- George Lemaitre, a Belgian astrophysicist, proposed the *big bang theory*.
- First vaccine for tuberculosis.
- First vaccine for tetanus.

1928
- A television set with a 3" x 4" screen was introduced by GE.
- The first television was sold for $75 – a Daven.
- The first cartoons with synchronized sound was introduced by Walt Disney - *Steamboat Willie*.
- The radio classic, *Amos 'n' Andy* was created. (It was canceled in 1943 after 15 years and more than 4,000 consecutive shows.)
- Coolant chemicals for air conditioners and refrigerators was invented by Thomas Midgley, Jr.
- The electric refrigerator was invented.
- Sir Alexander Fleming discovered Penicillin; it did not become available in therapeutically usage form until 1940.

1929
- In Nov – Dec, stock market prices plummet; U.S. securities lost $26 billion, marking the first financial disaster of the Great Depression.
- William S. Paley founded CBS.
- Penicillin was first used to fight an infection.

1930
- Pluto, the ninth planet, was discovered by astronomers. (See 2006.)
- The chemical structure of the vitamin thiamine was determined by Robert R. Williams.
- The first analog computer – "differential analyzer" was built by Vannevar Bush.
- $1 in 1930 was equivalent in purchasing power to $15.14 in 2018.

1931
- "The Star-Spangled Banner" officially became the national anthem.
- General Motors's Frigidaire made refrigerators safe for household use.
- The xenon flash lamp for high-speed photography was invented by Harold E. Edgerton.

1932
- May 20-21, Amelia Earhart became the first woman to fly Atlantic solo.
- Cost of a first-class stamp went from $0.02 to $0.03 on Jul 6.
- The atom was split for the first time by physicists Sir John Douglas Cockcroft and Ernest Walton.
- Researchers discovered riboflavin/vitamin B3.

1933
- Prohibition was repealed.
- Frequency modulation (FM), a static-free method of transmission was introduced by Edwin Armstrong.
- The first men's magazine, *Esquire*, made its debut.
- The Hammond organ was introduced by Laurens Hammond.
- A. A. Michelson's work on the speed of light was completed posthumously.
- New Deal in U.S. was signed by F. D. Roosevelt. The New Deal included the development of public housing.

1934
- The turning point in the great depression in America; unemployment decreased to 22%.
- Congress passed the Jones-Connally Farm-Relief Act to help struggling farmers.
- Vitamin K was discovered by Henrik Dam.
- Federal Savings & Loan Association was created.
- Donald Duck appeared for the first time in "The Wise Little Hen."
- At five years old, Shirley Temple became famous when she sang "The Good Ship Lollipop" in the film *Bright Eyes*. *(She started acting at age 3.)*
- By 1934, mechanical televisions were obsolete; all televisions had been converted into the electronic system.

1935
- The second phase of Roosevelt's New Deal in U.S. opened, calling for social security, better housing, equitable taxation, and farm assistance.
- Technicolor was accepted.
- Nylon (the first completely synthetic fabric) was created by Du Pont chemist Wallace Hume Carothers.
- The first radar was developed by a team of scientists headed by Sir Robert Alexander Watson-Watt; utilized this discovery and built on the Doppler Principle.
- Protonsil, the first sulfa drug was discovered by Gerhard Domagk; it was used to treat infections caused by streptococcus.
- A group of consumer advocates broke away from Consumers' Research Inc. to begin a rival organization, Consumers' Union; they began to publish their own magazine, *Consumers' Union Reports* (now known as *Consumer Reports*).
- First vaccine for yellow fever.

1936
- The British Broadcasting Corp. (BBC) made its debut; the world's first television service with three hours of programming a day.
- Electric guitars debut.
- The first artificial heart was developed by Alexis Carrel and Charles Lindbergh.
- The Boulder Dam was completed; was the largest artificial reservoir in the U.S.-provided power to 1.5 million people.
- The first successful helicopter flight was made.
- New York optometrist William Feinbloom introduced scieral lenses; made of a combination of glass and plastic that were significantly lighter than older glass-blown contacts.

1937
- May 6- the dirigible "Hindenburg" exploded at Lakehurst, N.J., killing 36.
- Amelia Earhart and co-pilot Fred Noonan vanished over the Pacific Ocean on their Round-the-World Flight.
- Edgar Bergen and his puppet Charlie McCarthy made their radio debut on NBC.
- The Glenn Miller Band debut in New York.
- The first full-length animated feature, *Snow White and the Seven Dwarfs,* hit theaters.
- "Fallingwater" was built by Frank Lloyd Wright.
- A prototype "antihistamine" was produced to treat allergies.
- The first blood bank was started by Bernard Fantus at Cook County Hospital in Chicago, using a 2% solution of sodium citrate to preserve the blood. Refrigerated blood lasted ten days.

1938
- *War of the Worlds* was broadcast; it was Orson Welles' adaptation of H. G. Well's original. This broadcast on Oct 30 created a nationwide panic since listeners believed that aliens had actually landed in N. J.
- Minimum wage was established by the Fair Labor Standards Act.
- The principle of photocopying was invented by Chester F. Carlson; produced the first xerographic print.
- A nonstick plastic coating called Teflon was accidentally invented by Roy Plunkett.

1939
- World War II began.
- First food stamp program in Rochester, N.Y. began; Program was started by the U. S. Department of Agriculture - it ended in 1943.
- The premiere of *Gone with the Wind* movie; it was one of the longest films – 231 minutes.
- The Batman cartoon was introduced by Robert Kane.
- The first truly practical helicopter was built by Igor Sikorsky.

1940
- First Social Security benefit checks were paid out on Jan 30.
- The Pennsylvania Turnpike opened; it was the first multilane U.S. superhighway.
- The first McDonald's hamburger stand opened in Pasadena, Calif.
- CBS demonstrated color television in New York.
- The first regularly operated television station (estimated 10,000 viewers) made its debut –WNBT in N.Y.
- Superman radio show made its debut.
- The first Bugs Bunny cartoon showed.
- Freeze drying was adapted.
- Plasma was discovered to be a substitute for whole blood in transfusions.
- Rh factor in blood was discovered by Karl Landsteiner and Alexander Weiner.
- Sir Alexander Fleming discovered penicillin in 1928 but it did not become available in a therapeutically usable form until 1940. Howard Florey and Ernst Chain developed a method to produce a usable form of penicillin; a year later, first clinical trials of the drug show it had remarkable ability to cure life threatening infections.

1941
- U. S. joined World War II after Japanese attack Pearl Harbor.
- U.S. President Franklin D. Roosevelt was inaugurated for his 3rd term as US President.
- A new simplified electron microscope that magnifies up to 100,000 times was demonstrated by RCA.
- The United Service Organizations (USO) began operations providing coffee, donuts, and entertainment to US military forces.
- A bill created the fourth Thursday in November as Thanksgiving Day.

1942
- Women's military services were established.
- Casablanca premiered in theaters.
- "White Christmas" song from the film *Holiday Inn* was released by Bing Crosby.
- Glenn Miller's million-copy-seller *Chattanooga Choo Choo* was sprayed gold by RCA Victor; this created the first "gold record."
- Radar came into operational use.

1943
- Prices, salaries, and wages were froze by the President to prevent inflation.
- Withholding tax on wages was introduced.
- The Pentagon was completed and became the largest office building in the world.
- Streptomycin was discovered by Selman Waksman; he used the now popular term antibiotic. This drug was then used in the treatment of tuberculosis and other diseases.

1944
- The GI Bill of Rights was signed into law, providing benefits for armed-service veterans.
- The first occurrence of network censorship -- The sound was cut off on the Eddie Cantor and Nora Martin duet, "We're Having a Baby, My Baby and Me."
- The first automatic, general-purpose digital computer was constructed by scientists at Harvard University.
- Oswald Avery isolated DNA.

1945
- A form of desk-sized memory store called Memex was used by U.S. government scientist Vannevar Bush; it had some of the features later incorporated into electronic books and the World Wide Web (WWW).
- ENIAC (Electronic Numerical Integrator and Calculator) was completed; it was the first all-electronic computer.
- Oral penicillin was developed by Raymond Libby.
- Folic acid (abundant in green leafy vegetables, liver, kidney, and yeast) was discovered by American Cyanamid.
- First vaccine for influenza.
- The first successful, commercially produced **ballpoint pen** to replace the then-common fountain **pen** was introduced by Milton Reynolds in the United States.

1946
- University of Pennsylvania dedicated the first automatic electronic digital computer – ENIAC.
- Radar contact with the moon was made for the first time by the U.S. Army.

1947
- Percy Spencer of the U.S. invented the microwave oven.
- The transistor was developed by John Bardeen, Walter H. Brattain, and William B. Shockley (US). It allowed electronic equipment to be made much smaller and led to the modern computer revolution.

1948
- Columbia Records introduced the 33 1/3 LP ("long playing") record at New York's Waldorf-Astoria Hotel. It provided 25 minutes of music per side, compared to 4 minutes per side of the standard 78rpm record.
- The "Big Bang" theory was exhibited by George A. Gamow (US) to explain the origin of the universe.
- The Polaroid Land camera was invented by Edwin Land of the U.S.
- The all-plastic gas permeable (GP) contact lenses were introduced by optician Kevin Tuohy of California.

1949
- Cable television made its debut; brought better reception to rural areas where conventional TV signal was weak.
- 45 rpm records were sold in the U.S.
- Barcodes (striped patterns that are initially developed for marking products in grocery stores) was patented by Bernard Silver and N. Joseph Woodland.

1950
- Saturday morning children's programming began.
- The first pay-per-view service, became available - Phonevision.
- The *Peanuts* comic strip was introduced by Charles Schultz.
- Sep 22 - Col. David C. Schilling (USAF) made the first nonstop transatlantic jet flight - 10 hrs. 1 min.
- The first Xerox machine was produced.
- The first self-service elevator was installed by Otis Elevator in Dallas.
- Jun 25 - North Korean Communist forces invaded South Korea; Jun 27 -Truman ordered U.S. forces into Korea.
- Stanford Ovshinksy developed various technologies that made renewable energy more practical, including practical solar cells and improved rechargeable batteries.

(1950)
- Percy Spencer accidentally discovered how to cook with microwaves --inventing the microwave oven.
- Seat belts - Early in the 1950s, Dr. Hunter Shelden's ideas for retractable seat belts were introduced to the automotive industry.   (Seat belts were actually first used in 1885 to prevent ejection from horse-drawn carriages; the restraints were used later on airplanes and in race cars.)
- $1 in 1950 was equal to $10.49 in 2018.

1951
- 22nd Amendment to the U.S. Constitution was ratified on Feb 27; it limited the number of terms a president may serve.
- Color television was introduced in the U.S.
- The first business computer, to handle both numeric and alphabetic data, was introduced - UNIVAC (Universal Automatic Computer).
- The U.S. Atomic Energy Commission built the first nuclear power plant.

1952
- Debut of *Today Show* on NBC - Dave Garroway was host; television's first magazine-format program.
- *The Jackie Gleason Show (The Honeymooners) made its* debut on CBS; it continued for two-decades.
- A major polio epidemic swept the United States.
- The first experimentally safe dead-virus polio vaccine was developed by Jonas E. Salk of the U.S.
- An external cardiac pacemaker was developed by Boston cardiologist Paul M. Zoll.

1953
- Dr. Jonas Salk successfully tested the polio vaccine.
- Apr 3 - The first issue of *TV Guide* was sold in newsstands in 10 cities; a circulation of 1,560,000.
- Lucille Ball gave birth to Desi Arnaz, Jr. on same day the fictional Little Ricky was born on *I Love Lucy*.
- *Playboy* magazine became available at newsstands; a nude Marilyn Monroe was on the cover.
- The first successful open-heart surgery was performed in Philadelphia.
- Late in 1953, the FCC adopted the RCA compatible system, commonly referred to as the NTSC system.

1954
- Racial segregation was unanimously banned in public schools on May 17 by the Supreme Court.
- The World Series was broadcast in color for the first time.
- Polio vaccine was administered to the first children.
- The first 15-inch screen color television sets were sold; later in 1954, 19-inch sets were made and by 1955 all sets were made with a 21-inch picture tube.
- Television's first prime time network color series was *The Marriage*, a situation comedy broadcast live by NBC; NBC's anthology series *Ford Theatre* became the first network color filmed series.
- Photovoltaic technology was born in the United States when the silicon photovoltaic (PV) cell was developed at Bell Labs by Daryl Chapin, Calvin Fuller, and Gerald Pearson; it was the first solar cell capable of converting enough of the sun's energy into power to run every day electrical equipment.
- Indian physicist Narinder Kapany was the pioneer of fiber optics.
- The first kidney transplant was performed between identical twins by Dr. Joseph E. Murray.

1955
- U.S. began sending aid to Vietnam - $216 million.
- Dec 1 – Rosa Parks refused to sit at the back of the bus in protest of the Montgomery, Ala. segregated seating law; after a chain of events, desegregated service began Dec 21, 1956.
- Gunsmoke made its debut on CBS; became television's longest-running western.
- The first Sony transistor radio made its debut; Sony also made a series of moderately successful portable cassette recorders.
- Seat belts were offered as an option in all Ford vehicles.

1956
- Elvis Presley appeared on The Ed Sullivan Show; his song hit the US music charts for the first time, with " Heartbreak Hotel. "
- *The Wizard of Oz* had its first airing on TV.
- Rocky Marciano retired as the only undefeated Heavyweight Champion of the world with a perfect record.
- The first half-hour serial "As the World Turns" began on CBS.
- First hard disk (5MB) invented by IBM.
- Black-and-white portable TV sets hit the market.
- The first commercial videotape recorder the VR-1000 from Ampex Corp went on sale.

1957
- The Space Age began -- Russia launched Sputnik I, the first earth-orbiting satellite.
- *Leave It to Beaver* premiered on CBS; it was the first of what became an era of television shows that depicted the ideal American.
- Internal pacemaker was invented by Clarence W. Lillehie and Earl Bakk (US).
- First round-the-world nonstop jet plane flight (a flight of three Boeing B-52 bombers, led by Maj. Gen. Archie J. Old, Jr. -USAF) went around the world in 45 hours, 19 minutes.
- Dec - The Shippingport Reactor became the first commercial nuclear generator to become operational in the United States.

1958
- Jan 31 - Army's Jupiter-C rocket fired the first U. S. satellite, Explorer I, into orbit.
- Cost of a first-class stamp: $0.03 ($0.04 as of 8/1/58)
- Elvis Presley was inducted into the U.S. Army (Mar 24).
- First transatlantic jet passenger service started by BOAC - a New York to London route.
- Project Mercury was initiated by NASA - aimed at putting a man in space within two years.
- The integrated circuit was developed.
- Volvo's first chief safety engineer, Nils Bohlin, patented the first 3-point seatbelt (one piece, lap/shoulder belt).

1959
- Jan 3 - Alaska and Aug 21 – Hawaii became the 49th and 50th states.
- The first Grammy Award ceremony for recorded music was sponsored by The National Academy of Recording Arts and Sciences.
- IBM and General Motors developed Design Augmented by Computers-1 (DAC-1), the first computer-aided design (CAD) system.
- The US Navy launched the satellite *Vanguard*.
- The *Lunik II* probe (USSR) reached the moon; Lunik III photographed the dark side of the moon for the first time.

1960
- Seventy million people watched the presidential debate between Sen. John F. Kennedy and Vice President Richard Nixon; Kennedy defeated Nixon in a close presidential race.
- Ninety percent of U.S. homes had a television set.
- Alfred Hitchcock's movie *Psycho* made its debut.
- T. H. Maiman (US) built the first working laser.
- The first communications satellite, Echo I, was launched.
- The first weather satellite, Tiros I, was launched by NASA.
- $1 in 1960 was equal to $8.54 in 2018.

1961
- U. S. broke diplomatic relations with Cuba on Jan 31.
- The Berlin Wall between East and West Berlin was erected Aug 13 by East Berlin; it was built to stop the "flood of refugees."
- First U. S. astronaut traveled 116.5 miles up in a 302-mile trip - Navy Cmdr. Alan B. Shepard, Jr. on the *Freedom 7*. Virgil Grissom became the second U. S. astronaut the same year; he traveled 118-mile-high, 303-mile-long rocket flight over the Atlantic.
- Major Yuri A. Gagarin was Moscow's first man put in orbit around earth.
- U.S. Public Health Service began large scale use of the oral Sabin vaccine developed by Albert Sabin. (The first polio vaccine was the inactivated polio vaccine developed by Jonas Salk; it came into use in 1955 while the oral polio vaccine came into commercial use in 1961.)

1962
- Cuban Missile Crisis – the USSR was to build a missile base in Cuba, but Kennedy orders Cuban blockade which he lifted after Russia backed down on their plans.
- Telstar (communications satellite) was launched. The first transatlantic television transmission occurred through the Telestar Satellite; this made worldwide television and cable networks a reality.
- Johnny Carson became the host of *The Tonight Show; a position he held until 1992 - 30 years.*
- *The Mariner II reached Venus; it was the first interplanetary probe.*
- *The first industrial robot was introduced.*
- *Lt. Col. John H. Glenn, Jr. was the first American to orbit Earth; he made three orbits in 4 hours 55 minutes.*

1963

- An artificial heart was implanted in a human for the first time at Houston hospital.
- The U. S. Supreme Court ruled that no locality could require recitation of Lord's Prayer or Bible verses in public schools.
- Civil rights rally, "March on Washington," was held by 200,000 blacks and whites in Washington, D.C.
- Martin Luther King delivered his "I have a dream" speech.
- President Kennedy was shot and killed in Dallas, TX. – viewed on live TV. Lyndon B. Johnson became President the same day.   Lee Harvey Oswald was accused of Kennedy's assassination; he was shot and killed by Jack Ruby as viewers were tuned into NBC – the first live telecast of a murder following President Kennedy.
- Cost of a first-class stamp: $0.04 ($0.05 as of 1/7/63)
- Beatlemania hits the U.K.   The Beatles band was composed of John Lennon, George Harrison, Ringo Starr and Paul McCartney.
- The Rolling Stones band emerged as the anti-Beatles; their music was an aggressive, blues-derived style.
- Julia Child, the French Chef, made her debut on educational television.
- Marten Schmidt (US) discovered Quasars - one of a class of blue celestial objects having the appearance of stars when viewed through a telescope; they are believed to be the most distant and most luminous objects in the universe.
- The first liver transplant was performed.
- Sketchpad was developed by Ivan Sutherland; it was one of the first computer-aided design programs.
- Magnetic cassette technology began; Phillips, a Netherlands-based electronics firm, created it for use by secretaries and journalists.

1964

- The U.S. Supreme Court ruled that Congressional districts be as equal in population as possible.
- Psychedelic bands came on the scene; songs celebrating the counterculture of the 60s were sung by such groups as The Grateful Dead and Jefferson Airplane.
- The Beatles appeared on The Ed Sullivan Show.
- *Peyton Place* premiered on ABC; the first prime-time soap opera.
- Color televisions began to make their way into U. S. homes.
- *The Ranger VII* took 4,316 high-resolution pictures of the moon.
- The U. S. Surgeon General Luther Terry confirmed that cigarette smoking caused cancer.
- First vaccine for measles.
- An airline ticket reservation system, SABRE, was introduced with the help of IBM.
- The first computer mouse was publicly unveiled; it was invented by Douglas C. Engelbart.   (It was not included with computers until 1984 with the shipment of the first Apple Macintosh computer.)

1965

- The first US combat troops arrived in Vietnam.   By the end of 1965, there were 190,000 American soldiers in Vietnam.
- *The Sound of Music* movie premiered.
- An unprecedented $32 million was paid by ABC for a four-year contract with the NCAA to broadcast football games on Saturday afternoons.
- The "Big Bang" theory was confirmed by Arno A. Penzias and Robert W. Wilson's (U.S.) with their discovery of cosmic background radiation.
- The first commercial communications satellite, *Early Bird,* was launched.
- The first rendezvous with another spacecraft was performed; it was with Wally Schirra and Thomas Stafford on *Gemini VI* and Frank Borman and James Lovell on *Gemini VII*.
- The first spacewalk was performed by the Soviet cosmonaut Aleksei Lenov in mid Mar.
- Edward White II became the first American to walk in space the first of Jun.
- The portable defibrillator for treating cardiac arrest patients was developed.
- Medicare and Medicaid legislation were created and passed by U. S. Congress.
- The law requiring a label on cigarette packages was passed by U. S. Congress: "Warning: Cigarette Smoking may be Hazardous to your Health."

1966

- Jul 1 – Medicare began.
- Sep 8 - The first Star Trek episode was broadcast - "The Man Trap."
- Jul – The Mercury Record Company, the U.S. affiliate of Philips, introduced music cassettes to the U.S.

(1966)
- Congress introduced the earliest bills recommending use of electric vehicles; a means of reducing air pollution. A Gallup poll indicated that 33 million Americans were interested in electric vehicles.
- Congress passed the National Traffic and Motor Vehicle Safety Act requiring all automobiles to comply with certain safety standards. It included the first seat belt law, Title 49 of the United States Code, Chapter 301, which took effect on Jan 1; it required all vehicles (except buses) to be fitted with seat belts in all designated seating positions.

1967
- Astronauts Col. Virgil I. Grissom, Col. Edward White II, and Lt. Cmdr. Roger B. Chaffee were killed in a fire during a test launch.
- PBS was created by Congress.
- *Rolling Stone* and *New York Magazine* debut.
- Amanda, a division of Raytheon, produced the first domestic microwave oven.
- First coronary bypass operation (using a patient's vein) was performed by Surgeon Rene Favaloro in Cleveland, Ohio.
- First vaccine for mumps.

1968
- Martin Luther King, Jr. was slain in Memphis. James Earl Ray was indicted for his murder; sentenced to 99 years.
- Jun 5 - Sen. Robert F. Kennedy was shot and critically wounded in a Los Angeles hotel after winning the California primary; he died Jun 6.
- Cost of a first-class stamp: $0.05 ($0.06 as of 1/7/68)
- CBS airs *60 minutes*; it has been the longest-running prime-time newsmagazine.
- The rating system for movies was started - G, PG, R and X.
- The rock musical *Hair* opened on Broadway.
- The largest reservoir of American petroleum was discovered in Alaska.
- The first people to orbit the moon were Commander Frank Borman, Command Module Pilot James Lovell, and Lunar Module Pilot William Anders aboard *Apollo 8*.
- 911 service was started in the U.S. in New York. (Britain began a 999 emergency number in 1937.)

1969
- Nixon began withdrawing troops and transferring the responsibility and direction of the war effort to the government of South Vietnam - "Vietnamization."
- The nuclear nonproliferation treaty (NPT) was signed by the United States, USSR, and about 100 other countries.
- Jun 28 - The gay rights movement was started with the Stonewall riot in New York City.
- Jul 20 - Neil A. Armstrong and Edwin E. "Buzz" Aldrin, Jr., Apollo 11 astronauts, took the first walk on the Moon.
- Aug – Woodstock. More than half a million people gathered in Bethel (near Woodstock, N.Y.) for four days of rain, sex, drugs and rock 'n' roll. Janis Joplin, Jimi Hendrix, The Who, Joan Baez, Crosby, Stills, Nash and Young, Jefferson Airplane and Sly and the Family Stone were some of the performers.
- *Sesame Street* was introduced by Children's Television Workshop.
- All cigarette advertising was ban on television and radio by the FCC.
- ARPA (Advanced Research Projects Agency) went online in Dec; this connected four major US universities. It was the foundation upon which the Internet would be built. ARPA was designed for research, education, and government organizations.
- The scanning electron microscope was developed.
- Alan Kay worked on developing his idea of Dynabook, an electronic book - the predecessor to portable computers.

1970
- US troops invaded Cambodia.
- Jimi Hendrix and Janis Joplin both died of drug-related deaths at age 27.
- The FCC regulations required separate ownership of television networks and studios.
- Monday Night Football made its debut on ABC; Howard Cosell, Frank Gifford, and Don Meredith were the announcers.
- The floppy disk was introduced by IBM.
- First vaccine for rubella/German measles.
- $1 in 1970 was equal to $6.52 in 2018.

1971
- The U. S. Supreme Court ruled unanimously that busing of students may be ordered to achieve racial desegregation.
- The voting age was lowered to 18 with the Twenty-sixth Amendment to U. S. Constitution.
- Cost of a first-class stamp: $0.06 ($0.08 as of 5/16/71)
- CBS made the debut of *All in the Family*; started a trend in socially conscious programming.
- Jim Morrison died in Paris at age 27; his death ended the Doors band's career together.
- The Allman Brothers' Duane Allman died in a motorcycle accident at age 24.
- The microprocessor was introduced by Intel.
- Excellent pictures of the surface of Mars was taken by *Mariner IX*.
- Nick Sheridon, at Zerox PARC, pioneered electronic ink.
- The first single-chip computer/microprocessor was built by Ted Hoff.

1972
- Watergate scandal - 5 men were apprehended by police in attempt to bug the Democratic National Committee headquarters in Washington, D.C.'s Watergate complex.
- The first pay cable network – HBO – was transmitted by Time Inc.
- Gloria Steinem's *Ms* magazine made its debut.
- M*A*S*H premiered on CBS.
- Atari introduced the arcade version of *Pong*, the first video game. (The home version came out in 1974.)
- RCA (U.S.) developed the compact disk.
- The video disk was introduced by Philips Company (Netherlands).
- Electronic mail was introduced.
- The last manned moon landing - *Apollo XVI* returned to Earth; it brought back 250 pounds of lunar samples.
- In response to the 1970 Federal Clean Car Incentive Program, the first full-powered, full-sized hybrid vehicle was built by Victor Wouk, the "Godfather of the Hybrid." He used a 1972 Buick Skylark which was provided by General Motors.

1973
- Involvement of American ground troops in Vietnam War was ended when a ceasefire is signed Jan 28.
- Aug 15 - U. S. bombing of Cambodia ended; this marked an official halt to 12 years of combat activity in Southeast Asia.
- Nixon accepted responsibility on national TV, but not blame, for Watergate.
- Spiro T. Agnew resigned as Vice President; he also pled no contest to charges of evasion of income taxes while he was Governor of Maryland.
- Ethernet was developed by Robert Metcalfe; it was a simple way of linking computers together. Many computers that are connected to the Internet nowadays use Ethernet.
- Transmission Control Protocol/Internet Protocol (TCP/IP) was developed; the standard for communicating between computers over the Internet. (Several other TCP/IP prototypes were developed at multiple research centers between 1978 and 1983.)
- NMR – Nuclear Magnetic Resonance was developed; it is the technology behind MRI scanning.
- The first American space station, Skylab, was launched.
- The first handheld cellphone/mobile phone was developed by Martin Cooper.
- A renewed interest in electric cars from both consumers and producers arose due to concerns about the soaring price of oil -- peaked with the Arab Oil Embargo of 1973.

1974
- Aug 8 - Richard M. Nixon became the first President to announce he would be resigning; he resigned the next day. Vice President Gerald R. Ford was sworn in as 38th President of the US on Aug. 9. Ford granted "full, free, and absolute pardon" to ex-President Nixon on Sep 8.
- Cost of a first-class stamp: $0.08 ($0.10 as of 3/2/74)
- *People* magazine made its debut; Mia Farrow was on the cover.
- The first grocery-store purchase was made of an item coded with a barcode.
- Required new food labeling that specified full listing of all ingredients in each product was started by the Food and Drug Administration.
- First vaccine for chicken pox.
- Vanguard-Sebring's CitiCar made its debut at the Electric Vehicle Symposium in Washington, D.C. It had a top speed of over 30 mph and a reliable warm-weather range of 40 miles. By 1975 the company was the sixth largest automaker in the U.S. but is dissolved only a few years later.

1975
- Apr 30 - The Vietnam War ended with the surrender of the city of Saigon; the remaining Americans evacuated.
- Jul 15 - Apollo and Soyuz spacecrafts took off for US-Soviet link-up in space.
- Cost of a first-class stamp: $0.10 ($0.13 as of 12/31/75)
- A "family hour" was created by ABC, CBS and NBC; it was an early evening time slot free of violence and sex.
- *Saturday Night Live* premiered on NBC; George Carlin hosted the show.
- Home videotape systems (VCRs) were developed in Japan by Sony (Betamax) and Matsushita (VHS).
- Consumers could now build and program their own personal computers with Altair home computer kit.

1976
- *Viking I* landed on Mars.
- Cosmic string theory was first postulated by Thomas Kibble.
- The Apple I was launched by Steve Wozniak and Steve Jobs.
- The Environmental Protection Association dropped the 1970 Federal Clean Car Incentive Program program......but Congress passed the Electric and Hybrid Vehicle Research, Development, and Demonstration Act.   This law was intended to spur the development of new technologies including improved batteries, motors, and other hybrid-electric components.

1977
- The first woman Episcopal priest was ordained.
- The previously unknown bacterium that was the cause of mysterious "legionnaire's disease" was identified by scientists.
- Vietnam war draft evaders were pardoned by President Carter.
- Star Wars opened in theaters for the first time.
- The disco era started with the movie – *Saturday Night Fever*.
- The space shuttle *Enterprise* made its first test glide on the back of a 747.
- First successful human-powered aircraft, *Gossamer Condor,* was developed by Paul MacCready (U.S.).
- The first fusion reaction was initiated with the use of lasers.
- First vaccine for pneumonia.

1978
- The U. S. Senate approved the Panama Canal neutrality treaty (Mar 16); the treaty would turn the canal over to Panama by 2000.
- Cost of a first-class stamp: $0.13 ($0.15 as of 5/29/78)
- The first portable stereo, *Walkman*, was introduced by Sony.   (See 1979.)
- Balloon angioplasty was developed (treats coronary artery disease).
- The first test-tube baby was born in the U.K.
- First vaccine for meningitis.

1979
- Three Mile Island - An overheated reactor at the Three Mile Island nuclear facility in Pennsylvania threatened to melt down; it did not, but 144,000 residents of Middletown were evacuated.
- Jul 1 – The Sony Corp. introduced the Sony Walkman TPS-L2 - a 14 ounce, blue-and-silver, portable cassette player with chunky buttons, headphones, and a leather case; it even had a second earphone jack so two people could listen at one time.
- Some parts of mainland U. S. saw a total eclipse of the Sun on Feb 26. (See 1918, 2017.)

1980
- Diplomatic ties were broken with Iran.
- Former Beatles member, John Lennon was shot dead in New York City.
- CNN, the first all-news network, was launched by Ted Turner.
- Janice Brown, a former teacher, made the first long-distance solar-powered flight in the *Solar Challenger.*
- *Voyager I* reached Saturn; returned data on its 14 moons as well as more than 1,000 rings.
- World Health Organization (WHO) announced smallpox was eradicated.
- $1 in 1980 was equal to $3.07 in 2018.

1981
- The Space Shuttle made its maiden voyage.
- President Reagan was wounded by a gunman, with press secretary and two law-enforcement officers.
- The first woman on the U.S. Supreme Court was nominated by Reagan – Judge Sandra Day O'Conner of Arizona.
- Cost of a first-class stamp: $0.15 ($0.18 as of 3/22/81; $0.20 as of 11/1/81)
- MTV started to air around the clock music videos, debuting with "Video Killed the Radio Star."
- Television cameras were allowed in courtrooms by a Supreme Court ruling.
- Pacman became the popular video game in the country.
- AIDS was first identified. (see 1983)
- First vaccine for hepatitis B.
- Laser eye surgery for removing cataracts was developed by Patricia Bath.
- IBM introduced its first personal computer (PC), using the Microsoft Disk Operating System (MS-DOS).
- Fujio Masuoka filed for a patent for flash memory—a type of reusable computer memory that could store information even when the power was off.
- The use of the artificial sweetener aspartame (NutraSweet) was approved by the FDA.

1982
- John Belushi died of a drug overdose at age 33.
- The play *Cats* opened on Broadway.
- Dr. Barney B. Clark implanted a permanent artificial heart in a human for the first time at University of Utah Medical Center in Salt Lake City.
- *Columbia* made its first mission; it deployed two communications satellites.
- The first genetically-engineered plant was approved for sale – the Flavr Savr tomato developed at Washington University in St. Louis.
- Phillips and Sony co-developed and released a digital optical disc data storage - compact disc (CD). It was first publicly demonstrated in 1981 on the BBC program Tomorrow's World with the Bee Gees' album Living Eyes played. The first commercial compact disc was produced in Aug.

1983
- New Roman Catholic code incorporating changes was signed by Pope John Paul II.
- U.S. invaded Grenada.
- Apr - Maiden voyage of second space shuttle, Challenger; the first U.S. spacewalk in nine years occurred.
- Jun – The first U.S. woman astronaut, Sally K. Ride, was a crew member aboard space shuttle Challenger.
- Vinyl records began a drastic decline after the introduction of noise-free compact discs.
- Motorola was authorized by the FCC to begin testing cellular phone service in Chicago.
- Karen Carpenter died of complications from anorexia nervosa at age 32.
- The last episode of M*A*S*H; watched by more than 125 million viewers.
- "Crack" cocaine was developed in the Bahamas; soon appeared in the United States.
- The virus, HIV, that causes AIDS, was identified. (See 1981.)
- Front seat belt wearing regulations for drivers and passengers (both adult and children) came into force.

1984
- The Supreme Court ruled that taping television shows at home on VCRs did not violate copyright law.
- The user-friendly MacIntosh personal computer was introduced by Apple.

1985
- Public school teachers were barred from parochial schools by a U. S. Supreme Court ruling.
- Cost of a first-class stamp: $0.20 ($0.22 as of 2/17/1985)
- The first major movie star died of AIDS – Rock Hudson, age 59.
- Laser printers and computers became much more affordable and inexpensive; therefore, desktop publishing began to be more commonly used.
- An enormous hole found to have opened in the earth's ozone layer over Antarctica was reported by British scientists.

1986
- Jan 28- Space shuttle Challenger exploded after launch at Cape Canaveral, Fla.; all 7 aboard were killed.
- The first nonstop flight around the world without refueling was made by Dick Rutan and Jeana Yeager in the *Voyager;* it flew 24,986 miles around the world, from Edwards AFB, California; it took 216 hours, 3 minutes, and 44 seconds.
- Images of Uranus, its moon, rings, atmosphere, interior and magnetic field were returned by The *Voyager 2* probe.
- Fox, the fourth television network, was created by Barry Diller, head of News Corp.; it offered 10 hours of prime time programming a week.
- *The Oprah Winfrey Show* made its debut.
- The first reference work was published on CD-ROM – The Academic American Encyclopedia.
- Nintendo video games were introduced in the U. S.
- FDA gave approval of the first genetically engineered vaccine for hepatitis B.

1987
- Ruling by the U.S. Supreme Court – Rotary Clubs must admit women.
- Televangelist Jim Bakker scandal.
- First Criminal convicted using DNA evidence occurred in England.
- Oct 19 - U. S. stock market crashed with a 508-point drop/22.6%; stock markets around the world followed with fails by the end of Oct.
- Clive Sinclair launched the Z88 Portable Computer weighing under 2 lbs.
- 1987 is shortened by 1 second to adjust to the Gregorian calendar.
- Disposable Contact Lenses became available for commercial distribution.
- Jun 11 - a rare earthquake, 5.0 on Richter scale, affected 14 states in the Midwest and parts of Canada.
- The U.S. population was estimated at 244.6 million; the world's population at approximately 5 billion.

1988
- U. S. and Canada reached a free trade agreement.
- Cost of a first-class stamp: $0.22 ($0.25 as of 4/3/88)
- Ninety-eight percent of U. S. households had at least one television set.
- Sales of CDs topped that of vinyl records for the first time.
- Turner Network Television (TNT) was started by Ted Turner; he bought MGM's film library.
- Congress was warned of the dangers of global warning and the greenhouse effect by NASA scientist James Hansen.
- G.M. teams up with California's AeroVironment to design what would become the EV1, which one employee called "the world's most efficient production vehicle;" Roger Smith, CEO of G.M., agreed to fund research efforts to build a practical consumer electric car. Some electric vehicle enthusiasts had expressed that the EV1 was never undertaken as a serious commercial venture by the large automaker.

1989
- After 28 years, the Berlin Wall was opened to the West.
- The ruptured tanker, Exxon Valdez sent 11 million gallons of crude oil into Alaska's Prince William Sound.
- The term virtual reality was coined, and Jaron Lanier produced the equipment to experience it.
- While working at CERN, the first World Wide Web server and browser was developed by Tim Berners-Lee (England).
- As *Voyager 2* passes by Neptune, it made startling discoveries about the planet and its moons.
- The Simpsons - the shorts became a part of The Tracey Ullman Show on Apr 19, 1987; after three seasons, the sketch was developed into a half-hour prime time show.
- Wearing rear seat belts became compulsory for children under 14.

1990
- 90% of American households have at least one radio, with five being the average.
- *Seinfeld* made its debut on NBC.
- The Hubble Space Telescope was launched.
- The Clean Air Act was signed by President Bush; it mandated a variety of pollution-reducing changes in the automobile and fuel industries.
- U. S. Congress passed the Nutrition Labeling and Education Act; it required standardized listing of ingredients and serving sizes on food products.
- All vehicles were required to have either automatic seat belts or driver side air bags.
- $1 in 1990 was equal to $1.93 in 2018.

1991
- Persian Gulf War ends with a cease-fire; UN forces are victorious.
- Cost of a first-class stamp: $0.25 ($0.29 as of 2/3/91)
- Fox Broadcasting was the first network to permit condom advertising on television.
- The University of Minnesota created Gopher, the first user-friendly internet interface; named after the school mascot. Gopher becomes the most popular interface for several years.
- The first version of Linux, a collaboratively written computer operating system, was created by Linus Torvalds.

1992
- Feb 1 - A formal end to the Cold War was proclaimed by Bush and Yeltsin.
- Compact discs took over cassette tapes as the preferred medium for recorded music.
- Americans have 201 million of the estimated 900 million television sets in use around the world.
- Johnny Carson hosted his last The Tonight Show after 20 years.
- A text-based Web browser is made available to the public.
- First vaccine for hepatitis A.

1993
- The Pentium microprocessor was introduced by Intel.
- Windows NT 3.1 was released by Microsoft.
- The World Wide Web was born at CERN.
- Dyson sells the first bagless cyclonic vacuum cleaner.
- Islamic Fundamentalists bomb World Trade Center.
- Clinton agreed to compromise on military's ban on homosexuals.
- Beanie Babies were launched.
- Brady bill requiring background checks of prospective buyers was signed into law.
- Severe Blizzard strikes the eastern U.S., bringing record snowfall and other severe weather all the way from Cuba to Québec.

1994
- 95 million viewers watched O. J. Simpson & Al Cowlings drive Los Angeles freeways in low-speed chase.
- For the first time in history, chain bookstores outsold independent stores, starting what many feared to be the death of smaller booksellers.
- *ER* and *Friends* made their debut on NBC.
- The term "spamming" began -- White House launched a Web page -- Initial commerce sites were established and mass marketing campaigns were launched via email.
- Dr. Ned First (US) cloned calves from cells of early embryos.
- The first genetically-engineered food product was approved by the FDA – the Flavr Savr tomato.
- John Daugman perfected the mathematics that made iris scanning systems possible.
- VoIP was invented for sending telephone calls over the Internet.
- Driver side airbags became mandatory on all passenger vehicles in model year 1995.

1995
- U. S. shuttle docked with Russian space station Mir.
- Cost of a first-class stamp: $0.32 (as of 1/1/95).
- The Rock and Roll Hall of Fame Museum opened in Cleveland; designed by architect I. M. Pei.
- The world's first cloned sheep were created from embryo cells - Megan and Morag.
- eBay auction website was launched.

1996
- The first female U. S. Secretary of State was appointed by Clinton - Madeleine Albright.
- Broadcasters and television and PC manufacturers agree on a standard for HDTV (high-definition digital television).
- Of the total estimated 45 million people worldwide, approximately 30 million North Americans (U. S. and Canada) were using the Internet.   43.2 million (44%) of US households owned a personal computer.
- Global warming reaches a new record high.
- The first cloned sheep from adult cells was born in Jul – named Dolly.
- The first high-definition television (HDTV) signal in the United States was broadcast by WRAL-HD.

1997
- U. S. shuttle joined Russian space station. (Jan 17).
- The controversial television ratings system debuted on cable stations and broadcast networks. The ratings, TV-Y, TV-G, TV-Y7, TV-PG, TV-14 or TV-M, appear for 15 seconds in the upper left-hand corner of the screen at the beginning of each show, except news and sports programs, which are not rated.
- Electronics companies agreed to make Wi-Fi a worldwide standard for wireless Internet.

(1997)
- J. K. Rowling's *Harry Potter and the Philosopher's Stone* is published in the U.K. It comes to U.S. in 1998 as *Harry Potter and the Sorcerer's Stone*.
- Scientists at Oregon Regional Primate Research Center (US) created the first primates —two rhesus monkeys named Neti and Ditto— from DNA taken from cells of developing monkey embryos.
- Comet Hale-Bopp was the closest it will be to Earth until 4397 (Mar 22).
- US spacecraft began exploration of Mars (Jul 4).
- Toyota unveiled the Prius in Japan -- the world's first commercially mass-produced and marketed hybrid car. (See 2001.)

1997 - 2000
- A few thousand all-electric cars (such as Honda's EV Plus, G.M.'s EV1, Ford's Ranger pickup EV, Nissan's Altra EV, Chevy's S-10 EV, and Toyota's RAV4 EV) were produced by big car manufacturers, but most of them were available for lease only. All the major automakers' advanced all-electric production programs were discontinued by the early 2000s.

1998
- President Clinton was impeached by the House; along party lines on two charges, perjury and obstruction of justice.
- Seinfeld's last episode was watched by an estimated 76 million viewers.
- The *Athena* probe found frozen water on the moon. Scientists state that ice crystals mixed with soil could provide fuel for rockets exploring solar system.
- Astronomers detected giant explosion in deep space; said to be second in force only to the "Big Bang."
- Senator John Glenn, at age 77, returned to orbit in the space shuttle *Discovery. (He was the first American to orbit the earth.)*
- First vaccine for Lyme disease.

1999
- About 75 million Americans were using the internet; worldwide users reached 150 million.
- Y2K bug – many in the world awaited the consequences when drastic millennial theorists warned of an Armageddon with the upcoming 1999 turning to 2000.
- Cost of a first-class stamp: $0.33 (as of 1/10/99)
- The Melissa and Chernobyl viruses afflicted computers worldwide; it forced several large corporations to shut down their e-mail servers.
- Ford acquired Volvo.
- The human population of the world surpassed six billion.
- The U. S. Senate acquitted President Bill Clinton of perjury and obstruction of justice.
- *SpongeBob SquarePants* premiered on the Nickelodeon cable network.
- The West Nile Virus first appears in the U. S.
- Bluetooth was announced.

2000
- Beginning of the end of the Internet stock boom as wary investors cause a stock plunge.
- Time Warner, the nation's largest traditional media company, was bought by America Online for $165 billion. This was one of the biggest mergers in the country's history. The mega-deal reflected "the growing dominance of the Internet in areas including publishing, music, film, and broadcasting. It also served to validate the Internet, proving that the Web is likely here to stay and somewhat justifying the value of Internet companies that have yet to turn a profit but are worth billions" of dollars on paper.
- The NEAR spacecraft became the first to orbit an asteroid.
- The "I love you" virus caused disruption of computers worldwide.
- The first draft of human genome (the whole of its hereditary information encoded in its DNA) was announced; the finalized version wouldn't be released until three years later.

2001
- The online encyclopedia, Wikipedia, was founded by Larry Sanger and Jimmy Wales.
- Toyota's Prius was introduced worldwide.
- Nov 16 – Harry Potter and the Sorcerer's Stone opened in 8,200 theaters nationwide.
- Sep 11 (9/11) - Terrorist hijackers rammed jetliners into the twin towers of New York City's World Trade Center and the Pentagon; a fourth hijacked plane crashed 80 mi at Shanksville, outside of Pittsburgh. The Islamic militant Osama bin Laden and al-Qaeda terrorist network were identified as the parties behind the attacks. Thousands were killed or injured in the attacks.

(2001)
- Oct 7 - U. S. and British forces launched a bombing campaign on Taliban government and al-Qaeda terrorist camps in Afghanistan in response to Sep 11 attacks.
- iPod MP3 music player was unveiled by Apple; this revolutionized music listening.

2002
- iRobot Corporation released the first version of the Roomba® vacuum cleaning robot.
- "The United States' seventh largest airline, US Airways filed for bankruptcy. After declaring bankruptcy, a judge granted the corporation $75 million in emergency financing and $500 million in debtor financing. In 2004, US Airways filed for bankruptcy again; it merged with America West in 2005; in 2013 merged with American Airlines; and in 2015, American Airlines discontinued use of the US Airways brand name."
- Kmart Corp became the largest retailer in American history to file for Chapter 11 bankruptcy protection.
- WorldCom, a telecommunications giant, filed for Chapter 11 bankruptcy protection in the largest such filing in United States history.
- Queen Elizabeth, the Queen Mother of the UK died.
- 36 people were killed when tornadoes struck a number of southern states from Louisiana to Pennsylvania on Veterans Day.
- Former United States President Jimmy Carter was awarded the Nobel Peace Prize.
- Jun 7 - George Bush created the Department of Homeland Security to fight threats of terrorism.
- The No Child Left Behind Act was passed; President George W. Bush signed it into law.

2003
- Mar 19 - The U. S. and Britain launched war against Iraq.
- May 1 - The U. S. declared official end to combat operations in Iraq.
- Feb 1 - Space shuttle Columbia exploded; killed all 7 astronauts.
- A massive crack down came about by The Recording Industry Association of America on people illegally downloading more than 1,000 songs over the Internet; lawsuits were filed against hundreds of people, including a 12-year-old girl.
- iTune Music Store was developed; made affordable and easy by Apple Computer; downloaded tunes cost 99 cents each.

2004
- U.S. handed over power to Iraqi interim government.
- Bush proposed a new space program that inclued flights to the Moon, Mars, and beyond.
- Massachusetts began gay marriages, the first state in the country to legalize such unions.
- The number of songs and albums downloaded from the Internet continued on a large scale; Apple's iTunes sold their 200,000,000th song.
- Aug - The founders of Google, Sergery Brin and Larry Page, became instant billionaires when the company went public.
- A planetoid named Sedna was discovered and confirmed the most distant object ever identified in our solar system; it was the largest object discovered since Pluto in 1930.

2005
- Astronomers at the California Institute of Technology find another object larger than Pluto which may in fact be another planet (Jul 29).
- Hurricane Katrina stuck the Louisiana, Mississippi, and Alabama coastal areas.
- Oil prices rise sharply throughout the year caused by Trouble in the Middle East and Hurricane Katrina.
- "YouTube" was founded.

2006
- After a seven-year, three-billion-mile expedition, NASA's *Stardust* spacecraft capsule landed in the Arizona desert; it had particles captured from Comet Wild-2.
- The *New Horizons* spacecraft was launched; it traveled three billion miles over nine years to study Pluto's atmosphere and surface.
- A group of scientists reported finding the fossil of a 375-million-year-old fish that has early signs of limbs; the find suggested the missing link between fish and land animals.
- Pluto lost its status as a planet after the International Astronomical Union voted to redefine the solar system; Pluto was reclassified as a dwarf planet. (See 1930.)
- Tesla Motors publicly presented the ultra-sporty Tesla Roadster at the San Francisco International Auto Show; it would be sold in 2008 with a base price listing of $98,950.

2007
- The U.S. began its "surge" of some 30,000 troops to Iraq; caused increasingly deadly attacks by insurgents and militias.
- President Bush signed an energy bill that required passenger vehicles sold in the U.S. to have fuel economy standards of 35 mpg by 2020, a 40% increase over the current standard.
- *Discovery* was launched for a 14-day mission to the International Space Station; astronauts would add a "room" to the station and move a 17.5-ton solar array and truss.
- Kindle electronic book (e-book) reader was launched by Amazon.com.
- The Apple iPhone touchscreen cellphone made its debut.

2008
- United States Presidential Election 2008 Barack Obama (Democratic) Defeats John McCain (Republican).
- "The space shuttle *Atlantis* delivered the Columbus science laboratory to the International Space Station (ISS). The $2 billion laboratory has room for three astronauts and ten experimentation racks that can simulate gravity for biotechnical and medical research."
- The National Bureau of Economic Research stated that the U.S. had been in a recession since Dec 2007.
- President Bush signed the $700 billion bailout; Rescue package bill (Emergency Economic Stabilization Act of 2008) was signed into law.
- Apple began to sell the new ultra-thin MacBook Air notebook; it was less than an inch thick and turned on the moment it was opened.
- Microsoft was attempting to buy Yahoo for $44.6 billion.

2009
- Barack H. Obama became the first African American to be elected to the presidency; he served two terms.
- Michael Jackson died at age 50.
- Chrysler filed for bankruptcy protection; entered into a partnership agreement with Fiat.
- General Motors filed for bankruptcy; announced it would close 14 plants in the United States.
- President Obama signed his first bill into law - the Lilly Ledbetter Fair Pay Act, an equal-pay act.
- 20 cases of swine flu in the United States were confirmed; the U. S. declared the outbreak a public health emergency.
- Cost of a first-class stamp: 44 cents
- Scientists announce that water was found on the Moon during NASA's Lcross mission.
- Nissan introduced its new electric car, the LEAF ("Leading, Environmentally Friendly, Affordable, Family Car"); it was capable of a maximum speed of more than 90 mph, could travel 100 miles on a full charge, and had a battery that can be recharged to 80% of its capacity in 30 minutes. The first production LEAFs was scheduled to go on sale in Japan, Europe, and the U.S. in the fall of 2010.

2010
- The health-care overhaul bill, called the Patient Protection and Affordable Care Act, was signed into law by President Obama.
- The U.S. was experiencing its worst economic period since the Great Depression. A 15-year high percentage of Americans were living below poverty line ($10,830-individual;$22,050-a family of four).
- President Obama announced the end of Operation Iraqi Freedom with a withdrawal of combat troops; this was seven years after the war in Iraq had begun. The U.S. will continue to be a presence in Iraq, mainly with civilian contractors but also with a smaller military contingent of approximately 50,000 troops. The remaining troops are scheduled to leave Iraq by the end of 2011.
- The touchscreen tablet computer – iPad – was released by Apple.
- 3D TV started to become more widely available.

2011
- May 5 - Heavy rains caused flooding in the Mississippi and Ohio River valleys.
- Aug. 5 – "For the first time in history, the U.S. had its credit rating lowered. Credit agency Standard & Poor's lowered the nation's credit rating from the top grade of AAA to AA+, removing the U.S. from its list of risk-free borrowers."
- Jul 8 - The *Atlantis* space shuttle was launched into space for the last time from the Kennedy Space Center; this was the 135th and final flight of the space shuttle program started in 1981 (it ended with the return of the Atlantis two weeks later). For its final mission, the *Atlantis* carried 8,000 lbs. of spare parts and supplies to the International Space Station.

2012
- Feb. 9 – "The Pentagon announced that women would now be permanently assigned to battalions. Many women already serve in those battalions due to demand in Iraq and Afghanistan. The new ruling only made the job assignments official and upheld the ban on women serving in combat."
- May 17 - Data was released by the Census Bureau showing over the last 12-month period ending Jul 2011, Asians, blacks, Hispanics, and mixed races made up just over 50 percent of all births; this was the first time in the history of the United States.
- Cost of a first-class stamp: 45 cents
- An outbreak of meningitis spread throughout the U. S.; more than 30 people died. The cause was linked to a contaminated steroid drug used on patients for back pain – first used in Framingham, Mass.
- Hurricane Sandy made landfall in Atlantic City, N.J.; it was re-classified as a post-tropical cyclone. There were at least 100 deaths and an estimated $30 billion in damages caused by Sandy; this made it the second costliest hurricane in the U. S. since Hurricane Katrina.
- *Curiosity*, a plutonium-powered rover, successfully landed on Mars; it was to spend two years examining the land.

2013
- President Obama was sworn in for a second term. He became the first president to say the word *gay* in an Inaugural Address when he compared the battle for same-sex marriage to past battles over gender and racial equality.
- Cost of a first-class stamp: 46 cents

2014
- "The Obama administration announced that the federal government would recognize the marriages of the 1,300 same-sex couples in Utah even though the state government had currently decided not to do so. With federal approval, same-sex couples would be able to receive spousal benefits, like health insurance for federal employees and filing joint federal income tax returns.
- The Supreme Court ruled that police need a warrant to search the cellphone of anyone that they arrest.
- Cost of a first-class stamp: 49 cents
- For the first time ever, a probe named Philae landed on Comet 67P, located 310 million miles from Earth; it was launched from the mother ship Rosetta.

2015
- Supercomputers were determined to be only 30 times less powerful than human brains; they were classified as the world's fastest computers.
- Baby boomers lost their position as the country's largest generation, a title held for decades. It was projected the U. S. would have 75.3 million millennials (those between the ages of 18 and 34) in 2015 - 74.9 million boomers (51-69) - and roughly 66 million Gen-Xers (35-50).

2016
- President Obama became the first sitting U.S. president to visit Cuba since the 1920s.
- American voters elected the most diverse congress; the total number of women of color in the Senate went from one to four.
- One of the most talked about Presidential elections occurred with Donald Trump winning.
- The musical artist, Prince died at the age of 57.
- American Idol ended its shows after 15 seasons.

2017
- Quantum computing showed signs of becoming a practical technology.
- Investigations began into Russian interference in the 2016 presidential campaign.
- America's opioid epidemic became a national emergency.
- Worse hurricane season on record - Hurricanes Harvey, Irma and Maria plowed through southeast Texas, Florida and the Caribbean.
- Late Aug - A total solar eclipse shifted across the U.S.; it was the first total solar eclipse to cross the U.S. since 1918. The next total solar eclipse from a location in the contiguous U. S. will be on Apr 8, 2024. (See 1918, 1979.)

~ ~ ~

INDUSTRIAL BUSINESSES

In the fall of 1986, Center Township officials made a very good attempt to create an industrial park in the municipality. They wanted to take advantage of the flow of growth from the Greater Pittsburgh International Airport along the Beaver Valley Expressway. The property being considered was in the area off the Expressway near Pleasant Drive. The officials had their hands more or less "slapped" when residents eagerly expressed their dislike for the plan to convert 26 acres of undeveloped property from a mixed-residential classification to industrial. This conversion involved rezoning many of their properties and they accused the township of giving little or no thought to the quality of life that creating this industrial park would cause for all adjacent residents.

The proposed acreage involved disrupting the lives of 30 some residents who lived in the vicinity of Pleasant Drive, Main Street, Center Street, and West Shaffer Road. These residents were very concerned that if the township rezoned the area, then their homes and properties could easily be affected as eminent domain would be enforced. (Eminent domain is the right of a government to take private property for public use.) The officials tried to satisfy the residents by stating that their property values would increase greatly and if they chose to make a profit, they could easily sell, or if they chose to live where they were, they could live there forever. The residents stated that even if their homes remained, the value would not increase, but rather decrease. There were also many other concerns such as what type(s) of industry would be approved for the area and how would the current roads handle the traffic conditions an industrial park would create.

Sadly, the concerns of the citizens fell on deaf ears once again and the area is now considered "industrial park property." These residents like so many in the township fell victim to the officials' "decisions" and once again relocation, inconvenience, devaluing, condemning, and/or excessive traffic replaced the reason these residents originally chose the location of their homes. This is just another example of how the residents of Center Township have had disruption to the once rural area.

Another example of disregard to how most residents may feel. Recently the massive land moving, and removal of even more open, undeveloped land has occurred. This includes properties from Potter Township and along the river into Center Township with all of the hillside property between the Beaver Valley Mall and the Ohio River, as well as all the commercial properties encircling the Lowe's plaza. Some may say there were previously other industrial business in that same area, which is true, but, there was much more acreage affected by this approval! Whether actually industrial based or commercial based, it is all the great loss of the rural atmosphere that drew many to this area. To save typing, the increased pollution (air and light), wear and tear on roadways, and stupidly increased flow of traffic won't even be discussed.

Fact: As of 1950, Center Township was without any type of industry.

From the onset of industrial companies coming to the areas around Center Township through previous years, it cannot be denied that many, many of the township residents found employment with these industries. For this reason, I have included information on several of the larger industries adjacent to the township who would have employed residents of Moon/Center Township (along with Potter Township and Monaca residents, too) through so many of the years.

A E S Beaver Valley Cogeneration Plant – 394 Frankfort Road (Potter Township)
1942 to 2015
This plant was originally a coal-fired plant built in Potter Township plant in 1942, during WWII times. At its on set, it was to serve as a power generator for the Koppers plant. It was built as a "bomb proof facility."

AES was founded in 1981, with their Headquarters in Arlington VA. They bought this coal-fired facility in 1981, with an agreement between NOVA Chemicals (see further). The AES Beaver Valley Plant was a 120-megawatt coal-fired facility and was under a long-term contract to provide electricity to the West Penn Power Corporation and steam to ARCO Chemicals. This company once employed more than a hundred people and provided power to nearly a hundred thousand homes. They were at one time, considered the world's largest global power company. They had five plants in operations or under construction, totaling 860-megawatts.

BV Partners, managed by AES Beaver Valley, acquired the powerhouse in 1985, from ARCO Chemicals. The Partnership refurbished the existing facility and installed a new steam turbine and related electric and steam generating equipment, with the total project cost of $120 million. At last report, AES employed approximately seventy-five men and women at the AES Beaver Valley Plant and was essentially a supplier of low-cost electricity to public utilities and steam to independent companies. The AES Corporation employed approximately forty-thousand people around the world. The company always stressed that all employees were to conduct all the company's business activities in accordance with the corporate values of integrity, fairness, fun, and social responsibility with special emphasis on environmental sensitivity.

The plant was to close in 2017, but this was accelerated, and closure began in 2015. It was expected to take until 2018 for the last of the demolition of the external buildings to be completed. Chemicals had the responsibility of demolishing the plant. The 10-acre site is expected to be converted to a sustainable Brownfield Area.

Under construction – 1943.

View of AES from the Ohio River.

Aerial view of AES plant.

Fun fact: The area of this AES plant was formerly the site of the Hostetter mansion and estate. (See Summer Homes section.)

St. Joseph Lead Company – 300 Frankfort Road - along south bank of Ohio River, Potter Twp.
1930 to 1987

The St. Joseph Lead Company was founded in 1864, for the mining and smelting of lead in Missouri, receiving its name from a well-known county where mining started. This was St. Francois County which was formerly known as St. Joseph's Parish. As of 1940, that area was proven to contain the greatest lead deposit in the United States. Early pioneers benefited from extracting a little metal from surface workings, but it was not until after the Civil War for any real efforts to develop a commercial industry.

The original company concentrated on the mining and milling of lead from mines. In the mid 1920s, the company made the decision to enter into the zinc smelting field. Engineers in Missouri were then required to develop the necessary process to accomplish this new line of work. By the end of the 1920s, the company was interested in finding a new location to put the smelting division into production. They chose Potter Township, Beaver County, PA. This site was chosen due to the proximity to markets, power, water, fuel, and skilled labor. The Zinc Smelting Divisions plant in Potter Township was being erected in Jun/Jul 1930. As of Jul 5, 1930, the foundation construction had been completed and a large amount of structural steel had been delivered to the site. Mr. George F. Weaton was the first Division Manager.

In the fall of 1930, construction work on the new Pittsburgh & Lake Erie railroad branch line began. It was a 3 ½ mile line branch from Monaca to Raccoon Creek costing $500,000. It was being built to connect with the new $3,000,000 plant of the St. Joseph Lead Co.

From 1931 until 1936, the principal product produced was zinc oxide – a white pigment used extensively by the rubber, paint, and ceramic industries. In 1936, Mr. Weaton and Mr. H. K. Najarian (design engineer and later General Plant Superintendent) invented and put into operation a "vacuum condenser" for the profitable smelting of zinc metal. As of 1939, the company stated the total lost time of the plant's personnel for all cases of accident and sickness amounted to only about 1.3% of the total time worked. As of 1940, the company also still had a policy that provided free insurances, pensions, and many other benefits to their employees. For 20 years there were practically no amendments necessary to satisfy and maintain the offerings to employees. The plant was expanded over the years, as was the diversity of product. The plant started with seven original oxide producing furnaces and expanded to sixteen furnaces by 1965.

In 1953, there were several hundred surrounding areas' residents making up the approximately nine hundred employees at St. Joseph Lead Company in Potter Township. It was considered one of the major industries of the county. They had also recently done a huge expansion program. Zinc metal, cadmium metal, sulphuric acid, and zinc oxide were produced at the smelter.

Mr. Weaton* retired in 1954, and the management of the Division was passed on to Mr. John Wehn*. Mr. Wehn was succeeded by Mr. Charles D. Henderson in 1963. As of 1965, the company stated that the smelter had operated since its beginning thirty-four years ago without a work stoppage and had grown to the position of the largest zinc smelter in the country. The company's name was changed in 1971, to St. Joseph Mineral Corps. Unexpectedly, the plant announced on Nov 1, 1979, they would have a permanent shut down in Jan 1980. In 1987 they merged with the New Jersey Zinc Company to form The Zinc Corporation of America (ZCA). By Sep 1987, St. Joseph Mineral Corp. sold their properties in Potter Township for $2,600,000 to Horsehead Industries, Inc. The ZCA filed for bankruptcy in 2002, Sun Capital purchased the company in 2003, and it became one of the three divisions of Horsehead Corporation.

*The Wehn's were former residents of the township. Their home and property were located were the Gee Bee, now Walmart Plaza is located. The Weaton family was residents of Potter Township.

Fun fact: St. Joseph had but one shut down in 1936 due to flooding of the Ohio River.

Fun fact: As of 1946, St. Joseph Lead Company had their own "park" area for employee picnics and activities, the "St. Joseph Lead Company Park."

Found information: As of 1959, together, St. Joseph Lead Company and Koppers Company owned 92.3% of all taxable real property situated in Potter Township, each owning and operating large manufacturing establishments. "Each owns and operates an independent water supply system which is adequate for all its needs, present and contemplated."

Dec 1943
(note the address of the company in this ad – "Josephtown, PA")

1953
This picture shows the office building with part of the plant in the background.

General view of the plant

QUITE A RECORD!!
Continuous, Uninterrupted Operation Since 1930!!

*ONLY WORK STOPPAGE IN 23 YEARS CAUSED BY FLOOD OF 1936

ST. JOSEPH LEAD CO.

1953 ad

Horsehead Zinc Smelting Plant – 300 Frankfort Road, Potter Township
1987 to c2013

ZCA had taken over the plant and property of the former site of St. Joe Minerals/Lead. Then Sun Capital purchased the bankrupted Zinc Corporation of America in 2003, renaming it Horsehead Corporation. Horsehead was a producer of specialty zinc and zinc-based products and a leading recycler of electric arc furnace dust.

In 2011, Horsehead made an official announcement the company would be moving to Rutherford County, N.C. and they would be closing the Potter Township plant. Jim Hensler was Horsehead president and chief executive officer at that time. The reason for not continuing operations at their Potter Township plant was not revealed at the time the company made the statement of moving to N.C. Later, it was stated the reason for moving was due to "electrical power costs, logistics and the incentives provided by state and local government." The Potter Township plant was kept up and running into 2013 while the new plant in N.C. was completed. While in Potter Township, Horsehead employed more than five hundred people. The plant and land were sold to Shell c2013. The last well-known landmark was the smokestack of the plant which was demolished in 2015.

(Poor Farm)   Horsehead Plant

Part of St. Joseph Lead and Horsehead Corporation included the ...

George F. Weaton Power Station
1958 to 2012

I found an article that provided information on a specific coal-fired power plant located in Potter Township that was formerly owned by Horsehead Corportion completed in 1958, by Kaiser Engineers, later ICF International. It was described as the "George F. Weaton Power Station" and said to have cost $30 million to erect. It was constructed to supply power to the Horsehead company's zinc smelting operation nearby. All excess electricity could be sold to the "local grid market". This plant contained steam generators, tandem compound double flow steam turbines, and Westinghouse genrators.

George F. Weaton was a former manager of the St. Joe Lead company. He was then assigned to oversee the construction of this power plant. There was said to be a picture of Mr Weaton that hung in the main office stairwell until the plant closed; the picture dipicted him turning one of the turbine throttle valves when it first opened. The Weatons had their home in Potter Township. Mr. Weaton died shortly after the power plant was completed. The plant was leased by Horsehead to Cinergy Solutions, Inc. of Cincinnati in 2004. Cinergy also discontinued the use of eastern bituminous coal at the G. F. Weaton Station and chose a cheaper, low-sulfur subbituminous coal supply. Horsehead regained control of the facility's operations after the lease had ended and retained control until its closure. In 2010 there was a terrible and fatal explosion of one of the plant's two substations when a high pressure auxiliary steam line ruptured. Horsehead announced in Jun 2011, that the operations at the George F. Weaton station would be indefinitely idled. Most of the employees of this plant were then laid off or transferred. The plant stopped operations in Sep 2011, and then officially closed in Jul 2012. The plant was demolished in 2014/15, along with all other buildings after Shell purchased the property.

Kobuta   aka   Koppers Company   aka   Sinclair–Koppers   aka   ARCO Polymers   aka   NOVA Chemicals - 400 Frankfort Road/Route 18, Potter Twp.
1942 - 2012

One of the major industries in the area was the Kobuta plant of the Koppers Company, Inc. The Beaver Valley Plant of Atlantic Richfield began in the early years of WWII. Even before officially entering the war, the United States government was formulating plans for developing a synthetic rubber industry following the invasion of southeast Asia by Japanese troops. The U.S. government realized that this invasion caused the loss of our major source of rubber. They purchased acreage in Potter Township to erect a synthetic rubber producing facilities. Koppers Company of Pittsburgh was chosen by the Defense Plant Corporation since they had a strong background in construction of chemical plants that specifically processed by-products of the coke industry. At the government's behest, Koppers Co., Inc. built the plant to begin manufacturing the needed styrene butadiene monomer which was needed to make a form of synthetic rubber for the WWII defense endeavor.

The site along the Ohio River was chosen to produce styrene and butadiene (two essential ingredients for making Buna S rubber, the best type of synthetic rubber at that time) and first became known as Kobuta, located in Potter Township. The name "Kobuta" was formed for **Ko**ppers and **buta**diene. The plant was built very rapidly due to the pressure of the war. The first boiler was "fired up" one year and a day later, ground had been broken on Jun 22, 1942. Eighteen months later (Dec 17, 1943), it was in full operation. The total cost for this plant was $61 million. There were more than twenty thousand men and women who helped build Kobuta and in the summer of 1943, as many as seven thousand, three hundred and seventy-five people were employed at one time. Even with all the expense, labor, and time to build Kobuta, the plant was totally shut down in less than two years once the war had been won. (See Housing Area section for much more on the community of *Kobuta*.)

Following the war, the Surplus Property Act of 1944 permitted the government to dispose of any property they used for the purpose of war productions. In a 1955 report on disposal of government owned synthetic rubber producing facilities, it was stated the Kobuta plant was sold by the government to the Koppers Co., which had no antitrust* history. Koppers Co., Inc., apparently did not want the whole plant but is said to have purchased it in its entirety just to get the power plant and utilities. This was said to be the only transaction by the government at that time with a company having no antitrust* history. (*preventing or controlling trusts or other monopolies, with the intention of promoting competition in business)

Following the sale to Koppers Co. Inc., the plant continued to produce styrene which was used to make polystyrene plastic. The market for plastics grew and Unit 3 of the plant was put back into operation around Jan of 1951, after being in "mothballs" since the war ended. By the mid 1950s, Koppers was expanding and producing many types of products including introducing high density polyethylene to the U. S. market. At the end of 1955, Koppers had a backlog of orders well over one hundred million dollars.

1952 aerial view   from University of Pittsburgh/Historic Pittsburgh

Photo courtesy Beaver County Historical Research and Landmarks Foundation – BCHR&LF

(Also see the previous aerial photograph of the area under Horsehead.)

Two of the distillation columns in the styrene processing section of the plant as seen from the Styrene laboratory. The laboratory (begun by the Chemical Division) was adjacent to the newly development plant. They developed a new "toughy" in the field of plastics, an improved polyethylene plastic.

1953

Photos courtesy BCHR&LF

Fun fact: Does anyone, like me, still have at least one of the round, lidded barrel type containers (make for excellent storage) that many employees just seemed to gain possession of from the Kopper's plant?

In Jan 1956, Fred C. Foy was the President of the Koppers Company, Inc. He made a lengthy statement of how Koppers would be investing approximately $25,000,000 to continued their five-year expansion program that was started in 1955. Koppers was planning not only to expand and improve existing facilities but would be constructing new plants. They acquired six different companies; all were engaged in the manufacture of products closely related to Koppers' own operations. Koppers joined with The Firestone Tire & Rubber Co. and along with certain Brazilian interests, they even helped form a new company to construct and operate a styrene monomer plant in Cubatão, Brazil.

Also, in 1956, Koppers purchased all the government-owned facilities adjacent to the Kobuta plant including butadiene units, a steam and power producing plant, a water treating and pumping plant, docks, coal handling facilities, office and laboratory facilities, and plant maintenance shops. They officially announced that it was exploring activities in the nuclear energy field and had established the Nuclear Products Section of Central Staff Production Department.

The Sinclair Oil Company purchased a one-half interest in the former Kobuta plant from Koppers in 1965. This purchase formed a merger that benefited both companies and the company became known as Sinclair-Koppers. The trademark was modified for both and became a "SK" surrounded by Koppers' familiar octagon. Numerous Kopper employees continued to work at the plant as in the past since there was little change with them after the merger. Then the Atlantic Richfield Company (ARCO) purchased the bulk of the assets of Sinclair Oil in 1970. In 1974, Koppers began to feel the effects of this purchase by ARCO. As ARCO continued to purchase shares, eventually Koppers' share of Sinclair-Koppers, Inc were bought up and once again the plant's identity changed. The sign at Koppers was changed and read "Beaver Valley Plant, ARCO Polymers, Incorporated." A UPI article in a Pittsburgh paper the end of Oct 1975, stated, "Koppers Company, Inc finalized its merger with Sprout, Waldron & Co, Inc., of Muncy. The merger involved the exchange of 428,352 shares of Koppers common stock for all outstanding common stock of Sprout-Waldron, a firm manufacturing industrial equipment for grain processing, pure food, chemical and paper industries."

In mid-June 1996, NOVA Chemicals, Inc. announced they were going to be purchasing ARCO Chemical Company's plastics business which included the Beaver Valley Plant in Potter Township. NOVA Chemicals, Inc. (formerly ARCO Chemicals) was celebrating being fifty-six years old as of the first of Feb 1998. Since 2009, NOVA Chemicals had been a subsidiary of International Petroleum Investment Co. of Abu Dhabi, United Arab Emirates. NOVA is said to have had 2,400 employees worldwide. The company planned on acquiring Royal Dutch Shell's styrenics business which would make NOVA Chemicals the largest producer of plastic resins in the hemisphere and second in Europe. The Monaca NOVA Plant produced plastic resins used in packaging, insulation, and beverage cups. NOVA completed a planned sale of the facility to PFB International of Calgary, Canada in May 2012.

With the plant a key producer in the WWII synthetic rubber program, it meant there were large quantities of butadiene, made from high proof alcohol. Each unit of the plant, when in full production, converted more than two million gallons of alcohol into five million pounds of synthetic rubber a month. Ethylene is derived from crude oil and benzene is a coke oven by-product. Even before the Korean War, the plant took great precautions against fire. Workmen entering the plant were required to leave behind all matches or anything else that could start a fire. Yet the plant still did not escape three incidents of quite severe fires. (Koppers Company also had a styrene plant it owned located nearby, but it was not involved or damaged by any fires.)

Through the years there were three serious explosions at the Kobuta/Koppers plant, all resulting in significant fires.

FIRE 1949 – There were only a few notations of a serious fire at the Kobuta plant in 1949. Two men were reported of receiving burns. No other information was found regarding this fire.

FIRE - Mar 6, 1951 - A severe explosion and fire caused estimated damages of $500,000. There was a call for help to battle the fire, with the appeal for volunteer fire companies made over the Beaver Falls radio station WBVP. There were more than two hundred firemen from twenty communities in a ten-mile radius involved in fighting this fire, including two companies from Pittsburgh. The initial blast from this incident was heard as far as two miles away and flames were said to be shooting at least a hundred feet into the air. The fire originated in one of the four butadiene lines of the plant, with the fire centered in the tanks outside No. 3 unit located on the south side of the building. It was reported, the tanks included twenty-five steel cylinders, approximately seventy-five feet high, and they contained butadiene.

With aide of constant flows of water being streamed onto the blaze and surrounding areas, as well as a sprinkler system, a series of safety valves and other safety devices, all was soon under control. The plant's giant pumping system was the main source of water, providing thousands of gallons of river water. It was later reported that all the water was not needed to put out the existing fire itself, but rather was used to cool down the area and to protect exposure to the surrounding areas. (Once butadiene is ignited, it is almost impossible to extinguish without certain dry powder chemicals.) "The stills, tanks, pipes and other equipment of the burned unit were twisted into fantastic shapes by the heat." It was originally feared the nearby Koppers Co.'s styrene plant might have been involved with the explosion, but it was soon discovered it was not affected.

There were no firemen seriously injured, but two of Kopper's employees were hospitalized with second degree burns. One of these employees stated the first blast occurred because of a leak in a pump. He also stated the packing broke loose and the pressure pushed out butadiene gas that then burst into flames.

Photo by Howard Moyer, Press Staff

Photo by Martin Herrmann, Press Staff

FIRE - Sep 12, 1957

The major fire at the Koppers plant in Sep 1957 did an estimated $850,000 in damages. The blast reportedly rocked homes and factories throughout the adjacent Beaver Valley districts and caused some heavy property damage. The blast knocked down unnumbered workers in the immediate area within the plant, and there were flames that shot over a hundred feet into the air. The initial explosion and fire were centered in a tower-like heat exchanger situated on the top of a one-storey brick hydro-pump room. This unit was in the center of the plant, adjacent to the power building supplying the whole operation. The heat exchanger unit's purpose was to keep down the temperature of chemicals that were used to make the quite flammable ethyl benzol. The Federal Bureau of Investigation and State Police fire marshals began an immediate probe to the cause of the fire to determine if it was intentional or accidental. The cause of the initial blast was determined to be the rupture of a six-inch line which carried ethyl benzene at elevated temperatures and very high pressures.

There were more than a dozen fire companies from the area, including firemen and apparatus from Center, Potter, Monaca, Aliquippa, Beaver, New Brighton, Rochester, North Rochester, Raccoon, Hopewell, Patterson, White, and Pulaski (all under the organized disaster plan that was in effect). Despite how terrible of a blast occurred, followed by just as severe of a fire, none of the one thousand one hundred workers at the plant were injured, nor were any of the more than three hundred volunteer firemen or the plant's fire fighters.

The plant's manager, W. K. Todd, stated that the fire was confined to a small area of about a hundred fifty square feet which was such a small area compared to the two hundred seventy-five acres of the whole plant. There were over forty strong water streams on the fire and closer areas during all the fire-fighting actions. The massive supply of water was obtained by the plant which drew the water from the Ohio River.

photo from Post Gazette

Fun fact: Area high schools would take science-oriented students to Koppers to view and tour the laboratory facilities of the plant.

Fun fact: Anyone that frequently used Frankfort Road/Route 18 through Potter Township and was a nature lover will remember that in the grassy area between the roadway and NOVA Chemicals facilities' site entrance road*, you could always get to see numerous ground hogs there. Even as an adult, I would look forward to driving past that site just to see how many groundhogs were out that day. (*This entrance road was on the right, not too far along Frankfort Road after passing over the Potter Bridge. The entrance to the plant later being marked by a traffic light.)

Polysar Latex – Frankfort Road, Potter Township
1980 - 1988
This facility opened in 1980. It was one of four styrene-butadiene latex manufacturing facilities operated by Polysar in North America. They supplied carboxylate latex used to coat paper and mix with concrete for bridge deck overlays. They also supplied laboratory and technical services to the paper industry. In 1984, it had invested three million dollars upgrading its facilities and employed sixty-five people. In 1988, BASF purchased the Latex division of Polysar LTD. This purchase included the facility on Frankfort Road.

BASF Chemicals Co. – 370 Frankfort Road, Potter Township
1954 - current
I have included a quote from the BASF web site to describe their company. "At BASF, we create chemistry for a sustainable future. We combine economic success with environmental protection and social responsibility. Through science and innovation, we enable our customers in nearly every industry to meet the current and future needs of society. BASF Corporation is the largest affiliate of BASF SE and the second largest producer and marketer of chemicals and related products in North America." They list their products and uses at this plant as being Acronal® polymers: adhesives, non-woven and textile coatings, paints, primers, sealants, paper coatings, and construction chemicals; Basonal® polymers: paper coatings; Basoplast® agents: surface sizing agents used in the production of paper, paperboard, and other paper products; Butofan® polymers: specialty adhesive applications and paper coating adhesion; Coater Ready®: adhesives; Joncryl® polymers: inks for overprint varnish of paper based substrates; Styrofan® polymers: carpet backing, vinyl flooring backing; Styronal® polymers: binder in paper coating to provide gloss and printability. They list employment of one hundred thirty people.

For orientation, the Ohio River is along the left of this photograph and Frankfort Road runs along the bottom portion.

Shell Ethane Cracker Plant – Frankfort Road, Potter Township
In c2012, rumors began that Shell was interested in building a cracker plant in Potter Township, including smaller properties in Center Township. By 2013, Shell had purchased the Horsehead Corporation property and continued to purchase other properties, businesses, structures, and homes in a vast area surrounding this first purchase. Shell moved in heavy land moving equipment and completely changed the look of all the land in the area of what was said to become the new site of this Shell Cracker Plant. They redirected roadways, added overpasses for their own usage, installed massive overhead cables/wiring and poles, created new ramps of the Expressway, rerouted Frankfort Road, and as stated, just completely changed the former landscaping of the whole area. Even with all the massive land moving and construction work, from 2013 until into 2016, Shell never made a solid commitment for erecting their plant until early in Jun 2016. Then, as the majority of people in the area already strongly suspected, Shell officially notified the general public that it would indeed be erecting the plant. The Pennsylvania Shell ethylene cracker plant is owned and operated by Shell Oil Company, the American subsidiary of supermajor oil company Royal Dutch Shell.

Anyone who was born and raised in the area or was familiar with the area of Potter Township beginning at the Potter bridge over Raccoon Creek and coming into Center Township, will tell you that nothing is recognizable nowadays. Shell moved existing hillsides and created massive new ones, altered and even eliminated familiar roadways, leveled all landmarks and even historic buildings, and continues to do more as they inch their way up the Ohio River toward the area below the Beaver Valley Mall and even along Raccoon Creek. As of 2019, the company has been bringing in massive structural components and the erection of the plant is underway. The future of all surrounding areas adjacent to the facility, as well as across the Ohio River, seems quite questionable once this new company becomes operational. As several persons shared with me – "now we wait………………."

~ ~ ~

Though located in the Borough of Monaca, listed below are several of the larger companies since there were quite a few residents of Moon/Center Townships who listed their occupation as working for one of these factories. (There are complete histories and pictures of these businesses in my *Monaca aka Phillipsburg* book.) Also, see Volume II of this book on Center Township for some information on early brick companies, glass companies, sawmills, grain mills, and oil/gas companies where township residents could have easily sought employment.

Colonial Steel Company – east Monaca
1901, 1953, 1962   They were located near Opalite Tile and US Sanitary Company by RR tracks. Specialized in tool and die steels. John Auth started with the company at age 17 helping clear off the site for construction of the mill. During his employment, he invented two improved processes, one for the manufacture of cooper-clad products and the other for removing cores from drilled rods. The company merged with Vanadium in 1928, making it a division of Vanadium-Alloys Steel Co. of Latrobe, PA
    became known as …
Colonial Steel Division of the Vanadium Alloys Steel Co.
In 1962, the company made extensive improvements and added a new sheet mill.

Colona Division of Ampco-Pittsburgh Steel Co.   aka   **Colona Thread Protector Division**
1916, 1924, 1979, 1986   aka **Colona Steel**
They manufactured and reconditioned thread protectors for the oil industry, cold finished steel bars. Closed in Dec 1986 by the parent company - Ampco-Pittsburgh Corp. At the time of closing, there were fewer than twenty people employed and no production for quite some time. The Ampco-Pittsburgh Corp became known as Wyckoff Steel Inc. Wyckoff was sold Apr 29, 1987.

Colona Manufacturing Company
1908, 1916, 1924, 1929   On Pennsylvania Avenue, Monaca. Began operations in 1908. They made pipe, fittings, and valves.
    became known as …
Pittsburgh Screw and Bolt Corporation plant
1929, 1953, 1954   On Pennsylvania Avenue, with some land associated previously with Moon Township. Feb 1929 – merged and consolidated with Colona Manufacturing Co.

Imperial Manufacturing Company
1906   Located south Monaca, near 2060 Pennsylvania Avenue - by Pittsburgh Tube Co.

Monolith Steel Company
Feb -1909, fall of 1911, 1912   On Pennsylvania Avenue; were manufacturers of steel reinforcing bars for concrete work, girder bars, and spiral banded columns.

Nichols Wire Co.   aka   **Nichols Steel & Wire Company**
1923, 1937, 1941   Came to Monaca in 1923; on Pennsylvania Avenue near Seventeenth Street).
    Property was purchased in 1941, reorganized, and incorporated to become …
W. A. Laidlaw Wire Company of Pennsylvania
1941, 1956, 1979, closed by 1980   Was reorganized Dec 7, 1941. In 1979/early 1980, the former Laidlaw Wire Co. building was used by Phoenix Glass Co. as a warehouse while they were rebuilding from the massive fire in their plant.

Pittsburgh Tool Steel Wire Co.
1902, 1955, 1966, 1991   Located at Sixteenth Street and P & LE railroad line (which would put it on Beaver Avenue, to right of bottom of Fourteenth Street Hill). Founded Apr 3, 1902; Jul 1955, merged with Vanadium-Alloys Steel Co. of Latrobe, PA; became part of Teledyne Inc. of Century City, Calif. in 1966. Was often called "the wire mill." American Glass Specialty Co. had property right beside them. They purchased the property and planned to expand and to raze all but two of the older buildings for their use. All the "wire mill" buildings were razed in 2016.

Pittsburgh Tube Company
1902, 1929, 1953, 1978, 1998   At 2060 Pennsylvania Avenue, Monaca; built in 1902. Originally known as Pittsburgh Tube Company of Delaware, later "of Delaware" was dropped. John P. Gangwisch purchased a small mill next door to his plant in Monaca; together Mr. Gangwisch and four other men completed arrangements to take over the name, business, assets, and liabilities of the Pittsburgh Tube Co. Company; it was later named PTC Alliance Corporation. This particular plant would have had to been completely dismantled to be modernized and become productive, but, instead, with 50 percent of the employees eligible for retirement at the time of closing, they received packages that included severance pay, life insurance, and health insurance for life, while others were to receive severance packages and benefits extending a period beyond the date of the plant closing. Jul 31, 1998, they closed the antiquated 75-year-old manufacturing plant. The Beaver County Corporation for Economic Development (BCED) purchased the large building and planned to utilize it as a multi-tenant facility.

The Penn-Monaca Steel Products, Inc.
1927, 1944, 1954   Located at 1746 Pennsylvania Avenue; a welding service; owned by C. C. McCreary.

Pittsburgh Hanger Company
1944, 1965

Superior Drawn Steel Company   aka   Standard Steel Specialty Co.
1925, 1942, 1954, 1963, 1965, 1983, 1992   At 1585-1600 Beaver Avenue. Originally, the Bakers, Morris, Mellon, Baldwin, Alcorn, Eckert, Jackson and Ferguson farms had all been adjacent or in the immediate area of this location. Closed the business in Monaca Aug 31, 1992.
  Reopened as………………

BVHT Inc. aka Beaver Valley Heat Treating Inc.
1992   At 1585-1600 Beaver Avenue. Took over when the Superior Drawn Steel Company left on Aug 31, 1992. Metal Heat Treating plant. Moltrup Steel Products, Inc. (Beaver Falls) purchased the facility and Beaver Valley Heat Treating Inc. making the BVHT a subsidiary.

Not steel mills, but a few other factories in Monaca included:

United States Sanitary Mfg. Co. (aka Tub Works)
1901, 1912, 1943   At 1729-1731 Pennsylvania Avenue, in south Monaca (called Colona); located by the Pgh. Tube Company and the Pgh. Screw and Bolt Co. and the P & LE RR. There was an estimate of 125 men employed in the beginning. Manufactured a complete line of cast-iron enameled plumbing fixtures until Jun 1942 when the facilities then became devoted to production of war work where possible. Dec 3, 1943, the company and stock were sold to The Richmond Radiator Company of Uniontown – a subsidiary of the Reynolds Metals Company.
  became……………

Richmond Radiator Company of Monaca
1943, 1959, 1989

Beaver Valley Alloy Foundry Company
1919, 1953, 1967, current   At the end of Pennsylvania Avenue Ext.; also an entrance listed on Atlantic Avenue Ext. which reflects an entrance to the plant from the "boat launch area."

~ ~ ~

and ….

As early as the 1900 and 1910 censuses, several of the Moon Township residents simply had "mill," "factory," or "industry" listed as their employer. At first, it was thought they were referencing a saw or grist mill or even one of the glass related businesses in Monaca, but after discovering some of my ancestors were employed in mills in Aliquippa/West Aliquippa, I furthered my research. Much information surfaced regarding other mills or factories in what was considered Hopewell Township, then Aliquippa (West Aliquippa), as early as the 1890s. For this reason and the fact that I love sharing local history information, I have chosen to include not only information on Jones and Laughlin Steel, but facts found of the other mills/factories. They are included because some of the Moon/Center Township residents were most likely employed or connected with at least one of them. (Census sheets simply listed "mill" or "factory" with no proper name listed.) These other mills/factories were in what is now the West Aliquippa area which some of Moon and Center Township residents were employed or connected with.

Most of these businesses were found in the area of what is now on or adjacent to the First Street area in West Aliquippa, close to the Ohio River and the railroad tracks. One publication's description of these early businesses stated --- "*...industrial plants are on the banks of the river excepting the brewery. Named in order from First Street and the Kidd Brother's Mill downstream along the Ohio River -- Vulcan Crucible Steel, Russell Shovel, and Crucible Steel Works.*"

Kidd Brothers Burgher Wire Co. / Kidd Brothers Burgher Steel Wire Co./ Precision Kidd Steel Company

Edwin, William, Jr., Walter Scott, Harry Kidd came to America separately between 1869 and 1880 in hopes of taking advantage of the rapid spurt of the steel industry. Edwin was the first to start a steel business in America with Rutherford Burgher later becoming a partner. In 1885, Wm., Jr. joined Edwin and Rutherford. They incorporated, transformed an abandon flour mill in Harmarville, PA to their factory, and started the *Kidd Steel Wire Co*. In 1892, they built an enlarged modern factory in Sharpsburg and Harry Kidd was persuaded to come join the business. Almost immediately, the brothers began to squabble. The result was a breakup of the business and the forming of two rival businesses. Edwin and a partner formed one company, Walter, Wm., Harry, and Rutherford formed the other and won the battle over the rights to use the name *Kidd*. The latter incorporated as *Kidd Brothers and Burgher Steel Wire Co*. In 1898, Harry died of tuberculosis, Wm. left the company and went out west and became a minister, and Walter Kidd and Rutherford Burgher continued with the growing business. In 1902, a burglar is credited with starting a fire which destroyed the entire factory in Sharpsburg.

Walter and Rutherford immediately set out to find a new site for their business and chose an area in what was then considered part of Hopewell Township, now known as West Aliquippa, PA. The location was beneficial for the growing industry being adjacent to/abutting the P&LE railroad and the river. In 1902/1903, they built a fire-resistant brick factory equipped with a modern sprinkler system. The Aliquippa plant encouraged many men to give up farming and begin working in the new factory, including many men from Moon Township.

The company immediately prospered and began to produce polished drill rod in 1903. Prior to joining the steel industry in 1892, Walter had been a minister and was never wholeheartedly interested in steel, so in 1904, he decided to sell his interest in the business to Burgher. Walter then turned to establishing a greenhouse and flower business. As with all businesses, there are periods of "booms" and periods of decline. The Kidd Brothers and Burgher Steel Wire Company was no different. Having made it through family feuds, fire, death, and resignations, they were forced to declared bankruptcy. In 1910, the company went into receivership with H. W. Sutton, the treasurer of the First National Bank of McKeesport, appointed receiver and operator of the business. In 1912, a trusted manager of the company left Aliquippa, taking with him company dies, machinery, and three key employees. With these stolen assets he started his own company in the East Liberty section of Pittsburgh. With the important assets now missing, the McKeesport Bank had no choice and were forced to close the Aliquippa plant. The bank was about to write off Kidd Brothers and Burgher as a total loss, but then events far from Aliquippa changed things for the wire company. The war in Europe created abnormal demand for steel products and it became a sellers' market for steel producers. The bank, not knowing how to run a steel business, decided to approach Walter Kidd on Apr 1, 1914, at his greenhouse and asked him to reopen the plant. Walter felt obligated to help and agreed. He brought his son Walter, Jr. with him and they re-incorporated as *Kidd Drawn Steel Company*.

Fun fact: Walter Kidd, Jr. attended college at the Beaver College, Beaver, PA. where he was the only male graduate of that well-known school for women.

By 1958, stockholders of the Kidd family agreed to sell the firm to the H. K. Porter Company. The new owners merged Kidd Drawn Steel Company with Vulcan Crucible Steel Company, which Porter had purchased earlier, creating the *Vulcan-Kidd Steel Division of the H. K. Porter Company*. (See Vulcan Crucible Steel further.) H. K. Porter only operated the Kidd Division for a few more years. Tom Milhollan (of Precision Industries), being fascinated with the history of the Kidd family and business and how they manufactured drill rod in Aliquippa, decided to purchase the original Kidd Drawn Steel Company, and over a two-month period in 1966, he negotiated to acquire the plant. Tom named the new company *Precision Kidd Steel Company*. The factory remained in Aliquippa, and he personally interviewed and hired every employee. By 1966, even more of Center Township residents were employed not only in Precision Kidd Steel Co., but other steel mills of the area. In 1992, Precision Kidd Steel Co., Inc was incorporated as a stand-alone business located at One Quality Way, Aliquippa (West Aliquippa), PA.

Kidd Brothers and Burgher Steel Wire Company   c1898

J. C. Russell Shovel Company aka Russell Shovel Company

This company was started in 1891 in a cross over or grey area of West Aliquippa and Hopewell Township (now West Aliquippa). On numerous deeds, they were stated as owning a little over 4 acres adjacent to the property of the Aliquippa Steel Company (see further) and the Kidd Brothers and Burgher Steel Wire Company properties (see previous). There were a couple Moon Township men who stated on the census they were employed by a shovel company and although no company name was listed, it could have easily been this very company. The company employed about forty men and were in business between 1891 until into 1928. They were forced to close due to labor disputes. In Aug 1928, John Hubbard was president of the Russell Shovel Company and once approved by the directors of the company, he deeded the company's property and gas wells to John Seyler. (See Vulcan Crucible Steel Company.)

Fact: While Russell Shovel was digging massive ditches for their company, they came upon ancient Native American burial grounds. These types of burials were very common in the area but remained undisturbed until development occurred. The remains that were found included one of two skeletons that were said to be over twelve feet in length (see the Aug 23, 1892 Pittsburgh Dispatch for more information). The fate of these particular skeletons and any other burials of the area is unknown, but if they were reburied anywhere in that immediate area, it is a fact that they would have been disturbed once again with the construction of the soon to be J & L Steel company.

Vulcan Crucible Tool and Steel Company aka Vulcan Crucible Steel Company

Located in what was Hopewell, now West Aliquippa at 100 First Street. It was founded in 1901, by Walter S. Kidd, Sr., Rutherford Burgher, and W. A. Shaw. Although fabricated elsewhere, the tool steel produced at the company was made into various machine shop products including lathes, planers, files, chisels, drills and punches. They employed approximately one hundred and fifty men.

Beginning in Dec 1902, the Vulcan Crucible Steel Company made several purchases of property, some were of private lots. One of the properties was a 4-acre lot from the Ohio River Improvement Company (who owned most of the land of that area). All the properties were adjacent or in the area of First Street, Main Avenue, the P&LE railroad, and the J. C. Russell Shovel Company. In Sep 1928, John Seyler also deeded the property and gas wells he had purchased (not more than a month earlier) from Russell Shovel Company to the Vulcan Crucible Steel Company. "The Vulcan Crucible Steel Company was one of a number of American companies chosen to process uranium for use in the development of atomic weapons. In 1948-49, the company rolled uranium billets into rods for use in nuclear breeder reactors. This work was part of a nationwide fabricating effort immediately after World War II to create atomic weapons as part of President Harry Truman's 1947 Cold War policy of military supremacy over Russia." As a result of the use of uranium, it involved "clean up" of the area due to residual contamination left in and around the mill. So, after one and a half years of handling uranium, after the clean-up, Building 3 of the Vulcan Company was returned to entirely producing tool steel once again.

During the Atomic Energy Commission contract period, the Vulcan Crucible Steel Company owned the site. Then in 1955, the facility was bought by H. K. Porter Company and became Vulcan Crucible Steel of H. K. Porter. In 1958, after the Porter Company bought the nearby Kidd Drawn Steel Company, both were combined, and the American Iron and Steel Institute records indicate the name was changed to Vulcan-Kidd Steel of H.K. Porter Company. Beginning 1966, the next owner was Universal Cyclops, Inc. In 1981, the plant was closed. By 1987, the Aliquippa Forge bought the plant, using it for limited production. In 1991, the plant closed again and then became owned by American Specialty Metals.

Vulcan Crucible Steel Company   Historic American Engineering Record (Library of Congress)

Aliquippa Tin Plate Company – Hopewell Township - Aliquippa/West Aliquippa
This company was only in the area for a few years. In Jun 1893, the Aliquippa Tin Plate Company bought an approximate 300' by 205' parcel from the Ohio River Improvement Company in (then) Hopewell Township, now Aliquippa/West Aliquippa. This was a separate company from the Aliquippa Steel Company because within a deed, their property is described adjacent to the J. C. Russell and that of the Aliquippa Steel Co. They are listed as not turning out any tin plate in 1895, so, the company was evidently faltering by that time. By 1896, their properties were sold at a Sheriff's sale.

Aliquippa Steel Company – Hopewell Township – now Aliquippa/West Aliquippa
The Aliquippa Steel Company purchased 15+ acres from the Ohio River Improvement Company in Dec 1891. There is not much information found on this company except that in Aug of 1900, the stockholders of Aliquippa Steel Company passed a resolution and sold their business to Crucible Steel Company for $100,000. This sale included their property in (then) Hopewell Township together with all the buildings, machinery, engines, equipment, tools, apparatus, fixtures, appliances, and devices attached to, in, or on the premises.

Crucible Steel Works – Aliquippa/West Aliquippa
The Crucible Steel Company of America was formed from the merger of thirteen crucible-steel companies in 1900. In Aug 1900, Crucible paid $100,000 and purchased the Aliquippa Steel Company (see previous). In Mar 1913, a deed stated, the Crucible Steel Company sold interests in the 15+ acres, equipment, and steel plant to several men, Josiah Thompson (8/20th interest), Isaac Semans (7/20th interest), James Hustead 3/20th interest) (they were all of Fayette County), and Quin Hibbs (2/20th interest) (of Washington County). There was no other specific company or business name found as associated with any of these men. Evidently, Crucible Steel no longer needed this

facility after their Midland purchase and these people took over the buildings for another business purposes, but I have no name or association of such. It gets a bit "muddy" after this 1913 deed. J. Thompson filed for bankruptcy and his's shares went to Gallatin Land Co. in 1920. I. Semans also filed for bankruptcy and his shares went to Nelson Rodgers in 1921. J. Hustead's shares went to his heirs and then in 1924, to Woodlawn Land Co. Q. Hibbs was a widow, and her shares also went to Woodlawn Land Co. in 1924. From this point, I did no further research, but Crucible Steel Company is lost in the deeds for this particular property from 1913, as is any usage of the buildings.

Not a steel related mill............
(Note, there were several brewing companies in the area, I chose to provide information on this particular one since there were a few township residents who were known to work at a brewing company, but no specific brewing company's name was ever mentioned.)

Mutual Union Brewing Company
1907 to 1920

This brewery was located on a large area of individual lots in the Erie Avenue, Main Street, Fifth and Sixth Street area, adjacent/ close to the railroad tracks in what was originally part of Hopewell, now West Aliquippa. The company began to formulate plans to start their business in 1905 and is credited with being in business at this location from 1907 until 1920. Prohibition most likely played a part in their decline/closing. The company is said to have distributed steins to all who attended their grand opening. The Mutual Union Brewer Company purchased all their various lots of properties over a period of a few years beginning as early as 1905. They began selling this same property in 1921, making three sales of limited areas/lots of their property to three different individuals. Their final sale of the buildings and remaining/majority of the property and the plant was in Nov 1927, to J & L Steel. They actually had sold the entire businesses in 1921, to Mutual Beverage Company / Liberty Products Company for $205,000. But the Mutual Beverage Company failed to make proper payments, lost it all, the Mutual Union Brewing Company became owners again, then resold it to J&L.

During its time of operation, it was considered a massive plant and one of the largest establishments in Pennsylvania. Some say it was capable of producing 250,000 barrels per year, others have stated 100,000 barrels. The plant was built with plans by Chicago Brewery Architect and Engineer, William Griesser. The plant was erected for the brewing and bottling of beer and consisted of one six-storey brick and steel main brewing building, one one-storey bottling house, one one-storey concrete and brick storage building, one two-storey concrete and brick storage building. The list of all the machinery, equipment, and apparatus found throughout the buildings was quite lengthy and detailed. This list had details of numerous wood and steel storage tanks, vats, stokers, pumps, refrigerating machines, engines, motors, boilers, piping, et cetera. They employed an average of one hundred people. The two main known brands they produced at this plant were *Aliquippa Beer* and *Pennsy Select Beer*. It has been stated that when Jones and Laughlin Steel purchased the building and property, they moved offices into the former brewery building. I found no dates or verification of this.

There was also the Mutual Union Brewery Workers Beneficial Association of Aliquippa, PA who made purchases of a couple lots adjacent to the brewery plant. They had appointed trustees and were considered an unincorporated society. They sold their property during the same year(s) as the brewery company. I found no other information on this society/ association.

early 1900s depiction of the Aliquippa plant (extracted from a stock bond)

Aliquippa Beer bottle

Pennsy Select Beer

Beaver County Genealogy and History Center
view of the Mutual Union Brewing Company in Aliquippa in the early 1900s, now West Aliquippa

Jones & Laughlin Steel Corporation   aka   LTV Corp. – Aliquippa Borough and Center Township
1906 to 1984

Although most of this company was truly based in the Borough of Aliquippa, a small portion of the property crossed over into Center Township. There were many, many of the residents of Moon/Center Township who became employed by the company through the years. J & L played an important part in the growth of Center Township since it provided so many people with employment over the years as occupations were waning from farming.

Benjamin Franklin Jones entered into a partnership with Bernard Lauth in 1852/53, known as Jones, Lauth & Company and they operated puddling furnaces on the south side of Pittsburgh. This was the beginning of what fondly became known as J & L Steel (often just called J & L, with locals pronouncing it more like "Jane-ell"). Mr. Lauth sold his interest to James H. Laughlin in 1854, and Jones & Laughlin was organized in 1861 with their headquarters at Third & Ross in Pittsburgh. Fifty-four years later J & L found it necessary to expand and purchased a piece of land on the Ohio River at Aliquippa, formerly known as Woodlawn. In 1907, a blast furnace was constructed, and this was the start of the Aliquippa Works Division of Jones & Laughlin Steel Corporation.

A large section of the original 475 acres of land was first that of a picnic area and amusement park known as Aliquippa Park. (See Entertainment section for much more on this park.) Adjacent to the site of the park was the former farm and homestead of river boat Captain John H, Douds. The Douds home then served as an office building for the Aliquippa & Southern Railroad which was a J & L subsidiary. The Aliquippa Works consisted of the North Mills and South Mills sections. It was stated, "The flow of materials at the Aliquippa Works is always in one direction, from the North Mills in the direction of the South Mills, or from the receipt of raw materials to shipment of finished products."

J & L stretched for approximately seven miles along the riverfront. It was a welcomed company in the valley, helped expand Aliquippa, and contributed to the building of homes to accommodate the workers. What was known as Woodlawn was renamed to Aliquippa in 1928. What was first known as Aliquippa then became West Aliquippa (because the P & LE railroad considered it "west" of the actual town of Aliquippa). During the Great Depression of the 1930s, the J & L sustained control over the community because rather than doing layoffs, they instead, reduced work hours and kept all employees earning some amount of money. Also, to help workers thrive in those hard times, they provided a system of garden areas on some of their unused property of a then adjacent island for the workers and families to use as vegetable gardens. They also established a "company store" – the Pittsburgh Mercantile Store. (See Grocery section in Volume II for more on the store.)

Courtesy B.F. Jones Memorial Library
Barges served as a bridge to link residents of West Aliquippa and Aliquippa to Crow Island where the gardening areas were located.

By the early 1940s, thanks to J & L, the populations swelled to over 27,000. The Aliquippa Works employed as many as 9,000 people. They also were instrumental in the development of the Aliquippa Hospital. (See Medical section.)

J & L Steel made several acquisitions and a merger through the years – they acquired Youngstown Sheet and Tube in 1978, and McLouth Steel Products in Detroit in 1981, then merged with Republic Steel in 1984. After the merger with Republic Steel, J & L Steel then became known as LTV Steel. LTV issued a statement in 1984, disclosing they were going to be closing most of the Aliquippa Works and laying off approximately 8,000 workers. As sudden as this massive layoff was, so was LTV's reorganizational bankruptcy. Demolition of the blast furnaces began in 1990, they were all built between 1910 and 1919. As of 2000, LTV Corp. sold the tin mill which was the only remaining section of the plant that was still operating. LTV closed the tin mill, and 400 more steel workers were laid off. One report stated that J & L Steel Corp. had the bulk of their properties in Aliquippa and Hopewell Township, but there were also two undeveloped parcels (433 acres and 55 acres) situated in Center Township.

late 1970s

pre-1928

Note – the former entrance originally went over the railroad tracks.

Entrance to J & L   Jul 1938   Rothstein, Arthur, photographer
Historic American Engineering Record (Library of Congress)

Fun Fact: Growing up knowing that J & L was a staple in the area during all those years, it was fun to read so many articles from 1907, 1908, and into 1909 that stated "the <u>new</u> J & L Steel mill….."

Little known fact: After the Aliquippa Park closed, J & L moved the entire former Dance Hall building to the area of their business offices, raised it and set it upon a two-storey base building they had erected, and it became office and drafting areas of the Jones & Laughlin Steel Company.   J & L also added a recreation area and swimming pool to the property behind the building. The following two pictures show the front and rear of the building after it was moved and converted to office space.   The swimming pool can be seen in the second picture. (There is a picture in the Entertainment section of the original Dance Hall while it was located within the Aliquippa Park.)

Jones & Laughlin Steel Company General Office.

Jones and Laughlin Swimming Pool and office building.

Jones and Laughlin Steel Company Plant, Aliquippa, PA.
The pointer on the left is indicating the location of the former dance hall/General Office Building. The pointer on the right is indicating the "tunnel" to enter the plant area. Almost each and every one of the former buildings on the J & L property have been razed to-date.

"The Tunnel"   This became the only way to drive onto the property of J & L.   This area was fondly known as the *Wey*.

Unions and Industrial Groups

Plumbers and Steamfitters Local #47 – 186 Wagner Road, Monaca
1990

This building now houses a food distribution center – formerly known as Faith Restoration, now Families Matter Food Pantry.

U.S.W.A., Local Union 8183 – Production & Maintenance Employees of the Zinc Corp. of America
   In 1990, the officers included Jim Douglas-Pres, Dave Renner-Vice Pres, Buzz McKay-Rec Secy, Al Smith-Fin. Secy, and Tom Johnson-Treasurer.

Heat and Frost Insulators Local #2 – Business Complex – 109 Pleasant Drive
Current   Location of union offices and meeting hall.

~ ~ ~

HOUSING PLANS and AREAS

Currently in Center Township, it is so common to find former large pieces of properties now divided into small lots with homes on them, rather than to find residents with multiple acres included in their homesteads. What was once very large individual homesteads, made up of numerous acres of pastures, herds of livestock, cultivated acres, and/or undeveloped land, have disappeared. They have become the current growing aspirations, stockpiling, and voracity of landowners. All being approved for development by the approval from township supervisors. I have tried to identify as many of these already converted "areas" as possible. In listing the many areas in the township that have been subdivided and developed, there is no doubt that I have overlooked some areas. If any were overlooked or omitted, please know this was an oversight and was not intentional. It should be understood, as I sit and type these words for this book, there are pens being put to paper to make even more deals on selling acreage, more contractors plotting out new areas, construction of even more homes or businesses, and more concrete and asphalt being added to the township.

Perhaps a very sizeable tax break could be considered by the township and extended to residents who have their homes on multiple acres of property. This action might encourage homeowners to retain more acreage/"open" property and not be so anxious to sell it. Don't get me wrong, growth can be good, but this former "farm girl" can't help but ask, when is enough, enough? Why does every open plot of land have to be developed?

It is always said that by growing, this means more incoming tax revenue. It also means much more wear on existing roads, construction of additional/new township roads, added usage and wear on township equipment or a need for purchasing additional equipment, more overall maintenance hours required by the township in general, and more personnel to township departments. It also involves more water usage, more sanitation needs, and more congestion and traffic. This raises the train of thought, isn't it more of a "wash"? When matching the extra costs and line items needed/required (supplies, equipment, personnel), how much money is really generated by the new tax revenue?

More importantly, and often never considered, there are additional things seriously affected with this type of growth and development of communities, including Center Township. These things involve generating much more air, noise, and light pollution. These three pollutions have a very serious, much longer, and sometimes irreversible affect to the environment and people! So, why do our officials keep approving to use up the township's precious land resources and acreage, to further compromise the quality of air and add to the noise and light pollution?

Compared to surrounding areas, in 1990 and 2000, Center Township was considered one of the few Beaver County municipalities to have noticeable growth in their census counts, a 7% increase from 10,742 people to 11,492. There was also an 11% increase in housing units, from 3,997 to 4,438. In 2001, Center Township had 23 subdivisions approved, 303 affected lots/units, and a little more than 326 affected acres with 21 land developments that involved 64.02 acres. This may not seem like a lot, but those 21 developments in Center made up the majority of the 36 TOTAL land developments <u>countywide</u> in 2001. In comparison, the same year, the next highest township listed for land developments was New Sewickley with a mere 3 developments. Center Township also was ranked first in the county in building permits. They had 183 total, which included 61 single-family homes and 27 commercial permits. Again, in comparison, only four other communities had triple-digit total numbers of permits. They were New Sewickley-170, Chippewa Township-156, Economy-139, and Brighton Township-128. Note, all were lower than Center!

Within the listings further are some of the earlier "mini communities" that were or are not actual "housing complexes", but rather just "areas" which were familiarly known within Moon/Center Township. Others listed are or were definitely developed as housing plans. Again, what I have listed is only to give the reader an idea of just how vast the growth has been in Center Township and how quickly a former farm and/or homestead would be subdivided leaving no trace of the former farmland.

Readers will notice many of these areas, although sold purely for profit and most likely not with the purpose of self-recognition being desired, traditionally usually became known by a specific name of either the owner or an earlier former family. Whatever the reasoning for the land being sold, developed, and turned into a housing area, the following information gives light to why or how the names of many of the areas were chosen. Many of the areas listed were sold by persons who either owned the land for multiple years or by heirs of the former owners. Many of the "sellers" were seemingly quite pleased with the amount of money received for the land. They did not realize the purchase was made at a quite conservative price by contractors. These contractors, being businesspersons, then subdivided, developed, resold, and thus received a comparatively much higher price as a housing type plan for their own investment ventures. Without doing extensive deed researching, information on each area will include as many details as could be found. Sometimes it was simply too lengthy to include a complete list of who previously owned and/or most recently owned all properties, who a developer may have been, et cetera. Again, I did not give much attention nor honestly even attempted to name all the areas that have been newly completed or are currently being developed, those are for the next adventurous person to include in a future look back at the township.

All this being said, continue on to read particulars of some very old areas that were found within the portion of Moon Township (now Center Township), along with many other areas which were added one by one to the township.

Baker's Landing

This was not a housing plan, but rather was a well-known area to all early local residents. Baker's Landing was located along the Ohio River at the far end of Monaca (heading toward Aliquippa). Moon Run creek empties into the Ohio River close to the former location of this area. Many times, Baker's Landing is associated with Monaca, but Baker's Landing was actually a part of Moon Township and the area is currently within Center Township boundaries.

Baker's Landing was sometimes even referred to as Baker's Yard. The word "landing" was associated with this area due to an actual boat "landing" which was at this location to access the Ohio River. It was a place where all types of cargo was not only sent out but delivered. I want to take a moment to remind readers, during the 1800s, workmen did not have the luxury of machinery to help in many of the tasks which needed done. This was also true on the docks and landings where they worked in the cold and snow of wintertime and the extreme heat of the summers to make sure all shipments were properly handled.

There was also a Post Office located at Baker's Landing*, located in what was a store called the Baker Trading Post. Postmasters at this location were: William Lawson-appointed Apr 20, 1883, Mrs. Jane (McGregor) Lawson-appointed May 3, 1886, Anna McDonald-appointed Oct 16, 1901. (See Grocery Store section and Post Office section.)

The original property was owned by brothers, Anthony and Jacob Baker* of Strasburg, Germany. They were the proprietors of Baker Trading Post. Direct members of this family (or relatives of this Baker family through marriage) are buried in the Baldwin / Baker Cemetery which is located adjacent to the former Baker's Landing location (to the south/far end of Monaca). This cemetery is situated on former family property. (See Churches and Cemetery section.)

Some of the names/families associated with living within the former Baker Landing's area or known to be in the post office's delivery area were: George and Sarah Baker, James and Elizabeth Barbour, Catherine Barto, Albert and Catherine Bloom, Caroline Hicks, Godfrey Carson, William and Julia Erbervein, Catherine Gillin, Thomas Hill, Morton Shorts, John and Lydia Stewart, Homer-Allen-Hiram Craig, David Wilson, Mrs. Mary King, Wm. Bowers, Henry Pink, Emil Vogt, Frederick Shively, John Brooks, Cain, Daniels, Keherar, Larkins, and John Baker. (See Miscellaneous and General Businesses section, Post Office section, and individual family information.)

> *Some more recent publications and articles have mistakenly expressed Baker's Landing as being located where the Baker family home was in Center Township and named after the George Baker family. Although Baker's Landing was indeed on property in Moon/Center Township and it did lend its name to "a" Baker family, that is all that is correct in this mistaken information. The Baker's Landing area and adjacent cemetery are associated with the *Anthony Baker's* family who settled in Moon Township on land located just past the southern area of the town of Monaca and closer to the Elkhorn Run Road area.
>
> Although the Anthony Baker family settled in and lived in Moon/Center Township, their family cemetery is a now defined to be on property that is within Monaca boundaries (across the road from the current Rome Monument plant at the far end of Monaca). Proof

of all this is found in maps, cemetery records, vintage historic documents, and publications. (Viewing township and borough maps will clarify the divisions of land for Moon/Center Township and the Borough of Monaca in this particular area.)

Beverly Hills Country Club Plan – loosely laid out between Schultz Drive and W. Shaffer Road. This area of homes was laid out in the vicinities of Malone Avenue, Sunset Boulevard, Charity Avenue, Lindberg Drive, Bennett Boulevard, Hilger Avenue, and Summer Avenue. This plan included land once owned by Louis and Mabel Goll and deeded to H. W. and Agnes Neiswonger in 1928. On the 1928 and 1929, plat maps of this subdivision of the land by H. W. Neiswonger, there were 380 lots laid out. I have no other information on H. W. or Agnes Neiswonger, nor did I find them as being residents of the township. (See Goll Family information.)

Mona Manor – off Brodhead (close to Union Cemetery and Penn State Beaver Campus)
This area of homes is still currently considered the area of houses on and around Lafayette Drive. It also formerly once included the few houses off the lower roadway that now leads into Penn State campus. In 1919, H. L. Grimmell, a real estate agent in Monaca, purchased 53 acres of the former 93+ acres of the Dr. Turnbull property/farm from the Carnegie National Bank. Howard L. and his wife May had their home on the back corner of the property above the current water treatment plant at the traffic lights where Brodhead Road meets Route 18 just outside Monaca. The Grimmells named their acreage/"estate" *Mona Manor (the word Mona probably short for "Monaca")*. The Grimmells' estate had a large frame home and a fishpond. Access to their home was on the now defunct Lincoln Road. (See section on Roads for additional information.)

In mid Apr of 1922, it was reported Mr. Grimmell had "completed the construction of a macadamized* road leading from the Brodhead Road to his residence, Mona Manor, in Center Township." By the date of information, it lends itself to this roadway probably being the now defunct Lincoln Road since it was not for a few years that the Grimmells would be subdividing all the property. *to pave by laying and compacting successive layers of broken stone, often with asphalt or hot tar.

In Jun of 1926, the Grimmells developed a plat map to subdivide their acreage. Howard laid out a plan of thirty lots on their property. The break down and approximate sizes of the lots included twenty-four at ½ to ¾ acre, one of 1 acre, one of 1.8 acres, one of 3.8 acres, one of 2.2 acres, one of 1.1 acres, and the lot that contained the Grimmell home had 4.3 acres. He named the whole area of subdivision after his "estate" - *Mona Manor* - which is still referenced as such nowadays. As early as the fall of 1928, Wm. Sinclair of Atlantic Avenue, Monaca was building his home in Mona Manor. Lincoln Road was still one of the entrances to Mona Manor into the 1930s, but eventually, the new entrance to his property became the current Lafayette Drive, which is off Brodhead Road.

On the original plat map of Mona Manor, the layout of lots is quite like that of nowadays. The biggest change over the years has been the roadways. The original plat map of the area only had Lafayette Road, Lincoln Road, and Lawrence Lane. Lafayette Road is still basically as it was in 1926. Franklin Road would have begun at the end of Lafayette and gone straight to just short of the current roadway of Penn State Beaver Campus. The original Lincoln Road was extended and would have had two entrances after the land was subdivided. It started with the original roadway that came up the hillside to the Grimmell home. Then, with the first plans of subdivision, it was lengthened and had another entrance added along Brodhead Road, not far from the current lower entrance to Penn State. Formerly, once Lincoln Road came up the hillside, it continued to the point where the first big curve currently occurs on Lawrence Lane, then it straightened out and exited onto Brodhead Road. This former extended portion of Lincoln Road became and is currently a private driveway to a single home. Lincoln Road has just "faded away" altogether and both the former entrances are also now defunct. Lawrence Lane was originally shorter and currently begins were Layfette ends. This current portion of Lawrence was once a portion/the beginning of Franklin Road which then would have extended straight and ended just short of coming out on the entrance of the Penn State Beaver Campus. (See Roads for a snippet of the Mona Manor plat map.)

There was one large remaining 20+ acre plot of land left when the Grimmell property was first subdivided into lots, and it remains mostly undeveloped. This section begins along Brodhead Road, between the entrance to the Penn State Beaver Campus and the current private driveway mentioned previously) on Brodhead Road. Then continues along the current Penn State property and goes over the hillside to the current divided Route 18 which leads into Monaca.

In 1938, the Grimmells deeded Dr. John A. Mitchell and his wife a large portion of property adjacent to the above-described undeveloped land. The Mitchells built a larger private home. The Mitchell's land was eventually subdivided a few times and what was Dr. Mitchell's private driveway now gives access currently to five homes. These five homes were built to the left side of Mona Manor and have since become severed from the original Mona Manor area. They are all now on a cul-de-sac road with access to these homes being off the current Penn State roadway.

In the 1940s, these names were listed as having homes and living within *Mona Manor*:

Moffett	Rambo	Savot/Sauret	High	Sinclair
Anderson	Feeley	Patterson	Streit	Calligan
Ademan	Lindsay	Embree	Elwood	Ahrend

Fun Fact: Edwin Ahrend, a Mona Manor resident, was very popular for the hobby he had from 1915 through at least 1958. He had a short-wave set, telegraph, and short-wave telephone. He even had a mobile short-wave unit in his car for a period of time. Edwin had to obtain government short wave licenses to be a "ham operator." His call letters were W3DV – the W indicated an American Station, the 3 was the district in the United States, and the DV were his personal call letters. Edwin would tell of being able to talk to airplanes and ships at sea. To do communicating all over the United States and in foreign countries involved him having a 60-foot antenna for his set. No amateur radio usage was permitted during the war, but he did use his radio during the Korean conflict since there was no ban during that time.

Fun fact: In 1937, Chris Lindsay was living in one of the homes within Mona Manor. Chris was a former baseball player for the big-league Detroit Americans.

Sylvan Crest

Sylvan Crest is a larger area in Center Township, situated adjacent to the current Lowe's plaza area, extending to the end of the Borough of Monaca and from the divided highway to along the hillside above the Ohio River. This was also once known as simply "Garland Heights" in the early 1900s. Some of the older directories would list this area as being located "north of Pennsylvania Ave. Extension." In the early 1900s, it was often just listed as "Monaca" for the location (probably because of the "post office" listing and proximity to the town of Monaca). If you look at township/borough maps, 99+% of Sylvan Crest is considered in Center Township but there is that 1% or less on the hillside closest to/adjacent to Monaca (toward the Alloy company) that shows up as being in the Borough of Monaca. To add to the confusion, for many years, there were homes in the Sylvan Crest area which received their water supply from the Monaca Borough. In May 1982, the Monaca Borough Council was asking for bids to supply approximately seventeen homes in the Sylvan Crest housing development in Center Township with water. These homes had their water traditionally piped through former private lines from Monaca since around 1926. Center Township eventually took over all sewage and water services to the area.

The entire area now referenced and known as the Sylvan Crest area was once farmland, had a stone quarry, and eventually the properties and estates for summer homes of a few prominent families. The summer homes were a place where "town folk" could escape the polluted air of the big cities, especially Allegheny City/Pittsburgh. For years, these city dwellers found the air was cleaner, there was very little noise, and open land, all a perfect surrounding for their summer getaways. These would be ideal locations for social events and affairs and/or an extended stay away from the hustle and bustle of work and city living. It provided all these "town folk" what they wanted plus the bonus of beautiful views of the river and surrounding valley.

Isaac and Elizabeth Lawrence were the first I found to own acreage in this area, 1812. They had 438+ acres which was broken into smaller parcels including 125 acres, 234 acres, and others. Eventually, after quite a few transactions and owners, by 1849 and 1860, Israel Wagner was deeded 109 acres and 125 acres of the original 438+ acres. (See Wagner Family information for more details.) After all the deeds made by the Wagner families, approximately 122+ acres ended up belonging to either James Welch's brick company or to James Welch for his own use. James erected a fourteen room, buff brick mansion on the property. After additional transactions, the next constant owner of the land became Simpson M. Powell of Allegheny County. Then enters the Tener and Garland families. (See Summer Homes section and information on the Garland families.)

In general, the first person to appreciate the value of the views from this location was James Welch. It is also obvious that he did not purchase all this land just to build a mansion and have a view. By purchasing the land of this "elevated" location it gave him ownership to all the mines UNDER the land which he could use for obtaining clay for his brick company. He also had the advantage of being able to look down upon his brick business property. Through all but a few of the transactions James Welch made in selling his property that is now part of Sylvan Crest, it was always stated that all coal, clay, gas, and mines found under the acreage would remain either his personally or that of the brick company.

After James Welch and then Simpson Powell, the property passed through the Tener family and next to the Garland families.   After the Garland brothers also sold the property, it eventually became owned by the Valley Land and Construction Company in the early/mid 1920s. In May 1925, approval was given by the township supervisors to the subdivision submitted by this company. They surveyed, subdivided, and laid out small individual building lots, retaining the name given to the area by the Garlands and officially calling this plan of lots *Sylvan Crest*.   With many zoning problems arising and no restrictions in place, the company never completed all their original plans, but they still managed to build many fine homes prior to pulling out of the project.   E. M. Love and Archie McConaughey of Pittsburgh come into the mix next and continued to sell lots.   From 1925 and into the 1940s, many areas of the Sylvan Crest area had been sectioned off into lots and a more stable and easier accessible roadway was added.   H. F. Morgan was one of the owners of much of the land in the mid 1940s and living in his own home in Sylvan Crest at that time. He advertised 50 x 150 lots for sale "on a good road……." "$150 per lot, $15 down, $5 per month."   As for the two former mansions, up until at least the 1980s, both mansions remained standing, but both have since been razed.   (Again, see Summer Homes section.)

1925 ad

During the time after the Valley Land & Construction Co. backed out of the development of Sylvan Crest, there appears to have been some tie between E.M. Love and Archie McConaughey with one or the other loaning or owing money to the other when this property was purchased.   When both men died, they stated in each of their wills that they owned and were transferring the same specific properties to each of their heirs.   None of this confusion surfaced until each of the men's wives and/or children started to sell properties, each selling the same properties but to different people.

Edwin M. Love is listed on the plat map for laying out the lots for Sylvan Crest Section "B" in 1941 and Sylvan Crest Section "C" in 1946.   Amid all the confusion of the deeds and ownership, the first plan was laid out and approved in 1941 and called *Sylvan Crest Section B*.   This property was basically from Grandview Avenue, all land to the left and to the right, and then down over the hillside to the river, too.   The second plan was laid out and approved in 1946. This plat map also stated it was laid out by E.M. Love, called *Sylvan Crest Section C.* It consisted basically of the properties from Grandview Avenue to the current divided highway and all to the left and to the right.   To add to the confusion of everything, on the plat map for Section C, in the space that would have been from Grandview Ave. to the river, is printed "Robert M. Garland to Archie McConaughey." (Robert M. being John W. Garland's son) AND...... then printed toward the bottom of the same plat map it has printed "land of E. M. Love."   Is it my imagination or did it just get "cloudier"?   Whatever went on in those earlier years and whoever really purchased and legally owned the property, the fact is that the courts worked it all out, and the current deeds appear to be free and clear of all the "clouds upon the titles."

Just for general purposes and my own curiosity, I investigated who these two men were to possibly find why both made claim to ownership of the land...

... Edwin M. Love (1869) married Flora Heffley, they had one daughter, Edna. Edwin M. and Edna seem to be the key to most of the purchases and/or selling of the properties. E. M. Love was originally from, married, and lived in Allegheny County. The 1910 through 1940 censuses show them having at least one servant living with them. His occupations included, 1910–secy/treas of a coal company, 1920–operator of coal company, 1930–president of Bessemer Coal & Coke Company, and 1940–coal operator. (Bessemer was a very large company known to mine coal and minerals in Allegheny County.) E. M. may have had the most interest in the land by association with his occupations -- coal.

... Arch(ie) McConaughey (1881) married Christina Nielson, they had two sons. I have no clue as to how or when or if he every made any connections with Mr. Love. The 1900 through 1940 censuses show Arch and family were from Washington County, PA. with no indication of servants.   His occupations included, 1900–(age 18) worked in coal mine, 1910–proprietor of pool room, 1920–book salesman, and 1930–auto dealer.   Arch died in 1939, so his occupation between 1931 and 1939 is unknown.

Just to help visualize the vast area that nowadays is still known as the *Sylvan Crest* area, this is a map of the land in the 1800s. It is included as an example of how they marked off acreage and land in that time period. Note the "Cherry" tree, "Hickory" tree, etc. Although these were excellent site lines at the time of a survey, goodness knows this would not hold up through the years ☺

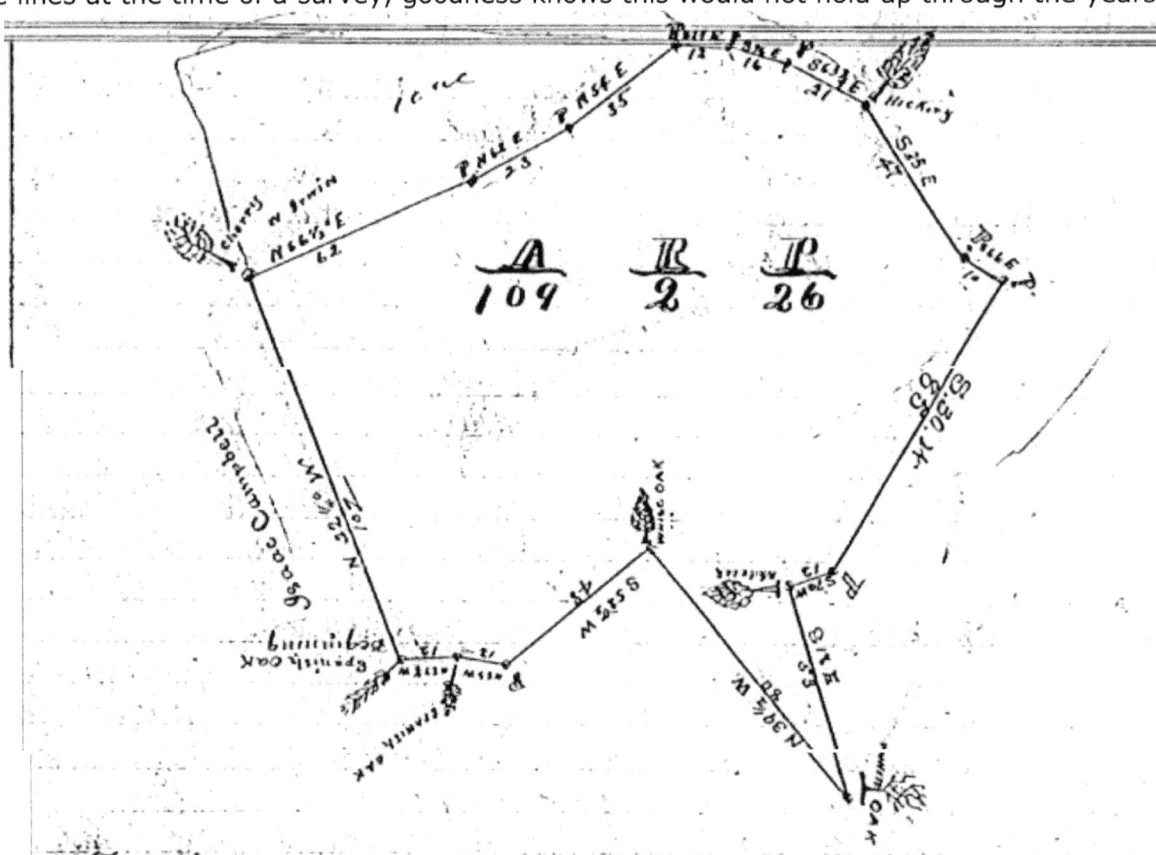

(This is only for part of the land which was once that of Isaac Lawrence and later Jacob/Israel Wagner.)

Next are divided copies of a Plat Map laid out in May of 1925 by E. M. Love and used by the Valley Land and Construction Company. As stated, they retained the Garland's estate name of *Sylvan Crest* for the name of the entire project. This copy of the plat map has been "pieced" together to allow it to fit onto a page and still be somewhat readable. To the right side of this first map would be closest to Monaca, the left side of the area that would be closest to the current Lowe's plaza. Not included on these maps was the area between Grandview Avenue and the current divided highway. It was sold by E. M. Love's daughter, Edna and then eventually subdivided into building lots.

When looking over this plat map of "Sylvan Crest," note they still included…

… two pools (indicated by pointers) which were of the Garlands' estates

… the stable structure (indicated by pointer) – again, of the Garlands' estates

… a pointer indicates the 5.14 acres with only one of the mansions (built by John W. Garland and last owned by Robert Garland) (this Garland home was last used as a private family home for many years by the Brewer family). Curiously, the former Welchmont mansion is not indicated but would have definitely still been standing. (The general location of the former Welch's mansion is indicated by a pointer to the right of the map.)

… there is also a "bridge" indicated on what was on, appropriately called, *Bridge Street*. There is still a section of Bridge Street where a small run passes under the roadway at the same location.

… on the far right of the map, there is an indication for "proposed steps." I found no explanation of why these steps would have been needed except for convenience for the new multiple residents of Sylvan Crest to be able to go to Monaca without using the roadway.

… the "brim of the hillside" is also indicated to help orient the whole area (I used a pointer on the map to indicate that line).

… the Ohio River, railroad tracks, and former Narrows Road were all indicated at the top of this map.

… the original roadway leading out of Monaca is seen on this map -- this is prior to that small section being straightening as the road was improved.

… there was a total of 178 lots subdivided by the land company. These did not include two very large plots of land that were not subdivided and considered "exceptions" during the subdivisions.

Compairing the roadways of Sylvan Crest nowadays to those on this first plat map from 1925, you will see that a few of the streets indicated on this map no longer exsist, some were altered/moved, and a few others still exist but had the names changed.

Roadways associated with Sylvan Crest:
- N to S   Shady Way,   Cross Street,   Carpenter Street,   Beaver Street … All new streets
- N to S   Bridge Street ….Is still there, except there is currently no formal "bridge."
- E to W   Grandview Avenue …. Originally was a U shape from the middle of Bridge Street, wrapping around and then along the edge of hillside to meet the other end of Bridge Street.
- N to S   Lash Street… Originally was longer, beginning on Grandview (as it still does), then went straight to join the other "U" shape of what was more Grandview.
- E to W   Beggs Avenue… Went from Bridge Street to Jones and appears to have been what is now Grandview from Bridge Street to about Cross Street.
- E to W   Union Avenue… This roadway appears to have faded away over time but would have run from Bridge Street to Jones (around the same site as current Carpenter Street).
- E to W   Sylvan Avenue…Was the entrance road that abutted to Bridge Street. It went straight and seems to become Franklin Avenue. Sylvan Avenue wound its way up the hillside and was the former private drive which was the entrance to the estates. (See pictures of this drive in the Summer Home section.)

- N to S Jones Street …Appears to have gone from what is now Wagner, straight back and ended short of the hillside and being close by the current Carpenter Street.
- E to W Franklin Avenue …In 1925, it was a continuation of former Sylvan Avenue.
- E to W Shirley Drive …Added after 1925. There originally was no roadway here, just lots.

This arrow indicates Narrows Road along the shore of the Ohio River.

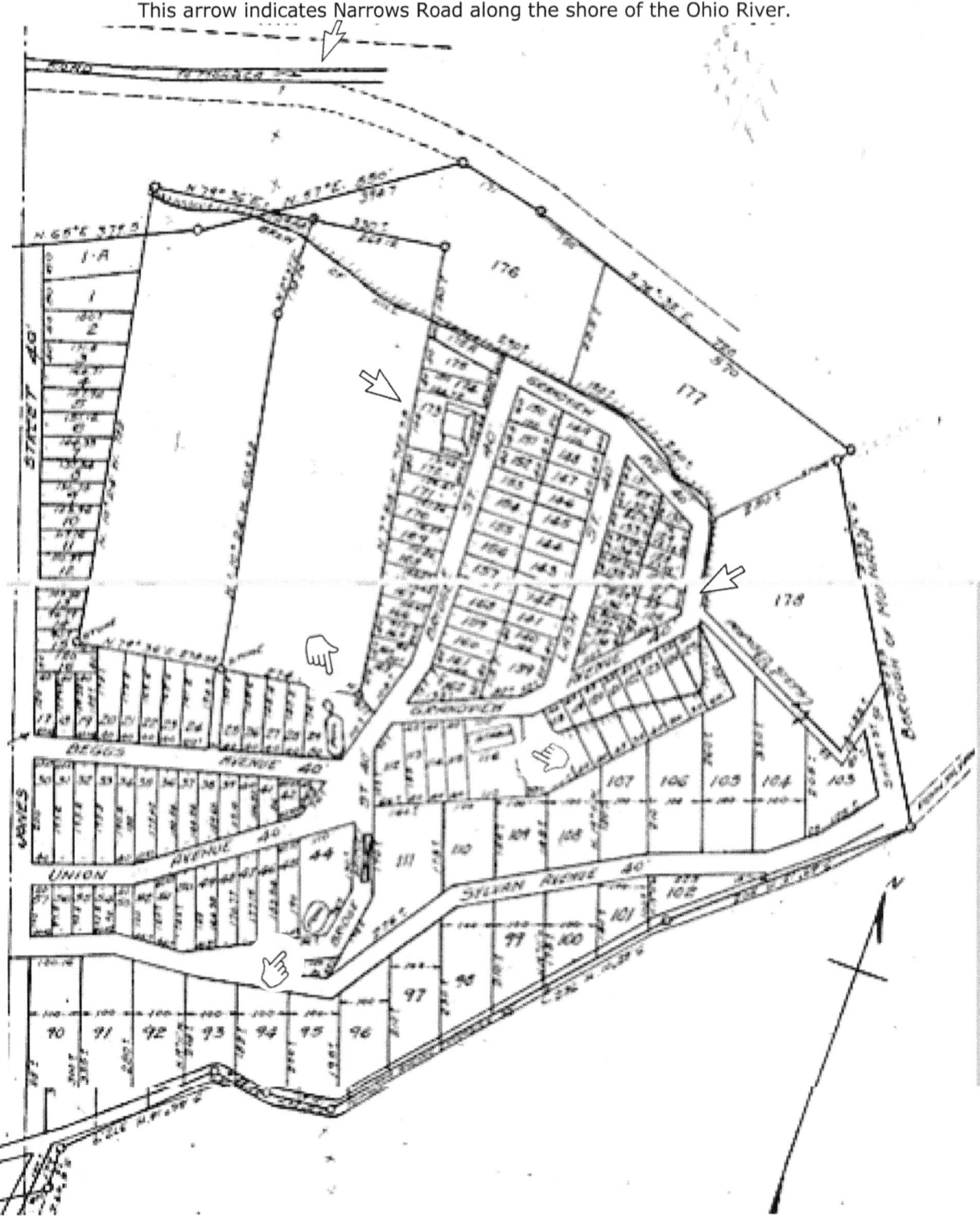

To the right of this 1925 plat map would be the current Beaver County Alloy Foundry Co. and Monaca. The arrow on the right indicates approximately where the former Welchmont mansion would have been located. The arrow toward the middle of the map indicates the former 5.14 acres and Garland mansion. The pointer in the middle of the map indicates one of the pools. The pointer toward the bottom, a little toward the right indicates the stables, and the bottom pointer, to the left indicates the second pool.

This is the continuation of the left side/portion of the previous plat map.

The Narrows Road is indicated here with the two solid lines, and simply labeled "Public Road to Monaca."

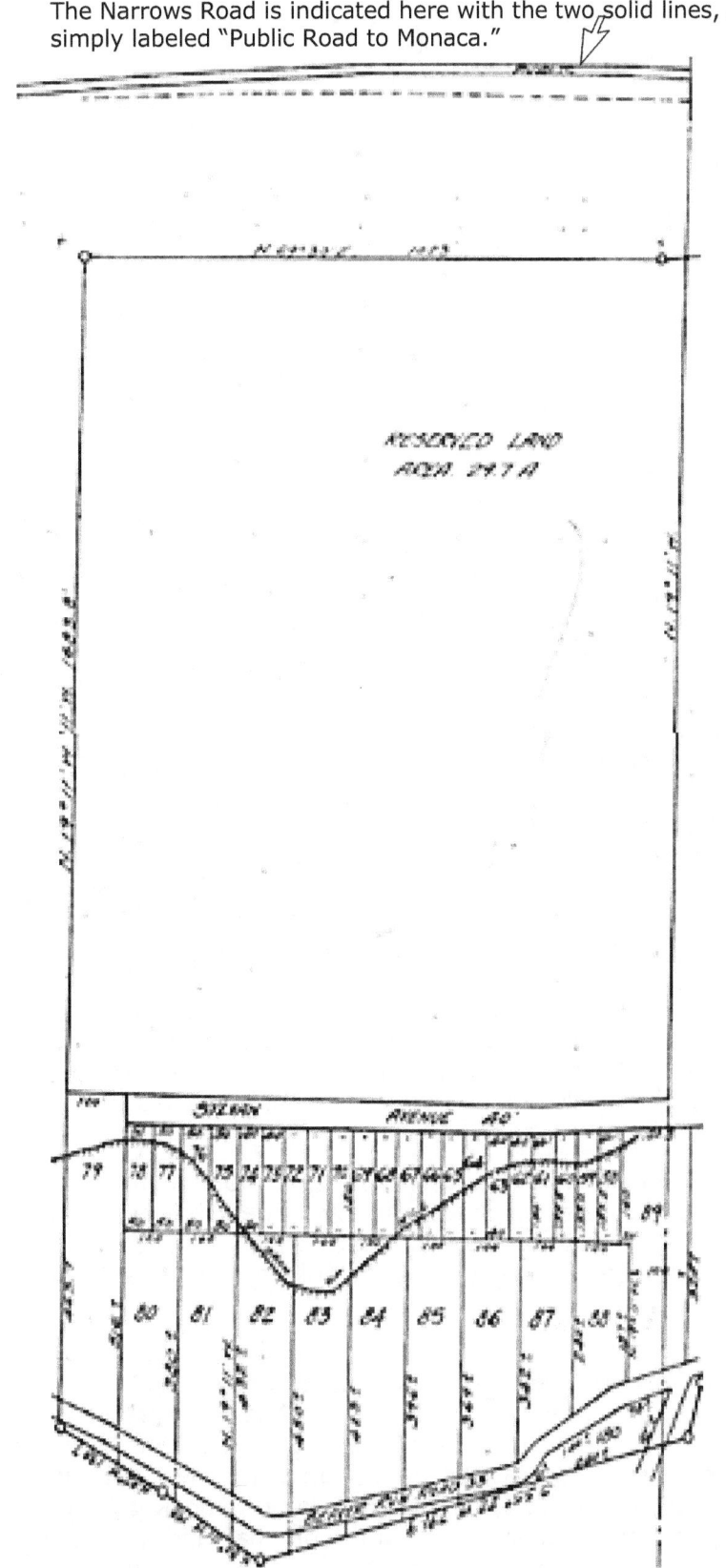

For orientation, the current Lowe's plaza would be to the left of this map. The current multilane, divided highway into Monaca would be past the bottom of this and the previous plat maps.

In those earlier years and even into the 1950s, Sylvan Crest was described as a place to see both the Beaver and Ohio Rivers, the traffic and railroad bridges, the towns of Monaca, Rochester, Beaver, West Bridgewater, Freedom, New Brighton, and Beaver Falls. It is hard to believe that around sixty years ago, a person could also see both the lights from the Northern Lights Shopping Center and the lights from the Greater Pittsburgh Airport depending where in Sylvan Crest you were standing and which direction you were looking. Viewing land, water, railroads, and air travel at one time was a selling point to prospective buyers once the land was subdivided for private homes. It also once was and may still be a popular place for artists and photographers to capture scenes.

Many newcomers to Center Township may not have heard of Sylvan Crest but in the late 1990s a very serious problem plagued the area's land owners -- mine subsidence. The subsidence was all a result of the numerous mines that were developed and used along the hillsides and under the entire area beginning in the 1800s. There were actually many early mines which were used not only under the Sylvan Crest area, but all along the area beginning at the end of Monaca and extending on past the current Beaver Valley Mall area and into Potter Township. These mines were originally used for extracting coal and clay which were the two most popular resources for several local companies and businesses in those earlier years. There were no problems under Sylvan Crest from all these abandoned mines for many years. Any memories of these mines had been forgotten, actually, most residents did not even know they existed. But by 1997 these mines began to collapse which severely affected many of the Sylvan Crest land owners' homes and properties.

Here are some snippets of articles published in the newspapers regarding the subsidences.

- Sixteen residents in Sylvan Crest found their homes were in danger of being destroyed in early summer of 1997 due to subsidence. The land under the homes in the area began to settle. Cracks appeared in walls. Foundations shifted. Gas and water lines were threatened. If that was not enough to deal with, most found out immediately that the values of the homes were greatly reduced and even though they were being forced out of the homes, they could not sell the homes and with most still financing the homes, they would have to continue to pay all loans and mortgages for the homes, yet not being able to live in or dispose of them.

- The federal government came to the rescue. It was determined that coal, along with clay, had been mined under the neighborhood. The Office of Surface Mining in Pittsburgh recommended the neighborhood be stabilized by pumping a mixture of concrete, fly ash, and sand into the crumbling mines. OSM's interpretation of the law was very generous!

- The OSM funds stabilization of mines is done by using money generated by a tax on coal. Funding is provided only when it is determined that coal was actually mined for a profit in any given area. Although in this case, clay for bricks was the main reason for the digging and mining, coal was also taken from the mines and used to fire the ovens, therefore, the reason for OSM's involvement.

The individual residents would never have been able to fund the stabilization project with their private funds. Only the state or federal government has the kind of money needed to undertake such a project. This is definitely a case where 'big government' cannot be criticized, rather gratitude should be extended, as well as a thank you for the speedy response by OSM.

Vankirk aka Stobo aka South Monaca area

In the early years, a large portion of the land in this area was at one time that of the McDonald and VanKirk families. Many have their own theory for how the name "Stobo" came to be. One stronger and continuous tradition is that the name came from the railroad who had a water stop for their steam engines located by the entrance of Elkhorn Run Road along the roadway outside Monaca. This water stop is a bit of a distance from the original lane/drive that is now known as Monaca Road, so I'm not sure of the valitity of this tradition, but the McDonald property could have easily spanned toward Elkhorn Run Road. The other well-known name of the area, "Vankirk," is a bit more self explanatory since William VanKirk was settled in that portion of Moon/Center Township as early as

1820. As stated, the McDonald families were also early to settle here and used a very narrow dirt road known as McDonald Road to access their homes. This road is now known as Monaca Road beginning/coming off Constitution Boulevard outside Monaca. Today, access to what is known as the Vankirk/Stobo area is one of three ways. One is by traveling the length of Center Grange Road until it intersects with Monaca Road, then making a left turn. Another is traveling out of Aliquippa, then onto Monaca Road. The third way would be coming onto Monaca Road off Route 51/Constitution Boulevard just past the end of Monaca.

Stobo/Vankirk is not a housing plan, it is rather a name people simply attached to the area which is still use to refer to this area. The people from this area do consider themselves as being more from this specific area first, and then from Center Township second. When asked where they live, these residents usually answer with "Stobo" or "Vankirk" and casually add "in Center Township."☺ The orignal heart of this area encompases properties on Summer Street, Grimm Street, Stobo Street, Noble Street, Lincoln Street, Dorothy Street, Vankirk Road, Washington Street, Locust Street, Gillin Drive, Eric Drive, Riverview Drive, all along Monaca Road. There are many more homes along and off Monaca Road that are now also considered in the Stobo/Vankirk area.

Another known name in the area to anyone who has lived in Center Township for numerous years is "Y McDonald." The intersection of Monaca Road and Center Grange Road form a "Y" shape and because of the McDonald property and family, this intersection became more of a landmark known as "Y McDonald" to all local people. (Also, see the section on Roads.)

There were two stone quarries that existed on the McDonald and Hicks properties. Both quarries were in operation in the 1800s, beginning prior to the P & L E railroad being built. The stone was brought out of the quarries by horse and wagon, much of it would be taken down to the river to be transported by boat to Pittsburgh. With the Ohio River being very shallow in the very early years, many people could easily drive a team of horses and wagon, go by horseback, and even at times walk across the river to do trading and/or shopping on the other side of the river. This was how the wagons of rocks were also, on occasion, as needed, transported across the river. Many of the rocks/stones that were quarried from this area would be crushed and used as bases for roads prior to the processes of surfacing roadways using brick, concrete, and/or asphalt.

There were originally only about four families that lived in this area. Today it has grown considerable with well over 150 current homes. Some of the more familiar past and possibly current families of the Vankirk area would be Erickson, Shively, Black, Weigle, Fath, Gillin, Shepard, Winkle, Hicks, Karlberg, Frank, Brooks, Forres, Sciaretta, Powell, Haller, and Summerville.

As mentioned above, originally, in the early years, access to the McDonald homestead was on a lane/drive off what is now Route 51/Constitution Boulevard, with the McDonald's home being the first house you would have come to on your left. The McDonald home was still standing in the late 1950s, but was empty and in a state of disrepair. I do not know whether it was purposely torn down, simply fell down and was then cleared, or may still be standing and was totally remodeled. (I personally did not locate it.) The view of the river and other communities from the McDonald property was said to be wonderful. I found an article that stated "a South Monaca plan of lots was laid out on the former McDonald farm;" the part regarding the lots being laid out would be true, and the part of being "south of Monaca," but the farm was actually within Moon/Center Township boundaries and not part of Monaca Boro. The farm and plan itself was laid out by Rev. and Mrs. Grimm in 1937. Mrs. Grimm was a former McDonald and heir to the property. They called this plan of subdivision *South-Monaca Plan*. It included land on Lincoln and Dorothy Street, and other drives in that immediate area. Back in 1937, the names of roads found on the plat map were McDonald Road (became Monaca Road), Hill Alley (defunct), Locust Drive (now Summer Street), Main Alley (most is gone, but one end of it is now an extension of Riverview Drive). (See Roads section.)

The Smith Hicks property was located in the same area as the Sciaretta service station and garage and several new homes (now Lynda Lane). The Alfred Erickson family had property and built their home close to 1900, as did the Spencer Powell family. All families of this area used the origial drive of the McDonald family. It was simply extended as the homesteads became more numerous. Eventually Center Grange was also extended as was the roadway leading into Aliquippa, both giving additional access to the Vankirk/Stobo area.

The Duquesne Slag Company had a slag dump adjacent to this area for many years. There were thousands and thousands tons of slag dumped into the great ravine along the Stobo/Vankirk area. There is also the very old Vankirk/McCullough cemetery located in the woods to the left of the last house on Vankirk Road. (See Cemetery section.)

Fun fact: An Atlas, published by Rand McNally in 1895, stated that Stobo was located 3 miles to the East from Bellowsville, it had railroad service and no post office.

~ ~ ~

There are three other locations that may interest readers. Throughout this book, there may be mention of a few locations or a few post offices that may sound foreign nowadays, therefore, by including the following information it may give some clarity and satisfy any curiosity.

All three of the following were very close to each other in proximity yet were also considered quite individualized. They were all once located in what became a massive earth moving project just across the Center Township line in Potter Township as you come off the Beaver Valley Expressway/ 376. Note -- All the buildings of the former County Home (along with the layout of its grounds) and the original land configurations of all these areas are all now gone, reshaped, and unrecognizable due to the former industrial plants, the construction of the Expressway, and most recently, the land moving project and erection of the Shell cracker plant going on in Potter Township. If you were or are at all familiar with various 'landmarks' in Beaver County, then the former ARCO, St. Joe Lead, Koppers, Horsehead plants and the current BASF plant may stir a memory or two and were/are located in the vicinity of what was once called and known as being in one these three distinctly different small communities: Bellowsville, Josephtown, and Kobuta.

Bellowsville
An 1877/78 report, by the Commonwealth of Pennsylvania, stated that in 1871, the northwest sub-district of Moon Township, petitioned the Legislature for an independent district. It was granted and the district was formed. This report is referencing the formation of Bellowsville. The Bellowsville village immediately addressed having a schoolhouse which was fashioned from one of the old buildings. The schoolhouse was soon remodeled, playgrounds were enlarged, and the property was enclosed with a nice fence. This school was among others to receive an annual income from the Alcorn family estate (see the Alcorn Family information and the Education section). The 1877/78 report went on to state "The school is now advanced to the front of enterprising, efficient schools, and will give a good account of itself."

Bellowsville was considered a small community yet had its own post office from 1874 to 1902 (see Post Office section). The formation of this post office is credited to Samuel Maxwell, a county industrialist who died in the early 1900s. The 1898 directory, *All Business and Professional Men and Official Guide of Beaver County, Penn'a* had Eliza S. Flocker as the Postmaster, J. C. Dunn as proprietor of an agricultural and farm implements business, and Frank J. Flocker as being the proprietor of a general merchandise building in Bellowsville. Ferry Street in Vanport, almost directly across the river, was the destination of the ferry which traveled to and from Bellowsville (see Ferry section).

Viewing of historic topo maps indicate Bellowsville's boundaries were in the area between the current Beaver Valley Expressway/Route 376, almost to Poorhouse Run creek, and from the Ohio River to the railroad tracks that paralleled most of Frankfort Road. Many references to Bellowsville are made along with another community known as Josephtown, so it is clear that these were very close to each other and may have even overlapped areas yet were considered separate communities. The Rand McNally Atlas shows that Bellowsville had a population of 46 people in 1895, but I also located some references made in 1900, stating an estimated 275, maybe 300 people. The differences in these population numbers is likely because it may have included residents of the County Home or the larger number may have been of a pure 'association' to Bellowsville and obtained from those who were being "serviced" by the Bellowsville post office (similar to residents of Center Township having a Monaca or Aliquippa address due to post office locations).

Just a very short distance up the Ohio River from Bellowsville (heading toward Monaca) along the shore of the Ohio River was a place known as Rag Run. This is where the Rag Run creek emptied into the Ohio. It does not appear that Rag Run was an actual community, but more of a port or point of location along the Ohio River in that area. Rag Run was also the site of a local ferry that would travel the Ohio River a short distance to Bellowsville. Many references state that the County Home (Poor Farm as it was often referenced) was situated close to the Ohio River and between the two small, now defunct, towns/communities of Bellowsville and Josephtown.

Some families that were said to live in the community area of Bellowsville were:
- Joseph Patterson
- Frank (Mary) Barnes
- Joseph B. Maxwell (ferry company)
- Robert (Margaret and Rosanna) Potter
- Samuel (Eliza) Maxwell (blacksmith & ferry company)
- Miller (Julia) Flocker (store)
- Joseph (Martha) Phibbs
- William (Eliza) Flocker (store)

See the maps in the section on Roads. There is a 1926 map which depicts former Route 115 and Route 76. Route 115 became Route 18 (Frankfort Road) and Route 76 became former Route 51, currently Brodhead Road. Not only is Bellowsville still indicated on this 1926 map, but there is also a 1941 map showing Routes 18 and 51 listed and this map also still has Bellowsville listed.

Also associated with Bellowsville was a once familiar home, that of Samuel Maxwell. His home was left standing after he died in 1894, it sat along the old Narrows Road which ran parallel to the Ohio River from the County Home to Monaca. Samuel's former large home stood abandoned for many years and became quite run down and overgrown with weeds and vines. Many considered this former home, and even the surrounding grounds, to be haunted.

> *Fun Fact:* Tales of hauntings included...
> Bellowsville is described many times as being a sleepy village along the Ohio River in Potter Township. But did you know that it was reported that ghosts were playing "queer pranks" on anyone that passed by on the old Narrows Road, especially at night?
> There were no longer any other of the Bellowsville village's houses or buildings standing, all being razed by the zinc plant except for the former County Home buildings and the former home of Samuel Maxwell which stood along the old Narrows Road, but it was terrible run down and overgrown. Travelers who passed by this rundown former home would all agree that there were "uncommon noises, flitting lights and wailing of banshees characterized the nocturnal activities in and about the Old Haunted House in Bellowsville." Many stated that they were all too glad when they reached their homes safely.
> The former Maxwell house supposedly was the meeting place of all ghosts from the area including those soles of persons who died while living in the adjacent County Home. These 'ghosts' were said to converge in Maxwell's former house and discussed various and sundry matters of interests to them alone. There were also reports of secret passageways and concealed trapdoors leading to underground rooms and hidden treasure in the then abandoned house.
> One specific incident occurred when a headless man frightened a traveler so much that he was unable to run away as the ghastly spirit walked toward him. The ghost vanished, but the traveler said he heard noises coming from the house as if someone was walking up a long staircase, then there was a crash, and all was quiet except the whisping of tree leaves and the sounds of the lapping waters of the river waves.
> Another incident was reported by a raccoon hunter who saw a spirit hobbling about the area on golden crutches catching fireflies in the moonlight. The ghost just disappeared when the hunter shouted.
> Prior to the Maxwell's house being razed, the consensus was that the only beings who were inhabiting this run-down house were from tramps and bootleggers that stayed there. Regardless of the truth, a newspaper reporter was quoted as saying "In spite of the accepted incredibility given to haunts, something unusual certainly inhabits the place."

Josephtown

The majority of the information provided or found recorded for the community and post office of Josephtown was associated with St. Joseph Lead Co. in Potter Township, PA. St. Joseph Lead Co. had their mailing address with "Josephtown, PA;" the St. Joseph Lead Company was located along Frankfort Road/Route 18. In the 1895 Rand McNally Atlas, there was no mention of *Josephtown*, but then St. Joseph Lead Company did not come to Potter Township/Center Township area until the 1920s, a bit after the atlas was printed. There would most likely still have been a few homes in the immediate area of Josephtown since there were homes and farms dotted throughout that entire area. So it was not uncommon in the 1930s and 1940s to find references to the P & L E railroad and other transportation media to state "between Monaca to Josephtown." (See St. Joseph Lead Co. in the Industrial section.)

The post office located in Josephtown was short lived, existing only from 1931 until 1933 when it was officially discontinued (see Post Offices section). Other than the St. Joe Lead Company having it as their address, I found no other residents having *Josephtown* as part of their addresses, but it was found to be included in several deeds from that area (see further).

In 1938 and 1939, the St. Joseph Company presented Potter Township with a school building they erected, the school was appropriately called "St. Joe School Building." This school had two classrooms, a storage room, a heater room, a small kitchen, and was supplied with well water. There was also a nice play area on the school grounds. This school was built in the area of the former Horsehead plant's scales which sat closer to Frankfort Road. It was also used by Beaver County for special education classes for a period, as well as a community center for several years before the building was turned back over to the lead plant (per stipulations made on the original deed).

Even with no post office, no railroad station, no signs that it ever really existed on many maps, I found that people still reference Josephtown for many years. Then, by the 1990s, sixty some years later, it seemed to have faded off into just memories. Yet, there was a 2000 report by the Raccoon Creek Watershed Association discussing watersheds and other topics which made a reference to Raccoon Creek stating "...until it discharges into the Ohio River near Josephtown in Beaver County."

Location of the St. Joseph Lead Company and area of Josephtown. (Note the Expressway bridge over the Ohio River in the top right corner.)

Josephtown was still being reverenced in this 1961 deed.

Fun fact: Even as late as 1965 to 1968 Josephtown and Kobuta were both used for the address of St. Joseph Lead and Sinclair Koppers Co. (respectively).

Kobuta

With the construction of the Koppers United plant and its operation that started in late 1942, there was the need for many men. As the Koppers plant was first being erected and into the early days of its operations, the community of Kobuta was already being formed along Frankfort Road/ Route 18. Kobuta was an unincorporated community in Potter Township, yet when references were made to the Koppers plant in Potter Township, the address would state "Kobuta, Beaver County, PA." Local lore states that the name Kobuta was formed from a combination of the words **Ko**ppers and **buta**diene (an ingredient used by Koppers Co. to produce synthetic rubber) (see Industrial section and War section). Kobuta has disappeared from modern maps but is still reflected within a few businesses' names and sometimes just for general orientation to the area.

The first workers of the plant were living in two smaller communities adjacent to the plant at the time. Eventually, there were three areas for the workers to reside in............

1) *Kobuta Village* which was the trailer camp and housed the workers who had their families with them. Kobuta Village filled to capacity very quickly with waiting lists on both the government owned trailers and the parking spaces for private trailers. There were 250 government owned units (90 were for families of 5 or more, 160 were for up to 4-person families) and an additional 30 private spaces.

2) *Camp Beaver* which was an area with barracks (mere huts) adjacent to the plant, used by the bachelors or married men who came to work at the plant without bringing their families. Both Kobuta Village and Camp Beaver were necessitated due to housing facilities in the area being sparse.

3) *Kobuta Homes* Soon, there was an additional housing option that was built on the property called *Kobuta Homes*. There were 300 dwellings constructed by the Public Housing Administration, acting for the Federal government, and were specifically built for the housing of families and individuals employed by Kobuta and engaged in the vital war work. This work was exactly what all the workers at Koppers United were considered to be doing.

In addition to the housing areas, the community of Kobuta had a modern cafeteria that was described as well lit, had glass on three sides, capable of seating 500 persons, and an up-to-date kitchen with a bakery. Most mornings it was not unusual for this cafeteria to serve breakfast to 1200 or 1300 persons along with over 2,000 meals a day being considered the average. There were also two canteens located within the plant.

The immediate area around this newly forming Kobuta community continued to grow. There was a recreation hall used by all the village residents, trailer residents, and the barracks men. The recreation hall was adjacent to the cafeteria, 80 feet long and 60 feet wide. It had a barbershop, a clock room, lobby area, soda fountain, auditorium, and large community area. Within a few months there was also a fire department, a Civilian Defense Council and a regular civic organization with functioning groups that met each Tuesday evening in the Kobuta recreation hall. Dances were held each Saturday night with musicians like The Kobuta Cowboys performing. There were also weekly movies shown. The children living at the village had a playground set up for them and there was also a railroad station located at Kobuta.

By November of 1943, Kobuta was considered the second largest war housing project in Beaver County, Van Buren Homes in Vanport, was the largest. On Nov 26, 1943, the Beaver County Housing Authority, Koppers United Company, the Housing Architects of Beaver County, County Commissioners, and other prominent county people were present for a dedication ceremony of the community building at the Kobuta Homes. There were town meetings held in the community hall every Monday evening so matters of the Kobuta community could be aired and discussed. They had an Improvement Committee to resolve all concerns, interests, and suggestions. These meetings were open to the public.

The community had its own unofficial small post office and mail was dispatched from it three times each day. It existed from 1944 to 1955 (see Post Offices section). There were laundry trailers and a 'drying yard' with clothes lines erected. A Navy physician would regularly visit at Kobuta village vaccinating all who asked for it and would attend to other health matters. Victory gardens were cultivated along the bank of the Ohio River by the village residents. Everything possible was done to make the men working at Kobuta, as well as their families, feel as much at home as could be done with this new community that was only a few months old.

School classes were first held in the community building for the children living in Kobuta until the completion of the planned project/community school building. The Kobuta School was eventually erected for the residents of the Kobuta Homes community. It was a very nice school building with a hallway the entire length of the building, four classrooms, a principal's office, a teacher's lounge, stock room, and bathrooms. There was also a playground to the rear of the building. The number of students soon overcrowded the school as more residents moved into the village. To aleviate the overcrowded conditions, seventh and eighth grade students were sent to Center Township's school and then to Monaca's schools. Even with the village having its own school, by 1950 there were sixty-five to seventy children who attended classes at the newly constructed Potter Township grade school and approximately ten others who attended classes at Monaca High School.

Kobuta School
Photo from Beaver County Yearbook

1943 view of a section of the Kobuta Homes.

These pictures courteousy Joann Bishop

This picture is of poor quality, but it depicts the one-storey building provided for the Kobuta Homes. It was a community center for these residents, containing a nursery room (to the extreme right), a meeting hall (in the center of the building), and to the left were management offices and maintenance quarters. The building had hardwood floors and was heated by coal. This picture is from 1943.

Since it was directly connected to the government and the war effort, coupled with the vital nature of the product Koppers United Company used (butadiene and styrene) for their production of synthetic rubber, it goes without saying that the plant was well-guarded against sabotage. The entire grounds, including the housing areas, were fenced and patrolled twenty-four hours a day by the Koppers plant police force. The guard force was organized shortly after construction of the plant was started in Jul 1942. The well-equipped guard force was under the jurisdiction of the Third Service Command, Fourth District, Military Police, U.S. Army. The guards had a genuine arsenal of weapons and ammunition and there was a rifle range and pistol range on site. There were also three "War Dogs," or as they were fondly called "guardettes," added to the force along with other canine guards. All were housed in a specifically built area with kennels at the plant.

Fun Fact: Like the men, the "guardettes" were all sworn in as Military Policeman.

Fact: All employees of Kobuta were photographed and fingerprinted and there were badges issued with restricted and unrestricted zones of various employees and/or visitors. There were even feminine guards on duty and in positions in the administration building. They checked identifications and kept the records of visitors. One of these women was a local resident - Mrs. Jane Hicks.

When the Kobuta Homes and the community were first constructed and developed in 1942/1943, it was expected to have the normal life span of seven years. In 1946, following the end of the war, the current residents in the housing units were told they had to find other homes of their own. Forty-eight of the housing units were then transferred elsewhere for veterans' housing. References were made into the 1950s with addresses of residents still living within these homes as *Kobuta Homes*. In Oct 1952, there were yet approximately one hundred and fourteen families living in the war housing project of the Kobuta community. These remaining residents were all notified they must now vacate their apartments and living quarters by 1953, due to the land of the community had been leased by a company that planned to dredge the site for sand and gravel. Although there were only these one hundred and fourteen families physically living in Kobuta in 1952, there was actually a record of two hundred and thirty-three family unit structures that were still located there. Once all residents evacuated, the homes were scheduled to be demolished.

Also found in the area known as Kobuta, there was a smaller hotel built at 427 Frankfort Road, located across the road from Koppers named appropriately - *Kobuta Hotel*. Additionally, there were two other former well-known watering holes/tap rooms/bars/taverns for the plant workers along Frankfort Road that should be mentioned – The Red Rooster Inn/Tavern and the Midway Bar (see the Hotel section and the Restaurant and Bar section).

Here are two similar 1944 aerial views of Kobuta showing the plant in the upper portion of the pictures and the housing plan areas (trailers, barracks, homes) in the lower portions.

Photo courtesy BCHR&LF

The top pointer is indicating the Kobuta plant. The bottom pointer is indicating the housing areas.

Photo courtesy BCHR&LF

The top pointer is indicating the Kobuta plant. The bottom pointer is indicating the housing areas.

So................ Even before the construction of the Expressway and the reconstruction and land moving of the area by Shell, almost every thread of evidence of the former Bellowsville, Josephtown, or Kobuta communities had already disappeared.

~ ~ ~

MISCELLANEOUS HOUSING PLANS

Now, on to the many other various housing plans in Center Township not previously described. There are so many different plans of homes and areas that have been developed and are still being developed. I repeat myself and say I make no claim to having included all areas, but I did make an earnest attempt to try to include as many as possible.

Baker Plan – off Bunker Hill Road, by Patton Drive.

Baker Place Plan – off Brodhead Road in both Hopewell and Center Townships
Includes Linden Street, Neish Street, Cemetery/Mt Carmel Lane, Orchard Street, James Street. All was at one time Cooper family farmland.

Brock Plan - The homes along the section of Woodlawn Drive that comes off Brodhead Road. Previously the land of the Baker family, then the Short family, and then named *Bye-Way* farm by the Blair family in the early 1900s.

Brodhead Heights Plan
More of an addition/extension of lots in the Sylvan Crest area. It includes lots between Shirley Drive, Wagner Street, Grandview Avenue, Beaver Street, to Carpenter Road. The Valley Land Company first subdivided parts of this area in 1926, then E. M. Love refined lots in the entire Sylvan Crest area in 1941 which his daughter, Edna continued in 1947/48.

Brookhaven Estates – Chapel Road and Geneva Drive
17-acre development - approved in 2001. No sidewalks or recreation land; cul-de-sac. entrance off Geneva Drive.

Bunker Hill Acres
In 1926, C. I. McDonald's farmland was subdivided into 22 building lots and one large lot that contained 37.47 acres. This property was all along what is now where Pleasant Drive comes out onto Brodhead (O. C. Cluss), going down past the current Center Exit Tire, and then over onto Bunker Hill Road and across the road from the Bunker Hill School/VFW. I have no further information as to when the property was purchased by the McDonalds, if the family lived on the property or rented/leased it out, et cetera. The property was bordered by Zimmerman, Good, Rok, and Springer families when it was subdivided.

Cedar Ridge Estates –Cedar Ridge Road off Chapel Road
Property was the former Dusold dairy farmland. 31-lot housing development was accepted the first of Jun 1978. The developer was Pave Enterprises, Inc. of Moon Township. There were a few different phases to this plan. In 1978, there were 30 homes. In 1987, there were 61, and more homes were built through the 2000s with a continuing phase.

Caymus Estates – 3348 Brodhead Road

Center Vue Manor – off Chapel Road, includes homes on Cherry Lane
The lots were laid out by Mike and Mary Sintay in 1955. They owned the land and it was deeded down through the years to other Sintay family members. The land was divided off into building lots.

Chapel Valley Plan   aka   Xenos area - on Chapel Road
Ulysses and Helen Xenos were listed as the owners of this land when it was laid out into building lots. They sub divided their property and gave specific uses and types of buildings that could be built on each lot (residential only). Mid Oct 1956, 91-acre, 300 homes, garden apartments. Developed by Xenos Brothers Builders of Ambridge, engineering done by Michael Baker Inc, Wallover, Petz, and St. Jean of Beaver Falls handled the layout work, and Steve Petz was the landscape architect. There was also a park area included which was more or less donated. It originally had 5 acres of ground for recreation and park facilities. This park area was used by Center Recreation for several years. There were many phases to this plan, one was a 50 lot Chapel Valley plan no. 3 in 1973. Mike and Stella Xenos sold some property to the Chapel Valley Swim Club, too.

Canterbury Manor – 500 Center Grange Road
Started as an apartment complex – William Demeson/developer. First approved in 1975. In the fall of 1983 the complex was owned by Herman Investment. It included a private pool and tennis court at this time. It was proposed in the fall of 1983 to convert the complex from rentals to individually owned townhouses with a homeowners association retaining the community building, pool, and community areas. As of 1984, 65 units were converted. In Jan 1984, the Canterbury Manor Townhouses changed. They totally relandscaped and made other changes to enhance the deveopment's country-like atmosphere. Instead of apartment units, residents could purchased units under a condominium-type agreement or investors could buy whole buildings to use as a rental investment. As of Jan 1984, the development was owned by Prudential Realty Co, Pgh.

This apartment complex was subdivided and remodeled to form...

Beaver Creek Apts / Beaver Creek Village – 500 Center Grange Road
In 1984 units were being sold as condominiums / townshouses.

 1985 ad

Center College Estates – off Brodhead Road at end of Christy Drive
Jul 1968 "new executive type homes and lots" were up for sale. 24 homes constructed by Ambridge firm – Mazzie & Colella Inc. The third plan/phase was underway in 1978, included storm sewer system.

Chateau Estates (condos) – off Chapel Road
Newer constructed condominiums – 2005. On Chateau Drive – across from Chapel Valley.

Cherrywood Grove – Moffet Run Road
Started in 1990 with 29 lot subdivision. It includes Cottonwood, Whitewood, and Buttonwood Drives.

Clover Manor – on Clover Drive off Brodhead Road
Located opposite Penn State entrance (pond area) and through to Chapel Road. This large tract of land was sold off in 1956 from the original farm by the Hartenbach family shortly after Henry C. Hartenbauch's death (1954). One of the original Hartenbach homes, a 2 storey, white farm house still stands and can be seen just behind the lower few homes on the right as you turn off Chapel Road. Clover Manor was approved to be a 32 plan of homes. There are currently 28 homes. Eugene and Ernest Nero / Nero Brothers were the contractors.

Colonial Arms Apartments – Milne Drive
This is an 84-apartment unit located adjacent to the former Gee Bee/ now Walmart Plaza area. They began leasing units in 1974.

Cooper Ridge Plan – off Brodhead Road, Ridgeview Drive
Laid out by Nicholas Plodenic, Jr. in 1942. Was part of 71 acres of Cooper family farmland.

Crabapple Chase Plan – Kennedy Drive off Gourley Lane
Theodore and Arlene Churovia requested variance in Oct 1987 to reduce minimum front yardage for the 10 lots in the plan.   There was a cul-de-sac in 2016 with 13 homes.

Davis Plan – begins along Center Grange Road
These are all the lots and homes beginning on Center Grange Road from just past the Lutheran Church to Woodlawn Drive, then all along Woodlawn Drive (off Center Grange Road), back to Evergreen Drive, then going to Chapel Road by Hall Road. All land involved being part of the early Davis family farms.

Doak Plan – off Baker Road
The plan of homes on your right off Baker Road just before entering the campus of Central Valley High School, includes homes on Truman Street and Roosevelt Drive. Originally the Doak farm.

Eagles Landing at Mateer Farms – Marshall Road
This is a three storey multi building complex of apartments developed in 2019; built upon the former Mateer farm which was located along both Brodhead Road and Marshall Road.

East Shaffer Estates – East Shaffer Road
Started in late 2002; 95-lot plan of homes; Joe Hall Excavating and Construction–developer.

Eben Estates – Chapel Road / past Hall Road
Selling of lots was handled by K. Hall Realty. Land was being landscaped and sewage lines being installed in 1988. There were a few phases to these estates. 1988, there were 47 lots available, then 1991 there were 74 lots.

Evergreen Estates – along Bunker Hill Road.
May 1983 - Approval to Theodore Churovia for subdivision in the estates. There were a few phases to these estates. 1980 there was first 47 lots; 1989 - 38 lots; 1991 - 12 lots.

Fernwood Estates aka extension of Lincolnshire Plan of Lots - currently Lincoln Drive
(See Humbert Plan, Lincolnshire, and Sylvester Plans further.)
Lincoln Drive was originally to be called Ruhe Street, then Lincolnshire Drive. Anthony Sylvester – developer. Began 1976 with Lincoln Drive as a cul-da-sac. Winwood Drive was added around 1978. There is also currently an Oakcrest Drive off Winwood, too. This land/ surrounding property was formerly owned by a Rev. W. J. Engle and/or Mr. Michael Baker.

Fronko Plan – along/off Brodhead Road. Laid out by M. K. Fronko in 1928.

Garden View Estates – along Bunker Hill Road (just past V.F.W.)
Started in spring of/to mid-2002. 102 carriage home community on 50 acres (main road – Patton Drive). Developed and built by TDS Group. Proposed by Richard Yoko of Raccoon Township. Phase I included about 60 units. The buildings are mostly duplexes and triplexes.

Gourley Plan – off Center Grange Road
Original lots were on Gourley Lane, now includes Kennedy Drive, Terry Lane, & Circle Drive. Laid out by G. Gourley in 1955.

Gross Plan - Gross Drive and Raccoon Street, along Brodhead Road
Lots were laid out in 1945 by John W. Gross.

Humbert Ruhe Plan – currently on Lincoln Drive
(See Fernwood Plan previous and Lincolnshire Plan and Sylvester Plan further.) Land of Lyle McCon in the mid 1950s was deeded to Eugene B. & Vera Humbert and Otto & RoseMary Ruhe who laid out subdivisions in 1957, then deeded to A. Secontine Sylvester. The name of the plan was a combination of both names, and the main road was originally named "Ruhe Street" then became Lincolnshire Drive – currently Lincoln Drive.

Kalinoske Plan - off Brodhead Road; lots and homes along Mulberry Lane.
Laid out by the Kalinoske family in 1956 – all was part of their parents' farmland (which was on both sides of Brodhead Road).

Lakeview Farms – former McCracken family property - off Chapel Road
Notice for the 60-lot plan of homes were started in Feb 1993– 1 mile south of the intersection of Chapel Road with Brodhead Road. There were continuing phases underway.

Lakewood Estates – on Edgewater Drive – between Todd Lane and Chapel Road
In Jun 1957 the Lakewood Estates plan of lots was approved; Steven Petz was to make preliminary inspections of plans for the subdivisions. A portion of the land was formerly of the McCracken family. A 1957 ad stated, "A distinguished address – LAKEWOOD ESTATES – On Chapel Road in Center Township." In 1961 there were still new homes being built and sold. In Feb 1976, there was a special zoning and planning meeting held to review business of revised information; it was stated it was a 15 to 29 lot plan. In the spring of 1976, there were realtors advertising "brand new" built homes for sale. In the past 10 years, there have been even more homes built along Edgewater.

LeGoullon Plan – Stone Quarry Road area
Laid out by Frank LeGoullon in 1939. Lots located along and off Stone Quarry Road including those on Woods Avenue, and lots laid out by F. A. LeGoullon in 1955, between Wagner Road and the current divided highway going into Monaca. The LeGoullons also previously owned and sold acreage/lots across from and adjacent to the current Wal-Mart plaza.

Lincolnshire - Lincoln Drive
(See Humbert Ruhe Plan and Fernwood Estates previous and Sylvester Plan further.)
This was originally known as the Humbert Ruhe Plan in the 1950s, then called Lincolnshire in 1965. The first and singular road in the 1950s was originally Ruhe Street but was changed to Lincolnshire Drive and is now known as Lincoln Drive.

Lincoln Homes - along Brodhead Road
See St. James Park further. Lincoln Homes was another earlier name used when referencing the St. James Park homes.

Nedde Plan - laid out in 1952 by Wm. Nedde and H. Lees – 10 lots along Christy Drive.

Oakland Heights - Biskup Lane
Final approval was given for a 25-home subdivision in c1991.
Developers – Sam and Eli Rebich of Aliquippa.

Old Orchard Estate – Oak Lane, off Brodhead Road at #3677
Smaller development with only 12 lots. The land was once part of the original property of Bryan, McCormick, Coombs, then the Smith families. The Smith family became involved as developers and part owners in selling the lots of this estate. It was started in 1986.

Orchard Grove Estates – off Center Grange Road
Lots included on/ adjacent to Gourley Lane and Terry Lane. Laid out in 1957. Originally part of the large 200+ acre farm of James and Janet Reed (early 1800s) prior to acreage being reduced and sold to quite a few other individuals. It was last owned and divided into lots by Geo./Jean Gourley, Larry Giammaria, Wm./Shirley Patton.

Olszanski Plan – along Bunker Hill Road
Land owned by the Olszanski family. It was laid out in 1997.

Paularon Plan - East Shaffer
Laid out in 1980. On Paula Drive. Plan was to build 14 homes.

Pine Crest Plan – lots along Brodhead Road
In/By the Pine and Locust Streets. Laid out in 1947.

Pinehurst Estates – off Chapel Road
1978 (final subdivision)   Had 14 lots when first developed by Chirichetti & O'Connor Development Co. Located across the road from Chateau Estates / condos and between Columbia and Geneva Drives.

Riverview Heights Estates – Sylvan Crest area
Located on the extenstion of Shirley Drive. Started in 1996.

Rolling Hills Plan – off Center Grange Road
Include 29 lots on Rolling Hills Drive and Ellen Avenue. Land owned by Mr. and Mrs. H. Glasser and laid out in lots designed by Stephen Petz in 1959, currently consists of 27 homes.

Roman Estates - 100-300 Capital Drive, off Brodhead Road (close to Center Bowling Lanes)
Luxury apartment complexes.

Roxview Estates – off Brodhead Road, on Jenny Lynn Drive.
Laid out by C. Betters in 1978. It is a 24-lot plan for homes.

Shadow Estates – extension of St. James
The road to these lots is an extension of York Way (one phase of plan) and an extension of Warrencliff (another phase of plan). Originally 30+ acres, formerly the Dockter homestead, then lastly, the Tilly Farm. Approximately 56 lots were subdivided for the two phases. Subdivision began c2005 and is currently still developing.

Sherwood Acres – off Brodhead Road

Approved in Nov 1975, to be a 121 unit housing development. Described as being on the former Mary Todora property. (Her property being a tract of land which extended from behind the former Barn tavern and going across Brodhead Road to Poplar Drive. Originally planned to be 319 townshouses, but developer, Dorme Land Co (Ernest Martin of EA Martin Real Estate, James McDonald of McDonald Real Estate in Hopewell, and Rudy Colella of Economy were owners of Dorme Land Co.) changed their plans and made it 121 single home plan. Has a 2nd exit/entrance off Poplar Drive. There is still a designated area for a playground in the center of the plan.

Fact: In Jan 1975, Center Township officials were considering the proposal of a 337- development by Dorme Land Co. It was to be located on the former Mary Todora property – a 43 acre tract of property behind "The Barn" and the "Sherwood Inn." The development was to consist of two and three bedroom units – most units being two and a half stories, a maximum of four units to each building, and the buildings would be clustered to allow for open space. The development was to also include a swimming pool, tennis courts, and a recreation building with some garage space to be provided. Cost to the buyers of the units would be $24,000 or more and each buyer would also pay dues to the a home association.

Sky View Plan – off Chapel Road, above Sky View Lounge, adjacent to Chapel Valley

Frank and Jenny Linko laid out the Sky View Plan in 1957. This land was in dispute as to owners with it going to Frank and Jenny. They owned 50 acres of the former land of Jacob Streit (1800s) and family. There was also a piece of township property off Sky View Drive that had been planned for a sewage treatment plant, but plans changed with it not being a "buildable lot" or even useable for recreation with the way it was laid out, the supervisors began to accept proposals for someone else to purchase the land (nothing further).

Smolanovich Plan – by Skyview Drive

Milton and Anna Smolanovich made some subdivision of one of their lands in 1991, being the same property they purchased in 1963. The property was located off Skyview Drive. In 2006, the plat map of the 84-acre Smolanovich Plan showed it spanning from along Elkhorn Road to Temple Road and on into a small portion of Hopewell Township. There is one older home on this plan that was built in 1860 and still has a Smolanovich family living in it.

South Monaca Plan of Houses –located along Monaca Road in the Vankirk/Stobo area

Included Dorothy Street, Grimm Street, Lincoln Street and Noble Street. It was laid out in 1937 by Kate (McDonald) Grimm and Rev. Joseph L. Grimm from part of the Grimm farm.

Sohn Farm Plan - off Brodhead Road

This is a very large plan, including lots along Main Street, Patterson Ave, Figley Avenue, Mengel Avenue, Locust Street. This was formerly the Sohn farm and was laid out in 1929 by John W. Patterson, D. Wilbert Figley, David S. Patterson, and Clarence A. Mengel. Need I mention where I believe the current names of streets in this area came from ☺

Solar Heights Plan – extension of Ridgeview Drive and Cooper Ridge Plan

Lots included on Ridgeview Drive, Solar Drive, and Richard Drive areas. Laid out by Ida Solkovy in 1949, phases continued through 1959.

Springer Plan – from W. Shaffer Road to near Oakhill Road

This plan had three different plat maps between 1937 and 1941 by members of the Springer family. The lots of this plan are all in the area involving West Shaffer Road on Center Street, Zimmerle Street, Winter Street. The land was originally from the farm of James H. and Mary Springer. The last of the Springer family to live on the land were three of their unmarried daughters – Sarah, Rebecka, and Mary (in 1930s).

St. James Homes – along/off Brodhead Road/Route 18

This plan of homes covers the area between the two large water storage tanks to North Branch Road. This land was formerly part of the farmland of Bryan-McCormick–Coombs families. In early 1958, Mr. Coombs sold this portion of the property, which consisted of around 43 ½ acres. It was purchased by John Cochran who sub-divided and developed it into a housing project (St. James Park) by the Union Supply Co., Ambridge. The plan for this development was approved mid Dec 1958, originally to be 146 home development by C. R. Martin, district manager of Style Builders of the Union Supply Division, U. S. Steel Corp. Steven Petz, Center Township landscape architect, planned the site design. In Mar 1963, there was a variance made due to some errors in the original plans, all changes were approved. Many "new" homes were still advertised and for sale in mid 1973. There were 180 homes listed in the plan by Jan 1973 when the Beaver County Planning Commission turned down plans for a shopping complex to go in across Brodhead Road from St. James Park.

This picture was taken before 1965 since the top left corner still shows the former golf course prior to the BV Mall being built in 1965.

Sunshine Valley Plan – by St. Francis Cabrini Church
These lots are in the area along Shadyside Drive, Trinity Drive, Lynn Way, Shadyside Drive, Whitehall Avenue. Laid out by Hall family members in 1961. Whitehall Avenue extension was added around 1978.

Sylvester Plan – (off Lincoln Drive) - on Winwood Drive and Oakcrest Drive
There are two plat maps (1963 and 1969) of these lots by A. Secontino & Mary Sylvester. In 1975 there is another plat map for adding Oakcrest Drive. (Also see Humbert Ruhe Plan, Lincolnshire, and Fernwood Plan previous.)

Walnut Grove - off Moffett Run Road
In 1990 it was to be a 40-lot subdivision, but in 1996, it was stated as an 84-lot subdivision off the Center Exit of Route 60. Ryan Homes began building houses in Jan 1996. Spiro Pappan was the developer. This plan is adjacent to Cherrywood Grove Plan.

Wedgewood Chase – off Brodhead Road
Approved in 1985/spring 1986. It is a 19-unit townhouse development. Architect was Ted Victor and developer/builder was Ted Churovia.

Wickham Manor – off Brodhead Road
This plan consists of the current lots and homes on Wickham Drive, Crest Drive, Chestnut Drive, Highland Avenue, and Elm Drive. All the acreage of this plan covered the lots beginning along Brodhead Road and going down to meet Chapel Road. The plan was laid out by Walter and Glenn Wickham, with W.A. Wickham and Sons Builders & Developers building the homes. It was often referred to as the "Nero Plan-Wickham Manor Plan" and was first laid out into lots in 1956. The Wickhams purchased the land from the Laubscher family. (As the crow flies, the Laubscher farmhouse sits almost directly below Chestnut Street.)

Woodhaven Estates – off Chapel Road (adjacent to Chapel Valley)
The original plat map was laid out by Stanley Brobeck, Samuel Milanovich, and David Jones in 1957. In May of 1959 the Confienti Real Estate and Insurance (J. Martin Confienti, owner) became exclusive brokers for the new subdivision. It was started with 58 large lots for homes. The buyers could use Confienti's or hire their own builders, but there were specific architectural requirements. The ad that was in a newspaper said, "located off Chapel Valley Road." There were several phases to this plan, including, in 1973, they were still selling

homes in the plan. In 1976, there were "newly constructed" homes being advertised. In 1982, 16 lots, in 1988, 30 lots and 41 lots, and in 1992, 22 lots.

Woodmont Estates -   off Center Grange, then off Reinish, on Woodmont Drive
   Laid out in 1988.   Was to be a 30-lot plan of homes.

Xenos – a portion of the area of land/homes in Chapel Valley
   There was a township playground in this area. (Also see Recreation section.)

(_?_ name) – off Chapel Road - now on Amy Drive
   Stated as a plan of 14 lots in 1976, in 2016 there were only 12 homes. Proposed by Matzzie and Colella Construction Co of Economy.

(_?_ name) - apartment complex - off Pleasant Drive near Beaver Valley Expressway
   Associated with the National Development Corp, Pgh.   220 apartments.

(_?_ name) – condo/apartment complex – rear of 3572 Brodhead Road
   Group of condos/apartments. Two sections of five units each, and one section of six units.

~ ~ ~

Center Township Senior Apartments – 3671 Brodhead Road
   Apartment complex was built in 2001, 4 stories, 47 units.   It is located across the Brodhead Road from St. James Park/Housing.

current

~ ~ ~

Baker's Trailer Court – Chapel Road
Started in c1950s, 1960s - located on the property behind the former Baker Store. No longer exists.

Center Manor   aka   **Tate's Trailer Court**   aka   **Mobile Manor** – off Brodhead Road
Started on a drive off Brodhead Road, now named Center Manor Drive. Mr. and Mrs. E. Tate were the original founders and owners.   They had their first trailer sales business in the 1940s on Sheffield Road in New Sheffield, Aliquippa. In Nov 1946, after purchasing the first club house and some acreage of the Raccoon/ Pettibon Golf (currently the site of Hampton Inn, former ToysRUs, and other surrounding Mall property), they converted the club house to their home, a portion of the property became their trailer sales, and another portion became their first trailer park.
   This first trailer park encircled the land beginning from the area past the Township's water authority building at the BV Mall, on down and onto the property of the former Toys R US and close to the former Humane Society location.   People could rent a space and "park" the trailers they purchased from the Tates on the designated space. The Tates would sometimes "park" a trailer they took in as a trade (for a new one that was purchased) onto one of the spaces. Being part of their trailer park, they would then rent the second-hand trailer. The entrance to the sales lot, the Tate's home, and to the "trailer park" was a long driveway that began close to the current main mall entrance and paralleled the current divided highway. (See additional information in the family section on the Tates, as well as some in the Recreation and Entertainment section with Raccoon Golf Course, and in the Miscellaneous Business section.)
   The current trailer court/park off Brodhead Road has existed since mid-1957.   The 1956 plans to improve the main township's intersection meant the Tates were going to have a large portion of their present trailer sales, park, and home taken by the state road department, therefore, Mr. and Mrs. Tate purchased the 16 acres of a wooded area off Brodhead Road.   Mr. Tate announced at the

Center Township Citizens Council meeting the end of Nov 1956, that he was planning to develop his trailer park. J. R. Thompson, pastor of North Branch Presbyterian Church was the largest adjacent property owner to the proposed site of the new trailer court in 1956. Mr. Thompson stated at the council meeting that he had no objection to Mr. Tate's proposed project, so, the officers of the Citizens' Council approved Mr. Tate's plans. By the end of May 1957, full-scale construction for the mobile home park had begun.

They planned for all possible luxuries to the prospective residents of the park. There was a service building, a recreation area, picnic facilities, a shuffleboard area, a badminton court, horseshoe courts, and a children's play area. Each trailer space/lot was 40 by 60 feet, with a concrete pad. There was to be room to accommodate 50 units and enough land to expand to include at least 50 more units. Two water connections (the 2nd connection being for lawn care and in case of fire) and sewage would be available to each unit, also. Rolfe Johnson of RD#1 Monaca was the engineer in charge of the project. All plans were made under the direction and guidelines of the Mobile Homes Manufacturer's Association's planning division. By the beginning of Jun 1958, mobile home owners were being invited to begin moving into the park.

mid 1958   Cement slabs being laid for lots in the park.

There was a contest in Mobile Manor in the summer of 1959. This is a photo of State Senator John Carl Miller of Aliquippa presenting one of the winning prizes to Mrs. William Florian, a $50 savings bond. The contest was held to select the best landscaped home in the manor. Other winners of bonds were Mrs. Denzil Cutright ($50), Donald Reed and Mrs. H. H. Burke ($25 each). The bonds were given by Mr. and Mrs. Tate.

~ ~ ~

Many of the homesteaders in the current Monaca Heights area had always been considered and included within all census and other records as part of Moon Township. As the larger portion of Moon Township was being settled and developing into Center Township, the remaining section of Moon Township (now the majority of Monaca Heights) was officially annexed and became a portion of the Monaca Borough. For this reason, it took quite some time for everyone to have the mindset of many of those families no longer being part of the newer Center Township.

Once the former section of Moon Township was annexed and part of the Monaca Borough, the borough reorganized and made this area the Fourth and Fifth Wards of the borough. It did not take long before some of the former larger homesteads of Moon Township, now Monaca Heights area, were being bought up. The Allaire Land Co., Colona Land Co. and several others began dividing the former farmland into suburban housing plans. Some of these plans became known as the Welsh Plan, Griffiths Plan, Eckert Plan, Allaire, and Docktor Heights. So, former Moon Township residents were also now moving into these newly developed Monaca heights housing plans.

To add to the confusion was not only that some parts of Monaca Heights were still within Center Township, but homes on one side of a street would be considered Monaca residents, while the other side may be Center residents. Also involved with this final division of the former Moon Township area came some confusion of boundaries to different areas in what was previously referred to as South Monaca. One area of South Monaca in this mix was known as Colona. Although considered in

South Monaca, a large portion of Colona was technically in what was Moon Township and therefore some portions became that of Center Township, too. The area of Colona received its name basically from the adjacent Colonial Steel Company.

~ ~ ~

Center Township continues to grow, and it seems during any given week there are new deals being made and former larger portions of land being sold and developed. Keeping up with all these transactions and developments would require a constant appendix to this book. What I have included is primarily prior developments tied in with the older lands and families of Moon/Center Township. The above section was included merely to give a taste of how rapidly the once vast and open farmlands of the township have been sold and developed. Remember to go through the Shopping Plazas section in Volume II on to see the transformation of even more of the former homesteads from farmlands, orchards, pastures, and lush greenery to a combination of even more concrete, bricks, steel, and massive parking lots.

An excellent example of this growth is by the time this book is published and available for sale, there will be another completed apartment/condo housing area available. The construction and occupancy of what is to become 180 apartments and 80 condominiums in the development project going on along the steeper hillside behind the former Sears Automotive Center at the BV Mall. The developer is calling the area on this hillside "Bluffs at Glade Path" which is said to include two medical facilities, two office buildings, and a large storage facility. (See Medical section.)

Ohio River is along the top of this illustration.

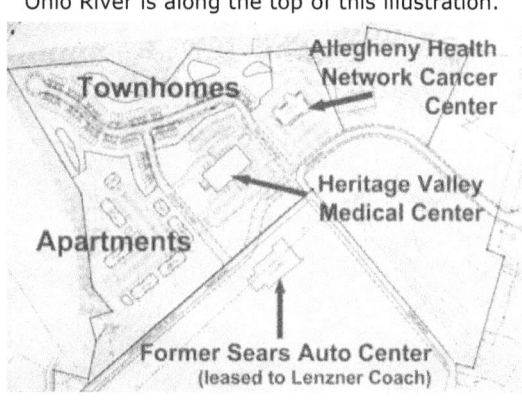

~ ~ ~

Although not a Housing Plan or Housing Area, there once was an "area" which "housed" individuals. Once you read further you will understand why it was not a "plan" of homes, nor was it located close to other homes/families, and definitely was not some place anyone chose on their own to live.

> *Elizabeth ("Gram") Todd Mateer relayed her memories of what was called "The Pest House."*
> *This place was used prior to the smallpox vaccination. It was said to be a house that was located somewhere back in the woods on the property of James Michael and Elizabeth P. (Todd) Mateer. Their homestead was located on the corner of Brodhead and Marshall Roads.*
> *There was an old road that went up the side of a hill from old Brodhead Road and into the woods to supposedly a place where people who had smallpox were taken either to live or more likely, to die. Other persons with known contagious diseases were also taken there to keep them away from others.*
> *I have no exact location, type of structure, or any further information regarding this particular pest house except what was related through the Mateer family. This was by far not the only pest house in the township or Beaver County, but I have no information on any other specific pest houses that may have existed.*

~ ~ ~

Contents for Volume II

The following sections are included in Volume II:

HOMES
   Looking back
   Life in Moon Township and early Center Township
   Older Homes
   Summer Homes and Estates
   Houses on the move
FARMS and DAIRIES
   Farms and Dairies
   Early Families of Moon/Center Township
GENERAL SERVICES, BUSINESSES, OCCUPATIONS, and/or ENTERPRISES
   BRICK WORKS
   GLASS BUSINESS
   SAW MILLS
   SALT WORKS
   GRIST MILLS and MILLERS
   STONE QUARRY and STONE MASONS
   ROPE MAKING
   BELLOWS SHOP
   LIVERYMEN
   TANNERS and CURRIERS
   BUTCHERING / SLAUGHTER HOUSES
   WAGON MAKERS
   BLACKSMITHS
   WEAVERS
   BASKET MAKERS
   TAILORS
   SHOE MAKERS
   THRESHERS
   VINEYARDS
   COAL BUSINESSES
   OIL BUSINESSES
   GARDENERS
   MERCHANTS / RETAIL / STORES
   DISTILLERY
   DRUGGISTS
   PHYSICIANS
   PHOTOGRAPHERS
   MUSIC
   PROF. OF MUSIC
   TEACHERS
   OCCUPATIONS RELATED TO THE RIVER
   MISCELLANEOUS OCCUPATIONS
ASSORTED OTHER BUSINESSES
   Associated with Animals
   Miscellaneous interests
   Sportsman businesses
   Landing strio for private airplane
AUTOMOTIVE RELATED BUSINESSES
   Bus Companies / Businesses
   Gasoline Rationing
   Gasoline Shortage

FOOD RELATED BUSINESSES
　　General / Smaller Grocery Stores
　　All other found grocery and convenient stores
　　Confectionary businesses
　　Convenience Stores
　　Larger Grocery Stores and Supermarkets
　　Trading Stamps
　　1975 – US Govt. Food Stamps
RESTAURANTS and   EATERY BUSINESSES
　　Public Houses OF Refreshment
　　Moonshine Whiskey and Wholesale Liquor
HARDWARE – HOME IMPROVEMENTS – ENGINERRING
　　CABINET MAKER and   CARPENTERS
　　PLUMBERS
　　CONTRACTORS / PAINTERS
　　Various other hardware/home improvement related businesses
　　NURSERY, FLORAL, GARDEN
　　LANDSCAPING and LAWN SERVICES
　　APPLIANCES
BARBERS and SALONS
REALTORS - INSURANCE - TRAVEL
TRAVEL AGENCIES
LEGAL
RETAIL BUSINESSES
SHOPPING CENTERS, MALLS, and PLAZAS
　　CENTER MARKET PLACE
　　TOWNSHIP MARKET PLACE PLAZA
　　STONE QUARRY COMMONS
　　GEE BEE / WAL-MART PLAZA
　　STRIP MALL AND OTHERS ACROSS FROM MALL
　　CENTER POINT SHOPPING CENTER
　　Free standing building to the left of above small plaza
　　BEAVER VALLEY MALL
　　SATELLITE BUILDINGS AT THE BEAVER VALLEY MALL
　　FREE STANDING BUSINESSES AT BEAVER VALLEY MALL
　　CENTER PLAZA / CENTER SQUARE
　　BONANZA STEAK HOUSE
　　GENTILE PROFESSIONAL BUILDING
　　LUCCI PLAZA
　　VILLAGE SHOPS
　　Across the road from the Village Shops
　　BRODHEAD COMMONS
　　Adjacent to Center Commons
　　CENTER PLACE
　　Along Pleasant Drive
　　VISTA PLAZA
In Closing...
REFERENCES (for both Volumes of book)

www.ingramcontent.com/pod-product-compliance
Lightning Source LLC
Chambersburg PA
CBHW081156230426
43666CB00016B/2837